Earliest Man and Environments in
the Lake Rudolf Basin

PREHISTORIC ARCHEOLOGY AND ECOLOGY

A Series Edited by Karl W. Butzer and Leslie G. Freeman

Earliest Man and Environments in the Lake Rudolf Basin

Stratigraphy, Paleoecology, and Evolution

Edited by

Yves Coppens, F. Clark Howell, Glynn Ll. Isaac,
and Richard E. F. Leakey

University of Chicago Press

Chicago and London

YVES COPPENS is professor of anthropology at the National Museum of
Natural History and deputy director of the Musée de l'homme in Paris.
He has worked as a paleontologist in various parts of Africa.

F. CLARK HOWELL received his Ph.D. from the University of Chicago,
where he taught for many years. He is professor of anthropology at
the University of California at Berkeley and has done fieldwork in
Western Europe and Africa.

GLYNN Ll. ISAAC received his Ph.D. from Cambridge University. He is
professor of anthropology at the University of California at Berkeley
and has spent many years in Kenya.

RICHARD E. F. LEAKEY is the director of the National Museums of Kenya
and has done extensive research in East Africa.

The University of Chicago Press, Chicago 60637
The University of Chicago Press, Ltd., London

Library of Congress Cataloging in Publication Data

Main entry under title:

Earliest man and environments in the Lake Rudolf
    Basin.

    (Prehistoric archeology and ecology)
    Proceedings of a workshop-symposium held in East
Africa, Sept. 9-19, 1973, sponsored by the Wenner-
Gren Foundation for Anthropological Research, N.Y.,
and by the National Geographic Society, Washington,
D.C.
    Bibliography: p.
    1. Stone age--Kenya--Lake Rudolf region.
2. Geology--Kenya--Lake Rudolf region. 3. Paleon-
tology--Kenya--Lake--Antiquities. I. Coppens, Yves.
II. Wenner-Gren Foundation for Anthropological Re-
search, New York. III. National Geographic Society,
Washington, D.C. IV. Series.
GN865.K4E17   967.6'27   75-5075
ISBN 0-226-11577-1

A Dedication to Camille Arambourg and Louis S. B. Leakey

Camille Arambourg, 1885-1969

Camille Arambourg was born in Paris in February 1885. He died there in November 1969, nearly eighty five years later.

He attended secondary school in Paris and continued his university education there. He was named Professor of Geology in the Institut national agronomique (1930-36) after which he served as professor (paleontology) in the Muséum national d'histoire naturelle (1936-56).

Although he spent nearly forty years of his life in Paris, many of his scientific researches took him to North Africa. He was a few months old when he first came with his family to Algeria, and it was in his father's vineyards near Oran that he first practiced as an agricultural engineer. He taught geology in the Institut agricole in Algiers before returning to Paris in 1930. Thereafter he traveled frequently to the Maghreb.

He considered the African continent a major center for the emergence, evolution, and dispersal of vertebrate species. A perusal of the 231 publications in his bibliography reveals the major role of Africa in his researches; more than 150 contributions over a period of fifty years are primarily devoted to that continent. The implications of his work there are touched on in 50 other papers. Of his publications 108 are devoted to North Africa and are concerned, for example, with fossil fishes from the Sahelian of Oran, fishes and reptiles from the Cretaceous and Eocene of Morocco, mammals from the Miocene of Algeria, Villafranchian vertebrates from Algeria and Tunisia, researches on the Middle Pleistocene locality of Ternifine (Algeria), and studies of the later Pleistocene coastal caves of Algeria.

In 1932-33 he led the Mission scientifique de l'Omo to southern Ethiopia. At that time he also investigated Miocene fossil occurrences in northern Kenya and visited Tanzania at the invitation of L. S. B. Leakey. When the international Omo Research Expedition was formed (in 1966) he participated in the initial field seasons in 1967 to 1969, until his death. Twenty-seven papers in his bibliography are concerned with this work in East Africa.

In the course of his paleontological researches he was inevitably led to a concern with Hominidae. He devoted 72 papers to this subject, including the australopithecines of the Omo, pebble-tool industries in Algeria, remains of *Homo erectus* in Algeria and Morocco, and *Homo sapiens* remains from the late Pleistocene caves of Algeria. These studies led him to publish several general articles on human evolution and to summarize his views in *La genèse de l'humanité*, in the Que Sais-je? series of the Presses Universitaires de France. An eighth edition of this very successful book appeared in the year of his death.

Arambourg was a field man, and a true naturalist. Through knowledge of the present he was enabled to recapture the past.

Without neglecting his endeavors in vertebrate systematics, he was concerned above all with the evolutionary processes effective in their phylogenetic history. His ideas in this respect were influenced by the works of Lamarck, and he viewed the effects of the environment, at the cellular and biochemical level, as of prime importance. He confirmed the constant direction of evolution toward more complex, better adapted forms, for him an "overall orthogenesis of the world of life." However, he also took note of the irregularity and discontinuous pattern of evolution. ·He sought to apply his ideas, perhaps in too dogmatic a fashion, to the evolution of Hominidae, which he envisioned as a series of successive and morphologically progressive stages, each corresponding to a distinctive morphology and an associated elaboration of prehistoric technology.

Finally, a personal remark on this man, Camille Arambourg. Warm, courteous, modest, and imbued with a profound devotion to scientific work associated with a remarkable energy, for him retirement was merely an arbitrary, administratively determined date. On a Saturday afternoon in November 1969, I discussed with him in his museum office plans for the forthcoming 1970 field season of the Omo Research Expedition. The following Wednesday he was dead.

Yves Coppens

Louis Seymour Bazett Leakey, 1903-72

Louis Leakey was born at Kabete in Kenya on 7 August 1903. He died at the age of sixty nine in London on 1 October 1972, while on his way to the United States to give a series of lectures on human origins.

Louis Leakey devoted his life and his restless exploratory energy to the study of man and nature in Africa. He was one of a missionary family, and a crucial part of his early education was growing up in rural Africa with a wealth of plant and animal life around him and the Kikuyu countryfolk as mentors. In spite of the isolation of his childhood and irregularities in his schooling, Louis was determined to become a scientist and to explore Africa's prehistoric past. He struggled for and achieved admission to Saint Johns College, Cambridge University, where he took part I of his first degree in modern languages and part II in archeology and anthropology, graduating with first-class honors in 1926.

Louis Leakey then led four successful expeditions to East Africa. His most intensive researches at this time were done in the Nakuru-Naivasha sector of the Kenya Rift valley, where he and his co-workers established the existence of an important stratigraphic sequence involving major fluctuations of lake levels and a rich and varied series of prehistoric industries. On the basis of these researches he was awarded his Ph.D. and a research fellowship at Saint Johns College. At this time, too, Louis made his first visit to Olduvai Gorge in the company of Dr. Hans Reck, from whom he took on responsibility for continuing research, an undertaking that was to engage him for the rest of his life. During work at Olduvai in the 1930s Louis Leakey recruited Mary Nicol into East African archeology; later they were married and had three sons. The combined impact of this family on paleoanthropology is now well known! Over the years Mary Leakey assumed increasing responsibility for the research operations at Olduvai, and she continues to direct this work.

Louis Leakey's African ties were too strong for him to remain based in Europe for long, and in 1937 he returned to Kenya to make a detailed ethnographic study of the Kikuyu. He and Mary made many important discoveries during the years that followed and worked on Hyrax Hill, Njoro River Cave, and Olorgesailie, as well as on the Miocene fossil localities of western Kenya.

Louis Leakey became curator of the Coryndon Museum in 1945 and built this up as a modern research institution with a strong tradition in paleontology and archeology. He left this post in 1961 and shortly afterward founded the affiliated Centre for Prehistory and Palaeontology--an institution that has been host to most of the participants in the recent wave of paleoanthropological research in East Africa. A lineal successor to the centre will be the Louis Leakey Memorial Institute for African Prehistory, for which funds have been raised and which will be built on the museum grounds in Nairobi.

A bibliography of Louis Leakey's writings has been published by P. V. Tobias in the *South African Archaeological Bulletin* (vol. 28, pp. 3-7), and a classified, annotated bibliography prepared by Shirley Coryndon (Savage) is in press for publication in a special issue of *Perspectives on Human Evolution* (vol. 3, 1975) which commemorates Louis's lifework (edited by G. Ll. Isaac and E. R. McCown). These bibliographies show the extraordinary breadth of the man's knowledge and scholarship. The entries span topics from prehistory to ethnography and from paleontology and natural history to politics and public affairs.

Louis Leakey did not himself do any extensive work in the Lake Rudolf basin, but he recognized very clearly its great potential. He sponsored Bryan Patterson's Harvard expeditions at the outset of their exploratory trips to Maralal, Kanapoi, and Lothagam. He also participated in the negotiations that led to the establishment of the international Omo Research expeditions. However, it is out of recognition of a more general debt that this volume is dedicated to him and Camille Arambourg. Louis and Mary Leakey put East African prehistory and hominid paleontology on the map. A considerable number of the participants in the Rudolf basin got their scientific start under Louis's guidance and inspiration.

For Louis Leakey Africa was home, and on Kenya's accession to independence he became a citizen. He campaigned throughout his life for proper recognition of Africa's contribution to human cultural development, but he was not a narrow nationalist or chauvinist. Louis saw the study of human origins as a cause that could and should unite people from all over the world in an endeavor of great interest and high importance. He did not hesitate to discuss the relevance of knowledge of man's past to an understanding of his present and future predicaments. The wide spectrum of research interests and the combination of East African and international involvement represented by this Rudolf basin symposium are built on foundations laid by Louis Leakey.

Glynn Ll. Isaac

CONTENTS

x   Contents

Part 2. *Paleontology and Paleoecology*, ed. Y. Coppens and F. C. Howell

*The papers marked by asterisks were prepared after the conference.

Late Cenozoic fossils were first discovered in the Lake Rudolf basin in 1902, when a selection of Pliocene forms was collected in the Omo valley of southwestern Ethiopia. Systematic work by Camille Arambourg in 1933 established a rudimentary geologic sequence there, and a massive paleontological inventory was published.

Detailed studies in the Omo began in 1966, with the encouragement of Emperor Haile Selassie, and led to an international Omo Research Expedition in 1967, initially based on the University of Chicago, the Musée de l'Homme, and the National Museums of Kenya. The American team was supported by the National Science Foundation as well as the Wenner-Gren Foundation and was led by F. C. Howell. They explored the Omo region in 1966-67 and have continued intensive work in the northern part of the Omo type area of Shungura since 1968. The Paris group, supported by the Centre national de la recherche scientifique and directed by Arambourg and, after his death at 84, by Yves Coppens, has worked south of Shungura since 1967. The Nairobi group, led by R. E. F. Leakey, spent one season in the Omo and then shifted activity to the eastern margins of Lake Rudolf, in Kenya. With support of the National Geographic Society and National Science Foundation, and ultimately including workers from Berkeley, Harvard, Iowa State University, Dartmouth, Birkbeck College, and Cambridge, the East Rudolf Expedition has operated annually since 1968. All together, more than 1.5 million dollars may have been expended in what is unquestionably the most comprehensive paleoanthropological enterprise to date.

Despite the usual preliminary reports, published information has not always kept pace with the successive field seasons. Furthermore, although relationships between the groups have been remarkably cordial over the years, scientific interchange and comparison of results have been less satisfactory. Consequently, with so much already invested, it is commendable that the Wenner-Gren Foundation and National Geographic Society deemed it desirable to sponsor an unprecedented "workshop" on *Stratigraphy, Palaeontology, and Evolution in the Lake Rudolf Basin*. This was organized by R. E. F. Leakey, Y. Coppens, G. Ll. Isaac, and F. C. Howell and was specifically designed to bring the key scientists together. Some 38 participants assembled at the National Museum, Nairobi, from 8 to 20 September 1973, interjecting a four-day field trip to East Rudolf and an additional day in the Shungura area of the Omo. Four days of discussion, based on preprinted and circulated papers, were focused on (*a*) stratigraphy, sedimentology, and geochronology; (*b*) evolutionary biology of the key nonhominid vertebrate taxa; (*c*) hominid morphology and evolution;

and (d) hominid activities and ecology. Following the excursions, a final day of general discussion concluded the conference.

The wealth of information presented in papers and discussion defied adequate summation, and it is fortunate that it has been possible to publish all the revised conference papers and several additional contributions in the Prehistoric Archeology and Ecology series. With the particular inclusion of two articles on Lothagam, where Bryan Patterson discovered the first fossil of an australopithecine in 1966, the volume provides an unusually complete and up-to-date survey of the entire Rudolf basin and its contributions to paleoanthropology. It is altogether remarkable that the basic results of so large and complex an effort should be readily available to a broad audience while the research is still continuing.

It would be incorrect to say that the original Nairobi conference was without its points of disagreement. For example, substantial differences in geological methodology presented interpretations of past depositional contexts that were at times difficult to reconcile. Similarly, the faunal successions of Omo and East Rudolf are discordant with the radiometric values currently assigned to the strata. Additional paleomagnetic studies included in these volumes emphasize that significant geochronological problems remain, and these will necessitate caution in evaluating the dating frameworks favored by individual authors. The relevance of taphonomic studies for late Cenozoic studies was perhaps first clearly realized during the advanced stages of the Rudolf basin research, but perhaps too late to provide a firmer contextual setting for the major hominid occurrences. Finally, the considerable time-depth and potential cross-checks provided by the paleontological records from the Omo and East Rudolf yield an unprecedented potential for understanding faunal evolution, but one which cannot yet be fully exploited. This is in part because of the remaining stratigraphic uncertainties and in part because possible hypotheses of geographically isolated macroenvironments or different ecological adaptations in contrasting settings could not be adequately explored on account of persistent difficulties of sedimentological interpretation.

The volume includes substantial, well-illustrated discussions of lithic artifact series recovered from stratigraphic contexts in both the Omo and East Rudolf areas. These reports, and the data on associations and distributions they present, are especially welcome to students of hominid behavior.

The often-explosive issues of hominid phylogeny have been approached with caution. Both in conference and in the final papers it is apparent that the physical anthropologists are sufficiently awed by the true complexity of the problems to adopt a pragmatic approach. This is a welcome development from all points of view, but is particularly important in that it will allow a wide audience of students and younger professionals access to analytical data uncolored by idiosyncratic interpretation. The detached, scientific attitude that prevails throughout the volume is in fact remarkable in view both of the broad range of disciplinary specializations and personalities involved and of the pertinence of the results for a substantially new understanding of human origins.

The volume marks a milestone in paleoanthropology that reveals the strengths and weaknesses of the art. Much has been gained over the traditional study of fossils in isolation, by working in multidisciplinary groups whose broad range of results is increasingly effective for integrated interpretations. Nonetheless, with the benefit of hindsight it is now apparent that multidisciplinary teams do not by themselves ensure a successful interdisciplinary approach. It could perhaps be argued that the vital, contributing earth scientists and biologists have not always had sufficient influence on decisions affecting expedition strategy. It is, for example, significant that the research priorities recommended by the workshop consist of a more comprehensive earth science program (geophysical investigations, regional mapping, sedimentology, and paleopedology) and development of limnological and palynological research in the area. This underscores the reality that all the effort expended on African Early Man studies in the fifty years since the discovery of the Taung juvenile has barely begun to demonstrate microenvironmental contexts characteristic of the still-elusive hominid lineages suggested by the fossil remains.

We wish to express our sincere thanks to the volume editors for their efforts to bring these papers together with such care, thus assuring a balanced and comprehensive coverage that is completely up to date. We are confident that a large and enthusiastic audience will be equally grateful.

Karl W. Butzer

Leslie G. Freeman

PREFACE

These volumes are the proceedings of a workshop-symposium organized by the four of us. The meetings were held in East Africa from 9 to 19 September 1973. This symposium, entitled "Stratigraphy, Paleoecology, and Evolution in the Lake Rudolf Basin," was sponsored and financed by the Wenner-Gren Foundation for Anthropological Research, New York, and by the National Geographic Society, Washington, D.C.[*]

The proceedings are dedicated as a memorial to two great Africanists whose researches pioneered the way to this symposium--Camille Arambourg and Louis Leakey. Although they are no longer with us, we all recognize how greatly indebted our science is to their contributions and their leadership.

The roots of the researches that culminated in this symposium go back to the great explorers of the turn of the nineteenth and twentieth centuries. They traversed the Rift valley and recognized it as a natural wonder rich in geological history. Early accounts of the Rift were published by Joseph Thomson (1881), J. W. Gregory (1896, 1921), the Count Samuel Teleki Expedition (von Höhnel 1894, von Höhnel et al. 1891), the Bottego Expedition (Vannutelli and Citerni 1897; Angelis d'Ossat and Millosevich 1900), and the R. Bourg de Bozas Expedition (B. de Bozas 1906). However, it was not until the 1930s that the paleontological opportunities perceived by some of these early travellers were pursued. The followup began effectively with the researches of Louis Leakey in the Kenyan and northern Tanzanian sectors of the Rift (Leakey 1931, 1951) and the explorations of Camille Arambourg in the Miocene of north Turkana and then in the lower Omo valley of southern Ethiopia (Arambourg 1943, 1947).

The first substantial effort to decipher the natural history of this area was the Cambridge Expedition to East African lakes led by E. B. Worthington in 1930-31, which undertook various geological researches along the western margin of the lake and on its islands (Fuchs 1934), made substantial zoological collections (published largely in the *J. Linn. Soc.*, London, and the *Ann. Mag. Nat. Hist.*, London), and undertook various limnological studies (Worthington 1932; Worthington and Worthington 1933). In 1934 the Lake Rudolf Rift Valley Expedition, led by V. E. Fuchs, carried out further geological and related surveys to the west, south, and southeast of the lake (Fuchs 1935, 1939). Also, during this time A. M. Champion (1935, 1937; Champion and Smith 1938), who served as

---
[*] While this volume was in press, the name of Lake Rudolf was changed to Lake Turkana by a decree of President Kenyatta of Kenya. We respect this change but it has not been possible to alter the name throughout the book.

provincial commissioner of the Northern Frontier province, provided the first accurate observations on the recent volcanic region at the south end of the lake. In recent years
the South Turkana Expedition of the Royal Geographical Society of London has continued
trigonometric, topographic, and geological surveys in this area, as well as a variety of
botanical, zoological, ecological, and land-use studies--preliminary reports of which have
appeared since 1969 in the *Geographical Journal*.

In 1939 the Missione Biologica Sagan-Omo, led by Edoardo Zavattari, undertook extensive zoological and botanical collecting in southern Ethiopia, including the lower valley
of the Omo (Zavattari 1941, 1946). Some limited paleontological collecting was done by an
assistant of L. S. B. Leakey in the Omo fossiliferous deposits while this area was occupied
by Allied forces in World War II. In 1943 Sir Frank Dixey carried out extensive geological
reconnaissances over the Northern Frontier District and Turkana, in conjunction with hydrographic surveys (Dixey 1948). Except for northern Turkana (Walsh and Dodson 1969), the
general geology of most of the area of the Rudolf Basin has remained until recently largely
unknown.

In the past two decades the tempo of researches all along the Eastern Rift has quick-
ened as scientists from many different disciplines have been recruited into the investigations.

In the late 1950s T. Whitworth continued paleontological, geological, and related
researches along the western margin of the lake in North Turkana. And in the mid-1960s
L. H. Robbins carried out archeological studies in South Turkana (Robbins 1972, 1974). For
general histories of research see Cooke (1958) and Bishop (1971), and for an overview of
the discovery and early exploration of the region see von Höhnel (1938) (see appended list
of publications).

The Lake Rudolf basin in particular became the theater of intensive work by many
scholars from widely dispersed institutional bases, working in different teams and doing
fieldwork in separate areas. It became apparent that a workshop meeting would be of immense value in promoting communication and in helping us take stock of the state of our
knowledge--or rather, one might say, the state of our ignorance.

The work with which the symposium was concerned stems largely from three major "expeditions" that have been active over much of the past ten years in the Lake Rudolf basin:
namely, the Harvard-Princeton expeditions, the international Omo Expedition, and the
National Museum of Kenya East Rudolf Expedition (East Rudolf Research Project).

The first expedition in this recent round of research was that initiated by Harvard
University at the invitation of Louis Leakey. In 1964, under the direction of Bryan
Patterson, this group, which initially worked to the east of the Rift in the Maralal area,
began exploring parts of the area to the southwest of the lake, initially near Ferguson's
Gulf and then to the south in the Kerio valley in South Turkana. In 1968 the work was continued with Vincent Maglio as field leader. Maglio joined the faculty at Princeton University in 1971 and later passed on responsibility for the project to David Kinsman, who is
coordinating continuing geological and paleontological work.

The second program of fieldwork has been organized as the international "Omo Research
Expedition," which has operated since 1966 at the north end of the basin, in Ethiopia. One
of us (F. C. H.) first visited this area in 1959 and recognized its great potential for
extensive interdisciplinary research. A joint enterprise with the late Camille Arambourg
was discussed, but the requisite authorizations were not forthcoming. Subsequently the
authorization for such research was obtained from the government of Ethiopia, largely

through the good offices of Louis Leakey. Initially this expedition was composed of three field groups: a C.N.R.S.-supported group under the overall direction of Camille Arambourg and the field direction of Yves Coppens; an N.S.F.-supported group under the direction of F. Clark Howell; and a National Geographic Society-supported group under the overall direction of Louis Leakey and the field direction of Richard Leakey. On the death of Arambourg in 1969, Coppens assumed responsibility for the C.N.R.S.-supported research effort. Richard Leakey initiated the "East Rudolf Expedition" in 1968 and in 1970 invited Glynn Isaac to join him as co-leader. The expedition has grown to become a consortium of research teams from Kenya, Britain, and the United States, working in conjunction with the National Museum in Nairobi. The expedition has renamed itself the East Rudolf Research Project, and its scientific policy is now coordinated through a council of senior members.

These research efforts within the Rudolf basin are in fact part of larger research movements all along a 2,000-kilometer stretch of Rift valley extending from the Red Sea to the Serengeti. This wave of scientific activity can be traced to two sources in particular. First, the discovery of "Zinjanthropus" by Mary Leakey in 1959 at Olduvai Gorge, Tanzania, provided a dramatic demonstration of Eastern Africa's potential as a source of fossils and paleoanthropological evidence. Subsequent results at Olduvai and at points all along the Rift have served to reinforce the promise held out by that momentous discovery. Second, the widespread surge of interest in plate tectonics has encouraged international participation in geological and geophysical researches throughout the Rift system. Thus in the Rift valley researches into the roots of humanity and into the structure of the earth's crust have become inextricably intertwined.

The paleontological gold rush that was started fifteen years ago by the discovery of "Zinjanthropus" has brought to light more fossil specimens of early man than had been discovered in the preceding hundred years. During the same period a start has also been made on measuring the age of the various fossil-bearing beds. This began with the work of Evernden and Curtis (1965), and the point has now been reached where in spite of gaps the ages of the fossil-bearing late Cenozoic sequences of eastern Africa are better established than any comparable series elsewhere in the world. In terms of fossils, dates, and contextual evidence this area has become the key to our understanding of human origins. In fifteen years it has been shown that australopithecines go back at least five million years and *Homo* two million years or more, and the antiquity of traces of cultural activity can now be seen to be twice as great as most previous estimates.

The antecedents of the conference itself are also complex. In 1968 one of us (Y. C.) conceived of the idea of convening a colloquium of researchers working in the Rift valley of Kenya and Ethiopia. While the project was being discussed with Richard Leakey it was suggested that the Wenner-Gren Foundation be asked if they would sponsor such a meeting. In 1970 Clark Howell and Yves Coppens went ahead and proposed a meeting, and Richard Leakey and Glynn Isaac also made a proposal. The coalescence of these projected conferences was amicably arranged and this volume reports the results.

The conference was a gathering of some forty primary research workers, all with first-hand knowledge of an aspect of the basin or its fossils. Papers were circulated in advance so there was no need for formal presentation. Four days of discussion opened the conference, each session being under joint chairmanship. This was followed by six days in the field in northern Kenya and southern Ethiopia, with the participants housed and well catered for at the East Rudolf main camp at Koobi Fora. In spite of the logistic difficulties of housing and feeding forty participants and transporting them by light aircraft and four-wheel-drive vehicles, we examined many important sections and localities. One final day in Nairobi was devoted to concluding discussions.

The proceedings of the workshop-symposium have been partitioned into three sections, each under the particular editorial responsibility of one or more of the organizers: (1) Geology and geochronology (G. Ll. Isaac); (2) Paleontology and paleoecology (Y. Coppens and F. C. Howell); and (3) Paleoanthropology (F. C. Howell and G. Ll. Isaac). Clark Howell, assisted by Martha Anne Booth, bore the brunt of the work of finally compiling the papers. Except for the paper by J. Chavaillon (translated by Barbara Isaac) all the contributions by French participants were translated by Howell. The other organizers express gratitude on behalf of all contributors to these two for their very considerable efforts. Final proofs were corrected by F. Clark Howell and G. Shoekkenbroek.

Each section is preceded by a short introduction in which the editor of the section comments on the background to the papers and on the scientific issues that engaged participants during the workshop-discussions.

In the closing sessions the assembled group of scientists discussed future research needs. It seemed very clear to us all that in spite of the wealth of data retrieved in the past decade the research so far had to be regarded as largely exploratory. In all disciplines careful followup studies are essential, both in the field and in the laboratory. The conference identified some particularly crucial needs for new investigations or major extensions of work that has been started:

1. The geophysics, structure, and tectonic history of the basin should be elucidated in detail through seismic profiling, magnetic and gravity surveys, and eventually through deep drilling.
2. The geomorphological history of the basin should be worked out.
3. Denudation and sedimentation processes specific to the basin should be observed and measured through studies of land forms, erosion, and recent sediments.
4. The paleolimnological and paleoecological history of Lake Rudolf itself should be worked out from fossils, sedimentary characteristics, and geochemical markers.
5. Further palynological work is urgent and should be coupled with studies of contemporary plant communities and modern pollen rain.
6. Large-scale topographic and geological maps should be prepared.

The acquisition of support for these kinds of research undertakings as well as for continued paleontological and archeological work is essential for full realization of the region's potential both for elucidating processes in the earth's crust and for throwing vivid light on the circumstances of human origins.

The initial phases of work have involved scientists from many parts of the world, and we hope that the international character of the research will continue and expand. However, increasing numbers of technical experts, scientists, and students from East Africa have also been involved as contributors and trainees. We hope that this trend too will continue.

We warmly thank the governments of Kenya and of Ethiopia, who have fostered the researches and who were hosts to the meeting and to the field visits. We are also grateful to the National Museum in Nairobi and its trustees, who provided congenial facilities for the conference and hospitality for the participants. The brunt of this part of the organization fell on Richard Leakey, assisted by Margaret Cropper Leakey. All the participants are very grateful to them for their efforts.

We also wish to express our gratitude to the organization that granted the funds that made these meetings possible. The conference was pleased to have Mrs. Lita Osmundsen, Director of Research of the Wenner-Gren Foundation, present as an observer at the meetings.

Research in the basin has been funded by numerous organizations--chief among which have been the National Science Foundation (USA), the Centre national de la recherche scientifique (France), the National Geographic Society (USA), the Wenner-Gren Foundation for Anthropological Research, and the National Environmental Research Council (Great Britain). On behalf of all the research workers we acknowledge our indebtedness to these supporters and to numerous others listed in the appendix that follows this preface.

Finally, the organizers wish to thank the participants for their efforts before, during, and after the conference, for their contributions, and for their good company.

Yves Coppens
F. Clark Howell
Glynn Ll. Isaac
Richard E. F. Leakey

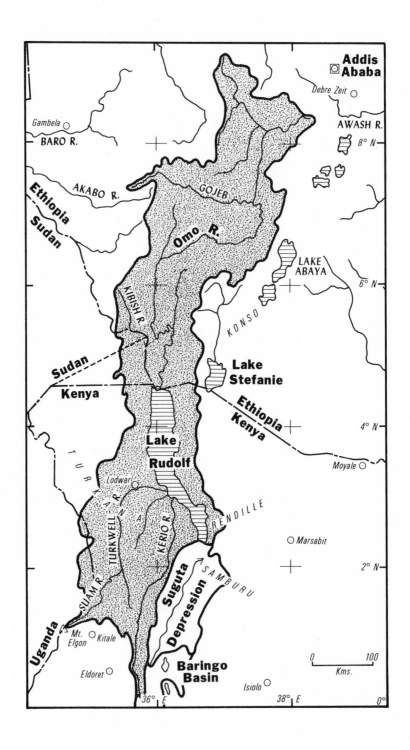

Part 1

GEOLOGY AND GEOCHRONOLOGY

Edited by G. Ll. Isaac

1. INTRODUCTION

G. Ll. Isaac

The papers in this section provide clear summaries of the basic facts pertaining to the geology and geophysical chronology of the several fossiliferous formations of the Lake Rudolf basin. Their titles speak for themselves, and little is needed in the way of an introduction. However, it may be useful to offer comments on some of the problems and areas of uncertainty that arise where the "facts" end and interpretation begins. The following is a partial list of issues which were probed by discussion at the conference in Nairobi and also during the field excursion:

1. Why do total sediment thicknesses differ from one part of the basin to another, even when the time spans are alleged to be almost equivalent?

2. To what extent were changes in the distribution of lake waters controlled by climate as opposed to tectonic deformation?

3. How were the beds of tuff emplaced in the Shungura and Koobi Fora Formations?

4. Can any of the tuffs or other rock units be matched between disparate areas such as the Omo and East Rudolf?

5. What has caused the great scatter of apparent K-Ar ages determined for several of the East Rudolf tuffs? Why are the dates for Shungura tuffs E, F, G, and I so tightly bunched, so that half the formation's thickness dated apparently between 1.8 and 2.1 m.y.?

6. Does the geological evidence of the East Rudolf area suggest a "disconformity" within the Koobi Fora Formation? Is the evidence even compatible with such a hypothesis?

7. What should stratigraphers and geochronologists do to resolve apparent discrepancies between time relations assessed from geophysics and time relations assessed from paleontological assemblages?

All of these questions should be borne in mind in reading the papers of this section. They were all discussed more or less directly in the meetings. The exchanges which took place served to clarify most of the questions, but did not provide simple answers that can be glibly set forth here.

There was general agreement at a meeting that sedimentary thicknesses might be expected to vary greatly from area to area and from period to period depending on relationships to zones of subsidence or to episodes of deformation within the basin. This view is set out in Fitch and Vondra's brief postconference synopsis of the "tectonic and stratigraphic framework," and it is implicitly accepted by de Heinzelin and Haesaerts and by

3

Brown in their interpretation of differences in sedimentation rates between segments of the Shungura Formation. However, the details of structure and the history of tectonic controls on sedimentation remain to be worked out more fully. Gravity surveys, magnetic surveys, and seismic profiling will be necessary before much advance can be made with these questions.

Uncertainty about the details of tectonic control also leaves unresolved the question of the relative importance of tectonic and climatic factors in determining observed changes in the extent of the lake waters. Many geologists with experience in the Rift valley feel that most major long-term shifts are likely to have been structurally determined, whereas oscillations may well reflect climatic fluctuations. However, opinion may be divided on this.

The prominent layers of pyroclastic deposits in both the Omo and the East Rudolf areas have a seemingly irresistible fascination for earth scientists. In many places the tuffs form spectacular, resistant beds which have been much studied and sampled--and yet there still exists uncertainty regarding the source of the eruptive materials and the relative importance of air fall, river transport, and wind action in their emplacement and reworking. Brown is inclined to believe that the Shungura tuffs derive largely from the volcanic complex of Mount Damota near Soddu, some 250 km northward up the Omo. The source, or sources, of the East Rudolf tuffs is still unknown, but for the most part Brown's petrographic and petrochemical analyses indicate that it was different from the source of the Shungura Tuffs. The only possible exception to this may be the Chari Tuff, which is indistinguishable from tuffs of the Kalam sector of the Shungura sequence. The K-Ar age determinations also do not differ significantly.

The meeting seemed to attach great interest to the possibility of a direct lithostratigraphic connection between the sections at this level near the top of both. It was remarked that there are general lithological similarities between the upper and part of the Ileret Member of the Koobi Fora Formation and members K and L at Kalam. De Heinzelin suggested that the similarities might be linked to increased importance of eolian transport around the north end of the lake at this time. This and other possible mechanisms causing convergence in sedimentary character need to be investigated. The faunal assemblages recovered from the uppermost beds of the two formations join the sediments in showing maximum similarity.

The tuffs are important, of course, both as mappable, isochronous units within each formation and as geophysically datable deposits. There were lively discussions and debates at the conference tables and in private over the reliability of the various "dates." During the weeks before the conference, it emerged that some paleontologists found strong similarities between the faunal assemblage of the Lower Member of the Koobi Fora Formation, that is, the *Mesochoerus limnetes* zone of Maglio (1972), and the faunas of members E, F, and G of the Shungura Formation. The chronologies of each formation which were being advanced on the basis of geophysics implied that the similarities should be with members B and C. The question of the relative reliability of the geophysical and the paleonotological data became the hottest single issue to be treated by the meetings. Figure 1 provides a graphic summary of the K-Ar age determinations involved in the discussion.

The workshop produced lively discussions of possible causes for the scatters of values that have been obtained for several East Rudolf tuffs. Fitch and Miller suggested in their paper that a major cause of scatter in the East Rudolf apparent ages has been a process of "overprinting" during complex alteration histories--probably involving hydrothermal

Frequency distributions of K-Ar determinations on tuffs from:
a) SHUNGURA FORMATION   b) KOOBI FORA FORMATION
   (from Brown, this volume)   (from Fitch & Miller this volume)

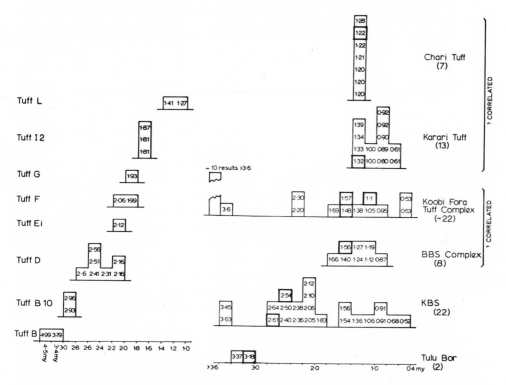

Figure 1. Frequency distributions of age determinations on tuffs from the Shungura Formation (a) and from the Koobi Fora Formation (b). The tuffs are shown in stratigraphic order,
except that some tuffs from different areas at East Rudolf have been named separately but
are now believed to correlate as shown. The dark boxes on the Koobi Fora section of the
diagram denote values derived by the ^{40}Ar/^{39}Ar step-heating method. As can be seen,
these form a series with a high degree of internal consistency, but the method itself is
regarded as controversial by some geophysicists. The diagram shows clearly the extent of
research efforts by the geochronology labs that have participated in the Rudolf basin research. (For details see Brown and Nash and Fitch and Miller, this symposium.)

metasomatism. In support of this view is a fission track date of 1.8 million years for a
vitric tuff in the upper part of the Kubi Algi Formation, which is known to be much older.
The date thus seems to be that of a period when the material underwent thermal annealing.
Several geologists expressed reserve over the metasomatism hypothesis, but no useful alternative explanation was offered. When the apparent discrepancy between the favored geophysical chronologies for the Shungura and Koobi Fora formations were discussed, the suggestion
was made that the older-dated Shungura sanidines might have suffered overprint distortion
of their K-Ar ages. Fitch and Miller have offered to do ^{40}Ar/^{39}Ar step-heating analyses to
try to detect such distortions, if they exist. Great importance was attached in the discussions to determining the paleomagnetic stratigraphy of the Shungura Formation. The
laboratory work has been done since the conference, and a summary of preliminary results by
Brown and Shuey is included in this volume. It will be seen that these workers found a
more complex reversal stratigraphy than would have been expected from the K-Ar chronology

and any published "standard" paleomagnetic time scale.

However, after some corrections for polarity differences that are specifically associated with lithological differences, Brown and his co-workers feel that there is good agreement between the paleomagnetic results and the K-Ar dates for all tuffs above Tuff B. Since these are postconference results they have not been fully discussed and evaluated by the other participants in the conference.

Inextricably bound up with the question of the reliability of the main chronologies was the question of whether "disconformities" could be recognized in either the Shungura sequence or the Koobi Fora sequence. Discussion was particularly lively on the matter of a disconformity at East Rudolf just above the KBS Tuff. It became clear that the physical, stratigraphic indicators of a break, if such there was, are partly ambiguous and are subject to different interpretation by different observers. Discussion then turned on whether a pause in deposition lasting 1/2 to 3/4 of a million years could have occurred without leaving clear traces. No poll was taken, but opinion was probably divided on this matter--with some geologists feeling that the stratigraphy is at least compatible with a time-gap hypothesis and others perhaps having reservations. The matter is further discussed in the paper on paleomagnetic stratigraphy by Brock and Isaac. De Heinzelin and Haesaerts report numerous minor pauses, weathering horizons and minor channeling within the Shungura Formation. The conference also discussed mounting evidence for more extensive channeling in Member D, perhaps amounting to a time gap or "disconformity." Perhaps coincidentally, this channeling occurs at a time equivalent to the start of the alleged post-KBS "disconformity"-- if one accepts both Brown's Shungura and Fitch and Miller's Koobi Fora chronologies.

As was already indicated, the most lively discussion arose from the sense of uncertainty over claims of discordance between chronologies being offered by various geophysicists and the perception of time relations indicated by several paleontologists. Many people saw two separate issues here. First, there is the need to test for this specific case, the reality of the apparent discrepancy: How reliable are the favored "dates"? how clear-cut are the paleontological patterns that are used to demarcate time lines? Second, for many present there was a sense that we need to preserve a clear conceptual separation between the paleontological record of changing biota and geophysical means of calibrating the timing of events in that record. If we start to bend geophysics to faunal indications or vice versa, we will lose much of the great advantage that Quaternary studies in East Africa began to acquire when Curtis and Evernden first made geophysical age measurements on the Olduvai rocks. To some of those present it seemed possible that what at first sight appeared as an embarrassing discrepancy between geophysics and paleontology might prove to be an exciting glimpse of the existence of prehistoric mosaics of spatial and ecological differentiation between the faunas of adjacent but environmentally contrasting regions.

Both the geophysics and the paleontology will have to be rigorously and independently checked before we can know whether this possibility is a reality.

The conference and the field parties also discussed a host of other particular and more or less technical questions including matters pertaining to sedimentological analyses, the recognition and classification of paleosols, and so forth. Many of these questions are partly covered in the contributions and they cannot usefully be broached here.

Several of the geological papers make important contributions to the reconstruction of paleogeography and of environments. Since this is a matter of wide interest, discussion kept reverting to it at the conference.

At the Calibration of Hominoid Evolution conference held in Austria in 1971, W. W.

Bishop recognized two groups of participants: producers of dates and consumers of chronology. In some senses a similar division applies in the Rudolf basin research. The geological studies of sedimentation and volcanism in and around the Rift valley would have great intrinsic value even if the sediments did not contain important fossils. However, the fact that the sediments are a source of evolutionary history does give the geology added interest and creates an eager throng of paleontological and archeological consumers clamoring for as much interpretation as can be squeezed out of the stones. Even when the rocks are dry these clients beg for more. It is a sign of progress and maturity in our field that research in the Rudolf basin has become a joint enterprise of scientists collectively concerned with earth history, evolution, and human origins. We work closely together in the field and comprehend both the insights and the limitations of each others' research better than used to be the case.

For reasons that have nothing to do with qualifications, it fell to me, a "consumer" of geology in the Rudolf basin, to edit the geology papers and write this introduction. I would like to take the opportunity to acknowledge the indebtedness of us consumers. We do recognize the efforts involved in working out stratigraphy, mapping, and dating, and we appreciate the patience with which geologists treat our haste for simple answers to complicated questions.

R. L. Hay gave valuable scientific advice, for which we are grateful, but the authors and editor remain responsible for such defects as may have escaped correction.

References

Maglio, V. J. 1972. Vertebrate faunas and chronology of hominid-bearing sediments east of Lake Rudolf, Kenya. *Nature* 239: 379-85.

2. TECTONIC AND STRATIGRAPHIC FRAMEWORK

F. J. Fitch and C. F. Vondra

Present-day Lake Rudolf (240 km long, 50 km wide) is an impressive accumulation of alkaline lake waters within a basin of inland drainage situated on the Kenya-Ethiopian border in East Africa (fig. 1). In the past the lake was much larger, and at times it has acted as a reservoir for the headwaters of the Nile. The lake lies within the Turkana depression, a complex faulted structural basin lying between the large Ethiopian and Kenyan domical upwarps of the African continental basement. The tectonic and volcanologic interest of the area is considerably enhanced by this intermediate position. Extending southward from a triple junction in the region of the Afar depression, the faults of the main Eastern Rift System can be traced across the two major domical swells. They are linked through the Turkana depression by a young rift and swell structure running across the southern end of Lake Rudolf toward Lake Stefanie. The East African Rift valleys are believed to indicate zones of crustal thinning and incipient plate disruption. There are, however, great contrasts in tectonic, volcanic, and sedimentological history between the central rift areas of the two major domical upwarps and the intervening Turkana depression. These contrasts, which are becoming clear from current work, may be of vital importance to interpretation of large-scale tectonic features.

The initiation of the present tectonic regime is represented by "end-Cretaceous uplifts" (400 m in central Kenya) and by early Tertiary flood basalt and ignimbrite volcanism in Ethiopia. Further arching of the major domes and related subsidence of the intervening areas occurred in the Miocene and was accompanied by a great extension of volcanism.

The Turkana depression first became a distinct feature at this time, and a thick sequence of basic and acid volcanics with interbedded fluvial and lacustrine sediments accumulated in a shallow faulted structural basin. In early Pliocene times major submeridional faulting extended across the floor of this shallow infilled structural depression, dividing it into a number of major west-tilted warped structural blocks or half-grabens. Intermittent volcanism and continental outwash and fluvial and lacustrine sedimentation have continued in the various sub-basins of the Turkana depression until the present. The combined effects of minor earth movements, climatic variations, and volcanism have resulted in numerous local unconformities, nonsequences, and facies changes within the stratigraphic record. The last major episodes of earth movement occurred in the early to mid-Pleistocene with the extension of the main Eastern Rift of Kenya northward through the Kino Sogo fault zone to join with the southern extension of the Ethiopian Rift south of Lake Stefanie. A local swell structure accompanies this connecting link between the two main sections of the

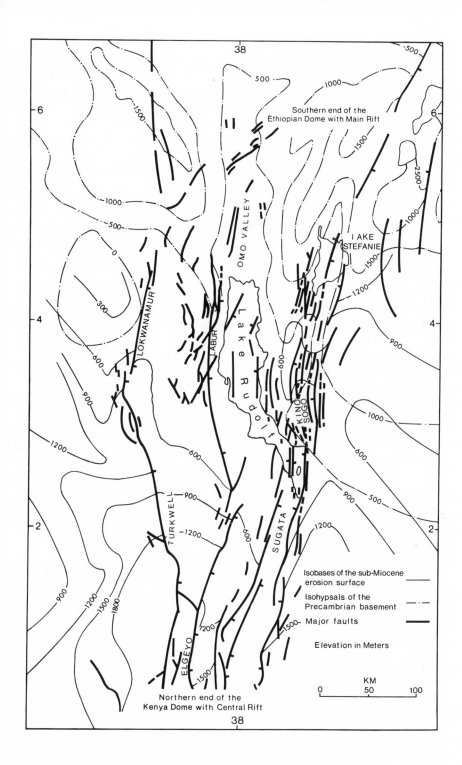

Figure 1. The greater Rudolf basin and its geologic structure

Eastern Rift system and is obviously related to the massive "end-Tertiary" uplifts of the major domes (1,500 m in central Kenya). The area continues to be tectonically and volcanically active.

Plio-Pleistocene deposits occur today in discontinuous pockets around the margins of the lake, attesting to a much larger body of water and variations in climates and tectonic activity. Preliminary studies of the stratigraphy of these sediments are under way in the Omo, East Rudolf, Lothagam, and Kanapoi areas, but almost nothing is known of the sediments in intervening areas.

The Omo area, situated to the north of the present northern shore of Lake Rudolf and along the rapidly subsiding axis of the Rudolf half-graben, was occupied by the lake during much of the Pliocene and Pleistocene. A large river flowing from north to south formed a broad alluvial plain and delta complex as it emptied into the lake. Over 950 m of interbedded lacustrine, deltaic, fluvial, and fluviodeltaic sediments accumulated (Butzer 1971; de Heinzelin, Brown, and Howell 1970).

The East Rudolf area in the northeastern sector of the Rudolf basin was occupied by a large embayment of the lake during essentially the same time. This was situated on the gently subsiding westward tilted eastern block of the Rudolf half-graben. At least two stream systems entered the embayment from the east, helping to form an interfingering and intercalated sequence of 325 m of fluvial, deltaic, transitional lacustrine, and lacustrine sediments.

Sediments accumulating on the margin of this basin were predominantly fluvial, with lacustrine or transitional lacustrine tongues extending eastward and thus documenting periodic lacustrine transgressions. The sediments coarsen vertically as well as laterally, indicating delta growth, lacustrine regression, and gradual infilling of the embayment (Bowen and Vondra 1973).

In the Lothagam area west of the lake, more than 700 m of dominantly fluvial sediments interbedded with lacustrine tongues has been recorded. This indicates local variations in source area and rates of sedimentation and records periodic uplift of local horst blocks and rapid subsidence of adjoining basins (Dennis Powers, pers. comm. 1973). A thin 70 m sequence of fluvial and lacustrine sediments occurs to the southwest of the present lake at Kanapoi.

Newly discovered sediments extending northward from Kanapoi to near Lothagam, sediments known farther north on the western lake margin, and sediments extending from Pori to Moti across the lake along its eastern shore have received only cursory examination. These may prove to be as fossiliferous as those in the other areas mentioned. If so they will undoubtedly be the focal point of future studies.

References

Baker, B. H.; Mohr, P. A.; and Williams, L. A. J. 1973. Geology of the East Rift System of Africa. *Geol. Soc. A., Spec. Paper,* no. 136.

Baker, B. H., and Wohlenberg, J. 1971. Structure and evolution of the Kenya Rift valley. *Nature* 229: 538-42.

Bowen, B. E., and Vondra, C. F. 1973. Stratigraphical relationships of the Plio-Pleistocene deposits, East Rudolf, Kenya. *Nature* 242: 391-93.

Butzer, K. W. 1971. Recent history of an Ethiopian delta. University of Chicago Department of Geography Research Paper 136: 1-184.

Dodson, R. G. 1963. Geology of the South Horr area. Geological Survey of Kenya, Report no. 60.

Gill, R. L. O. 1974. African swells, magmatism and plate tectonics. *Nature* 247: 25-26.

Heinzelin, J. de; Brown, F. H.; and Howell, F. C. 1970. Pliocene/Pleistocene formations in the lower Omo basin, southern Ethiopia. *Quaternaria* 13: 247-68.

Mohr, P. A. 1967. Major volcano-tectonic lineament in the Ethiopian rift system. *Nature* 213: 664-65.

Walsh, J., and Dodson, R. G. 1969. Geology of northern Turkana. Geological Survey of Kenya, Report no. 82.

3. THE MURSI, NKALABONG, AND KIBISH FORMATIONS,
LOWER OMO BASIN, ETHIOPIA
K. W. Butzer

Although the Plio-Pleistocene Shungura and Usno formations have provided the great
bulk of fossils recovered in the lower Omo basin, the fossil record is significantly com-
plemented both by the Yellow Sands fauna of the older Mursi Formation and by the early
sapiens hominids of the younger Kibish Formation. It is equally pertinent that the shorter
sedimentary sequences of the basin margins not only extend the stratigraphy from 770 to
1,160 m but provide different perspectives on regional depositional environments than do
sequences from the center of the basin. The purpose of this paper is to summarize the
available information from the Ethiopian peripheries of the lower Omo basin. A comprehensive monograph presenting the mapping, key profiles, and laboratory analyses is in preparation.

Since the history of exploration of the basin, its regional environment, the geological setting, and the contemporary delta landscapes have all been discussed at some length
in a previous publication (Butzer 1971*c*), no further introduction is offered here. However,
it should be noted that the sediment interpretations are based on extensive laboratory
studies and on a reasonably good personal knowledge of the modern Omo delta.

The Mursi Formation

The oldest sedimentary sequence known from the lower Omo basin is exposed under an
extensive basalt, southwest of the Nkalabong range, at elevations of 400 to 560 m (see
figs. 1-4). Defined as the Mursi Formation by Butzer and Thurber (1969; Butzer 1971*a*),
after the local tribe of that name, the type area of Yellow Sands (5° 24'N, 35° 57'E) lies
85 km north of the present shores of Lake Rudolf. The Mursi Beds were first recognized as
a sedimentary unit by the Kenyan Omo Expedition of 1967, which collected fossils in the
type area but did not carry out a geological examination. In 1968, assisted by Claudia
Carr, I studied the sequence in detail, mapping the type are at 1:10,500. I carried out
further field checks in 1969, at which time G. Eck and Y. Coppens collected more fossils.

The base of the Mursi Formation is not exposed, although it presumably rests on Mio-
Pliocene extrusives. It is represented by 143 m of deltaic and fluviolittoral deposits
that have potential counterparts in the modern Omo delta sensu lato. Whole rock samples
of the overlying basalt have yielded K-Ar dates of 4.4, 4.0, and 4.05 m.y. (Brown and Nash,
this symposium; Fitch and Miller, this symposium),suggesting eruption of the lavas ca.
4.18 m.y.

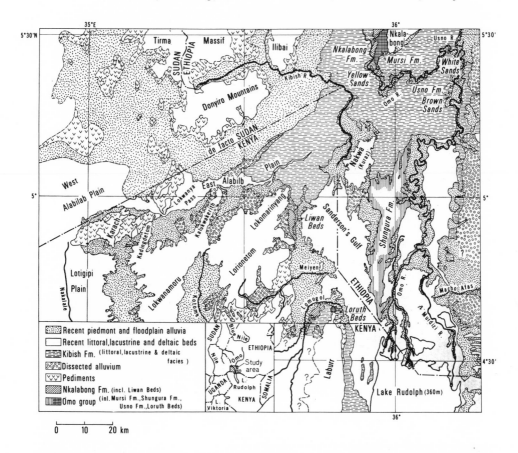

Figure 1. Surficial geology of the lower Omo basin, simplified from a 1:10,000 map (1968-69). (After Butzer 1971*a*, fig. 1.)

The deposits of Member I (over 43 m, 4 beds) are unusually sandy for typical deltaic sediments in the Omo delta, and individual lenses are far too extensive to represent mixed-grade channel beds. An alternation of massive-bedded, vertically structured units, including gypsum or sodium salts, with laminated or thin-bedded strata is also noteworthy. Each unit is intensively gleyed or ferruginized, with several horizons of carbonate or ferruginous cementation. Except for the steep foresets of unit Id, bedding was originally horizontal and inclined in a southwesterly direction. All together this suggests a broad fluviolacustrine environment of deposition, in which extensive fans from the Nkalabong piedmont contributed sands laterally to a delta-fringe environment of the Omo River. In this way suspended and bed-load sediments were mixed along a broad contact zone. Concretionary bands probably record intervals of partial emergence, and foreset complex of unit Id suggests the advancing core of a major tributary delta fan. The capping, fossiliferous crust implies partial emergence, possibly as a result of progradation, and the bone fragments speak for fluvial transport.

Member II (24 m, 6 beds) begins with extensive but thin beds of clayey silts and silty clays (IIa, IIb) suggesting a lacustrine environment and lake transgression. With unit IIc, conditions analogous to those coeval with Member I returned, namely, mixed fluviolacustrine sedimentation in fan proximity. Unit IId is similar, but the lenticular alluvial components

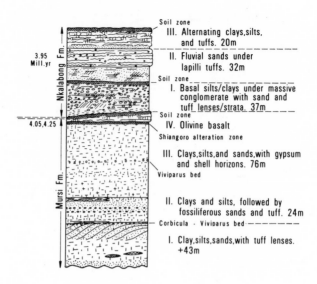

Figure 2. Generalized stratigraphic column of the Mursi and Nkalabong formation. (After Butzer 1971a, fig. 4.)

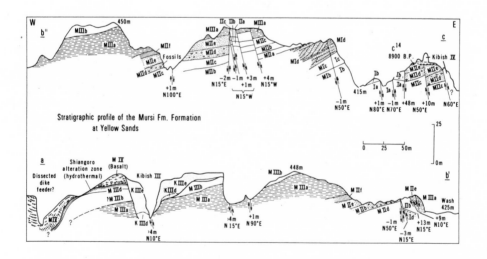

Figure 3. Stratigraphic profile of the Mursi Formation at Yellow Sands. Late Pleistocene-Holocene units of the Kibish Formation are shown in gray. (After Butzer 1971a, fig. 3.)

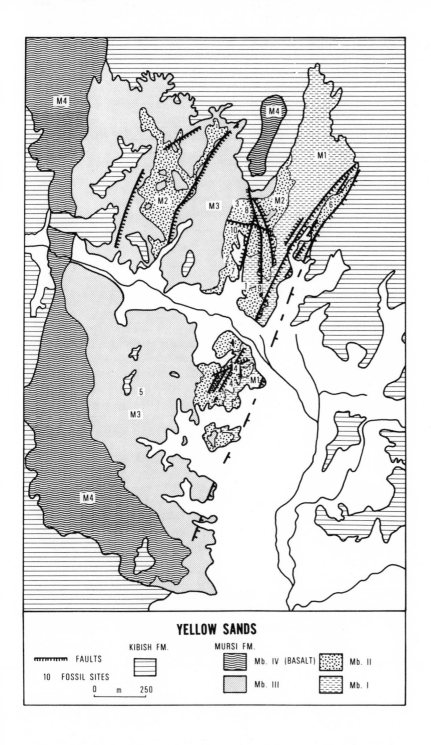

Figure 4. Surficial geology of Yellow Sands, 1968-69

are conspicuous, and the gravels thicken northeastward along the Nkalabong piedmont. Some 6.5 km NNE of Yellow Sands, at an elevation now 90 m higher, the IId gravels are 1 m thick, resting on some 20 m of grayish, yellowish, and reddish silty clays that are interbedded with conglomeratic horizons and terminate in a buried vertisol; the IId gravels are over-lain by 4.5 m of white and pale brown clayey silts and interbedded tuffs (IIe, IIf) and by a further 50 m suite corresponding closely to Member III and capped by the Mursi basalt. In other words, Members II and III can be traced laterally, with appropriate facies changes, to the foot of the Nkalabong range. Not surprisingly, the IId gravels here are much coarser, subrounded and heterogeneous in terms of rolling: a dominance of sliding motions is indicated. Consequently, the best facies analogues for the Yellow Sands fossil strata can be obtained from the mixed littoral-alluvial environment at the southeastern periphery of the modern Omo delta (see Butzer 1971c, pp. 85-86). The paleogeographical situation is also remarkably similar, with a zone of fluviolittoral interplay between piedmont alluvia to the east and north and a former Omo delta somewhere to the west. Units IIe and IIf in-dicate a new transgression with sedimentation in low-energy, relatively shallow waters. The key tuff (IIf) becomes tripartite on the Nkalabong piedmont and is everywhere sandy and moderately well sorted, suggesting direct air fall over open waters. In view of the pre-vailing winds (Butzer 1971c, pp. 29-34, 161-67) this speaks for a southeasterly origin, possibly from the Stefanie area. The origin of earlier tuffaceous units is much less con-clusive, as they are either greatly altered or reworked or both.

Member III (76 m, 6 beds) contrasts with earlier units in that massive, subhorizontal, deltaic clays are far more conspicuous. The basal bed is of this type, with abundant sodium salts and gypsum laminae or lenticles, suggesting interdistributary environments. Thereafter clays alternate with silts or sands, suggesting repeated shifts between the delta fringe and a mixed littoral-alluvial environment. Concretionary bands are found within the coarser units and in part coincide with shell horizons. These low-energy littoral-foreshore deposits in part suggest temporary emergence and agree with interpreta-tion of a *Viviparus* bed by "a calm body of water with abundant plant growth" (Van Damme and Gautier 1972, p. 27). Some of the terminal beds underlying the basalt flow include sizable proportions of fresh volcanic feldspar, probably sanidine (F. H. Brown, pers. comm.), that have been transported only short distances and may herald the subsequent eruption of the Mursi basalt.

Altogether the Mursi Formation differs fundamentally from the interpretation offered for the Shungura Formation by Brown, de Heinzelin, and Howell (1969) and de Heinzelin (1971). The Mursi sequence does not show cyclic-fluvial patterning. More significantly, lateral fluviolacustrine components are prominent in the Mursi Formation much as they are in East Rudolf, and, in my opinion, in the basal units of the Shungura Formation and in the Usno Formation. In particular, the gravel inclusions of the Usno "gravel sands sequence" at White Sands (de Heinzelin and Brown 1969) are primarily subangular to subrounded, and some of the sands can be described as subarkosic. A 128-specimen gravel count I made in 1967 consisted of 44% meso- and macrocrystalline quartz, 49% granite, "granitoid quartz" and pegmatite, and 7% granite-gneiss; in the eight 5-mm grade classes from 20-60 mm I used, the quartz maximum was in 31-35 mm, granite in 21-25 mm, and gneiss in 26-30mm. I feel that this does not suggest a floodplain (cf. de Heinzelin and Brown 1969, p. 45) so much as a piedmont alluvial fan derived from Basement Complex outcrops farther to the east and interfingering with a low wave-energy littoral environment.

The Mursi Formation was faulted at some point after extrusion of the terminal basalt member (typically 3-5 m thick) and its related dike feeders. A vector diagram for Yellow

Sands shows that the primary fault system strikes N50-60°E, with most of the faults normal and the eastern sides of the blocks downthrown. Maximum vertical throws exceed 58 m (see figs. 3-4) and, depending on the nature of the Mursi-Kibish interformational contact, may exceed 120 m. The minor fault systems (N15°W-15°E and N80°-100°E) have displacements of 5-17 m and 1-2 m respectively. Typical dips of initially subhorizontal Mursi strata are 4°-10° at Yellow Sands, increasing to 5°-15° farther north and 18°-25° at the southwestern terminus of the Nkalabong range; corresponding fault-plane angles decrease from 60°-90° at Yellow Sands to 36°-42° in the piedmont, and north-south fault trends become primary.

The Nkalabong Formation

The oldest undeformed beds of the lower Omo basin are exposed west of the Nkalabong range, primarily east of the Omo River at latitudes 5°23'-5°35'N (figs. 1-2, 5). Absolute elevation ranges from 405 to 475 m. The beds were defined as the Nkalabong Formation by Butzer and Thurber (1969; Butzer 1971a) after the mountain range of that name. The type sections are located in Neusi Korongo (5°25'54"N, 35°36'11"E), an area I first studied in 1968 and geologically mapped at 1:10,500 .

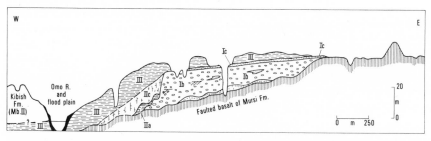

Figure 5. Generalized stratigraphic profile of the Nkalabong Formation at Neusi Korongo. (After Butzer 1971a, fig. 5.)

The base is formed by faulted, weathered, and eroded basalts of the Mursi Formation. Insofar as it can be reconstructed, the original land surface provided by the Mursi basalt seems to have been corrugated and step faulted, with individual segments dipping 3° to the west and northwest. The intact lava is primarily massive and prone to core weathering, with ropy interbeds. Zeolitic weathering is common, and the topmost 1.5 m forms a truncated (B)C horizon that preserves original rock structure despite intensive alteration. Several degrees of decomposition are apparent: (1) Hematite-discolored, mottled dusky red and dark gray zeolitic basalt, with zeolites intact but commonly coated with oxide rinds; (2) gray basaltic matrix with altered, pale yellow clayey zeolites; and (3) friable, pale yellow basalt with empty zeolitic hollows. The original solum was stripped by denudation, and channel cutting provided local surface slopes of 1°-10° and local relief of 18 m.

The late Pliocene Nkalabong Formation represents 88 m of fluvial, eolian, and lacustrine beds that generally fall outside the range of facies variation of the modern Omo delta.

Member I (37 m, 2 beds) records a succession from flood silts through bed-load deposits of an early Omo River to terminal units of tuffs and sands rich in volcanic ash. The coarse channel beds consist primarily of intensively gleyed conglomerates, interbedded with sands that interfinger laterally from local tributaries. Calcretion of the terminal unit may reflect on subaerial weathering, hydrothermal activity in the wake of local volcanism, or both. This floodplain sequence was followed by intensive dissection.

Member II (32.5 m, 3 beds) currently known from only one korongo, represents the filling of a tributary canyon that once drained the adjacent foothills. Basal sands of fluvial
origin were weathered and dissected before they were buried by a massive, unbedded lapilli
tuff of eolian origin, without reworking except for the lowest 50 cm.

Member III (18 m at the type section, 11 beds) is still different. A long succession
of alternating massive-bedded and laminated silts rests upon basal detrital strata with
derived lapilli tuff (IIc). Despite their consolidation, weathering--both 14 angstrom
units nonexpandable and 15-16.5 angstrom units expandable clays, (F. H. Brown, pers. comm.)
--and hydromorphic or terrestrial paleosols, these beds have a structure of more or less
primary tuffs interbedded with tuff derivatives and very rare lenses of spheroidal pumice
(<1 cm diameter). The disposition and regularity of these strata over a wide area, dipping
5° away from the foothills and thickening rapidly from 5-10 m to at least 22 m, appear to
argue for ash falls in a littoral-foreshore setting. All the beds are white or light gray,
with limited limonitic mottling but frequent pyrolusite discoloration; some horizons have
carbonate concretions. These additional features are possibly but by no means necessarily
explained by a former reducing environment. Cementation of the topmost bed, with some
carbonate concretions, reflects subsequent emergence. This noncyclic lacustrine-littoral
succession may reflect on repeated vulcanicity.

At Liwan (fig. 1) a sequence of detrital beds, overlain by at least 17 m of massive
white tuffs and interbedded, laminated, clayey strata, provides a close facies parallel to
Member III. These Liwan Beds, like the topmost Nkalabong sequence, are not faulted and
are found at an identical elevation over 50 km away, suggesting little or no differential
vertical displacement. They also dip to the center of the basin. In terms of facies,
Nkalabong III and the Liwan Beds appear to be linked to the Omo Group by lithologically
intermediate but faulted sediments near Loruth Kaado (see Butzer 1971a; De Heinzelin 1971),
north of the Labur range. It is therefore apparent that the upper, littoral sequence of
the Nkalabong Formation was once widely developed along the northern and western margins
of the Omo basin, marking the greatest expansion of Lake Rudolf, shortly after 3.9 m.y.

Since the basal Shungura Formation is believed to be fluvial (de Heinzelin 1971), the
entire Shungura Formation must postdate the regression of Lake Rudolf from Nkalabong III-
age shorelines along the Lokomarinyang and Nkalabong piedmonts. Thus there is no temporal
overlap between the Nkalabong and Shungura formations.

There is no evidence for postdepositional deformation of any Nkalabong Beds other
than a gentle tilting of the Nkalabong footslope region. The various episodes of faulting
which affected the Shungura and Loruth Kaado Formations were restricted to the east of a
line from Labur to Nakwa and thence to the eastern face of Nkalabong. They must be distinctly younger than the faulting of the Mursi Formation.

The Kibish Formation

Late Middle Pleistocene to mid-Holocene time in the Omo basin is adequately recorded
by the widespread littoral, deltaic, and fluvial beds of the tectonically undisturbed
Kibish Formation (figs. 1 and 6). Preliminary stratigraphic observations on these strata
were made by F. H. Brown and by R. E. F. Leakey in 1967, before I did a systematic study in
1967-69. The formation was defined by Butzer and Thurber (1969; Butzer 1969) and named
after the police posts of that name (at 5°19'N, 35°53'E). An interim report on the stratigraphy was provided by Butzer, Brown, and Thurber (1969), and a discussion of the

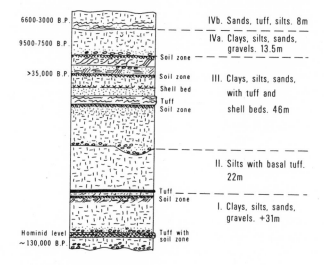

Figure 6. Generalized stratigraphic column of the Kibish Formation

depositional environments is given in Butzer (1970*a*). Finally, the correspondence of the
Holocene lake level fluctuations with those of other East African lakes has been discussed
by Butzer, Isaac, et al. (1972).

Member I has a cumulative thickness of at least 26 m with 7 beds. A single Th/U date
of 130,000 years tentatively suggests a late Middle Pleistocene age for a lake level that
was about 60 m higher than the present Lake Rudolf. Member I, which locally rests on the
strongly dissected Nkalabong Formation, records at least one complex transgressive-
regressive cycle (17 m of deposits in the Rhino Canyon-Kenya Camp type area), progressing
from channel sands and silts to delta-fringe beds (alternating clays and silts), terminating
with a calcareous paleosol. The basal beds (9 m), base unseen, probably mark a second but
incomplete cycle. They include channel conglomerates, subaqueous clays, and tuffs of complex origin, followed by emergence, calcification, and dissection.

Following at least 19 m of dissection by the Omo River in the type area, Member II
(22.5 m cumulative thickness, 2 beds) began with a tuff that mantled a highly irregular,
dissected delta plain. Frequent detrital components indicate colluvial working on slopes
(up to 20°), and gypsum laminae in depressions indicate subaqueous deposition near the
shores of the lake (interdistributary bays?). The following 22 m of laterally extensive
clay with silty interbeds and ferruginous horizons, or zones of carbonate and ferric concretions, indicates a delta-fringe environment, prone to shifts in the position of adjacent
distributaries and in the depth of standing water. This early Upper Pleistocene sequence
is, then, noncyclic in the sense of Brown, de Heinzelin, and Howell (1970). There is only
limited evidence of reduction.

At least 25 m of dissection preceded accumulation of Member III in the type area,
where a minimum ^{14}C date of greater than 37,000 years was obtained for the youngest beds.
Cumulative thickness is 45.4 m, subdivided into 12 beds. Two transgressive-regressive
cycles are recorded, each cresting with +60-70 m lake levels, separated by emergence and
a paleosol. The first 26.5 m of deposits range from distributary-channel beds up to
laterally extensive delta-fringe clays (interdistributary?) with silty units (channel or
channel-mouth shoals?). A terminal period of emergence is indicated by calcium carbonate

concretions and crack fillings, before deposition of a widespread tuff 2-3.5 m thick. This particular tuff, a well-sorted and fairly pure silt, is uniform and level over a stretch of 3.5 km across the modern valley and is certainly subaqueous. After a period of dissection, the second cycle (20 m) begins with thin but extensive sands or shell beds, with root drip, that suggest littoral-foreshore (and fluvial?) environments. Subsequent delta-fringe clays are followed by current-bedded channel or littoral sands and, finally, by massive, inclined clays related to channel/levee contacts.

The youngest Kibish Beds follow upon a long interval ca. 35,000-9500 B.P., during which Lake Rudolf must have been relatively low, and from which no contemporaneous deltaic or littoral sediments are preserved. Omo River dissection in the type area exceeded 15 m. Members IVa and IVb have cumulative thicknesses of 13 and 8 m respectively, preserve con-siderable surface morphology, are well exposed, and currently have 15 ^{14}C determinations. The initial transgressive sediments of Member IVa have not been identified, but the maximum level was attained by 9,500 years ago and the lake level fluctuated between about +60 and +80 m until a little after 7500 B.P., when Lake Rudolf shrank to about its present dimen-sions and the Omo River cut down its bed by 30 m. Member IVb records a transgression of Lake Rudolf that began shortly before 6600 B.P. and reached a high level of +65 to +70 m about 6200 B.P. This level was maintained until after 4400 B.P., then was followed by a temporary regression of unknown amplitude and a final transgression to +70 m a little before 3000 B.P. Lake Rudolf also has been relatively low since about 3000 B.P., with the level fluctuating rapidly within a range of over 40 m, and dropping from +15 to -5 m between 1897 and 1955 (Butzer 1971c).

Beach ridges, cuspate bars, and other shoreline features at +65 to +70 m indicate an interconnection between Lake Rudolf and the vast Lotigipi mud flats to the west through a low-level, swampy divide. The expanded lake must have periodically overflowed to the Lotigipi for much of the time about 6200 to 3250 B.P., with the threshold elevation essen-tially determining the maximum lake level. Temporary maxima near or above +80 m about 9500 to 7500 B.P. probably induced overflow across the flat watershed to the Pibor-Sobat River and ultimately to the Nile.

All of the Kibish mollusks described by Van Damme and Gautier (1972) derive from Member IV, and there are no stratigraphic grounds for distinguishing two faunal stages, since the microfaulted type site of their A1 assemblage has a ^{14}C date of 9300 B.P. nearby (Butzer 1972).

To overview, the Kibish Formation can be adequately interpreted in terms of contempo-rary depositional environments in the Omo delta. There are indeed some littoral and flood-plain deposits, but most of the sediments reflect a deltaic (sensu lato) environment. The delta-fringe deposits--including many fluvial beds of distributary origin--are best repre-sented and are certainly far better preserved than the littoral deposits so prominent in the surface expression of Member IVb.

Mountain Paleosols, Pediments, and Piedmont Alluvia

A great part of the 3.6 m.y. sedimentary hiatus between the Nkalabong and Kibish for-mations is spanned by the Shungura and Usno formations in the center of the lower Omo basin. The question remains to what extent the peripheries of the basin (see Butzer 1970b) provide independent evidence that may complement that of the dissected deltaic-lacustrine plains.

Most complete is the record east of Lorienatom, where the following sequence of devel-opment can be delineated for the Liwan piedmont and the Karenga valley entrant. The base is formed by an extensive piedmont surface cut across warped, late Tertiary basalts:

(*a*) 1.5 m. Accumulation of brown claystones, interbedded with subangular, coarse-grade conglomerates, filling in topographic irregularities and derived from reddish, argillic paleosol.

(*b*) 6 m. Aggradation of weakly stratified, nonhomogeneous reddish clay with basalt grit, sandy interbeds, and concentrations or lenses of coarse, subangular gravel. Inclined 3° to east and conformable with overlying tuffs.

(*c*) 17 m. Aggradation of stratified to laminated white tuffs with interbedded clays of tuff derivation and rare lenticles of sandstone or fine conglomerate. Lacustrine Liwan Beds (Nkalabong Member III, indicating apparent lake level of 450 m).

(*d*) Emergence may have been followed by pedogenesis of a reddish soil, implied by subsequent aggradation of 2 m pink to reddish or yellow silts and silty, gritty sandstones. These include tuff derivatives and suggest sheet and slope wash.

(*e*) Extensive denudation of surface, with at least 10 m stream downcutting.

(*f*) Aggradation of +30 m piedmont surface with more than 20 m of coarse to cobble-grade gravel with a brown, sandy matrix.

(*g*) Denudation of surface, with at least 20 m stream downcutting.

(*h*) Aggradation of +20 m piedmont surface (like *f*), contemporary with or followed by development of gravelly beach ridge at 460 m (Kibish Member III?).

(*i*) Development of a now degraded brown paleosol on both the piedmont alluvial fans (*f*) and (*h*). Original profile depth was 2.5-4.0 m, with strong brown (7.5YR 5/6) loams or clay loams in the B-horizon; parent material was basalt, rhyolite, and chert gravel in a matrix of quartz and ferromagnesian sands (coeval with Kibish Member III?).

(*j*) Denudation and mechanical eluviation of soil clays, with at least 20 m stream downcutting.

(*k*) Secondary calcification of the previous paleosol, with formation of a 5-cm Ca-horizon at -25 to -30 cm depth within the former B-horizon. The partly decomposed pebbles in the top 30 cm of such profiles were often split in situ by salt hydration, and surface lag is normally patinated.

(*l*) Aggradation of at least 7.5 m of fluvial and lacustrine beds, both horizontal and inclined, ranging from coarse to cobble-grade gravels to sands and silts, commonly limonitic, with abundant aquatic shells dominated by *Melanoides*. Lake level 425 m, equivalent to Kibish Member IV, grades upstream into fine-grained +12 m valley floor terrace.

(*m*) At least 8 m stream downcutting.

(*n*) Aggradation of fine-grained +3-3 m valley floor terrace.

(*o*) At least 4 m stream downcutting; development of modern noncalcic brown soil begins.

(*p*) Modern alluviation of gravelly alluvium, including small lateral fans. Pedogenesis continues.

The brown paleosols must record periods of longer or more intensive chemical weathering, since they contrast strongly with the zonal soil profiles found at lower elevations (below 1,500 m) today. At least two generations are indicated east of Lorienatom. However, the geomorphologic and pedogenetic record (Butzer 1970*b*) of the piedmont environments suggests that late Cenozoic climate has generally tended to be dry. The geomorphologic record indicates alternating pediment-cutting, aggradation of coarse alluvial spreads (by higher-competence rills and streams), and fill-dissection (by lower-competence watercourses). The equally variable pedogenetic record suggests contrasting trends such as rubefaction with intensive pedogenesis; noncalcic grassland soil formation; secondary calcification; salt-weathering; and patination. This suggests that ecological conditions have at different times been subhumid, semiarid, or arid.

General Interpretation

The geological records reviewed here provide two categories of evidence:

1. Transgressions and regressions of Lake Rudolf, as directly inferred from related lacustrine or littoral deposits or indirectly from deltaic or alluvial formations of the Omo River.

2. Piedmont or montaine phenomena, including alluvial fans and terraces, pediments, and paleosols.

The first type of evidence, which reflects on regional conditions over the entire drainage system (see Butzer 1971*c*, chap. 5), accounts for the great bulk of the Plio-Pleistocene record. The second category permits deductions about the more immediate, non-riverine setting but unfortunately is poorly represented in the predominantly deltaic sedimentary sequences of the basin floor.

Although the Rudolf-Omo drainage system has no outlet today, there is a low-level divide (at about 450 m elevation) to the west, beyond which lie a series of extensive mud flats that form the watershed to the Pibor-Sobat, a Nile tributary. The topography, the disposition and elevation of the various sedimentary formations, and the mollusks, fishes, and reptiles of the Rudolf-Omo system from the earliest times all indicate intermittent hydrographic links to the Nile system. Each of the formations culminates in 450-460 m elevations, that is, at the level of the Rudolf-Nile threshold, indicating that potential overflow across the divide set an upper terminus for littoral and deltaic sedimentation in the lower Omo basin.

The Plio-Pleistocene record indicates that the Omo River mouth was situated 90-120 km north of the present delta fringe (fig. 1) during the deposition of the Mursi Formation (Members I-III) and the later Nkalabong units (Member III, Liwan Beds). The present eleva-tion of these deposits supports the inference that almost the entire basin floor formed an extension of Lake Rudolf and that some kind of overflow to the Nile system existed. Regional climate must have been moister, although the alluvial sands injected into the Mursi sediments are more compatible with an adjacent piedmont alluvium and a semiarid climate. The terminal Nkalabong facies, marking the highest late Cenozoic transgression of Lake Rudolf (ca. 3.9 m.y.), is uniquely free of sandy wash from the adjacent uplands and may indicate a lack of torrential runoff because of an effective vegetation mat. The dissection of the Omo River before and after deposition of Nkalabong Member I (channel gravels and flood silts) indicates long-term lake regressions and presumably a drier climate, although the coarse conglomerates in Member I (ca. 4.0 m.y.) suggest a higher-competence stream. By contrast, present interpretation of the Shungura (Members A through F) and Usno formations suggests that the Omo delta was situated less than 50 km north of its present position, and the lake level may have been intermediate between that of today and that during Mursi times. The terminal Shungura units indicate a higher lake level, possibly at the overflow threshold to the Nile drainage, and may therefore again imply a moister climate. The various intra-zonal paleosols recorded within the Shungura and Usno formations (Brown et al. 1970) permit no paleoclimatic inferences, although the deep weathering evident after faulting of the

Mursi basalt does suggest a relatively moist climate at some time before aggradation of the first Nkalabong units. Unfortunately, no intact zonal soil profiles are preserved.

These apparent climatic changes may have been in part obscured or even simulated by tectonic deformation. It would be unrealistic to assume that modern elevations are meaningful for faulted strata, and other deformations have almost certainly affected the depth of the Rudolf trough and the relative level of the Rudolf-Nile divide. Thus, except for the Kibish Formation, no unequivocal paleoclimatic conclusions can be drawn from the geological evidence, although the broad inferences tentatively suggested above do seem to have some validity. Considering the rapid and significant recent changes in the level of Lake Rudolf (Butzer 1971c), the Plio-Pleistocene transgressions and regressions--as inferred from the horizontal delta displacements--do not necessarily imply *major* climatic changes. To all intents, the geology and geomorphology suggest that a semiarid climate has been characteristic throughout the late Cenozoic.

References

Brown, F. H. 1972. Radiometric dating of sedimentary formations in the lower Omo valley, Ethiopia. In *Calibration of hominoid evolution*, ed. W. W. Bishop and J. A. Miller, pp. 273-88. Edinburgh: Scottish Academic Press; Toronto: University of Toronto Press.

Brown, F. H., Heinzelin, J. de; and Howell, F. C. 1970. Pliocene/Pleistocene formations in the lower Omo basin, southern Ethiopia. *Quaternaria* 13:247-68.

Butzer, K. W. 1969. Geological interpretation of two Pleistocene hominid sites in the lower Omo basin. *Nature* 222:1133-35.

_____. 1970a. Contemporary depositional environments of the Omo Delta. *Nature* 226: 425-30.

_____. 1970b. Geomorphological observations in the lower Omo basin, southwestern Ethiopia. Carl Troll Festschrift, *Colloq. Geograph.* 12:177-92.

_____. 1971a. The lower Omo basin: Geology, fauna and hominids of the Plio-Pleistocene formations. *Naturwissenschaften* 58:7-16.

_____. 1971b. *Environment and archeology: An ecological approach to prehistory.* Chicago: Aldine.

_____. 1971c. Recent history of an Ethiopian delta: The Omo River and the level of Lake Rudolf. University of Chicago Dept. of Geography, Research Paper no. 136.

_____. 1972. Molluscan assemblages from the late Cenozoic of the lower Omo basin, Ethiopia: Comments. *Quat. Res.* 2:591.

Butzer, K. W.; Brown, F. H.; and Thurber, D. L. 1969. Horizontal sediments of the lower Omo valley: The Kibish Formation. *Quaternaria* 11:15-30.

Butzer, K. W.; Isaac, G. L; Richardson, R. L.; and Washbourn-Kamau, C. 1972. Radiocarbon dating of East African lake levels. *Science* 175:1069-76.

Butzer, K. W., and Thurber, D. L. 1969. Some late Cenozoic sedimentary formations of the lower Omo basin. *Nature* 222:1138-43.

Fitch, F. J., and Miller, J. A. 1969. Age determinations on feldspar from the lower Omo basin. *Nature* 222:1143.

Heinzelin, J. de. 1971. Observations sur la formation de Shungura (Vallée de l'Omo, Ethiopie). *C. R. Acad. Sci. (Paris)*, ser. D, 272:2409-11.

Heinzelin, J. de, and Brown, F. H. 1969. Some early Pleistocene deposits of the lower Omo valley: The Usno Formation. *Quaternaria* 11:31-46.

Van Damme, D., and Gautier, A. 1972. Molluscan assemblages from the late Cenozoic of the lower Omo basin, Ethiopia. *Quat. Res.* 2:25-37.

4. PLIO-PLEISTOCENE FORMATIONS OF THE LOWER OMO BASIN WITH PARTICULAR REFERENCE TO THE SHUNGURA FORMATION

J. de Heinzelin and P. Haesaerts, with
the assistance of F. C. Howell

The lower Omo basin was first visited by European explorers (Count Samuel Teleki von Szék and Ludwig Ritter von Höhnel) in 1888, after their discovery of Lake Rudolf (R. von Höhnel et al 1891; L. von Höhnel 1938). In 1896 Maurizio Sacchi, geographer with the ill-starred (second) Bòttego Expedition (Vannutelli and Citerni 1897, 1899; cf. Sclater 1899), was the first to note the existence there of flat-lying, undeformed sediments with fresh-water mollusks exposed to the north of the Omo delta. He lost his life in southern Ethiopia the next year, but his collections were subsequently studied and published by de Angelis d'Ossat and Millosevich (1900). These deposits have recently been investigated by the Omo Research Expedition (Butzer, Brown, and Thurber, 1969; Butzer and Thurber 1969) and defined as the Kibish Formation (Butzer, this symposium) of later Pleistocene to Holocene age.

Emil Brumpt, naturalist with the Bourg de Bozas Expedition (Bourg de Bozas 1903; 1906) was the first (in 1902) to recover vertebrate fossils from older, tectonically disturbed deposits underlying these largely horizontal sediments. Their importance for the study of the Cenozoic of sub-Saharan Africa, then practically unknown, was first noted by Haug (1912, p. 1727), who recorded the occurrence of silurid fish, crocodilians (2 species), chelonians, a hipparionine, rhinoceros, hippopotamus, a suid, various bovids, and deinothere and elephant. Subsequently the remains of the aquatic reptile *Euthecodon* (=*Tomistoma*) *brumpti* (Joleaud 1920*b*, 1930; Boulenger 1920), a deinothere and *Elephas* (Joleaud 1928), hippopotamus (Joleaud 1920*a*), and a hipparionine and *Equus* (Joleaud 1933) were described from Brumpt's collections, deposited at the Muséum national d'histoire naturelle, Paris.

The first geological reconnaissance and extensive paleontological prospection of these older fossiliferous deposits was made by the late Camille Arambourg between 30 January and 13 March 1933 as part of the activities of the Mission Scientifique de l'Omo (Arambourg and Jeannel 1933; Jeannel 1934). Arambourg (1943) subsequently reported on the geological re-sults of this work and on the substantial collection of fossil vertebrates, including fish (9 species), reptiles (6 species), and mammals (29 species) (Arambourg 1947). These de-posits, which Arambourg (1943) considered to extend some 90 km up the lower Omo valley, were informally termed "dépôts anciens du Lac Rodolphe" or "dépôts fluvio-lacustres de la vallée de l'Omo," or simply "Omo Beds."

A further reconnaissance of these fossiliferous sediments was made by Clark Howell in July-August 1959 and resulted in the recognition of the geological complexity of the

deposits and their vertebrate fauna (Howell 1968). In 1966 the formation of an international Omo Research Expedition was authorized by the Imperial Ethiopian Government. An
extensive geological reconnaissance of the area was made by F. H. Brown (1969) in 1966,
and various participants of the expedition have worked in the lower Omo basin each summer
since 1967.

Geologic Setting

The lower Omo basin, like the Rudolf basin to the south, is related to the Turkana
depression of the Eastern Rift valley (Baker, Mohr, and Williams 1972). It evidently represents a northward continuation of the depression into the southwestern margin of the
Ethiopian plateau. The Omo basin is considered a tectonic depression (Merla 1963), down-
warped and downfaulted after episodes of planation of the adjacent highlands during the
late Mesozoic and Paleogene. Although the structure of the highly folded and faulted area
to the southwest is known (Walsh and Dodson 1969), that of the lower Omo basin and of the
highlands to the northwest and to the east remains to be investigated (Butzer 1970). Projected gravity surveys in the lower Omo will help to resolve this problem. The Korath volcanics (Nakua), a low range of hills to the northeast of Sanderson's Gulf, represent a
series of basalt flows and a cluster of tuff cones (Brown and Carmichael 1969). They may
have been extruded in late Pleistocene times along a line of tensional faults, several of
which have been shown to fracture the Plio-Pleistocene deposits farther east.

The Amar-Kokke highlands form the eastern margin of the basin. They comprise Precambrian metamorphics, gneisses, and amphibolites, with intrusions of granite and pegmatite,
overlain by Tertiary (and Quaternary?) extrusive volcanics. The Nkalabong range, forming
the northern margin of the basin, is faulted along its southeastern margin. It exposes
crystalline basement overlain by a succession of interbedded basalts and rhyolites of early
Neogene, and probably earlier, age and an upper series of basaltic flows and dikes which
may be of Mio-Pliocene age (Brown and Nash, this symposium). Other, presumably Tertiary,
rhyolitic volcanic highlands, such as Mount Naita and Mount Tirma, form the northwestern
margin of the basin. To the southwest poorly exposed basement rocks are overlain by some
1,500 meters of extrusive volcanics, predominantly rhyolites and basalts, extremely folded
and faulted (Walsh and Dodson 1969). They range in age from mid-Oligocene to mid- (and
later?) Miocene (Reilly et al. 1966).

Stratigraphy

The Plio-Pleistocene succession exposed in the lower Omo basin has an aggregate thickness of nearly 1,100 m. The sediments outcrop discontinuously over an area of some 200 km^2
in four sectors of the basin (fig. 1). These exposed sediments have been given formational
status and named on a geographical basis, and together they make up the Omo Group (de
Heinzelin, Brown, and Howell 1970). All the formations have been surveyed and mapped on
aerial photographs (taken for the expedition by Robert Campbell in 1967 and 1970) at a
scale of 1:10,000 or smaller. The Omo Group can be defined as a set of somewhat consolidated
sediments (clays, silts, sands) and pyroclastics (tuffs and, rarely, extrusive lavas), in
most places tilted and locally faulted, which discordantly underlie horizontal sediments
comprising the Kibish formation. Their radiometric age (Brown and Lajoie 1971; Brown 1972;
Brown and Nash, this symposium), paleomagnetic record (Shuey, Brown, and Croes 1974; and
this symposium), and vertebrate fauna (Howell and Coppens 1974; Coppens and Howell 1974)

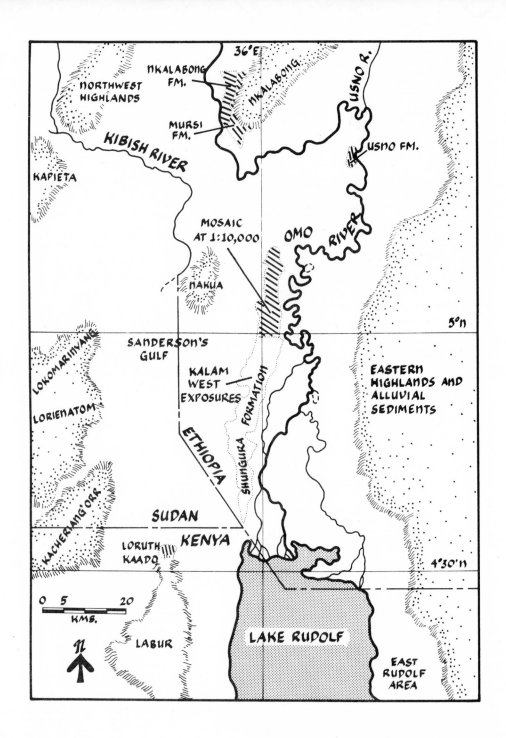

Figure 1. The lower Omo basin, southern Ethiopia, and situation of formations making up the Omo Group.

indicate a Pliocene and earlier Pleistocene age[1] for their accumulation.

Mursi Formation

This formation crops out southwest of the Nkalabong highlands at the Yellow Sands locality (5°24'N, 35°57'E). The locality was recognized in the course of aerial reconnaissance by Arambourg, Coppens, Howell, and R. E. Leakey in early June 1967. The locality was surveyed by R. E. Leakey in July-August 1967 and mapped by John van Couvering in August 1967, and its stratigraphy was studied by K. W. Butzer in August 1967 and July 1968. Further work during July 1969 was abruptly terminated by a destructive but not deadly helicopter crash (Butzer and Thurber 1969; Butzer 1971). The Mursi Formation is some 140 meters thick and comprises four semiconformable members, of which the uppermost is an extrusive basalt with radiometric age determinations of 4.05 m.y. (Brown and Lajoie 1970; Brown 1972; Brown and Nash, this symposium) and 4.4 to 4.1 m.y. (Fitch and Miller, this symposium).[2] We did further microstratigraphic work in the Mursi Formation in August 1973, coupled with a paleontological survey by Clark Howell. The results of this work will be reported elsewhere. The formation and its paleoenvironmental significance are discussed in some detail by Butzer (this symposium).

Nkalabong Formation

This formation crops out southwest of the Nkalabong highlands, a little to the north of the Yellow Sands locality where the Mursi Formation appears. The formation overlies unconformably the faulted basalt that makes up the uppermost member of the Mursi Formation. It consists of some 90 m of fluviolacustrine sediments and intercalated tuffaceous deposits comprising three members (Butzer and Thurber 1969; Butzer, this symposium). A lapilli tuff, overlying fluviatile sands of Member II, afforded a radiometric age of 3.95 m.y. (Fitch and Miller 1969). The formation and its paleoenvironmental aspects are discussed elsewhere (Butzer, this symposium).

Loruth Kaado Formation

This formation, which at this stage of research hardly merits formal status, outcrops at the northern end of the Labur massif. The deposits include tuffs, fine sediments and fanglomerates, and related fine sediments and tuffites. A small molluscan assemblage is taxonomically comparable with that obtained from the Basal Member, Shungura Formation (Van Damme and Gautier 1972; Gautier, this symposium), and suggests quiet water, perhaps a small embayment habitat. The occurrence has not yet been surveyed and investigated in detail.

Usno Formation

This formation crops out toward the northeastern margin of the basin, west of the confluence of the (seasonal) Usno stream and the Omo River (5°18'N; 36°12'E). The sediments occur on the upthrust side of a fault, with the Omo River meandering a short distance along

1. The Miocene/Pliocene boundary is here drawn at 5 m.y., and the Pliocene/Pleistocene (Tertiary/Quaternary) boundary at 1.8 my.y.

2. In 1967 Brown observed poor exposures of tuffs and sediments north of the Nkalabong highland, seemingly lacking in vertebrate fossils, which underlie or are intercalated with a substantial succession of thin basalt flows. These basalts unconformably overlie an older group of volcanics (F. H. Brown, pers. comm.).

the downthrust side. Active gullying has taken place along the scarp, and these deposits
are visible in a series of shallow exposures or along steep bluffs above the river. There
are eight major areas of exposure (fig. 2). The deposits are tilted WNW, with a general
strike of N 25° E and a general dip of 10° to 14° WNW.

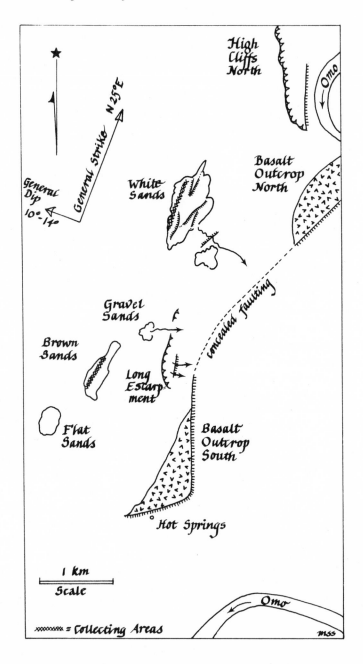

Figure 2. Principal exposures of the Usno Formation

De Heinzelin and Brown (1969), after the discovery and initial investigation of these localities in 1967, provisionally subdivided the Usno Formation into an informal ninefold succession. Further study by De Heinzelin and Haesaerts in 1973 has afforded a detailed microstratigraphy and led us to revise the previous informal subdivision. More than 10 m of sediments are exposed beneath the basalt, which varies in thickness up to 2.5 m and has afforded a whole rock age of 3.31 m.y. (Brown and Nash, this symposium). The main sedimentary sequence overlying the basalt has a measured thickness of 172 m. The basalt and these sediments have been subdivided into 20 units (U-1 to U-20, upward). The details of the stratigraphy will be published elsewhere. Units U-2 to U-6 are exposed at the High Cliffs North locality, Units U-6 to U-8 at the Gravel Sands and White Sands localities, Units U-9 to U-13 at the Brown Sands and White Sands localities, Units 14 and 15 between the Brown Sands and Flat Sands localities, and Units U-16 to U-20 at the Flat Sands locality. A tuff in Unit U-10, which underlies the main fossiliferous horizon (in Unit U-12) at the White Sands and Brown Sands localities, has afforded ages of 2.64 and 2.97 m.y.; the latter is regarded as the more reliable (Brown and Nash, this symposium). Older fossiliferous horizons occur at the Gravel Sands locality in Units U-6 and U-7, and also at the eastern margin of the White Sands locality. The youngest occurrence of vertebrate fossils is in Units U-19 and U-20 at the Flat Sands locality.

The age relation of the Usno Formation sediments to the protracted succession represented by the Shungura Formation has been a matter of concern since their discovery. On the basis of the initial radiometric measurement(s) of Usno pyroclastics, De Heinzelin, Brown, and Howell (1970) suggested that the most probable correlation was with lower Member C (the Usno basalt with Tuff C, and the three-part Usno tuff with a higher-lying subsidiary tuff in Member C). The recent detailed stratigraphic studies of the Usno Formation have shown this correlation to be unlikely, as has a more complete understanding of the respective assemblages of fossil vertebrates. The correlation now proposed is based on detailed comparisons of the sequences of deposits and their characteristics in the Shungura and Usno formations. The Usno Formation is now regarded as correlating with Shungura Formation Basal Member through Unit B-10 of Member B. This interpretation rests primarily on: the position and nature of the molluscan fauna (Gautier, this symposium; Van Damme and Gautier 1972) of the Usno U-3 and Shungura Basal Member-1 shellbeds, which indicate similar lacustrine environments; the close depositional similarities found between Shungura Tuff A and Unit A-1, and an Usno tuff (designated High Cliffs North Tuff) and Unit U-7; the similarity in position of a major and complex pedogenesis in Shungura Unit A-4 and Usno Unit U-9; the close depositional similarity between Shungura Tuff B and the Usno Unit U-10 tuffs; and the comparable relative situation of paleosoils in Usno Units U-16 to U-19 and Shungura Units B-6 to B-9. This correlation would thus equate the principal fossiliferous horizons (with Hominidae) of the White Sands and Brown Sands localities of the Usno exposures with the base (Unit B-2) of Shungura Formation, Member B. The younger fossil vertebrate assemblage from the Flat Sands locality would equate with that of Units B-9 and B-10 of Member B. This interpretation is consistent with vertebrate paleontological evidence, with available radiometric age determinations, and is not inconsistent with preliminary paleomagnetic determinations (by F. H. Brown and R. Shuey) on Usno Formation sediments.

Shungura Formation

This formation was first suggested as a stratigraphic entity by de Heinzelin and Brown (1969; cf. Butzer and Thurber 1969) and was formally defined by de Heinzelin, Brown, and

Howell (1970). It includes the ancient fluviolacustrine beds from which E. Brumpt, and subsequently C. Arambourg, made the "classic" Omo vertebrate fossil collection (Arambourg 1943, 1947). Its complexity, its substantial thickness, and the significance of its tuffs for radiometric dating and for extensive mapping were first demonstrated by Brown (1969). The formation crops out only on the west side of the Omo River, between 5° and 5°10'N, and comprises a series of fluvial, deltaic, and lacustrine sands, silts, and clays and a set of 12 principal, widespread tuffs (labeled A to L), as well as numerous subsidiary inter-calated tuffs. These deposits are faulted and tilted to the west and are of late Neogene to earlier Pleistocene age. The measured aggregate thickness of the formation (base un-known, and top unconformably overlain by Kibish Formation) is 850 m, although the base is not exposed and the top is truncated by the disconformity on which the Kibish Formation rests.[3] The thickness of the principal exposures, east of Korath (Nakua) Hills, is 670 m (extending from the Basal Member through middle Member J). The thickness of the exposures south of Korath Hills and west of Kalam police post (from upper Member C to the top of Member M) is 443 m. The differences in thickness are presumably related to differential subsidence (see below).

This sequence of deposits has been subdivided into a number of members through the occurrence of a series of widespread volcanic ash horizons which are usually readily dis-tinguishable. They are designated A to M from the base upward (de Heinzelin 1971). Each member (except the Basal Member) is represented by a major or principal tuff and its *over-lying* sediments (de Heinzelin, Brown, and Howell 1970).[4] The base of each principal vol-canic tuff is a true chronohorizon and is essentially isochronous over the whole lower Omo basin. Essentially the same interpretation was given and the same procedure followed by R. L. Hay at Olduvai Gorge and by Ian Findlater (this symposium) in East Rudolf. A member, as defined above, thus represents a lithozone (Moore 1958; also Forgotson 1957) or *assise* (cf. Dewalque 1882). The type sections of members have been measured along a type profile (located on 1:10,000 aerial photographs and on maps made from them,at 1:200 scale and sub-sequently analyzed, described, and reconstructed at the same scale in a vertical succession (cf. Visher 1965). Detailed profiles at scale 1:20 have been made wherever appropriate, as in the case of paleosoils, important fossil localities, and fossil (including hominid) excavations. (The stratigraphic situation of hominid remains recovered up to 1972 from the Shungura Formation is given in Bonnefille et al. [1973] and Howell, Coppens, and de Heinzelin [1974]). There is no single, simple east-to-west type section, owing to tectonic disturbance. However, exposures about a half-kilometer wide, extending west from the vicinity of Shungura village (on the river) toward the Korath Hills, include all members through Member J. South of the Korath hills and west of Kalam police post, the section ex-tends from Member C upward and includes extensive outcrops of Members G through M. It is in this area that the type sections of Members K, L, and M have been drawn. Mapping in 1972 and 1973 clearly demonstrated the interrelationships of these sets of sediments in the two major areas of exposure of the Shungura Formation and has permitted their correlation.

---

3. In the 1974 field season an additional 80 m of sediments, including Tuff M, was identified and measured in the Kalam area; this additional thickness is included in the total for the Shungura Formation but is not reflected in table 2.

4. This procedure (cf. Bonnefille et al. 1973), adopted for ease of mapping, since tuffs could be readily mapped from the prominent morphology of the tuff cuestas, replaced the initial informal terminology of the Omo Research Expedition (Arambourg, Chavillon, and Coppens, 1967, 1969), that of a "series" of sedimentary units *below* a capping tuff. Any initial designation of "series" is thus placed into this formal terminology by a lower letter designation (thus "series" H = Member G; "series" G = Member F, etc.).

A distinctive lithologic sequence occurs repeatedly through much of the Shungura Formation. The sequence consists of silt and clay overlain successively by coarse sand, medium sand, fine sand, silt, and clay. In general the sands are yellowish gray to light brown, poorly cemented, cross-bedded, and composed of fragments of quartz, feldspar, lithic fragments, and bits of chalcedony clasts. The clayey silts are brown to reddish brown and may contain gypsum or halite. There are also many minor tuffs in the succession, aside from the major tuffs which define the members. These minor tuffs occur only discontinuously along strike, but their position within a member is often constant. All tuffs are composed predominately of volcanic glass and have only a small admixture of other materials. In general the major tuffs are less contaminated than the minor tuffs. Pebbles and cobbles of pumice occur in many of the tuffs, but most of the material is of sand and silt size.

These repetitive sequences of coarser to finer sediments may vary in thickness and completeness but are basically similar. They are termed cyclic units and evidently represent sheets of deposits laid down by a meandering stream (Allen 1965a, 1970). They are defined as formal units in the type sections of members, and are numbered successively upward (B-1, B-2, etc.). In some cases exposure is such that units can be traced laterally for kilometers; but in many instances the accessible outcrops are disjunct, owing either to superficial cover or to faulting. However, correlations between more distant outcrops have been made by enumerating cycles between known marker horizons (customarily the major tuffs A-L) and by recognizing similar or identical sequences of deposits. The principle is of course well-established and forms the basis of much of stratigraphic geology (see Hedberg 1971, p. 13). In numerous instances it has led to the recognition of reliable chronosequences, and these have led to the definition of local chronozones (see Hedberg 1971, pp. 21-22), since the greater the complexity of events the greater the reliability of correlations based on apparent congruence. The units of the Shungura Formation can be considered chronozones, although they are somewhat diachronous, given their formation by the lateral displacement of a meander belt, and thus they should be considered, in a strict sense, parachronostratigraphic units.

The general outlines of the lower Omo basin were apparently delineated before the accumulation of Omo Group sediments (Butzer 1970; Butzer and Thurber 1969). The Mursi Formation sediments are similar to those of the Shungura Formation and represent deposits of an ancestral Omo river and of a proto- Lake Rudolf. The riverbed and lakeshore probably shifted substantially through time, as is also evident in the Ileret and Koobi Fora areas of East Rudolf. The basic geographical features of the lower Omo basin are thought to have been essentially as they are now, except that the Korath Range was probably absent, and it is possible that the adjacent highlands had a different elevation. Certainly there was a large river flowing over a broad plain from north to south, though its ancient course is not certainly known, and emptying into a lake. It is possible that the river's course was more direct and lacked the extensive easterly deviation past the Nkalabong highlands (F. H. Brown, pers. comm.). At any rate this was the general paleogeographic setting.

The principal characteristics of the members of the Shungura Formation are summarized in table 1.[5] Along with the description of the units within individual members, features

---

5. Sites are located on a composite air photomosaic according to four codes which partially overlap:
 Locality 28 = L. 28 = fossil locality worked under the direction of F. Clark Howell;
 Omo 28 = a different fossil locality worked under the direction of Y. Coppens and the late C. Arambourg;
 P. 28 = geological locality investigated by de Heinzelin and Haesaerts;
 F. 28 = a different geological locality investigated by F. H. Brown.

Table 1

Principal Characteristics of Members of the Shungura Formation

Shungura Formation Members	Thickness in Meters	Number of Units	Number of Subunits	Major and Minor Tuffs	Structured Paleosoils	Vertebrate Fossil Horizons	Molluscan Associations	Etheria Beds	Ostracod Beds
Mb. L	>48.60	9	15	6	5	4	4	1	4
Tuff L	0.40	1	1	1	-	-	-	-	-
Mb. K	26.40	4	>5	6	2	1	-	-	-
Tuff K	3.60	1	2	2	-	-	-	-	-
Mb. J	43.00	7	12	10	2	5	2	-	-
Tuff J	6.60	1	1	1	-	-	-	-	-
Mb. H	48.00	7	7	5	-	7	3	1	-
Tuff H	10.00	1	1	1	-	-	-	-	-
Upp. Mb. G	97.60	16	20	4	-	27	2	-	3
Low. Mb. G	112.60	13	28	11	2	16	-	3	-
Tuff G	6.00	1	2	1	-	-	-	-	-
Mb. F	35.50	5	9	2	-	5	-	-	-
Tuff F	7.20	1	4	1	-	3	-	-	-
Mb. E	35.00	5	13	5	1	6	-	2	-
Tuff E	2.00	1	2	1	-	1	-	-	-
Mb. D	37.00	5	11	5	1	5	-	-	-
Tuff D	4.00	1	2	2	-	1	-	-	-
Mb. C	78.00	9	32	12	3	12	1	4	-
Tuff C	1.80	1	3	2	-	1	-	-	-
Mb. B	84.40	12	44	13	8	16	1	2	-
Tuff B	13.00	1	4	4	-	2	-	-	-
Mb. A	31.60	4	10	5	2	2	-	-	-
Tuff A	3.20	1	1	1	-	-	-	-	-
Basal Mb.	>32.00	5	10	3	-	5	1	-	-
Total	>767.50	112	>239	104	26	119	14	13	7

indicating any development of land surfaces were recorded. These land-surface criteria
are grouped in seven categories as follows: 0 = sedimentary features only; 1 - sesquioxide
sheets, siderite concretions, and septaria indicating shallow water and groundwater regis-
tering Ph changes; 2 = desiccation cracks; 3 = mulching in silts, or slickensides in clays
and silty clays; 4 = rootcasts, substantial traces of rootlets or rhizomes; 5 = incipient
reduced soil, with or without calcic concretions and mottling; 6 = incipient oxidized soil,
with color or a brittle horizon, and polyhedral fracture; 7 = developed soil with structure,
peds, and with or without coatings.

Using these criteria, rather than the sedimentology proper, a general overview can be
given of the conditions of deposition in the Shungura Formation (cf. Visher 1965). The
members and units of the formation, and their respective land surface criteria, are summarized in figure 3. From this diagram the sequence can be divided into 17 successive sedimentary periods. In this respect the main tuffs, which form the basis for the stratigraphic
subdivision of the sequence, are extraneous and incidental, as are the numerous minor tuffs
which are incorporated in almost every unit.

Period 1: Basal Member up to BAS-4. The lower part of the lowest unit represents an
inshore lacustrine deposit of very shallow water origin. It contains only remains of
fish and 7 species of mollusks (Van Damme and Gautier 1972; Gautier, this volume).
The first evidence for land surface exposure appears in the upper part of Unit BAS-1
as desiccation cracks up to 3 inches deep. Subsequently cyclic fluviatile aggradation
was initiated, and mulching, slickensides, and rootcasts become recurrent features.

Period 2: Units BAS-4 to A-4. Initially there is a decrease in the development of
land surface features. Units BAS-5 to A-2 reveal only traces of mulching and slickensides. Tuff A accumulated in a calm body of water, during a brief interruption in the
normal fluviatile pattern of sedimentation. At least minor faulting occurred contem-
poraneously with the accumulation of this tuff. Unit A-3 initiates a transition to
the development of fully expressed alluvial floodplains with mature soils, and these
are fully developed in Unit A-4. There was enough precipitation during this interval
to induce illuviation of soils.

Period 3: Tuff B to Unit B-2. The complex events of the deposition of Tuff B initiate this period. Unit B-2 contains the first evidence of monotypic bioherms of
Etheria, indicating a perennial riverine situation with swift currents. In upper B-2
a mature floodplain is established and its surface bears several successive soils.
There is a possibility of hominid artifacts in lower B-2 (probable pieces of chipped
quartz from geological locality P. 912).

Period 4: Units B-3 to B-9. This interval is characterized by recurrent cyclic aggradation, with fluviatile transportation and deposition in a riverine floodplain, or
possibly at times transitional deltaic plain situations. There are relatively few
bone concentrations and no occurrences of mollusks. Between cycles sufficient time
elapsed for soil development, and precipitation was still adequate for illuviation.

Period 5: Units B-10 to C-2. Initially there was channeling on a grand scale, with
sand infillings, and brief intervening nonerosive intervals. The extent of dissection
may attain some 20 m. The capping surfaces bear reduced soils, or a pseudogley with

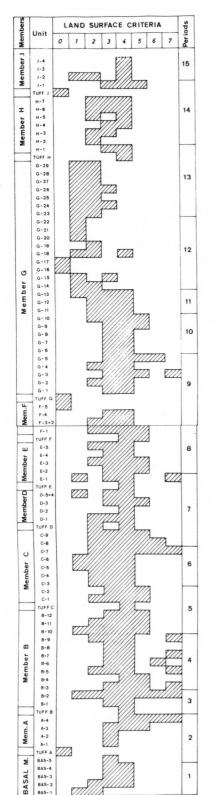

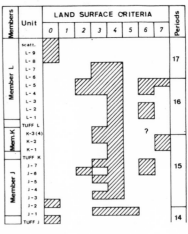

Figure 3. Land surface development (see text for key to criteria) and depositional periods of the Shungura Formation.

rootcasts and concretions, but no true soil weathering. An obliquely bedded coarse white sand in B-10-2 might represent a valley-side paleodune. The oldest hominid remains derive from B-10-1 (at L. 1 and Omo 28), and there are rich concentrations of micromammal fossils (see Jaeger and Wesselman, this symposium) and primates in lower B-10-3. A single hominid tooth is also known from the lower contact of Unit C-1. Surface occurrences of what may be derived artifacts have been noted in B-10 and the B-11 or B-12 contact, but situations suitable for excavation to prove artifacts are present have still to be located.

Tuff C is double and was deposited in a channel, and its occurrence is therefore limited by the channel's meandering shape. It is thought that a quartz flake and several small volcanic boulders, associated with rootcasts capping the surface of Tuff C-γ, could represent artifactual occurrences, but again situations suitable for excavation to prove artifacts are present have still to be located. The lower units of Member C are more aggradational and less erosional, and their surfaces bear incipient alluvial soils.

Period 6: Units C-3 to C-7. Recurrent cyclic aggradation occurred under floodplain conditions. Monotypic bioherms of *Etheria* are prominent in Unit C-6 (two sets) but are seldom present in Units C-4 or C-5. Vertebrate fossils are generally scattered in sands, seemingly near point bar situations. The alluvial soils consistently show mulching, slickensides, and rootcasts, but their weathering is quite immature. At one occurrence (L. 28) lower Unit C-7 afforded dwarf or juvenile specimens of *Caelatura* and *Cleopatra*, suggesting a very brief lacustrine incursion. The fluviatile, or perhaps upper deltaic, aggradational processes subsequently culminate in the extension of a well-expressed floodplain with its attendant levees. The silt and clay deposits have a thickness of about 10 m and were accumulated in two sets of flood basins and levees. Weathering horizons are locally preserved, but the soils are notably less evolved and less illuviated than in Periods 1 or 2 or 4, and this tends to suggest reduced precipitation.

Period 7: Units C-8 to E-1. The first half of this interval (to Unit D-2) witnessed a series of cyclic units in which land surfaces were decreasingly developed. Unit C-8 is capped by a color soil, Unit C-9 is capped by an incipient soil, and thereafter only rootcasts are related to surfaces. To judge from the palynological evidence (Bonnefille 1970, 1972, this symposium) depositional and climatic conditions during the accumulation of C-8 and C-9 were not unlike those of the present. Hominid remains are rather frequent in Units C-8 and C-9 (Arambourg and Coppens 1967, 1968; Howell, Coppens, and de Heinzelin 1974), and in situ artifacts were found by J. Chavaillon in 1974.

Tuff D was deposited on a low, even surface of waterlogged soils. It is double, and both portions (D-α and D-β) contain pumices. Each shows desiccation cracks, and both were vegetated shortly after deposition. Thereafter there was massive renewed channeling. The intervening phases are poorly indicated, as incipient soils have been detected only in upper Unit D-3. Several substantial tuff accumulations were discontinuously incorporated in channels as in Units D-3 and D-5 (formerly termed R tuffs; see de Heinzelin, Brown, and Howell 1970).

Tuff E was accumulated over a broad, even surface and is widespread and continuous. Its sharp basal contact exhibits nests of baked argillite, molds of vegetation, and other biogenic traces or turbations, including bird tracks. When the tuff was accumulated subaqueously it occurs in its stratified facies (E'). A structured soil caps Unit E-1; the absence of illuviation again suggests a relatively dry climate.

Period 8: Units E-2 to F-1. This interval was characterized by recurrent cyclic aggradation with only short intervening land surface exposures. The hominid site L. 338y, which yielded a partial juvenile hominid cranium and a humeral diaphysis in situ with a diversity of fossil vertebrates, and the nearby L. 338x are both situated in lower Unit E-3 at the onset of an aggradation. The situation of the former locality was perhaps a watering place along a shallow embayment, since paleosurfaces show turbations of animal footprints. That of the latter locality is a point bar undercutting. In lower Unit E-4 monotypic bioherms of *Etheria* occur infrequently. By this time there is palynological evidence for a substantially drier climate (Bonnefille, this symposium). There may be archeological occurrences in Member E (Chavaillon 1970, 1971), but situations suitable for excavation have still to be found.

Tuff F was deposited, usually, on the surface of a fresh silt with rootcasts. When found deposited, or redeposited subaqueously, it occurs in its stratified facies (F'). Lower Tuff F' contains rich pumices, baked argillite, and several rich and diverse bone concentrations, some (like Omo 33 and L. 398; Chavaillon and Merrick, this symposium) yielding a number of fragmented hominid specimens. Part of the biostratonomic processes involved in these accumulations could have been the action of ashflows. The completion of the rather thick cover of Tuff F-F' resulted in an overall leveling of the landscape slightly above the water table, and gley soils are common. The renewed aggradation of Unit F-1 was initiated with gullying and cut-and-fill processes. Locality 28, which has afforded hominid teeth as well as a microvertebrate assemblage (Jaeger and Wesselman, this symposium), is a gravel situation in lower F-1-2. Perhaps the widespread presence of pervious sandy soils on surfaces of shallow relief was favorable to hominid occupation. At any rate, apparently for the first time, there are frequent occurrences of flaked quartz, rarely in situ in F-1-1, but almost invariably derived at the base of the next subunit, a sand sheet deposited by a braided river (as at L. 204, and Omo 57). The completion of the floodplain of Unit F-1 resulted in the extension of clayey alluvial soils. Some hominid occupations are known (as at L. 396), but the surfaces were certainly less attractive (Merrick et al. 1973; Merrick, this symposium).

Period 9: Units F-2 to G-5. Unit F-2 is frequently absent. Hereafter there are some notable differences in thickness between sediments in the northern and southern reaches of the Shungura Formation exposures. These presumably were the consequence of tectonic events affecting the shape of the basin. The sediments of upper Member F, often with interlayered sands and silts with driftwood, reflect a tendency toward deltaic fringe conditions. The occurrence of Omo 123, in Unit F-3, affords here the first such dense in situ artifactual situation (Chavaillon, this symposium), undisturbed except for cracking of sediments. It was apparently situated close by a desiccating flood basin.

Tuff G is in many respects similar to Tuff F and has a broadly comparable thickness. However, the depositional undersurface was different, devoid of any vegetation and perhaps under shallow water. Land surfaces are rare up to Unit G-2. Subsequently, from Units G-3 to G-5, the return of braided river conditions distributed thick bodies of fluviatile sands and gravels. In G-3 and in G-5 there are soils with some structure. Vertebrate fossils, including hominid remains and some derived artifacts, are common in these levels.

Period 10: Units G-6 to G-10. Conditions were overall similar to those of middle Member C. The aggrading units are those of a meandering stream, and monotypic bioherms of *Etheria* are present in Unit G-8. The accumulation of each cyclic unit was followed by only brief exposure, however, scarcely of sufficient duration to initiate soil development.

Period 11: Units G-11 to G-13. There is a gradual transition toward deltaic fringe conditions. Some fossiliferous concentrations are very rich, and hominids are known (as at Omo 75).

Period 12: Units G-14 to G-22. This interval represents a sequence of shallow lacustrine deposits. However, there is still an ill-defined rhythm to the sedimentation. Unit G-14, a gypsic clay, is everywhere a consistent marker bed. It was apparently deposited and dried up in a permanently drowned embayment similar to Sanderson's Gulf. Unit G-15 is less reduced and less gypsiferous; its capping surface still reveals slickensides. Units G-16 and G-17 were fully subaqueous, although the waters were undoubtedly shallow. Ostracod beds appear in Unit G-17 and persist through Unit G-19. In Units G-18 and G-19 there are occasional traces of desiccation and of the bases of tree trunks. Units G-20 to G-22 are shallow subaqueous deposits with some concentrations of bones of fish, fecal pellets, and opercula of gastropods. Remains of mammals are associated, incidentally, but are indeed rare. During periods 9 to 12 there occurred a differential subsidence in the basin, more rapid in the Shungura than in the Kalam area. The lacustrine incursion was accordingly caused by tectonics.

Period 13: Units G-23 to H-1. The rhythmic character of the sedimentary process resumes increasingly, but not markedly. The rather regular sedimentation of silts is interrupted by quite short episodes of emersion evidenced by desiccation cracks; slickensides were noted only in one instance. Remains of fish vastly outnumber those of mammals, shells are poorly preserved, and bioturbations are infrequent or absent. A deltaic fringe or a prodeltaic situation seems to be indicated. The youngest and only hominid fossil remains known from this interval are a largely complete upper dentition and cranial vault parts from Unit G-28 (L. 894). Driftwood is unexpectedly common in the lower portion of Unit G-29.

The very rapid deposition of a 10 m thickness of volcanic ash, represented by the fairly widespread (when not buried under the Kibish Formation) Tuff H, evidently must have raised the overall land surface above water level. There are evidences of vegetation in the top part of Tuff H. Unit H-1 shows mulching and slickensides, its top representing a land surface of short duration without any dectectable signs of soil development.

Period 14: Units H-2 to J-1. Evidence of land surfaces are infrequent through most of Member H.[6] Only desiccation cracks and rootcasts are known through Unit H-6. Shellbeds occur in Units H-4, H-5, and H-6 (mainly the latter), with 9 molluscan species (Gautier, this symposium; Van Damme and Gautier 1972). A monotypic *Etheria* bed is also known in Unit H-4. In general these sediments reveal a predominance of fish over mammalian remains. The environment of deposition is regarded as shallow shore in a transitional lacustrine to prodeltaic area. The surfaces of Units H-6 and H-7 are capped with alluvial soils with slickensides and rootcasts.

The apparently sudden deposition of Tuff J, 7 m thick, raised the general surface of the landscape. The surface of Unit J-1 was evidently exposed for some time, since it bears an incipient reduced soil.

Period 15: Units J-2 to K-2. Gradually there are successively longer intervals between sedimentary units, and consequently the development again, after the prolonged preceding lacustrine and estuarine/prodeltaic episode, of structured soils. Units J-2 to J-5 show rootcast traces and rootlet pores. The overlying Units J-6 and J-7 exhibit the first real soils with porous, friable structure.

Members J, K, and L are most adequately exposed southwest of the principal Shungura Formation outcrops, west of the Kalam police post. This area was first surveyed in detail by F. H. Brown, and he established the correlations of these outcrops with the latter extensive exposures on the basis of reconnaissance and correlative mapping on aerial photographs. That correlation has been fully confirmed by our own observations (in 1972 and 1973).

Units K-1 and K-2 bear fully developed soils. However, these are completely different from those of members A or C; illuviation does not appear to have occurred, and the climate must have been correspondingly dry. Incipient reduced soils are no longer evidenced, there are no longer backswamps and flood basins, and there are scarcely any indications of point bar situations. Rather than a fluviatile to deltaic sedimentary regime, conditions are increasingly dry with emphemeral streams and even evidences of aeolian phenomena.

Period 16: Units K-3(4) to L-5. The sedimentary regime is essentially as before, terminating again with land surfaces in rather dry climatic conditions.

Tuff L is exceptionally thin, continuous, and abundant in pumices; dense mats of rhizomes occur at its lower contact.

Period 17: Unit L-6 upward. There is evidence of progressive lacustrine incursion, with the appearance of ostracods and shellbeds (Gautier, this symposium). In Units L-7 and L-8 reduced rootcasts reappear, but reduced soils are absent. Ultimately, the thick, extensive shellbeds (Gautier, this symposium) of Unit L-9, unconformably overlain by the Kibish Formation on the easterly margin of Sanderson's Gulf, clearly

---

[6]Member H was originally distinguished from Member I (Brown 1969; de Heinzelin, Brown, and Howell 1970). However, after detailed mapping the tuffs and sediments of "I" came to be subsumed, for stratigraphic and sedimentary reasons, within Member H. Consequently there is a Member H, more inclusive than initially recognized, and an overlying Member J.

suggest the near shore conditions of a substantial lake. The factors which may have
controlled this lacustrine transgression into the basin are still quite unknown.

Depositional Environments and Taphocoenoses

The sediments of the Omo Group are predominantly fluviatile with a subordinate proportion of lacustrine deposits. One fluctuating lacustrine episode occurred in the early
parts of the sequence, over 4 and again around 3 m.y.; two others toward the end around
1.85, and between 1.6 and 1.4 m.y.

The Mursi Formation reflects deltaic and fluviolittoral deposition before 4.1 m.y.
(Butzer, this symposium). The stratigraphy and sedimentation were also recently restudied
by de Heinzelin and Haesaerts. The depositional environment was initially lacustrine prodeltaic and offshore, with shellbeds and mud flats; subsequently there was deposition in a
delta distributary channel (with rolled macrovertebrate fossils), ultimately abandoned and
filled with vitric tuff; delta fringe conditions and desiccation of closed basins ensued,
followed by a return to lacustrine prodeltaic and offshore environments with shellbeds and
mud cracks, and evidence of drowned trees, persisting until the return of distributary
channel conditions. The end of the sedimentary sequence is truncated by the development of
a massive structured paleosol, after which there were basalt extrusions.

The Mursi Formation affords the oldest of the few major vertebrate fossil assemblages
from a marginal lacustrine distributary channel situation. This assemblage is distinctive
in that only a relatively few larger species are represented (Coppens and Howell, this
symposium), often by postcranial parts. Three proboscideans are present, a gomphothere
(*Anancus*) being very rare; hippo is not uncommon; rhino is infrequent; two bovid genera
are common; and a single suid (*Nyanzachoerus*) is very abundant.

The upper member (III) of the Nkalabong Formation again reflects the recurrence of
shallow littoral lacustrine conditions, at about 3.9 m.y., in association with ash falls
from explosive volcanism (Butzer, this symposium). Butzer (this symposium) considers the
Liwan Beds, exposed at the eastern edge of Lokomarinyang along the western margin of the
basin, to represent a penecontemporaneous occurrence indicating lacustrine conditions along
the northwestern periphery of the lower Omo basin. Vertebrate fossils are unknown in the
Nkalabong Formation and in the Liwan Beds as well.

Lacustrine conditions are subsequently evidenced in the lowest unit of the Basal
Member of the Shungura Formation. Fragmentary vertebrate fossils, representing only a few
identifiable taxa, and mollusks are recorded from the very restricted exposures of this
sedimentary unit. These sediments show normal remnant magnetization and are considered to
represent the base of the Gauss Normal Epoch, about 3.3 m.y. (Brown and Shuey, this symposium). It is possible that the decalcified and cemented shellbed overlying the Usno Formation basalt also reflects shallow lacustrine conditions, perhaps of short duration, at a
comparable time.

Lacustrine sedimentation, under delta fringe and prodeltaic conditions, is again reflected in the middle third (Units G-14 to G-22) of Member G of the Shungura Formation.
These shallow lacustrine deposits show several phases of reversed and normal polarity which
are considered to span the pre-Olduval event portion of the Matuyama Reversed Epoch (Brown
and Shuey, this symposium). These are largely silts and clays, finely laminated and often
gypsiferous. Abundant limonitic and calcareous septaria and ostracod-bearing sands are
present.

Some coarser sediments, intercalated with these clays and silts, could have been deposited as river mouth bars and in delta distributary channels. Silicified wood is often abundant in these deposits, and fish remains and Crocodilia are commonly found, the former often well preserved. Remains of higher vertebrates, particularly mammals, are uncommon to rare, and almost always fragmentary (as in Units G-16, G-20, and G-21). However, in the transitional fluviolacustrine sands, interbedded with silts, at the base (Unit G-13) of this sequence a number of localities afford substantial concentrations of a diversity of vertebrate taxa. These occurrences sometimes include associated portions of individual skeletons, preserved in beds considered to be transitional deltaic sediments. One hominid occurrence (Omo 75) is known in such a unit.

In upper Member H (Units H-2 to J-1), transitional lacustrine to prodeltaic conditions are recorded, usually with poor vertebrate fossil associations. In upper Member L, at the end of the Shungura succession, near-shore lacustrine situations are evidenced, again with very sparse occurrences of vertebrates.

With these exceptions most of the Plio-Pleistocene sedimentation and related fossil occurrences in the lower Omo basin reflect alluvial landscapes. Fluviatile settings pre-dominate in the lower portions (Members I, II) of the Nkalabong Formation (Butzer, this symposium), in the Usno Formation, and in essentially all of the Shungura Formation (through lower Member G). There are, however, important differences and variations within this general setting.

The Usno Formation comprises 19 sedimentary units above the extrusive basalt (Unit U-1). After the brief episode of shallow lacustrine conditions (Unit U-3-1) the succession reveals a prolonged period of fluviatile and fluviodeltaic sedimentation, including marsh and swamp situations, comparable in many respects to that recorded in the lower three mem-bers of the Shungura Formation (fig. 4). Significant vitric tuff accumulations occur at three horizons in the succession (Units U-6, U-10, and U-11) and appear to be the counter-parts of Tuffs A and B of the Shungura Formation.

Subsidiary tuffs, associated with other fine sediments, occur higher in the succession (Units U-12, U-17, and U-20), and these, at least in part (like U-20), have equivalents in the Shungura Formation (e.g., the B-10-1 tuff). The successive accumulations of relatively coarse clastic products, which generally incorporate vertebrate fossils at four localities, all reflect to a greater or a lesser extent the proximity of piedmont alluvial fans, drained by the Usno and related streams along the eastern margin of the basin and affording quantities of Basement Complex detritus.

The Gravel Sands, Brown Sands/White Sands, and Flat Sands deposits represent three successively younger concentrations of vertebrate fossils in the Usno Formation. Gravel Sands (in U-6 and U-7), which we think probably equates with the upper part of the Basal Member, Shungura Formation, is not particularly fossiliferous and only a dozen identifiable specimens have been collected there (mostly bovid, and a few hippo, *Giraffa*, cercopithecoids, and *Protopterus*). Flat Sands, the youngest occurrence (in U-19 and U-20) which we think probably equates with the upper part (probably about Unit B-9) of Member B, Shungura Forma-tion, has produced substantially more vertebrates, from fluviatile sands interbedded with floodplain silts and with clays. More than 50 identifiable specimens have been collected, about half bovid and hippo, some cercopithecoids and suids, a few proboscideans, including deinothere, and an equid. By comparison the Brown Sands and especially the White Sands occurrences are extremely productive of vertebrates, yielding more than 1,500 identifiable specimens. At these sites two subunits of Unit U-12, a light gravel and medium sands, and

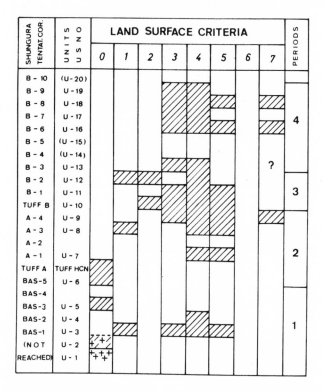

Figure 4. Land surface development (see text for criteria) for units of the Usno Formation and proposed correlation with the lower members of the Shungura Formation.

an underlying gravelly sand are interbedded with clay silts, a laminated tuff, and strati-fied sands with silt and clay lenses. In some instances the finer sands and silts yield more complete specimens, and even associated skeletal elements of individuals may occur (e. g., bovids, suids, elephant, cercopithecoids). In the coarser sediments at both locali-ties specimens are usually disarticulated, incomplete, or fragmentary. Both localities have yielded a substantial diversity of vertebrate taxa, including fishes, aquatic and other reptiles, and nearly 50 species of mammals (see Coppens and Howell, this symposium), and 21 hominid teeth (Howell and Coppens, this symposium).

Most members of the Shungura Formation are deposits of a large meandering river system. Its sinuosity was undoubtedly substantial, perhaps even on the order of some meander belts of the present lower Omo River; but details of the ancient hydrographic system have still to be elucidated. In many respects the present lower Omo River can presumably serve as an appropriate model for much of the Plio-Pleistocene situation in the lower Omo basin.

The fining-upward sedimentary cycles (Allen 1965b, 1970) characteristic of the Shungura Formation merit further consideration. The basal coarse sands are moderately sorted, frequently cross-bedded, and composed predominantly of quartz and of feldspar with fragments of chalcedony and chert. The measured attitudes of cross-beds generally indi-cates north-to-south currents. Reefs of the river oyster *Etheria* suggest a stable bed, with a persistent supply of fresh, flowing water, which these mollusks require. Such con-ditions obtain only in a fluvial situation along the river channel below the dry-season watermark. The coarse sands at the base of these units are thus thought to represent fairly well sorted, coarse sediments accumulated at or near the bottom of the channel and on the point bars of meander bends.

The overlying medium and fine sands are mineralogically similar and have similar bedding features, and are moderately sorted. They may contain interbeds of silt. They could represent the higher levels of point bar deposits, formed by hydraulic sorting. Or they might be the consequence of rises in lake level leading to coarse sand and pebble gravel deposition upstream and finer sands in their former place.

The finer silts and clays presumably represent levee and overbank deposits on the river floodplain. The clays are in places reduced and show root casts and calcareous concretions suggesting standing water in river edge flood basins. Silty sediments of levees can be overlain by clays of flood basins if the river migrates in one direction, especially if there is a simultaneous rise in lake level.

Paleosols are recognizable at the tops of many silt beds. Soil development is generally weak and the grade of oxidation moderate, generally having Munsell values of 7.5-10 yr, occasionally attaining 2.5-5 yr values. Recognized B-horizons are characterized by prismatic and polyhedric structure with coatings. Units are frequently terminated by reduced clays, with colors near 5 y, root casts, and calcareous concretions. These have been interpreted as swamp soils. Sometimes the porous tops of tuffs contain concretions and abundant root casts, and even mammalian remains, and here weak soil profiles are developed.

Very extensive channeling is evidenced during two main intervals in this fluviatile succession. In upper Member B three major episodes of cut-and-fill attended the accumulation of Unit B-10, which attains a cumulative thickness nearly double (about 40 m) its actual thickness (20 m), with dissection on the order of 20 m. Subsequently, the sediments of Member D were largely accumulated in a series of substantial channels, with dissections reaching several meters.

On at least two occasions the meandering river seems to have been replaced by braided channels or by branching distributaries that resulted in the accretion of rather thick and extensive bodies of sand.

This occurred during the deposition of Unit F-1 and again in Units G-3 to G-5. In such situations the riverine floodplain was less continuous and permanent than before and channel banks were shallower and broader. In both instances, such conditions were seemingly favorable for hominid activities, judging from the number of bones and derived artifacts recovered (see Chavaillon, Merrick this volume).

Most sediments are fluviatile or shallow-water deposits, and as they compose more than 800 m of section, the area of deposition must have been subsiding. In this situation the river could migrate back and forth across its floodplain without completely removing deposits accumulated previously. Truncated cyclic units are known in many instances, and well-preserved channels are evident. (Tuff F shows several such instances, with channels infilled with fine pebble gravel and coarse sands overlain by medium to fine sand. The distinctive tuff lithology makes the channel relations particularly apparent.)

There is substantial diversity of depositional environments within such a riverine system (Leopold, Wolman, and Miller 1964; Allen 1965a). They include channels with point bars enclosed between meander loops; floodplains and their abandoned and weathered terraces; levees with crevasses and crevasse splays; alluvial ridges with abandoned channels and meander loops, and associated ox-bow lakes, backswamps, marshes and mud flats; and floodbasins which are sometimes ill-vegetated and sometimes more permanently watered, with denser, more established vegetation. Microstratigraphic studies at the unit and intraunit level in members of the Shungura Formation reveal the varied microsedimentary situations with which the abundant Omo vertebrate assemblages are associated. As a consequence it has been possible to obtain the data needed for taphonomical studies both from surface occurrences and from a series of excavated situations (see Johanson, Boaz, and Splingaer, this symposium).

Some of these varied fossil occurrences include:

a) Those on or in a paleosoil, with the fossils protected from dissolution and cracking by their incorporation in calcic concretions. Land mammals including cercopithecoids and hominids make up the bulk of the faunal assemblage; such is the situation of the L. 7A-125 hominid mandible in upper G-5 and of the L. 345 baboon and hippo remains in middle Member C (see Johanson, Boaz, and Splingaer, this symposium).

b) Those included in the porous top of major tuffs. The assemblages are similar to the preceding ones. Various occurrences were collected from the top of tuffs D, E, F, and G especially.

c) Those on grayish reduced horizons which represent ancient swamp soils. The faunal assemblages comprise land mammals including primates as well as hippopotamus, aquatic reptiles, and fishes; such is the situation of the lower contact of L. 338X in lower E-3 and of the L. 396 artifactual occurrence in F-1-3.

d) Those incorporated at some stage of the floodplain construction, in many instances close to the transition from medium sand to silt and trapped in temporary ponds and ephemeral small bodies of water. The resulting faunal assemblages are as a rule rather rich and varied, and they are also more frequent than might be suspected. Bones are very friable indeed and are destroyed as soon as they are exposed on the surface. These assemblages can be effectively recovered only by excavations like those of L. 345, L. 626, and L. 338Y.

The situation of the Omo 123 archeological site is similar (see Chavaillon, this symposium).

e) Those reworked in gentle washouts and derivatives of paleosoils. In some instances the washout of levees or shallow consolidated embankments results in a concentration of small bones, including remains of micromammals. The best-demonstrated instance is the lower contact of B-10-3 at L. 1 North, but there are other occurrences at the lower contacts of C-8 and of B-2.

In other instances, it seems that incipient floodplains were washed over and then buried under sheets of river sands. Diverging channel deposits resulted in rather even dispersal of coarse elements and mixed pellets. This is a common situation at the base of F-1-2, where extensive artifactual occurrences have been detected (L. 204, Omo 57, and Omo 58, for example).

f) Those in small pebble gravels where the sorting is particularly favorable for vertebrate tooth concentrations. Examples are known in lower B-10-1 (Omo 28) and in lower G-3 (L. 628).

g) Those in erosional channels, cross-bedded sands, and even in coarse gravels which yield allochthonous large and small vertebrate skeletal parts and some in situ aquatic reptiles. Omo 18 and Omo 57 are typical examples. Bones can be associated laterally to *Etheria* beds but are very seldom in close contact with them. The assemblages are mixed, resulting mainly from the concentration of previously deposited material having already undergone some grade of diagenesis, epigenesis, or both.

The last two categories, *f* and *g*, afford the bulk of surface-collected vertebrate fossils. The resulting oryctocoenoses are meaningless in terms of local taphonomy but are certainly significant at the scale of large biogeocoenoses.

h) Those in erosional channels, with the peculiar circumstance that the channel was choked with vitric tuffs (as in D', E', F', and G' facies).

Two major bone concentrations have been excavated thus far in lower F': Omo 33 and L. 398. In both instances the assemblages are exceptionally rich and dense, including a diversity of vertebrates and a number of hominid teeth. The deposits are characterized by pumices and pellets of baked argillite. This peculiar association could be due to a direct action of ash flows, but there is as yet no complete demonstration of this.

There are somewhat similar, but much less rich, occurrences of bones in lower Tuff B-α and lower Tuff D.

Although the volcanic ash horizons played a decisive role in stratigraphy and mapping, the details of their own depositional history are still only partially understood. These horizons are the result of the episodic and swift intercalation of foreign pyroclastics into the local sedimentary regime at any place in the lithologic sequence. Extreme situations vary from lenses in cross-bedded channel sands to extensive and massive cover of bioturbated silt and clay or laminated lacustrine beds.

More than 100 distinct intercalations of volcanic ashes have been counted in the Shungura Formation, and there may be still others. This represents a mean of 1 tuff/7.50 m of sediment, or minimally 1 tuff/20,000 years on the chronological scale of Brown and Shuey (this symposium).

Differences between major (or principal) and minor tuffs are not so much differences of lithology and composition as of lateral continuity. Both consist largely of volcanic glass shards, with fresh grains that are angular and unabraded and often show small glass bubbles or elongated vesicles; fresh angular sanidine is sometimes found associated as in Units B-10-1 and D-3.

No nearby volcanic source is known from which these volcanic ashes could have been ejected. Known volcanics inside the Rudolf basin have a different chemical composition. Sources in the middle reaches of the Omo drainage basin, and possibly on Mount Damota (near Soddu, Sidamo Province, some 275 km distant), whose rocks are silica-rich and peralkaline, appear most likely (Brown and Nash, this symposium). Pantelleritic ignimbrites occur extensively over much of central Ethiopia, including the upper Omo basin (Mohr 1968). These ignimbrites are of (inferred) late Tertiary age, and presumably they fall at least partly within the same time span as the Omo Group.

Some tuffs are regarded as primary ash falls over shallow lacustrine or littoral foreshore situations, as Butzer (this symposium) recognizes for the laminated tuff (IIf) of the Middle Mursi Formation and those tuffs of the upper member (III) of the Nkalabong Formation. In the Shungura Formation Tuff A and several occurrences of minor tuffs are also laminated and diatomitic. Tuffs H, J, K-β, and a number of minor tuffs in upper Member G, Member K, and Member L are more massively stratified and are regarded by us as primary ash falls.

Aerial transportation of pyroclastic ash falls (of Sparks and Walker 1973) cannot adequately account for the many medium- to coarse-grained tuffs or for those which contain large pebbles, cobbles, or even boulders of pumice (as do Tuffs D, E, F, G, G-3, J-2, I-4, and L) or large lumps of red baked argillite (as in Tuffs B-α, D-3, E, E-3, F + F', and G-3).

Two means of transport can be envisioned, both possibly successive and complementary. Initially, a flowage (Smith 1960; Ross and Smith 1961) or transportation of a fluidized mass; and second, redistribution by water (Transporttuffe in German). Two processes of flowage have been recognized, depending on the relative density of the fluidized mass. The ratio of gas to fragments of pyroclastics is relatively low in pyroclastic flows and higher in ground surges (Sparks and Walker 1973). To what extent these processes contributed to the deposition of tuffs in the Omo Group is not always clear. Table 2 gives an overview of the current terminology as pertinent to the following discussion.

Table 2

Current Terminology of Pyroclastic Deposits

Mechanism		Pyroclastic Deposit	
Airborne Pyroclastic fall		Ash fall Pyroclastic fall deposit	
Nuées	Ash-flow Pyroclastic flow	Ash-flow sheet Ash-flow tuff Ignimbrite (welded or not)	Pure
Ardentes	Ash hurricane	Ground surge deposit	
Transportation from a primary source by streams, rill-wash or otherwise.		Derived tuff Transporttuffe (German)	
		Tuffite	Impure

SOURCE: Ross and Smith 1961; Smith 1960; Sparks and Walker 1973.

Many tuffs, such as Tuffs F and G, have large current cross-bedding or climbing ripple marks indicative of rapid deposition by running water. They have been regarded as derived and essentially fluviatile (de Heinzelin, Brown, and Howell 1970). The purity of the tuffs may simply be the result of dilution of the normal sediment load by vast quantities of ash, or as partly a consequence of the hydraulic characteristics of the glass fragments, since glass is less dense than the sediments normally carried by the river.

Although the fluviatile transportation hypothesis might hold for a substantial number of cases, there is contradictory evidence to suggest that this explanation is not wholly adequate.

It has been repeatedly demonstrated that the same tuff was deposited simultaneously in a variety of lateral situations, including active channels, in abandoned meanders, on the cracking clays of backswamps and on bioturbated land surfaces. The basal contact of the tuffs, except those in active channels, is usually not erosional but is sharp to very sharp. The transition with the underlying sediments is less than 1 mm, especially in the case of Tuffs B-*a*, D, E, F, G, and L. Where the underlying sediment is silt and clay, the top suffers a peculiar physical modification of some 10 to 20 cm, becoming hard and brittle and being affected by a diagonal breakage. Dense networks of root casts are common features near both lower and upper contacts. Animal footprints and trails (Tuff E), grass and other plant impressions (Tuffs F, G), and calcified mats of small rhizomes (Tuff L) have sometimes been detected at the lower contact. Individual beds of utterly pure, massive vitric tuff can be traced over kilometers, particularly in Tuffs D, E, F, G, K-χ, and L. Beds of vitric tuff can change to tongues of pisolitic tuff, as in Tuffs C-4, E, and, sporadically, several others. In addition, pumices and lumps of red baked argillite, unrolled scoriae, and cobbles of lava may be associated, as in Tuffs C-, C-4, and C-9.

Tuff E deserves specific mention. In this tuff the two same basal beds of pure vitric ash ("doublet") can be mapped over a distance of 20 km. Locally it changes to tongues of pisolitic tuff or, in channels, to stratified tuffite. Hollow casts of stems, radiating roots, and identifiable footprints are quite distinct in places, and nests of red baked argillite are found concentrated in former fissures or depressions.

These observations, and their congruence, are totally unfamiliar in fluvial situations known to us. They are more likely explained by the direct action of pyroclastic flows or ground surges over the area.

It must be admitted that a variety of mechanisms were doubtless responsible in the repeated inflow and deposition of vast quantities of volcanic ashes into the basin of the lower Omo. The case is quite exceptional and especially beneficial to stratigraphy, but it is not yet completely understood.

References

Allen, J. R. L. 1965a. A review of the origin and characteristics of recent alluvial sediments. *Sedimentology* 5:89-191.

_____.1965b. Fining-upwards cycles in alluvial successions. *Liverpool Manchester Geol. J.*, 4:229-46.

_____.1970. Studies in fluvial sedimentation: A comparison of fining-upwards cyclothems, with special reference to coarse-member composition and interpretation. *J. Sed. Petrol,* 40:298-323.

Angelis d'Ossat, G. de, and Millosevich, F. 1900. Studio geologico sul materiale raccolto da M. Sacchi. Secondo spedizione Bòttego (Afrique orientale). Rome: Società Geògrafica Italiana.

Arambourg, C. 1943. *Mission scientifique de l'Omo (1932-1933): Géologie-Anthropologie.* Vol. I, fasc. 2, pp. 60-230. Mémoire, Muséum national d'histoire naturelle (Paris).

_____.1947. *Mission scientifique de l'Omo (1932-1933): Paléontologie.* Vol I, fasc. 3, pp. 231-562. Mémoire, Muséum national d'histoire naturelle (Paris).

Arambourg, C.; Chavaillon, J; and Coppens, Y. 1967. Premiers résultats de la nouvelle mission de l'Omo (1967). *C. R. Acad. Sci. (Paris),* ser. D, 265:1891-96.

_____.1969. Résultats de la nouvelle mission de l'Omo (2e campagne 1968). *C. R. Acad. Sci. (Paris),* ser. D, 268:759-62.

Arambourg, C., and Coppens, Y. 1967. Sur la découverte dans le Pléistocene inférieur de la vallée de l'Omo (Ethiopie) d'une mandibule d'australo-pithécien. *C. R. Acad. Sci. (Paris),* ser. D, 265:589-90.

_____.1968. Découverte d'un australopithécien nouveau dans les gisements de l'Omo (Ethiopie). *S. Afr. J. Sci.,* 64:58-59.

Arambourg, C. and Jeannel, R. 1933. La mission scientifique de l'Omo. *C. R. Acad. Sci. (Paris),* 196:1902-4.

Baker, B. H.; Mohr, P. A.; and Williams, L. A. J. 1972. Geology of the Eastern Rift System of Africa. *Geol. Soc. Am., Spec. Paper,* no. 136.

Bonnefille, R. 1970. Premiers résultats concernant l'analyse pollinque d'échantillons du Pléistocène inférieur de l'Omo (Ethiopie). *C. R. Acad. Sci. (Paris)*, ser. D, 270:2430-33.

_____. 1972. Considérations sur la composition d'une microflore pollinque des formations plio-pléistocènes de la basse vallée de l'Omo (Ethiopie). In *Palaeoecology of Africa*, ed. E. M. van Zinderen Bakker, 7:22-27. Cape Town: A. A. Balkema.

Bonnefille, R.; Brown, F. H.; Chavaillon, J.; Coppens, Y; Haesaerts, P.; de Heinzelin, J.; and Howell, F. C. 1973. Situation stratigraphique des localités à hominidés des gisements Plio-Pléistocènes de l'Omo en Ethiopie. *C. R. Acad. Sci. (Paris)*, 276:2781-84, 2879-82.

Boulenger, G.-A. 1920. Sur le gavial fossile de l'Omo. *C. R. Acad. Sci. (Paris)*, 170:913-14.

Bourg de Bozas, R. 1903. D'Addis-Abbabá au Nil par le lac Rodolphe. *Géographie* 7:91-112.

_____. 1906. Mission scientifque du Bourg de Bozas de la Mer Rouge à l'Atlantique à travers l'Afrique tropicale, Octobre 1900, Mars 1903. Paris: F. R. de Rudeval.

Brown, F. H. 1969. Observations on the stratigraphy and radiometric age of the "Omo Beds," lower Omo basin, southern Ethiopia. *Quaternaria* 11:7-14.

_____. 1972. Radiometric dating of sedimentary formations in the lower Omo valley, southern Ethiopia. *Calibration of hominoid evolution*, ed. W. W. Bishop and J. A. Miller, pp. 273-87. Edinburgh: Scottish Academic Press; Toronto: University of Toronto Press.

Brown, F. H., and Carmichael, I. S. E. 1969. Quaternary volcanoes of the Lake Rudolf regions: 1. The basanite-tephrite series of the Korath range. *Lithos* 2:239-60.

Brown, F. H., and Lajoie, K. R. 1971. Radiometric age determinations on Pliocene/ Pleistocene formations in the lower Omo basin, southern Ethiopia. *Nature* 229:483-85.

Butzer, K. W. 1970. Geomorphological observations in the lower Omo basin, southwestern Ethiopia. In *Argumenta Geographica*, Carl Troll Festschrift, ed. W. Lauer. *Colloq. Geograph.* 12:177-92.

_____. 1971. The lower Omo basin: Geology, fauna and hominids of Plio-Pleistocene age. *Naturwissenschaften* 55:7-16.

Butzer, K. W.; Brown, F. H.; and Thurber, D. L. 1969. Horizontal sediments of the lower Omo basin: The Kibish Formation. *Quaternaria* 11:15-29.

Butzer, K. W., and Thurber, D. L. 1969. Some late Cenozoic sedimentary formations of the lower Omo basin. *Nature* 222:1132-37.

Chavaillon, J. 1970. Découverte d'un niveau Olduwayen dans la basse vallée de l'Omo (Ethiopie), *C. R. Soc. Prehist. Franc.* 1:7-11.

_____. 1971. Etat actuel de la préhistoire ancienne dans la vallée de l'Omo (Ethiopie). *Archéologia*, no. 38, pp. 33-43.

Coppens, Y., and Howell, F. C. 1974. Les faunes de mammifères fossiles de formations Plio-Pléistocène de l'Omo en Ethiopie (Proboscidea, Perissodactyla, Artiodactyla). *C. R. Acad. Sci. (Paris)*, ser. D, 278:2275-78.

Dewalque, G. 1882. Sur l'unification de la nomenclature géologique: Résumé et conclusions. *Congrès Géologique International, 2e session, Bologna*, 1881:549-59.

Fitch, F. J., and Miller, J. A. 1969. Age determinations on feldspar from the lower Omo basin. *Nature* 222:1143.

Forgotsen, J. M. 1957. Nature, usage, and definition of marker-defined vertically segregated rock units. *Bull. Am. Assoc. Petrol. Geol.* 41:2108-13.

Haug, E. 1912. *Traité de géologie.* 2. *Les périodes géologiques.* Paris: Armand Colin.

Hedberg, H. D. 1971. Preliminary report on chronostratigraphic units. (International Subcommission on Stratigraphic Classification, Report no. 6). International Geological Congress, 24th session, Montreal, 1971.

Heinzelin, J. de. 1971. Observations sur la formation de Shungura (vallée de l'Omo, Ethiopie). *C. R. Acad. Sci. (Paris)*, ser. D, 272:2409-11.

Heinzelin, J. de, and Brown, F. H. 1969. Some early Pleistocene deposits of the lower Omo valley: The Usno Formation. *Quaternaria* 11:31-46.

Heinzelin, J. de; Brown, F. H.: and Howell, F. C. 1970. Pliocene/Pleistocene formations in the lower Omo basin, southern Ethiopia. *Quaternaria* 13:247-68.

Höhnel, R. L. von; Rosiwal, A; Toula, F.; and Suess, E. 1891. Beiträge zur geologischen Kenntnis des östlichen Afrika. *Denkschr. Akad. Wiss. Wien, Math.-Naturw. Kl.* 58:1-140.

Höhnel, L. von. 1938. The Lake Rudolf region: Its discovery and subsequent exploration (1888-1909). *J. Roy. Afr. Soc.* 37:21-45, 206-26.

Howell, F. C. 1968. Omo Research Expedition. *Nature* 219:567-72.

Howell, F. C., and Coppens, Y. 1974. Les faunes de mammifères fossiles des formations Plio/Pléistocènes de l'Omo en Ethiopie (Tubulidentata, Hyracoidea, Lagomorpha, Rodentia, Chiroptera, Insectivora, Carnivora, Primates). *C. R. Acad. Sci. (Paris)*, ser. D, 278:2421-24.

Howell, F. C.; Coppens, Y., and Heinzelin, J. de. 1974. Inventory of remains of Hominidae from Pliocene/Pleistocene formations of the lower Omo basin, Ethiopia (1967-1972). *Am. J. Phys. Anthropol.* 40(1):1-16.

Jeannel, R. 1934. *Un cimetière d'éléphants*. Paris, Société des Amis du Muséum national d'histoire naturelle.

Joleaud, L. 1920a. Contribution à l'étude des hippopotames fossiles. *Bull. Soc. Geol. France*, ser. 4, 20:13-26.

_____. 1920b. Sur la présence d'un gavialidé du genre *Tomistoma* dans le Pliocène d'eau douce de l'Éthiopie. *C. R. Acad. Sci. (Paris)*, 170:816-18.

_____. 1928. Eléphants et dinothériums Pliocènes de l'Éthiopie: Contribution à l'étude paléogéographique des proboscidiens africains. *Int. Geol. Cong., Madrid, 14th session*, 3:1001-7.

_____. 1930. Les crocodiliens du Pliocène d'eau douce de l'Omo (Ethiopie): Contribution à l'étude paléobiogéographique des *Tomistoma* et des crocodiles à museau de gavial. *Soc. Geol. France, Livre Jubilaire, 1830-1930*, 2:411-23.

_____. 1933. Un nouveau genre d'equidé quaternaire de l'Omo (Abyssinie): Libyhipparion ethiopicum. *Bull. Soc. Geol. France*, ser. 5, 3:7-28.

Leopold, L. B.; Wolman, M. G.; and Miller, J. P. 1964. *Fluvial processes in geomorphology*. San Francisco and London: W. H. Freeman.

Merla, G. 1963. Missione geologica nell' Etiopia meridionale del Consiglio nazionale delle ricerche 1959-1960. Notizie geo-morfologiche e geologiche. *Giorn. Geol.*, ser. 2, 31:1-56.

Merrick, H. V.; Heinzelin, J. de; Haesaerts, P; and Howell, F. C. 1973. Archaeological occurrences of early Pleistocene age from the Shungura Formation, lower Omo valley, Ethiopia. *Nature* 242:572-75.

Mohr, P. A. 1968. The Cenozoic volcanic succession in Ethiopia. *Bull. Volcanol.* 32:5-14.

Moore, P. F. 1958. Nature, usage, and definition of marker-defined vertically segregated rock units. *Bull. Am. Assoc. Petrol. Geol.* 42:447-50.

Reilly, T. A.; Musset, A. E.; Raja, P. R. S.; Grasty, R. L; and Walsh, J. 1966. Age and polarity of the Turkana lavas, northwest Kenya. *Nature* 210:1145-46.

Ross, C. S., and Smith, R. L. 1961. Ash-flow tuffs: Their origin, geologic relations, and identification. U.S. Geol. Survey Professional Paper 366.

Sclater, P. L. 1899. Results of the second Bottego expedition into eastern Africa. *Science* 10:951-55.

Shuey, R. T.; Brown, F. H.; and Croes, M. K. 1974. Magnetostratigraphy of the Shungura Formation, southwestern Ethiopia: Fine structure of the lower Matuyama polarity epoch. *Earth Planet. Sci. Lett.* 23:249-60.

Smith, R. L. 1960. Ash flows. *Bull. Geol. Soc. Am.* 71:795-842.

Sparks, R. S. J., and Walker, G. P. L. 1973. The ground surge deposit: A third type of pyroclastic rock. *Nature-Phys. Sci.* 241:62-64.

Van Damme, D., and Gautier, A. 1972. Molluscan assemblages from the later Cenozoic of the lower Omo basin, Ethiopia. *Quat. Res.* 2(1):25-37.

Vannutelli, L., and Citerni, C. 1897. Relazione preliminare sui risultats geografici della seconda spedizione Bòttego. *Bull. Soc. Geograf. Ital.* ser. 3, 10:320-30.

_____. 1899. *Seconda spedizione Bottego. L'Omo. Viaggio di esplorazione nell'Africa orientale.* Milan: Vottoepli.

Visher, G. S. 1965. Use of vertical profile in environment reconstruction. *Bull. Am. Assoc. Petrol. Geol.* 49:41-61.

Walsh, J., and Dodson, R. G. 1969. Geology of North Turkana. *Kenya Geol. Surv. Rept.* 82:1-42 pages (1:500,000 map).

5. RADIOMETRIC DATING AND TUFF MINERALOGY
OF OMO GROUP DEPOSITS

F. H. Brown and W. P. Nash

Introduction

Through the efforts of the Omo Research Expedition and the East Rudolf Research Group, a large number of vertebrate fossils have been collected from the sedimentary deposits near the northern end of Lake Rudolf in Kenya and in the lower Omo valley in Ethiopia. The hominid fossils collected in this area have attracted the most attention, but the associated mammalian fossils are of equal importance, since they provide clues to the environment in which early man lived. Because these large collections of well-preserved material are extremely useful for correlation and for ascribing ages to other deposits, dating them is critical. In this chapter we try to describe some of the problems encountered in dating the deposits in the lower Omo valley, to assess some of the possible problems, and where possible to apply other controls to the radiometric dates. The work is not yet finished, and it may be many years before the final words are written on the age of these deposits. The following text is merely a summary of our knowledge to date.

Mineral Analyses

The stratigraphy and nomenclature of the sediments of the lower Omo valley have been discussed by de Heinzelin, Brown, and Howell (1970). A number of tuffs in the Shungura Formation have proved useful for obtaining radiometric dates and for dividing the formation into members. For a review of the nomenclature and stratigraphic position of these tuffs, see de Heinzelin, Brown and Howell (1970) and figure 6 of this paper.

We prepared samples of feldspar separated from the Omo Tuffs for electron microprobe analysis in order to determine the compositional variation within each sample and thus assess the possible effect of error in the potassium analyses on the ages of the samples.

The standard used for microprobe analysis potassium and sodium potassium was anorthoclase 5748, which is similar in composition to all of the samples analyzed (K_2O = 5.92%; Na_2O = 7.46%). The standard used for calcium was Crystal Bay bytownite (15.5% Ca). Barium and iron were analyzed using a synthetic barium silicate glass (46% BaO) and olivine YS-24 (11.54% FeO) respectively.

Data are presented in the form of histograms (fig. 1) and in tabular form where flame photometer analyses may be compared with the microprobe means. One hundred points approximately 10μ in diameter were taken on each sample, and the analyses were checked by converting the oxide percentages of Na_2O, K_2O, and CaO to albite, orthoclase, and anorthite,

50

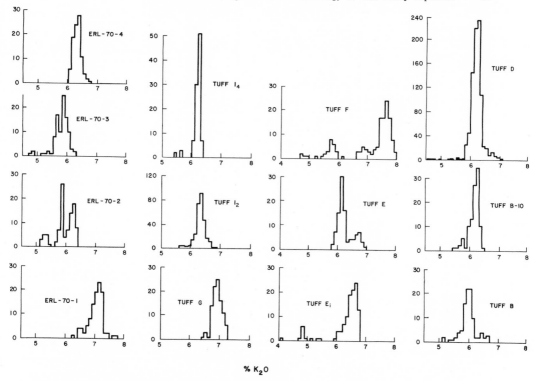

Figure 1. Histograms of potassium content of feldspars from various tuffs. The tuffs were grouped in 0.1 % intervals. On each plot the abscissa represents K_2O content and the ordinate represents the number of samples.

respectively. Since the barium component is small (less than 0.1% celsian), the sum of the feldspar molecules should be near 100%. Accordingly only analyses whose totals were between 98.5 and 101.0% were used in the plots and in calculating the means. For assessing the variation in Fe and Ba, only 50 points were analyzed.

In addition to the feldspars from the Omo tuffs, feldspars from tuffs from East Rudolf were analyzed, and the results of these determinations are presented in table 1 and figure 1 along with the Shungura results. The microprobe analyses of a number of samples of Tuff D are presented separately in table 2. Because of the similarity in age and composition of the feldspar, we suspected that Tuff D and the Tool Site Tuff at Koobi Fora (KF-2A;ERL-70-4) represented the same volcanic event. On the basis of potassium, sodium, and calcium contents, there is no way to distinguish the two feldspars, but the barium and iron contents may be used to establish that the two are distinct. In figure 2 the barium content of feldspars from the Tool Site Tuff is plotted against the iron content; a similar plot was made for the feldspars from Tuff D. On this diagram, it can be seen that although there is a small area of overlap, the two are distinguishable, the feldspar from the Tool Site Tuff having in general less iron and more barium than feldspars from Tuff D of the Shungura Formation.

In fact, the diagram in figure 3 shows that plotting barium content against iron content may be useful in distinguishing feldspars from various tuffs, since each of the four tuffs examined from East Rudolf has a distinct field when plotted on such a diagram. This is not true for the Omo tuffs, however, in which the feldspars from various tuffs plot in

Table 1

Analyses and Calculated Molecules of Feldspars from Various Tuffs

	B	B10	D*	Ei	E	F	G	I_2	I_4	L	KF-2	ERL-70-1	ERL-70-2	ERL-70-3	ERL-70-4	S1	S2	S5	S6
K_2O	6.03	6.10	6.19	6.36	6.26	6.61	6.96	6.32	6.18	5.91	6.22	7.01	5.92	5.67	6.27	7.21	6.39	6.40	6.56
Na_2O	7.50	7.56	7.47	7.17	7.37	7.07	6.88	7.37	7.45	7.39	7.48	6.90	7.67	7.78	7.43	6.76	7.33	7.36	7.26
CaO	0.17	0.15	0.06	0.14	0.08	0.13	0.03	0.07	0.10	0.38	0.10	0.01	0.02	0.13	0.08	0.01	0.01	0.07	0.01
BaO	0.01	0.06	0.01	0.08	0.01	0.03	0.01	0.03	0.04	0.19	0.04	0.01	0.16	0.30	0.04	0.03	0.01	0.04	0.03
Fe_2O_3	0.34	0.69	0.68	0.64	0.61	0.78	0.64	0.47	0.69	0.52	0.43	2.00	0.62	0.34	0.42	1.05	1.27	0.49	1.52

Calculated feldspar molecules (percentage by weight)

	B	B10	D*	Ei	E	F	G	I_2	I_4	L	KF-2	ERL-70-1	ERL-70-2	ERL-70-3	ERL-70-4	S1	S2	S5	S6
Or	35.63	36.05	36.58	37.61	37.00	39.07	41.13	37.35	36.52	34.91	36.76	41.42	34.99	33.51	37.06	42.63	37.78	37.81	38.76
Ab	63.47	63.98	63.21	60.67	62.36	59.83	58.21	62.38	63.04	62.49	63.30	58.38	64.90	65.83	62.87	57.23	62.00	62.24	61.45
An	0.84	0.74	0.30	0.69	0.40	0.64	0.15	0.35	0.50	1.88	0.50	1.05	0.10	0.64	0.40	0.05	0.05	0.33	0.05
Cs	0.02	0.15	0.02	0.20	0.02	0.07	0.02	0.07	0.09	0.47	0.10	0.02	0.39	0.73	0.10	0.08	0.03	0.11	0.08
Total	99.96	100.92	100.11	99.17	99.78	99.61	99.51	100.13	100.15	99.75	100.66	99.87	100.38	100.71	100.43	99.99	99.86	100.49	100.34

Electron microprobe and flame photometer K^+ values

	B	B10	D*	Ei	E	F	G	I_2	I_4	L
Probe	5.01	5.06	5.14	5.30	5.20	5.49	5.78	5.25	5.13	4.91
F.P.	4.659	5.074	5.097	5.080	5.186	6.101	5.912	5.124	5.095	3.35
	4.964	5.054	--	--	--	6.233	5.886	5.182	5.010	3.13
	--	--	--	--	--	--	--	5.111	4.99	--

*Average value for Tuff D.

Table 2

Analyses and Calculated Molecules of Feldspar Separates from Tuff D

	F142	Tuff D	Tuff D	F160	UD-2	UD-3	208-12	LD-1	14D
K_2O	6.20	6.21	6.17	6.11	6.16	6.04	6.24	6.37	6.18
Na_2O	7.52	7.46	7.45	7.54	7.44	7.55	7.42	7.34	7.53
CaO	0.02	0.03	0.09	0.05	0.05	0.08	0.08	0.11	0.05
BaO	n.d.	n.d.	0.02	0.01	0.01	0.01	0.01	0.01	0.01
Fe_2O_3	0.73	0.72	0.58	0.71	0.71	0.58	0.71	0.64	0.64

Calculated feldspar molecules (percentage by weight)

	F142	Tuff D	Tuff D	F160	UD-2	UD-3	208-12	LD-1	14D
Or	36.66	36.70	36.49	36.12	36.41	35.70	36.89	37.62	36.52
Ab	63.67	63.09	63.03	63.76	62.92	63.89	62.79	62.08	63.72
An	0.10	0.14	0.43	0.26	0.23	0.40	0.41	0.53	0.25
Cs	--	--	0.05	0.01	0.03	0.01	0.01	0.03	0.01
Total	100.43	99.93	100.00	100.15	99.59	100.00	100.10	100.26	100.50

Electron microprobe and flame photometer K^+ values

	F142	Tuff D	Tuff D	F160	UD-2	UD-3	208-12	LD-1	14D
Probe	5.15	5.15	5.12	5.07	5.11	5.01	5.18	5.29	5.13
F. P.	--	--	5.03	--	5.182	4.984	5.139	--	5.151

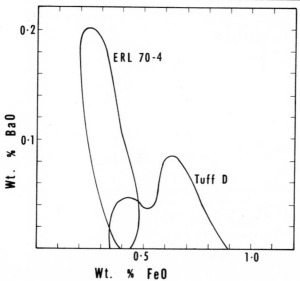

Figure 2. Barium content of feldspars separated from ERL-70-4 (KBS tuff) and Tuff D of the Shungura Formation plotted against iron content of the same.

the same general field. Such data might be useful if a tuff occurs where the stratigraphic situation is not well known, allowing one to eliminate some of the possible correlations.

The only possible correlation noted between the Omo tuffs and those of East Rudolf is between KNW2 and the specimen labeled ERL-70-3 from the Ileret area (Chari Tuff). Such a correlation gains support from the data presented in figures 4 and 5 and tables 1 and 3. In figure 4 the barium content of both feldspars is plotted against the iron content. The two sets of data are not separable on such a plot, nor are they separable in figure 5, where the iron content of the feldspar is plotted against the potassium content. In addition, the only mafic mineral noted in these two tuffs was a pyroxene; partial analyses of pyroxenes from each tuff are given in table 3, where it can be seen that the composition is strikingly

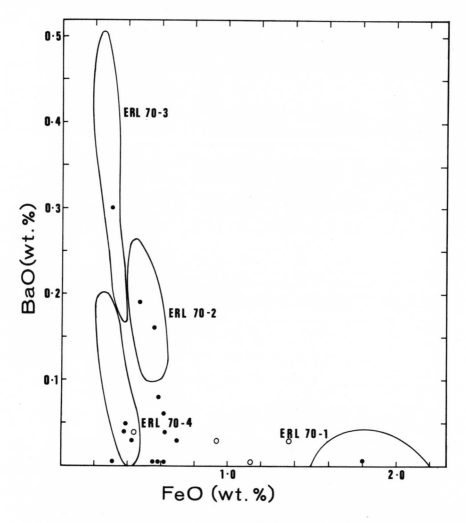

Figure 3. Barium content plotted against iron content of feldspars from various tuffs from East Rudolf. (See Appendix for sample locations.) *Open circles*, average values from Mount Damota feldspars; *closed circles*, average values from Shungura Formation tuffs.

similar. If individual pyroxene analyses are plotted in the pyroxene quadrilateral (diopside-hedenbergite-enstatite-ferrosilite), the trends of the two are again indistinguishable. This is not surprising, since most of the pyroxenes from the Omo and East Rudolf tuffs plot along the same trend, and the feature is not generally diagnostic. Some tuffs can be distinguished on such a diagram, however, and the method should not be overlooked.

Still another common feature between KNW2 and ERL-70-3 is the feldspar trend on the ternary feldspar diagram. Here again, the two prove indistinguishable, although the range in composition observed for KNW2 is somewhat larger than that for ERL-70-3. This greater range in composition probably accounts for the poor agreement between flame photometer values and the microprobe analyses for potassium (table 1), since a correspondingly larger number of data points is needed to define the mean over a larger range of composition. The

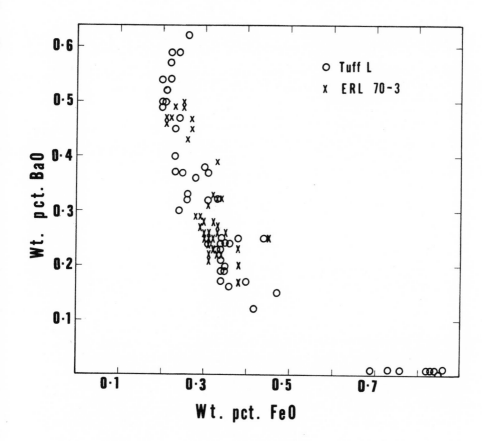

Figure 4. Barium content plotted against iron content of feldspars from Tuff L and ERL-70-3. (See Appendix for location of East Rudolf samples.)

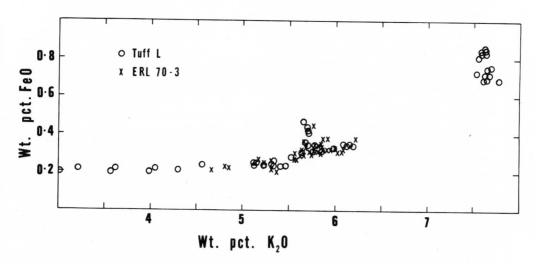

Figure 5. Iron content plotted against potassium content of feldspars from Tuff L and ERL-70-3. (See Appendix for location of East Rudolf samples.)

Table 3

Pyroxene Analyses

	L	ERL-70-3	S1
SiO_2	--	--	48.6
TiO_2	0.3	0.3	0.33
Al_2O_3	0.4	0.3	0.23
FeO	23.7	25.6	29.0
MnO	1.65	1.68	2.68
MgO	4.6	3.1	0.89
CaO	19.0	19.3	17.4
Na_2O	0.6	0.6	1.30
Total			100.43

analyses of feldspars from other East Rudolf tuffs fall into other areas of the ternary feldspar diagram and appear to be diagnostic for each tuff.

All the evidence given in the preceding paragraphs is permissive only. That is, a correlation between KNW2 and ERL-70-3 cannot be ruled out; nor can a correlation be considered proved. The real tests lie in comparing the major and trace element contents of the two glasses as well as their radiometric ages and associated fauna. Should the correlation prove to be real, it will provide a welcome tie between the two sequences on direct stratigraphic grounds, even though the correlation is near the top of both sedimentary sequences.

Potassium-Argon Dates

The potassium-argon dates which have been run on samples from the lower Omo Valley are presented in table 4. Some of these dates have been published previously (Brown and Lajoie 1971; Brown 1972). A number of additional ones are included, and one date has been deleted from earlier lists (KA-2176), for reasons discussed below.

Potassium-argon ages have been obtained for three new stratigraphic horizons in the Shungura Formation. For stratigraphic details on previously published dates see de Heinzelin, Brown, and Howell 1970; only the newly dated stratigraphic levels are discussed below.

Tuff B-10 is a minor tuff about 20 cm thick which is locally preserved at the base of submember 10 in Member B of the Shungura Formation. The only known outcrops of this tuff are at Locality 1. The glass in this tuff is completely altered to clay, but remnants of the structure can be seen. Large crystals of anorthoclase (to 4 mm) occur. We separated these and made two determinations of the argon and potassium contents on splits of the purified feldspar. The resulting dates are in good agreement (2.93 and 2.96 m.y.) and yield an average age of 2.95 ± 0.1 m.y.

The dates on samples KNW2 are on anorthoclase from a tuff collected near the top of the section, in the western exposures. The approximate position of this tuff with respect to Tuff G is shown in the schematic diagram in figure 6. We approximated this stratigraphic position by calculating from the outcrop width on the map, and it may be in considerable error. The potassium analyses are in good agreement, but the argon determinations vary by

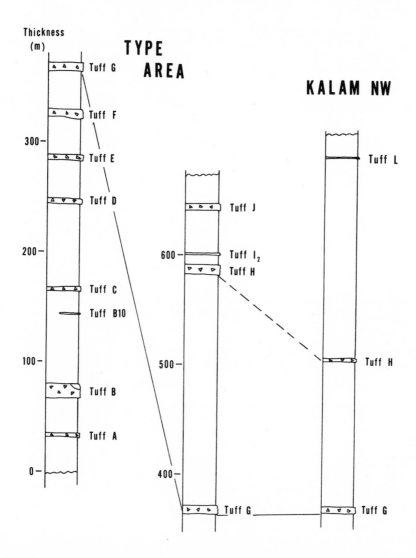

Figure 6.   Schematic diagram of the stratigraphy of the Shungura Formation in the type area and in the exposures northwest of Kalam.

about 10%, leading to the rather large difference in the two ages (1.27; 1.41 m.y.). The average of these is 1.34 m.y., and we prefer to use this average rather than argue the merits of one age or the other. The most immediate use of this date is to roughly define the upper time limit on the Shungura Formation as something less than about 1.34 ± 0.15 m.y.

During reconnaissance mapping a hominid molar was found in the Kalam West exposures, and approximately 15 m below this in the section a pumiceous tuff was found and dated. The hominid molar thus appears to be only about 1.4 m.y. old, and therefore much younger than most of the hominid material from the Shungura Formation.

We also found a rich fossil locality near Namaruputh, and the date for a tuff stratigraphically within a few meters of the fossil horizon yielded an age of 1.51 ± 0.1 m.y. The fauna of F8 is of roughly this age also, and helps to place it stratigraphically, as no

Table 4

Potassium-Argon Ages and Related Data

Horizon	Lab. No.	Wt. (gm)	K^+ (%)	Ar^{40}_{atm} (%)	Ar^{40}_{rad} ($\times 10^{-11}$ moles)	Ar^{40}_{rad}/gm ($\times 10^{-11}$ moles)	K^{40}/gm ($\times 10^{-8}$ moles)	Calculated Age ($\times 10^6$ years)
Tuff L	KA-2504	3.35558	4.510	71.2	3.4075	1.0155	13.72	1.27 ± 0.10
Tuff L	KA-2505	3.13131	4.490	72.9	3.5283	1.1268	13.66	1.41 ± 0.10
F223	KA-2521	3.01333	4.140	79.0	3.1771	1.0543	12.59	1.43 ± 0.10
KAR OLO	KA-2516	3.33791	4.246	71.1	3.7980	1.1380	12.92	1.51 ± 0.10
Tuff I_2	KA-2509	3.0537	5.124	24.5	5.032	1.648	15.59	1.81 ± 0.09
Tuff I_2	KA-2187	5.2886	5.182	54.8	8.824	1.668	15.77	1.81 ± 0.09
Tuff I_2	KA-2085	5.0010	5.111	--	--	--	15.55	1.87 ± 0.09
Tuff G	LKA-9	1.9868	5.899	59.3	4.0173	2.022	17.95	1.93 ± 0.10
Tuff F	LKA-11	1.6682	6.101	66.4	3.597	2.156	18.56	1.99 ± 0.10
Tuff F	LKA-21	2.0586	6.101	48.2	4.595	2.232	18.56	2.06 ± 0.10
Tuff E_1	LKA-14	2.3350	5.010	49.1	4.4136	1.890	15.24	2.12 ± 0.11
Tuff D	KA-2519	2.93381	5.139	44.0	5.795	1.975	15.64	2.16 ± 0.11
Tuff D	LKA-23	1.80134	5.151	52.4	3.557	1.975	15.67	2.16 ± 0.11
Tuff D	LKA-22	1.64782	5.151	37.3	3.490	2.118	15.67	2.31 ± 0.11
Tuff D	KA-2510R	2.99531	4.984	46.7	6.411	2.141	15.16	2.41 ± 0.12
Tuff D	KA-2511	3.06549	5.182	30.9	7.084	2.311	15.77	2.51 ± 0.12
Tuff D	KA-2067	5.00225	5.151	51.0	11.70	2.340	15.67	2.56 ± 0.12
Tuff D	ℓ1040	1.6675	5.030	34.0	3.882	2.328	15.31	2.60 ± 0.12
Tuff B10	KA-2458	3.10180	5.002	35.7	8.0881	2.608	15.22	2.93 ± 0.10
Tuff B10	KA-2441	3.04414	5.064	60.0	8.1045	2.674	15.41	2.96 ± 0.10
Tuff B	KA-2096	6.0050	4.625	50.3	18.74	3.120	14.07	3.79 ± 0.20
Tuff B	ℓ1029	1.2379	4.474	44.5	4.9259	3.9792	13.62	4.99 ± 0.2

SHUNGURA FORMATION

Formation	Unit	Sample							Age
USNO FORMATION	Triple Tuff	LKA-25	0.77656	2.830	91.6	1.0163	1.3087	8.61	2.64 ± 0.92
	Triple Tuff	ℓ1027	1.5878	2.640	89.8	2.292	1.4434	8.03	2.97 ± 0.3
	WS Basalt	KRL-2	10.8442	0.7074	84.5	4.2487	3.9179	2.152	3.11 ± 0.15
	WS Basalt	LKA-20	6.3263	0.7074	90.7	2.7958	4.419	2.152	3.51 ± 0.70
MURSI FORMATION	Yellow Sands Basalt	KA-2094	10.1667	0.828	75.4	6.067	0.5967	2.520	4.05 ± 0.2
	Nkalabong Basalt	KA-2508	1.81778	0.515	56.3	3.367	1.852	1.567	20.1 ± 2
	Nkalabong metamorphic	KA-2515	0.00516	10.969	43.8	5.1232	992.9	33.379	451 ± 20

direct connection has been found between the exposures southwest of Kalam and the type section to the north.

Brown (1969) originally published two dates for Tuff D (KA-2067 and KA-2176). While compiling the data for the table of dates which appears in this chapter, we noticed that the potassium content of KA-2176 was exceptionally high compared with the other samples. The published value was $K^+ = 5.432\%$ (= 6.544% K_2O). Since this is much higher than the mean value determined by microprobe, the value was checked from the original run sheets. It was found that the calculations were correct, and that since sodium had been run at the same time, the analysis could be checked for internal consistency. This was done by converting to feldspar molecules (see above) and summing. The resulting total was 95.63%; adding in the average anorthite and celsian contents brings the total to less than 96%. Clearly something is amiss, and the best procedure seems to be to delete the date from the list.

The remaining dates obtained on Tuff D are presented in order of age in table 4. One can immediately see that the relation between potassium content and age is obscure, but that the variation of age with argon content is nearly linear. This strongly suggests that the variation in the measured ages results from a variation in argon content. In any case, the spread in ages cannot be attributed solely to potassium error. For example, the potassium content of KA-2519 and LKA-23 would have to be only 5.57% K_2O if the age is to be brought up to the mean (2.4 m.y.). A glance at figure 1 will convince the reader that a potassium content this low is unlikely for any sample of Tuff D.

If the potassium determinations are not the source of error, then the problem must lie in the argon determinations or the argon content. Similar values of argon content for feldspars from Tuff D have been reported from Lamont and Berkeley (LKA-23 and KA-2519), and also from the United States Geological Survey at Menlo Park and Berkeley (compare ℓ1040 and KA-2067). This leads to the suspicion that the determinations are not in error, leaving one with the conclusion that the argon content is variable.

The question then arises whether from a geochronological point of view the low values or the high ones are in error. High argon values could be caused by extraneous argon from a number of sources; low values might result from leakage.

In 1971 we found that there were two distinct levels of pumice in Tuff D, and it was suggested that perhaps part of the reason for the large spread in ages was that pumice had been collected from these different levels. The feldspar from both levels is of the same composition, and this may be taken as evidence that the tuff represents a single volcanic event. It may also be argued that the two levels represent two separate volcanic events but that the feldspar happens to be of the same composition. In any case the dates KA-2510R and KA-2511 fall into the older category rather than into the young set, and both are from the upper pumice level. De Heinzelin (pers. comm.) has suggested that the pumices of the lower level were exposed to some grade of incipient weathering, with possible consequent loss of argon, whereas those of the upper pumice level "look indeed fresher, and are expected to be more reliable."

A second date (4.99 m.y.) has now been determined for Tuff B (see table 4), which is in marked disagreement with the earlier date (3.79 m.y.). The data on both dates have been reexamined, and there seems to be no reason to doubt either of the argon determinations or the potassium determinations. The possibility of contamination by older feldspar is much greater for Tuff B than for any of the other tuffs, and although care was taken to avoid this, the pumice clasts from Tuff B are small and contamination cannot be considered impossible. Paleomagnetic data indicate that both dates may be in error.

A second date has also been obtained on the thick tuff underlying the fossiliferous deposits of the Usno Formation. This date is considered more reliable than the earlier date, and it is likely that the age of the fossils from this formation are slightly older than the previous estimate given by Brown (1972). At that time, the only date available was 2.64 ± 0.92 m.y., and the fossils were supposed to be approximately 90,000 years younger than this. Assuming that the newer date is more nearly correct, the fossils at White Sands and Brown Sands should be about 2.9 m.y. in age.

Two other dates of interest are those of KA-2515 and KA-2508. Of the three groups of rocks exposed in the Nkalabong range, the oldest is the crystalline basement; its outcrops restricted to the lower reaches of a narrow canyon which lies almost due southeast of the peak of the range and debouches onto the plain of the northern lower Omo basin. The rocks consist of folded gneisses which have been subsequently cut by pegmatites and aplites made up dominantly of alkali feldspars, quartz, and accessory muscovite. A sample of orthoclase from one of the pegmatites yielded an age of 451 ± 20 m.y. It must be emphasized that this date represents a minimum estimate because the specimen records the latest event recognizable in the metamorphic complex and because the feldspar is perthitized. Perthitized feldspars are known to give low ages relative to biotite from the same rock; typically the ages are 20 to 30% too low, but they may be as much as 85% too low (see Dalrymple and Lanphere 1969, p. 168).

Overlying the crystalline basement is a group of lavas and pyroclastic rocks which make up the bulk of the mountain. The lavas consist dominantly of fine-grained basalt and porphyritic rhyolites and trachytes. Basaltic flows here seldom exceed 12 to 15 m in thickness and are often less than 6 m thick. In contrast, the rhyolites are rather thick, single flows often exceeding 60 m. The total thickness of this volcanic sequence is probably greater than 1,500 m. The oldest flows rest directly on the metamorphic complex and are basaltic. Feeder dikes which cut the metamorphic rocks are well exposed in the canyon mentioned above. It appears that the succession consists of basalts overlain by rhyolites and trachytes, followed again by a sequence of basalt, and finally rhyolite. Near the top of the range, a thick tuff breccia occurs overlain by a sodic rhyolite.

The southwestern portion of Nkalabong is made up of massive rhyolites and rhyolitic tuffs. Silicified wood similar to that noted by Fuchs (1939) near Naramum in the Lorienatom range is common on these western slopes.

The overall petrographic and structural similarity leads one to suspect that the older volcanic sequence on Nkalabong might correlate with the Tertiary lavas of Lorienatom and Lokwanamur to the southwest. These lavas are mapped as Tertiary olivine basalts and rhyolites by Walsh and Dodson (1969), and Reilly et al. (1966) have obtained potassium-argon ages of 23 m.y. on the upper basalt sequence (Tvb_2) of Walsh and Dodson. We separated plagioclase from a porphyritic basalt found near the middle of the older volcanic sequence on Nkalabong and obtained a date of 20.1 ± 2 m.y. This lends credence to the supposed correlation between the two sets of volcanic rocks.

The third group of rocks on Nkalabong is a series of thin basalt flows exposed on the northwestern side of Nkalabong. The flows dip gently to the west and often exhibit columnar jointing. The basalts are nonporphyritic and consist of interlocking laths of medium plagioclase, clinopyroxene, and ilmenite in roughly equal-sized grains, with turbid altered glass filling the interstices. Olivine grains are occasionally seen, of hortonolitic to chrysolitic composition. Dikes cut the flows, but petrographically are exactly the same. The most distinctive feature of these lavas is their regularity in grain size and mineralogy. It is not possible to distinguish a lava from the top of the sequence from one at the bottom, nor is it possible to distinguish a dike from a flow by petrographic means.

The basalt which occurs at Yellow Sands is of this petrographic type, as is the basalt at the White Sands fossil locality. The dates of these basalts, 3.3 m.y. and 4.1 m.y., perhaps represent the latter part of the volcanism. Occasional lenses of tuff and coarse gravels occur intercalated with the lavas on the northern slopes of Nkalabong, and it is possible that these in some way correlate with the Yellow Sands sequence of sediments described by Butzer and Thurber (1969).

Possible Source Area of the Tuffs

Brown (1972) suggested that Mount Damota near Soddu in Ethiopia might be a likely source for at least some of the tuffs of the Shungura Formation. Petrography of a small collection of rocks from this mountain indicates that the lavas are silica-rich and peralkaline. All samples contain phenocrysts of quartz and anorthoclase. In addition they contain alkali amphibole, enigmatite, sodic hedenbergite, fayalite, and manganese-rich ilmenite. In all of these features, the Damota rocks are similar to the Shungura tuffs.

Average analyses of feldspars from the Damota rocks are given in table 1 (sample numbers S1 to S6), and an average pyroxene analysis is given in table 3. Average BaO and FeO contents of feldspars from Soddu are plotted in figure 3. In terms of $CaO-Na_2O-K_2O$ contents, feldspars from Soddu lie on the compositional trend of those from the Omo tuffs and, with one exception, fall within the most common compositional variation limits of the tuff feldspars.

The amphiboles in the Soddu samples are richer in iron than those analyzed from the Omo tuffs. They are also richer in Ti and Na and depleted in Mg and Ca. Although basically similar, the Soddu amphiboles are more highly evolved in terms of magmatic differentiation. Similarly, the pyroxenes are generally more iron-rich than most of those from the Omo tuffs, although they do fall at the iron-rich end of the Omo $CaO-MgO-FeO$ compositional variation trend.

The similarity in rock types and mineralogy of Shungura tuffs and the lavas from Mount Damota indicates that the latter is a possible source for the tuffs. As an example, feldspars from sample S5 strongly resemble feldspars from tuffs I_2, KF-2, and ERL-70-4. However, none of the Soddu samples can be positively correlated with a specific Shungura tuff at this time.

Summary and Conclusions

The sediments of the lower Omo basin span an age range from somewhat greater than 4 m.y. to somewhat less than 1.4 m.y, excluding the younger sedimentary accumulations (Bourillé and Kibish formations). Although most potassium-argon ages are supported by the paleomagnetic evidence collected so far, problems have been noted, and it is possible that some revisions in age estimates may become necessary as more work is done.

Acknowledgments

The cooperation of the governments of Ethiopia and Kenya in making research possible in the lower Omo valley is gratefully acknowledged. Similar thanks are due to the National

Science Foundation and the Wenner-Gren Foundation for Anthropological Research for financial assistance. Support for microprobe analyses was provided by National Science Foundation grant GA-37088 and by the Institutional Fund of the University of Utah. A. K. Behrensmeyer provided the samples of pumice from the East Rudolf tuffs on which some of the work was done, and we thank her for these specimens.

Appendix: Locality Data for East Rudolf Tuffs

ERL 70-1   Pumice from lacustrine tuff, Koobi Fora area (Upper Member, Koobi Fora Tuff)

ERL 70-2   Pumice from lacustrine tuff, Sibilot area (Kubi Algi Formation, lower tuff)

ERL 70-3   Pumice from lacustrine tuff, Ileret area (Ileret Member, Chari Tuff)

ERL 70-4   Pumice from the "Tool Site Tuff," Koobi Fora area (KBS Tuff)

KF 2   Pumice from fluvial tuff, Koobi Fora area (Koobi Fora IIA) (KBS Tuff)

For an explanation of stratigraphic nomenclature and maps, see Vondra and Bowen, Findlater (this symposium).

References

Brown, F. H. 1969. Observations on the stratigraphy and radiometric age of the Omo Beds, lower Omo basin, southern Ethiopia. *Quaternaria* 11:7-14.

Brown, F. H. 1972. Radiometric dating of sedimentary formations in the lower Omo valley, Ethiopia. In *Calibration of hominoid evolution*, pp. 273-87. Edinburgh: Scottish Academic Press; Toronto: University of Toronto Press.

Brown, F. H., and Lajoie, K. R. 1971. K-Ar ages of the Omo group and fossil localities of the Shungura Formation, southwest Ethiopia. *Nature* 229:483-85.

Butzer, K. W., and Thurber, D. L 1969. Some late Cenozoic sedimentary formations of the lower Omo basin. *Nature* 222:1138-43.

Dalrymple, G. B., and Lanphere, M. A. 1969. *Potassium-argon dating.* San Francisco: W. A. Freeman and Co.

Fuchs, V. E. 1939. The geological history of the Lake Rudolf basin, Kenya Colony. *Phil. Trans. Roy. Soc. London,* ser. B, 229:219-74.

Heinzelin, J. de; Brown, F. H.; and Howell, F. C. 1970. Pliocene/Pleistocene formations in the lower Omo basin, southern Ethiopia. *Quaternaria* 13:247-68.

Reilly, T. A.; Musset, A. E.; Raja, P. R. S.; Grasty, R. L.; and Walsh, J. 1966. Age and polarity of the Turkana lavas, northwest Kenya. *Nature* 210:1145-46.

Walsh, J., and Dodson, R. G 1969. Geology of Northern Turkana. Mines and Geological Department of Kenya, Report no. 82.

6. MAGNETOSTRATIGRAPHY OF THE SHUNGURA AND USNO FORMATIONS,
LOWER OMO VALLEY, ETHIOPIA

F. H. Brown and R. T. Shuey

Introduction

The Shungura Formation is situated in the Omo basin in the southwestern corner of
Ethiopia, and consists of about 850 m of well-exposed late Pliocene and early Pleistocene
fluvial and lacustrine sediments. The Usno Formation is exposed about 25 km to the northeast of the Shungura Formation and consists of about 210 m of similar sediments. The
stratigraphy of these formations is described elsewhere in this volume by de Heinzelin and
Haesaerts, and the terminology used in this chapter is consistent with theirs. Please
consult their chapter for details of stratigraphy and nomenclature. A small collection of
samples taken in 1972 indicated that the sediments of the lower Omo valley were quite
suitable for detailed magnetostratigraphic work, and therefore in 1973 we made a survey of
the entire Shungura and Usno formations.

Fieldwork

Paleomagnetic samples were taken from shallow pits dug at stratigraphic intervals of
1 to 2 m. In each pit three cubes about 2 cm^2 were cut with knives and hacksaws. Cubes
were oriented north by compass, and level with the bedding by eye. We estimate the accura-
cy of sample orientation to be ± 5°. All lithologies were collected, and only in a few
coarse sands was sampling unsuccessful. All samples were encapsulated in household cement
while still moist. This step was essential, for otherwise the clayey samples cracked and
the sandy ones sloughed.

Samples up to the middle of Member J of the Shungura Formation were taken within a
few kilometers of the American camp (fig. 1). Above Member J-5 the Shungura Formation near
the American camp is covered by late Pleistocene lake deposits. Hence the top of the formation was sampled some 20 km to the south, near the village and police post of Kalam
(fig. 1). Figures 2, 3, and 4 show the actual stratigraphic levels sampled. The Usno Formation was sampled at its outcrop area (fig. 1), and the stratigraphic levels sampled are
shown in Figure 5.

A report of this work has previously been published by Shuey, Brown and Croes (1974).

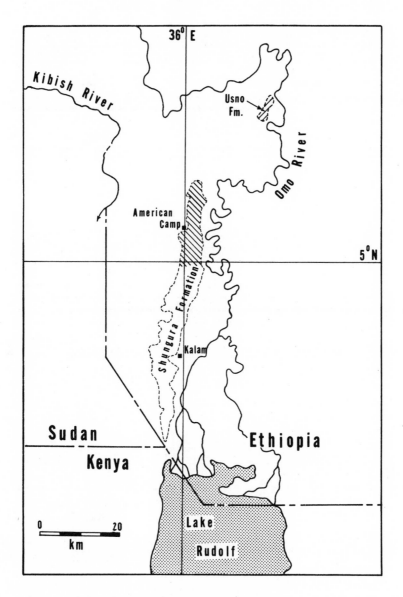

Figure 1. Index map of the lower Omo basin, southwestern Ethiopia, showing principal outcrop areas of the Shungura and Usno formations.

Laboratory Work

Remanent magnetization was measured on a DIGICO spinner magnetometer. Initial intensities were typically 10-30 x 10^{-6} emu/cc. The rough magnetostratigraphy was worked out in a few days by two-spin measurements on one cube per site. Subsequent measurements used the full six spins. Each sample was measured at least five times and was progressively demagnetized in alternating fields increased in steps of 25 or 50 gauss to 200 gauss or more. It was then classified as "normal," "reverse," or "indeterminate," with the

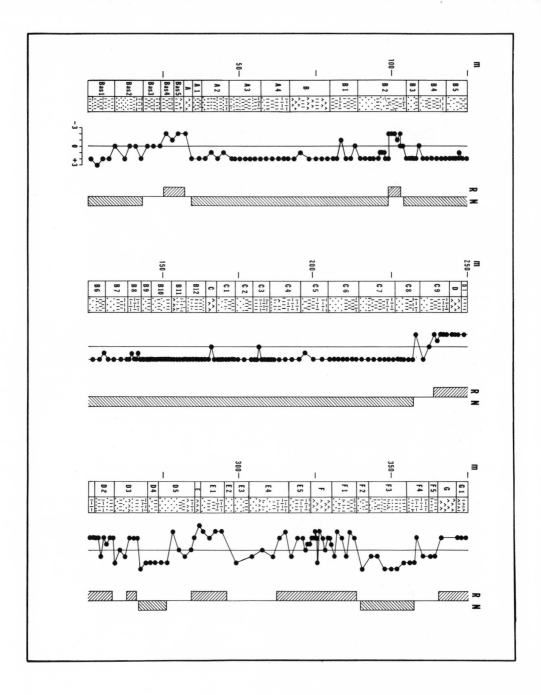

Figure 2. Paleomagnetic log of the lower Shungura Formation as sampled east of the American Camp. Left column shows measured thickness in meters, member and submember designations, and simplified lithology. (See fig. 3 for key to lithologic symbols.) Center column shows stratigraphic levels sampled and the "total polarity" described in text. Arrows mark sites where polarity determinations conflict.

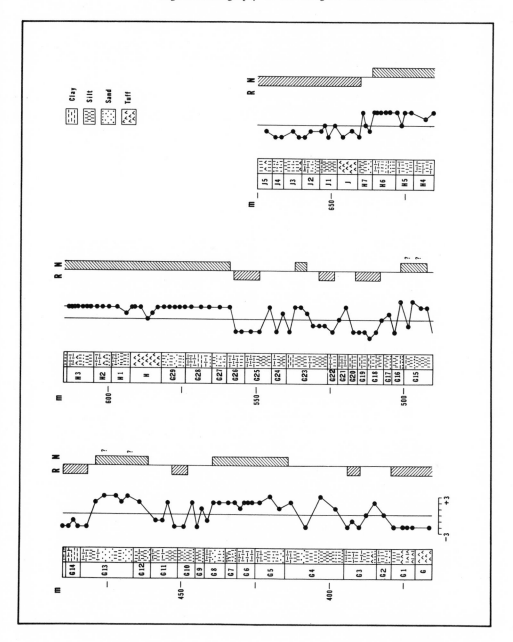

Figure 3. Paleomagnetic log of middle Shungura Formation. See fig. 2 for further explanation.

condition for definite polarity being a reproducible magnetization of coercivity more than 150 gauss directed within a cone of 30° half-angle with the axis horizontal and north-south. Since the area is located at 5° N latitude, mean inclination was actually positive for normal samples and negative for reverse samples.

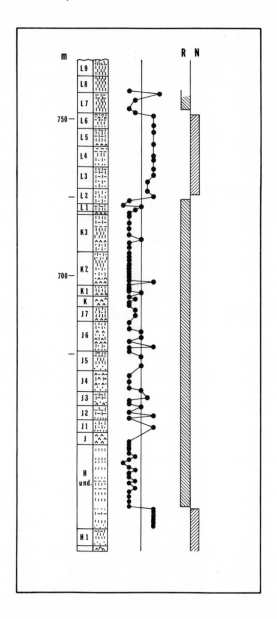

Figure 4. Paleomagnetic log of upper Shungura Formation as sampled west of Kalam. See fig. 2 for further explanation.

Of the 1,500 cubes originally collected from the Shungura Formation, we have actually measured only about 1,070. We did not measure the third cube from a site whenever the first two gave a definite polarity in agreement with each other and the polarity at stratigraphically adjacent sites. Outstanding in this respect were Members A, Upper Member B, and Members C, F, and H. Of the 240 cubes collected from the Usno Formation we have measured only about 160, since the others are being kept for thermal demagnetization.

The quality of our paleomagnetic samples showed no apparent relation to primary lithology but was strikingly correlated with topographic slope. The troublesome samples

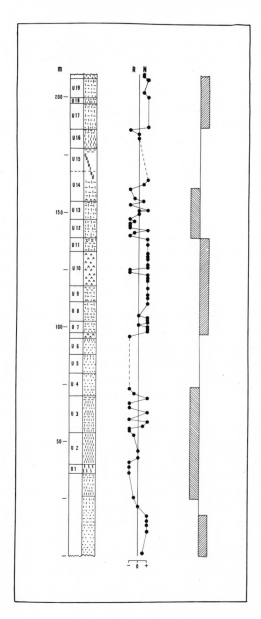

Figure 5. Paleomagnetic log of Usno Formation. (See fig. 2 for further explanation.)

generally came from a nearly horizontal surface, where erosion is slow. This effect had not been fully appreciated during the sampling. Thus a future field expedition might be able to obtain better samples at many of the stratigraphic horizons where polarity is still uncertain.

Of the 1,230 cubes measured, about 140 were classified as indeterminate. In some cases the direction was stable but outside our 30° limit, but more often most of the natural magnetization was removed by relatively low alternating field, and no repeatable hard component could be identified. Whenever two or more samples from the same site had a definite polarity, this was almost invariably consistent between samples. At only 18 sites were there conflicting polarities. A few of these might be caused by labeling error.

Magnetostratigraphy

After completing the measurement process described above we performed an algebraic sum for each of the 500 sampling sites. We counted "+1" for a normal sample, "-1" for a reversed sample, and "0" for an indeterminate sample. This total polarity is shown in figures 2, 3, 4, and 5 for the various sites. A zero value may represent indeterminate or conflicting measurements. In either case we cannot assign a polarity to the site. Where all is well we have either "+2" or "-2."

The polarity log was smoothed to arrive at a preliminary magnetostratigraphy. This is shown in figures 2, 3, 4, and 5. In this smoothing process any isolated sites in conflict with a long sequence above and below were simply ignored. Where the polarity log alternated in sign or was zero at successive sites, no polarity was shown on the smoothed magnetostratigraphic column. The result is preliminary since further sampling would be desired to fill in the gaps and to trace laterally those polarity subzones presently based on only three to five sites.

The various magnetozones shown on figures 2 through 5 differ greatly in the certainty with which the present data define their upper and lower stratigraphic limits and even their existence. The results from the lower and upper parts of the section are clear on the diagrams and need little discussion, but we will review the status of the zones in the middle part of the section in detail. The small reversed part of the section in Member B-2 is recorded by samples which seem quite reliable magnetically, and there is little reason to doubt its existence. It could well represent a reversed event out of proportion to its stratigraphic thickness, because the transition from normal to reverse is at a minor erosional surface separating units B-2-4 and B-2-5, and the magnetic field could have been reversed during all of the time period of nondeposition and erosion.

The magnetostratigraphy of the middle part of the Shungura Formation--members D, E, F, and G is much less clear than in the upper and lower parts, and consequently we discuss the portion of the section from Tuff D to G-26 in detail.

Tuff D and submembers D-1 and D-2 seem reversed, although at one site in D-2 we had two indeterminate samples and one normal sample. The samples from three sites in lower D-3 were all rather dubious magnetically, although several were classified normal by our criteria. Since three consecutive sites above these gave stable reverse readings, we rather suspect a continuous reverse magnetozone. The upper part of this zone includes a yellow tuff probably equivalent to the "sanidine sand" designated in table 1. There is a very definite transition from reverse to normal, apparently at the minor diastem separating D-3-2 and D-3-3. The normal zone includes the silt of D-3-3, the graded bedding of D-4, and the concreted sand of D-5-1. All samples from these beds are quite stable magnetically, and there seems no reason to doubt the existence of the normal zone. It is not clear from our present samples whether D-5-2 is included in the normal zone. In any case the time represented is fairly short, perhaps a few tens of thousands of years. Tuff E and submember E-1 are definitely reversely magnetized. The samples from E-2 disintegrated and those from E-3 and lower E-4 were rather scattered magnetically. But all samples from the uppermost two sites in E-4 had stable reverse magnetization. This sort of result continues through submember F-1, and we suspect that the entire interval from Tuff E to submember F-1 is a single reverse magnetozone.

Table 1

K-Ar Dates on Tuffs of the Shungura and Usno Formations

Tuff	No. of Dates	Age Range (m.y.)
L	2	1.27-1.41
I_2	3	1.81-1.87
G	1	1.93
F	2	1.99-2.06
E_i	1	2.12
D	7	2.16-2.60
B-10	2	2.93-2.96
B	2	3.79-4.99
U-10	2	2.64-2.97
U-1 (basalt)	2	3.11-3.51

SOURCE: Brown and Nash, this symposium.

There is a definite transition from reverse to normal between F-1 and F-2, and all of F-3 is normal. This zone may extend to the top of Member F. The submembers involved, F-2, F-3, F-4, and F-5, are mostly silt and sand. Each has a marked lateral variation in thickness, and F-2 is frequently absent. Thus the time represented by this normal zone is probably rather less than might be supposed from the total thickness shown in figure 2.

Tuff G and submember G-1 are definitely reversed, and no results were obtained from the one site in G-2. We consider G-3 all reversed, although two of three samples from the basal sand gave normal directions. In submember G-4 we suspect a hard secondary magnetization, since the basal concreted sand is again normal but there is an overlying reversed site. All samples from G-5, G-6, and G-7 are normal and offer no reason to doubt the existence of a normal magnetozone, although its limits are obscure. Submembers G-9 and G-10 again show the phenomenon of normal directions in the base and reverse magnetization in the top. We hypothesize the primary magnetization is reverse. Submember G-11 has mixed polarity, but without a definite vertical pattern. The thick block of normal sites in G-13 is mostly concreted sand, and in view of the pattern described above the existence of a normal magnetozone is highly questionable. The top clay of G-13 and the tuffaceous clay of G-14 are reversely magnetized. Submember G-16 shows the pattern of normal bottom and reversed top, and so the existence of the normal magnetozone shown on the smoothed polarity log is doubtful. In fact, the only firm evidence in our present data for normal primary magnetization anywhere from Tuff G to submember G-26 is in G-23. Here in a thick section of lacustrine clayey silt all samples between two minor diastems are normal. Several linear kilometers of exposure are available, so a future expedition to the Omo could readily test this possible normal magnetozone. Even should it prove out, the time involved is necessarily short, probably less than 10,000 years.

At submember G-26 there is a definite transition from reverse to normal, and this normal zone continues through Member H, ending somewhere before Tuff J. In the section near camp (fig. 3) the transition is in H-7.

All of Members J and K are considered reversely magnetized. The upper limit of this reversed zone is apparently at a fossiliferous concretionary layer in Member L-2. The middle part of Member L is normal, and the very top of the Kalam exposures is again reversely magnetized.

The lowest part of the Usno Formation has not been formally described, but samples from this part of the section are of normal polarity. There appears to be a transition from normal to reverse about 10 m below Member U-1, a basaltic lava flow. The basalt is reversely magnetized, and although the data are poor we consider Members U-2, 3, and 4 reversely magnetized. The two reversed samples in U-10 are attributed to labeling error, since they occur in the middle of a thick tuff for which twelve other samples gave normal polarity. A transition from normal to reverse polarity occurs at the minor diastem between U-11 and U-12, and this reversed magnetozone extends through U-12, U-13, and U-14. The upper boundary of this magnetozone is poorly defined, and could lie anywhere between upper U-14 and the top of U-16. The top of the section (U-17, U-18, U-19, and U-20) is of normal polarity. The poor quality of the data is probably due to the shallow exposures, which were also noted in the samples from the Shungura Formation.

Radiometric and Faunal Data

In order to correlate the magnetostratigraphy of the Shungura Formation with the standard polarity scales (Dalrymple 1972; Cox 1969) some independent chronological data are needed. Table 1 gives the K-Ar determinations available for the interbedded tuffs, and a fuller discussion of these dates will be found in Brown and Nash, this volume. Since the dates are all fairly repeatable and in stratigraphic order, they cannot be grossly in error. The K-Ar data implies that we are dealing with the Gauss and Matuyama polarity epochs.

More than 20,000 mammalian fossils have been recovered from the Shungura Formation. Faunal arguments from many different families may be used to correlate the upper part of the Shungura Formation (Members H and J) with Bed I and Lower Bed II at Olduvai Gorge, which has become the standard section for East Africa. These beds are also the type locality for the Olduvai normal polarity event, and are now thought to span 1.7-1.9 m.y. (Gromme and Hay 1971). Three examples of such faunal arguments are: (1) the stage of evolution in the *Mesochoerus limnetes-Mesochoerus olduvaiensis* lineage (Cooke and Maglio 1972); (2) the stage of evolution of *Elephas recki* (Maglio 1970); (3) the stage of evolution of *Kobus sigmoidalis-Kobus ellipsiprymnus* (A. W. Gentry, pers. comm.).

Brief Review of the Lower Matuyama Epoch

Chronological interpretation of the Shungura magnetostratigraphy is made difficult by a serious uncertainty in the number of global polarity reversals which occurred in the lower Matuyama reversed epoch. We wish to review this situation as we see it.

In deep-sea cores, the lower Matuyama has only one normal event, called either the Olduvai or the Gilsa. On the hypothesis that there indeed is only one event, Opdyke (1972) proposes 1.71 and 1.86 m.y. as best estimates for its boundaries. The compilation by Dalrymple (1972) of reliable K-Ar dates on volcanics of measured polarity shows only normal data in the age range 1.65-1.82 m.y. More recent K-Ar data suggest that the temporal limits of this event should be ca. 1.6-1.8 m.y. If this is indeed the case, then both the Gilsa and Olduvai type lavas represent this same event, which would also be the one seen in deep sea cores. The compilation by Dalrymple (1972) shows only reversed data in the age range 1.86-1.93 m.y., and Fleck et al. (1973) have reported a reversed lava at 1.86 m.y. Thus there seems to be a definite reversed interval preceding the Gilsa/Olduvai event postulated above.

There is abundant evidence of a plurality of short normal events in the lower Matuyama epoch preceding the major one just described. Attempts at high-resolution analyses of oceanic profiles have repeatedly suggested such events. The classic work of Heirtzler

et al. (1968) reported a persistent anomaly "X" preceding the Gilsa/Olduvai anomaly.
Emilia and Heinrichs (1969) assigned an age of 2.3 ± 0.1 m.y. to this anomaly. They also
identified a "W" anomaly centered at 1.97 m.y., and subsequently (Emilia and Heinrichs
(1972) a third anomaly at 2.17 m.y. Deep-towed magnetometer data also suggest several
short normal events prior to 1.9 m.y. (Klitgord et al. 1974).

The K-Ar data seem to give a picture quite like that of the oceanic magnetic anomalies.
McDougall and Aziz-ur-Rahman (1972) have fixed the age of the Gauss-Matuyama boundary at
2.41 ± 0.01 m.y. This implies that the normal lava of Valencio, Linares, and Villas (1970)
at 2.31 ± 0.09 m.y. could represent a brief normal event, correlative with the "X" anomaly.
Dalrymple's compilation (1972) shows two normal lavas at 2.08 and 2.09 m.y. Cox (1969)
had designated this as the older Olduvai event, but Grommé and Hay (1971) redesignated it
the older Reunion event. However, the Reunion sample first dated 2.08 m.y. has now apparently been assigned an age of 2.04 ± 0.02 m.y. (McDougall and Watkins 1973). From radiometric and paleomagnetic work on numerous flows of known stratigraphic order, McDougall
and Watkins (1973) concluded that the true Reunion event has a mean age of 2.02 ± 0.02 m.y.
Fleck et al. (1973) report a normal lava at 2.04 ± 0.02 m.y. and an underlying intermediate
lava at 2.06 ± 0.03 m.y., which probably records the bottom of this Reunion event. The
question of an "older Reunion event" near 2.1 m.y. remains open. In addition, there are
two normal lavas dated 1.95 ± 0.10 m.y. and 1.96 ± 0.04 m.y. from the Pribilof Islands
(Dalrymple 1972) which might represent a short event between the Reunion and the Gilsa/
Olduvai. All these normal lavas between 1.95 and 2.09 m.y. are to be correlated with the
"W" magnetic anomaly.

It might seem that we have been inconsistent in analyzing the radiometric data, play-
ing "lumpers" in the 1.6-1.9 m.y. time range and "splitters" in the 1.9-2.4 m.y. time
range. But such a bias seems to be dictated by the marine anomalies and the deep-sea
cores. Both show a big event which is dated by interpolation and stacking as younger than
1.9 m.y. There are quite a few normal lavas which must be in the range 1.9-2.2 m.y., if
the radiometric error analyses are taken seriously. If these were all in one event, it
would be most strange that such an event never turns up in deep-sea cores. But if the
polarity in the time interval 1.9-2.2 m.y. had an alternating character, with several short
normal events taking perhaps half as much time as the intervening reversed periods, then
all data would be accounted for.

Magnetochronology

Let us now consider correlation between the standard polarity scale(s) and the
polarity zones we have identified in the Shungura Formation. We will begin with correlations that seem rather unambiguous and proceed to speculations that demand additional
fieldwork.

The most striking feature of the magnetostratigraphy is the long normal zone from B-3
through C-8. We consider that this can only be the upper part of the Gauss normal epoch.
The two short reversed zones below it are then identified as the Mammoth and Kaena events.
Using the boundaries estimated by McDougall and Aziz-ur-Rahman (1972), we can then assign
dates to the lower part of the Shungura Formation as in figure 6. These "paleomagnetic
dates" make the bottom of the section rather younger than suggested by the K-Ar dates of
table 1. In particular, Tuff B is assigned an age of about 2.95 m.y., whereas the two K-Ar
dates for it are 3.79 and 4.99 m.y. Of course the gross discrepancy between the two K-Ar
runs makes one willing to consider them both bad. We believe that putting the long normal

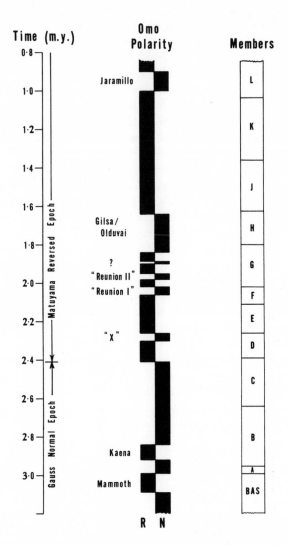

Figure 6.   Interpreted magnetochronology of the entire Shungura Formation.   See text for details of reasoning by which this figure was constructed from figs. 2-4.

zone anywhere other than in the upper Gauss epoch makes unreasonable demands on the sedimentation rate when the entire magnetostratigraphy has to be fitted to the standard polarity scales.   Such unreasonable demands had in fact been made by the K-Ar dates on Tuff B.

The "paleomagnetic date" for Tuff D is exactly the mean K-Ar date, which is ironic in that the K-Ar runs for Tuff D were more scattered than for any other tuff except Tuff B.

The next most certain identification is of the normal zone in Member H with the normal zone in Bed I at Olduvai Gorge.   This is completely consistent with the K-Ar dates and almost demanded by the faunal evidence.   We also find it a rather certain result of any attempt to match our magnetostratigraphy to the standard polarity scale(s) while being consistent with the geologic evidence of de Heinzelin and Haesaerts.

The question then arises whether the normal zone in Member L is the Jaramillo event (about 0.9 m.y.) or the Gilsa event (about 1.6 m.y.). We definitely favor the former interpretation for the following reasons. The radiometric dates on Tuff L range from 1.27 to 1.41 m.y., and a tuff approximately 20 m below Tuff L has yielded an age of 1.43 m.y. (F223 in Brown and Nash, this volume). Since the normal magnetozone lies above these dated horizons, the implication is that it must be the Jaramillo event. In addition, "compression" of Members J and K into 50,000 years would imply a sedimentation rate greater than 200 cm/1,000 yrs, which is a factor of 5 greater than the computed rates in fluvial parts of the section near camp (table 2), and a factor of 7 greater than the computed rate near Kalam in the lower part of the section. On the other hand, "stretching" this part of the section out to 0.5 m.y. results in a sedimentation rate of about 20 cm/1,000 yrs, which is much closer to (although lower than) other computed rates. Additional evidence comes from a statistical analysis of all Shungura fauna (to be published elsewhere). By assuming a constant rate of evolution we have derived a faunal time scale for the Shungura Formation. This matches the paleomagnetic time scale only if the upper part of the section is stretched as just described. Thus all three lines of evidence--radiometric, sedimentological, and faunal--agree that the uppermost normal magnetozone is the Jaramillo event. It should be recalled that oceanic profiles show no evidence for a separate "Gilsa" event preceding the main anomaly, and a high resolution study by Opdyke, Kent, and Lowrie (1973) of the top of the Olduvai event also showed no separate Gilsa. The identification of the normal zone in Member L as the Jaramillo event rather implies that the Gilsa and Olduvai events are the same, and figure 6 is so labeled.

Table 2

Average Sedimentation Rates in the Shungura Formation

Time period (m.y.)	Area	Rate (cm/1,000 yrs)
3.2-2.4	Camp	40
2.4-1.6	Camp	50
2.4-1.6	Kalam	30
1.6-0.9	Kalam	20

The above interpretations fairly well define the chronology of the Shungura Formation. Combination with measured stratigraphic thicknesses gives the mean sedimentation rates presented in table 2. Note that spatially the rate is greater to the north and east (toward the source), whereas temporally it is greater in the middle of the formation.

It remains to discuss the several normal zones interpreted to correspond to events in the lower Matuyama epoch before the major one. For the zone in the middle of Member D, there are two alternative interpretations. Its proximity to Tuff E_i with one K-Ar date of 2.12 m.y. would suggest that it should be called a Reunion event. But if the effective sedimentation rate is kept reasonably constant at the levels in table 2, this normal zone would be dated around 2.3 m.y. We therefore identify it with the "X" magnetic anomaly of Heirtzler et al. (1968) and the lava of Valencio, Linares, and Villas (1970). This implies that the K-Ar date on Tuff E_i is too young by 0.12-0.20 m.y. It should be added that the stratigraphy of Member D is complex and has not been worked out in full detail.

The magnetostratigraphy shows two other substantial normal events, in Member F and in lower Member G. Either one could be correlated with the "true" Reunion event shown to be somewhere in the period 2.00-2.05 m.y. by McDougall and Watkins. Accordingly we have labeled them in figure 6 as Reunion I and Reunion II. This is perhaps the greatest ambiguity in correlating the Shungura magnetostratigraphy with the standard magnetochronological data. The radiometric dates are better fit by taking our Reunion I as the true Reunion, and figure 6 is so arranged.

There remains one normal zone which seems to be real in the data available so far. It is shown with a question mark in figure 6 because its validity as a magnetozone in the Shungura Formation requires further sampling.

Correlation of the Shungura and Usno Formations

As in the case of the Shungura Formation, some independent chronological data are needed in order to identify the magnetozones recognized there. The K-Ar determinations available for the Usno Formation are given in table 1, and range from 3.5 ± 0.7 m.y. (U-1) to 2.97 ± 0.3 m.y. (U-10). A fuller discussion of these dates can be found in Brown and Nash, this volume. These data imply that we are dealing with the lower part of the Gauss polarity epoch. The radiometric data are given support by faunal correlation, which indicates that the Usno Formation is somewhat older than B-10 of the Shungura Formation.

The only two reversed events known in the lower Gauss normal epoch are the Kaena and Mammoth events, and we identify the reversed magnetozones of the Usno Formation with these events. Accepting this interpretation results in the correlation shown in figure 7. The bulk of the fauna from the Usno Formation (U-12), lies near the base of the Kaena event, and thus is assigned an age of about 2.9 m.y. It is correlative with the fauna of upper B-2 of the Shungura Formation. Fossils from U-19 and U-20 (Flat Sands) are probably equivalent in age to fossils from upper Member B of the Shungura Formation.

The Shungura and Usno formations differ strikingly in the relative thicknesses of the Gauss magnetozones (table 3). This is due to nonuniform sedimentation rates, and we have

Table 3
Thickness or Time for Mammoth and Kaena Events, Relative to Intervening Interval

	Mammoth	Kaena
Cox (1969)	3.0	2.5
Usno	1.7	0.9
Opdyke (1972)	0.85	0.8
Shungura	0.17	0.09

already discussed how the reversed events are truncated at minor unconformities in the Shungura Formation. The implication is that in terrestrial sequences such as these, events 0.1 m.y. long are fairly sure to be detected but only with poor fidelity in their duration. The situation is worse in deep-sea cores. Harrison (1974) lists 24 cores that have penetrated the whole of the Gauss normal epoch. Of these only 11 had two reversed zones; 6 had one zone; 6 had no zones; and 1 had three zones.

Conclusions

The paleomagnetic sampling of the Shungura and Usno Formations has had several results. Most importantly it has provided a rather definite chronology for these formations which basically confirm the dates previously assigned to major fossil localities, at least within the temporal resolution of faunal evolution. The major difference between the K-Ar and

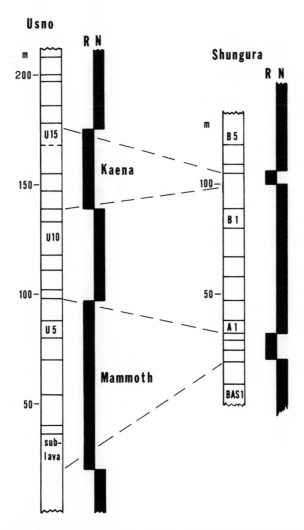

Figure 7. Correlation proposed between the Usno and Shungura formations on the basis of magnetic boundaries

paleomagnetic age assignments is that the lowest part of the Shungura Formation is now thought to be only about 3.2 m.y. old whereas previously it was thought to be about 4 m.y. in age. In addition the paleomagnetic samples have clarified the stratigraphic relations between the Usno and Shungura formations and resulted in independent evidence for the age of the Usno fauna.

Acknowledgments

Special thanks go to Jean de Heinzelin and Paul Haesaerts, without whose careful work the detailed stratigraphy of the Shungura Formation would still not be complete, and to John Munyoki Mutua and Christopher Wambua, without whose help the sampling could not have been done in the time available. Marc Croes is thanked for his assistance in the laboratory work. The work was supported financially by National Science Foundation Grant GA38686.

References

Cooke, H. B. S., and Maglio, V. J. 1972. Plio-Pleistocene stratigraphy in East Africa in relation to proboscidean and suid evolution. In *Calibration of hominoid evolution*, ed. W. W. Bishop and J. A. Miller, pp. 303-29. Edinburgh: Scottish Academic Press; Toronto: University of Toronto Press.

Cox, A. 1969. Geomagnetic reversals *Science* 163:237-46.

Dalrymple, G. B. 1972. Potassium-argon dating of geomagnetic reversals and North American glaciations. In *Calibration of hominoid evolution*, ed. W. W. Bishop and J. A. Miller, p. 107. Edinburgh: Scottish Academic Press; Toronto: University of Toronto Press.

Emilia, D. A., and Heinrichs, D. F. 1969. Ocean floor spreading; Olduvai and Gilsa events in the Matuyama epoch. *Science* 166:1267-69.

_____. 1972. Paleomagnetic events in the Brunhes and Matuyama epochs identified from magnetic profiles reduced to the pole. *Marine Geophys. Res.* 1:436.

Fleck, R. J.; Mercer, J. H.; Nairn, A. E. M.; and Petersen, D. N. 1973. Chronology of late Pliocene and early Pleistocene glacial and magnetic events in southern Argentina. *Earth Planet. Sci. Lett.* 16:15-22.

Grommé, C. S., and Hay, R. L. 1971. Geomagnetic polarity epochs: Age and duration of the Olduvai normal polarity event. *Earth Planet Sci. Lett.* 10:179-85.

Harrison, C. G. A. 1974. The paleomagnetic record from deep sea sediment cores. *Earth-Sci. Rev.* 10:1-36.

Heirtzler, J. R.; Dickson, G. O.; Herron, E. N.; Pitman, W. C.; and LePichon, X. 1968. Marine magnetic anomalies, geomagnetic field reversals and motions of the ocean floor and continents. *J. Geophys. Res.* 73:2119-36.

Klitgord, K. D.; Huestis, S. P.; Mudie, J. D.; and Parker, R. L. 1974. The geomagnetic time scale 0 to 5 m.y. b.p. *EOS* 55:237.

Maglio, V. J. 1970. Early Elephantidae of Africa and a tentative correlation of African Plio-Pleistocene deposits. *Nature* 225:328.

McDougall, I., and Aziz-ur-Rahman. 1972. Age of the Gauss-Matuyama boundary and of the Kaena and Mammoth events. *Earth Planet. Sci. Lett.* 14:367-80.

McDougall, I., and Watkins, N. D. 1973. Age and duration of the Reunion geomagnetic polarity event. *Earth Planet. Sci. Lett.* 19:443-52.

Opdyke, N. D. 1972. Paleomagnetism of deep sea cores. *Rev. Geophys. Space Phys.* 10:213

Opdyke, N. D.; Kent, D. V.; and Lowrie, W. 1973. Details of magnetic polarity transitions recorded in a high deposition rate deep sea core. *Earth Planet. Sci. Lett.* 20:315-24.

Shuey, R. T.; Brown, F. H.; and Croes, M. K. 1974. Magnetostratigraphy of the Shungura Formation, southwestern Ethiopia: Fine structure of the lower Matuyama polarity epoch. *Earth Planet. Sci. Lett.* 23:249-60.

Valencio, D. A.; Linares, E.; and Villas, J. F. 1970. On the age of the Matuyama-Gauss transition. *Earth Planet. Sci. Lett.* 8:179-82.

7. PLIO-PLEISTOCENE DEPOSITS

AND ENVIRONMENTS, EAST RUDOLF, KENYA

C. F. Vondra and B. E. Bowen

Introduction

Geologic investigation of the East Rudolf basin was initiated by A. K. Behrensmeyer in 1969 (Leakey et al. 1970), and a survey of regional geology was undertaken. In 1970 fundamental rock units were established and mapped at a scale of 1:24,000 by a team from Iowa State University as a part of the National Museums of Kenya Expedition, and the study has been continued to date (Vondra et al. 1971; Bowen and Vondra 1973). More than sixty critically situated exposures were measured, described, and sampled to determine the lithology, major stratigraphic relationships, and depositional history of the Plio-Pleistocene sediments. "Marker beds" were delineated for use in local correlation and for the stratigraphic documentation of fossils. Detailed laboratory analyses--mechanical, microscopic, X-ray, and mass-spectrometer--of samples collected have been initiated to supplement the fieldwork and to provide a basis for paleoenvironmental interpretations.

Geologic Setting

The East Rudolf basin is located at the northern end of the Kenya Rift system. The main graben forms the Suguta valley at the southern end of Lake Rudolf and trends across the lake in a north-northeasterly direction. The northward continuation of the trend is the Kinu Sogo fault zone east of Lake Rudolf and the Stefanie graben on the Ethiopian border (Baker, Mohr, and Williams 1972). The area studied lies on the northwestern flanks of this trend (see Fitch and Vondra, this symposium).

The Suregei cuesta forms the northeastern and eastern margins of the East Rudolf basin. It is upheld by a series of westward-dipping interbedded Miocene (11.6 ± 0.5 m.y.) basalt flows and associated paleosols, ignimbrites, tuffs, and sediments that form a basement upon which the Plio-Pleistocene sediments were deposited. The Miocene volcanics were tilted westward by early Pliocene faulting and folding, forming an asymmetrical fault basin or half-graben bounded on the west by a major fracture system and on the east by a fractured monoclinal flexure. Along the southeastern and southern portion of the basin a complex of volcanics of Pliocene age is exposed down dip of the outcrop of Miocene volcanics. Lower Pliocene volcanics occur as isolated relief features which have been surrounded and partially buried by Upper Pliocene fissure eruptions. They are highly varied, consisting of a complex of faulted ignimbrites and associated agglomerates (as at Sibilot), volcanic plugs (Kubi Algi and Derati), and acidic flows and obsidian intrusions (Shin). (See fig. 1.) The

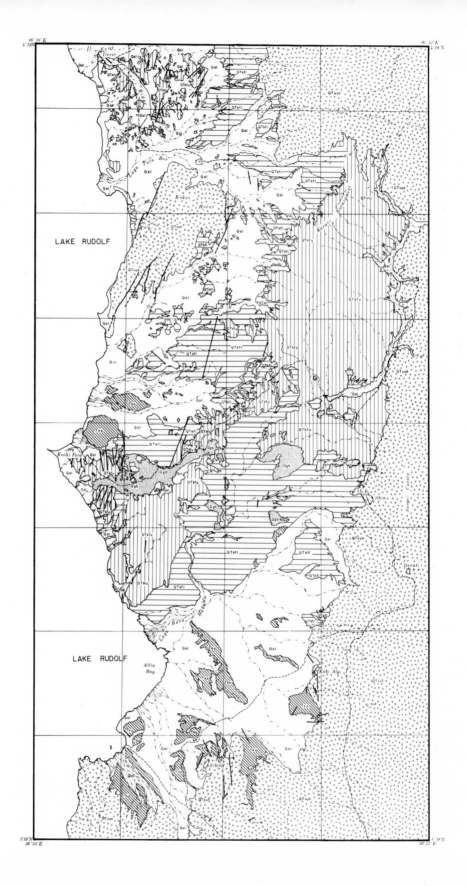

GEOLOGIC MAP of the EAST RUDOLF AREA

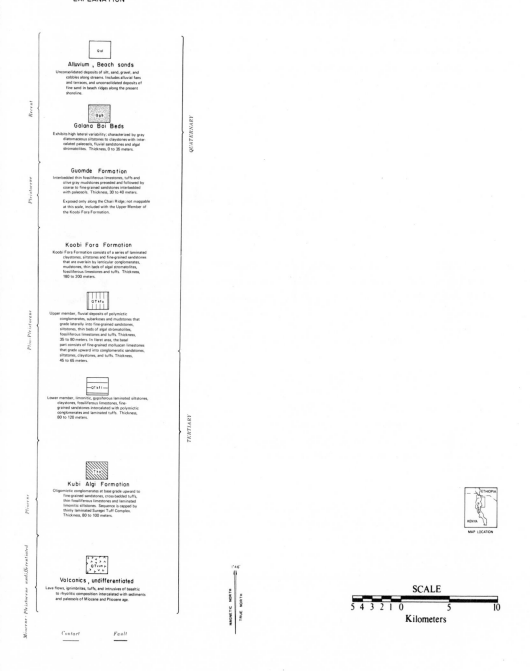

EXPLANATION

Alluvium , Beach sands

Unconsolidated deposits of silt, sand, gravel, and cobbles along streams. Includes alluvial fans and terraces, and unconsolidated deposits of fine sand in beach ridges along the present shoreline.

Galana Boi Beds

Exhibits high lateral variability; characterized by gray diatomaceous siltstones to claystones with intercalated paleosols, fluvial sandstones and algal stromatolites. Thickness, 0 to 35 meters.

Guomde Formation

Interbedded thin fossiliferous limestones, tuffs and olive gray mudstones preceded and followed by coarse to fine-grained sandstones interbedded with paleosols. Thickness, 30 to 40 meters.

Exposed only along the Chari Ridge; not mappable at this scale, included with the Upper Member of the Koobi Fora Formation.

Koobi Fora Formation

Koobi Fora Formation consists of a series of laminated claystones, siltstones and fine-grained sandstones that are overlain by lenticular conglomerates, mudstones, thin beds of algal stromatolites, fossiliferous limestones and tuffs. Thickness, 180 to 200 meters.

Upper member, fluvial deposits of polymictic conglomerates, suberkoses and mudstones that grade laterally into fine-grained sandstones, siltstones, thin beds of algal stromatolites, fossiliferous limestones and tuffs. Thickness, 35 to 80 meters. In Ileret area, the basal part consists of fine-grained molluscan limestones that grade upward into conglomeratic sandstones, siltstones, claystones, and tuffs. Thickness, 45 to 65 meters.

Lower member, limonitic, gypsiferous laminated siltstones, claystones, fossiliferous limestones, fine-grained sandstones intercalated with polymictic conglomerates and laminated tuffs. Thickness, 80 to 120 meters.

Kubi Algi Formation

Oligomictic conglomerates at base grade upward to fine-grained sandstones, cross-bedded tuffs, thin fossiliferous limestones and laminated limonitic siltstones. Sequence is capped by thinly laminated Suregei Tuff Complex. Thickness, 80 to 100 meters.

Volcanics , undifferentiated

Lava flows, ignimbrites, tuffs, and intrusives of basaltic to rhyolitic composition intercalated with sediments and paleosols of Miocene and Pliocene age.

Recent · Pleistocene · Plio-Pleistocene · Pliocene · Miocene-Pleistocene and Undiferentiated

QUATERNARY · TERTIARY

Contact   Fault

MAGNETIC NORTH · TRUE NORTH · 1°46'

ETHIOPIA
KENYA
MAP LOCATION

SCALE

5 4 3 2 1 0   5   10

Kilometers

Figure 1. Geologic map of the East Rudolf area

northeast-southwest trending Kokoi horst complex to the north of Koobi Fora is a sequence
of faulted and uplifted Pliocene basalt flows and interbedded lacustrine sediments and
tuffs. Faults in the area, although numerous, are of minor importance. They form small
half-graben, graben, and horsts with a general northward trend paralleling that of the
present lake basin. Shallow echo sounder reflections, provided by A. J. Hopson of the Lake
Rudolf Fisheries, indicate that the present lake basin consists of a series of northward
trending graben.

Stratigraphy

Regional Setting

The Plio-Pleistocene of East Rudolf consists of 325 m of fluvial, deltaic transitional
to lacustrine, and lacustrine sediments deposited unconformably on the late Miocene and
Pliocene volcanics. The sediments occur in a band 10 to 40 km wide and 80 km long extending along the lakeshore south of the Ethiopian border. Outcrops show little relief, are
discontinuous, and are generally mantled with fluvial terraces or eolian sand. Except for
reversals due to faulting, the sediments dip gently toward the lake and off the Kokoi horst.

Researchers originally separated the sedimentary exposures into three areas because of
the difficulty of making stratigraphic correlations between them (Vondra et al. 1971). The
exposures at Ileret, the northernmost area, are separated from those along the Koobi Fora
ridge, the central area, by the Kokoi horst structure and a large Holocene alluvial plain
complex to the east of the Kokoi. The Holocene floodplain deposits of the intermittent
stream, Laga Bura Hasuma, separate the Kubi Algi area, which is southernmost, from the
Koobi Fora area. This separation has led researchers to devise two sets of stratigraphic
terms. In the Ileret area the sedimentary sequence has been divided into three unconformable units designated as the lower, middle, and upper units. In the Koobi Fora-Allia Bay
area the sequence has been divided into four units designated as Koobi Fora I, II, and III,
and Galana Boi (Behrensmeyer 1970; Vondra et al. 1971).

Marker beds were subsequently established in the sediments and traced between the
Ileret and Koobi Fora-Allia Bay areas. After the correlation was established, the current
stratigraphic nomenclature was developed and formalized (Bowen and Vondra 1973). (See
fig. 2.)

Kubi Algi Formation

The predominantly coarse-grained Pliocene strata in the East Rudolf basin which lie
unconformably on Miocene or Pliocene volcanics or are in fault contact with the volcanics
and are conformably overlaid by fine-grained Plio-Pleistocene strata were named the Kubi
Algi Formation (Bowen and Vondra 1973). The Kubi Algi strata vary laterally across the
basin but have unifying features which make mapping possible. The most unifying features
of the strata are their position with respect to both older and younger rocks; the tendency
for each unit to become finer upward by grading from pebble conglomerates with large cut-
and-fill structures up to laminated claystones; and the high percentage of volcanic rock
fragments contained in the coarse sediments. The base of a complex of laminated bentonitic
tuffs and claystones, named the Suregei Tuff complex (Bowen and Vondra 1973), marks the
upper boundary of the Kubi Algi Formation. The formation is 90 m thick at the type locality, which was designated at 3°45'N latitude and 36°19'E longitude along a terrace trending
toward Kubi Algi, a prominent butte 20 km east of Allia Bay. The unit crops out extensively
in the area south of the Laga Bura Hasuma and west of Kubi Algi to the southern margin of
the East Rudolf basin. North of the Laga Bura Hasuma, exposures of the Kubi Algi Formation

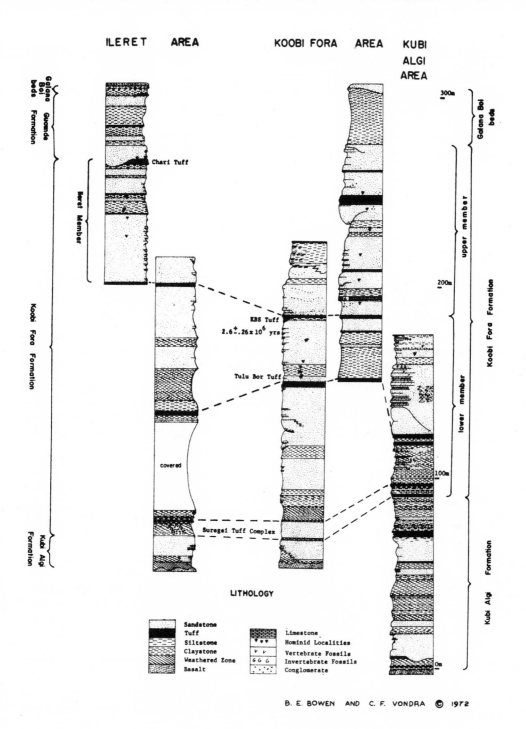

Figure 2. Generalized stratigraphic section, East Rudolf basin

are limited to the western margin of the Suregei cuesta and a small area between the Kokoi
horst and the Koobi Fora ridge. The Kubi Algi Formation as proposed by Bowen and Vondra
(1973) is equivalent to the lower portion of the informal Koobi Fora I (Vondra et al.
1971). [The Pliocene age of the formation is established from its faunal contents (Maglio
1972) and the scatter of associated K-Ar dates between 3.8 and 4.9 (Fitch and Miller, this
symposium) Ed.]

Koobi Fora Formation

The Koobi Fora Formation comprises these sedimentary strata which lie between the
basal contact of the Suregei Tuff Complex and the upper contact of the prominent Chari Tuff
exposed along the Ileret ridge, or the basal contact of the Holocene gray, diatomaceous,
predominantly lacustrine siltstones (Bowen and Vondra 1973). The exposures situated near
Koobi Fora spit at 3°56'N latitude and 36°15'E longitude (HBH6136, East Africa Grid) best
illustrate the lithology of the formation and were designated as the type locality (Bowen
and Vondra 1973). The unit as defined includes upper portions of the informal Koobi Fora
I; the Koobi Fora II and III units of Behrensmeyer (1970) and Vondra et al. (1971); and
the lower unit at Ileret as defined by Vondra et al. (1971). The formation crops out
throughout the East Rudolf basin north of Derati and the Laga Bura Hasuma and attains a
thickness of approximately 200 m. It has been subdivided into two members in the Ileret
and Koobi Fora areas.

Lower Member The Lower Member as designated by Bowen and Vondra (1973) is the portion of
the Koobi Fora Formation below the upper contact of the KBS Tuff. It is characterized by
alternating limonitic siltstones and claystones, ripple-laminated sandstones, and molluscan
limestones. The unit crops out extensively east of the Ileret ridge to the Suregei cuesta
and south of the Kokoi horst to Derati. It reaches a thickness of 140 m.

Upper Member The upper portion of the Koobi Fora Formation above the KBS Tuff is characterized by large-scale trough cross-bedded sandstones and conglomerates intercalated with
flaser-bedded siltstones, algal stromatolite beds, and ostracod sandstones. It was designated the Upper Member by Bowen and Vondra (1973) in the Koobi Fora area. It crops out
along the Karari and Koobi Fora ridges and south to Shin and the Laga Bura Hasuma. At
Koobi Fora the unit is 90 m thick.

Ileret Member The beds in the Ileret area which were formally designated the "lower unit"
(Vondra et al. 1971) are a homogeneous sequence of fine-grained sandstone and siltstone.
They are geographically restricted to the Ileret ridge. The term Ileret Member was proposed for these beds lying between the upper contact of the KBS Tuff in the Ileret area and
the top of the Chari Tuff which caps the Koobi Fora Formation (Bowen and Vondra 1973). The
outcrops in the Ileret area at 4°16'N latitude and 36°15'E longitude (HBH6173, East Africa
Grid) were designated as the type exposures. The maximum thickness of the Ileret Member
is 66 m.

Although individual beds of the Ileret Member cannot be traced from the Ileret to the
Koobi Fora area, the Chari Tuff can be equated with the Karari Tuff along the Karari escarpment on the basis of radiometric dating (Fitch and Miller, this symposium) and total
elemental oxygen isotope ratio analysis of the glass shards (Cerling, this symposium). The
Chari Tuff and the Karari Tuff may correlate with the Koobi Fora Tuff exposed on the Koobi
Fora ridge. Although the radiometric dates of the Chari and Karari tuffs do not match that
of the Koobi Fora Tuff, the analysis of the total elemental content and oxygen isotope
ratios of the glass shards suggests a correlation between the tuffs (T. E. Cerling, pers.

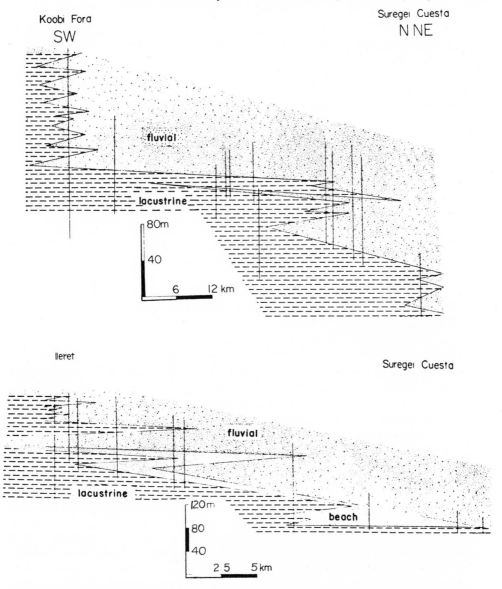

Figure 3. Interpretative cross sections of the Upper Cenozoic sediments of the East Rudolf area, showing shifts in the facies boundaries: *a*, a diagrammatic section from Koobi Fora northeastward to the Suregei cuesta; *b*, a diagrammatic section from Ileret eastward to the Suregei.

comm., 1973). Since the Koobi Fora Tuff is 12 m thick and is a highly varied complex of intercalated sandstone, relatively unweathered tuff, and weathered tuff, the disparity in radiometric dates may be a problem involving sampling.

Guomde Formation

The strata overlying the Chari Tuff and underlying the sequence of Holocene gray diatomaceous siltstones were named the Guomde Formation (Bowen and Vondra 1973). The unifying features of this unit are the dark gray laminated siltstones and intercalated thin molluscan limestones. This predominantly lacustrine sequence, 34 m thick, is capped by an unnamed thin gray tuff.

The name of the formation is taken from Kolum Guomde, a tributary of the Laga Tulu Bor which dissects the southern end of the Ileret ridge. The formation is restricted to the Ileret ridge and is most exposed along the eastern flanks of the ridge. The exposures at 4°18'N latitude and 36°15'E longitude (HBH625752) best illustrate the lithology of the formation and were designated as the type locality (Bowen and Vondra 1973). The Guomde comprises the middle unit at Ileret, as originally defined by Vondra et al. (1971).

Galana Boi Beds

The gray diatomaceous siltstones which cap the Guomde Formation in the Ileret area and the Koobi Fora Formation in the Koobi Fora and Allia Bay areas are termed the Galana Boi beds. Although the lithology and stratigraphic position for the widely distributed strata assigned to this unit are similar, their exact lateral relationships are not yet fully known. [^{14}C dates for some horizons in these beds range from 9,880 to 4,390 (Vondra et al. 1971) and Johnson and Raynolds (pers. comm.) Ed.]

Petrography

Conglomerates

The Plio-Pleistocene sediments of the East Rudolf basin contain extraformational as well as intraformational conglomerates. Extraformational types are represented by three distinct suites:

1. Polymictic conglomerates, which occur mainly in the Ileret area and consist of microcline, orthoclase, quartz, and metamorphic rock clasts in a coarse-grained arkose matrix usually cemented by calcite. The coarse clasts are moderately well sorted and well rounded, granule- to pebble-sized and disk-shaped or spherical.

2. Polymictic conglomerates, which occur primarily along the Karari escarpment and Koobi Fora ridge and consist predominantly of volcanic, metamorphic, and plutonic igneous rock clasts in a coarse-grained sublitharenite matrix. The gravel clasts are well rounded and subspherical, granule- to cobble-sized.

3. Oligomictic conglomerates, occurring in the Allia Bay area, consist of basalt, rhyolite, or ignimbrite fragments in a matrix of clay or coarse-grained sublitharenite cemented by iron oxide. The clasts are generally well sorted, well-rounded, subspherical, and boulder-sized.

Intraformational conglomerates, although relatively common, do not constitute a large volume of the sediments. They occur as thin, lenticular sheets of angular to well-rounded limonite clasts in a very calcareous, fine-grained sublitharenite matrix. The clasts are derived from plate-shaped limonite nodules which occur in the underlying siltstones. They range from granule- to cobble-sized pebbles.

Sandstones

The sandstones vary in composition from arkose in the Ileret area to sublitharenite in the Koobi Fora and Allia Bay areas. The average composition of the arkoses in the Ileret area is 29% quartz, 17% orthoclase, 7% microcline, 14% plagioclase, 13% rock fragments, 13% heavy minerals, and 7% miscellaneous chert and fossil fragments. That of the sublitharenites in the Koobi Fora area is 30% quartz, 9% orthoclase, 18% plagioclase, 21% rock fragments, 15% heavy minerals, and 7% fossil fragments. Analysis has not yet been completed for the sandstones in the Allia Bay area.

The quartz grains of the sandstones generally display strong undulose extinction (>5°). Less than 1% exhibit straight extinction (>1°), a condition that suggests more of a plutonic igneous or metamorphic source rather than a volcanic one. Internal features of the quartz grains include vacuoles, bubble trains, and microlites. Etching by calcite is common, but there is a noticeable lack of silica overgrowths. Quartz particles are common, predominantly subangular, but there are a few well-rounded, spherical grains. Metaquartz is found in semicomposite and composite grains with intragranular units separated by sutured boundaries and displaying separate, strongly undulose extinction; it composes up to 16% of the quartz in the sandstones.

The feldspar content of the sandstones decreases toward the south, from 38% in the Ileret area to 27% in the Koobi Fora area. Grains of orthoclase appear fresh and un-weathered and grains of microcline generally exhibit sericite alteration. Extinction angles of albite twin planes in plagioclase grains indicate compositions ranging from sodic to calcic, with the calcic (laboradorite) predominating. The amount of plagioclase in the sandstones increases southward from Ileret, indicating the increasing influence of an extrusive volcanic source terrane.

Rock fragments make up an increasing percentage of terrigenous grains in the sand-stones from the Ileret area south to the Koobi Fora area. Those in the Ileret area are derived predominantly from plutonic igneous and metamorphic source terranes, and those in the Koobi Fora area are derived from extrusive volcanic and metamorphic source terranes. The rock fragments range in size from medium to very coarse (sand) and are generally well rounded and spherical.

Accessory minerals include species derived from plutonic igneous, metamorphic, and volcanic source terranes. These include magnetite, common hornblende, oxyhornblende, augite, aegirine-augite, hematite, spodumene, zircon, tourmaline, leucoxene, pyrite, olivine, and kyanite. Mineral percentages fluctuate, laterally increasing in basaltic varieties southward from Ileret and vertically increasing in metamorphic varieties.

The plutonic igneous and metamorphic mineral suites in the Ileret area and the vol-canic mineral suites in the Koobi Fora and Allia Bay areas indicate two different source areas. Precambrian metamorphics crop out northeast of Ileret in Ethiopia near the northern limit of Lake Stefanie. These may have been the source of the Ileret terrigenous sediments. The ignimbrite and basaltic rock fragments in the sediments near Koobi Fora indicate both a local volcanic source and one to the east. The Allia Bay sediments are composed of locally derived material. Calcite is the major cementing agent of the sandstones, making up 1 to 50% of the rock. Sparry crystals of calcite form an interlocking mosaic within a disrupted granular framework. Iron oxide and silica cement occur less commonly and generally make up less than 1% of the rock.

Mudstones

Quartz and clay minerals are the dominant constituents in the siltstones, claystones, and mudstones of the East Rudolf basin. Montmorillonite is the most abundant clay mineral, with vermiculite, illite, and chlorite occurring in minor amounts. Little difference in clay mineral composition was noted among beds of different colors or from one area to another within the basin. Chemical components, however, show slight variations within the different sediments. Free iron and free manganese are more abundant in the light brown argillaceous sediments than in the drab (yellowish gray) and yellow varieties. Carbonate minerals are more abundant in the yellow and light brown argillaceous sediments than in the drab varieties.

Tuffs

The tuffs consist of glass shards and sanidine, hornblende, biotite, quartz, and pumice fragments. Some locally contain a significant amount of terrigenous material and authigenic montmorillonite clay. Considerable variation in texture and degree of alteration is evident within the same tuff as well as between tuffs. The glass shards range in diameter from 250μ to less than 2μ, but average around 95μ (the size of very fine sand). Index of refraction is 1.497 for most of the shards. The primary minerals are highly angular and are usually in the same size range as or slightly smaller than the associated shards. Pumice fragments are locally abundant. They vary in diameter from 1 to as much as 450 mm and are well-rounded spherical to roller-shaped particles. They often contain a considerable amount of secondary calcite.

Facies and Environments of Deposition

Four major lithofacies (microfacies) have been recognized in the Plio-Pleistocene sediments in the East Rudolf basin. These are: (1) the laminated siltstone facies; (2) the arenaceous bioclastic carbonate facies; (3) the lenticular fine-grained sandstone and flaser-bedded siltstone facies; and (4) the intertongued, lenticular, conglomerate, sandstone and mudstone facies. These possess properties indicative of four major depositional environments: (1) prodelta and shallow-shelf lacustrine; (2) littoral lacustrine-- beach and barrier beach and associated barrier and supralittoral lagoons; (3) delta plain-- distributary channel and interdistributary flood basin; and (4) fluvial channel and floodplain.

The facies are complexly interbedded and intertongued. Their position at any given time was related to the level of the lake, which in turn was controlled by variations in climate and tectonic activity. In general the four major facies occur in north-south trending belts which migrated to the west during the Plio-Pleistocene, recording a general regression of the lake. Figure 1 diagrams the shifts in depositional environments.

Laminated Siltstone Facies

The laminated siltstone facies is exposed along the base of the Koobi Fora ridge and along stream cuts to the west of Shin. Here it constitutes nearly all of the Lower Member of the Koobi Fora Formation. It interfingers laterally with and grades vertically into the arenaceous bioclastic carbonate facies to the east and north along the margin of the East Rudolf basin.

The facies consists of thick sequences of laminated, yellowish gray, limonitic, argillaceous siltstones interbedded with thin beds of laminated grayish orange sandstone (sublitharenites) and light gray bentonitic tuffs. The siltstones contain thin lenses of sandstone and conglomerates consisting of pebbles of bioclastic carbonates. Thin, plate-shaped limonite nodules, parallel to laminae and subvertical to horizontal veins of gypsum, generally less than 5 mm in thickness, are common.

The laminated siltstones generally occur in units between 2 and 4 m thick, although units as thick as 18 m have been found in exposures at Koobi Fora near the present lake margin. Their basal contacts are usually sharp but nonerosional, whereas their upper boundaries are gradational. The facies is locally ripple laminated and in rare instances bioturbated. Fossils are rare in this facies compared with the other facies with which it is interfingered. They usually consist of scattered small lenses of lacustrine gastropods.

The fine-grained nature and lamination of the siltstones indicate deposition under low-energy conditions, and occasional ripple lamination suggests sporadic current activity.

This, along with its relationship to interfingering facies, suggests that the facies was deposited in a distal prodelta or shallow lacustrine shelf environment.

Arenaceous Bioclastic Carbonate Facies

The geographic extent of this facies is difficult to define because it is so intimately interbedded with other facies. It is exposed throughout the basin and occurs intermittently in the entire Plio-Pleistocene sedimentary sequence. Eastward it interfingers with and passes vertically into the lenticular, fine-grained sandstone and flaser-bedded siltstone facies.

This facies consists of sandy gastropods or biosparites, or both, that are characteristically dark yellowish orange to moderate yellowish brown. These may grade laterally into very calcareous, fossiliferous fine- to medium-grained sandstones (sublitharenties) or into carbonates with algal stromatolite structures (biolithites). The sandstones are usually yellowish gray and the carbonates grayish orange. Individual beds vary in thickness from 5 cm to 3 m, and all diminish in thickness and pinch out to the east. Vertically they usually display a sequence of primary structures. The basal portion of each unit is a laminated, silty, fine-grained sandstone which is gradational with the underlying laminated siltstone. It contains vertical burrows and occasional internal molds of the bivalve *Mutela*. This becomes a ripple-laminated and trough and planar cross-bedded, fine- to medium-grained sandstone or bioclastic carbonate in the middle portion, and a fine-grained sandstone in the upper portion, which is structureless except for occasional root casts and ripple marks in the upper portion.

The upper half of the middle portion is often found packed with the shells of gastropods or ostracods. Disarticulated fish remains, fragments of algal mats or spheroids, occasional fragments of bivalves as well as complete organisms, and relatively rare abraded mammalian bones may also occur. Laterally as well as vertically, this portion in some places gives way to thin algal biolithites which locally display a variety of forms.

The carbonates and sandstones of this facies are often associated with beds of massive pale yellowish brown siltstone 1 to 2 m thick. It has a gradational lower contact and is sandy at the base, becoming very argillaceous at the top. The siltstone contains calcareous concretions, calcareous root casts, and thin, subvertical veins of gypsum.

Studies of recent shallow marine deposits and recent littoral deposits of Lake Rudolf indicate a sequence of sedimentary structures similar to those of the arenaceous bioclastic carbonate facies occurring in barrier beaches. The three distinct units of the sandstones and bioclastic carbonates of this facies correspond in texture and structural features to the sediments accumulating as the shoreface, beach, and sand-dune environments described by Dickenson, Berryhill, and Holmes (1972) for barrier islands. We observed the same types of units for the beaches at Lake Rudolf, where they were deposited by shoreward-migrating submergent bars or megaripples and barrier beaches, and the massive siltstones accumulated in low-energy lagoons behind the barriers. Algal stromatolites formed in associated very shallow-water littoral or lagoonal environments.

Lenticular Fine-Grained Sandstone and Flaser-Bedded Siltstone Facies

This facies, which occurs throughout the basin, usually constitutes the upper portion of each formation. It interfingers laterally with the lenticular conglomerate sandstone and mudstone facies.

The facies consists of lenticular channels of grayish orange fine- to medium-grained sandstone which grade laterally into sheets of pale yellowish brown, flaser-bedded, coarse-grained siltstone between 1 and 2 m thick. Sandstone bodies often display a sequence of structural features ranging upward from channel lag pebble conglomerates through large-scale trough and planar cross-bedding to horizontal bedding and ripple lamination. Contorted bedding, slump structures, and load casts are common. Root casts are very abundant locally. The sheets of siltstone are very sandy and possess lenses of sandstone adjacent to the channel, becoming increasingly finer grained and more argillaceous normal to the axis of the channel. They contain abundant mud cracks as well as root casts associated with capping caliche horizons. Vertebrate fossils are numerous in this facies.

The lithologies, sedimentary structures, and vertebrate fauna suggest deposition in a low energy fluvial-delta plain environment. The sandstones have structures similar to recent distributary channel point bar deposits, and the siltstones are analogous to interdistributary floodplain sediments.

Lenticular, Conglomerate Sandstone and Mudstone Facies

This facies occurs along the eastern margin of the East Rudolf basin in the lower portion of the Kubi Algi Formation and in the upper portion of the Koobi Fora Formation.

The facies is the most heterogeneous of the four described. It consists of a complex variety of microfacies which grade laterally and vertically into one another, wedge in, thicken, thin, and pinch out. The facies is composed mainly of lenses of grayish orange, granule to cobble conglomerate and fine- to coarse-grained sandstone (arkose or sublitharenite), occurring in channels or sinuous depressions eroded into older deposits. It also includes finer-grained sediments, namely, pale orange to grayish orange siltstones, claystones, and mudstones and light gray tuffs. The conglomerates are most abundant to the east along the basin margin and in the basal axial portion of channels, or in the basal portion of fining-upward lenses. They diminish in grain size toward the center of the basin as well as vertically within individual channels. The sandstones display a variety of primary structures, but two basic sequences predominate. The first occurs in sandstone lenses several meters thick with a basal surface eroded in older deposits. This sequence begins with large-scale trough cross-bedded fine- to coarse-grained sandstone giving way vertically to horizontally bedded fine- to medium-grained sandstone and ripple-laminated, silty, very fine-grained sandstone. Lenses or banks of the freshwater oyster *Etheria* occasionally occur within these units. The second sequence is present in lenses which are usually not more than 1 m thick. The basal erosional surface is succeeded by large-scale trough cross-bedded medium- to coarse-grained sandstone. The trough sets diminish in size upward and are usually planed by erosion or are occasionally draped with a thin veneer of clay. This is overlain by large-scale planar cross-bedded fine- to medium-grained sandstone, often followed by a thin cap of laminated or ripple-laminated fine-grained sandstone. This in turn is eroded and is followed by another, similar sequence in which *Etheria* is absent.

Laterally the sandstones grade and interfinger with siltstones, claystones, and mudstones, which locally contain calcareous root casts with accompanying concretions or caliche, mud cracks, and incipient fossil soil horizons.

This facies is analogous with recent fluvial deposits described by Frazier and Osanik (1961), Allen (1965), Royse (1970), Williams (1971), and many others. Permanent meandering streams with point bar and related thick floodplain deposits are documented by channel sandstones displaying the first sequence of structural features. Ephemeral streams with large-scale ripples and migrating transverse channel bars are indicated by channel sandstones possessing the second sequence. The siltstones, claystones, and mudstones were deposited in a variety of minor floodplain environments, some immediately proximal to the

channel (levee?) and others distal to the flood basin. Tuffs were deposited and preserved
as usually lenticular beds in ephemeral streams and in backwater and cutoff channel segments, swales, and flood basin depressions associated with ephemeral as well as permanent
streams.

Tectonic and Paleogeographic History

The tectonic development of the Rudolf basin began in the Miocene. Subsequent
Pliocene arching of major domes to the east and faulting to the west in the Turkana depression created a shallow, asymmetrical, westward tilted north-south trough or half-graben in
which the Plio-Pleistocene sedimentary wedge accumulated. The uplift was accompanied by
intrusion and obsidian and ignimbrite eruption, followed by basaltic volcanism.

The East Rudolf basin was occupied by a large embayment of the lake during much of
the Pliocene and Pleistocene. This developed first during the Middle Pliocene in the Allia
Bay area and then extended northward during the late Pliocene. Two major perennial streams
and several ephemeral ones entered the embayment. The perennial streams headed to the
northeast and east and received sediments from Precambrian plutonic igneous and metamorphic
rocks exposed on the flanks of the Stephanie Arch and from volcanics on the Suregei cuesta.
The sediments were deposited in the East Rudolf basin as two fluvial and prograding deltaic
complexes, one near Ileret and the other near Koobi Fora. Sand-bed ephemeral streams
draining the Suregei cuesta and local volcanic uplands to the southeast formed small fans
along the edge of the basin in the Ileret, Koobi Fora, and Allia Bay areas. Thin lenses
of littoral lacustrine deposits were intercalated with the sediments of the two delta
plains at the margins of the basin, documenting periodic short-lived lacustrine transgressions. Distal prodeltaic and shallow-shelf deposits accumulated within the basin.

The sediments tend to coarsen upward in the center of the basin, indicating delta
growth and lacustrine regression through time. Periodic coarsening, cut-and-fill structures, and unconformable relationships with underlying sediments are characteristic of the
fluvial deposits at the basin margin. These features are attributed to climatic change
and uplift of the source area.

The fluvial deposits along the present lake shoreline indicate that major regression
occurred near the end of the deposition of the Koobi Fora Formation. Fluvial conditions
persisted in the Allia Bay and Koobi Fora areas until the advent of a major Holocene transgression recorded by Galana Boi lacustrine deposits (Vondra et al. 1971). In the Ileret
area, however, the Pleistocene Guomde Formation represents a limited lacustrine transgression and regression before the Holocene transgression and Galana Boi deposition.

Acknowledgments

This report was made possible by National Science Foundation grants GA-25684 and
GS-37813 to Carl F. Vondra and in part by National Geographic Society grants to R. E. F.
Leakey. The work was aided by the assistance and cooperation of the National Museums of
Kenya and the Kenyan government. Appreciation is extended to the members of the East
Rudolf Research Group, particularly to H. Acuff, R. Bainbridge, A. K. Behrensmeyer, F. J.
Fitch, I. C. Findlater, H. J. Frank, G. L. Isaac, and G. D. Johnson, for their assistance
and many helpful suggestions.

This is paper no. 52 in the East Rudolf Research Project catalogue of publications.

References

Allen, J. R. L. 1965. A review of the origin and characteristics of recent alluvial sediments. *Sedimentology* 5:89-191.

Arambourg, C. 1947. *Mission scientifique de l'Omo (1932-1933)*. Vol. 1. *Géologie-Anthropologie*, fasc. 1-3, pp. 1-562. Mémoire, Muséum d'histoire naturelle (Paris).

Arnal, R. E. 1961. Limnology, sedimentation and microorganisms of the Salton Sea, California. *Bull. Geol. Soc. Am.* 72:427-78.

Athill, L. F. 1920. Through southwestern Abyssinia to the Nile. *Geograph. J.* 56:347-70.

Axelsson, V. 1967. The Laitaure delta: A study of deltaic morphology and processes. *Geograf. Ann.* 49:1-127.

Baker, B. H.; Mohr, P. A.; and Williams, L. A. J. 1972. Geology of the eastern rift system of Africa. *Geol. Soc. Amer., Spec. Paper*, no. 136.

Behrensmeyer, A. K. 1970. Preliminary geological interpretation of a new hominid site in the Lake Rudolf basin. *Nature* 226:225-26.

Bowen, B. E. and Vondra, C. F. 1973. Stratigraphical relationships of the Plio-Pleistocene deposits, East Rudolf, Kenya. *Nature* 242:391-93.

Brown, F. H. 1969. Observations on the stratigraphy and radiometric age of the Omo beds, Lower Omo Basin, Southern Ethiopia. *Quaternaria* 11:7-14.

Butzer, K. W. 1970. Contemporary depositional environments of the Omo delta. *Nature* 226:425-30.

Butzer, K. W.; Brown, F. H.; and Thurber, D. L. 1969. Horizontal sediments of the lower Omo Valley: The Kibish Formation. *Quaternaria* 11:15-30.

Butzer, K. W., and Thurber, D. L. 1969. Some Late Cenozoic sedimentary formations of the lower Omo basin. *Nature* 222:1138-43.

Carver, R. E., ed. 1971. *Procedures in sedimentary petrology*. New York: John Wiley.

Dixey, F. 1956. The East African rift system. *Colon. Geol. Suppl. Ser. Bull.* Suppl. 1, 71 pp.

Frazier, D. E., and Osanik, A. 1961. Point-bar deposits, Old River Locksite, Louisiana. *Trans. Gulf Coast Assoc. Geol. Soc.* 11:121-37.

Fuchs, V. E. 1934. The geological work of the Cambridge expedition to the East African lakes, 1930-31. *Geol. Mag.* 71:97-112; 145-66.

_____. 1935. The Lake Rudolf Rift Valley Expedition, 1934. *Geograph. J.* 86:114-42.

_____. 1939. The geological history of the Lake Rudolf basin, Kenya colony. *Phil. Trans. Roy. Soc. Lond.*, ser. B, 229:219-74.

Glennie, K. W. 1970. *Desert sedimentary environments*. Amsterdam: Elsevier.

Harrison, J. J. 1901. A journey from Zeila to Lake Rudolf. *Geograph. J.* 18:258-75.

Heinzelin, J. de, and Brown, F. H. 1969. Some early Pleistocene deposits of the lower Omo valley: The USNO Formation. *Quaternaria* 11:31-46.

Heinzelin, J. de; Brown, F. H.; and Howell, F. C. 1971. Pliocene/Pleistocene formations in the lower Omo basin, Southern Ethiopia. *Quaternaria* 13:247-68.

Hohnel, L. R. V.; Rosiwal, A.; Toula, F.; and Suess, E. 1891. Beitrage zur geologischen kenntniss des Ostlichen Afrika. *Denkschr. Kaiserl. Akad. Wissensch. (Wien), Math-Naturw. Kl.* 58:447-584.

Howell, F. C. 1968. Omo Research Expedition. *Nature* 219:567-72.

International Subcommission on Stratigraphic Terminology. 1960. Stratigraphic classifica-
    tion and terminology. *Intern. Geol. Cong. Rept.* 25:7-38.

Isaac, G. L. L.; Leakey, R. E. F.; and Behrensmeyer, A. K. 1971. Archeological traces of
    early hominid activities, east of Lake Rudolf, Kenya. *Science* 173:1129-34.

Kamp, P. C. van de. 1973. Holocene continental sedimentation in the Salton Basin,
    California: A reconnaissance. *Bull. Geol. Soc. Amer.* 84:827-48.

Leakey, R. E. F. 1971. Further evidence of Lower Pleistocene hominids from East Rudolf,
    North Kenya. *Nature* 231:241-45.

_____. 1972. Further evidence of Lower Pleistocene hominids from East Rudolf, North
    Kenya, 1972. *Nature* 242:170-73.

Leakey, R. E. F.; Behrensmeyer, A. K.; Fitch, F. J.; Miller, J. A.; and Leakey, M. D. 1970.
    New hominid remains and early artifacts from Northern Kenya. *Nature* 226:223-30.

Leakey, R. E. F.; Mungai, J. M.; and Walker, A. C. 1971. New Australopithecines from East
    Rudolf, Kenya. *Am. J. Phys. Anthropol.* 35:175-86.

Maglio, V. J. 1972. Vertebrate faunas and chronology of hominid-bearing sediments east of
    Lake Rudolf, Kenya. *Nature* 239:379-85.

Maud, P. 1904. Exploration in the southern borderland of Abyssinia. *Geograph. J.* 23:
    552-79.

Mohr, P. A. 1971. Outline tectonics of Ethiopia. In *Tectonics of Africa*, pp. 447-60.
    Paris: UNESCO.

Patterson, B. 1966. A new locality for early Pleistocene fossils in northwestern Kenya.
    Nature 212:577-79.

Patterson, B.; Behrensmeyer, H. K.; and Sill, W. D. 1970. Geology and fauna of a new
    Pliocene locality in northwestern Kenya. *Nature* 226:918-21.

Pezzetta, J. M. 1973. The St. Clair River delta: Sedimentary characteristics and deposi-
    tional environments. *J. Sed. Petrol.* 43:168-87.

Reid, J. A.; Brooks, R. H.; and Simons, D. B. 1967. Variation of the characteristics of
    deltaic and stream bed deposits in laboratory studies. *Bull. Intern. Assoc. Sci.
    Hydrol.* 75:345-54.

Royse, C. F. 1970. A sedimentologic analysis of the Tongue River-Sentinel Butte interval
    (Paleocene) of the Williston basin, western North Dakota. *Sed. Geol.* 4:19-80.

Smith, A. D. 1896. Expedition through Somaliland to Lake Rudolf. *Geograph. J.* 8:221-39.

_____. 1900. An expedition between Lake Rudolf and the Nile. *Geograph. J.* 16:600-25.

Smith, N. D. 1971. Transverse bars and braiding in the lower Platte River, Nebraska.
    Bull. Geol. Soc. Am. 82:3407-20.

Vondra, C. F.; Johnson, G. D.; Behrensmeyer, A. K.; and Bowen, B. E. 1971. Preliminary
    stratigraphical studies of the East Rudolf Basin, Kenya. *Nature* 231:245-48.

Walsh, J., and Dodson, R. G. 1969. Geology of northern Turkana. Mines and Geological
    Dept. of Kenya, Rep. 82.

Williams, G. E. 1971. Flood deposits of the sand-bed ephemeral streams of Central
    Australia. *Sedimentology* 17:1-40.

Worthington, E. B. 1932. The lakes of Kenya and Uganda. *Geograph. J.* 79:275-97.

Yaalon, D. H., ed. 1971. *Paleopedology: Origin, nature and dating of paleosols.*
    Jerusalem: Israel Universities Press.

I. C. Findlater

Introduction

The stratigraphy of the East Rudolf Plio-Pleistocene sedimentary basin has been described by Behrensmeyer 1970; Vondra et al. 1971; and Bowen and Vondra 1973. This chapter
deals with the field characters of the tuff horizons within this succession and their use
as time-equivalent planes (isochronous surfaces) in the erection of a chronostratigraphy
for the basin. The available correlation methods and their problems are reviewed and, because of their importance in assessing the time lapse between eruption and deposition of
the tuffs, origin and transport factors are considered. The feasibility and reliability
of mapping the base of the tuff outcrop as an isochronous surface and the interpolation of
this surface where the tuff is no longer present are discussed. Throughout the paper the
field aspect is stressed.

Field Character of the Tuff Horizons

In the field the tuff horizons have a very varied aspect in thickness and continuity
along the outcrops, their color and structure reflecting the environments in which they
were deposited. Most of the tuffs show internal structures and have field relationships
which suggest deposition from an aqueous medium.

Typically a tuff horizon has a well-defined base resting on channel sands, fluvial
floodplain, deltaic, coastal plain, or lacustrine lithofacies. The basal facies may be
very fine grain (silt to clay grade), often with many thin intercalations of clay-grade
terrigenous sediment. Internal structure, though small in scale, includes cross-
stratification as well as ripple and plain laminations. This facies probably represents
air-fall dust blown or sheetwashed from the local landscape and introduced into the drainage
network and subsequently deposited in low energy environments under circumstances where the
ash becomes intercalated "normal" terrigenous sediment. Absence of this fine-grain facies
may indicate high-energy depositional environments in which the tuff was not deposited or
from which it was subsequently scoured. Locally these fine-grained ashes have altered to
bentonite.

Most of the deposit comprises one or more layers of fragmentary volcanic glass, each
incorporating a limited suite of primary volcanic crystal fragments, sanidine, a green
sodic amphibole, and ilmenite, with occasional bipyramidal high-temperature quartz (beta).
Mixed with these primary volcanic elements are found a varying proportion of nonvolcanic

detritus, lithic fragments from Miocene basalt and Precambrian crystalline terrains. Often
the basal deposits of tuff have a high degree of purity, suggesting either that the sediment source areas were heavily mantled by tephra or that locally the drainage was heavily
choked and that in both cases this newly deposited ash blanket had to be removed before
"normal" sediment again became available. Grain size varies from silt to medium sand grade.
Internal structures that may be present include large- and small-scale cross-stratification,
and ripple drift. Locally, strong contortions may result from dewatering and compaction.
Root and burrow casts are common from all except the lacustrine environment. Color varies
from chalk white through grays and blues to pale green and, in the tuffaceous horizons,
orange browns. Occasionally laterally extensive thin clay grade layers separate the tuff
horizons, suggesting that numerous layers of fairly pure tuff may have been deposited over
a period of time, recording consecutive flood stages of the drainage with increasing contamination by nonprimary volcanic detritus in the later deposits.

    Pumice lumps, well-rounded and subangular to subspherical, are common in the channel
and beach littoral complexes, but only locally abundant in fluvial and deltaic floodplain
depositional environments. They are absent in the lacustrine lithofacies and uncommon in
coastal plain deposits. Rounded pumice lumps range in size from granule gravel to boulder
gravel, with lumps in the latter category attaining a maximum diameter of 250 mm. Although
there is an apparent diminution in the size of the pumices from the basin margin toward
the present lakeshore, size variation at any locality is often great, and there can be
little doubt that floating was an important transport mechanism. A proportion of the
smaller pumice lumps appear to have been moved as part of the bed load, which accounts for
the inclusion of pumice within layers of tuff, in contrast to floated material, which becomes stranded in depressions on the top surface of a layer. Pumice is not common in the
early layers of a multilayered deposit, often occurring in concentrations on the upper surface only. Stranded on the upper surfaces of initial deposits at the recession of flood-
waters, the pumice would dry out and if not partly buried would float downstream during the
next high water. This mechanism would tend to concentrate the pumice toward the top of a
multilayered unit. In some tuffs, notably the Karari, this seems to have occurred, but in
other examples what are probably bed load pumices are enclosed within individual layers.

    The pumice contains phenocrysts of sanidine and a green sodic amphibole, usually in
complex intergrowth. Often associated with these intergrowths are crystals of limenite,
and in some horizons bipyramidal high-temperature quartz is an accessory. The pumice and
the phenocrystic potassium-rich sanidine feldspar crystals have special significance in the
studies at East Rudolf, since they offer the best available material for K-Ar dating.

    The upper boundary between the tuff horizons and the "normal" terrigenous sediment is
gradational. Reworking of the upper surfaces by wind and bioturbation mixes tuff and overlying deposits, resulting in a blurred contact. Deposits overlying the tuff are initially
rich in glass and crystal debris, but the availability of these clasts appears to have
diminished fairly rapidly in the source areas so that "normal" sedimentation was soon re-
established. The blurring of the upper contact by local reworking occurs in a few inches,
but beds of tuffaceous sediment may be up to 2 or 3 m thick. The tuffs are usually easily
identifiable in the field, often forming obvious bench features or capping prominent
topographic features.

    The Suregei Tuff complex differs from all the other tuffs so far examined in that it
may well have fallen from the air into standing water where it settled below wave base.
Although the grain size is variable from clay to silt grade, the tuff is always composed

of thin laminations, from 0.1 mm to 3 m thick. Except for local warping of the laminations due to dewatering and compaction, there are no other internal structures. Immediately above and below are found typical quiet-water lacustrine deposits. It is apparent from the enclosing lithofacies that at the time of the deposition of the Suregei Tuff complex, Lake Rudolf extended much farther to the east, reaching its present boundary between sediment and basin margin volcanics.

Diagenetic modification appears to be very important locally. Since deposition, there has been considerable movement of carbonates, resulting in extensive caliche and concretion development throughout the succession. This is particularly conspicuous in the younger, mainly fluviatile deposits. Within the tuffs carbonate is present, though its distribution is easily modified by weathering on exhumation. This is well displayed by the pumice: exposed pieces may be completely leached of soluble carbonate, whereas partly or totally buried pumice lumps from the same locality may be solid with carbonate.

X-ray diffraction analysis reveals that some bentonites are completely sodic, whereas elsewhere they are potassium-rich. Cation exchange may have resulted from deposition in sodium-rich lake waters, or the exchange may have occurred during later, mildly thermal metasomatic events. In this connection it is of interest that heated groundwaters are still present in the Lake Rudolf region as hot springs on the eastern shore of Lake Stefanie (Grove and Goudie 1971) and at Loiyengalani. Fumarolic activity occurs both at the south end of the lake and on North Island. A serious effect of postdepositional alteration is the initiation of argon loss from the sanidine crystals. Although at present the exact mechanism is not fully understood, the loss would explain some of the low ages obtained in the K-Ar dating program (for full discussion see Fitch and Miller, this symposium). On the basis of laboratory analyses by R. L. Hay, Isaac reports the presence of zeolites as a cementing medium in eolian tuff at the KBS archeological excavation, where eolian reworking into an abandoned delta channel seems to have occurred. Elsewhere the tuffs are not particularly indurated, though they often prove more resistant to weathering than do the enclosing lithologies.

Origin and Transport Factors

As was already discussed, a "typical" tuff deposit has three distinct facies from the bottom to the top. Initially, silt to clay grade ash may be deposited on a sharply defined basal surface; the bulk of the tuff follows as a single bed or a succession of layers, at first of high purity but becoming contaminated toward the top by "normal" detrital sediment. The middle facies thus grades into the third and uppermost facies, which, though sharing the same depositional structures as the second facies, is a tuffaceous sediment. Only rarely is the boundary between the second and third facies sharp, and this in turn gives way upward gradationally to nontuffaceous detritus.

The initial basal facies probably represents the fine ash and dust dispersed as primary air-fall deposits being reworked from the landscape into the drainage system either within or upstream from the East Rudolf basin. If the drainage was permanent, it is possible that quite substantial deposits were sedimented (locally up to 80 cm) between over-bank stages. After an eruption it is during the flood stage, either seasonal or at some other interval, that silt- to sand-grade ashes and associated pumice are transported. The well-rounded, subspherical shape of the pumice lumps strongly suggests that they have been transported over a fair distance, possibly by successive floods. We do not know where the ash was initially deposited. It could have been deposited within the basin, with primary air falls of ash being reworked locally by sheetwash and floodwaters and then transported over only short distances. However, it seems more probable that the ash was carried into the basin from initial deposition sites well upstream. As the ash was stripped from the landscape by successive rains the "normal" terrigeneous sediment would again become avail-able to contaminate the later tuff deposits of the upper facies.

It is not possible at present to trace the Plio-Pleistocene drainage patterns upstream from the East Rudolf basin to the source areas, since as yet we lack knowledge of the evo-lution of the regional topography. The gross sedimentological history of the basin and the areal distribution of depositional environments strongly support the hypothesis that a sub-stantial river must have entered the basin where the Stefanie Gap is today. Upstream of the Stefanie Gap, tectonism and erosion may well have radically altered the landscape in the last three million years. It seems that the fluviatile deposits at the Omo and those at East Rudolf are different drainage systems. If, as seems probable from the character of the tuffs and their overlapping age ranges, some of the tuffs are common to both areas, then some of the source vents must have been along a common drainage divide.

Emission of the ash could have been by either Plinian, vulcanian, or ash-flow vol-canism. Plinian and vulcanian eruptions are dependent on wind directions and strength to determine the distribution of their ash blankets. If the prevailing wind was from the southeast to east (see Brown 1972), the source of the Suregei primary air-fall tuff could have been many kilometers to the east or southeast of the basin, since no tuff fragments greater than silt grade have been found and most of the deposits are clay grade. None of the tuffs occurring stratigraphically above the Suregei tuff complex show evidence from sorting, internal structures, or topographic blanketing to suggest major primary air-fall deposition. The available evidence supports the hypothesis that most of the ash was car-ried into the basin by streams. At present it is not possible to say whether upstream the initial deposition was dominantly by air fall or ash flow. Certainly the second mechanism is very attractive, as ash-flow volcanism would lead to the local massive choking of the drainage by thick deposits of ash which would have to be swept away before the drainage could again function efficiently, this leading to circumstances in which the sediment load would be almost entirely ash. These ashes would later be sedimented out as deposits of high purity. Still later the proportion of nonvolcanic detritus would increase.

It is clear that whichever mechanism was responsible the time lapse from eruption to final sedimentation of the tuffs was short, probably at the most a few years, and therefore in the terms of K-Ar resolution, an instant in time.

Tuff Correlation and Correlative Methods

The sediments within much of the basin are flat-lying, with tectonic dislocation and tilting being significant only in a zone a few miles wide along the present lakeshore. However, uplift and erosion have caused a major physical gap in sediment outcrops across the Kokoi horst structure (map, fig. 2). Firm correlation of the Ileret and Koobi Fora sedimentary sequences has been determined for beds older than and including the KBS tuff (Bowen and Vondra 1973), but correlations of later tuffs, such as the BBS tuff and younger ones, are still tentative. As was already discussed, there is a great lateral variation in depositional environments, and because of this and also because of penecontemporaneous erosion, the tuffs are not continuous along the strike. If the outcrops are widely spaced, facies variation in the sediments between tuff occurrences can make correlation difficult. The faunal zones erected by Maglio (1972) allow gross correlation, but resolution is not

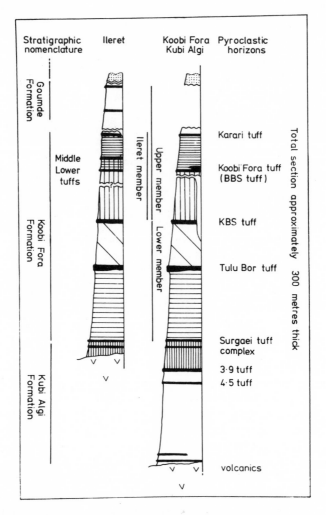

Figure 1. Generalized sections showing tuff horizons, the basal surfaces of which are used to define isochronous surfaces. Correlation above the KBS is provisional only.

good enough when tuff horizons are separated by time intervals of less than 250,000 years or when not enough fossils are present to identify the zone. Neither the field character of the tuffs nor their petrography shows unique features that are specific to individual horizons and could be used for correlation.

Of the correlation methods requiring laboratory analysis, the most useful will probably be the paleomagnetic reversal chronology, assuming that sufficiently complete and geologically understood columns can be sampled. Although suitable material is widespread, the increasing grain size in the younger sediments which are dominated by fluviatile flood-plain channel lithologies may complicate paleomagnetic determinations. Initial studies are very promising, however; for further details see Brock and Isaac, this symposium. In the absence of unique features at the transition between polarity zones it is necessary to identify polarity intervals by a chronometric dating method. At East Rudolf this need is supplied by K-Ar age determinations.

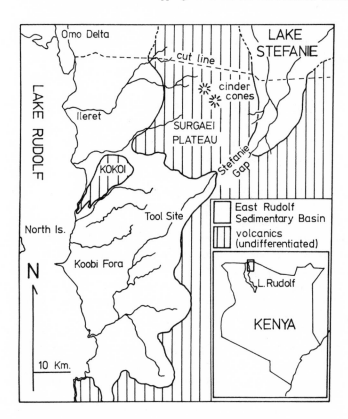

Figure 2. Map detailing locations of features mentioned in text. The East Rudolf sedimentary basin extends south from the outline marking the Ethiopia/Kenya frontier.

Oxygen isotope analysis of the tephra has proved to have some significance for correlations, though the extent to which observed values are determined by pre- or posteruption circumstances is not fully known. (See Cerling, this symposium).

Neutron activation analysis to determine the amounts of trace elements in the tephra will also be attempted, but problems rather similar to those just mentioned will probably be found here also. If the temperature in the magma body before eruption was inhomogeneous, it is very unlikely that trace element distribution would be homogeneous. Work done by Ewart (1966) suggests that variation is to be expected in the essential mineralogy, indicating that before eruption the magma body (in Ewart's study an ignimbrite) is not in equilibrium. There are many further studies that reflect the disequilibrium conditions in magma bodies before eruption (Rittman 1933; Curtis 1968). Evidence of gravity separation and inhomogeneity of volatile distribution are well documented, the results being most noticeable when great volumes of magma are erupted.

The geochemical methods discussed above share the problem of metasomatic alterations in the composition of the glass caused by leaching or precipitation under the influence of circulating groundwaters. This may lead to isotope fractionation and, as appears to have occurred in some of the bentonites, ion exchange. As with any geochemical study of this sort, much depends on the scale of these processes. There may still be enough variation between tuffs to allow geochemical fingerprinting, and since compositional variation in volcanic glasses is reflected in variation in refractive index, I would hope to be able to use this as a correlative parameter. However, initial results are not promising.

It is apparent from the discussion above that no one method can provide a simple basis for correlation and discrimination. But the integration of various approaches will probably lead to reliable solutions for most field correlation problems.

Isochronous Mapping Units and the Validity of the Mapped Pyroclastic Horizons as Time Markers

To be of practical use as a time marker a sedimentary unit must be laterally extensive, must have been deposited in a brief period of time, and should be readily recognizable in the field. It is also helpful if its age is known, either by determination on the unit itself or by inference from age data for the enclosing sediments.

Of the East Rudolf sediments the tuff horizons are the obvious choice. The sedimentary record at East Rudolf involves a prograding deltaic complex which advanced from the basin margin volcanics westward. The resulting depositional environments produce abrupt lateral facies variation at any stratigraphic level. Although the tuffs reflect these facies changes, their obvious lithologic difference from the enclosing sediment makes them easily recognizable in the field. As a matter of convenience the sharp basal contact of the tuff is taken as an isochronous surface. The top surface of the tuff is usually gradational and has often been removed by erosion.

The eruption, transport, and deposition was probably very rapid and though inevitably there must have been some time lag during transport into the basin and dispersion of the tuff within the basin, this is insignificant when compared with the best resolution available from the dating methods that can be applied. The problem of age determinations on the unit itself is complicated in the East Rudolf tuffs because the age determinations are on sanidine phenocrysts from pumice lumps enclosed within or associated with the tuffs. Various geochemical and optical techniques are being tried, to ascertain whether an individual tuff horizon and its associated pumice are coeval. It is possible that pumice from earlier eruptions may have been incorporated with later pyroclastics.

Because the tuffs are not continuous along the strike, it is necessary, by interpretation of the geology, to interpolate the equivalent time plane between tuff outcrops. On the detailed maps (figs. 3-5) the outcrops of the pyroclastic sediments are shown by solid dark lines, but where the tuff was absent the interpolated outcrop of the time plane is shown as a broken line. The reliability of the isochronous surface when the tuff is not present depends on the precision with which its stratigraphic level can be followed and mapped in the field. This in turn depends on the environments of deposition of the sediments through which the surface passes. In shallow lacustrine or coastal plain situations reliability is high, since the lithologies are laterally extensive. Sandy shell bands resulting from short-term lake transgressions are particularly useful in this respect, since they have great lateral continuity and are of known short duration. Similarly, shallow-water bands and other sand/shell concentrations are often extensive and useful stratigraphic markers. In deltaic and fluviatile floodplain regimes, individual lithologies are not so extensive, and it becomes more difficult to follow the isochronous surface laterally in the absence of the tuff horizon. Soil profiles and other lithologic variation resulting from short-term change of deposition environment may be useful, but bioturbation and restricted lateral extension reduce the precision. In fluviatile channel complexes where incision into underlying sediments is an important factor, reliability is much lower. Given sufficient time and the generally excellent exposure at East Rudolf, we could

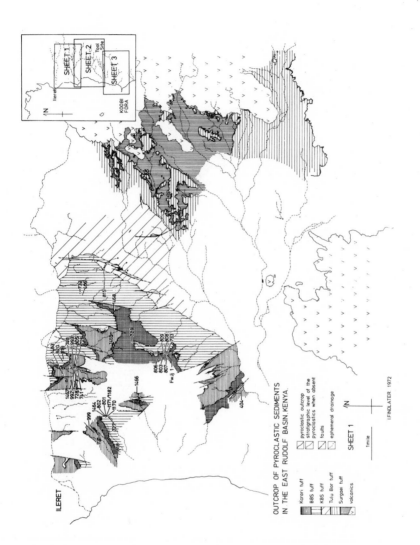

Figure 3

determine the boundary between channel base and underlying sediments. However, such microstratigraphic mapping consumes a great deal of time, and so it is hoped that persons using
the maps will, where channeling is an important factor, make their own local interpretations as to the position of the isochronous surface.

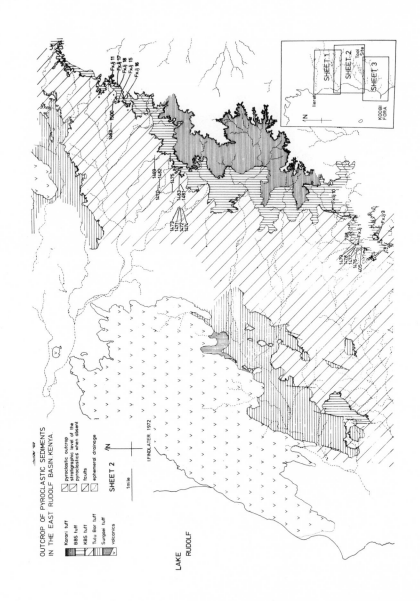

Figure 4

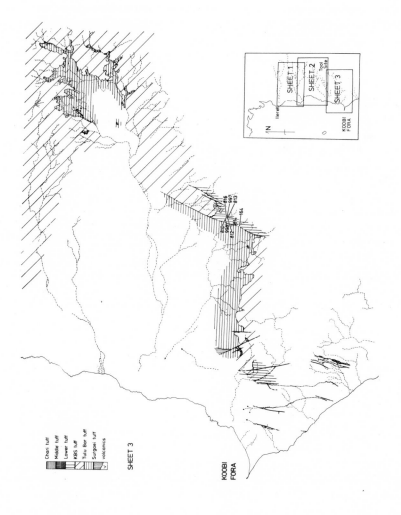

Figure 5

Acknowledgments

My thanks are due to F. J. Fitch and J. A. Miller, who have encouraged and are encouraging my study in both the field and the laboratory; to R. E. F. Leakey for making the East Rudolf Research Project a reality; to G. L. Isaac; to A. K. Behrensmeyer and B. E. Bowen for helpful discussion in the field; to R. Merriman for help with mineralogical studies, to Miss D. Boyd, who typed this and many other reports for me; and to the Royal Society and Natural Environmental Research Council, who are financing this study.

This is paper no. 53 in the East Rudolf Research Project catalogue of publications.

References

Behrensmeyer, A. K. 1970. Preliminary geological interpretation of a new hominid site in the Lake Rudolf basin. *Nature* 226:225-26.

Bowen, B. E., and Vondra, C. F. 1973. Stratigraphical relationships of the Plio-Pleistocene deposits, East Rudolf, Kenya. *Nature* 242:391-93.

Brown, F. H. 1972. Radiometric dating of sedimentary formations in the lower Omo valley, Ethiopia. In *Calibration of hominoid evolution,* ed. W. W. Bishop and J. A. Miller, pp. 273-88. Edinburgh: Scottish Academic Press; Toronto: University of Toronto Press.

Curtis, G. H. 1968. The stratigraphy of the ejecta from the 1912 eruption of Mr. Katmai and Novarupta, Alaska. In *Studies in volcanology,* pp. 152-210. Geological Society of America, Memoir 116.

Ewart, A. 1966. Mineralogy and petrogenesis of the Whakamaru ignimbrite in the Maraetai area of the Taupo volcanic zone, New Zealand. *New Zealand J. Geol. Geophys.* 8:611.

Grove, A. T., and Goudie, A. S. 1971. Secrets of Lake Stefanie's past. *Geograph. Mag.* 43:542-47.

Maglio, V. J. 1972. Vertebrate faunas and chronology of hominid-bearing sediments east of Lake Rudolf, Kenya. *Nature* 239:379-85.

Rittman, A. 1933. Petrologic descriptions of the plutonic and eruptive rocks of Somma and Vesuvius and the evolution and differentiation of their magmas. *Z. Vulkanol.* 15:8-94.

Vondra, C. F.; Johnson, G. D.; Behrensmeyer, A. K.; and Bowen, B. E. 1971. Preliminary stratigraphical studies of the East Rudolf basin. *Nature* 231:245-48.

9.   OXYGEN-ISOTOPE STUDIES OF THE EAST RUDOLF VOLCANOCLASTICS
T. E. Cerling

Introduction

Preliminary investigations of the various tuffs in the East Rudolf basin did not yield conclusive correlations of the ash units within the basin. Because of the discontinuous nature of the outcrops and the lithologic changes within sedimentary units, field mapping could not link the sedimentary sequence at Ileret with that at Koobi Fora. Laboratory studies of the tuffs, including indexes of refraction, heavy mineral analysis, and neutron activation analysis, indicated that the tuffs were complex. Because of their largely fluvial nature, they had been contaminated with other sediments, and in some cases might actually be multicomponent ashes (see Findlater, this symposium).

Measurements have been made of O^{18}/O^{16} ratios in the volcanic glasses to help solve this problem. It was thought that different ashes might have characteristic oxygen-isotope ratios either because of different initial O^{18}/O^{16} ratios or because of different amounts of alteration in ashes of different age. Results showed that the latter process was of great importance in this particular area.

Description of Specimens

The geology of the East Rudolf basin is discussed in detail elsewhere in this volume (Vondra and Bowen), as are the ash units (Findlater, this symposium) and the dating of the tuffs (Fitch and Miller, this symposium). Therefore these units will be discussed only briefly.

The stratigraphic occurrence of the ash units studied is shown in figure 1.

Tulu Bor Tuff Samples were collected from the Tulu Bor Tuff from east of the Kokoi horst and along the Koobi Fora ridge. An unknown tuff thought to be the Tulu Bor Tuff was collected near Bura Hasuma (sample 6). Two pumices were collected from a tuffaceous channel just below the Tulu Bor Tuff (samples 5 and 7). A description of each specimen is given in table 1 and the locations of the samples are shown in figure 2.

KBS Tuff Samples of this unit were collected along the Koobi Fora ridge and along the Karari escarpment. One specimen was collected near the Il Eriet River (sample 8). This tuff was thought to be the KBS Tuff, although the correlation is not a firm one based on field mapping. One sample of pumice from a coarse tuffaceous channel several meters above the KBS Tuff was also collected (sample 16).

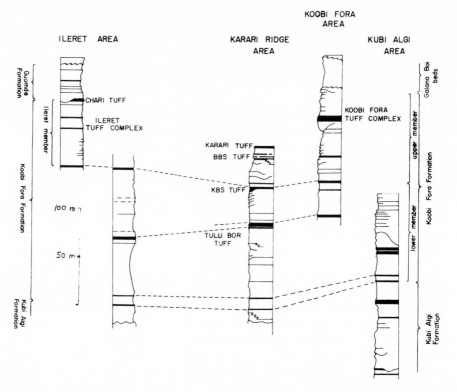

Figure 1. Generalized stratigraphic section, East Rudolf basin. Modified from Bowen and Vondra (1973).

The rest of the samples were collected from known tuffs, and their locations and descriptions are straightforward. They are listed in table 1 and shown on the map in figure 2.

Basis for Isotope Studies

The study of O^{18}/O^{16} ratios has shown that the content of O^{18} varies over a range of 10% (100 units per thousand) in natural systems (Garlick 1972). Comparisons of oxygen-isotope studies show that ultrabasic and high-temperature minerals are deficient in O^{18} compared with lower-temperature minerals. Weathering of these rocks causes increased fractionation, so that there is an enrichment of O^{18} in the weathered material (Lawrence and Taylor 1972). In this study I have used the standard procedure for computing oxygen-isotope ratios in geologic materials:

$$\delta O^{18} = \left(\frac{R_{sample} - R_{standard}}{R_{standard}} \right) \times 1,000$$

The standard in common use today is SMOW (Standard Mean Ocean Water).

Taylor (1968) has shown that unaltered volcanic glasses have constant δO^{18} values throughout the same flow unit. (Studies on many different unaltered volcanic glasses showed a range from +6 to +8 O^{18}.) He also found that altered glasses could be enriched up to +10 per mil in O^{18}; the total enrichment was greater in older rocks.

Garlick and Dymond (1970) studied the effect of ocean water exchange with volcanic

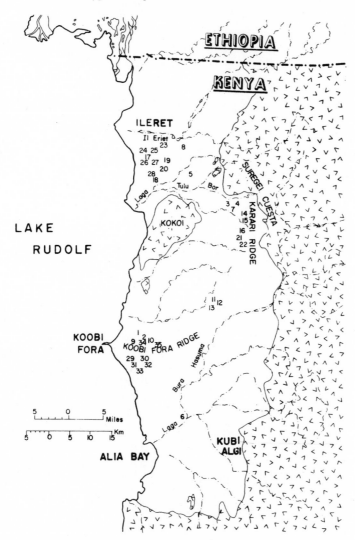

Figure 2. Location of samples within the East Rudolf basin

glass; they found a significant correlation of enrichment in 0^{18} with increasing age. The exchange with seawater was homogeneous in that the same ash unit encountered in different cores had a constant $\delta 0^{18}$ value. Exchange with seawater was found to be relatively simple in that many variables were held constant (e.g., temperature).

These observations were used as the basis for this study. Because unaltered glass has $0^{18}/0^{16}$ ratios characteristic of the parent magma, and altered glasses have $0^{18}/0^{16}$ ratios characteristic of their particular alteration history, each tuff should have $\delta 0^{18}$ values peculiar to its individual history.

Sample Preparation

The samples analyzed in this study were collected in the 1972 field season. Most were collected by Bruce Bowen, Ian Findlater, or myself from known tuff horizons that could be traced into detailed stratigraphic sections.

Table 1

Field Location of Samples and Results of O^{18}/O^{16} Analysis

Locality and Bed Number[a]	Field Correlation	Comments	O^{18}/O^{16} Ratio Relative to Tank Oxygen	O^{18}/O^{16} Ratio Relative to SMOW
1 102-0420	Tulu Bor Tuff	Collected from known Tulu Bor Tuff locality along the base of Koobi Fora Ridge	-13.73	+14.94
2 102-04310	Tulu Bor Tuff	Collected from Tulu Bor Tuff along the base of Koobi Fora Ridge	-14.11	+14.55
3 130-0409	Tulu Bor Tuff	Collected from Tulu Bor Tuff along the base of Koobi Fora Ridge	-12.28	+16.43
4 130-0505	Tulu Bor Tuff	Collected from Tulu Bor Tuff along the Laga Tulu Bor	-13.53	+15.14
5 012-0211Aa		Pumice collected from a tuff in stratigraphic position similar to that of Tulu Bor Tuff along the Suregei cuesta	-21.29	+ 7.16
6 125-0101		Collected from a tuff in stratigraphic position similar to that of the Tulu Bor Tuff along the Laga Bura Hasuma floodplain	-21.45 / -21.49	+ 7.06 ± 0.03 (2)
7 130-0402Ap		Pumice collected from a tuff about 4 m below the Tulu Bor Tuff along the Laga Tulu Bor	-19.42	+ 9.09
8 010-0315	KBS Tuff	Collected from tuff in stratigraphic position similar to that of the KBS Tuff; near the base of the Ileret Section along the Il Eriet River	-19.35	+ 9.16
9 102-0445	KBS Tuff	Collected from the KBS Tuff along the base of Koobi Fora Ridge	-19.28	+ 9.23

Table 1—Continued

10	104-0342	KBS Tuff	Collected from a tuff in a stratigraphic position similar to that of the KBS Tuff near eastern end of Koobi Fora Ridge	-19.01	+ 9.51
11	105-0006	KBS Tuff	Collected from KBS Tuff	-19.32	+ 9.18
12	105-9203	KBS Tuff	Collected from KBS Tuff	-19.89 -19.62 -19.26	+ 8.91 ± 0.31 (3)
13	105-9203A	KBS Tuff	Pumice from same bed as 105-9203	-15.77	+11.84
14	130-0203	KBS Tuff	Tuff collected from KBS Tuff along the Karari Ridge	-18.58 -19.93	+ 9.25 ± 0.95 (2)
15	130-0212	KBS Tuff	Tuff collected from KBS Tuff along the Karari Ridge	-19.38 -19.67	+ 8.98 ± 0.21 (2)
16	131-0011A		Pumice collected from an orange tuff several meters above the KBS Tuff along the Karari Ridge	-19.95	+ 8.54
17	006A-0538	Ileret Tuff Complex	Tuff that occurs at the top of the Ileret Tuff Complex along the Ileret Ridge	-20.92	+ 7.54
18	007-9805	Ileret Tuff Complex	Tuff from near the middle of the Ileret Tuff Complex	-20.22	+ 8.26
19	008-0406	Ileret Tuff Complex	Pumice from pumice channel near middle of tuff complex	-22.55	+ 5.86
20	008-9902	Ileret Tuff Complex	Tuff from near base of the Ileret Tuff Complex	-21.86	+ 6.57
21	130-0015	Karari Tuff Complex	Tuff collected from the top of the Karari Tuff Complex along the top of the Karari Ridge	-22.20 -22.63	+ 6.00 ± 0.30 (2)
22	131-0301	BBS Tuff Complex	Tuff collected from the base of Karari Ridge	-21.82	+ 6.62
23	001-9902CC	Chari Tuff	Pumice collected from Chari Tuff along the Ileret Ridge	-20.74	+ 7.72
24	006-0561F	Chari Tuff	Collected along Ileret Ridge	-21.45	+ 7.00

Table 1--Continued

Locality and Bed Number[a]	Field Correlation	Comments	O^{18}/O^{16} Ratio Relative to Tank Oxygen	O^{18}/O^{16} Ratio Relative to SMOW
25 006-0561H	Chari Tuff	Pumice collected from Chari Tuff along the base of Ileret Ridge	-20.34	+ 8.14
26 006A-0561c	Chari Tuff	Collected from the Ileret Ridge	-21.21	+ 7.24
27 006A-0561e	Chari Tuff	Pumice collected from Chari Tuff	-21.34	+ 7.11
28 007-9822	Chari Tuff	Collected along the southern end of the Ileret Ridge	-21.41	+ 7.04
29 101-0215	Koobi Fora Tuff Complex	Collected from the base of the Koobi Fora Tuff Complex along the Koobi Fora Ridge	-21.62	+ 6.82
30 101-0221	Koobi Fora Tuff Complex	Pumice collected from complex along the Koobi Fora Ridge	-20.93	+ 7.53
31 101-0222	Koobi Fora Tuff Complex	Collected along the Koobi Fora Ridge	-21.88	+ 6.55
32 101-0223	Koobi Fora Tuff Complex	Collected along the Koobi Fora Ridge	-21.44	+ 7.01
33 101-0224	Koobi Fora Tuff Complex	Collected along the Koobi Fora Ridge	-21.76	+ 6.68
34 102-0461A	Koobi Fora Tuff Complex	Pumice collected from near the base of the complex	-21.52	+ 6.92
35 102-0464	Koobi Fora Tuff Complex	Collected along the Koobi Fora Ridge	-21.43	+ 7.02

[a]All sample numbers have the prefix "ER72."

Pumice fragments and glass shards were separated by hand picking, as were pumice fragments of different compositions (e.g., light-colored pumice from dark, vesicular pumice, or calcareous pumice from noncalcareous pumice). The samples were disaggregated by gentle grinding with a mortar and pestle, unless they were well indurated, in which case more vigorous action was required. The samples were dry sieved and the material measuring 63 to 125μ was collected.

The fragments of glass (shards and ground pumice) were isolated from the heavier mineral fraction by heavy liquid techniques. (The separation was made with a bromoform-toluene mixture of 2.49 gm/cc.) The samples were then washed with acetone and allowed to air dry for several days. Each sample was also dried in a vacuum at 100°C for 24 hr before analysis.

Procedure: O^{18}/O^{16} Analysis

A more detailed description of the process used to analyze the O^{18}/O^{16} ratios is in preparation, but a brief discussion should be given here.

The standard techniques for analyzing silicates for oxygen-isotope ratios involve fluorinating the samples with bromine pentafluoride or with fluorine gas. Since both procedures involve handling dangerous liquid and gaseous fluorides, a new technique was explored. Flesch, Svec, and Staley (1960) found that cobalt trifluoride (CoF_3) could be used to evolve oxygen from chromates, since gentle heating of the solid CoF_3 causes the evolution of fluorine gas. Therefore a safe, easy-to-handle solid-solid mixture of CoF_3 and volcanic glass was prepared for analysis.

Gentle heating of this mixture resulted in the evolution of O_2 gas, which was then analyzed for O^{18}/O^{16} ratios. Again a digression was made from standard procedure: the O^{18}/O^{16} ratios were determined by analyzing O_2 gas instead of passing the gas over hot carbon and analyzing the resulting CO_2. Analysis was made on a double collecting Nier-type mass spectrometer operating with an accelerating voltage of 47 v.

Results

Using this method I obtained O^{18}/O^{16} ratios within about ± 0.3δ units. The results are reported in the standard manner:

$$\delta O^{18} = \left(\frac{R_{sample} - R_{standard}}{R_{standard}} \right) \times 1{,}000$$

Tank oxygen was used as a standard. Because this gas is not used in reporting oxygen-isotope ratios in the literature, the results were standardized to Standard Mean Ocean Water (SMOW) by measuring the oxygen-isotope ratio of NBS #28 (+10.06 relative to SMOW; Friedman and Gleason 1973) relative to tank oxygen. NBS #28 was found to be -18.47 relative to tank oxygen. Therefore:

$$\frac{R_x}{R_{SMOW}} = \frac{R_x}{R_{tank}} \times \frac{R_{tank}}{R_{NBS}} \times \frac{R_{NBS}}{R_{SMOW}}$$

and

$$\delta_{x/SMOW} = 1.02907 \, \delta_{x/tank} + 29.07.$$

112   T. E. Cerling

These values are reported in table 1 and plotted in figure 3. The results of the Karari Tuff, the BBS complex, and the Ileret Tuff complex are shown, although there are very few samples for those particular horizons. The tuff horizons in figure 3 are plotted against relative age on the basis of their stratigraphic position (fig. 1, and Fitch and Miller, this symposium).

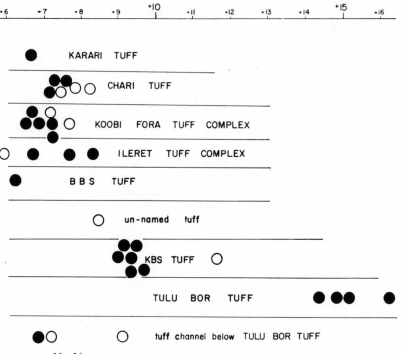

Figure 3. O^{18}/O^{16} ratios plotted relative to SMOW. Open circles represent pumice.

Two very important observations can be made about these data: first, in general there is an enrichment in O^{18} with increasing age; and, second, the pumice in general has had greater O^{18} enrichment than the tuff. Both factors indicate that the observed differences are due primarily to differences in the total amount of alteration of the glass within the sediments. The enrichment in O^{18} is residual.

In general, this study shows that the Tulu Bor Tuff can be distinguished from the KBS Tuff and the younger tuffs, and that the KBS Tuff differs from the younger tuffs. However, this technique does not provide the necessary precision to separate all the younger tuffs from each other. The samples studied of the Ileret Tuff Complex, the BBS Tuff Complex, and the Karari Tuff Complex were too few to define the range of the O^{18}/O^{16} ratios characteristic of these units; they will not, therefore, be discussed in detail, nor will the data obtained be used to make definitive statements.

It should also be noted that the O^{18}/O^{16} ratios obtained from pumice generally are substantially higher than those obtained from the glass of the tuffs. Thus the characteristic δO^{18} ranges should be considered on the basis of the tuff values or the pumice values, but not both. Because the pumice have different values, even in the younger units, it is concluded that all δO^{18} values are due to alteration and there possibly are no δO^{18} values characteristic of the original O^{18} composition.

There are several deviations from the general pattern of $\delta 0^{18}$ with increasing age. The most obvious is the very low values obtained for several samples associated with the Tulu Bor Tuff (samples 5, 6, and 7). Sample 7 occurred several meters below sample 3 in a different tuff bed, but in the same outcrop. Sample 5 is thought to be equivalent to this unit because pumice fragments have not been observed in the massive Tulu Bor Tuff, although numerous pumice fragments have been found in the associated underlying channel. The alteration of these pumices is markedly less than that in the overlying tuff. I cannot explain this at present. Sample 6 was attributed to the Tulu Bor Tuff but came from an outcrop several miles away from definitive outcrops of the Tulu Bor or KBS tuffs. There could be an error in field correlation. However, because of the distance from the other samples the discrepancy could be due to deposition in a different environment, or to a different alteration history.

The members of the KBS Tuff assemblage are tightly grouped, indicating a similar amount of alteration in the glass shards. The only sample that had not been correlated by tracing the KBS unit (sample 8) fell into this grouping. It is concluded that this correlation of the KBS Tuff to the Ileret area is valid.

The Chari Tuff and Koobi Fora Tuff have very similar $\delta 0^{18}$ ranges, although the values of the Chari Tuff are consistently higher than the Koobi Fora Tuff Complex. The conclusions drawn from this data, then, are that the alteration histories of the two tuffs are different, although no statements can be made concerning their relationship in time, since both have similar ranges, since alteration processes may differ in different burial environments, and because of the proximity to the Gregory rift. Both units show only slight alteration, because the range of unaltered tuffs is from +6 to +8 relative to SMOW (Taylor 1968).

This study shows that there is significant alteration of the glasses within the volcanic ash units of the East Rudolf basin owing to the isotope exchange with groundwaters. Although this does not mean that equivalent exchange has occurred within the feldspars, it is possible that there has been some exchange. Any exchange would be expected to be much smaller because of the high susceptibility of glass to alteration.

Summary

The oxygen-isotope ratios were determined by extraction of oxygen with cobalt trifluoride and analysis by mass spectrometer.

Results showed that the older tuffs were significantly enriched in 0^{18} relative to the younger ashes, which showed only a minor increase in 0^{18} from unaltered glasses. The two oldest units were distinct from each other and from the younger tuffs, which could not be differentiated from each other. Alteration of the tuff varied from an enrichment of about +8 to +10 per mil to a very slight enrichment (still within the range of the unaltered tuffs).

These results concur with the studies of Taylor (1968) and Garlick and Dymond (1970), which demonstrate that volcanic glass shows significant enrichment in 0^{18} with time. It also indicates that these amounts of exchange can be used as a tool in correlating ash units.

This is paper no. 54 in the East Rudolf Research Project catalogue of publications.

References

Bowen, B. E., and Vondra, C. F., 1973. Stratigraphical relationships of the Plio-Pleistocene deposits, East Rudolf, Kenya. *Nature* 242:391-93.

Flesch, G. D.; Svec, H. J.; and Staley, H. G. 1960. The absolute abundance of the chromium isotopes in chromite. *Geochim. Cosmochim. Acta* 20:300-309.

Friedman, I., and Gleason, J. D. 1973. A new silicate intercomparison for 0-18 analysis. *Earth Planet Sci. Letters* 18:124.

Garlick, G. D. 1972. Oxygen isotope geochemistry. In *The encyclopedia of geochemistry and environmental sciences,* ed. R. W. Fairbridge, pp. 864-74. New York: Van Nostrand Reinhold.

Garlick, G. D., and Dymond, D. 1970. Oxygen isotope exchange between volcanic materials and ocean water. *Geol. Soc. Am. Bull.* 81:2137-42.

Lawrence, J. R., and Taylor, H. P., Jr. 1972. Hydrogen and oxygen isotope systematics in weathering profiles. *Geochim. Cosmochim. Acta* 36:1377-93.

Taylor, H. P., Jr. 1968. The oxygen isotope geochemistry of igneous rocks. *Contrib. Mineral. Petrol.* 19:1-71.

10. LATE CENOZOIC ENVIRONMENTS OF THE KOOBI FORA FORMATION:
THE UPPER MEMBER ALONG THE WESTERN KOOBI FORA RIDGE

G. D. Johnson and R. G. H. Raynolds

Introduction

Tuff, tuffaceous silts, diatomaceous silts, calcarenites, lithofeldspathic sands, and
mudstones dominate in a sequence of Plio-Pleistocene terrestrial and lacustrine sediments
in the East Rudolf basin area of Kenya.

The reconstruction of the paleoenvironment is indeed complex for such a varied and
interdigitated sequence as is found in most of the East Rudolf area. Although most of the
sequences of the western part of the basin show predominantly lacustrine conditions throughout most of the Plio-Pleistocene, several regressions of the lake waters are associated
with intervals of fluvial and fluvial-deltaic sedimentation. These intervals are the subject of most of the research of the East Rudolf project. The present study involves one
area in the extreme western part of the Koobi Fora ridge in which several intercalated sequences of lacustrine and fluvial lithosomes are found. The interval spans the time from
approximately 2.6 m.y. to slightly less than 1.5 m.y.[1]

Within the East Rudolf Research Project, the Dartmouth College geological research
team has taken responsibility for large-scale mapping (1:3,000) and detailed stratigraphic
studies at the western end of the Koobi Fora ridge (i.e., areas 101, 102, and 103 in par-
ticular--see fig. 1). The work was done in 1972 and 1973, with the assistance of G. Hahn
and R. Wood. This paper offers a brief summary of the stratigraphy recorded in the area
and of the paleoenvironments represented.

Both the Lower and the Upper members of the Koobi Fora Formation are well exposed at
the western end of the Koobi Fora ridge, but this report is concerned primarily with the
Upper Member, the stratigraphic interval from the KBS Tuff through the Koobi Fora Tuff Complex to the unconformity that separates the Koobi Fora Formation from the overlying Galana
Boi Beds (see figs. 2 and 3, and Vondra and Bowen, this symposium).

The aggregate thickness of the Upper Member in areas 102 and 103 is 155 m, which represents an appreciably greater thickness than is preserved farther east in areas 105, 130, or
131. The character of the sediments also contrasts with the Upper Member of the eastern
areas with which this report is concerned, which consist of alternating lacustrine, deltaic
and generally low-energy fluvial deposits.

The Upper Member sedimentary section at the western end of the Koobi Fora ridge is of

1. These dates concern the best radiometrically dated material from the KBS Tuff and
the Koobi Fora Tuff complex (see Fitch and Miller, this symposium, and Findlater, this
symposium).

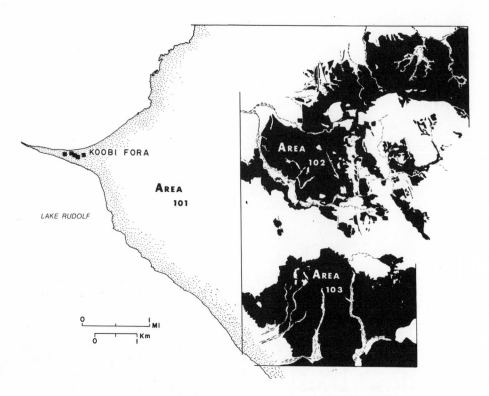

Figure 1. Outline map of western portion of Koobi Fora ridge showing East Rudolf collecting areas 101, 102, and 103. Outcrop distribution of Kubi Algi and Koobi Fora formations shown in black for areas 102 and 103.

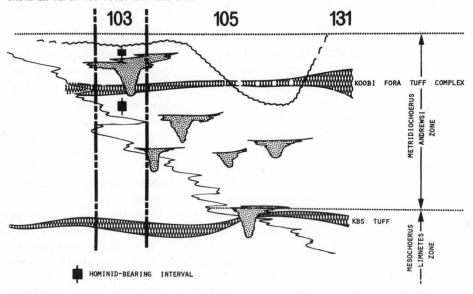

Figure 2. Generalized lithostratigraphy of the Upper Member of Koobi Fora Formation, along the Koobi Fora ridge. Biozonation from Maglio (1972). Details of Area 103 are covered in this report.

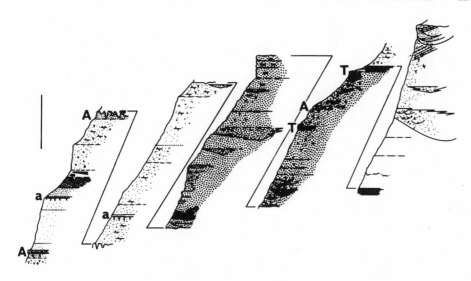

Figure 3. Schematic stratigraphic section of middle portion of Upper Member of Koobi Fora Formation, western Koobi Fora ridge. Cyclical sedimentation is illustrated by repetitive occurrence of algal stromatolites (A), algal boundstones (a) and repetitive character of interbedded mudstones and sandstones. The Koobi Fora Tuff Complex (*stippled*) is similarly characterized by transgressive-regressive facies and contains two well-defined tuff horizons (T) in addition to a well-developed stromatolitic layer (A). The important hominid-bearing intervals of Area 103 occur approximately 5 m above the uppermost algal boundstone (a), second column from left. Length of vertical bar, 2.5 m.

interest and importance for a number of reasons. First, it provides information crucial to the reconstruction of the paleogeography of the region during the time interval represented. Second, various units within the interval have yielded a rich mammalian fauna, including important hominid fossils such as KNM/ER 403, 730, 734, 736, 737, 1808, and 1820.

Areas 102 and 103 were collected by V. Maglio, who used the samples obtained as part of the basis for establishing the *Metridiochoerus andrewsi* peak zone and its related vertebrate assemblage (see Maglio 1972, and this symposium). The beds also contain abundant molluscan fossils which have been studied by P. Williamson, but details of this work are not yet available.

Lithology and Field Relations

The Upper Member of Koobi Fora Formation (variable thickness, maximum 155 m exposed), is composed of interbedded distributary, interdistributary, littoral, lacustrine, and strand lithosomes.[2] Lithologies vary, but coarse fraction sediments (> .5 mm) are predominantly lithofeldspathic ($Q_{35}F_{32}L_{33}$),[3] with subordinate amounts of pyroclastic detritus throughout the section. The formation as exposed in areas 101-103 develops a cyclic style of deposition characterized by distinct and rapidly transgressive littoral lacustrine sequences followed by fluctuating recessional strand and fluvial/deltaic complexes. The Upper Member,

---

2. A lithosome can be defined as a three-dimensional rock mass with specific lithologic character

3. The $Q_xF_yL_z$ quantitative serial designation of sandstones is a convenient way of annotating contained mineralogies. Q is total quartzose grains, F is total feldspar grains, and L is total unstable lithic fragments in the sandstone framework where $Q+F+L = 100$.

interpreted on the above character, can be locally mapped on the basis of these cycles. Well-developed algal biolithites or stromatolites (see below) constitute laterally continuous lithologies "occurring in" many cycles (Johnson 1974). These have been utilized as marker beds differentiating sedimentary cycle boundaries; the formation can be subsequently discussed in terms of these deposition cycles. The lowest portion of the Upper Member overlies the KBS Tuff, which is described briefly.

KBS Tuff. (Defined by Behrensmeyer 1970; Vondra et al. 1971; Bowen and Vondra 1973). This is of variable thickness (0-1 m), moderately indurated, medium- to coarse-grained reworked white tuff with locally developed small-scale cross-bedding. Root casts, thin parallel laminae, and a siltier composition characterize the upper portion of the tuff. This general character is quite persistent, but locally small interbeds of slightly more silty character are prominent.

Upper Member, Koobi Fora Formation

1. Above the KBS Tuff lies a variable lacustrine sequence giving way to mixed floodplain sediments characterized by sands and silts, with small calcareous concretions, flasers of coarse material, and root casts. This is in turn capped by proximal lacustrine gastropod-bearing sandstones (up to 1.3 m thick), evidencing minor lacustrine transgressions. In all there are 8 gastropod units, varying in thickness from several centimeters to >1 m. The "gastropod sands" are separated by variable thicknesses of silts and sands, often with scattered invertebrates, cross-bedding, root casts, and weathered surfaces.

Two thin but laterally continuous tuffs occur in this sequence. The first, a very thin (1 to 3 cm) pinkish tuff occurs 18-20 m above the KBS. The second, a thicker (0.25-1 m) white finely ripple-laminated tuff, occurs 26-28 m above the KBS.

The alternating "gastropod units" are overlain and partially cut into by a channel complex 10 m thick. This channel system is continuous across 102 and 103 and is an important marker horizon. Basal deposits of the channel contain coarse gravels, with a characteristic light green pumice in well-rounded pebbles up to 6 cm in diameter. The horizon weathers into white, quartz- and feldspar-sand-filled valleys, and so its outcrop pattern is conspicuous on aerial photographs.

The channel complex is overlain by a paleosol up to 2.5 m thick, showing mottles of green (reduced) and red (oxidized) muddy sand.

2. In general the above predominately lacustrine sequence of fine-grained mudstones and interbedded beach sands gives way upward to several fluvial/lacustrine transitional cycles (fig. 3). These represent a phase of sedimentation in proximity to sources of sediment input with its subsequent influence on littoral lacustrine facies variability. Three cycles of transgression-regression are noted in this portion of the member; the style of sedimentation does not vary much among them. Each cycle, 16 to 18 m thick, is characterized by rapidly transgressive laterally extensive algal stromatolitic beds giving way upward to interbedded lacustrine silts and minor channel sands. The mineralogical character differs little within each cycle. Pedogenic alteration (soil formation) of most of the fluvial lithosomes appears to be present and varies considerably. This is interpreted as representing the differing hydromorphic influences of the varied topographic elements of the original depositional landscape.

3. Koobi Fora Tuff Complex (ca. 15 m thick, but varies owing to downcutting of the channel complex mentioned below) (Bowen and Vondra 1973). A 15-m interbedded tuffaceous silt and pumice pebble conglomerate and tuff interval is collectively known as the Koobi

Fora Tuff Complex. Best exposures occur in Area 103 in the upper portion of the Upper Member of the Koobi Fora Formation. The first phase of the deposition of this complex is characterized by an arenaceous interval of quartzose silts and lithofeldspathic sandstones giving way upward to interbedded pumice pebble conglomerates which are well developed in channel lag and point bar types of structures. Lateral to the main "channel" body are tuffaceous intervals composed of very fine grained pumice fragments and shards. The entire sequence continues to fine upward until a facies of interbedded fine-grained littoral silts and interdistributary mudstones is attained. Midway through the section is an algal bound-stone containing a mixed invertebrate faunal assemblage in which *Etheria* sp. is a dominant component. Fish remains as well as other vertebrate faunal remains occur throughout the silt intervals. Locally, sandstone lenses are common, some of which are quite pumice-rich.

Midway between the lower and upper boundaries of the Koobi Fora Tuff Complex are ex-posed two intervals of tuffaceous clay which are irregularly persistent laterally. The intervals generally are characterized by light gray (N7.5) clays having a lack of internal bedding. The outcrop can be traced laterally for several tens of meters and irregularly across the entire Area 103 terrane for approximately 2.5 km. A hard mixture of amorphous clays and montmorillonite allows for the soft-textured appearance of the clay intervals, but enough shards are present to make a relatively rough texture. Intermediate between the two light gray tuffaceous clays is a 30 cm thick bed of oolitic carbonate. This is inter-bedded with a tuffaceous clay sequence very similar to the marker beds below and above. The oolitic particles are mostly between 2 and 6 mm in diameter, occurring with some algal oncolites ranging in size from 5 to 15 cm in diameter.

4. Overlying the Koobi Fora Tuff Complex is a small (7-m) interval of littoral lacus-trine mudstones. This represents one of the last major phases of lacustrine sedimentation for the exposed sequence in Area 103. The mudstones are truncated by an extensive distribu-tary sand body which gives way upward to supralittoral muds, which again show evidence of hydromorphic pedogenesis (soil formation). A minor period of lacustrine transgression fol-lows with the development of a 0.5-m calcarenite containing oolites and scattered oncolites (type SS, spheroidal algal stromatolites) interspersed throughout the bed. This unit is subsequently replaced by terrestrial conditions characterized by supralittorial mudstones and minor channel sands. The aggregate thickness of the Upper Member of the Koobi Fora Formation in areas 102 and 103 is 155 m.

Algal Biolithites

Probably the most interesting features of specific lithosomes within the entire upper member of Koobi Fora Formation are the extensive biolithites created by the entrapment and binding of sediment by filamentous algae. Throughout most known lacustrine sequences, cal-careous algae play a significant part in providing a sediment baffling mechanism within the shallow margins of "such" lakes. Ancestral Lake Rudolf was no exception.

Nonskeletal, organic sedimentary structures (stromatolites) which are produced by this mechanical accretion of carbonate and other particles are common in the upper Koobi Fora Formation. For the most part these occur as laminated rocks in which the cellular detail of the algae responsible for entrapment is not preserved. Prior work on Holocene and modern, marine and lacustrine algal stromatolites (Logan, Rezak, and Ginsburg 1964; Kendall and Skipwith 1968; and Gebelein 1969) generally considers three dominant geometric forms of stromatolitic growth: hemispheroids, spheroids, and mats. The environmental response is influenced by various conditions of turbulence, turbidity, and desiccation in the littoral

or supralittoral environment. Comparing the growth form of various Koobi Fora algal
stromatolites suggests several distinct environmental facies (discussed in Johnson 1974)
which are illustrated in figure 4. In addition, the form and distribution of algal stromatolites in East Rudolf areas 102 and 103 seem to be controlled by subsequent reworking
of the littoral lacustrine environment.

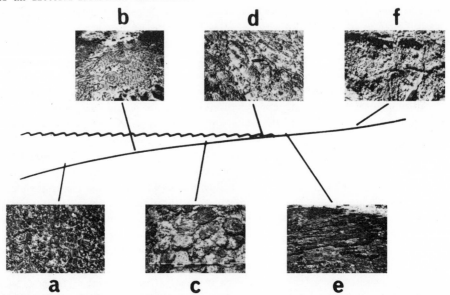

Figure 4. Spatial distribution of algal stromatolite facies variability within the Upper
Member of Koobi Fora Formation, western Koobi Fora ridge. Unit which is mapped is represented in figure 4 as the basal major algal unit (A) in the lower portion of the left-hand
column. Major variability within this bed is related to proximity of strand conditions
in ancestral Lake Rudolf. Of particular importance are growth forms and relationship to
channels developed perpendicular to the ancient strand. Several growth forms are illustrated: (a) Spheroidal stromatolites occurring in extreme distal (deeper-water lacustrine)
segment of stromatolitic beds. These give way laterally to (b) laterally coalesced type
of vertically stacked hemispheroidal stromatolites in medial position between distal and
proximal facies; (c) vertically stacked hemispheroidal stromatolites which become more
coalesced in their proximal position; (d) and (e) stromatolites which reflect major influence of channels developed perpendicular to lacustrine strand. Within the channel, many
stromatolites are not in growth position, having been overturned; (f) Supralittoral stromatolitic laminations showing evidence of desiccation and a profuse gastropod epifauna
(Bellamya).
     Lateral facies variability extends 1 km in areas 101, 102, and 103.

Tectonics

     The structural geology displayed in the western Koobi Fora Ridge is complex. Intense
normal faulting N5°W affects the entire geologic column, including some of the Holocene
Galana Boi Beds. Faulting in the Koobi Fora Formation cuts the Galana Boi Beds near the
base of the beds at several locations, displacing it >1' without disturbing the stratigraphically superior sediments. A series of depositional hiatuses which in several localities are associated with minor faulting occur in areas 102 and 103. Structural displacements of up to 1 m have been observed which are overlain by disconformable and laterally
extensive lacustrine strand and distributary sand bodies. In Area 106, but considerably
lower in the section, a similar hiatus exists approximately 5 m above the top of the KBS
Tuff. Although the relief associated with these unconformities in the western part of the

East Rudolf basin is low, there may be a correlation between these hiatuses and those affecting the interval above the KBS Tuff farther to the east (Behrensmeyer, this symposium; Vondra and Bowen, this symposium).

Approximately 14 m above the top of the KBS in the extreme northern portion of Area 102, a 5-cm clastic dike composed of derived gastropod-bearing sands is injected approximately 5 m into underlying sediments. The trend of the dike is en echelon with the set of N5°E faults which predominate in the area.

Summary

Facies relationships within the Upper Member sediments of the Koobi Fora Formation are varied in the western Koobi Fora ridge. Cyclic sedimentation is characterized by rapid lacustrine transgressions followed by irregular and sedimentologically varied regressive lithosomes. Hominids occur here within regressive strand and supralittoral lithosomes (lake fringe), with some association found with distributary lithosomes.

The Lower Member in areas 102 and 103 contrasts with the Upper Member by showing much more stable lacustrine conditions. From the work of Bowen and others it is known that the shoreline zone in Lower Member times was commonly situated many kilometers to the northeast, in areas 130 and 131. During Upper Member times the shoreline zone had clearly shifted out to the west so that the area with which this report is concerned experienced alternating fluvial and lake margin conditions. Initial sedimentation above the KBS Tuff reflects shallowing conditions in ancestral Lake Rudolf but generally evidences the cyclical sedimentation so characteristic of the Upper Member. Midway in the Upper Member an increase in clastic input suggests proximity to sedimentary distributary sources from the east and hence a restriction in lacustrine development such that there is a general regression of sedimentary lacustrine lithosomes to the west. This regressive character persists through most of the remaining portion of the Upper Member of the formation. Here many well-developed algal biolithites reflect both transgressive and regressive events within the section. They are associated with delta fringe, interdistributary, and distributary lithosomes and numerous intervals of fluvial sediments yielding important vertebrate faunal associations.

The principal sources of paleontological collections are considered to be fluvial and lacustrine beach strand in character through most of areas 102 and 103. The general character of prograding terrestrial facies from east to west throughout the East Rudolf sequence is a character noted at Ileret, Koobi Fora, and Koobi Algi terrane (Vondra and Bowen, this symposium; Findlater, this symposium).

This is paper no. 55 in the East Rudolf Research project catalogue of publications.

References

Behrensmeyer, A. K. 1970. Preliminary geological interpretation of a new hominid site in the Lake Rudolf basin. *Nature* 266:225-26.

Bowen, B. E., and Vondra, C. F. 1973. Stratigraphical relationships of the Plio-Pleistocene deposits, East Rudolf, Kenya. *Nature* 242:391-93.

Gebelein, C. D. 1969. Distribution, morphology and accretion rate of Recent subtidal algal stromatolites, Bermuda. *J. Sed. Petrol.* 39:49-69.

Johnson, G. D. 1974. Cainozoic lacustrine stromatolites from hominid-bearing sediments East of Lake Rudolf, Kenya. *Nature* 247:520-23.

Kendall, C. G., and Skipwith, P. A. 1968. Recent algal mats of a Persian Gulf lagoon.
    J. Sed. Petrol. 38:1040-58.

Logan, B. W.; Rezak, R.; and Ginsburg, R. N. 1964. Classification and environmental sig-
    nificance of algal stromatolites. *J. Geol.* 72:68-83.

Maglio, V. J. 1972. Vertebrate faunas and chronology of hominid-bearing sediments east of
    Lake Rudolf, Kenya. *Nature* 239:379-85.

Vondra, C. F.; Johnson, G. D.; Behrensmeyer, A. K.; and Bowen, B. E. 1971. Preliminary
    stratigraphical studies of the East Rudolf Basin, Kenya. *Nature* 231:245-48.

11. CONVENTIONAL POTASSIUM-ARGON AND ARGON-40/ARGON-39 DATING OF VOLCANIC ROCKS FROM EAST RUDOLF

F. J. Fitch and J. A. Miller

The East Rudolf Area

In nothern Kenya, to the east of Lake Rudolf, extensive segments of the Miocene to Recent rock succession are extremely well exposed. The East Rudolf sedimentary basin extends some 1,200 km^2 to the east of the present lake and contains a full, varied, and abundantly fossiliferous sequence of sediments and tuffs, late Pliocene to mid-Pleistocene in age. Less extensive outcrops of late Pleistocene and more recent superficial and high-level lake deposits are also exposed in this area. Rising as faulted periclinal upwarps through the sediments at East Rudolf and generally occupying the ground to the east of the sedimentary basin are complex volcanic highlands in which an interdigitation of basic and acid volcanics with various local sedimentary sequences suggests a Miocene to Recent geological history dominated by repeated volcanic eruption and explosion. The geochronological evidence to be obtained from the sedimentary basin and the volcanic highlands is complementary. A detailed and precise geochronology for the rocks of the Plio-Pleistocene sedimentary basin is urgently required as a time framework in which to view the important archeological, paleoanthropological, and paleontological finds that have been made in the East Rudolf area. This chapter is an interim report on our attempts to provide such a geochronology.

Geochronology and Geochronometry

Geochronology is earth history presented as an ordered sequence of events seen against a calibrated time scale. Geochronometry is the science of dating rocks by various physical methods. Analytically precise "apparent ages" obtained in the laboratory may be incorrect, however, for a variety of geological reasons (see Fitch 1972). Thus, before the geochronology of an area can be satisfactorily deciphered, a considerable amount of geological work must be done, and the basic rock stratigraphy, mapped field relationships, petrology, and structure must be known in detail. In erecting a geochronology all relevant evidence is used, including that from stratigraphical relationships (e.g., "way-up" evidence, sequence of deposition, structural sequence, and cross-cutting intrusive relationships); from the irreversible sequence of evolutionary change (paleontological evidence); from paleomagnetism (particularly geomagnetic reversal chronology); from dendrochronology, varved clays, and similar evidence; as well as that from radioisotopic geochronometry and detailed petrographic analysis of the dated samples. Our conclusions are therefore a tentative synthesis

123

of numerous lines of evidence provided both by our own investigations and by the work of others.

Geochronometric Methods

The principal radioisotopic dating methods applicable to the rocks found at East Rudolf are: (1) carbon-14 dating; (2) fission track dating; (3) conventional total degassing potassium-argon dating; (4) total degassing argon-40/argon-39 dating; and (5) argon-40/ argon-39 isochron and age spectrum dating. Detailed descriptions of each of these methods, with evaluations of their significance and of the problems of interpretation, can be found in Bishop and Miller (1972); Fitch, Forster, and Miller (1974); and Fitch and Miller (1973).

Geochronological Synthesis

When the evidence obtained from related geological, paleontological, paleomagnetic, and geochronometric studies is synthesized, it can be presented in one or all of three forms: (1) as a calibrated stratigraphical column (or columns) summarizing the geological history of an area; (2) as a descriptive account; or (3) as a "geochronological map" on which dated isochronous surfaces (e.g., thin tuff horizons or mapped geomagnetic transitions) are indicated in addition to the more usual delimitation of rock stratigraphy. Eventually we hope to provide a synthesis for East Rudolf in each form. This chapter presents only the current geochronometric evidence. The supporting geological, paleontological, paleomagnetic, and other evidence for the synthesis can be found in the chapters by our colleagues in the East Rudolf Research Project and in the references contained therein. The stratigraphic position of the various tuffs which have been dated is shown diagrammatically in figure 3.

Geochronometric Results from East Rudolf

The work being done by the Fitch-Miller rock dating research group in their London and Cambridge laboratories is summarized here. No ^{14}C dates have yet been obtained from East Rudolf rocks. The fission track dating technique is being applied to a number of samples of volcanic glass, but only one of these experiments has been completed so far (Hurford 1974). This preliminary investigation, on glass shards from a vitric tuff in the upper part of the Kubi Algi Formation, shows that fission track dating of East Rudolf tuffs is practicable and that in appropriate circumstances various kinds of information can be obtained. In fact, it was found that at the sampled locality the tuff investigated had suffered complete track annealing during a mild thermal event around 1.8 m.y.

Table 1 contains a summary of the basic geochronometric data obtained from conventional K-Ar, total degassing ^{40}Ar/^{39}Ar, and ^{40}Ar/^{39}Ar age spectrum-age determination analyses of about one hundred rock and mineral samples from the Lake Rudolf basin and from a sample of basalt from Olduvai Gorge. The analytical data and interpretative description of ^{40}Ar/^{39}Ar isochron and age spectrum determinations is exceptionally voluminous and cannot be presented in full. The primary data can be inspected on application to our Cambridge laboratory.

Geological Interpretation of the Geochronometric Data

Potassium-argon age determinations are subject to both under- and overestimates, and argon losses due to the effects of subsequent geological events are the most common cause of discrepancy. Most of the ages quoted in table 1 for lavas and intrusive rocks are derived from fresh samples unaffected by major alteration effects other than those that could be judged deuteric. Thus these ages are generally thought to be geologically correct. Nevertheless, initial contamination or subsequent events can result in severe disturbance of the isotopic systems of even quite fresh-looking rocks. The basalts from Kanapoi and the Olduvai Gorge provide examples of the difficulties that can be encountered.

Dating tuffs, especially reworked or epiclastic tuffs, is extremely difficult. It involves a number of specific geological problems not encountered in dating lavas and intrusive rocks. Field and petrographic evidence being gathered at East Rudolf has made it clear that the following possible sources of error must be considered when any attempt is made to date tuff horizons in the Rudolf basin:

1. Contamination of the tuffs by older volcanics and bedrock eroded by the rivers carrying each new flood of volcanic debris into the sedimentary basin. Because most of the East Rudolf tuffs are demonstrably *not* primary air-fall or ash-flow deposits, this is a very likely source of contamination.

2. Contamination by xenoliths and xenocrysts incorporated as a result of explosive eruption through the basement complex and through an overlying pile of volcanic rocks older than the current eruption. This also is a likely source of error at East Rudolf.

3. Retention of unusually high initial ^{40}/Ar/^{39}Ar ratios by rapidly cooled crystals ejected from deep-seated magma chambers. This is a possible but unlikely source of error (Fitch and Miller 1971).

4. A flood of new volcanic debris resulting from a specific volcanic event in the source area. The overall geology of the East Rudolf sedimentary basin and the adjacent source areas makes it reasonably certain that each of the major tuff horizons represents such a flood. Nevertheless, division of some tuffs into various separate leaves and possible delays in the arrival of tuff floods could be envisaged as related to such factors as river capture or sudden draining of lava-dammed lakes in the source area.

Any one of the above-mentioned sources of error would cause an excess age discrepancy in the dating results.

5. Weathering during various stages of transport and before final sedimentation and burial (during contemporaneous soil-forming processes, for example) and a variety of diagenetic processes occurring after sedimentation, including the partial or complete devitrification of volcanic glass. These conditions might result in argon losses from tuffs. As far as possible in the dating work, we have avoided rocks that are severely weathered because they are near the present land surface or ancient erosion surfaces.

6. Groundwater metasomatism caused by the passage of hot aqueous solutions through porous tuff horizons. In an area in which rocks are unaffected by regional metamorphism, this is likely to be the major cause of potassium-argon age discrepancy. Geothermal groundwater metasomatism can produce a combination of argon-loss discrepancy and aberrant apparent ^{40}Ar/^{36}Ar initial ratios, depending upon the nature and temperature of the solutions involved. The highly alkaline nature of the groundwaters in the East Rudolf area might be important. It is possible to envisage various groundwater systems, driven by either solar or volcanic heat energy with either the proto-Lake Rudolf or a primary volcanic source as a reservoir supplementing the water derived directly from rainfall.

This second group (numbers 5 and 6) of possible sources of error could produce low age discrepancies, but under certain conditions hot groundwater metasomatism can lead to more complex errors arising from interference with the apparent ^{40}Ar/^{36}Ar initial ratios of the various age components of the minerals in a rock.

Table 1

Geochronometric Data on Samples from the Lake Rudolf Basin and Olduvai Gorge, East Africa

Sample Reference	Method	K_2O (%)	Atmospheric Contamination (%)	V/M	Apparent Age and Error (m.y.)
A. LAVAS, IGNIMBRITES, AND INTRUSIVE ROCKS					
F733 basalt, plateau variety, N. side of Buluk Gap	K-Ar T.R. 50/70 mesh	1.02 1.02	96.1 96.0	7.39×10^{-5} 7.54×10^{-5}	2.17 ± 0.44 2.22 ± 0.44 Average = 2.20 ± 0.44
FM 7052 basalt, Kokoi uplift	K-Ar T.R. 50/70 mesh	0.98 0.98	81.1 79.8	1.19×10^{-4} 1.17×10^{-4}	3.64 ± 0.36 3.59 ± 0.36 Average = 3.62 ± 0.36
FM 7053, basalt, overlaid (?) by Kubi Algi Formation rocks	K-Ar T.R. 50/70 mesh	1.15 1.15	73.1 74.2	1.46×10^{-4} 1.45×10^{-4}	3.82 ± 0.38 3.78 ± 0.38 Average = 3.80 ± 0.38
ER58W basalt, volcanic center ENE of Derati	K-Ar T.R. 50/70 mesh	0.92 0.92 0.92	86.5 85.7 84.7	1.09×10^{-4} 1.20×10^{-4} 1.24×10^{-4}	3.5 ± 0.4 3.9 ± 0.4 4.0 ± 0.4 Average = 3.8 ± 0.4
FMA 74 basalt, Yellow Sands	K-Ar T.R.	1.01 1.01	93.0 92.2	1.471×10^{-4} 1.385×10^{-4}	4.4 ± 0.3 4.1 ± 0.3 Average = 4.25 ± 0.3
ER10RW peralkaline rhyolite, Kubi Algi	K-Ar T.R. 50/70 mesh	4.84 4.84 4.84	91.3 89.8 89.2	1.17×10^{-3} 1.22×10^{-3} 1.22×10^{-3}	7.3 ± 0.7 7.6 ± 0.8 7.6 ± 0.8 Average = 7.5 ± 0.8
FM 7040 basalt, Suregei margin	K-Ar T.R. 40/50 mesh	1.41 1.41 1.41	39.1 43.6 38.7	5.56×10^{-4} 5.36×10^{-4} 5.45×10^{-4}	11.8 ± 0.5 11.4 ± 0.5 11.6 ± 0.5 Average = 11.6 ± 0.5
ER19RW obsidian, Shin	K-Ar T.R. 50/70 mesh	5.40 5.40 5.40	52.7 56.7 56.1	2.06×10^{-3} 2.18×10^{-3} 2.12×10^{-3}	11.4 ± 0.9 12.1 ± 1.0 11.8 ± 0.9 Average = 11.8 ± 0.9

Table 1—Continued

Sample	Method				Age (Ma)
ER38RW basalt, Suregei area	K-Ar	0.84	81.2	3.47×10^{-4}	12.4 ± 1.2
	T.R.	0.84	89.8	3.12×10^{-4}	11.1 ± 1.7
	50/70 mesh	0.84	79.3	3.78×10^{-4}	13.5 ± 1.4
				Average =	12.3 ± 1.4
FM 7051 basalt, Suregei margin	K-Ar	0.68	57.8	3.13×10^{-4}	13.8 ± 1.4
	T.R.	0.68	63.8	3.26×10^{-4}	14.4 ± 1.4
	50/70 mesh			Average =	14.1 ± 1.4
ER46RW sanidine conc. ignimbrite, Gum Dura area	^{40}Ar/^{39}Ar age spectrum analysis revealed:-			an isochron age of and minor overprinting around ~	16.07 ± 0.14 1.0 (i.e., 1.42)
ER47RW sanidine conc. ignimbrite, Gum Dura area	^{40}Ar/^{39}Ar age spectrum analysis revealed:-			an isochron age of	16.22 ± 0.10
ER43RW obsidian plug to vent, Gum Dura area	^{40}Ar/^{39}Ar age spectrum analysis revealed that this former volcanic glass had suffered severe soda- and silica-metasomatism and is now virtually non-potassic				
ER52RW basalt, F ra W.H.	K-Ar	0.66	82.3	3.98×10^{-4}	18.1 ± 1.8
	T.T.	0.66	86.4	3.69×10^{-4}	16.8 ± 1.7
	50/70 mesh	0.66	82.2	4.15×10^{-4}	16.8 ± 1.9
				Average =	17.2 ± 1.8
F732 basic lava N. side Buluk Gap	K-Ar	1.24	66.2	7.17×10^{-4}	17.4 ± 1.4
	T.R.	1.24	62.7	7.10×10^{-4}	17.2 ± 1.4
	50/70 mesh			Average =	17.3 ± 1.4
FM 7004 basalt, Kanapoi	K-Ar	0.925	82.5	9.44×10^{-5}	3.06 ± 0.21
	T.R.	0.925	81.0	9.40×10^{-5}	3.05 ± 0.21
				Average =	3.06 ± 0.21
	^{40}Ar/^{39}Ar Age spectrum analysis revealed severe argon loss errors			Average of "2-point" plateau =	4.0 ± 1.0
FM 7013A basalt, Olduvai Gorge	K-Ar	1.06	92.7	6.03×10^{-5}	1.71 ± 1.7
	T.R.	1.06	92.2	6.37×10^{-5}	1.80 ± 1.8
	50/70 mesh	1.06	89.9	6.04×10^{-5}	1.71 ± 1.7
	preheat			Average =	1.74 ± 1.7

Table 1--Continued

Sample Reference	Method	K_2O (%)	Atmospheric Contamination (%)	V/M	Apparent Age and Error (m.y.)
FM 7013B basalt, Olduvai Gorge	K-Ar T.R. 50/70 mesh	1.06	92.7	6.59×10^{-5}	1.86 ± 1.9
	K-Ar T.R. 50/70 mesh preheat	1.06	95.2	6.56×10^{-5}	1.85 ± 1.9
		1.06	94.6	6.60×10^{-5}	1.87 ± 1.9
		1.06	90.0	6.59×10^{-5}	1.87 ± 1.9
					1.86 ± 1.9
				Average =	1.86 ± 1.9

B. TUFF HORIZONS WITHIN THE EAST RUDOLF BASIN

Chari Tuff

Sample Reference	Method	K_2O (%)	Atmospheric Contamination (%)	V/M	Apparent Age and Error (m.y.)
FM 7041A sanidine conc. from pumice	K-Ar 20/70 mesh	5.22	62.4	2.12×10^{-4}	1.22 ± 0.06
		5.22	58.7	2.08×10^{-4}	1.20 ± 0.06
		5.22	58.0	2.11×10^{-4}	1.21 ± 0.06
				Average =	1.21 ± 0.06
	$^{40}Ar/^{39}Ar$ total degassing		92.8		1.20 ± 0.23
			91.7		1.20 ± 0.23
				Average =	1.20 ± 0.23

$^{40}Ar/^{39}Ar$ age spectrum analysis revealed possible contamination and argon loss error, but apparent age of "peak" on spectrum = 1.28 ± 0.32
Apparent minimum age of main component = 1.28 ± 0.23
Apparent age of overprint = 0.56 ± 0.15

Sample Reference	Method	K_2O (%)	Atmospheric Contamination (%)	V/M	Apparent Age and Error (m.y.)
FMA 280 sanidine	$^{40}Ar/^{39}Ar$ age spectrum analysis revealed both contamination excess argon and argon loss error to be present. Sector analysis suggests apparent age of juvenile component to be near				1.22 ± 0.01

Lower/Middle Tuff Complex, Ileret

Sample Reference	Method	K_2O (%)	Atmospheric Contamination (%)	V/M	Apparent Age and Error (m.y.)
FMA 278 sanidine conc. from pumice	$^{40}Ar/^{39}Ar$ total degassing		90.72		1.48 ± 0.17

Karari Tuff

Sample Reference	Method	K_2O (%)	Atmospheric Contamination (%)	V/M	Apparent Age and Error (m.y.)
FMA 202 sanidine conc. from pumice	$^{40}Ar/^{39}Ar$ total degassing		90.4		0.92 ± 0.16
			90.3		0.92 ± 0.16
FMA 213 sanidine conc. from pumice	$^{40}Ar/^{39}Ar$ total degassing		97.8		0.61 ± 0.30
			95.0		0.61 ± 0.30

Table 1--Continued

Sample	Method				Age
FMA 214 sanidine conc. from pumice	$^{40}Ar/^{39}Ar$		93.6		0.90 ± 0.32
	total degassing		92.9		1.00 ± 0.33
FMA 215 sanidine conc. from pumice	$^{40}Ar/^{39}Ar$		88.3		0.89 ± 0.15
	total degassing		88.2		1.00 ± 0.17
FMA 216 sanidine conc. from pumice	$^{40}Ar/^{39}Ar$		76.3		1.34 ± 0.11
	total degassing		76.4		1.33 ± 0.11
FMA 219 sanidine conc. from pumice	$^{40}Ar/^{39}Ar$		94.9		0.80 ± 0.30
	total degassing				
FMA 290 sanidine conc. from pumice	$^{40}Ar/^{39}Ar$		84.8		1.39 ± 0.11
	total degassing				
	$^{40}Ar/^{39}Ar$ age spectrum analysis revealed both contamination excess argon and argon loss effects. Apparent age of major age component = <1.32 ± 0.01				
Koobi Fora Tuff					
FM 6953 pumice	K-Ar	2.97	93.0	5.87×10^{-4}	6.3 ± 1.2
	T.R.	2.97	92.8	9.72×10^{-5}	1.05 ± 0.13
	Decalc. core with many zenoliths removed				
	$^{40}Ar/^{39}Ar$ age spectrum analysis revealed contamination and argon loss errors. Apparent age of youngest component = 1.1 ± 1.7				
FM 6954 tuffaceous clay	K-Ar	1.99	91.1	1.016×10^{-3}	15.35 ± 1.54
	$^{40}Ar/^{39}Ar$ total degassing		92.6		15.60 ± 1.56
	$^{40}Ar/^{39}Ar$ age spectrum analysis revealed severe contamination errors				
FM 6955 sanidine conc. from pumice gravel area 103	K-Ar	4.99	52.0	7.40×10^{-4}	4.44 ± 0.22
		4.99	49.9	7.36×10^{-4}	4.42 ± 0.22
	$^{40}Ar/^{39}Ar$ total degassing		82.6		4.32 ± 0.21
	$^{40}Ar/^{39}Ar$ age spectrum analysis revealed both contamination and argon loss errors. Apparent age of youngest component ~ 2.35				
	Average apparent age of mixture				4.31 ± 0.33

Table 1--Continued

Sample Reference	Method	K_2O (%)	Atmospheric Contamination (%)	V/M	Apparent Age and Error (m.y.)
FM 7037A pumice lump from gravel area 103	K-Ar T.R. decalc. and cleaned of xenoliths	1.90	90.4	2.81×10^{-4}	4.4 ± 0.4
FM 7037B single pumice lump from gravel area 103	K-Ar T.R. decalc. and cleaned of xenoliths	2.67 2.67	97.1 97.2	1.97×10^{-4} 2.01×10^{-4}	2.2 ± 0.7 2.3 ± 0.7 Average = 2.25 ± 0.7
FM 7037C single pumice lump from gravel area 103	K-Ar T.R. decalc. and cleaned of xenoliths	1.72	94.2	2.07×10^{-4}	3.6 ± 0.5
FM 7037D single pumice lump from gravel area 103	K-Ar T.R. decalc. and cleaned of xenoliths	2.03	75.8	1.19×10^{-3}	17.6 ± 0.7
FM 7037E single pumice lump from gravel area 103	K-Ar T.R. decalc. and cleaned of xenoliths	3.06	93.5	6.02×10^{-3}	5.90 ± 0.9
FM 7042A sanidine conc. from pumice area 101	$^{40}Ar/^{39}Ar$ total degassing		91.3		1.69 ± 0.39
FM 7042B sanidine conc. from pumice area 101	$^{40}Ar/^{39}Ar$ total degassing		97.8 96.2		0.53 ± 0.30 0.53 ± 0.28
	$^{40}Ar/^{39}Ar$ Ar age spectrum analysis revealed both contamination and argon loss errors. Average apparent age from spectrum				1.48 ± 0.23
FM 7042C sanidine conc. from pumice area 103	$^{40}Ar/^{39}Ar$ total degassing		87.3		4.40 ± 1.27

Table 1--Continued

Sample	Measurement	%	Age ± error
FM 205 area 102	$^{40}Ar/^{39}Ar$ total degassing	82.6	1.38 ± 0.17
FM 222 area 102	$^{40}Ar/^{39}Ar$ total degassing	94.6	0.95 ± 0.30
FMA 270 area 102	$^{40}Ar/^{39}Ar$ age spectrum analysis revealed several age components. Apparent age of sanidine crystallization. Apparent age of major overprint		1.57 ± 0.00 1.0
BBS Tuff Complex			
FMA 208 sanidine conc. from pumice	$^{40}Ar/^{39}Ar$ total degassing	88.1	1.27 ± 0.20
FMA 209 sanidine conc. from pumice	$^{40}Ar/^{39}Ar$ total degassing	83.8	1.19 ± 0.12
FMA 210 sanidine conc. from pumice	$^{40}Ar/^{39}Ar$ total degassing	85.9	1.40 ± 0.17
FMA 223 sanidine conc. from pumice	$^{40}Ar/^{39}Ar$ total degassing	79.9	1.12 ± 0.09
FMA 224 sanidine conc. from pumice	$^{40}Ar/^{39}Ar$ total degassing	87.3	1.24 ± 0.17
FMA 228 sanidine conc. from pumice	$^{40}Ar/^{39}Ar$ total degassing	92.6	0.87 ± 0.22
FMA 266 sanidine conc. from pumice	$^{40}Ar/^{39}Ar$ total degassing	82.6	1.66 ± 0.01
	$^{40}Ar/^{39}Ar$ age spectrum analysis revealed two age components. Apparent age younger component. Apparent age older component		1.56 ± 0.02 1.70 ± 0.04
FMA 235 clay tuff	$^{40}Ar/^{39}Ar$ total degassing	91.6	26.47 ± 2.86
FMA 236 clay tuff	$^{40}Ar/^{39}Ar$ total degassing	87.4	30.38 ± 1.70
FMA 237 clay tuff	$^{40}Ar/^{39}Ar$ total degassing	89.2	29.90 ± 2.09

Table 1--Continued

Sample Reference	Method	K_2O (%)	Atmospheric Contamination (%)	V/M	Apparent Age and Error (m.y.)
KBS Tuff					
Leakey I (A) crystal-vitric tuff	K-Ar T.R. 30/50 mesh cleaned	1.79 1.79 1.79	62.7 63.4 62.0	1.37×10^{-2} 1.40×10^{-2} 1.39×10^{-2}	219 ± 7 223 ± 7 221 ± 7 Average = 221 ± 7
Leakey I (B1) pumice	K-Ar T.R. 30/50 mesh	0.70 0.70	99.6 91.1	8.49×10^{-5} 5.61×10^{-5}	3.63 ± 2.1 2.40 ± 1.0 Average = 3.02 ± 1.6
	$^{40}Ar/^{39}Ar$ total degassing		97.9		3.45 ± 1.2
Leakey I (B2) sanidine conc. from pumice	K-Ar 30/50 mesh	6.04 6.04	81.2 80.5	4.79×10^{-4} 4.76×10^{-4}	2.38 ± 0.3 2.36 ± 0.3 Average = 2.37 ± 0.3
	$^{40}Ar/^{39}Ar$ total degassing without preheating		94.9		2.64 ± 0.29
	total degassing with preheating		96.2		2.50 ± 0.50
	$^{40}Ar/^{39}Ar$ age spectrum analysis revealed slight contamination and argon loss error. Average apparent age "4-point plateau"				2.61 ± 0.26
FM 7054 pumice gravel, sanidine conc. from crushed and decalc. pumice	K-Ar 30 mesh	6.64 6.64	53.4 52.9	1.91×10^{-3} 1.82×10^{-3}	8.63 ± 0.52 8.22 ± 0.49 Average = 8.43 ± 0.51
	K-Ar 30/70 mesh	6.21 6.21 6.21	32.1 28.9 28.7	3.48×10^{-3} 3.84×10^{-3} 3.56×10^{-3}	16.8 ± 0.8 18.6 ± 0.9 17.2 ± 0.9 Average = 17.5 ± 0.9
FMA 201 sanidine conc. from pumice	$^{40}Ar/^{39}Ar$ total degassing		95.5 94.3		0.91 ± 0.54 0.91 ± 0.53
	$^{40}Ar/^{39}Ar$ age spectrum analysis revealed severe argon losses around 1.5-2.5 m.y. and later				

Table 1—Continued

Sample	Analysis		Age
FMA 203 sanidine conc. from pumice	^{40}Ar/^{39}Ar total degassing	96.8 83.5	0.52 ± 0.33 1.56 ± 0.19
FMA 206 sanidine conc. from pumice	^{40}Ar/^{39}Ar age spectrum analysis revealed complete overprinting at		1.75 m.y.
FMA 207 sanidine conc. from pumice	^{40}Ar/^{39}Ar total degassing	82.2	2.10 ± 0.19
FMA 211 sanidine conc. from pumice	^{40}Ar/^{39}Ar total degassing	85.5	1.83 ± 0.19
FMA 218 sanidine conc. from pumice	^{40}Ar/^{39}Ar total degassing	82.6	2.06 ± 0.19
FMA 220 sanidine conc. from pumice	^{40}Ar/^{39}Ar total degassing	92.6	1.06 ± 0.29
FMA 221 sanidine conc. from pumice	^{40}Ar/^{39}Ar total degassing	91.9	0.68 ± 0.17
FMA 225 sanidine conc. from pumice	^{40}Ar/^{39}Ar age spectrum analysis revealed complete overprint around		1.07 m.y.
FMA 226 sanidine conc. from pumice	^{40}Ar/^{39}Ar total degassing	79.6 87.2	1.54 ± 0.12 1.36 ± 0.14
FMA 227 sanidine conc. from pumice	^{40}Ar/^{39}Ar age spectrum analysis revealed complete overprint around		1.75 m.y.
FMA 294 sanidine conc. from pumice	^{40}Ar/^{39}Ar total degassing	79.12	2.12 ± 0.10
	^{40}Ar/^{39}Ar age spectrum analysis revealed severe overprinting on at least two occasions. Apparent ages of first overprint		2.05 ± 0.00 1.97 ± 0.06
	Apparent age of second overprint		1.02 ± 0.03
FMA 274 sanidine	^{40}Ar/^{39}Ar age spectrum analysis revealed a minimum apparent age of and severe overprinting at		>2.54 ± 0.23 2.42 ± 0.02 and later

Table 1--Continued

Sample Reference	Method	K_2O (%)	Atmospheric Contamination (%)	V/M	Apparent Age and Error (m.y.)
Tulu Bor Tuff					
FMA 233 clay tuff	$^{40}Ar/^{39}Ar$ total degassing		100		27.2 ± 7.7
FMA 255 sanidine conc. from pumice	$^{40}Ar/^{39}Ar$ total degassing		62.2		3.37 ± 0.07
	$^{40}Ar/^{39}Ar$ age spectrum revealed two apparent age components.			Average age	3.15 ± 0.10
				Apparent age minor component	4.04 ± 0.10
				Apparent age major component	3.22 ± 0.09
				Accepted "best age"	3.18 ± 0.09
Kubi Algi Formation Tuffs					
FM 7036 crystal-vitric tuff	$^{40}Ar/^{39}Ar$ total degassing on biotite conc.		45.6 53.6	Average = 186	186 ± 5 186 ± 5
	$^{40}Ar/^{39}Ar$ total degassing on glass shards		87.3 83.4		4.81 ± 0.36 4.95 ± 0.49
	K-Ar glass shards 70/100 mesh	3.56 3.56 3.56	64.0 64.2 90.5	5.22×10^{-4} 5.50×10^{-4} 4.55×10^{-4}	4.40 ± 0.22 4.63 ± 0.23 3.80 ± 0.4
	$^{40}Ar/^{39}Ar$ age spectrum on glass shards revealed both contamination and argon loss errors. Apparent age older component ~ 6.7 Apparent age younger component ~ 3.9				
FM 7035 pumice gravel	$^{40}Ar/^{39}Ar$ total degassing on xenolith removed from one pumice lump		23.8		283 ± 9
	$^{40}Ar/^{39}Ar$ total degassing on sanidine conc. from pumice lump FM 7035A		71.0		3.93 ± 0.20

Table 1—Continued

		Apparent age major component 4.6 ± 0.1
$^{40}Ar/^{39}Ar$ age spectrum analysis revealed both contamination and argon loss errors.		
$^{40}Ar/^{39}Ar$ total degassing on sanidine conc. from pumice lump FM 7035B	82.9	3.08 ± 0.19
$^{40}Ar/^{39}Ar$ age spectrum analysis revealed both contamination and severe argon loss errors.		
FMA 246 sanidine conc. from pumice lump — $^{40}Ar/^{39}Ar$ total degassing	64.09	3.71 ± 0.09

C. OTHER TUFFS DATED

Feldspar conc. from Nkalabong Fm., Omo — $^{40}Ar/^{39}Ar$ total degassing	67.2 67.1	3.90 ± 0.10 3.99 ± 0.12 3.95 ± 0.11
		Average = 3.95 ± 0.11

Constants used: $\lambda e = 0.584 \cdot 10^{-10} \, yr^{-1}$;
$\lambda \beta = 4.72 \cdot 10^{-10} \, yr^{-1}$.

V/M = volume of radiogenic argon-40 $(mm)^3$ NTP per weight of sample, grams.

T.R. = total rock sample.

Sieve mesh size limits quoted when T.R. sample analyzed in crushed form.

Despite rigorous care in the collection and preparation of dating samples, the presence of geological errors of various kinds makes the interpretation of much of the analytical data from East Rudolf tuffs difficult and even controversial. For example, contamination errors clearly mar the results from pumice samples FM 6953 and FM 7037A-E; from all the impure clay-grade tuffs or bentonites; from some sanidine concentrates, including FM 6955, FM 7042C, and FM 7054; and from the crystal-vitric tuffs Leakey I(A) and FM 7036. The vast majority of the samples can be shown to be slightly to severely affected by subsequent argon loss overprinting. Thus most of the total degassing apparent ages can be regarded as minimum values for the required date of the horizon to which they refer. Nevertheless, there will be exceptions to this generalization. It is our experience that argon-40/argon-39 age spectra obtained from appropriate samples can sometimes be used to resolve some of these problems. The date of initial volcanism can be obtained by this method of analysis when, as for example in the sanidine concentrate Leakey I(B1), subsequent overprinting is not complete. When argon loss is complete, however, only the date of overprinting will be obtainable by any of the potassium-argon methods. Samples FMA 206, FMA 225, and FMA 227 are examples of this situation. In suitable circumstances, the individual component ages contained in a sample of mixed age composition can be resolved by $^{40}Ar/^{39}Ar$ age spectrum analysis. This proved to be possible, for instance, with the sanidine concentrate FMA 255.

Interpretation of $^{40}Ar/^{39}Ar$ Age Spectra

$^{40}Ar/^{39}Ar$ age spectrum geochronometry[1] is a development of the $^{40}Ar/^{39}Ar$ dating technique in which the isotopic composition of the gas being released from an irradiated sample of a rock or mineral is analyzed repeatedly over a series of heating steps toward complete fusion (stepwise degassing). The data obtained are most usefully presented as plots on a graph, in which the isotopic ratios measured at each heating step are compared, and as plots upon which "apparent ages" and "atmospheric correction" at each step are recorded. Even within perfect crystals of a single mineral phase there are locales with different argon diffusion characteristics. In addition, the relative diffusivity or retentivity of the locales in any one mineral phase may change in response to different external stimuli. The presence of flawed, damaged, or partially altered crystals and of crystals of more than one size generation in a given sample or rock specimen further extends this variability.

During stepwise degassing experiments argon is released from any individual locale either at one step or over a small number of successive heating steps. The isotopic analysis of the gas released at successive heating steps produces a succession of "apparent K-Ar ages" from the sample which is referred to as its "apparent age spectrum." Single-generation minerals with a history uncomplicated by slow cooling or by such geological accidents as deuteric or subsequent alteration, reheating, or stress episodes produce virtually identical apparent ages from all their constituent locales. The age spectrum from such a sample is called an "argon-40/argon-39 isochron." Isochrons defining the crystallization-cooling age of a mineral generation may still be obtainable by $^{40}Ar/^{39}Ar$ age spectrum analysis from rocks that have been involved in subsequent weak geological events not intense enough to disturb the argon isotopes in any but the least retentive locales. Total degassing analysis of partially overprinted samples produces discrepant mixed

---

1. $^{40}Ar/^{39}Ar$ age spectrum dating is a relatively new geochronometric method, and the interpretative technique outlined here, although supported by our own experience over the past seven years, is still controversial in certain aspects.

ages of slight value. Any event, however, which is intense enough to cause total or near-total diffusion of argon from all the component locales in a given mineral generation will destroy the crystallization isochron and will replace it by an "overprint isochron" defining the age of the overprinting event. Potassium-argon age overprinting occurs in response to metamorphic, metasomatic, or stress processes under various environmental parameters. Significant amounts of "introduced argon" of variable isotopic ratio, for example, may characterize certain kinds of overprint. The presence of introduced argon can be recognized from the apparent intercepts made by ^{40}Ar/^{39}Ar isochrons on the axes of the ^{40}Ar/^{36}Ar versus ^{39}Ar/^{36}Ar plots and from the general characteristics of the other isotopic ratio plots obtained. Argon incorporated during initial crystallization can be recognized in the same way. Otherwise, the only extraneous argon present will be from modern atmospheric contamination, and the isochron will intercept the ^{40}Ar/^{39}Ar axis at a ratio of 296.

Total rock or mixed mineral samples lacking initial argon and with uncomplicated geological histories will, like single crystals, produce simple isochrons from ^{40}Ar/^{39}Ar age spectrum analyses. So will overprinted rock or mixed mineral samples that were totally overprinted in an environment which did not favor incorporation of significant amounts of introduced argon. Under certain conditions, the various component locales within a rock, mixed mineral, or single mineral sample may react in different ways to the introduction of argon during overprinting, and different amounts may be taken into each locale. From such a rock or mineral sample a set of closely related parallel isochrons is obtained instead of a single isochron.

Rock, mixed minerals, and single mineral samples of complex geological history which have suffered partial overprinting on perhaps more than one occasion since initial crystallization or since a major episode of total overprinting will reveal the ages of all the various facets of their history in their age spectra only under certain optimum conditions. The principal requirement is that the argon-release patterns of the various "apparent age components" or, in the case of rocks and mixed minerals, "compound apparent age components," do not overlap significantly during progressive heating of the sample in vacuo. Fortunately, the problem of overlap of argon release patterns is not as restrictive in practice as it appears from theoretical considerations. It frequently happens that the same apparent age component is found in a variety of samples of different mineralogy and degree of partial overprinting; it is clear that in each of them there can be no significant overlap of argon release between the locales revealing this age component and locales with different age indications. Even from samples that do have extensive argon release overlap problems it may be possible to deduce the ages of certain major events in their history. Interpretation of these difficult spectra is greatly assisted, of course, by comparing results from different samples of identical history. Analysis of complex ^{40}Ar/^{39}Ar age spectrum data in an attempt to separate the major apparent age components is called "sector analysis." A full treatment of one example of an age spectrum analysis is set out below as an illustration of the characteristics of the method and its results.

Outline Interpretation of One Age Spectrum
(See Tables 2 and 3)

Sample FMA 255 is a cleaned sanidine concentrate separated from pumice lumps contained within the Tulu Bor Tuff. It was collected and prepared by I. C. Findlater.

Two "average" apparent ages were obtained for this sample: first, 3.37 ± 0.07 m.y. from a total degassing age determination, and, second, 3.15 ± 0.01 m.y. by treating the entire age spectrum obtained by stepwise degassing as an analytically imprecise isochron.

Table 2

Summary of Analytical Data

Sample and Reactor Phial Nos.	$^{39}Ar/^{36}Ar$	$^{39}Ar/^{37}Ar$	$^{38}Ar/^{37}Ar$	$^{38}Ar/^{39}Ar$	R*	Q†	Atmospheric Contamination (%)	Apparent Age (m.y.)	Analytical Error (m.y.)
Results of Total Degassing $^{40}Ar/^{39}Ar$ Age Determination									
FMA 255	285.5579	60.58282	0.74612	0.01232	0.61124	0.00179	62.22	3.37	0.07
Results of $^{40}Ar/^{39}Ar$ Age Spectrum Analysis									
$J = 0.003151$‡									
Sample 255 RF nos.§									
RF00×	0.2904	1.60518	1.43818	0.89596	1.23509	0.00389	99.87	7.32	67.22
RF10	0.9451	2.29388	0.84515	0.36844	-1.06670	-0.00336	100.33	-6.35	46.80
RF20	13.3008	13.47626	1.31334	0.09746	0.07274	0.00023	99.58	0.43	6.76
RF30	82.1941	34.96576	0.73719	0.02108	0.64385	0.00203	84.46	3.82	0.87
RF40	223.0215	50.69160	0.66542	0.01313	0.66787	0.00210	65.91	3.96	0.28
RF50	361.9805	45.2457	0.57444	0.01270	0.53439	0.00168	59.66	3.17	0.16
RF60	481.5352	25.93103	0.31768	0.01225	0.51400	0.00162	53.55	3.05	0.15
RF70	779.4875	44.57782	0.52190	0.01171	0.53542	0.00169	40.68	3.18	0.09
RF75	262.9285	53.62120	0.63443	0.01183	0.51591	0.00163	67.82	3.06	0.16

* R = ratio of radiogenic ^{40}Ar to neutron induced ^{39}Ar corrected for argon isotopes generated from calcium, utilizing values of neutron-induced ^{37}Ar.

† $Q = (e^{t/Y} - 1)$

‡ J = constant of proportionality at reactor sites occupied by standards and corresponding samples.

§ RF number = step heating control level.

The above results are displayed graphically in figures 1 and 2.

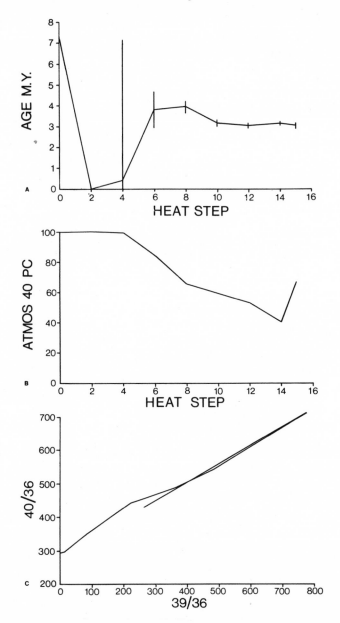

Figure 1. Results of argon-40/argon-39 age spectrum analysis of Tulu Bor sanidine sample FMA 255.

Examining the apparent age versus heat step plot (fig. 1*a*) and the principal argon-ratio plot (fig. 1*c*), and comparing these plots with the other data makes it clear that at least three age components are present. The age spectrum begins with a spuriously high apparent age obtained from minute amounts of loosely held surface argon. Low values suggesting a late minor age component resulting from overprinting (possibly metasomatic?) follow. From RF30 onward the "plateau" feature has two successive sectors, one apparently rising to near 4 m.y., the other averaging around 3.12 m.y. This dual nature of the later

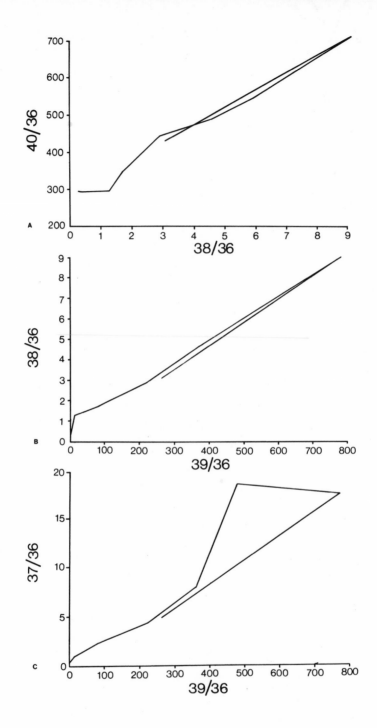

Figure 2.   Results of argon-40/argon-39 age spectrum analysis of Tulu Bor sanidine sample
FMA 255.

Table 3
Sector Analysis Results (^{40}Ar/^{36}Ar *versus* ^{39}Ar/^{36}Ar *Plot)*

Sample	Apparent Age and Error (m.y.)	Intercept on ^{40}Ar/^{36}Ar Axis
RF0 to RF75	3.15 ± 0.10	298.33 ± 5.83
RF30 and RF40	4.04 ± 0.01	292.42 ± 0.00
RF50 to RF75	3.22 ± 0.09	288.36 ± 7.42

part of the spectrum is clear from all the plots. It shows as two successive near-isochron sectors on the ^{40}Ar/^{36}Ar versus ^{39}Ar/^{36}Ar plot (fig. 1) and must indicate that the sample is a mixture of two primary age components; that is, "sanidines" of two generations, not distinguishable beneath the binocular microscope, have been concentrated from the pumice lumps to form the dating sample. The required date for the Tulu Bor Tuff is obviously that of the younger feldspar generation. Fortunately, the two age components are not present in equal proportions and do not have identical argon diffusion characteristics. They may be alkali feldspars of slightly different composition or structural state. Or the older generation may have been considerably affected by the later volcanism.

At steps RF30 and RF40 argon gas release was predominantly from the older feldspar component. Sector analysis of this portion of the spectrum suggests an apparent age of 4.04 ± 0.01 m.y. for the older feldspar component. The virtually normal intercept value of 292.42 further supports the validity of the date. Gas release from steps RF50-75 was dominated by much more voluminous amounts of argon derived from the younger feldspar component. Sector analysis of this portion of the spectrum suggests an apparent age of 3.22 ± 0.09 m.y. for the younger component. This important sector of the principal argon-ratio plot is not a perfect isochron, however, and the intercept obtained was farther from the normal value of 296. It is probable that at one or more of the steps there was slight overlap, with argon released from the older feldspar component (e.g., RF50) and from late, partially overprinted locales (e.g., RF75). The step at which argon release was most voluminous, most likely to be derived from the younger feldspar component, and at which atmospheric contamination was at its lowest value was RF70. The apparent age derived from this step is 3.18 ± 0.09 m.y.

Considering all the relevant factors, we could say from the data currently available that the best interpretation of the age of the younger feldspar component in the Tulu Bor Tuff pumice (presumably the age of Tulu Bor volcanism) is 3.18 ± 0.09 m.y. This age is consistent with its stratigraphical position below the KBS Tuff and with its occurrence within an episode of normal geomagnetic polarity.

Provisional Summary of Geochronology of the East Rudolf Area

Chari Tuff

A variety of work done on a sanidine concentrate from the single pumice lump FM 7041A suggests a minimum age of 1.2 m.y. from K-Ar and ^{40}Ar/^{39}Ar total degassing age determinations and a minimum age of 1.28 ± 0.23 m.y. from ^{40}Ar/^{39}Ar age spectrum analysis *as long as* excess age contamination is regarded as minimal. There is, in fact, no reason to think otherwise. Age spectrum analysis of a sanidine concentrate from pumice FMA 280 indicates three major age components, including both excess age contamination and partial overprinting effects, but sector analysis permitted the apparent age of the juvenile feldspar component to be estimated with reasonable certainty at 1.22 ± 0.01 m.y. From this it can be concluded that the best apparent age currently available for the Chari Tuff is around 1.22 ± 0.01 to 1.28 ± 0.23 m.y.

Lower Middle Tuff Complex, Ileret

An apparent age of 1.48 ± 0.17 m.y. has been obtained from $^{40}Ar/^{39}Ar$ total degassing analysis of a sanidine concentrate from pumice FMA 278. Without confirmatory age spectrum work, this apparent age must be regarded as a maximum/minimum age for the tuff horizon. The best apparent age currently available for the Lower/Middle Tuff Complex, Ileret, is 1.48 ± 0.17 m.y.

Karari Tuff

The results of $^{40}Ar/^{39}Ar$ total degassing age determinations on seven sanidine concentrates from pumice (FMA 202, 213, 214, 215, 216, 219, and 290) range in apparent age from 0.6 to 1.39 m.y. If excess age discrepancy due to contamination is not present, these results could be assumed to indicate variable partial overprinting alone; thus the oldest apparent age obtained could be assumed to be a close minimum estimate for the age of the sanidine concentrate. If contamination is present, however, this close minimum age estimate for the concentrate must also be regarded as a maximum age for the tuff. Age spectrum analysis of the sanidine concentrate from pumice FMA 290, which produced the highest apparent total degassing age of 1.39 m.y., revealed that contamination excess argon errors are present in this sample. Thus the highest total degassing apparent age of 1.39 ± 0.11 m.y. must be regarded as a maximum/minimum age for the tuff. Fortunately, a very close maximum age of 1.32 ± 0.01 m.y. can be derived from the age spectrum. The best apparent age currently available for the Karari Tuff is 1.32 ± 0.10 m.y. It appears that the Chari Tuff can be correlated with the Karari Tuff with reasonable certainty.

Koobi Fora Tuff

Considerable dating work over several years before 1973 failed to produce a convincing estimate for the age of this group of closely related tuff horizons. Contamination of the samples by xenoliths, volcanic accessory and detrital material, and a variable degree of partial overprinting effects make most of the apparent ages obtained useless or suspect. The results from sample FM 6953 suggested a very imprecise apparent age of 1.1 ± 1.7 m.y. Total degassing $^{40}Ar/^{39}Ar$ apparent ages range from 1.53 to 1.69 m.y. As contamination was undoubtedly present in samples FM 6954, 6955, 7037A, 7037B, 7037C, 7037D, 7037E, and 7042C, arguments similar to those outlined for the Karari Tuff indicate that the highest apparent age of 1.69 ± 0.39 m.y., obtained from sanidine separated from pumice FM 7042A, must be regarded as a maximum/minimum apparent age for the tuff. An age spectrum study of a sanidine concentrate from pumice FM 7042B produced an average apparent minimum age of 1.48 ± 0.23 m.y. Further age spectrum analysis undertaken on sanidine concentrated from pumice FMA 270 revealed several age components. The apparent age of sanidine crystallization was identified at 1.57 ± 0.00 m.y., and there was evidence of severe overprinting around 1.0 m.y. The best apparent age currently available for the Koobi Fora Tuffs is 1.57 ± 0.00 m.y.

BBS Tuff Complex

Apparent ages obtained from a number of total degassing $^{40}Ar/^{39}Ar$ age determinations made on sanidine concentrated from pumice FMA 208, 209, 210, 223, 224, 228, and 266 range from 0.87 to 1.66 m.y. The apparent age of 1.66 ± 0.10 m.y. obtained from sample FMA 266 must be regarded, therefore, as a maximum/minimum age for the BBS Tuff Complex. Age spectrum analysis of sanidine concentrated from pumice FMA 266 showed it was a mixture of two feldspar components of apparent age 1.70 ± 0.04 and 1.56 ± 0.02 m.y. Argon loss partial overprinting was minimal in this sample. The best apparent age currently available for the BBS Tuff Complex is 1.56 ± 0.02 m.y. It appears that the Koobi Fora and BBS Tuff complexes can be correlated with certainty.

KBS Tuff

Work done on samples from the KBS Tuff falls into three categories: (1) K-Ar and ^{40}Ar/^{39}Ar total degassing analysis of samples such as Leakey 1(A), Leakey 1 (B1), and FM 7054 in which contamination error is clearly present; (2) total degassing age estimates from sanidine concentrates Leakey II (B2), FMA 201, 203, 207, 211, 218, 220, 221, 226, and 294, which range in apparent age from 0.52 to 2.64 m.y.; and (3) several ^{40}Ar/^{39}Ar age spectrum analyses. Using the same arguments outlined above, the highest total degassing apparent age of 2.64 ± 0.29 m.y., from a sanidine concentrate from pumice Leakey I (B2), would have to be regarded as a maximum/minimum age for the KBS Tuff. However, though all the age spectra revealed overprinting of various intensities at various times, it does appear that the sanidine concentrates from the KBS Tuff are free from major contamination error and therefore can be regarded as a reasonably close estimate for the age of the KBS Tuff.

The principal age components identifiable from the seven age spectra of KBS sanidine concentrates (Leakey I [B2], FMA 201, 206, 225, 227, 294, and 274) are as follows:

Crystallization	2.61 ± 0.26 m.y.
	> 2.54 ± 0.53 m.y.
Overprints	2.42 ± 0.02 m.y.
	~ 1.75 m.y.
	1.07 m.y. and 1.02 ± 0.03 m.y.
	(say ~ 1.0 m.y.)

The best apparent age currently available for the KBS Tuff is 2.61 ± 0.26 m.y.

Tulu Bor Tuff

See "Outline Interpretation of One Age Spectrum," above, ^{40}Ar/^{39}Ar age spectrum obtained from sanidine concentrated from pumice FMA 255. The best apparent age currently available for the Tulu Bor Tuff is 3.18 ± 0.09 m.y.

Suregei Tuff

No dating results are available.

Kubi Algi Formation Tuffs

A considerable amount of work has been done on two tuff horizons within the Kubi Algi Formation. Dating analysis of samples from both these tuffs was shown to be complicated by contamination excess argon errors and argon loss discrepancies leading to partial overprinting. The best age obtainable from a ^{40}Ar/^{39}Ar age spectrum analysis of the younger of the two tuffs is ~3.9 m.y. This estimate was made from glass shards FM 7036 (fission track dating of the same sample revealed overprinting at 1.8 m.y.). ^{40}Ar/^{39}Ar total degassing analysis of sanidine concentrates from pumice samples FM 7035 and FMA 246 from the older of the two tuffs produced apparent ages from 3.08 to 3.93 m.y. The highest apparent age of 3.93 ± 0.20 m.y., from samples FM 7037A, must be regarded as a maximum/minimum age for the tuff. A rather imprecise age spectrum sector analysis suggested an age of 4.6 m.y. for a major sanidine component in this same tuff. Of course, a major crystalline component in such a tuff is not necessarily of the same age as the tuff.

More work needs to be done on the tuffs in the Kubi Algi Formation. The best estimates of the apparent ages of the two tuffs examined currently stand at ~3.9 and ~4.6 m.y., but these dates urgently require confirmation.

Plio-Pleistocene and Mid-Pliocene Basalts

North of Buluk Gap
  F733 (?) overprint ca.   2.20 ± 0.44 m.y.
Kokoi
  FM 7052 extrusion ca.   3.62 ± 0.36 m.y.
Fora Shield
  ER50RW extrusion ca.   3.8 ± 0.4 m.y.
  FM 7053 extrusion ca.   3.80 ± 0.38 m.y.

Miocene Volcanics

Kubi Algi group
  ER10RW extrusion before Shin   7.5 ± 0.8 m.y.
  ER19RW intrusion ca.   11.8 ± 0.9 m.y.
Suregei area basalts
  FM 7040 extrusion ca.   11.6 ± 0.5 m.y.
  ER38RW extrusion ca.   12.3 ± 1.4 m.y.
  FM 7051 extrusion ca.   14.1 ± 1.4 m.y.
Gum Dura ignimbrites
  ER46RW extrusion ca.   16.07 ± 0.14 m.y.
  ER47RW extrusion ca.   16.22 ± 0.10 m.y.
Buluk Gap-Fora W.H. basalts
  ER52RW extrusion ca.   17.2 ± 1.8 m.y.
  F732 extrusion ca.   17.3 ± 1.14 m.y.

Conclusions

The geochronological data listed above suggests the following provisional summary of the geological history of the East Rudolf area:

The oldest cover rocks seen in the East Rudolf area are basalts and lacustrine sediments at the base of a thick sequence of Miocene volcanics exposed in eroded and dissected portions of the volcanic highlands. Paleosols are well developed at certain levels. The Miocene sequence includes pantelleritic ignimbrites, basalt lavas, and a variety of sedimentary intercalations. It is part of the Miocene fill of the Turkana basin and is generally comparable to volcanic successions known elsewhere in Turkana, the Suguta Valley, and the Nkalabong Hills. The earliest basalt lavas overlie basement rocks along the Kenya Ethiopia border and extend far south of the East Rudolf area, where an alkali-olivine-basalt lava at Fora Waterhole (ER52RW) has been dated at 17.2 ± 1.8 m.y.

Intercalated with the basalts in the upper part of the Ileret River drainage basin are the products of a complex of small pantelleritic ignimbrite volcanoes typically seen as low rings of agglomerate, agglutinate, and viscous lava, each about 0.5 to 1.0 km in diameter. Some of these vents may have contained crater lakes. Most of them are plugged by intrusions of flow-folded obsidian. From these small vents were erupted voluminous plinian air-fall tuffs and numerous ash flows now represented by thin sheets of welded eutaxitic and nonwelded crystal-vitric ignimbrite. Fossil wood is common in some of the tuffs, and around certain vents of this age at East Rudolf it is sufficiently abundant to warrant the term "fossil forest." The two ignimbrites that have been dated from this area (ER46RW and ER47RW) are just over 16 m.y. old. Contemporaneous fumerolitic and subsequent hydrothermal activity has caused intense alteration and silicification at and near some of the centers. The partial overprinting seen in the age spectrum of ER46RW near 1.0 m.y. may be related to one of these episodes of late hydrothermal activity.

In the Buluk Gap area the oldest rocks are basalts overlaid by a sequence of lacus-trine sediments in which one can clearly see the overwhelming of an extensive early Miocene lake by acid volcanism. The acid volcanic rocks are generally very similar to those ex-posed farther north on the upper Ileret River-Gum Dura intercalation. Small vents, fossil fumeroles, and fossil forests cut down by ash flows are common. Thick units of bedded tuff fill the lake and are covered by ash-flow and air-fall tuffs interbedded with basic and intermediate lava flows. One such lava (F732) is the oldest Miocene rock dated so far from East Rudolf, at 17.3 ± 1.14 m.y. The extensive thin sheets of welded ignimbrite form marked horizons outlining the subsequent gentle fold-fault structure of this area. We sus-pect that subsequent hydrothermal activity was also important. Along the Suregei cuesta the sub-basin sediments' unconformity is cut by alkali-olivine basalts and related rocks that range in age from 11.6 ± 0.5 m.y. (FM 7040) through 12.3 ± 1.4 m.y. (ER38RW) to 14.1 ± 1.4 m.y. (FM 7051). Some thin, not persistent, and highly altered siliceous/ calcareous fragmental horizons are seen within the basalts east of the Suregei cuesta, sug-gesting the former presence of hot springs, ephemeral volcanic lakes, and a variety of pyroclastic, outwash river, and lacustrine deposits.

South of the Buluk Gap, around Shin and at Sibilot (which is included in this group on petrographic grounds) is another extensive ignimbrite intercalation within the Miocene basalts. The numerous pantelleritic flows of this group are typically thick, massive, coarsely eutaxitic welded ignimbrites. They are associated with a variety of air-fall tuffs, fossil fumaroles, sediments, fossil wood, and flow-folded subsurface intrusions. The obsidian margin of a sill-like intrusion at Shin (ER19RW) is dated at 11.8 ± 0.9 m.y. Soon after the emplacement of this acid intrusion, the accumulation of Miocene basalts and ignimbrites at East Rudolf ceased.

At Kubi Algi and Derati there are intrusive/extrusive centers of a peralkaline rhyolite-granophyre-microgranite granite. The rock at Kubi Algi (ER10RW) is dated at a minimum age of 7.5 ± 0.8 m.y. Kubi Algi appears to be an irregularly shaped rhyolite dome center, flanked by sheets of rhyolite talus and ladu breccia.

Late Miocene and early Pliocene times[2] at East Rudolf saw the initiation of a proto-Lake Rudolf in something like its present form as a result of large-scale warping and the extension of major submeridional faults across the former Turkana basin. The faulted half-graben that is the basic structure of East Rudolf was started at this time, and erosion controlled by the new base levels of the lake began to cut back extensively into the up-warped Miocene volcanic area to the east.

A large complex shield volcano of Pliocene basalts was built to the east of Fora in

---

2. The Miocene/Pliocene boundary is here taken to be 5.25 m.y., after van Couvering (1972).

early to mid-Pliocene times. Lava flows of this age flooded an irregular topography cut in the Miocene volcanics, as is seen dramatically in a number of valleys south of the Buluk Gap and in the Shin-Derati-Kubi Algi area. Some lava flows from the Fora Shield reached into the sedimentary basin, as at Kubi Algi. In the complex faulted periclinal uplift of the Kokoi, lavas of this age (or slightly later) and probably from a local center are interbedded with lacustrine sediments and acid tuffs. Three lavas of this Pliocene volcanic episode have been dated at 3.8 ± 0.4 m.y. (ER50RW, from a basaltic center east of Derati), 3.80 ± 0.38 m.y. (FM 7053, basalt within Kubi Algi Formation), and 3.62 ± 0.36 m.y. (basalt on margin of Kokoi structure). A minimum date of 2.20 ± 0.44 m.y. has been obtained from the plateau basalts capping the escarpment north of the Buluk Gap. This might suggest that the thin sheet of basic lavas capping the volcanic highlands in this area is either Plio-Pleistocene or late Pliocene, but this date will require confirmation.

The sedimentary record of the Koobi Fora Formation indicates that a major river system began to enter the East Rudolf basin from the east in mid-Pliocene times. Maybe its course ran between the older Fora basalt shield to the south and another (possibly later) area of basalt eruption to the north of the Buluk Gap.

From earliest Pliocene times acid volcanic tuffs are intercalated with East Rudolf sediments. Our present conclusions regarding the dating and correlation of these tuffs are outlined in figure 3. The source vents of these tuff horizons have not been identified with certainty. Having eliminated all possible source vents within the basin margin volcanic highlands, we now think that the most probable source area is somewhere within the main rift belt that runs from the Sugata Valley north-northeast through Kino Sogo to Lake Stefanie. The extent, character, and correlation of the tuffs in the sedimentary basin are currently being investigated by I. C. Findlater. The volcanic geology of the eastern highlands from the Kenya/Ethiopia border southward to the Buluk Gap is being studied in detail by another of our associates, R. T. Watkins, and much fuller accounts of the volcanic geology will be presented elsewhere. It is notable that some of the major episodes of overprinting identified in the dating work (at 2.4, 2.0, 1.75, 1.0, and 0.5 m.y.) can be correlated with episodes of uplift and erosion in the basin and with important events occurring elsewhere along the Gregory Rift valley.

This is paper no. 56 in the East Rudolf Research Project catalogue of publications.

References

Baker, B. H.; Mohr, P. A.; and Williams, L. A. J. 1972. Geology of the Eastern Rift system. Geological Society of America, Special Paper 136.

Bishop, W. W., and Miller, J. A., eds. 1972. *Calibration of hominoid evolution*, ed. W. W. Bishop and J. A. Miller. Edinburgh: Scottish Academic Press; Toronto: University of Toronto Press.

Couvering, J. A. van 1972. Radiometric calibration of the European Neogene. In *Calibration of hominoid evolution*, ed. W. W. Bishop and J. A. Miller, pp. 247-71. Edinburgh: Scottish Academic Press; Toronto: University of Toronto Press.

Fitch, F. J. 1972. Selection of suitable material for dating and the assessment of geological error in potassium-argon age determination. In *Calibration of hominoid evolution*, ed. W. W. Bishop and J. A. Miller, pp. 77-91. Edinburgh; Scottish Academic Press; Toronto: University of Toronto Press.

Fitch, F. J.; Forster, S. C.; and Miller, J. A. 1974. Geological time-scale. *Rept. Prog. Phys.* 37:1433-96.

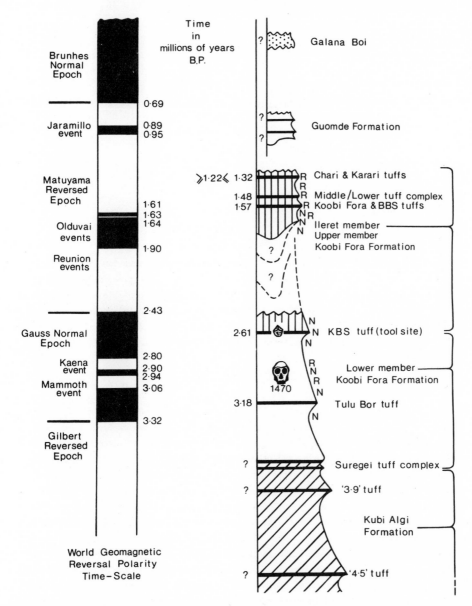

Figure 3. Dated tuffs in the East Rudolf sedimentary basin. Paleomagnetic data on East Rudolf rocks from Brock and Isaac, and stratigraphic nomenclature from Bowen and Vondra (this symposium).

Fitch, F. J., and Miller, J. A. 1971. Atmospheric argon correction in the K-Ar dating of young volcanic rocks. *J. Geol. Soc. London* 127:533-34.

_____. 1973. Dating granites by the potassium-argon method. In *Granite '71*. Geological Society of South Africa, Special Volume 3.

Hurford, A. J. 1974. Fission track dating of a vitric tuff from East Rudolf, Kenya. *Nature* 249:236-37.

Reversals of the earth's magnetic field have been known for some time, and in recent years a time scale for these reversals has been established. This time scale, which covers the past five million years, makes magnetic polarity correlation possible within this time span. In favorable circumstances the polarity pattern recorded in rock sequences can be used not only for correlation but also for dating. This chapter discusses the application of the technique to sediments of the Koobi Fora Formation, East Lake Rudolf.

The Reversal Time Scale

The construction of time scales and their development over the past few years is well described in review papers by Watkins (1972), Opdyke (1972) and Dalrymple (1972). The last is particularly useful, appearing as it does in a previous Wenner-Gren symposium volume, and gives much more detail than we can include here. Recent scales appear to be converging toward a common pattern, and other earth scientists are beginning to use them for correlation and dating. In an attempt to achieve uniformity in this area a sub-commission of the international Commission on Stratigraphy has been set up to recommend nomenclature and usage (see the May 1973 issue of *Geotimes*); but there are still differences in detail between versions of the time scale, and the subcommission has not yet endorsed any one scale.

Perhaps the most widely used scale is that originally proposed by Cox (1969) in an article in *Science*. It is shown here in figure 1, but the names of the polarity episodes are given according to the scheme of Grommé and Hay (1971). Dalrymple (1972) discussed this scale and points out that it suffers from a rather poorly determined value for the age of the Matuyama-Gauss boundary. Fortunately, recent data from Norfolk Island presented by McDougall and Aziz-ur-Rahman (1972) yield a rather good determination for the age of this boundary of 2.41 ± 0.01 m.y., very close to Cox's original estimate of 2.43 m.y. McDougall and Aziz-ur-Rahman also give slightly revised ages for the boundaries of the Kaena and Mammoth events. These modifications are shown in figure 1 alongside the original Cox scale.

Cox's scale and others like it are derived primarily from a study of the paleomagnetism of dated lava flows. Data from deep sea cores is also used but plays a minor role. Such scales therefore depend upon another physical dating method--the K-Ar method--and are not fully independent. However, the scale is compiled from a large number of dates from many

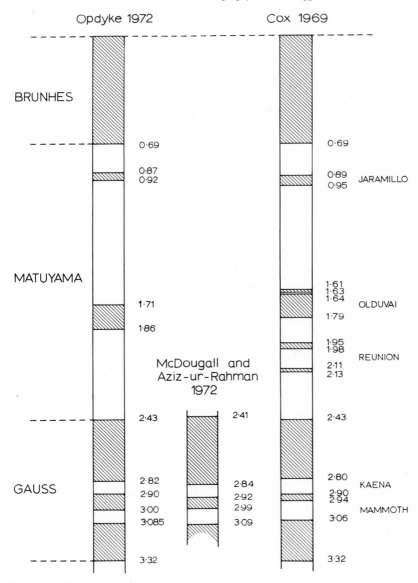

Figure 1. Some recent geomagnetic polarity time scales

different formations, and the dates themselves have to meet strict selection criteria (see Dalrymple 1972 for details). The ages of the polarity boundaries are therefore usually much better determined than ages for any single rock unit and are unlikely to suffer from the kinds of errors that can afflict such single determinations.

The scale given by Opdyke (1972) differs from the scales described in the previous paragraphs in that it puts much greater weight on the polarity record from deep sea cores (see fig. 1). It omits some of the shorter polarity episodes, because many of the deep sea cores have very low sedimentation rates and are thus unable to resolve them. However, it is generally accepted that short polarity episodes do occur, and it is therefore advisable to use the scale which best represents this feature. Accordingly, Cox's scale, with the nomenclature recommended by Grommé and Hay, is used in this chapter.

Reversal Stratigraphy

If a sedimentary column is effectively continuous, its polarity record may be matched on a one-to-one basis with the polarity time scale to provide a chronometric dating of the sequence. With formations that are not well dated by other means the value of the method is obvious, and in richly fossiliferous sequences the method can provide a calibration of evolution which will allow worldwide comparisons.

Such is the aim at Koobi Fora, but the conditions for achieving it are formidable. First, the rocks must be sufficiently magnetic to be measurable, and their magnetism must be stable enough for the measurements to yield the original polarity state rather than some secondary one. Next, one must have a sufficiently long uninterrupted column so that one can recognize a unique pattern which can be matched to the time scale. And finally, one should ideally have some confirmation in the form of independent isotopic dates from some part or parts of the column.

In practice, the rocks may be either weak or unstable or both. The sedimentary column is rarely continuous; time breaks may be present, and even when they are absent, sedimentary rates may be impossible due to the lack of suitable material or may vary widely through the column. Isotopic dating may be impossible because there is no suitable material or may yield conflicting results. At Koobi Fora all these difficulties are present in some degree, but, as so often happens in the earth sciences, careful, detailed work makes progress possible even without "ideal" conditions.

Time breaks are probably the most difficult features to accommodate. But if their presence is recognized (this is crucial) the polarity pattern usually allows only a very limited range of solutions. In deciding between these, other evidence must be used, and often an isotopic age will provide the required solution. In such a case, however, the dates concerned play a central role in the method rather than acting as independent confirmatory evidence. Sometimes we must appeal to faunal evidence to settle this type of problem, but such appeals should be made with care. Faunal correlation is a perfectly acceptable method in stratigraphy, but since the aim of this work is to provide an independent age calibration for the sediments and their associated fauna, there is a danger of using circular arguments. All these points are well illustrated in the construction of a magnetic chronology for the Koobi Fora Formation.

The Koobi Fora Formation

The stratigraphy and nomenclature of the Koobi Fora Formation have been summarized by Bowen and Vondra (1973) and Vondra and Bowen (this symposium). Paleomagnetic samples have been taken from four stratigraphic columns in the formation: Ileret areas 6 and 8, the Karari escarpment areas 130 and 131, the KBS ridge Area 105, and Koobi Fora Area 103 (see figures in Findlater, this symposium). When the paleomagnetic work was started the KBS Tuff was the only unit for which an apparently reliable K-Ar date had been obtained.

The chronological interpretation of the paleomagnetic stratigraphy that we put forward here involves the hypothesis that in many, if not all, sections considerable time gaps separate fossiliferous sediments below the KBS Tuff from any fine-grained, fossiliferous sediments above it. This possibility was first recognized by A. K. Behrensmeyer in her mapping of Area 105 (Behrensmeyer 1970; Isaac, Leakey, and Behrensmeyer 1971). The hypothesis appeared to receive support from the contrasts found between faunal samples collected

from above and below the KBS Tuff in areas 105 and 103 (Maglio 1972). Subsequent work by
G. Johnson has revealed evidence of tectonic disruption, mild erosion, and an influx of
coarse material in the equivalent interval of sections closer to the basin center (Area 103;
Johnson, this symposium). It should be stressed that the hypothesis of local "disconformities" existed before the paleomagnetic work was undertaken and before the chronology of
the Lower Member of the Koobi Fora Formation became a matter of keen debate. As will be
seen below, we are confident of its validity and have incorporated it in our suggested correlation of observed polarities with the global time scale. (Further discussion on the
"disconformity" is contained in a supplementary note at the end of this chapter.)

Paleomagnetism

A small preliminary collection was made in the 1971 field season, but the main sampling
was done during the 1972 season, a total of 247 samples being collected. The rocks are all
rather soft sediments, and so the traditional paleomagnetic techniques of collecting blocks
or drilling cores in situ were impossible. Instead the samples were collected in small
plastic boxes (2.4 cm^2), using a simple magnetic compass and inclinometer, then removed and
sealed. Where necessary hardener and glue were used to set the more friable material. At
each horizon three samples were usually taken a few meters apart. The vertical spacing was
variable, being governed by the nature of the outcrop and the time available for fieldwork.
In the more closely sampled sections the vertical spacing was typically a few meters, but
elsewhere it was often as large as 10 m.

The oriented cubes were measured in the paleomagnetism laboratory of the Physics Department, University of Nairobi, using a 5 H spinner magnetometer of the type described by
Foster (1966), and were then subjected to the usual alternating field partial demagnetization processes. Initial NRM intensities were of the order of 10^{-4} gauss (fairly high for
sedimentary material), and the subsequent partial demagnetization was therefore easy to
carry out. In most cases secondary components were removed by demagnetization in peak alternating fields of 100 oersted. The initial directions of magnetization were classified
as normal (N), reversed (R), or intermediate (I). Intermediate directions were arbitrarily
defined as those which departed from the dipole field axis for Koobi Fora (D = 0°, 180°,
I = ±8) by more than 50°. The same classification was used for cleaned directions except
that in a few cases the cleaning gave rise to erratic directional changes due to instability.
Such samples were described as showing no clear result. Of the 247 samples 75 changed their
classification after cleaning. The cleaned polarity results are shown on the sampling
columns in figure 2. It can be seen that the polarities at each sampling horizon are
generally consistent. The occasional discrepancies could be due to orientation errors,
hard secondary components not removed by cleaning, or discordant ages of magnetization.
These possibilities raise the general question of the reliability of the paleomagnetic
results.

If the cleaned paleomagnetic directions are to be used for correlation with the polarity time scale we must be assured that they do reproduce the original directions of magnetization. Paleomagnetism has a number of internal tests for judging reliability and
stability, and several of these were applied. One test is to study both the intensity and
the direction of the demagnetization behavior. Demagnetization curves are useful indicators
of stability, and by these criteria the behavior of the Koobi Fora specimens was generally
good. More detailed laboratory studies of the magnetic properties of these specimens are
still under way.

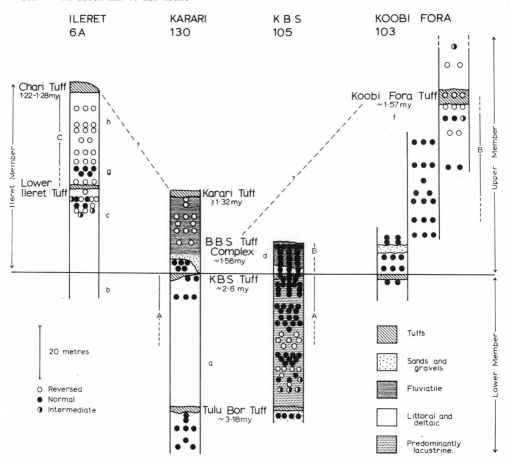

Figure 2. The four paleomagnetically sampled columns shown in their field stratigraphic relations, together with the cleaned polarity results. Approximate positions of the faunal zones A-C and fossil sets (a-h) are shown.

Field tests can be also used. One test is simply to seek internal consistency at each sampling horizon, and this is why we collected several samples at each horizon. In one area the conglomerate test was applied. In Area 105 in the Lower Member there are several horizons of bedded limonite concretions. These concretions have the same polarity as the softer lacustrine sediments in which they lie. At one point a local episode has eroded and redeposited previously formed concretions into the "Gold Pebble Conglomerate." Oriented samples collected from the conglomerate showed an initial magnetization which was normal although rather scattered. This is due to secondary magnetization acquired recently. After partial demagnetization the directions become random. These directions are those of the original magnetization of the pebbles and are random because of the redeposition process. This is a classic test in paleomagnetism, and it shows that the original magnetization must have been formed before the conglomerate was deposited and remained stable since that date. It also shows that the partial demagnetization treatment is able to separate the primary and secondary components. All these tests taken together suggest that for most of the Koobi Fora samples the cleaned directions do indeed represent an original rather than a secondary magnetization, and that the age of the original magnetization is not very different from the age of deposition. However, it remains a possibility that there is some time lag between deposition and magnetization, and further work is planned to study this. If present, the time lag is not sufficient to blur the recognition of the Kaena and Mammoth events, which are clearly resolved in the 105 column. Since these events are of the order of 10^5 years in length, the time lag is probably of an order of magnitude less than some 10^4 years. It should not therefore present any serious problems in attempts to correlate with the known time scale, but it does provide a possible explanation for the occasional occurrence of mixed polarity within a single horizon.

Figure 2 shows the results placed on the sampling columns, in relation to the known marker beds, and thus represents the state of knowledge in early 1973, after the paleomagnetic measurements had been completed on the 1971 and 1972 collections. The next step was to attempt a correlation of the magnetic polarity patterns with the time scale of figure 1.

Correlation

Since none of the columns extend to the present, the correlation needs a starting point, and we used the previously published age of 2.61 ± 0.26 m.y. for sanidines from pumice pebbles found in the KBS Tuff (Fitch and Miller 1970). The polarity of samples from in or near KBS Tuff is everywhere normal, which is entirely consistent with the quoted age, and this was therefore used as a fixed point in the correlation. The polarity of the Lower Member from the KBS Tuff downward remains predominantly normal, but in Area 105 two short reversed events occur in a stratigraphic position which suggests that they represent the Kaena and Mammoth events in the Gauss Normal epoch. The spacing of events and their vertical distance from the KBS Tuff implies a net sedimentation rate of about 10 cm in 10^3 years in this part of the column (compared with a rate of the order of 0.5 cm in 10^3 years for deep sea cores). If this rate is assumed it is possible to predict an age of between 3.1 and 3.2 m.y. for the Tulu Bor Tuff. Stratigraphic mapping has traced the Tulu Bor and KBS tuffs through most areas of the Koobi Fora and Karari regions, and to the extent that this has been done the above correlation can be assumed to hold in those areas also, although it was established only in Area 105.

The placing of the KBS and Tulu Bor tuffs of the Lower Member in the Gauss Normal epoch, and the recognition of the Kaena and Mammoth events within the column seem to us the most secure parts of the paleomagnetic chronology. The positions of the Upper Member and the Ileret Member in relation to the time scale require rather more careful argument. It is necessary to make some use of faunal evidence, and for this we use Maglio's chronology for the Koobi Fora Formation based upon fossil mammal zones (Maglio 1972).

Maglio recognized three faunal zones in the Koobi Fora Formation, each based on a distinct group of vertebrates. By comparison with the isotopically dated deposits of the Shungura Formation in the Omo Valley and with those of Olduvai, Maglio was able to suggest mean ages and age ranges for each of these zones and thus to suggest a chronology for the Koobi Fora deposits. The zones and their ages as estimated by Maglio are summarized in table 1. The actual values of the ages are less important for our purpose than the recognition of distinct zones with implied time differences between them.

The *Mesochoerus limnetes* zone (A) is defined by an assemblage of fossils from the upper part of the Lower Member which has normal polarity. Table 1 shows a best fit age of 2.3 m.y. with a range of uncertainty of 3.0 to 2.0 m.y. for this zone. The paleomagnetic evidence for this part of the Lower Member favors placing it below the 2.43 m.y. boundary. Combining this with the K-Ar determination for the KBS Tuff, we suggest that the best age estimate for the zone be revised upward to about 2.7.

Table 1

Age of Maglio's Faunal Zones

Zone	"Best Fit Age" (m.y.)	Range of Uncertainty (m.y.)
C *Loxodonta africana*	1.3	1.6 ⁼ 1.0
B *Metridiochoerus andrewsi*	1.7	1.9 ⁼ 1.5
A *Mesochoerus limnetes*	2.3	3.0 ⁼ 2.0

The fossils used to define the *Metridiochoerus andrewsi* zone (B) come from outcrops of the Upper Member above the KBS Tuff in which the polarity is predominantly normal. The simplest paleomagnetic solution for this part of the column would be to regard it as an upward continuation of the Gauss Normal epoch, and thus to assign an age greater than 2.43 m.y. But, as we have seen, in areas 105 and 103 a disconformity is believed to exist just above the KBS Tuff, and there is a change of faunal zone across the disconformity. Both factors imply some degree of time loss. If a time loss is accepted, then the normal polarity forces the zone above the disconformity to correspond with the Olduvai event. As it happens, this fits Maglio's age for zone B rather well, but the argument does not depend on this fit; rather, it depends on the simple dichotomy created by the polarity evidence: either the normal polarity is near the end of the Gauss or it is in the Olduvai; either there is no time gap or there is a large one: Compromise situations are not possible. In Area 103 the normal polarity region is followed by a rather ragged upward transition of reversed polarity, and this transition, which coincides with the Koobi Fora Tuff, is assumed to mark the end of the Olduvai event.

Maglio's youngest zone, *Loxodonta africana* (C) is represented only in the Ileret Member above the lower tuff. The paleomagnetic column starts just below the lower tuff with a rather mixed polarity pattern, changing upward into a consistently reversed section to which the main fossil assemblage belongs. A long reversed section extends upward to the Chari Tuff. Since this zone represents a rather later stage than the *Metridiochoerus andrewsi* zone, and since the polarity is mainly reversed, perhaps the column belongs to the upper part of the Matuyama with the end of the Olduvai event being recorded at about the level of the Lower Tuff. This placement is reasonably in accord with the faunal age and best satisfies the polarity evidence, but the column needs to be extended downward for full confirmation.

The Upper Member in Area 130 gave consistently reversed polarities from the local disconformity to the Karari Tuff. On polarity grounds this section must be placed in the Matuyama, but it is not clear whether it should be older or younger than the Olduvai event. Few mammal fossils have been recovered from these beds, although they do contain many archeological sites. However, there are some geological grounds for correlating the Karari Tuff with the Chari Tuff at Ileret and the BBS Tuff Complex with the Koobi Fora Tuff in Area 103. An age after the Olduvai event for this part of the Area 130 column would then provide the best fit, and this is adopted in our chronology.

The suggested placements of the sampled columns are given in the diagram (fig. 3), which shows the main marker horizons and the polarity results correlated with the polarity time scale. The faunal zones (A-C), the hominid fossil sets (a-h), and the main industries are shown in their correct stratigraphic position on the columns. Since the columns themselves are placed according to the polarity data, this diagram acts as calibration for the other data, on the assumption that the suggested polarity chronology is correct (see table 1).

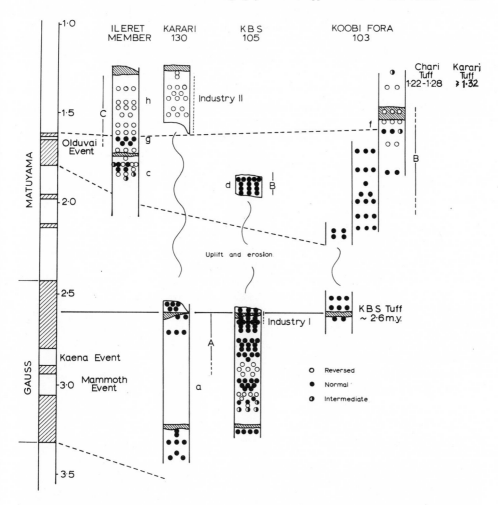

Figure 3. The suggested correlation of the sampled columns with the geomagnetic polarity time scale of Cox (1969).

We arrived at this chronology early in 1973, and the above treatment is an expanded version of that presented in our paper in *Nature* (Brock and Isaac 1974). Later in 1973 a new set of isotopic dates became available from the Fitch-Miller dating group. (Fitch and Miller, this symposium; Findlater et al. 1974). These ages have been added to the relevant tuff horizons in figure 2. The diagram was of course constructed so as to give the KBS Tuff an age of 2.61 m.y., but the consistency between the polarity scheme and the other five isotopic ages is reassuring.

It is interesting to note that had the new dates been available earlier, other "starting points" could have been chosen, but all would have led to essentially the same proposals. The general agreement between the two types of data is very impressive, and we believe that the joint evidence greatly strengthens the proposed chronology.

Alternative Chronology

In constructing the scheme of figure 3 we used, among other things, Maglio's faunal chronology first published in 1972. Since then new faunal evidence has been presented, much of it in this symposium, and some of it implies conflict between the East Rudolf and the Omo chronologies. In particular, faunal correlation of the suids between Omo and East Rudolf can be taken to suggest that if the Omo dating is correct, the ages for the Lower Member at East Rudolf are too high. We will not attempt to tackle the faunal evidence itself, but instead will discuss the paleomagnetic consequences of alternative chronologies. If the KBS Tuff is required to be appreciably younger than 2.61 m.y., its normal polarity forces it to be placed somewhere in the Olduvai event, which is the next youngest substantial episode of normal polarity. Indeed, the whole of the sampled part of the Lower Member would also have to be placed in the Olduvai event, since it is predominantly normal. We here discount the possibility that such a thickness could have been preferentially deposited during the very brief Reunion events (see Postscript). We would thus compress the whole section from below the Tulu Bor Tuff to the BBS Tuff within the Olduvai event. The 200,000 year Olduvai event would then involve some 120 m of section, including the two distinct faunal zones. In addition, two previously unknown, short reversal polarity episodes would have to be postulated. None of these are impossible, but in combination they seem to us to present a vastly less likely state of affairs than the chronology presented here.

Arguments like these can be brought to bear on other alternatives, and they nicely illustrate the character of paleomagnetic "dating." It is rare that an actual age can be produced, but the polarity data will almost always narrow the possibilities to manageable levels and will often rule out otherwise plausible alternatives. Thus the large block of normal polarity at and near the KBS Tuff makes it impossible for it to have an age of, say, 2.2 m.y. And unless the polarity data is itself suspect, we must bow to this verdict. A blunt but very compelling argument!

Discussion

To assist the discussion in other areas of study we suggest that figure 2 be used as a quick "time" reference. It can be supplemented by table 2, which lists all the hominid finds to the end of the 1972 field season in relation to the main marker beds. This table and the corresponding diagram are offered as an interim calibration of the Koobi Fora Formation. Future geophysical work may well change it: current faunal studies already suggest some conflict with other areas. But since the aim of the study was an independent calibration of evolution we suggest that it be used as such, even though it is neither as complete nor as independent as we wish. If the proposed calibration is accepted it will have implications for geology, archeology, and fossils. These are discussed in several other contributions to this symposium, and we make only brief remarks on the topics.

As we have seen, it is necessary to propose a time break in the sequence in order to accommodate the paleomagnetic and faunal evidence. There was preexisting geological evidence for a disconformity (Behrensmeyer 1970; Isaac, Leakey, and Behrensmeyer 1971), but the nature of the evidence and the extent of the disconformity are still under debate. However, if the paleomagnetic evidence is accepted, the disconformity must not only be present in the sampled area but must involve time loss of the order of 0.7 m.y. There will then be consequences for the sedimentary and tectonic history of the area, and it is important to test the hypothesis and to seek clarification of the processes involved.

In the field of hominid paleontology one of the more important specimens is KNM-ER 1470 from Area 131. It was found at a level some 38 m below the KBS Tuff, and by comparing thicknesses with the equivalent column in Area 105 it was possible to suggest an age of

Table 2

Relation of Hominid Fossils to Marker Beds

	Ileret Areas 1,2,6,7,8,10,12	Karari Escarpment Areas 130, 131		KBS Ridge Area 105	Koobi Fora Ridge — Area 104	Koobi Fora Ridge — Area 103	Suggested Age
h	Chari Tuff 404 725 728 731 739 740 741 805 992 993 1463 1465 1466 1467	Karari Tuff Industry II					1.4 - 1.6
g	Middle Tuff 729 733 803 806 807 808 809 818 1468 Industry II Lower Tuff	BBS Tuff					
c	Lower Tuff 406 407 727 732 801 802 815 819 820 1170 1171 1464 1591 1592 KBS Tuff		d	405 738 1476 1477 1478 1479	e 164 810 812 813 814 816 997 998	f Koobi Fora Tuff 403 730 734 736 737	1.6 - 1.8
b	KBS Tuff 1590 1593	KBS Tuff Industry I 1462 1469 1470 1471 1472 1473 1474 1475 1481 1482 1483 1500	a	KBS Tuff Industry I			2.7 - 3.0
	Tulu Bor Tuff	Tulu Bor Tuff		Tulu Bor Tuff		Tulu Bor Tuff	

406 = cf. *Australopithecus boisei*   806 = cf. *Homo* sp.   998 = affinities indeterminate

All numbers are Kenya National Museum East Rudolf catalog numbers (KNMER). Basic information on the fossils has been published by Leakey and others. See fig. 3 for the relationships of sets *a - h* to the paleomagnetic columns.

about 2.9 m.y. Preliminary results from the 1973 collection allow us to modify this estimate. The 1470 site appears to be stratigraphically *below* the Mammoth event in the Gauss
Normal epoch, and it therefore has an age greater than 3.09 m.y. Since it lies above the
Tulu Bor Tuff, which has been isotopically dated at 3.18 ± 0.09 m.y., its age is now well
bounded, and on this evidence a figure of 3.1 m.y. should be a good estimate of the age of
this important specimen.

There are also implications for paleomagnetism. The accumulation rate in the Lower
Member is of the order of 10 cm in 10^3 years, and in parts of the Upper Member it may be
as high as 30 cm in 10^3 years. This is at least an order of magnitude higher than that in
the deep sea cores, and these sediments therefore have a much higher resolving power for
short events. In principle, events as short as 10^4 years should be detectable. Against
this must be set the practical difficulties of sampling at the required density. However,
it should be noted that in both those columns which include the upper boundary of the
Olduvai event there is some complexity, with a suggestion of an N-R-N-R pattern. Of the
published time scales, Cox's is the only one to show a short event at this point; but if
it is real, our sediments probably record it in some detail. The relevant sections would
then qualify for extremely dense sampling. Paleomagnetic work in areas such as Koobi Fora
could thus lead to improvements of the time scale by showing up fine detail which other
methods miss. But for the moment the emphasis will probably remain on the inverse problem--
namely, use of the existing time scale to provide an age calibration for the sediments.
There is much still to be done in this area.

Supplementary Note on the "Disconformity"

The problem of the "disconformity" has been discussed and debated among members of the
East Rudolf Research Project over several years. Since the geological contributions to the
symposium do not treat the question directly, we will offer a brief summary in this epilogue.
Discussion has turned on two issues: First, there has been debate on whether there is evidence for a "time gap" just above the KBS Tuff in many or most sections--that is to say,
whether there was a substantial time interval during which little or no deposition occurred
over large parts of the structural "shelf" on which the Koobi Fora Formation rests. The
second point that has been debated is whether such "time gaps," if verified, can be linked
between areas and given the label "disconformity."

Arguments in favor of the existence of important time gaps include the following:
1. In eastern areas (105, 108, 130 and 131) a sharp, mappable contact occurs between sediments encasing the KBS Tuff and overlying deposits. The upper beds pertain to a fluvial
regime with much higher energy characteristics than those associated with the KBS Tuff.
The contact appears to be an erosion surface.
2. In Area 105 there are marked contrasts between the faunal samples recovered from the
beds just below the KBS Tuff and from beds just above the KBS Tuff. The contrasts both in
species composition and in the stage of evolution of suids, elephants, and hippopotamids is
great relative to the small thickness of sediments separating the horizons sampled (Maglio
1972; Coryndon and Cooke, this symposium).
3. The K-Ar determinations chosen by Fitch and Miller as the most reliable results indicate an age of 2.61 ± 0.26 for the KBS Tuff and 1.56 ± 0.02 for the BBS Tuff Complex. In
many parts of the Karari escarpment these two units are separated by only 5 to 10 m of deposits, in spite of a putative difference in age of a million years. The intervening deposits are predominantly coarse channel sands and conglomerates.

4. Many, perhaps all, sections show an interval of coarse deposits (sands or gravels) between the KBS Tuff and the sediments yielding the *Metridiochoerus andrewsi* faunal assemblage. This is consistent with a "time gap" hypothesis but is not in itself proof of it.

Arguments against the necessity to hypothesize any major "time gap" include the following:

1. The sedimentary sequence merely shows a tendency to coarsen upward and the development of cut-and-fill contact relationships between upper units and lower units should be expected in such a sequence.

2. The scatter of K-Ar apparent age values obtained for the KBS and BBS tuffs overlaps to such an extent that one cannot be confident that there really is a major time difference between them.

Clearly the question of whether to call the time gap a "disconformity" largely depends on determining the real existence of such a gap and on measuring its magnitude.

The geologists who have worked at East Rudolf generally agree that the evidence of the field geology alone is inconclusive regarding the existence or the magnitude of any pause or gap in sedimentation. However, they also recognize that the absence of totally unambiguous evidence for a time gap in a sedimentary sequence does *not* mean that there was no interruption of deposition. We are thus thrown back on other means for gauging time differences between fossiliferous zones in the Koobi Fora Formation. If one accepts the findings of Maglio, since supported by S. Coryndon and other paleontologists, that the *Metridiochoerus* zone is separated from the *Mesochoerus* zone by about one-half to three-quarters of a million years, it follows that in some areas the two zones are separated by a period of retarded deposition or even of erosion. The same conclusion follows if one accepts Fitch and Miller's interpretation of the K-Ar results. Taken in combination, the case in favor of a post-KBS Tuff period of retarded deposition and gentle erosion seems very strong, but it clearly must remain a matter for investigation and testing.

The current model of sedimentation during the deposition of the Koobi Fora Formation involves sediments being laid down on a gently sloping "shelf" forming the eastern margin of a half-graben (Fitch and Vondra this symposium, Vondra and Bowen, this symposium). Streams and rivers issuing onto the shelf from higher ground to the east and northeast dropped much of their sediment load on the shelf, and the water and the finest sediment made their way out to the lake which filled the deepest part of the trough. Given this model, it is not difficult to envisage perturbations which could reduce the propensity of streams and rivers to spread their sediment load on the shelf--or even to cause them to become incised and gently strip preexisting sediment covers. The following set of factors is not regarded as exhaustive, and clearly these factors could operate singly or in combination.

Tectonic

1. Subsidence of the graben center lowers base level and creates a new sump to be filled with sediment. Deposition on the shelf would recommence when the enlarged sump had been filled.

2. Westerly tilting of the shelf increases gradients and reduces net deposition. Infilling of the basin would eventually reduce gradients again.

3. Downwarping of catchment areas reduces the sediment load of the streams.

Climatic

4. Lowering of lake level through a change in evaporation/influx balance leads to erosion of existing sediments.

5. Increase in vegetation cover in the source areas reduces sediment loads, to the point where streams traversing the shelf cease to deposit or even begin to erode the sediment cover.

If the indications are accepted that there was a break in deposition lasting on the order of half to three-quarters of a million years, it seems to us very likely that tectonic changes were at least partly involved in disrupting the Lower Member regime.

Some Recent History and Many Acknowledgments

Paleomagnetic polarity work in sediments on land (as opposed to deep sea cores) is comparatively recent, and it is of some interest to describe how it came about in East Africa. The Nairobi Palaeomagnetic Laboratory, which is a part of the Physics Department at the University of Nairobi, was basically interested in the paleomagnetism of volcanic rocks, but in the period 1969-72 it had acquired instruments suitable for measuring sediments. During this period the laboratory undertook a few polarity measurements for Mary Leakey and Richard Hay on samples from Olduvai Gorge. Workers at East Rudolf thus became aware that polarity work might also be useful in their area, and the first few samples were provided by Alan Walker. These showed that the rocks contained measurable magnetization, and as a result one of us (Isaac) initiated a field collection program on a reconnaissance basis in 1971 and on a larger scale in 1972. Encouraged both by Richard Leakey and by Isaac, Brock undertook to measure the resulting specimens in his laboratory. Thus there grew up a very fruitful collaboration between physics, geology, archeology, and paleontology.

The resulting work owes much to many other people, and our list of acknowledgments must be long. We thank in particular the students who undertook the tedious collection work in the field under the general direction of Isaac: Dan Stiles in 1971, Fred Lucas in 1972, and Joab Ndombi and Jack Hillhouse in 1973. Joab Ndombi also helped with the laboratory measurements.   Alan Cox visited the project in 1972 and gave much useful advice. The collection programs owe much to the geologists, and we thank the Iowa, Birkbeck, and Dartmouth groups for their advice and assistance to the sample collectors. Richard Leakey provided essential field support and background assistance; he also encouraged us greatly by his enthusiasm as a "consumer" of paleomagnetic data--we could not have wanted a better customer. The work was supported by the following: the National Science Foundation (grant GS 28607), the National Geographic Society, the Donner Foundation, the Miller Institute of the University of California, and the Deans' Committee of the University of Nairobi.

Postscript

Since this paper was written, results have become available from the extensive paleomagnetic sampling program in the lower Omo basin which was undertaken in 1973 (Brown and Shuey, this symposium). We feel that a postscript will promote the development of understanding better than any attempt to rewrite our paper after the fact.

Brown and Shuey have discovered in the Shungura Formation a far more complex reversal stratigraphy than might have been expected on the basis of the K-Ar dates for Shungura tuffs and standard paleomagnetic time scales such as those of Cox (1969) and Opdyke (1972). Brown and Shuey point out that this extra complexity can be accommodated in a number of ways. One would be to stretch the Shungura chronology to cover a longer range of the polarity time scale. This leads to age estimates for the lower Shungura Formation that seem highly improbable on faunal grounds. It also would imply seemingly unlikely variations in sedimentation rates. The alternative they suggest is that the polarity time scale itself needs to be revised in the time range 2.4 to 1.6. Notably they suggest that the "Olduvai event" is only one of a complex of early to middle Matuyama normal events. Their Omo polarity time scale shows predominantly normal polarity from about 2.1 to 1.6 m.y. This solution seems reasonable to us but will have to be evaluated in a wider forum of geophysical evidence than that furnished by the Lake Rudolf basin.

The possibility of important errors in the standard paleomagnetic time scales was one we did not discuss in our paper.

If there was a longer, complex period of normal polarity from 2.1 to 1.6 m.y., then we must consider the possibility that the normal polarity of the Lower Member, attributed by us to the Gauss Normal epoch, may in fact pertain to the lower part of the complex (Reunion and "X" events). Some, but not all, paleontologists may favor this alternative match as a way out of the alleged discrepancies between the K-Ar chronology of the Shungura faunal sequence and the East Rudolf faunal zones. Accepting this alternative means rejecting the dates favored by Fitch and Miller for the KBS Tuff. Given the scattered values obtained, that step may not seem unreasonable, but it also means rejecting the date for the Tulu Bor Tuff, which is not known to be subject to the same complicating factors. In our view these uncertainties can be resolved only by taking the following steps:

1. Verification of the revised polarity time scale proposed by Brown and Shuey.
2. Further K-Ar determinations on both the Shungura and Koobi Fora formations to test the chronologies now favored for each.
3. Careful evaluation of faunal evidence that seems to imply discrepancies between the chronologies. Since we are dealing with "fine-grained" correlations, explanations of similarities and difference other than the facile "time-equivalence explanation" need to be considered.

In addition we need to extend the paleomagnetic sampling program at East Rudolf.

In the meantime it seems to us that the balance of geophysical evidence still rests in favor of the correlation shown in figure 3. We propose that it be continued as the best working hypothesis and that it be tested with all possible vigor.

(Further sample columns have since been collected by J. Hillhouse and by Joab Ndombi in 1973 and 1974. Work on these is still in progress, but some preliminary results indicate that the polarity stratigraphy of the Lower Member may, at least in some cases, include a larger proportion of strata deposited during times of reversed geomagnetic field. Some revision of the proposed correlation to the standard time scale may be necessary if this is confirmed.)

This is paper no. 57 in the East Rudolf Research Project catalogue of publications.

References

Behrensmeyer, A. K. 1970. Preliminary geological interpretation of a new hominid site in the Lake Rudolf basin. *Nature* 226:225-26.

Bowen, B. E., and Vondra, C. F. 1973. Stratigraphic relationships of the Plio-Pleistocene deposits, East Rudolf, Kenya. *Nature* 242:391-93.

Brock, A., and Isaac, G. Ll. 1974. Palaeomagnetic stratigraphy and chronology of hominid-bearing sediments east of Lake Rudolf, Kenya. *Nature* 247:344-48.

Cox, A. 1969. Geomagnetic reversals. *Science* 163:237-46.

Dalrymple, G. B. 1972. Potassium argon dating of geomagnetic reversals and North American glaciations. In *Calibration of hominid evolution*, ed. W. W. Bishop and J. A. Miller, pp. 107-34. Edinburgh: Scottish Academic Press; Toronto: University of Toronto Press.

Findlater, I. C.; Fitch, F. J.; Miller, J. A.; and Watkins, R. T. 1974. Dating of the rock succession containing fossil hominids at East Rudolf, Kenya. *Nature* 251:213-15.

Fitch, F. J., and Miller, J. A. 1970. Radioisotopic age determinations of Lake Rudolf artefact site. *Nature* 226:226-28.

Foster, J. H. 1966. A palaeomagnetic spinner magnetometer using a fluxgate gradiometer. *Earth Planet. Sci. Letters* 1:463-66.

Grommé, C. S., and Hay, R. H. 1971. Geomagnetic Polarity epoch: Age and duration of the Olduvai normal polarity event. *Earth Planet. Sci. Letters* 10:179-85.

Isaac, G. Ll.; Leakey, R. E. F.; and Behrensmeyer, A. K. 1971. Archeological traces of early hominid activities east of Lake Rudolf, Kenya. *Science* 173:1129-34.

McDougall, I., and Aziz-ur-Rahman. 1972. Age of the Gauss-Matuyama boundary and of the Kaena and Mammoth events. *Earth Planet. Sci. Letters* 14:367-80.

Maglio, V. J. 1972. Vertebrate faunas and chronology of hominid-bearing sediments east of Lake Rudolf, Kenya. *Nature* 239:379-85.

Opdyke, N. D. 1972. Palaeomagnetism of deep-sea cores. *Rev. Geophys. Space Phys.* 10:213-49.

Watkins, N. D. 1972. A review of the development of the geomagnetic polarity time scale and a discussion of prospects for its finer definition. *Bull. Geol. Soc. Am.* 83:551-74.

13. LOTHAGAM HILL, KANAPOI, AND EKORA:

A GENERAL SUMMARY OF STRATIGRAPHY AND FAUNAS

A. K. Behrensmeyer

Lothagam Hill is an isolated, westward-tilted fault block in the plain adjacent to
Lake Rudolf between the Kerio and Turkwel rivers (fig. 1). Although small in area (about
14 km^2), this locality has produced an important fauna which helps to extend knowledge of
the Lake Rudolf basin into a time period between 4.0 and 6.0 m.y., which predates the
oldest deposits of the Omo Group. The Lothagam fauna thus serves as an important link between the paleontologic history of the Rudolf basin and that of the Baringo basin, which is
currently providing faunal information from still earlier time ranges (Bishop et al. 1971).

The Mio-Pliocene fauna of Lothagam was first noted by L. H. Robbins during his archeological study of Holocene deposits overlying the older Lothagam units. Paleontological
collecting and preliminary geological work were first conducted in 1967 by a Harvard University expedition led by Bryan Patterson. Additional collecting and more detailed geologic studies were done by V. J. Maglio and A. K. Behrensmeyer in 1968. Maglio resumed
this work at Lothagam during an expedition arranged by Princeton University in 1972. Paleontologic and geologic research is now being continued by C. Smart and D. Powers of the
Department of Geological and Geophysical Sciences at Princeton (this symposium).

The stratigraphic sequence of Lothagam Hill can be divided into six major lithostratigraphic units, as defined by Behrensmeyer (unpublished manuscript based on fieldwork done
in 1968).

1. 0-10 m Holocene "220" lake beds: sands, silts, and clays, light browns, buffs, and
grays (10 YR 8/2-6/2), poorly consolidated, with abundant mollusk remains,
vertebrate remains, and artifacts (Robbins 1967, 1972). Lower contact an
angular unconformity.

2. 100+ m *Lothagam 3*: gravels, sands, silts, and clays, red brown, green, and gray
(5Y 7/2, 5YR 5/6, 10 YR 7/4-6/2), size-ranges and sedimentary structures indicating fluvial deposition, vertebrate bone, and *Etheria* banks present. Lower
contact conformable.

3. 75-90 m *Lothagam 2*: silts and clays with minor sands, drab grays, olive greens, and
yellow browns (5Y 7/2, 10 YR 6/2, 7/4, 6/6), gypsiferous, beds of gastropods
including *Cleopatra, Bellamya ("Viviparus")* (A. Verdcourt, pers. comm.), and
rare vertebrate remains. Lower contact assimilated by the Lothagam sill,
lowermost units above sill hydrothermally altered.

4. 30-80 m Lothagam sill: olivine basalt, fine-grained and homogeneous, with horizontal
flow structures and spheroidal weathering. Lower contact irregular and occasionally discordant with underlying sedimentary bedding, on hydrothermally
altered sediments of Lothagam 1. K-Ar date of 3.73 ± 0.41 m.y. (Berkeley
KA-2262).

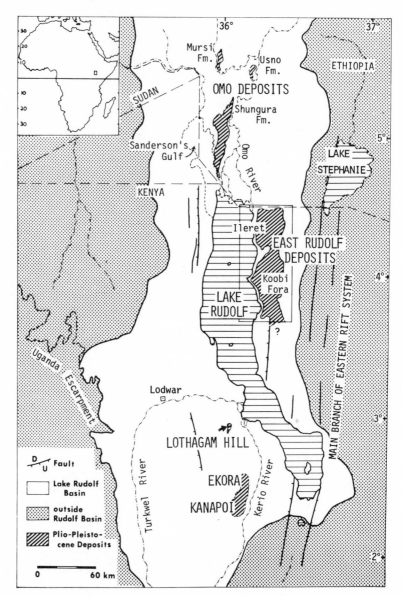

Figure 1. The Lake Rudolf basin, showing the important Plio-Pleistocene fossil localities.
The area now draining into the lake is shown in white.

5. 350-480 m *Lothagam 1*: boulder conglomerates, gravels, sands, silts, and clays, red
orange, light brown, gray, greenish gray (10 R 4/6, 5YR 5/6, 10 YR 5/4'7/4,
5GY 6/1), with particle characteristics and sedimentary structures indicating
fluvial and fluviodeltaic deposition; analcime present in fine fraction of
red-colored sediments; vertebrate bone abundant, *Etheria* banks. Lower contact an erosional unconformity.

6. 400 m+   Undifferentiated Miocene-Pliocene volcanics: interbedded basalts, phonolites,
pyroclastics, and lacustrine clays, overlaid unconformably by basalt flows,
interbedded coarse clastics and waterlaid tuffs. Base not exposed. Date on
a phonolite below the unconformity, 16.8 ± 0.5 m.y. (Geochron R-0906 (K-Ar)).
K-Ar date on basalt above the unconformity, 8.31 ± 0.25 m.y. (Berkeley JA-
2294).

The Mio-Pliocene sedimentary sequence, Lothagam 1, 2, 3, has been previously designated as the Lothagam Group (Patterson, Behrensmeyer, and Sill 1970). The total exposed
thickness of the Lothagam Group is 650-720 m. Number and letter designation of the sedimentary units has been used because there are no local names to serve as a base for stratigraphic nomenclature. When further work is done in the area, it may be possible to assign
more regionally significant formation names to Lothagam 1 through 3.

Lothagam 1 is approximately 480 m thick and can be conveniently divided into three
members, designated A, B, and C, on the basis of lithologic differences (fig. 2). Member
A (the lowest stratigraphically) consists of nonfossiliferous conglomerates and sandstones
derived from local volcanic source areas and deposited in alluvial and fluvial environments.
Member B is generally finer-grained, with sandy-silt beds ranging from 1 to 4 m thick intercalated with thinner conglomerates and sand lenses. The bedding sequence, cross-
stratification, and sediment textures indicate deposition in fluvial and fluviodeltaic environments, possibly representing periods of cyclic sedimentation comparable to those
described for the Shungura Formation of the Omo Group (de Heinzelin, Haesaerts, and Howell,
this symposium). Member C is generally better sorted than A or B and is characterized by
clearly expressed channel and overbank facies indicating a fluvial environment of deposition. Members B and C include the bulk of the Lothagam 1 section, with B approximately
185 m thick and C close to 240 m thick. The top of B is designated as the contact between
the laterally continuous "red marker bed" and an overlying pink agglomeritic tuff. The
fossil assemblage constituting the "lower fauna" of Lothagam has been recovered from members
B and C. A hominid half-mandible (*Australopithecus* cf. *africanus*) (Patterson, Behrensmeyer,
and Sill 1970, and manuscript in preparation) discovered by the Harvard Expedition in 1967
was a surface find from the upper half of Member C.

The sediments included in Lothagam 2 clearly indicate a period of lacustrine deposition which intervened between the fluvial phases represented in Lothagam 1 and 3. The proposal by Powers and McIntosh (pers. comm.) that the upper part of Lothagam 1C may correlate
stratigraphically with Lothagam 2 and 3 is difficult for me to accept owing to (*a*) the vertical stratigraphic sequence from Lothagam 1 to 3 which is apparent in the field; (*b*) the
faunal differences between Lothagam 1B/C and Lothagam 3; (*c*) the rapid facies change required from the homogeneous lake clays of Lothagam 2 to the coarse clastics of Lothagam 1C
over a distance of 300 to 500 m along an outcrop length of 6+ km and through a stratigraphic
thickness of 75 to 90 m. More work on the paleomagnetics and sediments is required before
this proposed correlation should be used as a basis for faunal or geologic interpretations.

Radiometric dates for the Lothagam sequence consist of four K-Ar determinations, as
indicated in table 1 and figure 2. The Lothagam Group is younger than the lava dated at
8.3 ± 0.25 m.y. and presumably older than the age of the intrusive basalt sill, 3.73 ±
0.41 m.y. It is possible that the sill was implaced during deposition of Lothagam 3, although the paleomagnetic evidence tends to argue against this (Powers and McIntosh
(pers. comm.) The sill postdates most of Lothagam 2, since the lake clays show hydrothermal
alteration and are often incorporated as xenoliths in the top of the sill. More refined
radiometric dating of the Lothagam group is probably not possible using present techniques.
The agglomeratic tuff at the base of Lothagam 1C yielded a wide scatter of dates on crystal
concentrates, indicating a mixture of older pyroclastics from 12 to 24 m.y. in age (FM
Consultants, rept. no. FMK/721). None of the dated components of this tuff can be reasonably related to its time of deposition. Other tuffaceous units occur in the Lothagam Group

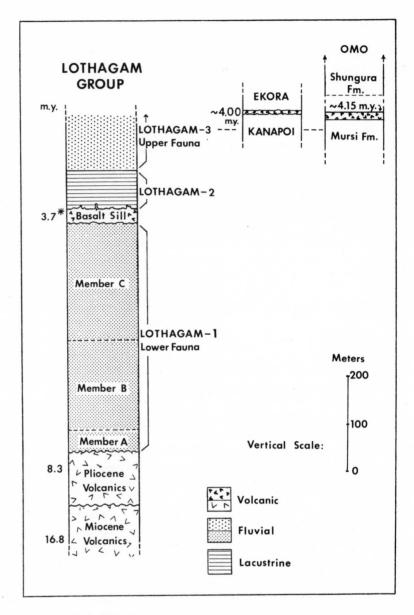

Figure 2. A generalized stratigraphic section of Lothagam Hill, with K-Ar dates indicated to the left of the lithologic section. The date of 3.7 on the basalt sill is starred because it represents the age of the intrusion of the sill between Lothagam 1 and 2. Hence, the sill is younger than Lothagam 2 and may also postdate Lothagam 3. The indicated correlations between Lothagam 3, Kanapoi, and the Mursi Formation are based primarily on faunal evidence. The currently accepted dates for the Lothagam sill, the Kanapoi basalt, and the basalt capping the Mursi Formation support the faunal correlations.

Table 1

Radiometric Dates of the Lothagam Hill and Kanapoi Localities

Locality	Sample No.	Method	Lab No.	Age(m.y.)
Lothagam				
Basalt sill	MCZ S178-68K	Whole rock K-Ar	Berkeley KA-2262	3.73±0.41
Basalt flow Upper Mio-Plioc. volcanics	MCZ S1-69K	Whole rock K-Ar	Berkeley KA-2294	8.31±0.25
Phonolite Lower Mio-Plioc. volcanics	MCZ LS7-67K	Whole rock K-Ar	Geochron R-0906	16.8 ±0.5
Welded tuff Lower Mio-Plioc. volcanics	MCZ LS8-67K	Feldspar concentrate K-Ar	Geochron F-0958	14.6 ±2.5
Kanapoi				
Kanapoi basalt	S (1966)	Whole rock K-Ar	Geochron R-0554	2.9 ±0.3
Kanapoi basalt	S (1966)	Whole rock K-Ar	Geochron R-0554	2.5 ±0.2
Kanapoi basalt	S (1966)	Whole rock K-Ar	Berkeley KA-2261	2.71± .26
Kanapoi basalt	S (1966)	Step-heating $^{40}Ar/^{39}Ar$	FM Consultants, pers. comm. to B. Patterson	~4.00

but are so obviously reworked and altered that there seems little hope that they will yield reliable dates.

The lower mammalian fauna of Lothagam is distinctly older than the upper fauna according to Patterson, Behrensmeyer, and Sill (1970), who estimate an age of 5.0 to 5.5 m.y. for Lothagam 1 and a time lapse of 1.0 to 1.5 m.y. between Lothagam 1 and 3. These estimates are based primarily on the evolutionary stages of the Proboscidea. Maglio (1973, p. 20) has noted that molars of *Stegotetrabelodon orbus* from Lothagam 1 can be matched with fragmental teeth from the Kaparyon beds (age about 5.0 m.y.) or the Mpsida beds (7.0 m.y.) in the Baringo sequence. Hooijer and Maglio (1974) have recently placed the age of Lothagam 1 at 6.0 m.y. and indicate that it is not likely to be much younger than this. However, as is noted by Smart (this symposium), much of the faunal material used for comparative purposes is derived from Lothagam 1B, and the fauna from 1C may be somewhat younger than 6.0 m.y. It is obviously important to think of the Lothagam 1 fauna as representative of a relatively long time span, since it derives from more than 300 m of section.

The Lothagam 3 fauna, although sparse, can be correlated with faunal assemblages from the Mursi Formation and the lower Shungura Formation of the Omo Group, the Chemeron beds of the Baringo succession, and the Kubi Algi Formation of East Rudolf (Patterson, Behrensmeyer, and Sill 1970; Maglio 1973) (fig. 3). This indicates an age of about 4 m.y. for Lothagam 3, based on faunal and radiometric criteria (Maglio 1973, p. 69).

Kanapoi and Ekora are two separate but adjacent localities some 50 to 75 km south of Lothagam Hill near the Kerio River (Patterson 1966; Patterson, Behrensmeyer, and Sill 1970) (fig. 1). Both have yielded Pliocene vertebrate fossils, and Kanapoi in particular has produced an extensive fauna collected by the Harvard expeditions of 1966 and 1967. The most up-to-date faunal lists for Kanapoi and Ekora are presented in table 2. The distal portion of a hominid humerus was collected from Kanapoi in 1967, and it has been assigned to cf. *Australopithecus* (Patterson and Howells 1967).

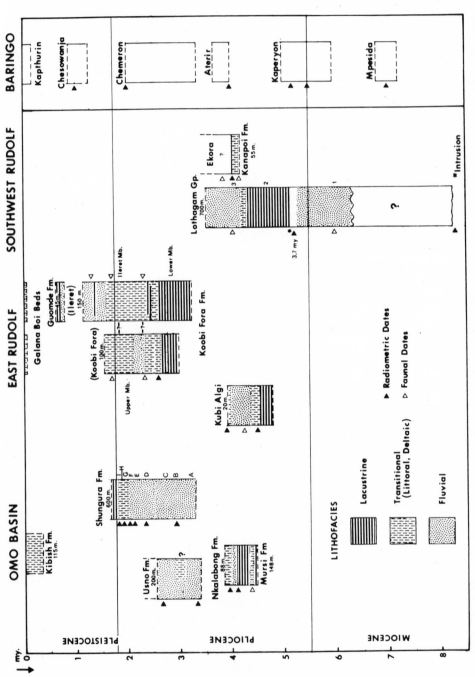

Figure 3. Stratigraphic correlations for the Rudolf basin as currently understood from faunal and radiometric evidence. Black triangles indicate radiometric dates; open triangles indicate inferred faunal ages. The vertical span of each section represents the length of time recorded by the sedimentary deposits, not the thickness of the deposits. [For further information and alternative chronological interpretations, see various other papers in the symposium.--Ed.]

Table 2

Faunal lists for Lothagam 3, Kanapoi, and Ekora

Lothagam 3	Kanapoi
Simopithecus sp.	*Parapapio jonesi*
Loxodonta adaurora	cf. *Australopithecus*
Hipparion (Stylohipparion) sp.	*Lepus* sp.
Hippopotamidae indet.	*Hystrix* sp.
Nyanzachoerus plicatus[1]	*Tatera* sp.
Notochoerus cf. *euilus*	*Enhydriodon* sp. nov.
Tragelaphus sp.	*Hyaena* sp.
Bovidae indet.	Machairodontinae indet.
Crocodylus sp.	*Deinotherium bozasi*
Euthecodon sp.	*Anancus* sp.
Podocnemis sp. nov. A	*Loxodonta adaurora*
Trionychidae indet.	*Elephas ekorensis*
Fish, indet.	*Ceratotherium praecox*[2]
	Hipparion primigenium[3]
Etheria elliptica	*Nyanzachoerus pattersoni*[1]
	N. plicatus[1]
	N. spp.[1]
Ekora	*Notochoerus* cf. *capensis*
	Not. cf. *euilus*
Anancus sp.	*Hippopotamus* sp. nov.
Loxodonta adaurora	*Giraffa* sp. nov.[4]
Elephas ekorensis	*Giraffa* sp.
Ceratotherium praecox[2]	*Tragelaphus* sp.
Nyanzachoerus cf. *plicatus*	Reduncini ? sp.
Euthecodon sp.	*Crocodylus* sp.
Podocnemis sp. nov. A	*Euthecodon* sp.
Geochelone sp.	*Podocnemis* sp. nov. A
Fish indet.	*Geochelone* sp.
Mollusca indet.	Fish indet.
	Mollusca indet.

SOURCE: Lists taken from Patterson, Behrensmeyer, and Sill, except footnoted items.

NOTE: For the faunal list from Lothagam 1, see Smart, this symposium.

1. Cooke and Ewer 1972.   3. Hooijer and Maglio 1974.

2. Hooijer (this symposium).   4. Savage (this symposium).

The stratigraphic section at Kanapoi consists of about 70 m of fluvial and lacustrine sediments capped by a basalt. This has been designated as the Kanapoi Formation in Patterson, Behrensmeyer, and Sill (1970). The Kanapoi basalt initially yielded three dates ranging from 2.9 to 2.5 m.y. (table 1) and a reversed polarity (Patterson 1966; Powers and McIntosh, this symposium). Patterson noted (1966) that there is "no evidence of any marked lapse of time" at the contact between the basalt and the underlying, fossil-iferous sediments. However, the dates were considered too young to be in accord with the fauna (Patterson, Behrensmeyer, and Sill 1970). A redating of the Kanapoi basalt by FM Consultants has yielded an age of about 4.0 m.y. (F. Fitch, pers. comm. to B. Patterson), which is in better agreement with the faunal evidence. Further work in the Kanapoi area by D. Powers may help to clarify the relationship between the basalt and the sediments as well as provide a paleomagnetic chronology.

The Ekora sediments are poorly exposed and thus are less well known than those of Kanapoi and Lothagam. They consist of coarse clastics and finer fluvial to lacustrine deposits overlying a basalt which was assumed by Patterson, Behrensmeyer, and Sill (1970) to be a continuation of the Kanapoi basalt.

The Kanapoi and Ekora faunas are considered to be essentially contemporaneous (Patterson, Behrensmeyer, and Sill 1970). Maglio (1973, p. 69) regards the Kanapoi fauna as indistinguishable from that of Lothagam 3, dating both at about 4.0 m.y. Ekora is dated by Maglio's faunal estimates as slightly younger than 4.0 m.y., which would be reasonable if the fauna does in fact come from above the Kanapoi basalt (see Powers and McIntosh, pers. comm.). It should be emphasized, however, that the dating of Kanapoi and Ekora is based primarily on faunal correlations with areas other than southwest Rudolf, with the one K-Ar date of about 4.0 m.y. on the Kanapoi basalt used as supporting evidence that the faunal determinations are correct.

This paper is offered as a summary of the findings of the first research teams in the area. The paper by Smart provides greater detail on current geologic and faunal research in the southwest part of the Rudolf basin.

References

Bishop, W. W.; Chapman, G. R.; Hill, A.; and Miller, J. A. 1971. Succession of Cainozoic vertebrate assemblages from the northern Kenya Rift Valley. *Nature* 233:389-94.

Cooke, H. B. S., and Ewer, R. F. 1972. Fossil Suidae from Kanapoi and Lothagam, northwestern Kenya. *Bull. MCZ* 143:149-295.

Hooijer, D. A., and Maglio, V. J. 1974. Hipparions from the late Miocene and Pliocene of northwestern Kenya. Zool. Verhandelingen no. 134 (Leiden).

Maglio, V. J. 1973. Origin and evolution of the Elephantidae. *Trans. Am. Phil. Soc.*, n.s., 63:1-149.

Patterson, B. 1966. A new locality for early Pleistocene fossils in northwestern Kenya. *Nature* 212:577-81.

Patterson, B.; Behrensmeyer, A. K.; and Sill, W. D. 1970. Geology and fauna of a new Pliocene locality in northwestern Kenya. *Nature* 226:918-21.

Patterson, B., and Howells, W. W. 1967. Hominid humeral fragment from early Pleistocene of northwestern Kenya. *Azania* 2:1-15.

Robbins, L. H. 1967. A recent archaeological discovery in the Turkana District of northern Kenya. *Azania* 2:1-15.

_____. 1972. Archaeology in the Turkana District, Kenya. *Science* 176:359-66.

Part II

PALEONTOLOGY AND PALEOECOLOGY

Edited by Y. Coppens and F. C. Howell

14. INTRODUCTION

Y. Coppens

The following contributions to the symposium are devoted to paleontology in the broader sense, including vertebrate and invertebrate paleontology, palynology, and taphonomy and their biostratigraphic and paleoecological significance.

The sequences of sediments at the three principal fossiliferous areas of the Rudolf basin--the Kerio valley and environs to the southwest, the vast exposures to the east of the lake, and the Omo valley to the north--encompass the past six million years of geologic time. The localities to the southwest--Lothagam, Kanapoi, and Ekora (Smart, this symposium)--are the oldest, apparently representing the 6 to 4 m.y. interval, whereas those to the east and to the north broadly represent the time range after 4 m.y. These areas have proved extremely rich in vertebrate fossils and, although the precise yield to date is still not totaled, it is probably not an exaggeration to surmise that nearly a hundred thousand fossil specimens have been recovered from these parts of the basin over the past decade.

Evidently this is not a common situation, and its uniqueness should be recognized. It is so not only because of the particular geologic situations in this part of equatorial Africa, but also because systematic, intensive, and prolonged fieldwork has been done, including that devoted to paleontological survey and collecting. In particular, the Omo and East Rudolf expeditions have been enabled, through requisite and continued financial support, to conduct fieldwork with a diversity of participating scientists, numerous support personnel, and modern technology, including four-wheel-drive vehicles, light aircraft for logistic and photographic purposes, and on occasion (in the Omo), a helicopter for reconnaissance and survey, and even (once again in the Omo) light earthmoving equipment to expedite overburden removal at excavations. Indeed, on occasion upwards of an aggregate of 150 to 200 personnel, of whom some 50 have been scientific staff, have participated in summer field research in the Omo and at East Rudolf. Particular attention has been devoted to detailed geological mapping, and in conjunction with intensive fossil collecting this work has produced results rarely if ever achieved before. In these more northerly parts of the basin fieldwork has been most prolonged and intensive, partly because of the thickness, extent, and fossil (including hominid) yield of the sediments and the opportunities for radiometric age determinations on volcanics and for paleomagnetic sampling. However, nothing could have been accomplished had there not been the most favorable encouragement of these researches by the governments of Kenya and Ethiopia.

Initially, in the field, paleontological collecting of surface specimens has usually been undertaken without the benefit of small-scale geological mapping. This has indeed often been the case in the Rudolf basin where detailed cartographic and stratigraphic observations, in tectonically disturbed situations, have not always preceded such paleontological collecting. However, with thoughtful, consistent recording, annotation, and designation of localities, and with subsequent followup, it is possible for geological mapping and precise stratigraphic recording of localities to furnish the requisite data on provenance. This systematic spatial and stratigraphic delimitation of paleontological data is a necessary and relatively new aspect of such explorations in previously little known regions of Africa and Asia. Such procedures afford extremely useful and important data for taphonomical analysis (Behrensmeyer, this symposium). After such prospections, generally recorded on specially prepared aerial mosaics, excavation of particularly appropriate fossiliferous localities or horizons (see Johanson, Splingaer, and Boaz, this symposium), has afforded detailed taphonomic data on the mode of occurrence, taxonomic diversity, and composition of vertebrate fossiliferous areas, including sedimentary environments, species representation and diversity, frequencies, distribution patterns, orientation, and size classes. I suspect that the impetus toward precision in collecting and excavating paleontological and taphonomic evidence stems in part from procedures developed in prehistoric archeology.

The systematic search for remains of micromammals--insectivores, bats, rodents, and the smaller carnivores--has also become important (see Jaeger and Wesselman, this symposium). Many accumulations of such remains have been found on certain land surfaces and in some sedimentary situations at Olduvai Gorge during intensive excavations to expose hominid occurrences. In the Rudolf basin such excavations were initiated by J.-J. Jaeger and then pursued on a massive scale by H. B. Wesselman (during 1972-73). Some occurrences are now also known in the East Rudolf area. Merely ascertaining the presence of such suspected remains in an appropriate microfaunal source usually entails accumulating,kerosene-reducing, washing and sieving, and ultimately, handsorting perhaps as much as half a ton of raw sediment. At least in the Omo situation, if the occurrence contains microvertebrate fossils, ten times this amount must subsequently be processed to retrieve an adequate sample. Compared with most macrofaunal elements, these are much more suggestive, if not always representative, of overall paleoenvironmental and paleoclimatic conditions, and they are almost as sensitive a paleoenvironmental indicator as is pollen.

What is the destiny of such a massive accumulation of fossils? Surely, no one person can cope with such a diversity and wealth of vertebrate fossils! Only specialists experienced in the identification, taxonomy, and evolutionary history of particular taxa are capable of dealing with such problems--as we see in these symposium contributions.

Initially, such studies require, rightfully following tradition, the taxonomic identification, so far as possible, of the fossil collections. As a consequence there is an impressive list of species, some new to science and others recorded for the first time perhaps in this subcontinent. The dynamic nature of the fauna over several million years is in some way ascertained: its transformation, its evidence of immigration and disappearance, perhaps its indications of paleoenvironmental/paleoclimatic adjustments in the course of several million years. Finally, some biozonational aspects of species and their associations may be detected and hence a provincial,even a regional biostratigraphy, may be realized.

As a consequence of the field procedures other less conventional procedures have been made possible and are in process. All aspects of the stratigraphic and spatial provenance of fossil specimens, their specific and body part identification having been determined, these data are appropriately recorded and prepared for computerization (an elaborate recording and retrieval system having been first devised for the Omo collections by F. H. Brown and G. G. Eck). Consequently it is feasible to determine readily the presence or absence of taxa, their nature and frequency, and their occurrence in particular associations. The features of particular life associations, thanatocoenoses or even sometimes biocoenoses, may be discovered through such procedures. Biological insights are gained when the paleontological data thus compiled are brought into conjunction with various geological studies (Behrensmeyer, this symposium).

The collection and subsequent analysis of invertebrate, particularly molluscan, assemblages (Gautier, this symposium) has afforded an important new basis for paleoecological interpretation, as well as a significant local biostratigraphy.

The initial results of palynological analyses (largely in the Omo, but now in East Rudolf as well) have afforded a measure of both allochthonous and authochthonous plant communities (Bonnefille, this symposium). They also document an important and presumably significant change in the paleoenvironmental situation ~2 m.y. ago. Because of uneven preservation in tropical situations, such researches, which have meaning only in the perspective of the diversity of modern communities (cf. C. J. Carr, this symposium), have proved difficult and often frustrating; however, even rare successes are clearly crucial to the overall research goals. The low frequency of preserved and identifiable pollen in sediment samples is a major problem. However, the initial results of such researches indicate the necessity to pursue them arduously and intensively. Although detailed collections have been made of fish, birds, and diatoms and other algae of which fossil examples exist, they generally are not mentioned here, since they are waiting to be studied by specialists. They will surely add substantially to our understanding of the natural history of this part of the world during the Plio-Pleistocene.

Five days of discussion (in Nairobi) and six days of excursion (in northern Kenya and southwestern Ethiopia) gave all symposium participants an opportunity to examine the geological setting and ecological circumstances of the research materials.

However, as was indicated in the introduction to part 1 of the symposium, the most active paleontological discussions concerned interareal correlation. In fact, after the presentation of stratigraphic evidence and the radiometric and (initial) paleomagnetic evidence from the areas east and north of the Rudolf basin, it became evident that there was an obtrusive discrepancy in the correlation of the sequences, especially between middle sectors of the stratigraphic columns. Certain mammalian groups--especially Proboscidea (Beden), Suidae (Cooke), Bovidae (Gentry and Harris), and Equidae (Eisenmann), but perhaps also Carnivora (M. G. Leakey, and Howell and Petter) and Cercopithecoidea (M. G. Leakey and G. G. Eck)--were found to have different characteristics and species compositions in parts of the sections that might be presumed equivalent on the grounds of radiometric dates.

A number of explanations for this discrepancy were considered. To some it seemed possible that there had been distortion of radiometric characteristics at either East Rudolf or the Omo or both. However, should both sets of radiometric determinations be ultimately and independently confirmed, paleontological identifications and particularly their biostratigraphic implications will have to be carefully checked. Since biostratigraphic comparisons are not often employed for detecting small-scale time differences, this is a new opportunity for comparative paleobiological studies. Others suggested in symposium discussion and in papers (especially J. M. Harris and M. G. Leakey) that if the dates are correct, ecological differences between the northern and eastern portions of the basin could partly explain the differences in the composition of mammalian assemblages.

If the results of radiometric determinations for the Omo and East Rudolf successions are considered as a whole (cf. the introduction to part 1 by G. Ll. Isaac), it at once becomes apparent that there is a widespread overlap in the scatters of apparent ages of many units, so that the discrepancy may turn out to be less marked than it has appeared. However, if the taxonomy is correctly understood, there are differences in evolutionary stages between several mammalian lineages in East Rudolf and the Omo, and these differences still must be explained (see chapters by Cooke, by Gentry, and by Harris, this symposium).

This conference and its scientific participants have not sought to resolve these and other attendant problems. An advantage of such a gathering of fellow scientists is in fact the recognition and open discussion of such differences of interpretation, which can in many cases be resolved only by future research.

Most important, this gathering has displayed a new pattern of concerted research, in field and laboratory, among scientists of diverse nationalities, traditions, specialties and, perhaps, study methods. Thanks to thoughtful governments and to foundation resources, they have been able to work with fewer than usual constraints of time and money. Their research over the past decade has allowed the development of attitudes and a new set of goals of international consequence and of immediate relevance for the study of man's evolution and its natural setting everywhere.

15. MAMMALIAN FAUNAS OF THE OMO GROUP:
DISTRIBUTIONAL AND BIOSTRATIGRAPHICAL ASPECTS

Y. Coppens and F. C. Howell

The Omo Group comprises several fossiliferous formations with an aggregate thickness of more than 1,000 m and spans a time range of some 3.5 m.y. This conference affords the opportunity to review some aspects of its mammalian biostratigraphy, as thus far known, on the basis of the work of the various specialists[1] entrusted with the study of fossil collections assembled by the Omo Research Expedition.

Previous Biozonation

Shortly after fieldwork was started in the lower Omo basin it appeared to one of us (Coppens, in Arambourg, Chavaillon, and Coppens 1967, 1972) that there were notable transformations of the vertebrate fauna through the long Omo succession. As an initial attempt at subdivision the fauna was grouped in four associations on the basis of four type localities.

The earliest locality (Omo 20-4), in Member B, Shungura Formation, was characterized by the association of *Elephas africanavus* (here *Loxodonta adaurora*), *Elephas recki* (here *E. recki* stage I), *Deinotherium bozasi*, *Hippopotamus protamphibius* (here *H.* sp. nov. D), *Metridiochoerus andrewsi* (here *Metridiochoerus jacksoni*), *Tragelaphus nakuae*, *Dinopithecus brumpti* (here *Theropithecus* sp.), *Crocodilus niloticus*, *Euthecodon brumpti*, Chelonia, and Siluridae.

The second oldest locality (Omo 18), in Member C, Shungura Formation, was characterized by *Elephas recki* (here *E. recki* stage IIA), *Deinotherium bozasi*, *Hippopotamus protamphibius*, *Omochoerus heseloni* (here *Mesochoerus limnetes*), *Aepyceros melampus* (here *Aepyceros* sp.), *Tragelaphus nakuae*, *Giraffa gracilis*, *Dinopithecus brumpti* (here *Theropithecus* sp./*brumpti*), *Paraustralopithecus aethiopicus* (here Hominidae), *Crocodilus niloticus*, *Euthecodon brumpti*, "*Rhinoceros*," Chelonia, and Siluridae.

The third oldest locality (Omo 6), in lower Member G, Shungura Formation, was characterized by progressive *Elephas recki* (here *E. recki* stage IIB), *Deinotherium bozasi*, *Diceros* cf. *bicornis*, *Hippopotamus protamphibius*, *Metridiochoerus andrewsi*, *Notochoerus capensis* (here *N. scotti*) *Omochoerus heseloni* (here *Mesochoerus limnetes*), *Aepyceros melampus* (here

1. M. Beden, H. B. S. Cooke, Y. Coppens, G. G. Eck, V. Eisenmann, A. W. Gentry, J.-L. Grattard, C. Guerin, D. A. Hooijer, F. C. Howell, J.-J. Jaeger, M. G. Leakey, R. E. F. Leakey, G. Petter, S. C. Savage and H. B. Wesselman. For institutional affiliations, see List of Participants.

Aepyceros sp.), *Tragelaphus nakuae*, *Dinopithecus brumpti* (here *Theropithecus* sp./*brumpti*), *Crocodilus niloticus*, *Euthecodon brumpti*, Chelonia, and Siluridae.

The youngest locality (Omo 2) in uppermost Member G, Shungura Formation, was characterized by progressive *Elephas recki* (here *E. recki* stage IIB), *Stylohipparion albertense* (here *Hipparion ethiopicum*), *Hippopotamus protamphibius*, *Hippopotamus amphibius* (here *H. gorgops*), evolved Suidae, *Phacochoerus africanus* (here *P.* cf. *aethiopicus*), *Menelikia lyrocera*, *Crocodilus niloticus*, *Euthecodon brumpti*, Chelonia, and Siluridae.

Subsequently (Coppens, in Arambourg, Chavaillon, and Coppens 1969, table 1) these associations were refined and others were distinguished: a fauna with mastodont (*Anancus*) below the basalt in the Mursi Formation; and a fauna, represented in the Usno Formation localities and the lowermost members (Basal and A and B members) of the Shungura Formation, characterized by *Nyanzachoerus*, primitive *Omochoerus* (here *Mesochoerus*), and *Elephas africanavus* (here *Loxodonta adaurora*). A faunal transition appeared toward members C and D. A third set of associations, corresponding to the "classic" Omo fauna described by Arambourg (1947) was represented in members C, D, E, F, and lower G, with *Elephas recki*, *Omochoerus heseloni* (here *Mesochoerus limnetes*). A further change appeared in members F and G, with progressive *Elephas recki* in Member F (here *E. recki* stage IIB), and *Phacochoerus*, *Equus*, *Omochoerus* (here progressive *Mesochoerus* = *M. olduvaiensis*) in Member G. This long sequence ended, in members G, H, and J, with a large tetraprotodont hippo (here *H. gorgops*).

Thus it was possible to define a series of faunal zones and for the first time, owing to the exceptionally protracted and continuous Omo succession, to treat faunal transitions (Coppens 1972) (table 1).

The zone of Kaiso 1 (Zone VI) is characterized by *Primelephas*, *Elephas*, *Hipparion*, *Anancus*, *Stegodon*, *Nyanzachoerus*, hexaprotodont *Hippopotamus*, and, in broadly contemporaneous localities elsewhere, *Stegotetrabelodon*, *Deinotherium*, *Stylohipparion* (here *Hipparion*), *Libytherium* (here *Sivatherium*), and *Australopithecus*. It is to Zone VI that the faunal association of the Mursi Formation (Omo O) should be assigned.

The zone of Omo 1 (Zone V) corresponds to the faunal assemblages of the Basal Member and members A, B, and C (the last being in fact transitional between two zones), Shungura Formation. It is characterized by *Stegodon*, *Nyanzachoerus*, hexaprotodont *Hippopotamus*, *Deinotherium*, *Stylohipparion* (here *Hipparion*), *Libytherium* (here *Sivatherium*), *Elephas*, and *Australopithecus*. *Primelephas* and *Anancus* are no longer represented.

The zone of Omo 2 (Zone IV) corresponds to the faunal assemblages of members C, D, E, F, and lower G (the last being transitional between two zones) of the Shungura Formation. It is characterized by hexaprotodont *Hippopotamus*, *Deinotherium*, *Stylohipparion* (here *Hipparion*), *Libytherium* (here *Sivatherium*), *Elephas*, and *Australopithecus*. *Stegodon* and *Nyanzachoerus* are no longer represented.

Finally, the zone of Olduvai 1/lower II (Zone III) is characterized by *Deinotherium*, *Stylohipparion* (here *Hipparion*), *Libytherium* (here *Sivatherium*), *Elephas*, *Australopithecus*, and the appearance of *Equus* and of *Homo*. The hexaprotodont *Hippopotamus* is no longer represented. This zone, within which the faunal assemblages of members G (upper) and H and the uppermost members J, K, and L exposed in the Kalam area fall, constitutes the Omo 3 zone.

An Updated Biozonation

Some 100 genera and more than 150 species of Mammalia are thus far known from Omo Group formations, which makes possible some further refinement of the previous (1972) biozonation proposed by Coppens. It is based essentially on the presence or absence of

Table 1

Biozonation of the Omo Group

Members	1967 (type localities)	1969 (zones)	1971 (zones)
Shungura Formation L			
K			
J		IV	Olduvai 1 and lower II = Omo 3
H			
G	Omo 2		
F	Omo 6		
E			
D		III	Omo 2
C	Omo 18		
B	Omo 20	II	Omo 1
A			
Basal Member			
Mursi Formation		I	Kaiso 1 = Omo 0

SOURCES: Arambourg, Chavaillon, and Coppens 1967, 1969; Coppens 1972.

particular taxa and may well require further revision as certain families receive more detailed study. Ultimately, quantitative treatment of the assemblages according to sedimentary units (close to a hundred of which are known now from the 13 members of the Shungura
Formation) will permit a fuller appreciation of the relative proportions of the various
taxa represented through the succession.

An inventory of the mammalian taxa of the Omo succession is set out in table 2. From
this table the faunal associations of the four major zones (Omo 0, 1, 2, and 3) may be discerned, and they are briefly discussed below. The first appearance of a species appears to
be of greater significance than its extinction. The table shows the apparent time of initial appearance, apparent duration, and apparent time of disappearance or extinction, at
least in the Omo succession. For certain species this documentation may indeed reflect
actual first appearance and extinction times, at least in this part of Africa. In some instances, samples are large enough so we can statistically judge time of disappearance (for

Table 2

Distribution of Mammalian Taxa in Formations of the Omo Group, Southwestern Ethiopia

Taxon	Mursi Fm. (4.05)	Basal Mb.	Mb.A	Usno Fm. (2.97)	Mb.B (2.95)	Mb.C (2.39)	Mb.D (2.12)	Mb.E (2.03)	Mb.F (1.93)	Mb.G	Mb.H (1.83)	Kalam (1.34)
Anancus kenyensis	X											
Stegodon cf. kaisensis			?	X	X	?						
Loxodonta adaurora	X		X	X	X	?	?	?				
Loxodonta cf. atlantica							X					
Loxodonta sp.												X
Elephas recki stage I			X	X	X	?						
stage IIA					X	X	X	?	?			
stage IIB								?	X	X		X
stage III											X	X
Deinotherium bozasi	X		X	X	X	X	X	X	X	X	X	X
Ceratotherium praecox	X											
Ceratotherium simum				X	X	X	X	X	X	X		
Diceros bicornis	X					X	X		X	X		
Ancylotherium hennigi	X					X	X			X		
Hipparion turkanense	X											
Hipparion cf. albertense			X	X	X	X	?	?	X	X		
Hipparion cf. sitifense					?	?	?					
Hipparion ethiopicum								?	X	X	X	X
Equus sp. (large)										X	X	X
Equus sp. (small)									X	X	2 spp.	
Hippopotamus sp. nov. D	X		X	X	X							
Hippopotamus protamphibius						X	X	X	X	X	X	
Hippopotamus sp. A			X			X	X			X		

Table 2—Continued

Species							level unknown	
Hippopotamus gorgops	X					X	X	X
Hippopotamus sp. nov. B						X	X	X
Nyanzachoerus jaegeri			X	X				
Nyanzachoerus pattersoni	cf.	X	X	X	X	X		
Nyanzachoerus kanamensis			?	?				
Notochoerus capensis		X	X					
Notochoerus euilus		X	X	cf.	cf.			
Notochoerus scotti		cf.?	cf.	X	X	X	X	sp.
Notochoerus sp. nov.				X		X		
Mesochoerus limnetes		X	X	X	X	X	X	
Mesochoerus cf. *olduvaiensis*						X	X	X
Metridiochoerus jacksoni	?	X	X	X	X	X	X	
Phacochoerus cf. *aethiopicus*		?	?	?	?	X	X	X
Phacochoerus antiquus						X	X	
Metridiochoerus andrewsi		X	X	X	X	X		X
Stylochoerus nicoli						X	X	X
Stylochoerus meadowsi						X	?	X
Stylochoerus compactus							?	X
Sivatherium sp.		X	X	X	X	X		X
Giraffa cf. *jumae*		X	X	X	X	X		?
Giraffa nov. sp.		X	X	X	X	X	X	X
Giraffa gracilis	X	X	X	X	X	X	X	X
Camelus sp.		X	X	X	X	X		X
Taurotragus sp.								
Strepsiceros imberbis								X
Tragelaphus strepsiceros	X					X	X	
Tragelaphus sp.								X
Tragelaphus gaudryi			X	X	X	X	cf.	X
Tragelaphus ?*pricei*			X	X				

Table 2--Continued

K-Ar Ages

Taxon	Mursi Fm. (4.05)	Basal Mb.	Mb.A	Usno Fm. (2.97)	Mb.B (2.95)	Mb.C (2.39)	Mb.D (2.12)	Mb.E (2.03)	Mb.F (1.93)	Mb.G	Mb.H (1.83)	Kalam (1.34)
Tragelaphus sp.						X	X	X				
Tragelaphus nakuae				X	X	X	X	X	X	X	X	X
Syncerus sp.					X	X				X		
Pelorovis sp.						X			X	X		
?*Hemibos* sp.								X		X		
Bovini spp. indet.				X	X	X	X	X	X	X	X	X
Kobus sigmoidalis					X	X	X	X	X	X	X	X
Kobus ellipsiprymnus										X	X	X
Kobus kob							?	?		?		X
Kobus ?*patulicornis*					X							
Kobus sp.					X	X						
Kobus ancystrocera					X	X			X	X		X
Menelikia sp.						X	X			X		
Menelikia lyrocera								X	X	X		
Menelikia lyrocera subsp. nov.												X
Redunca sp.					X	X		X				
Reduncini sp. indet.	X										X	sp. nov.
Hippotragini sp. indet.						X						
cf. *Connochaetes* sp.				X								
Megalotragus ?*kattwinkeli*										X		X
Oreonagor/Connochaetes sp.					X							
Beatragus antiquus											X	
Parmularius altidens												X
Parmularius/Damaliscus sp.						X						
Alcelaphini spp. indet.				X	X	X	X	X	X	X	X	X
Aepyceros sp.				X	X	X	X	X	X	X	X	X
Aepyceros sp.	X			X	X	X	X	X	X	X	X	X

Table 2--Continued

Neotragini spp. indet.						
Antidorcas ?recki	X	X	X	X		X
Gazella praethomsoni	?	X	X			X
Antilope subtorta				X		
Antilopini indet.	X	X	X			X
Orycteropus sp.	X			X		
Gigantohyrax sp.			X			
Heterohyrax sp.	X					
Lepus sp.				X		
Mastomys cf. minor	X	X	X	X		
Pelomys sp.	X	X				
cf. Oenomys sp.		X				
Arvicanthis sp.	X		X	X		
Aethomys sp.			X			
Thallomys cf. quadriiobatus			X			
Grammomys sp.	X					
Mus (Leggada)/sp.	X					
Lemniscomys sp.	X					
Muridae indet.	X	X	X	X		
Tatera sp.	X	X	X			X
Gerbillurus sp.			X			
Dendromus sp.			X			
Jaculus cf. orientalis			X			
Xerus cf. erythropus	X					
Xerus sp.			X			
Paraxerus cf. ochraceus	X		X			
Sciuridae indet.	X		X			

Table 2--Continued

Taxon	Mursi Fm. (4.05)	Basal Mb.	Mb.A	Usno Fm. (2.97)	Mb.B (2.95)	Mb.C (2.39)	Mb.D (2.12)	Mb.E (2.03)	Mb.F (1.93)	Mb.G	Mb.H (1.83)	Kalam (1.34)
Heterocephalus sp.												
Thryonomys cf. *swinderianus*					X				X			X
Xenohystrix cf. *crassidens*					X							
Hystrix cf. *makapanensis*				X		X		X		X		
Hystrix cf. *cristata*										X		X
Eidolon cf. *helvum*					X							
Taphozous sp.					X							
Coleura sp.									X			
Hipposideros sp. A					X							
Hipposideros sp. B									X			
Crocidura sp. A					X							
Crocidura sp. B					X							
Suncus cf. *infinitesimus*					X							
Helogale sp.					X				X			
Mungos sp.						X						
Herpestes sp.						X						
Viverra (Civettictis) sp.						X	X	X		X		
Viverra sp.							X	X				
Viverra leakeyi				cf.		X				X		
Pseudocivetta ingens										X		
Genetta sp.						X		X				
Genetta sp. nov.					X							
Mellivorinae indet. (large)											X	
Lutra sp.				X								
Enhydriodon sp. nov.				X	X	X		X	X			
Lutrinae indet.				X				X				

Table 2--Continued

	cf.									cf.	
Euryboas sp.											
Percrocuta sp.	X	X									
Hyaena aff. makapani	X	X		X			X	X			X
Crocuta crocuta							X			
Hyaenidae indet.	X		X				X			
Homotherium sp.	X	X	X	X			X	X		
Megantereon sp.	X	?	X				X	X		
Dinofelis sp.	X	X	X	X			X	X		
Panthera leo										X
Panthera pardus	X	X	X	X			X	X		
Panthera crassidens		X					X	X		
Acinonyx sp.								X		
Felinae indet. (large)	X	X	X				X	X		
Felis (lynx) caracal	X						X		X	
Felinae indet. (small)	X	X	X				X	X		
Galago cf. senegalensis	X									
Galago cf. demidoffi	X									
Galago sp.	X									
Colobus sp.										X
Colobinae gen. sp. indet. A	X	X		X						
Colobinae gen. sp. nov.	X	X	X	X	X		X	X		X
Colobinae gen. sp. indet. C							X	X	X	
Cercopithecus sp.	X	X		X						
Papionini gen. et sp. indet. A	X	X	X				X	X		
Papionini gen. et sp. indet. B	X	X		X			X	X		X
Papio sp.	X	X		X	X		X	X		X
Theropithecus sp.	X	X		X	X		X	X	X	X
Theropithecus brumpti			X				X	X		
Australopithecus sp.	X	X	X				X	X		
Hominidae gen. sp. indet.	X	?	X	?			X	X	X	X

example, *Anancus*) or initial appearance. However, in other instances the distribution largely reflects the occurrence of specific taxa at particular localities. This is so for the majority of micromammals, which are relatively abundant in two localities in members B and F which have been intensively washed for microfossils. These taxa are therefore of interest in a faunal association for their ecological and sometimes chronological significance; but their overall absence is at least in part more apparent than real.

Omo 0 Zone

The Omo 0 zone is represented by the vertebrates from the Mursi Formation which are older than 4 m.y. (Brown and Nash, this symposium). Thus far 12 genera and 13 species of mammals have been determined from the Yellow Sands locality where this formation crops out. Of the 13 species, 5 are apparently restricted to this formation: the gomphothere *Anancus kenyensis*; the extinct white rhino, *Ceratotherium praecox*; the primitive hipparion, *Hipparion turkanense*, probable ancestor of the hipparionines with ectostylids (*H*. cf. *albertense*, *H. ethiopicum*); an unnamed species of *Tragelaphus*, probably ancestral to *T. gaudryi* of the Shungura Formation; and an unnamed species of *Aepyceros*, more robust than, but perhaps ancestral to, the species of the Shungura Formation. There is also a hexaprotodont hippo, close enough to tetraprotodont *H. protamphibius* to represent an ancestral species; it recurs in Shungura Formation, Member B. Two species of *Nyanzachoerus* are represented, comparable to those found in older as well as younger localities. The primitive loxodont, *L. adaurora*, is represented, as is *Deinotherium*. Finally, there are some remains of a black rhino and perhaps a cheetah. This association might be conveniently characterized as the hexaprotodont *Hippopotamus protamphibius* zone.

Faunal List of Omo 0 Zone

Proboscidea-Gomphotheriidae: *Anancus kenyensis*; Elephantidae: *Loxodonta adaurora*; Deinotheridae: *Deinotherium bozasi*

Perissodactyla-Rhinocerotidae: *Ceratotherium praecox*, *Diceros bicornis*; Equidae: *Hipparion turkanense*

Artiodactyla-Hippopotamidae: *Hippopotamus* sp. nov. D; Suidae: *Nyanzachoerus jaegeri*, *Nyanzachoerus pattersoni*; Bovidae: *Tragelaphus* sp., *Aepyceros* sp., Reduncini sp. indet.

Carnivora-Felidae: cf. *Acinonyx* sp.

Omo 1 Zone

The Omo 1 zone is represented by the vertebrates from the lowermost members of the Shungura Formation (Basal Member, members A, B, and C, the latter transitional to zone 2) and those from the Usno Formation. The oldest localities of the latter (White Sands, Brown Sands) are now known to correspond with unit B-2 of the Shungura Formation., Member B (de Heinzelin, Haesaerts, and Howell, this symposium; Brown and Shuey, this symposium). The age of the zone extends from ~3.5 to 2.5 m.y.

Thus far 74 genera and 113 species of mammals have been identified from these horizons. A diversity of archaic elements are represented: *Stegodon, *Loxodonta adaurora*, *Elephas recki* stage 1, *Hipparion* cf. *albertense*, three species of *Nyanzachoerus*, two species of *Notochoerus*, an early form of *Mesochoerus limnetes*, *Tragelaphus pricei*, *Kobus patulicornis*, perhaps *Percrocuta*, *Hyaena* aff. *makapani*, and the hexaprotodont *Hippopotamus* sp. nov. D.

Other species, with variously protracted temporal distributions, such as *Deinotherium bozasi*, also occur, along with a new species of *Notochoerus* and *Notochoerus scotti*, *Metridiochoerus jacksoni*, *Sivatherium*, the first appearance of *Giraffa gracilis* and *G. jumae* as well as new small *Giraffa* sp., *Tragelaphus nakuae*, *Camelus*, and early Hominidae (referred to *Australopithecus* cf. *africanus*). This association, characterized by the species marked *, might be conveniently designated the *Elephas recki* stage 1 zone.

Faunal List of Omo 1 Zone

Proboscidea-Elephantidae: *Loxodonta adaurora*, *Elephas recki* st. 1, *Stegodon* cf. *kaisensis*, *Elephas recki* st. II A; Deinotheridae: *Deinotherium bozasi*

Perissodactyla-Rhinocerotidae: *Diceros bicornis*, *Ceratotherium simum*; Chalicotheridae: *Ancylotherium hennigi*; Equidae: *Hipparion* cf. *albertense*, *Hipparion ethiopicum*

Artiodactyla-Hippopotamidae: *Hippopotamus* sp. nov. D, *Hippopotamus* sp. A, *Hippopotamus protamphibius*, *Hippopotamus* sp. nov. B; Suidae: *Nyanzachoerus jaegeri*, *Nyanzachoerus pattersoni*, *Metridiochoerus jacksoni*, *Notochoerus euilus*, *Mesochoerus limnetes*, *Notochoerus capensis*, *Notochoerus* sp. nov., *Nyanzachoerus kanamensis*, *Notochoerus scotti*, *Phacochoerus* cf. *aethiopicus*, *Metridiochoerus andrewsi*; Giraffidae:*Giraffa gracilis*, *Sivatherium* sp., *Giraffa* sp. nov., *Giraffa* cf. *jumae*; Camelidae; *Camelus*; Bovidae: cf. *Connochaetes* sp., *Tragelaphus nakuae*, *Gazella praethomsoni*, Bovini spp. indet., Alcelaphini spp. indet., *Aepyceros* sp., *Oreonagor/Connochaetes* sp., *Kobus patulicornis*, *Kobus* sp., *Redunca* sp., *Synceros* sp., *Kobus ancystrocera*, *Antidorcas recki*, *Tragelaphus ? pricei*, *Parmularius/Damaliscus* sp., Hippotragini sp. indet., *Antilope subtorta*, *Menelikia* sp., *Tragelaphus* sp., *Tragelaphus gaudryi*, *Pelorovis* sp., *Kobus sigmoidalis*

Tubulidentata-*Orycteropus* sp.

Hyracoidea-*Heterohyrax* sp., *Gigantohyrax* sp.

Rodentia-*Hystrix* cf. *makapanensis*, *Grammomys* sp., *Mus* (*Leggada*) sp., *Lemniscomys* sp., *Xerus erythropus*, *Xenohystrix* cf. *crassidens*, Sciuridae indet., *Pelomys* sp. *Paraxerus* cf. *ochraceus*, *Arvicanthis* sp., *Mastomys* cf. *minor*, Muridae indet., *Tatera* sp., *Thryonomys* cf. *swinderianus*, cf. *Oenomys*

Chiroptera-*Eidolon* cf. *helvum*, *Taphozous* sp., *Hipposideros* sp. A

Insectivora-*Crocidura* sp. A, *Crocidura* sp. B, *Suncus* cf. *infinitesimus*

Carnivora-Felidae: *Acinonyx* sp., *Dinofelis* sp., Felinae (small) indet., *Homotherium* sp., *Megantereon* sp., *Panthera pardus*, Felinae indet. (large), *Felis* (*Lynx*) *caracal*, *Panthera crassidens*; Hyaenidae: *Percrocuta* sp., *Hyaena* aff. *makapani*, Hyaenidae indet.; Mustelidae: *Lutra* sp., *Enhydriodon* sp. nov.; Viverridae: *Viverra leakeyi*, *Genetta* sp. nov., *Helogale* sp., *Mungos* sp., *Herpestes* sp., *Genetta* sp., *Viverra* (*Civettictis*) sp.

Primates-Prosimii: *Galago* cf. *senegalensis*, *Galago* cf. *demidoffi*, *Galago* sp.; Cercopithecoidea. Colobidae: Colobinae gen. and sp. nov., Colobinae gen. and sp. indet. A, Colobinae gen. and sp. indet. C; Cercopithecidae: *Papio* sp., *Theropithecus* sp., *Theropithecus brumpti*, Papionini gen. and sp. indet. A, *Cercopithecus* sp.; Hominidae: *Australopithecus* sp., Hominidae gen. and sp. indet.

Omo 2 Zone

The Omo 2 zone is represented by the vertebrates from Member C (shared with those of Zone 1, with which it is transitional) and members D, E, F, and G (the latter shared with Zone 3, with which it is transitional) of the Shungura Formation. The age of the zone extends from ~2.5 to 1.9 m.y.

Faunal List of Omo 2 Zone

Proboscidea-Elephantidae: *Loxodonta adaurora, Elephas recki* st. I, *Elephas recki* st. II A, *Loxodonta* cf. *atlantica, Elephas recki* st. II B; Deinotheridae: *Deinotherium bozasi*

Perissodactyla-Rhinocerotidae: *Diceros bicornis, Ceratotherium simum*; Chalicotheridae: *Ancylotherium hennigi*; Equidae: *Hipparion* cf. *albertense, Hipparion ethiopicum, Hipparion* cf. *sitifense, Equus* sp. (large)

Artiodactyla-Hippopotamidae: *Hippopotamus* sp. A, *Hippopotamus protamphibius, Hippopotamus* sp. nov. B, *Hippopotamus gorgops*; Suidae: *Nyanzachoerus pattersoni, Metridiochoerus jacksoni, Notochoerus euilus, Mesochoerus limnetes, Notochoerus* sp. nov., *Notochoerus scotti, Phacochoerus* cf. *aethiopicus, Metridiochoerus andrewsi*; Giraffidae: *Giraffa gracilis, Sivatherium* cf., *Giraffa* nov. sp., *Giraffa* cf. *jumae*; Camelidae: *Camelus* sp.; Bovidae: *Tragelaphus nakuae, Gazella praethomsoni*, Bovini spp. indet., Alcelaphini spp. indet., *Aepyceros* sp., *Redunca* sp., *Syncerus* sp., *Kobus ancystrocera, Antidorcas recki, Tragelaphus* ? *pricei*, Hippotragini sp. indet., *Parmularius/Damaliscus* sp., *Antilope subtorta, Menelikia* sp., *Tragelaphus* sp., *Tragelaphus gaudryi, Kobus sigmoidalis, Pelorovis* sp., *Kobus kob, Menelikia lyrocera*, Neotragini spp. indet., *Hemibos* sp., *Tragelaphus strepsiceros, Kobus ellipsiprymnus, Megalotragus kattwinkeli*

Tubulidentata-*Orycteropus* sp.

Hyracoidea-*Gigantohyrax* sp.

Lagomorpha-*Lepus* sp.

Rodentia-*Hystrix* cf. *makapanensis, Pelomys* sp., *Paraxerus* cf. *ochraceus, Mastomys* cf. *minor, Arvicanthis* sp., Muridae indet., *Tatera* sp., *Thryonomys* cf. *swinderianus* cf. *Oenomys* sp., *Aethomys* sp., *Thallomys* cf. *quadrilobatus, Gerbillurus* sp., *Dendromus* sp., *Jaculus* cf. *orientalis, Xerus* sp., *Heterocephalus* sp., *Hystrix* cf. *cristata*

Chiroptera-*Coleura* sp., *Hipposideros* sp. B.

Carnivora-Felidae: *Acinonyx* sp., *Dinofelis* sp., Felinae indet. (small), *Homotherium* sp., *Megantereon* sp., *Panthera pardus*, Felinae indet. (large), *Felis (Lynx) caracal, Panthera crassidens*; Hyaenidae: *Hyaena* aff. *makapani*, Hyaenidae indet. *Hyaena hyaena, Euryboas* sp., *Crocuta crocuta*; Mustelidae: *Enhydriodon* sp. nov., Mellivorinae indet. (large), Lutrinae indet.; Viverridae: *Viverra leakeyi, Helogale* sp., *Mungos* sp., *Herpestes* sp., *Genetta* sp., *Viverra (Civettictis)* sp., *Viverra* sp., *Pseudocivetta ingens*

Primates-Cercopithecoidea. Colobidae: Colobinae nov. gen. nov. sp., Colobinae gen. and sp. indet. A, Colobinae gen. and sp. indet. C; Cercopithecidae: *Papio* sp., *Theropithecus* sp. (aff. *oswaldi*), *Theropithecus brumpti, Cercopithecus* sp., Papionini gen. and sp. indet. A and B; Hominidae: *Australopithecus* spp., Hominidae gen. and sp. indet.

Thus far 75 genera and 115 species of mammals have been identified from these horizons. The studies of M. Beden (Proboscidea, this symposium) and A. W. Gentry (Bovidae, this symposium) have shown that it is possible to divide this zone into two subzones at the level of Member E. The zone is characterized by *Elephas recki* stage II, type *Mesochoerus limnetes*, *Metridiochoerus andrewsi*, *Hippopotamus protamphibius* (tetraprotodont), hexaprotodont *Hippopotamus* sp. nov. A, *Tragelaphus gaudryi*, *T. nakuae*, *Kobus sigmoidalis*, *Menelikia* sp. (ancestral species), *Menelikia lyrocera*, *Theropithecus brumpti*, *T.* aff. *oswaldi*, as well as *Notochoerus scotti*, *N.* sp. nov., *Metridiochoerus jacksoni*, *Giraffa gracilis*, *Kobus ancystrocera*. In its earlier part some older elements (*Loxodonta adaurora*, *Nyanzachoerus pattersoni*, *Notochoerus euilus*) disappear, and in its uppermost part some new elements (*Equus*, *Hippopotamus gorgops*) appear for the first time. This association can be conveniently designated the tetraprotodont *Hippopotamus protamphibius* zone.

Omo 3 Zone

The Omo 3 zone corresponds to the first zone of Olduvai, representing Beds I and lower II (pre-Lemuta Member). It comprises the faunas of Member G (shared with Omo Zone 2) and those of members H, J, K, L, Shungura Formation. The age of the zone extends from ~1.9 to 1.0 m.y.

Thus far 53 genera and 85 species have been identified from these horizons. It is characterized by *Elephas recki* stage III, *Equus* spp., *Hippopotamus gorgops*, progressive *Mesochoerus limnetes/Mesochoerus olduvaiensis*, *Kobus ellipsiprymnus*, *Megalotragus kattwinkeli*, a progressive subspecies of *Menelikia lyrocera*, *Parmularius altidens*, *Beatragus antiquus*, *Stylochoerus nicoli*, *Notochoerus scotti*, *Deinotherium bozasi*, *Hipparion ethiopicum*, *Giraffa* cf. *jumae*, *Hystrix cristata*. Many species characteristic of Zone 2 seem to disappear in the course of or subsequent to (upper) Member G times: *Giraffa gracilis*, hexaprotodont *Hippopotamus* sp. nov. A, *Notochoerus* sp. nov. perhaps *Sivatherium*, *Giraffa* sp. nov. (small), *Tragelaphus nakuae*, *Gazella praethomsoni*, *Hystrix* cf. *makapanensis*, *Hippopotamus protamphibius*, *Metridiochoerus andrewsi*, *Tragelaphus gaudryi*, *Kobus sigmoidalis*, *Theropithecus brumpti*. This association can be conveniently designated the *Hippopotamus gorgops* zone.

Faunal List of Omo 3 Zone

Proboscidea-Elephantidae: *Elephas recki* st. II B, *Loxodonta* sp., *Elephas recki* st. III; Deinotheridae: *Deinotherium bozasi*

Perissodactyla-Rhinocerotidae: *Diceros bicornis*, *Ceratotherium simum*; Chalicotheridae: *Ancylotherium hennigi*; Equidae: *Hipparion ethiopicum*, *Hipparion* cf. *sitifense*, *Equus* sp. (large), *Equus* sp. (small)

Artiodactyla-Hippopotamidae: *Hippopotamus* sp. A, *Hippopotamus* sp. nov. B, *Hippopotamus gorgops*; Suidae: *Metridiochoerus jacksoni*, *Mesochoerus limnetes*, *Notochoerus* sp. nov., *Notochoerus scotti*, *Phacochoerus* cf. *aethiopicus*, *Metridiochoerus andrewsi*, *Phacochoerus antiquus*, *Stylochoerus nicoli*, *Stylochoerus meadowsi*, *Mesochoerus* cf. *olduvaiensis*; Giraffidae: *Giraffa gracilis*, *Sivatherium* sp., *Giraffa* sp. nov., *Giraffa* cf. *jumae*; Camelidae: *Camelus* sp.; Bovidae: *Tragelaphus nakuae*, *Gazella praethomsoni*, Bovini spp. indet., Alcelaphini spp. indet., *Aepyceros* sp., *Syncerus* sp., *Kobus ancystrocera*, *Antidorcas recki*, *Tragelaphus gaudryi*, *Pelorovis* sp., *Kobus sigmoidalis*, *Kobus kob*, *Hemibos* sp., *Menelikia lyrocera*, Neotragini spp. indet., *Tragelaphus strepsiceros*, *Kobus ellipsiprymnus*, *Megalotragus kattwinkeli*, *Beatragus antiquus*, *Menelikia lyrocera* subsp. nov., *Parmularius altidens*, *Taurotragus* sp.

Rodentia:*Hystrix* aff. *makapanensis*, *Mastomys* cf. *minor*, *Arvicanthis* sp., Muridae indet., *Tatera* sp., *Thryonomys* cf. *swinderanius*, *Hystrix* cf. *cristata*

Carnivora-Felidae: *Acinonyx* sp., *Dinofelis* sp., *Homotherium* sp., *Magantereon* sp., *Panthera pardus*, Felinae indet. (large), *Panthera crassidens*, *Panthera leo;* Hyaenidae: *Hyaena hyaena*, *Crocuta crocuta;* Viverridae: *Viverra leakeyi*, *Viverra (Civettictis)* sp., *Pseudocivetta ingens*.

Primates-Cercopithecoidea. Colobidae: Colobinae gen. and sp. nov., Colobinae gen. and sp. indet. C, *Colobus* sp.; Cercopithecidae: *Papio* sp., *Theropithecus brumpti; Theropithecus* sp., (aff. *oswaldi*), *Cercopithecus* sp., Papionini gen. and sp. indet. B; Hominidae: *Australopithecus* spp., *Homo* sp., Hominidae gen. and sp. indet.

Concluding Remarks

Table 3 gives a summary of the principal taxa characteristic of each major zone. Table 4 summarizes the stratigraphic distribution of those species taken as types for each Omo zone. Ultimately each of these distributions will be susceptible to further refinement as studies are intensified at the unit level and as the detailed frequencies of species are worked out. However, the very protracted, richly fossiliferous sequence provided by the formations of the Omo Group--well dated radiometrically and magnetostratigraphically-- already afford the critical comparative reference for other African fossil occurrences of Pliocene/Pleistocene age.

References

Arambourg, C. 1947. *Mission scientifique de l'Omo (1932-1933)*. Vol. 1. *Géologie-Anthropologie*, fasc. 3, pp. 231-562. Mémoire, Muséum national d'histoire naturelle (Paris).

Arambourg, C.; Chavaillon, J.; and Coppens, Y. 1967. Premiers résultats de la nouvelle mission de l'Omo (1967). *C. R. Acad. Sci. (Paris)*, ser. D. 265:1891-96.

_____. 1969. Résultats de la nouvelle mission de l'Omo (2ème campagne 1968). *C. R. Acad. Sci. (Paris)*, ser. D, 268:759-62.

_____. 1972. Expédition internationale de recherches paléontologiques dans la vallée l'Omo (Ethiopie) en 1967. *Actes du 6e Congrès panafricain de préhistoire et d'études du quaternaire*, Dakar, 2-8 December 1967, pp. 135-40.

Cooke, H. B. S., and Maglio, V. J. 1972. Plio-Pleistocene stratigraphy in Eastern Africa in relation to proboscidean and suid evolution. In *Calibration of hominoid evolution*, ed. W. W. Bishop and J. A. Miller, pp. 303-29. Edinburgh: Scottish Academic Press; Toronto: University of Toronto Press.

Coppens, Y. 1972. Tentative de zonation du Pliocène et du Pléistocène d'Afrique par les grands mammifères. *C. R. Acad. Sci. (Paris)*, ser. D. 274:181-84.

_____. 1973. Les faunes de vertébrés du Pliocène et du Pléistocène ancien d'Afrique. *Actes du Ve Congrès du Néogène mediterranéen*, Lyon, September 1971. Editions du B.R.G.M.

Coppens, Y., and Howell, F. C. 1974. Les faunes de mammifères fossiles des formations plio-pléistocènes de l'Omo en Ethiopie (Proboscidea, Perissodactyla, Artiodactyla). *C. R. Acad. Sci. (Paris)*, ser. D, 278:2275-78.

Coryndon Savage, S. C., and Coppens, Y. 1973. Preliminary observations on Hippopotamidae (Mammalia, Artiodactyla) from the Plio-Pleistocene of the lower Omo basin, Ethiopia. In *Fossil vertebrates of Africa*, ed. L. S. B. Leakey, R. J. Savage, and S. C. Coryndon, 3:139-57. London: Academic Press.

Table 3

Distribution of Principal Taxa Characteristic of Omo Faunal Zones

Taxon	Mursi Fm.	Basal Mb.	Mb. A	Usno Fm.	Mb. B	Mb. C	Mb. D	Mb. E	Mb. F	Mb. G	Mb. H	Kalam
K-Ar Ages	4.05				2.97	2.95	2.39	2.12	2.03	1.93	1.83	1.34
Anancus kenyensis	X											
Ceratotherium praecox	X											
Hipparion turkanense	X											
Tragelaphus sp.	X											
Aepyceros sp.	X											
Elephas recki st. I		X	X	X	?							
Notochoerus euilus		X	X	X	cf.							
Hipparion cf. *albertense*		X	X	X	X	?	?					
Notochoerus capensis				X								
Percrocuta sp.				cf.								
Stegodon cf. *kaisensis*				?	X							
Hyaena aff. *makapani*				X	X	X						
Nyanzachoerus kanamensis					?							
Kobus patulicornis					X							
Tragelaphus ? *pricei*						X						
Menelikia sp.						X	X					
Tragelaphus sp.						X	X	X				
Hippopotamus protamphibius						X	X	X	X	X		
Metridiochoerus andrewsi						X			X	X		
Tragelaphus gaudryi						X		X	X	X		
Kobus sigmoidalis						X	X	X	X	X		
Theropithecus brumpti						X	X	X	X	X		
Menelikia lyrocera								X	X	X		
Elephas recki st. II B								?	X	X		
Equus sp. (large)										X	X	X
Hippopotamus gorgops										X	X	X
Kobus ellipsiprymnus										X	X	X
Megalotragus kattwinkeli										X		X
Hystrix cf. *cristata*										X		X
Beatragus antiquus											X	
Stylochoerus nicoli											X	X
Elephas recki st. III												X
Mesochoerus olduvaiensis												X
Menelikia lyrocera subsp. nov.												X
Parmularius altidens												X

Table 4

Distribution of Type Species of Omo Faunal Zones

K-Ar Ages	4.05				2.97	2.95	2.39	2.12	2.03	1.93		1.83	1.34
Taxon	Mursi Fm.	Basal Mb.	Mb. A	Usno Fm.	Mb. B	Mb. C	Mb. D	Mb. E	Mb. F	Mb. G	Mb. H		Kalam
Hippopotamus-hexaprotodont-ancestral to *protamphibius*	X		X	X	X								
Elephas recki stage I			X	X	X	?							
Hippopotamus protamphibius						X	X	X	X	X			
Hippopotamus gorgops											X	X	X

Eck, G. G., and Howell, F. C. 1972. New fossil *Cercopithecus* material from the lower Omo basin, Ethiopia. *Folia Primat.* 18:325-55.

Howell, F. C. 1968. Omo Research Expedition. *Nature* 219:567-72.

————. 1972. Pliocene/Pleistocene Hominidae in eastern Africa: Absolute and relative ages. In *Calibration of hominoid evolution,* ed. W. W. Bishop and J. A. Miller, pp. 331-68. Edinburgh: Scottish Academic Press; Toronto: University of Toronto Press.

Howell, F. C., and Coppens, Y. 1974. Les faunes de mammifères fossiles des formations plio-pléistocènes de l'Omo en Ethiopie (Tubulidentata, Hyracoidea, Lagomorpha, Rodentia, Chiroptera, Insectivora, Carnivora, Primates). *C. R. Acad. Sci. (Paris),* ser. D, 278:2421-24

Howell, F. C.; Fichter, L. S.; and Wolff, R. 1969. Fossil camels in the Omo Beds, southern Ethiopia. *Nature* 223:150-52.

Leakey, M. G., and Leakey, R. E. F. 1973. New large Pleistocene Colobinae (Mammalia, Primates) from East Africa. In *Fossil vertebrates of Africa,* ed. L. S. B. Leakey, R. J. Savage, and S. C. Coryndon, 3:121-38. London: Academic Press.

EDITOR'S NOTE: *Hippopotamus* sp. nov. "B" has been formally named *H. aethiopicus* sp. nov. by S. C. Coryndon and Y. Coppens (*C. R. Acad. Sci. [Paris],* ser. D, 280 [1975]:1777-80).

16. PROBOSCIDEANS FROM OMO GROUP FORMATIONS

M. Beden

The Mursi, Usno, and Shungura formations of the lower Omo basin have afforded numerous remains of Pliocene and earlier Pleistocene Proboscidea, and only part of the collection assembled by the Omo Research Expedition has been studied. Seven extinct taxa have been recognized in the Omo succession.

The Omo formations abound in fossiliferous localities; more than 1,300 were sampled between 1967 and 1973, through a sedimentary sequence exceeding a thousand meters in thickness and spanning some 3 m.y. Over 200 localities have yielded a variety of proboscidean remains ranging from craniums, mandibles, teeth, and bones to more fragmentary material. The stratigraphic situation of these localities is well established, and the presence or absence of various proboscidean species in them is doubtless significant and must directly reflect whether those species existed when the deposit was accumulated. On the other hand, the temporal distribution of those species known from only a few fossil remains may well need revision as additional specimens are recovered. However, the large number of fossil localities, and their substantial spatial distribution over several hundred square kilometers, considerably reduces the chance that a species might be absent owing to locally unfavorable conditions.

The succession also gives us the opportunity to study long-term evolutionary changes (phyletic evolution)--as in the case of *Elephas recki*, for example--in a particular species over a protracted period of time and in a localized region.

The species which have been recognized and the number of specimens of each studied here are listed in table 1. The number of specimens varies considerably. Five species are represented by only a few specimens, whereas *Elephas recki* and *Deinotherium* are both common. For the most part the remains are molars or portions of molars. Here only molars, and in the case of Elephantidae only upper molars, are employed in the study. For Elephantidae M3's are most frequently collected and, because of their morphology and dimensions, are the best indicator among the molar series of individual, sexual, and morphological variation.

The stratigraphic occurrence of each species is shown in figure 1.

The anancine gomphothere *Anancus* has been documented only in the Mursi Formation. It does not seem to be present in the Usno Formation or the lowest part of the Shungura Formation. Thus mastodonts did not persist here after about 4 m.y. Stegodonts also seem to have disappeared early, but apparently later than gomphotheres, as they have been found at three localities in units B-10 and B-11 of the Shungura Formation.

Table 1

Proboscidean Species Found in the Omo Group Formations and the Number of Molars (Partial or Complete) in the Sample Studied Here

Taxon	Number of Localities	Number of Molars
Anancus kenyensis (Macinnes, 1942)	3	3
Stegodon kaisensis (Hopwood, 1939)	3	3
Loxodonta adaurora (Maglio, 1970)	3	5
Loxodonta cf. *atlantica* (Pomel, 1879)	1	2
Loxodonta sp.	1	1
Elephas recki (Dietrich, 1915)	110	360
Deinotherium bozasi (Arambourg, 1942)	130	370
Total	251	744

The most primitive known loxodont, *Loxodonta adaurora*, disappears about the same time. It occurs in the Mursi Formation and in members A and B, and perhaps C, of the Shungura Formation. Two other loxodonts, clearly more advanced species, also occur in the Shungura Formation, one in Member D and the other (represented by a single badly preserved molar) in Member J (Kalam exposures).

Elephas recki is the most common proboscidean in the Omo succession. It is present in the Usno Formation and throughout the Shungura Formation. On the basis of the material available to me now the presence of this species in the Mursi Formation is uncertain.

Deinotherium bozasi occurs in all the formations of the Omo Group and appears to persist throughout the Shungura Formation.

Gomphotheriidae Cabrera, 1829

Anancinae Hay, 1922

Anancus Aymard, 1859

Type Species: *A. arvernensis* (Croizet and Jobert, 1828)

Anancus kenyensis (Macinnes, 1942)

Remains of *Anancus* are exceptionally rare, and as far as I know only three specimens have been recovered, all from the Mursi Formation. Two species of anancine gomphotheres have been described from the later Cenozoic of Africa, *Anancus kenyensis* (Macinnes, 1942) and *Anancus osiris* Arambourg, 1942. The molar morphology of these two species is very similar, except that *A. osiris* seems to lack the supplementary tubercles present in *A. kenyensis*. They are also present in the specimens from the Mursi Formation (Yellow Sands locality); hence assignment to the latter species seems warranted. Arambourg also noted differences in molar proportions between the two forms, those of *A. osiris* being broader (85-88 mm) than those of *A. kenyensis* (76.5 mm), although their lengths are almost the same. The specimens from the Mursi Formation (fig. 2*a*) have breadths of 75-80 mm and 75 mm, and in this respect also are similar to *A. kenyensis*.

Stegodontidae Young and Hopwood, 1935

Stegodontinae Osborn, 1918

Stegodon Falconer and Cautley, 1847

Type Species: *S. cliftii, bombifrons?, ganesa; insignis* Falconer and Cautley, 1847

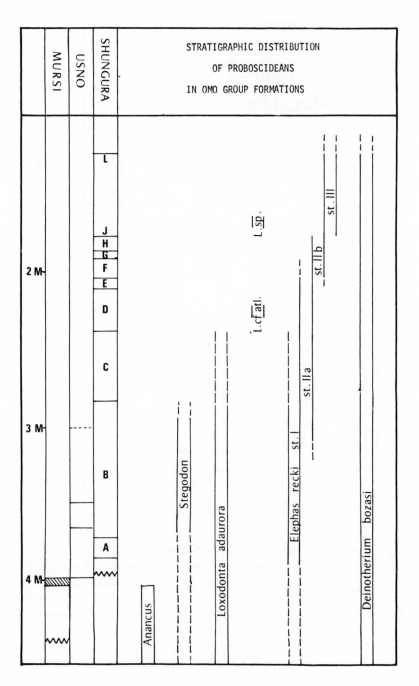

Figure 1

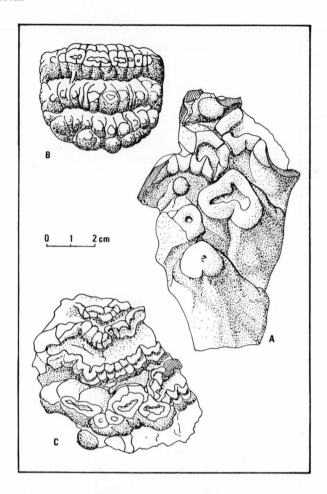

Figure 2. (a) fragment of *Anancus kenyensis* molar; (b) posterior part of milk molar of *Stegodon* cf. *kaisensis*; (c) fragment of M2 of *Stegodon* cf. *kaisensis*.

Stegodon kaisensis Hopwood, 1939

This stegodont is known only from three fragments of molar teeth from upper Member B of the Shungura Formation. The three specimens show typical stegodont features: plates with an increased number of enamel columns (8 to 13) separated by fine vertical grooves, deep V-shaped transverse valleys (with base of plates convergent), thick enamel, and very low hypsodonty. Without more complete specimens it is almost impossible to arrive at a more precise determination. However, the morphology of these specimens (fig. 2b,c) seems entirely comparable to molars of *Stegodon kaisensis* Hopwood recently described and figured by Cooke and Coryndon (1970, pp. 120-23, pl. 2), and they are therefore provisionally referred to that species.

Elephantidae Gray, 1821

Elephantinae Gill, 1972

Cuvier, 1827

Type Species: *L. africana* Blumenbach, 1870

Loxodonta adaurora Maglio, 1970

Among the proboscidean material examined thus far only a few specimens appear to represent this species. They include two hemimandibles, a maxilla fragment, and some partial molars. The specimens derive from the Mursi Formation and from members A and B of the Shungura Formation. This species does not appear to be represented in the Usno Formation.

The remains exhibit a number of primitive features. The mandible has a substantial symphyseal beak, the elongation being enhanced by the more forward situation of the symphysis compared with its position in *Elephas recki*. Thus, the posterior border of the symphysis is situated 4-5 cm anterior to the anterior border of M_2, whereas in mandibles of comparable age in *Elephas recki* the posterior border of the symphysis is situated almost even with the anterior margin of M_2.

Only the intermediate molar teeth are represented, and this hinders comparison. However, the molars appear primitive on morphological and dimensional grounds, with a few broad plates, scant hypsodonty, thick, scarcely folded enamel, rather prominent sinus, and low lamellar frequency. These features clearly distinguish these specimens from *Elephas recki*. They are very similar, however, to *Loxodonta adaurora* Maglio, the species established on the basis of material from Kanapoi (Kenya), to which Maglio (1969) has attributed molars from Laetolil (Tanzania). These teeth (dm_4, M_1, M_2) may be compared with their homologues in the Omo sample (table 2). The morphology of the Laetolil specimens is

Table 2

Comparative Dimensions and Indexes of Proboscidean Lower Molars Attributed to Loxodonta adaurora *from Laetolil and the Omo*

Characteristics	D_4		M_1		M_2	
	Laetolil	Omo	Laetolil	Omo	Laetolil	Omo
Number of plates	5	?	7	?	7/8	8[1]
Maximum length (cm)	126	-	155/165	-	200	200/210[1]
Maximum breadth (cm)	51/58	62	69/88	74/75[1]	81/88	78/79
Maximum height (cm)	-	-	67/80	-	80/87	-
Lamellar frequency	5/5.9	-	4.3/5.1	4.5/5.2	4.2/5	3.2/3.8
Enamel thickness (mm)	-	2.5/2.7	2.5/4	3/3.2	3.1/4.5	3.3/3.7

[1]Estimated.

essentially the same as that of the Omo specimens, and their dimensions are wholly comparable. In addition to the aforementioned features, noteworthy is the triangular shape of the plates (seen in cross-section), their thickness increasing markedly toward the base. Moreover, the median sinuses are clearly isolated from the plates in their upper part.

Loxodonta atlantica Pomel, 1895

Locality 161 in Member D (units D-3/4) of the Shungura Formation has afforded two M^{3}s which appear to represent a single individual. They differ markedly from all other molars of Elephantidae recovered from the Shungura Formation.

It is clear from the wear pattern of the crowns (fig. 3*b*) that these specimens should be referred to a species of *Loxodonta*. However, they are readily distinguished from *Loxodonta adaurora* by their more evolved morphology, especially with regard to the relatively thin enamel (2.4-3.2 mm), small maximum breadth (70 mm), and lamellar frequency (3.1-4.3). They cannot be assigned to *L. africana*, from which they differ in the much more folded enamel and greater number of plates (13 compared with 10 in the M^3 of *L. africana*). Maglio (in Cooke and Maglio 1972, p. 320) has attributed these specimens to *L. atlantica*. They are indeed similar in morphology to the latter species, but are substantially smaller (length = ~27 cm, breadth = 7.4 cm, for 13 plates) whereas these values are quite different for the North African species (length = 32.4 cm, breadth = 9 cm, for 14 plates--Pomel 1895). *L. atlantica* is a species typical of the Middle Pleistocene in North Africa, and its presence in the Omo, if confirmed, would substantially increase its temporal distribution in Africa. These specimens are only provisionally referred here to *L. atlantica*.

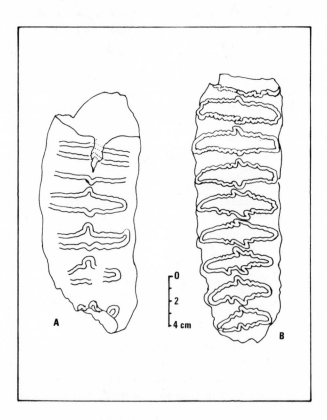

Figure 3.   Wear patterns in: (*a*) *Loxodonta adaurora*; (*b*) *Loxodonta* cf. *atlantica*

Loxodonta sp.

A badly preserved M_3 from Member J (Locality 994 in unit J-6) should probably also be attributed to Loxodonta. Its wear pattern is loxodont, with a large median sinus (though only slightly worn), the enamel is rather thin (0.29-0.34 mm), its maximum breadth low (~73 mm), its lamellar frequency 3.7-4.1, and its enamel grossly folded, though less regularly than in L. atlantica. It appears different from the specimens from Member D attributed to the latter species, but it is impossible to determine its affinities more precisely.

Elephas Linnaeus, 1754

Type Species: Elephas maximus Linnaeus, 1758

Elephas recki Dietrich, 1915

Elephas recki is the dominant proboscidean in the Omo succession. It is represented in the Usno Formation and throughout the Shungura Formation, including its uppermost member (L). It is also represented in the Mursi Formation.

Dietrich (1915) first described this form as a geographic race of Elephas antiquus Falconer and Cautley (1847) of Europe, but "recki" soon took on the rank of species. Its generic affinity was unclear for some time.[1] It is now evident that there is no basis for attributing this species to the loxodont proboscideans, as was once suggested on the basis of certain dental characters. This possibility was clearly excluded by the discovery at Kanapoi and Lothagam, in horizons largely or wholly antedating the Omo succession, of two skulls of the loxodont genus Loxodonta adaurora (Maglio 1970, 1973). Maglio demonstrated that the skull of Elephas recki (of which more than a dozen specimens are known) was markedly unlike that of loxodont species in many fundamental morphological features, as Arambourg (1942) had previously noted, and that in these respects it resembled the genus Elephas.

Analyzing the molar dentition particularly helps us appreciate specific and subspecific variations. In the Omo succession a series of morphological and dimensional changes can be elucidated which let us recognize several "forms" in the phyletic evolution of Elephas recki in the lower Omo basin. These may then be compared with the successive stages of Elephas recki recognized by Maglio (1970a): stage I from Kikagati (Uganda), stage II from the Omo succession, and stages III and IV from Olduvai (Tanzania). The type of Elephas recki, it should be recalled, derives from Olduvai Gorge Bed IV, and represents Maglio's stage IV.

It is well known that the upper molars of Elephantidae reflect morphological and dimensional variations, probably as a consequence of the plasticity of cranial structure, whereas the lower dentition is less expressive owing to the limitations of mandibular size and structure. For our purposes here only third molars have been studied in detail, and in particular (for the graphs) the upper third molars.

Of the features present in the permanent molars of Elephas recki some are relatively

---

1. This species was attributed successively to the following genera or subgenera: Elephas by Dietrich (1915); Pilgrimia by Osborn (1924); Elephas by Arambourg (1942); Palaeoloxodon by Osborn (1942); Elephas (Archidiskodon) by Arambourg (1947); Omoloxodon by Derinayagala (1955); Elephas (Hysudricus) by Vaufrey (1955); Palaeoloxodon by Cooke (1960); Elephas by Coppens (1965); Elephas by Arambourg and Coppens (1969); Palaeoloxodon by Aguirre (1968); Elephas by Maglio (1969, 1973); Elephas by Aguirre (1972), to cite only an incomplete list.

constant and represent the basic morphological pattern of the species, whereas other features show modification through time. The concept is exemplified in the folding of enamel. The axial zone of the plate is the site of most intense folding, and folding decreases in intensity outward and is intensified from the summit toward the base of the molar. This trend is reflected in the presence of anterior and posterior median sinuses, simple or more or less complex in the upper part of the plates and becoming less and less toward the base of the plates and progressively obscured by the enamel folding. It is worth noting that the enamel folding is often totally absent in the most inferior part of the plates.

Most other characters are progressively modified. They include the diminution of sinus size, sinus subdivision, increase in degree of enamel folding, increase in the amount of cement, and its progressively earlier appearance. Most morphological traits can be measured, and their modifications are consequently more readily appreciated. However, different features evolve at different rates; hence, a molar should be considered not as a single unit but as a set of elements evolving in more or less independent ways. Thus, some variable features concern the whole tooth and its general proportions (number of plates, maximum tooth length), other features are limited to the plates alone (maximum breadth and height), and other variables concern the enamel band itself (its thickness). These three sets of characters may evolve together or independently, and also at different rates.

There is a clear-cut increase through time in the number of molar plates. However, the overall length increases relatively much less, reflecting the increasing approximation of the plates (or increase in lamellar frequency, measured by the number of plates per 10 cm of length). Table 3 and figure 4 show three groupings of *Elephas recki* molars. The first group--molars with few plates and rather low lamellar frequency--derives from the Usno Formation and Shungura Formation Member B. The second group--comprising most specimens from Shungura Formation members B to G--shows an increased number of plates and a greater lamellar frequency. The third group--with even more plates and a greater lamellar frequency--derives exclusively from the uppermost horizons of the Shungura Formation, exposed west of Kalam.

Enamel thickness always decreases in a regular fashion but, it seems, through a series of successive steps (fig. 6*b*). This feature also distinguishes the three major groups of molar teeth in the Omo sample.

Table 3

Principal Dimensions and Indexes of M^3 *of* Elephas recki *from the Omo Succession*

Elephas recki	Stage 1	Stage 2 A	B	Stage 3
Number of plates	9-12	13-15	14-15	15-16
Maximum length (cm)	19-26.5	23-26.5	23-27	25-28
Lamellar ratio	2.20-2.55	1.60-2.10	1.50-2.00	1.65-2.00
Lamellar frequency	4-4.5	4.6-5.8	4.9-5.9	5.3-6.5
Maximum height (cm)	9.2-10.6	9-10.5	10.7-13.5	14.5-15
Maximum breadth (cm)	8.6-9.2	7.5-8.5	8.6-10.1	7.8-8
Hypsodonty index	107-115	115-131	119-156	181-187
Enamel thickness (mm)	0.32-0.45	0.28-0.36	0.24-0.32	0.18-0.28
	Mean=0.35	Mean=0.30	Mean=0.28	Mean=0.23

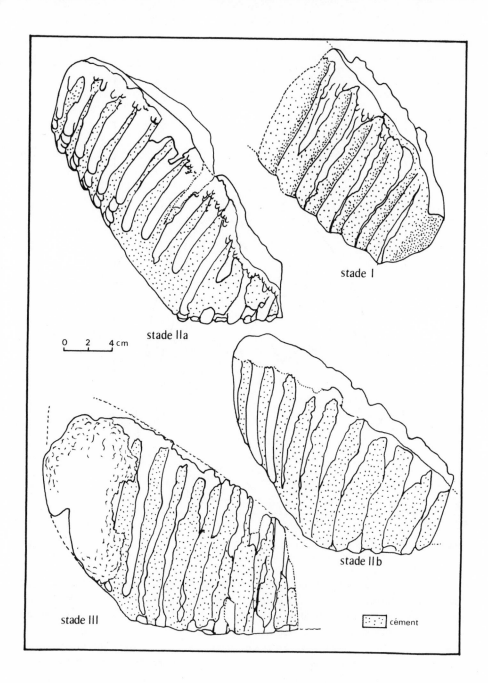

stade I

stade IIa

0 2 4 cm

stade IIb

stade III

cément

Figure 4. Lateral views of upper molars of *Elephas recki* stages 1, 2*a*, *b*, and 3 from the Omo succession.

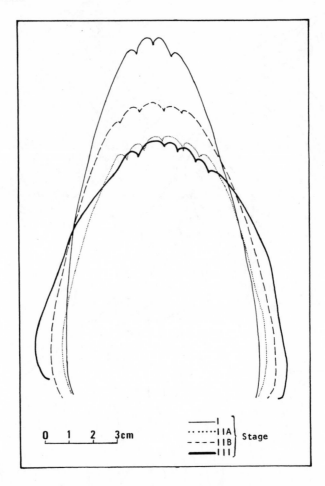

Figure 5. Cross-section diagrams of the form of the plates in *Elephas recki* upper molars according to the stages recognized in the Omo succession.

Are these three groups of molar teeth distinguishable on the basis of metrical aspects of the plates? Actually, if the most evolved group shows the greatest hypsodonty, which is logical, it is then almost impossible to distinguish the other two groups by this feature because of the great variability of the molar plates. It is especially the number of plates, the lamellar frequency, and the enamel thickness which separate the two groups of molars; on the basis of these features the oldest group appears clearly more primitive. For the second group, comprising specimens from members B to G (and H?), the hypsodonty is generally most marked on specimens found above Member E, but this increase is not substantial (fig. 6c), since height and breadth of the plates increase together, and the height increase is more clear-cut. Thus there are two subgroupings, having larger plates.

All the aforementioned characters indicate that these teeth should be attributed to *Elephas recki*. Maglio (1970b, 1973) has recognized four successive stages in the evolution of this species. The specimens from the Omo fall into three major groups, and it is necessary to inquire how these fit with Maglio's stages. The great majority of specimens, those of the second group, collected from localities in members B through G, represent Maglio's

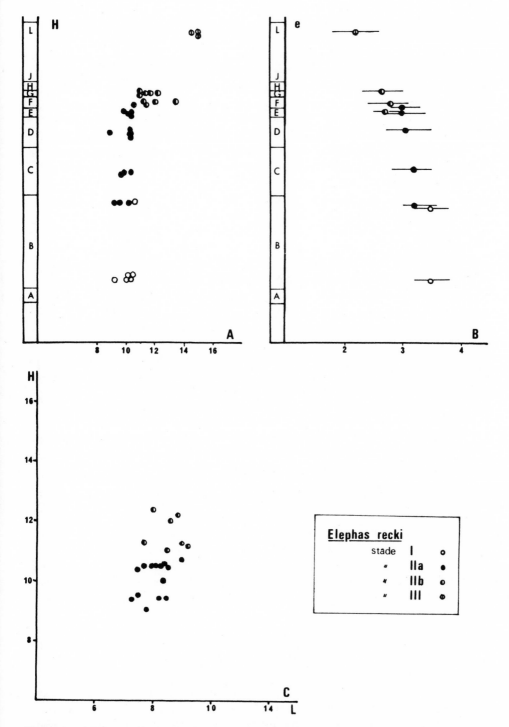

Figure 6. Graphs of the variation in some molar characters of *Elephas recki* following the stages recognized in the Omo succession: (*a*) variation in plate height through time (the ordinate shows the successive members of the Shungura Formation, their thickness drawn proportionate to their period of accumulation according to radiometric determinations); (*b*) variation (mean and range) of enamel thickness through time; (*c*) variation of hypsodonty index in stage 2 (ordinate = maximum height; abscissa = maximum breadth).

stage II (the type occurrence of which is the middle and upper portion of the Shungura Formation). Within this group two successive forms or subgroupings may be distinguished on the basis of the size increase of the plates. These are here distinguished as stages IIA and IIB, the latter appearing in Member F. Actually the limit between these subgroupings is still uncertain,since some specimens from Member E already are suggestive of the more evolved subgrouping IIB.

The molars in the first group are more primitive and, following their dimensions, can be compared with specimens from Kikagati (Uganda) as follows: number of plates = 12-13?; maximum breadth = 8.6 cm; maximum height = 10.3 cm; hypsodonty index = 119; lamellar frequency = 4.2; enamel thickness = 2.9-3.1 mm (cf. Maglio 1970, p. 24). Some of the observable differences could doubtless be due to the small sample.

The third group contains only two fairly complete molars. Their overall dimensions and morphology are clearly more advanced than in the other groups and closely approach *Elephas recki* stage 3 of Olduvai Gorge. However, the sample size is too small to be certain of their affinity, and more specimens are required to confirm it.

It is still uncertain whether there was a simple evolutionary progression of the *Elephas recki* lineage from stages 1 to 2 to 3. This matter could be clarified through detailed study of cranial morphology and of postcranial parts.

The several sedimentary sequences of East Rudolf, particularly those of Koobi Fora and Ileret, have also yielded remains of *Elephas recki*. Although the detailed correlation of this succession with that of the lower Omo basin is still being worked out, it does appear that there is substantial temporal equivalence and, in particular, that the uppermost part of the Upper Member of the Koobi Fora Formation (Ileret) corresponds closely in age to the uppermost members of the Shungura Formation (as exposed west of Kalam).

A number of remains of East Rudolf Proboscidea have still to be assigned precise stratigraphic provenances. However, I have selected 20 upper molars of *Elephas recki* for analysis and comparison with those of the Omo succession.

Maglio (1972) distinguished three successive faunal zones in the Koobi Fora Formation. They are designated (from oldest to youngest): *Mesochoerus limnetes* zone; *Metridiochoerus andrewsi* zone; and *Loxodonta africana* zone. *Elephas recki* is frequently found in this succession; the youngest occurrence being in the upper horizons at Ileret and the oldest from the sediments below the Tulu Bor Tuff (see Vondra and Bowen, this symposium). As in the Omo succession, both morphological and metrical evidence lets us recognize three groups or three temporally successive populations of *Elephas recki* in the East Rudolf sequence. The variations and changes observed are wholly comparable to those recognized in the Omo succession (table 4).

Thus, *Elephas recki* from the *Mesochoerus limnetes* zone is very like stage 2A from the Omo; the slight differences may result from the small size (3 specimens) of the East Rudolf sample. The morphological features, including degree of enamel folding, form of the sinus, and development of cement, are all very similar.

Elephas recki from the *Metridiochoerus andrewsi* zone is most like stage 2B from the Omo but seems to be slightly more advanced. The sample (10 specimens) is more hypsodont, with thinner and more folded enamel, more reduced sinus, and rather more extensive enamel than the Omo series. However, a larger sample is required to establish this conclusion.

.*Elephas recki* from the *Loxodonta africana* zone is still more advanced and closely resembles stage 3 from the uppermost part of the Shungura Formation. However, in each case the sample is too small (East Rudolf = 4; Omo = 3) to determine the closeness of the relationship.

Table 4
Principal Dimensions and Indexes of M^3 of Elephas recki *from the East Rudolf Succession*

| Elephas recki | Koobi Fora | | |
	Mesochoerus limnetes Zone	Metridiochoerus andrewsi Zone	Loxodonta africana Zone
Number of plates	12	14-15[1]	16-17
Maximum length (cm)	20-22	26-28[1]	-29
Lamellar ratio	1.66-1.83	173-200[1]	1.59-1.66
Lamellar frequency	4.5-5	4.9-6	5.2-6.5
Maximum height (cm)	9.8-10.5	11-13.8	13-14.5
Maximum breadth (cm)	7.6-8.2	8.5-9.5	7.8-9
Hypsodonty index	123-135	135-154	137-181
Enamel thickness (mm)	0.27/0.30/0.35	0.20/0.16/0.31	0.19/0.24/0.28

[1]Estimated.

Elephas iolensis Pomel, 1895

Maglio (1973) has attributed two fragmentary upper molars from localities termed Natodomeri, southeastern Sudan--lying near the margin of Sanderson's Gulf--to *Elephas iolensis*. This species is considered to represent a terminal species, both northern and southern African in distribution, in the evolution of the *Elephas recki* lineage. These remains, which I have not seen, are considered to derive from the later, but not youngest, part of the Kibish Formation (F. Clark Howell, pers. comm.). This would indeed represent a late survival of this species, which has not been previously recognized in eastern Africa.

Deinotherioidea Osborn, 1921
Deinotheriidae Bonaparte, 1845
Deinotherium Kaup, 1829
Type Species: *D. giganteum* Kaup, 1829

Deinotherium bozasi Arambourg, 1942

Deinotherium bozasi is common in all Omo Group formations. Although abundant, most of the fossil remains are fragmentary, and the variation observed in molars from various stratigraphic horizons is within the limits of individual difference. Hence it is unclear whether there is any evidence in the Omo succession of evolutionary change in this species.

Conclusions

The proboscideans from the Omo succession are of interest because of their associa- tions and the evidence for evolutionary change in the most common species, *Elephas recki*. Five patterns of associations can be recognized and correspond well with the stratigraphic succession (table 5).

In some instances the limits of the associations appear fairly well established, as with associations A and B, characterized by the extinction of *Anancus kenyensis*, a situa- tion well documented at several East African localities. However, the limits of the other associations are less well defined. The morphological and metrical features of molar teeth can and do change at different rates. Thus, some specimens of *Elephas recki* from Member F of the Shungura Formation are already more hypsodont than stage 2A but still preserve thick

Table 5

Proboscidean Associations in the Omo Succession

Association	Proboscidean Species	Formation
E	*Elephas recki* stage 3	Shungura (Kalam)
	Loxodonta sp.	(members H?L)
	Deinotherium bozasi	
D	*Elephas recki* stage 2B	Shungura
	Deinotherium bozasi	(members F, G, H?)
C	*Elephas recki* stage 2A	Shungura
	Loxodonta cf. *atlantica*	(members C, E, F?)
	Deinotherium bozasi	
B	*Stegodon* cf. *kaisensis*	Usno
	Loxodonta adaurora	Shungura
	Elephas recki stage 1	(members A, B, C?)
	Elephas recki stage 2A	
	Deinotherium bozasi	
A	*Anancus kenyensis*	Mursi
	Stegodon cf. *kaisensis* ?	
	Loxodonta adaurora	
	Elephas recki stage 1 ?	
	Deinotherium bozasi	

and less folded enamel. Also, the lack of specimens from Member H makes it impossible to determine precisely the limit between *Elephas recki* stages 2B and 3.

The *Elephas recki* specimens from East Rudolf corresponding to stage 3 suggest that the *Loxodonta africana* zone of the Upper Member of the Koobi Fora Formation is of the same age as the upper members (K, L) of the Shungura Formation. This is in keeping with the radiometric determinations on the Karari Tuff (East Rudolf) and Tuff L (Shungura Formation) and the paleomagnetic measurements of the respective sedimentary units. *Elephas recki* specimens from the *Metridiochoerus andrewsi* zone can perhaps be attributed to stage 2B, but there is some suggestion of an age more recent than members F-H(?) of the Shungura Formation. *Elephas recki* specimens from the *Mesochoerus limnetes* zone are attributable to stage 2A, suggesting that that zone is comparable in age to Shungura Formation members C-F(?). There appears to be no problem in relating the lower limits of these zones, but this is not the case for their upper limits. Thus, there are important differences between the absolute ages of the KBS Tuff (2.61 m.y.), forming the upper limit to the *M. limnetes* zone, and Shungura Formation Tuff F (2.04 m.y.), the upper limit of *Elephas recki* stage 2A. This discrepancy could be accounted for on methodological grounds (different methods of potassium-argon age determination) or on stratigraphic, ecological, or paleontological grounds. Only the last is of concern here. It is reasonable to expect the same evolutionary development in the same mammalian species, especially one so large and distributed between localities less than 100 km apart without significant intervening natural or climatic barriers. So a difference of a half million years in the time of appearance of similar characters between two such proximate situations is difficult to justify biologically.

For East Africa it is possible to establish correlations between local faunal zones and more comprehensive biozones like those proposed by Coppens (1972*b*) in biozonation of the East African Plio-Pleistocene (table 6). Coppens's Biozone V (=Omo Zone 1) probably can be usefully divided into an older subzone, characterized by the persistance of *Stegodon* cf. *kaisensis*, *Loxodonta adaurora*, and a primitive (stage 1) *Elephas recki*, and a more recent subzone from which these primitive species are absent. The limit between these subzones could be drawn within Member C of the Shungura Formation.

Table 6
Suggested Correlation, on Proboscidean Evidence, between the Omo and East Rudolf Successions

Omo		East Rudolf	East Africa
Association	Formations		
E	Shungura (Kalam) (members H?L)	*L. africana* zone	Zone III (Olduvai beds 1 and lower II)
D	Shungura (members F, H?)	*M. andrewsi* zone	Zone IV (Omo 2)
		?	
C	Shungura (members C, F?)	*M. limnetes* zone	Zone V (Omo 1)
B	Usno Shungura (members A, C?)		
A	Mursi		Zone VI (Kaiso 1)

References

Aguirre, E. 1969. Evolutionary history of the elephants. *Science* 164:1366-76.

Arambourg, C. 1934. Le Dinotherium des gisements de l'Omo (Abyssinie). *Bull. Soc. Geol. France*, Ser. 5, 4:305-9.

_____. 1942. *L'Elephas recki* Dietrich: Sa position systématique et ses affinités. *Bull. Soc. Geol. France*, ser. 5, 12:37-87.

_____. 1945. *Anancus osiris*, un Mastodonte nouveau du Pliocène inférieur d'Egypte. *Bull. Soc. Geol. France*, ser. 5, 15:479-95.

_____. 1947. Les mammifères pléistocènes d'Afrique. *Bull. Soc. Geol. France*, ser. 5, 17:302-10.

_____. 1947. *Mission scientifique de l'Omo (1932-1933)*. Vol. 1. *Géologie-Anthropologie*, fasc. 2. Mémoire, Muséum national d'histoire naturelle (Paris).

Arambourg, C.; Chavaillon, J.; and Coppens, Y. 1968. Résultats de la nouvelle mission de l'Omo, (2e campagne 1968). *C. R. Acad. Sci. (Paris)*, ser. D, 268:759-62.

Bowen, B. E., and Vondra, C. F. 1973. Stratigraphical relationships of the Plio-Pleistocene deposits, East Rudolf, Kenya. *Nature* 242:391-93.

Brown, F. H., and Lajoie, K. R. 1971. Radiometric age determinations on Pliocene-Pleistocene formations in the lower Omo basin, Ethiopia. *Nature* 229:483-85.

Butzer, K. W. 1971. The lower Omo basin: Geology, fauna and hominids of Plio-Pleistocene formations. *Naturwissenschaften* 58:7-16.

Cooke, H. B. S. 1960. Further revision of the fossil Elephantidae of southern Africa. *Paleontol. Africana* 7:46-58.

Cooke, H. B. S., and Coryndon, S. C. 1970. Pleistocene mammals from the Kaiso Formation and other related deposits in Uganda. In *Fossil vertebrates of Africa*, ed. L. S. B. Leakey and R. J. Savage, 2:107-224. London: Academic Press.

Cooke, H. B. S., and Maglio, V. J. 1972. Plio-Pleistocene stratigraphy in East Africa in relation to proboscidian and suid evolution. In *Calibration of hominoid evolution*, ed. W. W. Bishop and J. A. Miller, pp. 303-29. Edinburgh: Scottish Academic Press; Toronto: University of Toronto Press.

Coppens, Y. 1972a. Un nouveau proboscidien du Pliocène du Tchad, *Stegodibelodon schneideri* nov. gen. nov. sp. et le phylum des Stegotetrabelodontinae. *C. R. Acad. Sci. (Paris)*, ser. D, 274:2962-65.

————. 1972b. Tentative de zonation du Pliocène et du Pléistocène d'Afrique par les grands mammifères. *C. R. Acad. Sci. (Paris)*, ser. D, 274:181-84.

————. 1973. Les restes d'Hominidés des séries inférieures et moyennes des formations plio-villafranchiennes de l'Omo en Ethiopie (récoltes 1970-1971 et 1972). *C. R. Acad. Sci. (Paris)*, ser. D, 276:1823-26.

Heinzelin, J. de. 1971. Observations sur la formation de Shungura (Omo). *C. R. Acad. Sci. (Paris)*, ser. D, 272:2409-11.

Howell, F. C. 1968. Omo Research Expedition. *Nature* 219:567-72.

Leakey, L. S. B. 1965. *Olduvai Gorge, 1951-1961*. Vol. 1. *Fauna and background*. Cambridge: At the University Press.

Leakey, R. E. F. 1973. Further evidence of Lower Pleistocene hominids from East Rudolf, North Kenya, 1972. *Nature* 246:170-73.

Maglio, V. J. 1969. The status of the East African elephant *"Archidiskodon exoptatus"* Dietrich, 1942. *Breviora* 336:1-16.

————. 1970a. Early Elephantidae of Africa and a tentative correlation of African Plio-Pleistocene deposits. *Nature* 225:328-32.

————. 1970b. Four new species of Elephantidae from the Plio-Pleistocene of north-western Kenya. *Breviora* 341:1-27.

————. 1972. Vertebrate faunas and chronology of hominid-bearing sediments east of Lake Rudolf, Kenya. *Nature* 239:379-85.

————. 1973. Origin and evolution of the Elephantidae. *Trans. Amer. Philos. Soc.*, n.s., 63(3):1-149.

Osborn, H. F. 1942. *Proboscidea*. Vol. 2. American Museum of Natural History.

Pomel, A. 1895. Les éléphants quaternaires. *Publ. Serv. Carte Géol. Algérie, Alger, Paléontologie*.

17. EVOLUTION OF THE PERISSODACTYLA OF THE OMO GROUP DEPOSITS
D. A. Hooijer

The Perissodactyla, or odd-toed hoofed mammals, comprise the horses, the tapirs, and the rhinoceroses, all of which still have living representatives, as well as the extinct brontotheres and chalicotheres. The tapirs and the brontotheres are not found in Africa. The horses of Africa include two genera--the three-toed *Hipparion* and the one-toed *Equus;* the chalicotheres are represented by *Chalicotherium* and *Ancylotherium*; and the rhinoceroses include no fewer than seven genera: *Aceratherium, Brachypotherium, Chilotheridium, Dicerorhinus,* and *Paradiceros,* all extinct in Africa, and the living genera *Diceros* and *Ceratotherium*. Of these rhinocerotid genera, only *Ceratotherium* and *Diceros* occur in the Omo Group deposits; of the chalicotherids there is only *Ancylotherium*; and of the horses or equids we have both the extinct *Hipparion* and the living *Equus*. Thus we shall deal here with only five perissodactyl genera. The Omo Group deposits date back to 4 m.y., with the Mursi Formation, first discovered as the Omo Lower Level by Richard Leakey and his team in 1967, and range upward through the Usno and Shungura formations to the Kibish Formation, which is only about 5,000 years B.P. at the top. The collection on which my studies are based originates from all parts of this succession and was collected under the direction of F. Clark Howell (1967-74) and R. E. F. Leakey (1967).

Equidae

There are several forms of *Hipparion* in the Omo Group deposits (table 1):

Hipparion turkanense Hooijer and Maglio, 1973

The earliest species, *Hipparion turkanense*, recently described from Lothagam 1 in the Turkana district of Kenya, 6 m.y. old (Hooijer and Maglio 1973), appears to be represented by a single incomplete tooth from the Yellow Sands, Mursi Formation, apparently its latest occurrence, coeval with Kanapoi at the 4 m.y. level. *Hipparion turkanense* is devoid of a preorbital fossa and of ectostylids, with moderately plicated enamel on the cheek teeth. It is probably ancestral to *"Stylohipparion,"* the extremely hypsodont and otherwise special-ized *Hipparion* that we find in the Omo Group deposits from about Member F of the Shungura Formation, the 2 m.y. level, on upward.

Hipparion spec. indet.

The earlier Shungura and Usno Formation specimens of *Hipparion* are less advanced in structure than those of *Hipparion ethiopicum* and may represent intermediates between

Table 1

Distribution of Specimens of Equidae in Omo Group Formations

Level	Hipparion		Equus	
	Number of Localities	Number of Specimens	Number of Localities	Number of Specimens
K/L	2	1t, 1p	1	6t
J	1	1t	2	2t
H	1	1p	2	2t
G	27	60t, 3p	14	25t, 1m
F	16	34t, 2p		
E	12	16t		
D	6	11t		
C	17	32t, 2p		
B	6	26t, 1m, 1p		
Usno Fm.	16	21t		
A				
Basal Mb.				
Mursi Fm.	1	1t		

NOTE: t = teeth; m = mandibles; p = postcranials.

H. turkanense and *H. ethiopicum*. Unfortunately, the transformation is not as fully documented as one would wish, and as yet no skulls have been collected from the 4 to 2 m.y.
interval. The ectostylid is completely absent in one of three last lower molars from
Shungura Member B. The ectostylids may be small, only 2-3 mm wide at the base, in the Usno
Formation and Shungura Member D-5. Ectostylid height is 5-5.5 cm in Shungura members B and
C, compared with some 7.5 cm in Shungura Member G, with basal widths of 6-7 mm. This sug-
gests gradual increase in crown height and ectostylid expansion, which would link the Mursi
Formation *Hipparion* with that from Shungura members F and upward, but this needs to be sub-
stantiated by better material. Therefore it is best to leave the Shungura members B-E
Hipparion material without specific allocation for the time being.

Hipparion cf. *sitifense* Pomel

There are cheek teeth and incisors from Shungura members F and G that are indistinguishable from *Hipparion sitifense* Pomel, the pre-Villafranchian North African dwarf
Hipparion distinguished by the absence or rarity of ectostylids. The dwarf *Hipparion* teeth
found in Omo Group deposits are more hypsodont than those of a *Hipparion* occurring at
Lothagam and Kanapoi but have the same crown diameters and enamel patterns (Hooijer and
Maglio 1974). Unfortunately, the skull of the dwarf *Hipparion* is as yet unknown. It is
at any rate very different from the common, large *Hipparion* of the Upper Omo deposits that
I refer to:

Hipparion ethiopicum (Joleaud, 1933)

The hypsodont *Hipparion* with well-developed ectostylids was described from the Omo
deposits by Joleaud (1933). It is characterized not only by its high-crowned incisors and
cheek teeth, which are found in various Pleistocene beds in East Africa as well as in
northern and southern Africa, but also by cranial features known from skulls of Upper Bed
II at Olduvai Gorge in Tanzania. These suggest derivation from a species like *Hipparion
turkanense* Hooijer and Maglio, 1973, of Lothagam and Kanapoi. Various generic and specific

names have been applied to the advanced *Hipparion* of the African Pleistocene, but if a distinct generic or subgeneric name is considered necessary it should be *Eurygnathohippus* Van Hoepen, 1930, which has priority over *Stylohipparion* Van Hoepen, 1932; the two names refer to the same animal (Leakey 1965, p. 26). There may have been different geographic races or distinct species of the terminal *Hipparion* in various parts of Africa; this is not easily resolved on teeth alone. For the Upper Omo *Hipparion*, from Shungura Member F on up, I retain Joleaud's name. We have very characteristic incisors as well as cheek teeth that conform to Joleaud's material.

Equus spec. indet.

The large *Equus* teeth that we find in the Omo Group deposits from Shungura Member G on up defy determination of the species. There are many large named *Equus* species both in the New and the Old World, and there is much literature on details of the enamel pattern of the teeth, but even the long-upheld distinction between "caballine" and "zebrine" patterns breaks down. It is evident that one has to have the skull to arrive at a reliable specific identification (cf. Viret 1954, p. 145; Azzaroli 1965, p. 2). In the absence of skulls from the Omo Group deposits the species in question cannot be determined. Even a cf. determination may impart a false sense of precision and has been omitted. The protocones are short and the metaconid-metastylid valley V-shaped, but occasionally the protocone is long (14 mm in an upper third or fourth premolar, half the median length of the crown) and the lower internal valley U-shaped. It is not even certain that there is only one species of large *Equus* in the Omo beds, but characters may vary individually within the same species. *Equus stenonis* Cocchi, one of the two Villafranchian horses of the Upper Valdarno (Azzaroli 1965, pp. 5-9, pl. V, figs. 1-3), is very close to the Upper Omo *Equus* in the characters of both the upper and the lower cheek teeth, but on the basis of this evidence I am not prepared to accept conspecificity.

Chalicotheriidae

Ancylotherium hennigi Dietrich, 1942

In the American Omo collection I found three dental elements of this species, first described from Laetolil by Dietrich (1942, p. 105) (table 2). These are an upper left fourth premolar from Shungura Member D-5 and two fragments of upper molars from Shungura Member G. *Ancylotherium hennigi* has been described from Olduvai Bed 1 (Butler 1965, p. 226) and from the Chemeron Formation, locality J.M.511 (Hooijer 1972, p. 188; 1973, p. 152, pl. II, figs. 7-9).

Rhinocerotidae

Ceratotherium praecox Hooijer and Patterson, 1972

The presence of this species in the Mursi Formation is indicated by an upper fourth premolar and two upper molars collected by Richard Leakey in 1967 (Hooijer 1972, p. 187) as well as by two upper milk molars collected by F. Clark Howell in 1973. We (Hooijer and Patterson 1972) hold this to be the immediate ancestor of *Ceratotherium simum* (Burchell), the living white rhinoceros. *C. praecox* has been described, apart from Lothagam and Kanapoi, from the Chemeron Formation, locality J.M.507, the Aterir Beds, and the Mpesida Beds (Hooijer 1972, pp. 187, 189; 1973, p. 169) and occurs most abundantly at Langebaanweg in South Africa (Hooijer 1972) (table 3).

Table 2

Distribution of Chalicotheriidae in Omo Group Formations

	Ancylotherium hennigi	
Level	Number of Localities	Number of Specimens
K/L		
H		
G	2	2t
F		
E		
D	1	1t
C		
B		
Usno Fm.		
A		
Basal Mb.		
Mursi Fm.		

NOTE: t = teeth.

Table 3

Distribution of Rhinocerotidae in Omo Group Formations

	Ceratotherium praecox		Diceros bicornis		Ceratotherium simum	
Level	Number of Localities	Number of Specimens	Number of Localities	Number of Specimens	Number of Localities	Number of Specimens
K/L						
H						
G			6	6t, 2p	2	2t
F			3	4t	2	4t
E					4	4t, 2p
D			5	1t, 2m, 1c	3	1t, 1p
C			3	3t, 1p		
B			1	2p	2	3t
Usno Fm.			7	6t, 4p	7	7t
A						
Basal Mb.						
Mursi Fm.	1	2t	1	1t, 1p		

NOTE: t = teeth; p = postcranials; m = mandibles; c = craniums.

Ceratotherium simum (Burchell)

This species is not present in the Mursi Formation but appears very nearly everywhere else in the Omo sequence of deposits (Hooijer 1973, pp. 170-75). The earliest specimens, from Shungura Member B, are either incomplete or not sufficiently characteristic to show whether the early subspecies Ceratotherium simum germanoafricanum (Hilzheimer) is represented. This subspecies occurs in the Chemeron Formation, locality J.M.91 (Hooijer 1969, p. 76), and has teeth somewhat lower-crowned than the modern subspecies.   In the Usno Formation, a premolar definitely belongs to C. simum, so that the transition from C. praecox to C. simum must have taken place between 4 and 3 m.y.

Diceros bicornis (L.)

The earliest evidence of this species comes from the Mursi Formation--an upper right fourth milk molar less high-crowned than its recent counterparts (Hooijer 1973, p. 158-60). From Shungura Member D comes a very fine skull, completely modern in characters. An unworn lower fourth premolar from the same member shows that by this time, about 2 m.y., the recent stage of hypsodonty has already been attained. The *Diceros* group dates back in Africa to *Paradiceros* of Fort Ternan (Hooijer 1968), earlier than any *Diceros*, intimating an African origin of this group (Hooijer and Patterson 1972, pp. 24-25).

References

Azzaroli, A. 1965. The two Villafranchian horses of the Upper Valdarno. *Pal. Italica* 59 (n.s. 29):1-12.

Butler, P. M. 1965. Fossil mammals of Africa. No. 18. East African Miocene and Pleistocene chalicotheres. *Bull. Brit. Museum Geol.* 10(7):163-237.

Dietrich, W. O. 1942. Ältestquartäre Säugetiere aus der südlichen Serengeti, Deutsch-Ostafrika. *Palaeontographica*, ser. A, 94:43-133.

Hoepen, E. C. N. van. 1930. Fossiele Perde van Cornelia, O.V.S. *Pal. Navorsing Nas. Mus. Bloemfontein* 2:13-24.

_____. 1932. Die Stamlyn van die Sebras. *Pal. Navorsing Nas. Mus. Bloemfontein* 2:25-37.

Hooijer, D. A. 1968. A rhinoceros from the Late Miocene of Fort Ternan, Kenya. *Zool. Med. Museum Leiden* 43(6):77-92.

_____. 1969. Pleistocene East African Rhinoceroses. In *Fossil vertebrates of Africa*, ed. L. S. B. Leakey and R. J. G. Savage 1:71-98. London: Academic Press.

_____. 1972. A Late Pliocene rhinoceros from Langebaanweg, Cape Province. *Ann. S. African Museum* 59(9):151-91.

_____. 1973. Additional Miocene to Pleistocene rhinoceroses of Africa. *Zool. Med. Museum Leiden* 46(11):149-78.

_____. 1974. Hipparions from the Late Miocene and Pliocene of Northwestern Kenya. *Zool. Verhl. Leiden,* vol. 134.

Hooijer, D. A., and Patterson, B. 1972. Rhinoceroses from the Pliocene of Northwestern Kenya. *Bull. Mus. Comp. Zool.* 144(1):1-26.

Joleaud, L. 1933. Un nouveau genre d'Equidé quaternaire de l'Omo (Abyssinie): *Libyhipparion ethiopicum*. *Bull. Soc. Géol. France,* ser. 5, 3:7-28.

Leakey, L. S. B. 1965. *Olduvai Gorge 1951-1961*. Vol. 1. *A preliminary report on the geology and fauna*. Cambridge: At the University Press.

Viret, J. 1954. Le loess à bancs durcis de Saint-Vallier (Drôme) et sa faune de mammifères villafranchiens. *Nouv. Arch. Mus. Hist. Nat. Lyon* 4:1-200.

18. RHINOCEROTIDAE AND CHALICOTHERIIDAE (MAMMALIA, PERISSODACTYLA)
FROM THE SHUNGURA FORMATION, LOWER OMO BASIN

C. Guerin

Remains of rhinoceros and chalicotheres collected from the Shungura Formation, lower Omo basin, under the direction of Yves Coppens and the late C. Arambourg are briefly discussed here. Only specimens from the 1967, 1968, and 1973 field seasons have been examined thus far. Hooijer (1969, 1973, and this symposium) provides additional information on perissodactyls from the Mursi, Usno, and Shungura formations collected under the direction of F. Clark Howell.

Like most African mammalian localities of Pliocene and Pleistocene age the Omo succession has afforded faunal associations which have permitted continentwide correlation and the definition of a series of eight biozones (Coppens 1973). Most localities yield remains of Rhinocerotidae, but remains of Chalicotheriidae rarely occur. Although these perissodactyls have not yet played much of a role in the biozonation of African mammal faunas, they probably will do so once more extensive collections are available. Moreover, these large herbivores must have been dependent on well-defined plant communities which should afford indications of the paleoecology of the particular localities in which they occur.

The temporal distribution in the Shungura Formation of the remains studied thus far is shown in figure 1. They include a single chalicothere tooth and 20 specimens of rhino (4 of which are so worn or fragmentary that the genus cannot be determined). The chalicothere is referred to *Ancylotherium hennigi* (Dietrich). The rhinos represent the present species *Diceros bicornis* (black rhino) and *Ceratotherium simum* (white rhino). These are the usual rhinoceros species found in most African fossil localities of Pliocene to middle Pleistocene age, exceptions being *Brachypotherium lewisii* from the Pliocene of Lothagam, Kenya (Hooijer and Patterson 1972) and *Dicerorhinus africanus* from the "Villafranchian" of Lake Ichkeul, Tunisia (Arambourg 1968). *Ceratotherium* is more common than *Diceros* (13:3), as is usually true in Africa until the Upper Pleistocene, at which time the proportions are reversed (Hooijer and Singer 1960; Arambourg, Chavaillon, and Coppens 1967). On the other hand, in his recent discussion of Rhinocerotidae from the Omo succession, Hooijer (1973) notes that *Diceros* is more common than *Ceratotherium*.

Both genera show evolutionary changes during the Pleistocene, particularly in respect to increasing hypsodonty and certain variations in size (Hooijer 1969). However, Pleistocene representatives of the genus *Diceros* have never been separated specifically, or even subspecifically, from extant *Diceros bicornis*, in which six subspecies, one recently extinct, have been recognized (Zukowsky 1964; Groves 1967). The genus *Ceratotherium*, on the

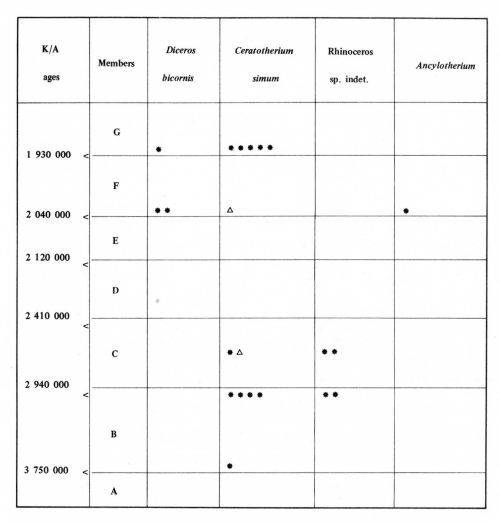

* teeth
△ postcranials

Figure 1. Stratigraphic distribution of rhinoceros and chalicothere remains in the Omo succession (collections of Y. Coppens and C. Arambourg).

other hand, is considered to have two living subspecies (*C. simum simum*, *C. simum cottoni*) and two extinct Pleistocene subspecies (*C. simum mauritanicum*, *C. simum germanoafricanum*) regarded as very different by Arambourg (1968). Hooijer and Patterson (1972) have also recognized a primitive ancestral species, *Ceratotherium praecox*, of Pliocene age, which also occurs in the earliest part of the Omo succession (Hooijer, this symposium).

All the Rhinocerotidae reported here derive from Shungura Formation members B, C, F, and G. There are no specimens from members D and E, but Hooijer (1973; this symposium) records three specimens of *Ceratotherium* from Member E (and none of *Diceros*) and lists both genera in Member D. Member G has afforded the most specimens of both rhinos and *Ancylotherium* (see also Hooijer 1973; this symposium).

The dentition is more often represented than the postcranial skeleton (although the latter is represented among collections made in years other than those discussed here). The postcranial skeleton is often neglected, and Dietrich (1945), Hooijer and Singer (1960) and Hooijer (1969) have suggested that such skeletal parts (in contrast to craniums and elements of the dentition) may not be specifically determinable. My own work on the "Pontian," Pliocene, and Pleistocene rhinos of western Europe has involved some detailed studies of the postcranial skeleton. A number of criteria (including size, proportions, and morphology of limb bones, carpals, tarsals, and metapodials) do permit separation of different species. The basis for the criteria has been a detailed comparative study of individual, sexual, and geographic variability in the five extant species of rhinoceros. However, a major problem is the general lack of postcranial skeletal parts in museum collections. (For example, there is only one mounted skeleton of *Ceratotherium simum* in France, and only two, one mounted and the other juvenile, in the British Museum of Natural History in London!) Nevertheless it has been possible to distinguish between the three species of *Dicerorhinus* in the Plio-Pleistocene of Western Europe (Guerin 1972) and the three species of rhinoceros in the Middle and Upper Pleistocene (Guerin 1973). Hooijer (1973), who has until recently considered it almost impossible to make specific differentiations on the basis of postcranial parts, now feels that it is possible, though difficult, to do so.

Diceros bicornis

The black rhino is represented by only three specimens of M^3, one of which is unworn. Figure 2 shows the breadth (taken parallel to the protoloph) to length (taken along the greatest length of the ectoloph) relations of this tooth in comparison with a modern *D. bicornis* sample (*N*=24). There are no differences between the samples either in dimensions or proportions.

The hypsodonty index[1] of the unworn M^3 (from Member G) is 100, compared with 120, 103.1, and 97.9 for three modern samples. Unfortunately, there are few comparative values of this index for modern rhinos (which would be most readily obtained with X ray in order not to damage specimens). At any rate there is no significant difference between the Omo value and that of modern samples of *D. bicornis*. Variability of this index on the order of 20% for M^3 is normal for European Pleistocene species.

Ceratotherium simum

The white rhino is represented by 13 specimens, 8 of which can be measured. They are two upper and three lower premolars, an upper molar, a fragment of metacarpal, and an astragalus.[2] The two teeth from Member B are too fragmentary to determine whether these represent *C. praecox* rather than *C. simum*. From Member C upward the specimens are clearly *C. simum*.

An unworn P^4 has a hypsodonty index of 138.8 compared with 185.1 in a recent specimen of *C. simum*. An M^3, very slightly worn, has an index of 118.

---

1. This index is 100 x H/L, where length (L) is along the greatest extent of the ectoloph and the height (H) is the maximum height of the ectoloph, perpendicular to the length. The length at the level of the neck is not used, since it is too imprecise when taken between two points of inflection.

2. One lower molar, collected in 1972, derives from a still undefined part of the uppermost Shungura Formation in the Kalam area. Arambourg (1947) described three upper and four lower cheek teeth and a fragmentary mandible from his collecting from the Shungura Formation in 1933.

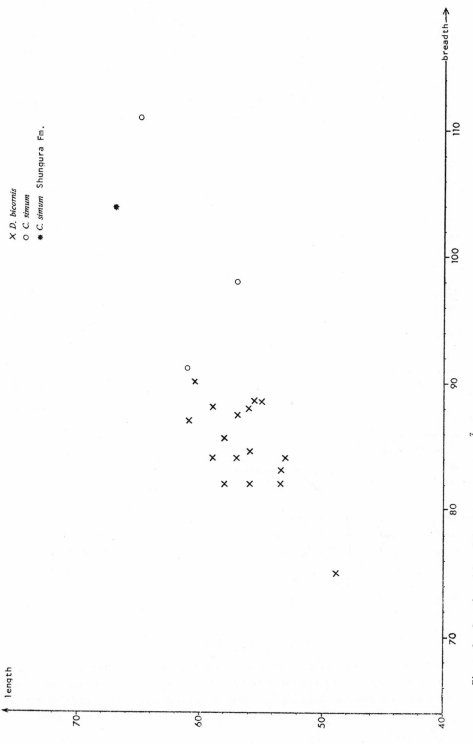

Figure 2. Length and breadth measurements of M^3 in *Diceros bicornis*

The metacarpal fragment represents the distal half. It shows characteristics distinctive of *C. simum*, including the shaft cross-section, which is thicker and more irregular than that of *D. bicornis*, with greater dimensions (even compared with the Cape subspecies of the latter) and the posterior face less depressed and the distal end more shortened.

An astragalus has the same dimensions and proportions (table 1; fig. 3) of a large *C. simum* individual and is very different from *D. bicornis*. It is also distinctive in its broader superior articular process and in the marked development and very different shape of the distal articular process.

Table 1

Comparative Dimensions of Rhinoceros Astragali

Dimension	Shungura Formation	Modern *Ceratotherium simum*			Modern *Diceros bicornis*		
		n	Mean	Range	n	Mean	Range
Breadth	104	3	100	91-111	17	84.91	75.90
Height	94	3	86	80-92	15	77.53	66-88
A-p diameter internal lip	67	3	61	57-65	17	56.29	49-61
Transverse diameter, distal articular surface	91.5	2	79.5	74-85	15	68.20	63.5-73
A-p diameter, distal articular surface	50.5	2	44.75	44-45.5	15	44.13	41-49.5
Trochlear width	76	2	67.5	67-68	15	63.37	57-70
Transverse diameter, distal portion	95.5	3	87.67	83-93	17	74.24	55-78

The relatively low hypsodonty index is typical of the subspecies *C. simum germanoafricanum*.

Ancylotherium hennigi

An unworn right lower molar, from Member F, is attributed to this chalicothere. It measures 52 mm (length), 24.5 mm (breadth), 35.5 mm (height), and has a hypsodonty index of 68.27. Dietrich (1942), Butler (1965), and Hooijer (1972) do not figure this tooth of this species, which appears to be the only such known from this time range. The morphology of the specimen is remarkably similar to an M_2 of *Phyllotillon* aff. *naricus*, described and figured by Viret (1961, pl. V, fig. 8), from La Grive-Saint-Alban. It also shows the two distinct points on the lingual face of the crown at the junction of the two lobes. However, the latter specimen is smaller (45 x 20.5 x 25.5 mm) and clearly more brachyodont (index 56.57) than the Omo specimen.

Conclusions

The Shungura Formation affords evidence of a chalicothere and of two species of rhino. The chalicothere is a very rare element of the fauna. The two rhinos are more common, the black being rarer than the white. It is impossible to distinguish the former from the living species, whereas the latter is represented by the extinct subspecies *C. simum germanoafricanum*.

These two rhinos clearly have (now) different biotopes. *Diceros bicornis* favors more or less wooded or bushy savannas or open woodland, whereas *C. simum* favors open savanna or

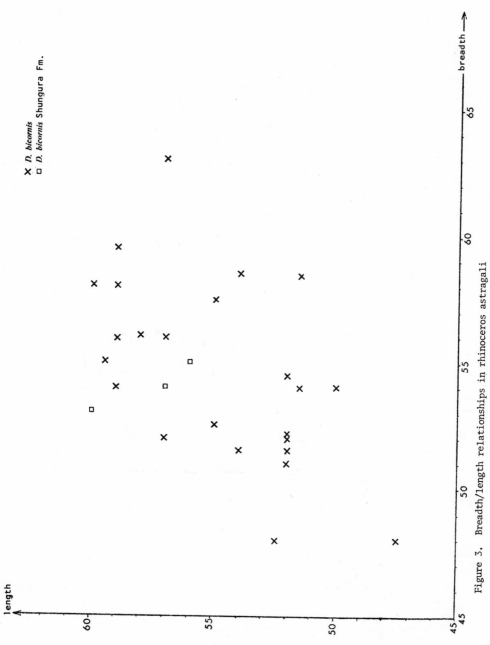

Figure 3. Breadth/length relationships in rhinoceros astragali

grassland. The frequency of each species throughout the Omo Group formations should reflect, in some way, the general nature of the vegetation cover at that time and place.
Thus it is probable that the coexistence of these two species, as well as chalicothere, in
Member G, should correspond to a more "closed" vegetation pattern than in other members of
the Shungura Formation in which *Ceratotherium simum* is thus far the only species represented. However, this is not confirmed by the palynological evidence (Bonnefille, this
symposium) or the microfaunal evidence (Jaeger and Wesselman, this symposium).

The two living species of African rhinoceros have existed for 3 or 4 m.y. without
significant morphological change. Each species is both ancient and remarkably stable. By
comparison, during the same range of time in western Europe six species of rhino appear
and vanish, to be replaced or to evolve rapidly over some hundreds of thousands of years;
only one persisted over some 2.5 m.y., and none of the other species persisted more than
1 m.y.

References

Arambourg, C. 1947. *Mission scientifique de l'Omo (1932-1933)*. Vol. 1. *Géologie-
Anthropologie*, fasc. 3, pp. 231-562. Mémoire, Muséum national d'histoire naturelle
(Paris).

_____. 1968. Les vertébrés du Pléistocène de l'Afrique du Nord. *Arch. Mus. Nat. Hist.
Nat.* (Paris) 10:1-126.

Arambourg, C.; Chavaillon, J., and Coppens, Y. 1967. Premiers résultats de la nouvelle
mission de l'Omo (1967). *C. R. Acad. Sci. (Paris)*, ser. D, 265:1891-96.

Butler, P. M. 1965. East African Miocene and Pliocene chalicotheres. *Bull. Brit. Mus.
Geol.* 10:163-237.

Coppens, Y. 1972. Tentative de zonation du Pliocène et du Pléistocène d'Afrique par les
grands mammifères. *C. R. Acad. Sci. (Paris)*, ser. D, 274:181-84.

_____. 1973. Les restes d'hominidés des formations plio-villafranchiennes de l'Omo en
Ethiopie. *C. R. Acad. Sci. (Paris)*, ser. D, 276:1823-26, 1981-84.

Dietrich, W. O. 1942. Ältestquartäre Säugetiere aus der südlichen Serengeti, Deutsch-
Ostafrika. *Palaeontographica*, ser. A, 94:43-133 (esp. pp. 105-7, figs. 33, 35, 37,
78, 80 and 83).

_____. 1945. Nashornreste aus dem Quartär Deutsch-Ostafrikas. *Palaeontographica*, ser.
A, 96:46-90.

Groves, C. P. 1967. Geographic variation in the black rhinoceros *Diceros bicornis* (L.,
1758). *Z. Säugetierkunde* 32:267-76.

Guerin, C. 1972. Une nouvelle espèce de rhinocéros (Mammalia, Perissodactyla) à Vialette
(Haute Loire, France) et dans d'autres gisements du Villafranchien inférieur européen:
Dicerorhinus jeanvireti nov. sp. *Docum. Lab. Géol. Fac. Sci. Lyon* 49:53-150.

_____. 1973. Les trois espèces de rhinocéros (Mammalia, Perrissodactyla) du gisement
pléistocène moyen de La Fage à Noailles (Corrèze, France). *Nouv. Arch. Mus. Lyon*
11:55-84.

Hooijer, D. A. 1969. Pleistocene East African Rhinoceroses. In *Fossil vertebrates of
Africa*, ed. L. S. B. Leakey and R. J. Savage, 1:71-98. London: Academic Press.

_____. 1972. A late Pliocene rhinoceros from Langebaanweg, Cape Province. *Ann. South
African Museum, Cape Town* 59:151-91.

_____. 1973. Additional Miocene to Pleistocene rhinoceroses of Africa. *Zool. Mededeel.,
Rijksmuseum Natuurl. Hist., Leiden* 46 (11):149-78.

Hooijer, D. A., and Patterson, B. 1972. Rhinoceroses from the Pliocene of northwestern
Kenya. *Bull. Mus. Comp. Zool. Harvard Coll.*, 144(1):1-26.

Hooijer, D. A., and Singer, R. 1960. Fossil rhinoceroses from Hopefield, South Africa. *Zool. Mededeel., Rijksmuseum Natuurl. Hist., Leiden* 37(8):113-28.

Viret, J. 1961. Catalogue critique de la faune des mammifères fossiles de la Grive-Saint-Alban (Isère), 2e partie. *Nouv. Arch. Mus. Hist. Nat. Lyon* 6:55-91.

Zukowsky, L. 1964. Die Systematik der Gattung *Diceros* Gray, 1821. *Zool. Garten, Dtsch.,* Leipzig. 30(Heft 1/2):1-104.

J. M. Harris

Introduction

The vertebrate fauna from the East Rudolf region has been discussed by Maglio (1972), who recognized four distinct faunal assemblages, which he assigned to four faunal zones. The oldest assemblage was collected from the Kubi Algi Formation and was termed the *Notochoerus capensis* zone. Faunal elements from this zone appear quite distinctive from specimens collected at stratigraphically higher levels at East Rudolf. The Kubi Algi region has, however, received less attention than the more northerly parts of the East Rudolf basin, and, perhaps as a result, the *N. capensis* zone has fewer taxa and fewer specimens than the younger faunal zones.

The bulk of the East Rudolf fauna has been collected from the Koobi Fora Formation in the Koobi Fora and Ileret regions. Three successive faunal zones younger than the *N. capensis* zone are recognized--the *Mesochoerus limnetes* zone, the *Metridiochoerus andrewsi* zone, and the *Loxodonta africana* zone. The *M. limnetes* zone occurs in the Lower Member of the Koobi Fora Formation from levels up to 35 m below the KBS Tuff. Very few specimens have so far been collected from earlier levels either immediately above or immediately below the Tulu Bor Tuff.

The *M. andrewsi* zone fauna occurs in the Upper Member of the Koobi Fora Formation at levels between the KBS and Koobi Fora tuffs. Relatively few specimens have been collected from levels immediately above the Koobi Fora Tuff. The *M. andrewsi* zone also occurs in the Ileret Member of the Koobi Fora Formation at levels between the KBS and Lower tuffs.

The *L. africana* zone fauna is so far confined to the Ileret region. Here it occurs in the Ileret Member of the Koobi Fora Formation at horizons between the Lower and Chari tuffs.

To date, very few fossils have been collected from sediments younger than the Koobi Fora Formation at East Rudolf.

Rhinoceroses are not common elements of the East Rudolf fauna and so far are restricted to the Koobi Fora Formation. Representatives of both extant genera are found in all three faunal zones. Most of the specimens are isolated teeth or jaw fragments, but some remarkably complete craniums have been collected. Very few postcranial elements have been recovered.

Diceros bicornis subsp.

The skull from East Rudolf is one of the few fossil black rhino skulls known. It is about as long as that of recent examples but is less wide, though this may be due to the

Table 1

Distribution of the East Rudolf Rhinocerotidae

Taxon	M. limnetes Zone	M. andrewsi Zone	L. africana Zone	Indet.
Diceros bicornis subsp.	2	7	1	
Ceratotherium simum germanoafricanum	2	9	3	2

relative immaturity of the specimen. The third molar is present but unerupted, and many of the sutures, especially in the facial region, are still open. Differences in morphology from modern skulls are minor and restricted mainly to the cranial region.

The occipital region of the extant black rhinoceros is wide and rounded, whereas that of the East Rudolf skull appears taller, squarer, and narrower. The widest part of the occiput in recent examples is formed by the ventral portion of the nuchal crest; the widest point on the occiput of the East Rudolf specimen is defined by lateral process from the paramastoid. Anatomical differences from modern black rhinoceroses are seen in the para-mastoid region, the auditory region, the glenoid fossa, and the postglenoid process.

The horizontal ramus of the mandible is deeper and stouter than that of modern forms, and the symphysis is wider.

There is no difference in dental morphology between the East Rudolf black rhino and the recent *D. bicornis*. Most of the fossil teeth are worn but appear slightly less hypso-dont than those of extant representatives.

The astragalus is similar in size to that of recent examples of *D. bicornis* and dif-fers in a number of minor features only.

Ceratotherium simum germanoafricanum

The white rhinoceros is a little more common than the black in the East Rudolf fauna. The remains include an adult and two immature skulls. In most respects the skull of the East Rudolf *Ceratotherium* is very similar to the extant subspecies *C. simum simum*. However, in the fossil skulls the postglenoid processes are shorter and less massive, the paraoccipi-tal region is more slender, and the nuchal fossa is more elevated above the foramen magnum. Also, the angle between the skull roof anterior to the nuchal crest and the plane of the occiput is more nearly at right angles in the East Rudolf specimens.

The mandible is deeper, longer, and wider than that of the extant form and also has a longer symphysis. The anterior edge of the ascending ramus is more nearly vertical, and the coronoid process is taller, more slender, and sited more anteriorly in relation to the condyle. The masseteric fossa is less deeply excavated than in *C. simum simum*.

Most of the upper teeth are heavily worn or incomplete. The only major morphological difference from the extant form is in the orientation of the metaloph, that of the fossil specimens being oriented more transversely. Hooijer (1969) showed that the teeth of *Ceratotherium* became progressively more hyposodont through the Pleistocene. The only teeth from East Rudolf that lend themselves to this form of analysis are from the *Loxodonta africana* zone, and according to Hooijer's criterion, seem closer to the modern subspecies than specimens from Upper Bed II at Olduvai.

Discussion

Groves (1967) recognized seven modern subspecies of *Diceros bicornis* that he defined by length and breadth parameters of the skull. A modern skull collected from East Rudolf in 1968 belongs to the smallest subspecies *D. bicornis michaeli*. According to Groves's criteria, the East Rudolf fossil black rhino skull is closest to *D. bicornis brucii* (the Somali black rhinoceros), which is intermediate in size between *D. bicornis michaeli* and the other black rhino common to northern Kenya--*D. bicornis ladoensis*. It is unfortunate that the partial skull of *D. bicornis* from Shungura Member C of the Omo (Hooijer 1973, pp. 161-62) may be too distorted laterally to provide an adequate comparison with either the East Rudolf specimen or modern subspecies.

The East Rudolf *D. bicornis* mandibles, all of which are from the *M. andrewsi* zone, are slightly deeper than a mandible from Shungura Member D-2 and than modern mandibles cited by Hooijer (1973, p. 164). Teeth from the *M. limnetes* zone are slightly larger than those from the *M. andrewsi* zone. However, more specimens are needed to establish the range of individual variation at different levels before any tentative conclusions on evolutionary trends within the East Rudolf succession can be formulated.

The astragalus (KNM-ER 1196) comes from the *M. limnetes* zone and is larger than recent examples. It is closer in size to an astragalus from Shungura Member E (Hooijer 1973, p. 160) than to examples from earlier in the Omo sequence.

Ceratotherium praecox is apparently absent from the Koobi Fora Formation. This species may perhaps have been expected to occur in the *Notochoerus capensis* zone, but so far no rhinos have been collected from the Kubi Algi Formation.

Ceratotherium simum germanoafricanum appears to be confined to the early part of the Pleistocene in East Africa and is recorded from Bed I at Olduvai and perhaps from the lower part of the Shungura sequence at the Omo (Hooijer 1969, 1973). The East Rudolf specimens are assigned to the fossil subspecies on the bases of dental and cranial morphology. The index of hypsodonty of some upper third molars from the *L. africana* zone suggests that some specimens from this level are intermediate between the fossil and the extant subspecies. The fossil white rhino astragalus (KNM-ER 1195) from the *M. andrewsi* zone is larger than any recent astragalus of *C. simum simum* in the osteology collections of the National Museum of Kenya.

In summary, the Rhinocerotidae appears to be a relatively stable family during the time period under consideration, and few evolutionary modifications are apparent within the succession of the Koobi Fora Formation at East Rudolf.

This is paper no. 58 in the East Rudolf Project catalogue of publications.

References

Groves, C. P. 1967. Geographic variation in the black rhinoceros *Diceros bicornis* (L. 1758). *Z. Säugertierk* 32:267-76.

Hooijer, D. A. 1969. Pleistocene East African Rhinoceroses. In *Fossil vertebrates of Africa,* ed. L. S. B. Leakey and R. J. Savage, 1:71-98. London: Academic Press.

————. 1973. Additional Miocene to Pleistocene rhinoceroses of Africa. *Zool. Med.* 46:149-78.

Maglio, V. J. 1972. Vertebrate faunas and inferred chronology of East Lake Rudolf, Kenya. *Nature* 239:379-85.

20. EQUIDAE FROM THE SHUNGURA FORMATION

V. Eisenmann

Material

The Omo collections of Equidae discussed here comprise those from the missions of Bourg de Bozas (1900-1903) and the late C. Arambourg (1932-33) and from the recent Omo Research Expedition, the last collected under the direction of C. Arambourg and Y. Coppens (collections of 1967, 1968, 1972, and 1973). The collections made after 1967 have precise provenance data. The specimens and their stratigraphic situations (where known) in the Shungura Formation are listed in table 1.

Hipparion

Members A and B

The lower members of the Shungura Formation have afforded fossil remains indicating the existence at this level of a large form of *Hipparion*. Its lower cheek teeth probably lacked an ectostylid. A rather damaged astragalus is evidently *Hipparion*, to judge from the junction of internal and posterior surfaces at a right angle, the proportion and form of the lower articular surface, the distance between that surface and the external lip, and the curvature of the internal lip (Gromova 1952, pp. 125 ff.). It is longer than the largest hipparionid astragali known--those of *H. longipes* Gromova of Pavlodar (table 2).

A lingual portion of a lower premolar appears distinctly larger than those from the upper part of the Shungura Formation. The double knot (conjoined metaconid-metastylid) and the entoconid are similar in size to a specimen from Ain Brimba which is 30 mm long (Arambourg 1970, plate XVIII, fig. 4). If a broadly similar size for the Member B specimen is assumed, it approaches in size remains from Langebaanweg and Laetolil (Boné and Singer 1965). It is larger than the P_4 from the earlier Kaiso (North Nyabrogo) (Cooke and Coryndon 1970). An M_1 or M_2 from Member B is also larger than those from the upper Shungura members but is smaller than those from Laetolil and Langebaanweg. A P_2 also from Member B is smaller than the aforementioned specimens, falling in the range of specimens from the upper Shungura.

The only intact lower molar, an M_1 or M_2 from Member B, lacks an ectostylid. In this respect it resembles some specimens from Laetolil, Langebaanweg, and earlier Kaiso and differs from those of Ichkeul and Ain Brimba, although the latter are of comparable size.

A damaged calcaneum and a phalanx are also known from Member A. The proximal phalanx, also damaged, has an estimated length of not more than 65 mm. It is therefore much smaller

Table 1

Stratigraphic Locations of Specimens from the Shungura Formation

Members	Localities	Hipparion	Equus
J	K 20		2 upper cheek teeth 1 fragment of metacarpal 3
H	11.2		1 astragalus
G	29 and 210, 35, 47, 113, 150, 187, 195 214, 215, 233, 235, 248, 252, 253, 256, VEO	4 upper cheek teeth 6 lower cheek teeth, 1 lower fragment 1 lower cheek tooth series 2 astragali, 1 incomplete tibia	5 upper cheek teeth 1 lower cheek tooth series 5 lower cheek teeth 1 fragment of radius 4 fragments of metacarpal 3 2 tibia fragments 1 astragalus 1 fragment of metatarsal 3 3 phalanges 1 2 phalanges 2
F	1 C, 76, 118, 130	2 upper cheek teeth, 1 upper incisor 1 lower cheek tooth series, 2 lower cheek teeth 1 metacarpal 3	
E	38, 108	1 upper cheek tooth, 1 upper fragment	
D	18 bis, 153, 216	1 upper cheek tooth 2 fragments metacarpal and metatarsal 3	
C	3.1, 18, 30, 53	1 upper cheek tooth 9 lower cheek teeth and fragments 1 fragment of metacarpal 3	
B	3, 28, 41	1 upper milk tooth, 1 upper fragment 3 lower cheek teeth, 1 cup	
A	127, 128	astragalus, calcaneum, phalanx 1	
Expeditions of Bourg de Bozas and Arambourg		1 upper incisor 3 upper cheek teeth and 2 fragments 7 lower cheek teeth	1 upper incisor 2 upper cheek teeth 3 lower cheek teeth 1/2 distal radius 1 fragment of metacarpal 3 1 phalanx 1 2 phalanges 2
Dental series		2	1
Isolated teeth and fragments		47	18
Postcranials		3	9
Fragments of postcranials		8	12
	Total	60	40

Table 2

Dimensions (mm) of Hipparion *Astragali*

Source	Specimen	Internal Height
Pavlodar	$n = 9$	59 to 63
Omo Member A	128-1972-12	69
Omo Member B	41-1973-991	56

than those described and figured by Boné and Singer (1965), the shortest of which is 70.2 mm. (According to their illustrations, phalanges L 1462 B and C come from an *Equus* and L 1462 A from a *Hipparion*, as does, possibly, L 1456.) On the other hand, the phalanx from Omo is much more gracile; but this might merely reflect the immaturity of the animal.

Members C through G

An ectostylid is present on all *Hipparion* lower premolars and molars from Member C upward. An exception is an M_3 which is a part of a dentition from Member F. The crown length of these teeth (tables 3 and 4) and the size of the postcranials (tables 2 and 5) are in general smaller.

The height (buccally, in mm) of a series of lower teeth of a young adult from Member F affords an indication of the degree of hypsodonty.

P_2	P_3	P_4^*	M_1	M_2	M_3
46	54	68	61	68.5	69

*Height slightly reduced by wear

The buccal half of a P_4 (Member E) already in wear, has a height of 71 mm. An unworn M^3 from the same horizon has a height of 59 mm.

Table 3

Length (mm) of Mandibular Cheek Teeth in Hipparion

Character	Source	P_2	P_3 and P_4	M_1 and M_2
Lacking ectostylids	Langebaanweg	33.5	28.3 to 32 ($n=5$)	26.5 to 29.3 ($n=6$)
	Laetolil	33	28.5; 29.5	27; 27
	Earlier Kaiso		26	18-20
	Shungura B	29	30?	25.5
Having ectostylids	Shungura G	28.5	25 to 26.5 ($n=4$)	20 to 24 ($n=5$)
	Shungura F	27.5	22; 23	20.5 to 22 ($n=4$)
	Shungura C	29; 29.5	24 (very worn)	25.5
	Ichkeul		28	
	Ain Brimba	33.5	30	28; 26

Discussion

An astragalus (from Member A) and two lower cheek teeth (from Member B) attest to the presence of a large *Hipparion* species in the lowest part of the Shungura Formation. The only intact lower tooth lacks an ectostylid. These remains are provisionally assigned to *Hipparion* cf. *albertense* Hopwood, a large form lacking an ectostylid.

Table 4
Length (mm) of Maxillary Cheek Teeth in Hipparion

Character	Source	P^2	P^3 and P^4	M^1 and M^2	M^3
Lacking ectostylids	Langebaanweg		27.5 to 30 (*n*=8)	20.5 to 27.8 (*n*=10)	23.6
	Laetolil	39	31; 31	27.3; 25	24.2
	Earlier Kaiso	(29)	29.5; (28.5)	21.5; 24	(20)
?	Later Kaiso		24.5		27.5
Having ectostylids	Shungura G		26; (26)	21; 23	
	Shungura F		23; 24		
	Shungura E		25		21
	Shungura D				22
	Shungura C			23	
	Ichkeul		26.5; 27	24 to 26 (*n*=4)	(24)
	Ain Brimba	41	28 to 32 (*n*=5)	27	28

The P_2 and first phalanx from members A and B are of more modest size. The P_2 is worn on the buccal side, and it is thus impossible to discern whether an ectostylid was present. Additional material is necessary to determine whether these remains can also be assigned to *Hipparion* cf. *albertense* or whether they might represent the *Hipparion* found from Member C upward. Hooijer (this symposium) regards the latter as *Hipparion* cf. *ethiopicum* (Joleaud), a generally more gracile form with lower cheek teeth, almost invariably having ectostylids.

Equus

The genus *Equus* appears for the first time at the base of Member G in the Shungura Formation.

The first phalanges (table 6) and the lower cheek teeth (table 8) from the Shungura Formation are near the upper limits of variability of *Equus grevyi*. However, an astragalus (113-1972-42) from Member G falls at the lower limits of the size range of *Equus grevyi* (table 7). The astragali of *Equus numidicus* from North Africa are also relatively small, a feature in common with the specimen from the Omo. Most remains indicate the presence of an *Equus* larger than most modern zebras, including possibly *Equus grevyi*. Its size was comparable to that of *Equus numidicus* Pomel from Ain Boucherit and Ain el Bey.

A distal metacarpal 3 from the lower units of Member G represents a very large species of *Equus*. This might well be the large *Equus* sp. nov. A, present in the Lower and Upper members of the Koobi Fora Formation, East Rudolf (see following chapter). Aside from the large species of *Equus* there are also some specimens collected by Arambourg (1947) and an astragalus recently collected from Member H which indicate the presence of an *Equus* similar in size to *Equus burchelli granti*. A left astragalus (1967-726), though damaged, clearly represents *Equus*. Its maximum height could not have exceeded 56 mm, and is well within the range of variability of *E. burchelli granti*, but not of *Equus grevyi* (table 7).

We cannot exclude the possibility that the specimen represents a young individual. (One newborn *Equus grevyi* had an astragalus height less than 60 mm, and an eight-month old individual had an astragalus height of 61 mm, larger than that of any *E. burchelli granti*.)

Arambourg (1947, p. 306, pl. X, fig. 4) collected an M_1 or M_2 (1933-9-397) which he hesitated to attribute to *Hipparion* or to *Equus*. It is in fact a small *Equus*, approximating

Table 5

Dimensions (mm) of Hipparion Metapodials

Source	Maximum Length	Proximal, Anterior-Posterior		Proximal Transverse	Mid-Shaft Transverse	Distal Anterior-Posterior	Distal Transverse	
		Articular Surface	Maximum				Articular Surface	Supra-articular Surface
Metacarpal 3								
Olduvai Bed II	206; 217; 223	36; 37; 37		44; 45; 46		33; 34; 36	42; (45); 48	
Shungura F	219	27.5	32	40.5	24.5	31	34	36.5
Shungura D						34	39.5	38
Shungura C		(30)		44	31.5			
Ichkeul	267	(33)		54	34	>37.5	>40.5	>45
Metatarsal 3								
Laetolil[a]						35	37	42
Olduvai Bed II[a]	242 to 266 (n=5)	37 to 41 (n=5)		45 to 48 (n=5)		32 to 38 (n=7)	43 to 48 (n=7)	
Shungura D					(31)	34.5	40	(42.5)
Ichkeul	267.5		>38	47	34.5	>33.5	>42	>44.5

[a]The transverse diameters of metatarsal 3 from Laetolil are from measured photographs published by Dietrich (1942), and the anterior-posterior diameter of this specimen, as well as those of the Olduvai Bed II specimens, are those given by Boné and Singer (1965).

the size of *Equus burchelli granti*. In figure 1 it is compared with a large specimen (252-1967-414) from Member G. The length of *Equus* lower premolars and molars from the Shungura Formation, as well as those from Ain Boucherit (Arambourg 1970) and those of modern *Equus grevyi* and *Equus burchelli granti*, are given in table 8.

Discussion

The size of phalanges, astragali, and lower cheek teeth of the large *Equus* from the upper Shungura Formation compare favorably with *Equus numidicus* Pomel from Ain Boucherit. A more interesting comparison might be made with *Equus* remains from eastern Africa, particularly Olduvai and East Rudolph. However, the collections from these localities have still to be studied in detail. Hooijer (this symposium) considers *Equus* teeth from Shungura Formation members G-I to be similar to those of Olduvai Bed II. Following this assumption, this large *Equus* is provisionally attributed to *Equus* cf. *oldowayensis* Hopwood. Another very large species of *Equus* is also represented in lower Member G.

The small form of *Equus* is too poorly known to identify at this point, but its presence is worth mentioning.

Coexistence of *Hipparion* and *Equus*

Equus and *Hipparion* coexisted in Member G of Shungura Formation and are found together at four localities:

Table 6

Maximum Length (mm) of First Phalanges of Equus

Specimen	Forelimb			Hind Limb		
	n	Mean	Range	n	Mean	Range
Equus burchelli granti	18	75.76	69.4-82.4	17	71.59	66.7-77.3
Equus zebra	7	79.74	75.8-83.4	7	75.51	71.2-79.6
Equus grevyi	9	86.33	82.0-91.1	9	81.33	76.4-87.0
Shungura G						
215-1973-2547		87.1				
253-1973-5116		86.2				
113-1972-42		>84.3				
Omo						
1933-9-741		84.2				
Equus numidicus						
(after Arambourg 1970)		85				78-81

NOTE: The minimum length of the phalanges varies between 70 and 73 mm, whereas the length of those from Olduvai varies between 64 and 69 mm (cf. Hopwood 1937 and his use of these measures).

Table 7

Maximum Height (mm) of Equus *Astragali*

Specimen	n	Mean	Range
Equus burchelli granti	26	56.44	52.2-60.0
Equus grevyi	10	63.60	60.5-67.5
Shungura H 1967-762			(56)
Shungura G 113-72-4			>61
Ain Boucherit *Equus numidicus* (Arambourg 1970)	4	61.25	57-64

29-- *Equus* 1 upper cheek tooth, 1 lower cheek tooth
    Hipparion 1 upper cheek tooth
215-- *Equus* 6 postcranial fragments, 1 upper cheek tooth
    Hipparion 1 astragalus
233-- *Equus* 1 lower cheek tooth
    Hipparion 1 lower cheek tooth
VEO-- *Equus* 1 upper cheek tooth and some teeth fragments, 1 proximal metatarsal 3, 1 tibia fragment
    Hipparion 1 tibia fragment

The coexistence of *Equus* and *Hipparion* has repeatedly been noted. The evidence from Europe and the Middle East bearing on this problem has recently been discussed elsewhere

Table 8

Mesiodistal Lengths (mm) of Equus Lower Cheek Teeth

Specimen	n	P_3 and P_4 Mean	Range	n	M_1 and M_2 Mean	Range	n	M_3 Mean	Range
Equus grevyi	12	28.55	25.8-31.0	15	26.38	23.1-31.0	6	30.53	26.8-33.8
Equus burchelli granti	108	23.78	20.1-26.1	110	21.72	18.5-25.7	52	24.21	21.5-28.0
Shungura Fm.									
252-1967-414			>31.3						
29-1968-1823			31.5						
195-1973-1353			>31.3						
233-1973-4129						28			
214-1973-4163									34
113-1972-40 (mandible)			31.5-32			28			33
1951-4-121			31						
1933-9-367			30						
1933-9-397						22			
Equus numidicus (after Arambourg 1970)			32			28-33.7			33.5-35

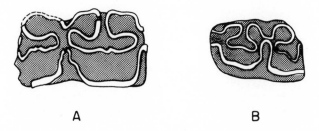

A   B

Figure 1. Lower molars of (B) a small species of Equus (1933-9-397) collected by Arambourg and (A) a large species from Member G, Shungura Formation (Omo locality 252-1967-414).

(Eisenmann and Brunet 1973). The collections from Ain Boucherit, Ain Hanech, and Ichkeul do not confirm such coexistence in North Africa, at least. In East Africa there is clear evidence that Equus and Hipparion coexisted at Olduvai Beds I and II (Leakey 1971, p. 293), at Koobi Fora and Ileret (Maglio 1972, and personal observations), and in the upper Shungura Formation, lower Omo basin.

Conclusions

Equids are present throughout the Shungura Formation. Hipparion occurs from Member A through Member G, and Equus appears from the base of Member G upward. Hipparion cf. albertense is present in members A and B. It is large, with lower cheek teeth probably almost invariably lacking an ectostylid, as in the samples from Laetolil and Langebaanweg. The large Hipparion from Ain Brimba and Ichkeul, Tunisia, is distinct in that an ectostylid is always present. From Member C upward, Hipparion cf. ethiopicum is the species commonly represented. It is smaller than the earlier species and almost always has an ectostylid.

For the moment the relationships of these two forms are unclear. It is thus impossible to know now whether *H.* cf. *ethiopicum* is a derivative of *H.* cf. *albertense* or if it is a new immigrant species, and it is also uncertain whether the two hipparionids may have coexisted before *H.* cf. *ethiopicum* ultimately replaced *H.* cf. *albertense*.

Equus cf. *oldowayensis* appears at the base of Member G about 1.9 m.y. (Bonnefille et al. 1973), or in the upper part of Zone IV as defined by Coppens (1972). In North Africa, the most ancient *Equus* known is *E. numidicus* from Ain Boucherit. According to J. J. Jaeger (pers. comm.) this occurrence is equivalent to Coppens's Zone III and probably to Olduvai Bed I. The findings from Omo, Olduvai, and Ain Boucherit are in agreement, showing that the genus *Equus* was already widespread in Africa about 1.9 m.y. in the upper part of Zone IV or Zone III. The first African appearance of *Equus* could be even older.

At Koobi Fora the skull of a large *Equus* has been recovered from below the KBS Tuff, which has a radiometric age of about 2.61 m.y. (Fitch and Miller 1970). This same very large species may also be present in lower Member G. In Europe *Equus* appears for the first time in localities which are dated at least 2.5 m.y.--including Roccaneyra (Eisenmann and Brunet 1973), and probably also Montopoli, Beresti, Malusteni, Grauceanu, and Moldavia (De Giuli 1972).

Besides *Equus* cf. *oldowayensis*, a small form of *Equus* is present in Member G. However, the paucity of material available does not permit us to determine its affinities or its biostratigraphic significance.

References

Arambourg, C. 1947. *Mission scientifique de l'Omo (1932-1933)*. Vol. 1. *Geologie-Anthropologie*, fasc. 3, pp. 231-562. Mémoire, Muséum national d'histoire naturelle (Paris).

_____. 1970. Les vertébrés du Pléistocène de l'Afrique du Nord. *Arch. Muséum Nat. Hist. Nat.* (Paris), 7th ser. 10:1-126.

Boné, E. L., and Singer, R. 1965. Hipparion from Langebaanweg, Cape Province and revision of the genus in Africa. *Ann. S. African Mus., Cape Town* 48(16):273-397.

Bonnefille, R.; Brown, F. H.; Chavaillon, Y.; Coppens, Y.; Haesaerts, P.; Heinzelin, J. de; and Howell, F. C. 1973. Situation stratigraphique des localités à hominidés des gisements plio-pléistocènes de l'Omo en Ethiopie. *C. R. Acad. Sci. (Paris)*, ser. D, 276:2781-84, 2879-82.

Cooke, H. B. S., and Coryndon, S. C. 1970. Pleistocene mammals from the Kaiso Formation and other related deposits in Uganda. *Fossil vertebrates of Africa*, ed. L. S. B. Leakey and R. J. G. Savage, 2:107-224. London: Academic Press.

Coppens, Y. 1972. Tentative de zonation du Pliocène et du Pléistocène d'Afrique par les grands mammifères. *C. R. Acad. Sci. (Paris)*, ser. D, 274:181-84.

_____. 1973. Les restes d'hominidés des séries inférieures et moyennes des formations plio-villafranchiennes de l'Omo en Ethiopie (récoltes 1970, 1971 et 1972). *C. R. Acad. Sci. (Paris)*, ser. D, 276:1823-26.

De Giuli, C. 1972. On the type form of *Equus stenonis* Cocchi. *Palaeontographica Italica* 68(n.s. 38):35-49.

Dietrich, W. O. 1942. Ältestquartäre Säugetiere aus der südlichen Serengeti, Deutsch-Ostafrika. *Palaeontographica*, ser. A, 94:43-133.

Eisenmann, V., and Brunet, J. 1973. Présence simultanée de cheval et d'hipparion dans le Villafranchien moyen de France à Roccaneyra (Puy-de-Dôme): Etude critique de cas semblables (Europe et Proche Orient). *International Colloquium on the Problem "The Boundary between Neogene and Quaternary."* Collection of Papers, 4:104-22.

Fitch, F. J., and Miller, J. A. 1970. Radioisotope age determinations of Lake Rudolf artefact site. *Nature* 226:225-28.

Gromova, V. 1952. Les hipparions (le genre *Hipparion*). *Trudy Paleontol. Inst. Akad. Nauk USSR* 36:1-475.

Hopwood, A. T. 1937. Die fossilen Pferde von Oldoway. *Wiss. Erg. Oldoway Exp.* 4:112-36.

Joleaud, L. 1933. Un nouveau genre d'equidé quaternaire de l'Omo (Abyssinie): *Libyhipparion ethiopicus*. *Bull. Soc. géol. France,* 5th ser., 3:7-27.

Leakey, M. D. 1971. *Olduvai Gorge*. Vol. 3. *Excavations in Beds I and II, 1960-1963.* Cambridge: At the University Press.

Maglio, V. J. 1972. Vertebrate faunas and chronology of hominid-bearing sediments east of Lake Rudolf, Kenya. *Nature* 239:379-85.

Pomel, A. 1897. Les Equidés. In *Monographies des vertébrés fossiles de l'Algérie,* 10:1-44. Publ. Serv. Carte géol. Algérie, Alger, Paléontologie.

21. A PRELIMINARY NOTE ON EQUIDAE FROM THE
KOOBI FORA FORMATION, KENYA

V. Eisenmann

The distribution of Equidae from localities in each of the faunal zones of Maglio (1972) of the Koobi Fora Formation, north Kenya, is given in table 1. The relative frequency of remains of *Equus* and of *Hipparion* is given in table 2.

Hipparion

Remains of *Hipparion* are fairly rare. Of 37 specimens recovered to date, 32 can be definitely referred to one of Maglio's three faunal zones (table 2). All lower cheek teeth (14 isolated finds and 17 associated in dental series) have generally well developed ectostylids. These teeth are the same size as or slightly larger than *Hipparion* cf. *ethiopicum* (Joleaud) from the Shungura Formation, Member C and upward. There does not seem to be any change in either tooth size or ectostylid size from one faunal zone to another. Table 3 gives the mesiodistal length (mm) of cheek teeth and their ectostylids in a *Hipparion* mandible from the Lower Member of the Koobi Fora Formation (*Mesochoerus limnetes* zone) and in a mandible from Member F of the Shungura Formation, Omo. An astragalus from the Upper Member of the Koobi Fora Formation (*Metridiochoerus andrewsi* zone) approaches in size a specimen from Shungura Formation, Member G. The former has a height of 55.2 mm and the latter a height of 56 mm.

In conclusion all these specimens from the Koobi Fora Formation can be referred to *Hipparion* cf. *ethiopicum*, species of moderate size with a constant ectostylid.

Equus

Remains of *Equus* are substantially more abundant than those of *Hipparion*. Of 178 specimens recovered to date, 135 can be definitely referred to one of Maglio's three faunal zones (table 2).

Equus sp. nov. A and *Equus* cf. *oldowayensis*

The Lower Member (*Mesochoerus limnetes* zone) of the Koobi Fora Formation has yielded a well-preserved and exceptionally large skull of *Equus*. The basal length is 20 mm larger than the largest of 23 specimens of *Equus grevyi* I have measured. The upper cheek teeth are also remarkably large. This appears to represent a new species which I provisionally designate as *Equus* sp. nov. A. There are also two upper molars from the Upper Member (*Metridiochoerus andrewsi* zone) of the Koobi Fora Formation which are similar in their great size (28.5 and 29.5 mm length).

234

Table 1

Areas of Occurrence of Specimens of Equidae in the Three Faunal Zones of the Koobi Fora Formation

Mesochoerus limnetes Zone	Equus	Hipparion	Indeterminate
102 0213	+		
103 0115	+		
01 15/23	+		
0222	+		
105 0101	+		
0109	+		
0205	+		
0209	+	+	
123			+
130	+	+	
131	+	+	
Mesochoerus limnetes zone?			
102 0201	+	+	
121	+	+	
130	+	+	

Metridiochoerus andrewsi Zone	Equus	Hipparion	Indeterminate
08 B 0306	+		
0308	+		
10	+		
10 1001	+	+	
1002		+	
1004		+	
12		+	
102			+
103	+	+	
103 0223/5	+		
0230/1	+		
0235/9	+	+	
0246/57	+	+	
0257/64	+		
0265/78	+	+	
104	+	+	+
104 B	+		
104 B 0114/6	+		
0120	+		
0121	+	+	
0126/9	+		
105 0121	+		
0222	+		
124	+		
129		+	
131		+	
Metridiochoerus andrewsi zone ?			
30	+	+	
102	+		
103	+		
123	+		
Above KBS tuff	+	+	

Loxodonta africana Zone	Equus	Hipparion	Indeterminate
01	+		
01 A	+		
01 0103	+		+
0104	+		
0107	+		
03 0106	+		
0107	+		
06 0101	+		
0104		+	
06 0301	+		
0308	+		
0309	+	+	+
0311	+		+
07			+
07 A	+		
08 0103	+		+
08 A 0302	+		
1105		+	
1106	+		
108	+		
Loxodonta africana zone ?			
01 0103			+

Table 2

Skeletal Parts of Equidae Recovered from the Three Faunal Zones of the Koobi Fora Formation

Specimen		*Equus*	*Hipparion*
Loxodonta africana zone			
Skull fragment		1	0
Isolated cheek teeth and fragments	(upper	20	1
	(lower	11	1
Limb bones and fragments		2	2
Metridiochoerus andrewsi zone			
Skull fragments		2	0
Mandibular fragments		2	1
Isolated cheek teeth and fragments	(upper	29	8
	(lower	14	12
Limb bones and fragments		17	2
Mesochoerus limnetes zone			
Skull		1	0
Mandibular fragments		1	1
Isolated cheek teeth and fragments	(upper	8	3
	(lower	5	1
Limb bones and fragments		22	0
Certain origin		135	32
Uncertain origin		43	5

Table 3

Length (mm) of Lower Cheek Teeth and of Ectostylids in Hipparion *Mandibles from the Lower Member of the Koobi Fora Formation (Kenya) and from Member F of the Shungura Formation, Omo (Ethiopia)*

Specimen	Total Length	Length of Premolar Series	P_2 Length	P_3-P_4 Length	P_3-P_4 Ectostylid Length	M_1-M_2 Length	M_1-M_2 Ectostylid Length	M_3 Length
KNM.ER 1626	145	74.5	28.2	23.9; 22.5	8.7	22; 22.2	5.8; 4.4	24.5
Omo 118.72.5	141	73.5	28	23; 22.5	6.5	21.5; 21	6; 4.5	24.5

All the other upper cheek teeth of *Equus* from the Koobi Fora Formation are smaller. They are the same size as two teeth from Member G of the Shungura Formation, Omo (see preceding chapter). This form from the upper members of the Shungura Formation has been attributed by Hooijer (this symposium) to *Equus* cf. *oldowayensis*. I am provisionally attributing most of the *Equus* upper cheek teeth from the Koobi Fora Formation to this same species. The upper cheek teeth of *Equus numidicus* from Ain Boucherit (Algeria) are larger than those of *Equus* cf. *oldowayensis* and smaller than those of *Equus* sp. nov. A (cf. table 4).

The attribution of lower cheek teeth and postcranial parts to one or the other of these two species of *Equus* from the Koobi Fora Formation is still an unresolved problem.

Table 4

Dimensions of Upper Cheek Teeth of Recent Equus grevyi *and Earlier Pleistocene Species of* Equus *from Koobi Fora, Omo, and Ain Boucherit*

Specimen		$P^3 - P^4$			$M^1 - M^2$		
		n	Mean and SD	Range	n	Mean and SD	Range
Equus grevyi		20	28.6 ± 1.53	25.8 - 31	23	25.3 ± 1.87	22 - 29.2
Equus cf. *oldowayensis*	Koobi Fora	35	28.7 ± 1.60	25.1 - 31.5	30	25.5 ± 1.38	22.5 - 27.9
	Omo (G)	1		29	1		26.5
Equus sp. nov. *A*	Koobi Fora	2		31.9 - 34.2	2		31.5 - 31.5
Equus numidicus	Ain Boucherit	8	30.9 ± 1.26	29 - 33	6	27.75 ± 1.44	27 - 29.5

Equus sp. nov. B?

There are some postcranial bones and a lower cheek tooth from the *Metridiochoerus andrewsi* zone and the *Loxodonta africana* zone which demonstrate the presence of an asinine species of *Equus*. From its size and proportions this *Equus* sp. nov. B? resembles *Equus tabeti* Arambourg (1970) from Ain Hanech (in Biozone III of Coppens 1972). However, the lack of sufficient material makes this attribution uncertain.

Conclusions

Equids are present in all the members of the Koobi Fora Formation.

Hipparion cf. *ethiopicum*, rather infrequent but present throughout the succession, always shows a well-developed ectostylid. Thus far there are no specimens referrable to the large hipparionine *Hipparion albertense*, which lacks an ectostylid and which is present at Laetolil, Langebaanweg, and in members A and B of the Shungura Formation, Omo.

An *Equus* similar to that characteristic of Shungura Formation, Member G, is present in all the members of the Koobi Fora Formation and is referred to *Equus* cf. *oldowayensis*. An exceptionally large skull with large upper dentition from the *Mesochoerus limnetes* zone apparently represents a new species of *Equus*. An asinine *Equus*, perhaps comparable to *Equus tabeti*, occurs in the *Metridiochoerus andrewsi* and *Loxodonta africana* zones, but its precise affinities are still uncertain.

Acknowledgments

I am grateful to the Wenner-Gren Foundation for financing my travel to Nairobi and to the C.N.R.S. (R.C.P. 292, under the direction of Y. Coppens) for supporting me there during the course of this work. Richard Leakey generously entrusted to me the study of the Equidae from East Rudolf, and John Harris was most helpful in regard to their stratigraphic provenance.

This paper is no. 59 in the East Rudolf Project catalogue of publications.

References

Arambourg, C. 1970. Les vertébrés du Pléistocène de l'Afrique du Nord. *Arch. Muséum Nat. Hist. Nat.* (Paris), ser. 7, 10:1-126.

Coppens, Y. 1972. Tentative de zonation du Pliocène et du Pléistocène d'Afrique par les grands mammifères. *C. R. Acad. Sci. (Paris),* ser. D, 274:181-84.

Maglio, V. J. 1972. Vertebrate faunas and chronology of hominid-bearing sediments east of Lake Rudolf, Kenya. *Nature* 239:379-85.

22. FOSSIL HIPPOPOTAMIDAE FROM PLIO-PLEISTOCENE SUCCESSIONS
OF THE RUDOLF BASIN

S. C. Coryndon

The Hippopotamidae of the Lake Rudolf basin were virtually unknown, except in the Shungura Formation of the Omo basin, until the mid-1960s. Until then most fossil hippopotamids recovered from African deposits could be allied to the extant species *Hippopotamus amphibius*, which ranged over most of Africa until historic times but is now restricted to well-watered areas south of the Sahara. This large, lumbering, splay-toed artiodactyl has four incisor teeth in each jaw (tetraprotodont), with the upper incisors positioned so that the lateral incisors are inserted posterior to the central; the cranium has elevated orbits and the lacrimal bone is large; the limbs are short and robust, ideally suited to a lacustrine environment. This hippopotamus spends most of the daylight hours in the water, coming to graze on land at dusk where grass is the chief item of diet, although it may eat other plants where grass is not freely available. *Choeropsis liberiensis*, the living pygmy hippopotamus of the West African forests, is a much rarer and morphologically very different animal with no known fossil connections. It has four incisors in the upper jaw but only two in the lower (diprotodont); the orbits are positioned on the side of the face and the lacrimal bone is small; the barrel-shaped body is supported by comparatively slender limbs. *H. amphibius* is the species with which fossil forms are mainly compared and has in the past been taken as the normal unspecialized form of *Hippopotamus*.

New discoveries from East Africa, mainly in the Baringo and Lake Rudolf basins, indicate that it is probably a distinct group which forms the basic hippopotamid pattern: These fossil hippopotamids have six incisor teeth in each jaw (hexaprotodont), orbits which are elevated little or not at all, an unspecialized facial bone arrangement with a small lacrimal bone, and comparatively long and slender limb bones. These hexaprotodonts probably arose at least 12 m.y. ago, that is, well into the Miocene (Bishop et al. 1971). They evolved and flourished as the stock from which all other hippopotamids both in and outside Africa arose, until their extinction in the late Pleistocene. The tetraprotodonts are a specialized group arising from the hexaprotodonts, probably about 4 m.y.

In the first half of the nineteenth century, Falconer and Cautley (1839) described a medium-sized hippopotamus from the Pleistocene deposits of the Asian Siwalik Hills as *Hexaprotodon sivalensis*. The generic name illustrated the fact that, unlike the living *Hippopotamus amphibius* or indeed any previously recognized fossil forms, this new species carried six incisors in each jaw. The morphology of the cranial bones, in particular those of the facial area, is not unlike that of the extant *Choeropsis liberiensis*. *H. sivalensis*

is found throughout the Pleistocene deposits of the Siwaliks, but becomes extinct before
the Holocene. During this time, a gradual evolution in the skull can be seen whereby the
second incisors in both jaws become smaller and the orbits are elevated so that in its most
advanced form as *H. sivalensis palaeindicus* in upper Pleistocene levels a skull approaching
the morphology of the extant *H. amphibius* is reached; many differences are still clearly
apparent in such details as the arrangment of the facial bones, position and number of the
incisor teeth, and shape of the canine teeth (Hooijer 1950). It is now clear that *Hexaprotodon* probably arose from an African hexaprotodont ancestor in the early Pliocene.

At the end of the nineteenth century, a collection of small, isolated hippopotamus
teeth were recovered from Bône in Algeria and described by Gaudry (1876) as *Hippopotamus
hipponensis*. This new species is known only from isolated teeth, and it was not until
sixty years later that Arambourg (1945) made a critical revision of the Bône remains and
demonstrated that *H. hipponensis* was a hexaprotodont hippopotamus, the first to be recognized in Africa.

The first hexaprotodont cranium recovered from the Lake Rudolf basin was found in deposits of unknown age near the Kalakol River, Ferguson's Gulf, in 1931, by a party under
Sir Vivian Fuchs. It was the only fossil mammal collected from these particular deposits
and was referred (Fuchs 1934) to *Hippopotamus imagunculus*, a species described by Hopwood
(1926) from the Plio-Pleistocene Kaiso Formation of Uganda. The Uganda specimens consist
mainly of isolated teeth, and no specimen from the type area shows for certain whether *H.
imagunculus* has a hexaprotodont dentition, although it probably is so in a species at this
late Tertiary level (Cooke and Coryndon 1970). Although the Kalakol specimen collected by
Fuchs may not be the same species as the Kaiso *H. imagunculus*, it is similar in size and
morphology, but rather more advanced. It consists of the rather broken but fairly complete
cranium of a small hippopotamid rather larger than *Choeropsis*. The six incisors are peglike, subequal in size, and positioned in a shallow arc in the premaxilla. The orbits are
slightly elevated and the cheek teeth rather higher crowned than those of *H. imagunculus*
from Kaiso, consistent with the Kalakol specimen's being a more evolved form, possibly from
deposits of later age.

Although the small hippopotamus from Kalakol, Ferguson's Gulf, was collected in 1931,
it was not recognized as a hexaprotodont until the mid-1960s. This decade saw increased
investigation of the Lake Rudolf area, starting with an expedition from Harvard University
to Loperot and Kanapoi, in the southwest of the basin (Patterson 1966; Patterson, Behrensmeyer, and Sill 1970). This latter Pliocene locality produced a very interesting and rich
mammalian fauna, with hippopotamids a relatively common element. The earlier deposits of
Lothagam to the north produced an even richer fauna; these two localities have produced
several specimens of a hexaprotodont hippopotamid larger than *H. imagunculus*, which shows
many characters not preserved in the Kaiso specimens.

The cranium of the Lothagam and Kanapoi species (fig. 1), referred to here as sp. "D"
nov., has orbits positioned at the side of the head, the pre- and postorbital portions of
the cranium nearly equal in length, and the canine teeth with a deep posterior groove. The
incisor teeth in each jaw are peglike with a tip-to-tip occlusion between upper and lower
producing a wear facet on one face only. The first upper premolar is double-rooted, one of
the distinguishing characters of the Siwalik *Hexaprotodon*. All the premolars are large and
pustulate, with the length of the premolar row P2-P4 nearly equal to the length of the
molar row M1-M3. In more advanced hexaprotodonts the premolars tend to become smaller and
the preorbital length of the cranium is extended. The limb bones of the species from

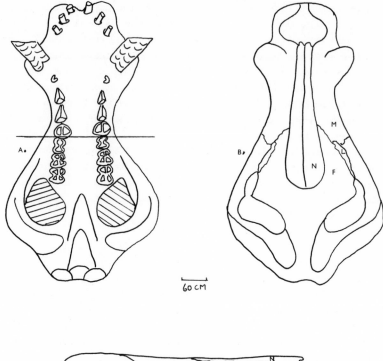

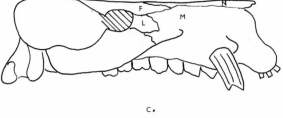

Figure 1. Cranium of hexaprotodont from Lothagam, sp. "D" nov.: (A) Occlusal, (B) dorsal, and (C) lateral views. *N*, nasal; *F*, frontal; *L*, lacrimal; *M*, maxillary.

Lothagam and Kanapoi are slender and gracile, resembling those of *Choeropsis* but considerably larger. Specimens of hippopotamids from these two areas represent the most complete specimens of early hippopotamids now known from anywhere in the world; they may be derived from ancestral forms represented by fragmentary hippopotamid remains recovered from the older (up to 12 m.y.) sediments in the Baringo basin to the south.

    With further exploration, discovery, and excavation of many fossil localities in the Lake Rudolf basin in the late 1960s many more specimens of fossil hippopotamids have been recovered. Only part of these specimens have been studied in detail, but it is clear that in the Rudolf basin there is a complex hippopotamus fauna of Plio-Pleistocene age containing several different species (fig. 2). *Hippopotamus amphibius* is the only living species found all round Lake Rudolf at present, and it is perplexing to understand why, during the previous 5 m.y. or more, so many different species flourished in the same area. Although the sediments of the Shungura Formation of the Omo and the Ileret Formation of East Rudolf are only a small distance apart, are of broadly similar age, and crop out near the present shores of the lake, each locality has a different species of fossil hippopotamid. Even in

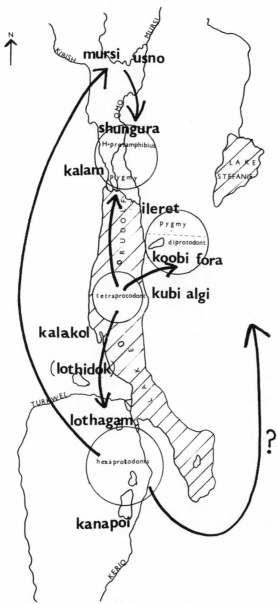

Figure 2. Lake Rudolf basin and some fossil hippopotamid localities

the most southerly of the East Rudolf exposures at Kubi Algi, where the sediments are
roughly contemporary with Kanapoi on the west of the lake, the hippopotamid is completely
different from the distinctive and unspecialized hexaprotodont of the Kanapoi and Lothagam
deposits. This contradicts evidence from other fossil mammal groups, for instance the
Suidae and the Proboscidea, where a continuity and evolution of species can be seen to link
many of the deposits around the lake basin.

The hippopotamus from the oldest sediments of the Omo basin in the Mursi Formation, roughly equivalent in age to Kanapoi sediments, is known from only a few specimens but appears to be very similar to the Kanapoi species. In the later sediments of the Usno Formation and the lowest (tuffs A and B) levels of the Shungura Formation a hexaprotodont hippopotamid is present (Howell, Fichter, and Eck 1969) which appears to be on the same line as the Mursi form and is probably ancestral to the much more common *Hippopotamus protamphibius* Arambourg (1947) of the Shungura Formation (tuffs C-G). From Tuff C upward this hippopotamid species is tetraprotodont in its anterior dentition (fig. 3), with the lower central incisor about twice the size of the lateral; the upper incisors are subequal in size and arranged in the premaxilla in a shallow arc as in the hexaprotodonts, not one behind the other as in the tetraprotodonts proper. The facial bones of the Shungura hippopotamus have the unspecialized arrangement seen in the hexaprotodonts, and although the orbits are slightly elevated they do not reach the specialization seen in the extant species. The limb bones are more slender than in *H. amphibius*, although more robust than in the Lothagam and Kanapoi species. Thus a single evolutionary line can be postulated to link the Lothagam species through Kanapoi, Mursi, and Usno, culminating in typical *H. protamphibius* of Shungura, Member G.

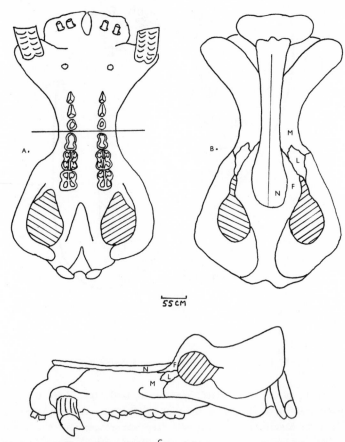

Figure 3. Cranium of *Hippopotamus protamphibius* from the Shungura Formation, Omo basin, Member C: (*A*) Occlusal, (*B*) dorsal, and (*C*) lateral views. *N*, nasal; *F*, frontal; *L*, lacrimal; *M*, maxillary.

The common hippopotamid from the lower levels of the East Rudolf deposits of Koobi
Fora--below the KBS Tuff (Vondra et al. 1971)--is superficially not unlike *H. protamphibius*
of the Shungura Formation, though it cannot be referred to this species as suggested by
Maglio (1971). It can be distinguished by the small canine teeth, small upper incisors,
large premolars, and the diastema between the lower central incisors. This hippopotamid is
probably the forerunner of a very specialized species found above the KBS Tuff in both the
Koobi Fora and Ileret formations, here referred to as sp. "C" nov., which has a diprotodont
lower dentition with only two very large incisors, probably I_1, having a large wear facet
on the upper surface only and separated by a wide midline bony protrusion. There are four
very small, peglike incisors in the upper jaw, set along the anterior edge of the premaxilla (fig. 4). The canine teeth are small and in the lower jaw are set in long slender alveoli (fig. 6*d*). The molars are very low crowned, fig. 5*b*, and the facial bone arrangement
is as in the hexaprotodonts; in specimens from the higher levels at Koobi Fora and Ileret,
the orbits become elevated to a remarkable degree, approaching the state seen in the large
tetraprotodont species from Olduvai Gorge, *Hippopotamus gorgops*. The East Rudolf diprotodont is quite unlike any other form known from other deposits of any age, and was probably
a browsing form rather than a grazer. Although the skull was rather larger than that of
H. protamphibius from Shungura, the limbs are very long and slender (fig. 6*b*) and very
suitable for a habitat in forest or bush country along a river valley, as envisaged by
Isaac (this symposium). They would, however, be quite useless in a muddy lacustrine environment.

In Area 105, Koobi Fora, a collection of hippopotamid and crocodile remains were found
in a small valley eroding from deposits below the KBS Tuff. The hippopotamus is the early
form of species "C," and the crocodile appears to be the riverine rather than the lacustrine species (Tchernov, pers. comm.), thus adding emphasis to the hypothesis of a

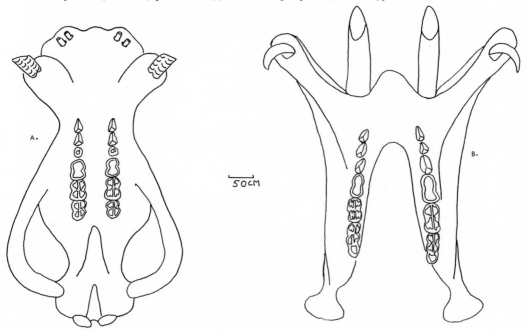

50CM

Figure 4. Diprotodont hippopotamus from above KBS Tuff, Koobi Fora, East Rudolf, sp. "C"
nov. Occlusal views of (*A*) cranium, (*B*) mandible.

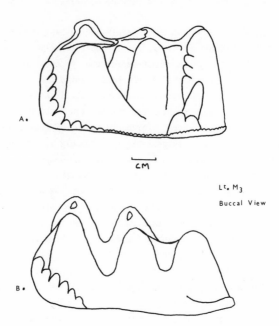

Lt. M₃

Buccal View

Figure 5. East Rudolf, Kenya. (A) Left lower third molar, *Hippopotamus* cf. *gorgops*, from above KBS Tuff; (B) left lower third molar, diprotodont, from above KBS Tuff.

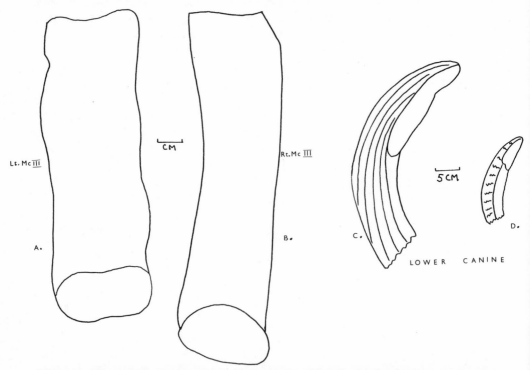

Figure 6. East Rudolf, Kenya. Fossil hippopotami. (A) Left third metacarpal, *Hippopotamus* cf. *gorgops*, from below KBS Tuff; (B) right third metacarpal, diprotodont, from above KBS Tuff; (C) lower canine, *Hippopotamus* cf. *gorgops*, from above KBS Tuff; (D) lower canine, diprotodont, from above KBS Tuff.

riverbank environment for the specialized form of hippopotamus. However, in this case, both forms are found in a deltaic to lacustrine sedimentary environment rather than a fluvial one, and their paleoecology cannot be considered firmly established until more environmental sampling can be done.

A second species, the tetraprotodont *H. gorgops*, is also found in East Rudolf deposits alongside the peculiar diprotodonts. It is rare in the sediments below the KBS Tuff but becomes more common with time until in the upper levels of the Ileret Formation it is dominant over the East Rudolf diprotodont. *H. gorgops* has high-crowned molars (fig. 5a), small premolars, orbits elevated to a marked degree, and a typical tetraprotodont arrangement of incisor teeth with facial bones as in *Hippopotamus amphibius*. The canines are large and strongly ridged (fig. 6c), and the limb bones are short and robust, as in the extant species (fig. 6a). *H. gorgops* was clearly suited to an aquatic life as a grazing animal, and thus the specialized browsing diprotodont species "C" could exist in the riverine habitats away from competition of *H. gorgops* in the lacustrine areas. The disappearance of the diprotodonts in the upper levels of the East Rudolf localities may well be due to some change in conditions causing expansion of Lake Rudolf by which *H. gorgops*, with its preadaption for an aquatic life, had a clear advantage over the diprotodont when the latter was driven from the riverine environment but could not adapt to the new lacustrine conditions.

A large hippopotamus similar to *H. gorgops* is present also in the upper levels of the Omo deposits and may have become the dominant species at Omo in the same way and at the same time as the *H. gorgops* of East Rudolf. Expansion of Lake Rudolf would affect the East Rudolf and Omo areas at the same time, and conditions would clearly favor the aquatic hippopotamus.

A third species common to both Omo and East Rudolf is present in the upper levels of both areas. This is a pygmy tetraprotodont (figs. 7, 8) described as "species B" by Coryndon and Coppens (1973), and cannot be referred to *H. imagunculus*. The remains from both Omo and East Rudolf are fragmentary, but they indicate a small form which probably was a lake dweller, though more evidence is needed before the true taxonomic position and environmental conditions for this small species can be assessed.

The hippopotamid fauna of the Lake Rudolf basin shows a marked diversification, with the oldest known generalized hexaprotodonts of Lothagam and Kanapoi giving rise to the hexaprotodonts of Ferguson's Gulf, the earliest forms from the Omo basin, and thence to the better known *Hippopotamus protamphibius* of the Shungura Formation. The diprotodonts of East Rudolf may also have arisen from the early hexaprotodonts, but this is not at all certain (fig. 9). It is interesting that a study of the bones at the possible butchery site at Koobi Fora 105 (Isaac, Leakey, and Behrensmeyer 1971), which produced artifacts among hippo bones at a level of the KBS Tuff, showed the hippopotamus species to be the early form of the East Rudolf diprotodont, species "C," thought to be a riverside dweller and not a lakeliving form.

One explanation for the diversity of hippopotamids could be that, in the Pliocene, Lake Rudolf was fragmented into several smaller lake basins, each with its own isolated species of hippopotamid; the terrestrial faunas, such as pigs, elephants, and bovids, were able to migrate from one basin to another with comparative ease. This theory for a fragmented proto-Lake Rudolf does not, however, fit the geological evidence. Investigation of the hippopotamid remains reveals that in almost all cases the specimens have comparatively long and slender limb bones, indicating that they would be perfectly capable of walking

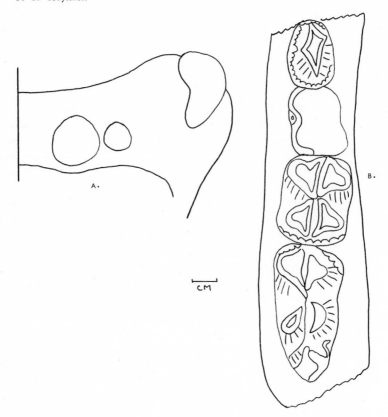

Figure 7. Omo basin, Ethiopia. Mandibular fragments of pygmy hippopotamus species "B."
(*a*) Outline of right side of symphysis to show position of incisors and canine. From
Kalam. (*b*) Right P_4-M_3. From Shungura Formation, Tuff C.

from one lake to another--far more easily, in fact, than the extant *H. amphibius*, which has
been known to travel up to 30 miles in a night.

The interpretation of hippopotamid diversification in the Lake Rudolf basin can be explained by the probable different habitats occupied by each species. The West African
Choeropsis liberiensis inhabits riverine areas, spending far less time in the water than
its larger common cousin. This little animal has comparatively slender limb bones and a
gait reminiscent of a large suid, obviously more suited to a bush or forest environment
than an aquatic one. Fossil hippopotamids from Lothagam, Kanapoi, Omo, and East Rudolf,
except for *H. gorgops*, all have more or less slender limbs which would enable each separate
species to move well on land but make them experience considerable difficulty in a muddy
lacustrine environment. It is most likely that it was the river systems which were the
confining areas for each species of hippopotamid, with the unspecialized hexaprotodont of
Lothagam and Kanapoi being near the basic stock from which other species were evolved
(fig. 2).

The lacustrine tetraprotodont *H. gorgops* was rare in early levels but became dominant
in the Pleistocene; it was present in the lake from about 3 m.y. and spread to all areas
when lake conditions were favorable. These large tetraprotodonts arose from a stock already living in the lake itself in Pliocene times and became dominant in the Pleistocene

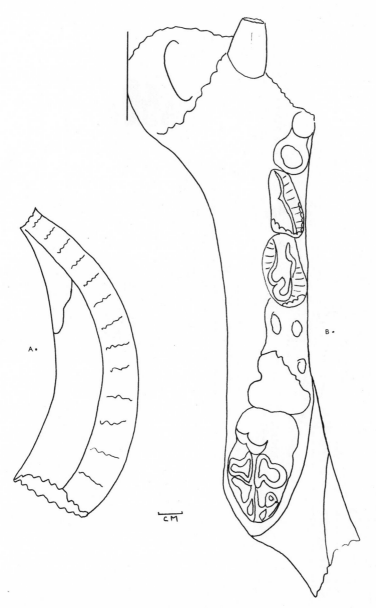

Figure 8. Pygmy hippopotamus from East Rudolf, Kenya. (*a*) Lower canine from Ileret 8;
(*b*) right mandibular ramus and symphysis from Koobi Fora, above KBS Tuff.

as Lake Rudolf expanded. The pygmy tetraprotodont from the same two areas is not common in
either locality, and the origin of this species is not at all clear; it might be comparable
and even possibly ancestral to one or another of the pygmy species known from some Mediterranean islands, but no one has yet attempted to investigate this hypothesis. The complexity
of the hippopotamid fauna of the Lake Rudolf basin is summed up in figure 10. I hope that
further investigation in this area will shed more light on the causes of speciation and the
history of the Hippopotamidae of the Lake Rudolf basin.

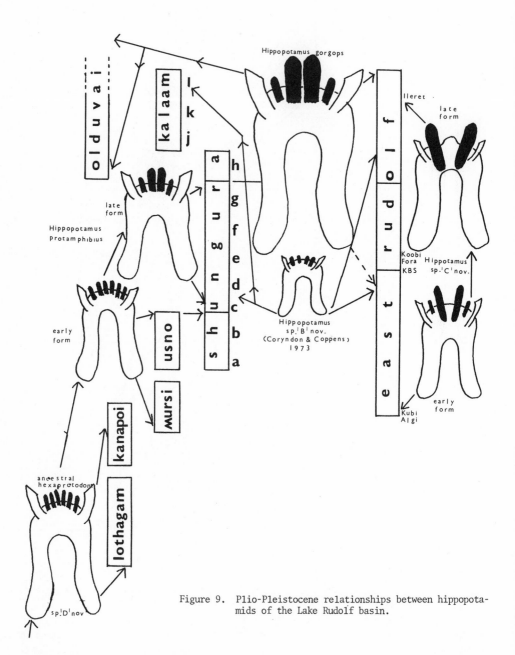

Figure 9. Plio-Pleistocene relationships between hippopotamids of the Lake Rudolf basin.

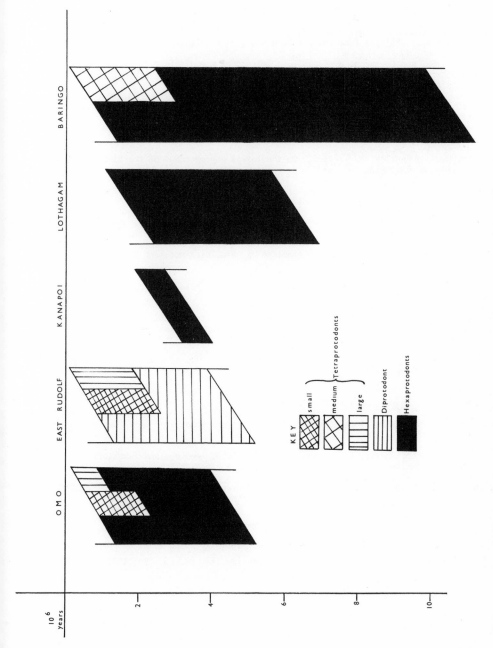

Figure 10.   Distribution of various hippopotamids in the Lake Rudolf and Baringo basins.

This paper is no. 60 in the East Rudolf Project catalogue of publications.

References

Arambourg, C. 1945. Au sujet de l'*Hippopotamus hipponensis* Gaudry. *Bull. Soc. Géol. France,* ser. 5, 14:147-53.

————. 1947. Contribution à l'étude géologique et paléontologique du bassin du lac Rodolphe et de la basse vallée de l'Omo. In *Mission scientifique de l'Omo* (1932-1933). Vol. 1. *Géologie-Anthropologie,* fasc. 3, pp. 231-562. Mémoire, Muséum national d'histoire naturelle (Paris).

Bishop, W. W.; Chapman, G. R.; Hill, A.; and Miller, J. A. 1971. Succession of Cainozoic vertebrate assemblages from the northern Kenya rift valley. *Nature* 233:389-94.

Cooke, H. B. S., and Coryndon, S. C. 1970. Pleistocene mammals from the Kaiso Formation and other related deposits in Uganda. In *Fossil vertebrates of Africa,* ed. L. S. B. Leakey and R. J. Savage, 2:107-224. London: Academic Press

Coryndon, S. C., and Coppens, Y. 1973. Preliminary report on Hippopotamidae (Mammalia, Artiodactyla) from the Plio/Pleistocene of the lower Omo basin, Ethiopia. In *Fossil vertebrates of Africa,* ed. L. S. B. Leakey, R. J. Savage, and S. C. Coryndon, 3:139-57. London: Academic Press.

Falconer, H., and Cautley, P. T. 1839. On the fossil Hippopotamus of the Siwalik Hills. *Asiatic Res.* 19:39-53.

Fuchs, V. E. 1934. The geological work of the Cambridge expedition to the East African Lakes, 1930-31. *Geol. Mag.* 71:97-112.

Gaudry, A. 1876. Sur un hippopotame fossile découvert à Bone (Algerie). *Bull. Soc. Géol. France,* ser. 3, 4:501-4.

Hooijer, D. A. 1950. The fossil Hippopotamidae of Asia, with notes on the recent species. *Zool. Verhandelingen* 8:1-124.

Hopwood, A. T. 1926. Fossil mammalia. In *The geology and palaeontology of the Kaiso bone beds,* ed. E. J. Wayland, 2:13-36.

Howell, F. C.; Fichter, L. S.; and Eck, G. 1969. Vertebrate assemblages from the Usno Formation, White Sands and Brown Sands localities, lower Omo basin, Ethiopia. *Quaternaria* 11:65-87.

Isaac, G. Ll.; Leakey, R. E. F.; and Behrensmeyer, A. K. 1971. Archeological traces of early hominid activities east of Lake Rudolf, Kenya. *Science* 173:1129-34.

Maglio, V. J. 1971. Vertebrate faunas from the Kubi Algi, Koobi Fora and Ileret areas, East Rudolf, Kenya. *Nature* 231:248-49.

Patterson, B. 1966. A new locality for early Pleistocene fossils in North-western Kenya. *Nature* 212:577-81.

Patterson, B.; Behrensmeyer, A. K.; and Sill, W. D. 1970. Geology and fauna of a new Pliocene locality in North-western Kenya. *Nature* 226:918-21.

Vondra, C. F.; Johnson, G. D.; Bowen, B. E.; and Behrensmeyer, A. K. 1971. Preliminary stratigraphical studies of the East Rudolf basin, Kenya. *Nature* 231:245-48.

———————

EDITOR'S NOTE: *Hippopotamus* sp. nov. "B" has been formally named *H. aethiopicus* sp. nov. by S. C. Coryndon and Y. Coppens (*C. R. Acad. Sci.* [*Paris*], ser. D, 280:[1975] 1777-80.

The Living Suidae

There now live in Africa three indigenous species of suid, each referred to a different genus. The Eurasiatic wild boar, *Sus scrofa*, existed in the Mediterranean littoral area in historic and prehistoric times, and because of the escape of domestic animals wild pigs occur locally in sub-Saharan Africa. The indigenous bush pig *Potamochoerus porcus* is the smallest of the African species and is a conservative form with a relatively unspecialized skull resembling that of *Sus*. It has brachyodont cheek teeth, three pairs of incisors, and short, sharply curved upper canines, whose tips are truncated at a steep angle by abrasion against the modest lower tusks. It inhabits areas with dense cover but at night ranges into more open areas to feed. It prefers soft vegetable matter and roots, which it digs up with its snout and short tusks while "kneeling." It is rare as a fossil except in upper Pleistocene deposits, where its presence may be the consequence of human predation. Its earlier record is obscure.

The giant forest hog *Hylochoerus meinertzhageni* is a large animal with a skull considerably bigger than that of the bush pig, having a broad occiput and wide, dorsally flattened braincase in contrast to the narrow occiput and rounded braincase of *Potamochoerus*. There is marked sexual dimorphism, and the male's zygomatic arches are strongly expanded laterally. The molars are low crowned, but the third molar is elongate and all the cheek teeth are specialized by thinning of the enamel pillars and strengthening by a thick coating of cement. The premolars are reduced. The upper canines are less rounded in cross-section than those of *Potamochoerus* but have a similar ventral band of ribbed enamel. They are much larger and curve gently to the sides to produce a broad wear facet against the lower canines, but the tips of the uppers remain intact. The forest hog, as its name implies, inhabits areas of tropical forest, including montane forest, and is largely a nocturnal feeder. Its diet consists mainly of soft plant vegetation, but it may also eat young grass.

The warthog, *Phacochoerus africanus*, has the braincase elevated and extended diagonally backward and upward so that the orbits lie much farther above the occlusal plane than in *Sus* or the other living African suids. There is a broad platelike area below the orbits, passing into the maxillary portion of the zygomatic arch. The added height of the maxilla accommodates specialized, very hypsodont molar teeth that consist of numerous rounded columns arranged in three longitudinal rows. The premolars are much reduced and are

251

present only in young animals, being shed early in life: many adults retain only the third molars. The upper canine is large, flares outward, is dorsoventrally flattened, and is devoid of enamel, except at the tip in juveniles; the long lower canines wear against the anterior surface of the uppers to maintain sharp tips, but the tips of the uppers are intact. The incisors are reduced to one pair in the premaxilla and three pairs in the lower jaw, although one or more of the latter are lost during adult life. Warthogs are daytime grazers in open grassland but also eat other vegetable materials such as berries and fruits. The high-crowned molars are well fitted to survive this harsh and abrasive diet. At night warthogs shelter in burrows and tend to avoid bushy country.

The Fossil Suidae

General

The fossil Suidae in East Africa can at present be divided into six generic groups as shown in figure 1; the ancestry of *Hylochoerus* is not clear, and *Potamochoerus* is not included. Discussion will be limited as far as possible to the species occurring in the Rudolf basin.

Nyanzachoerus

Nyanzachoerus is essentially a late Miocene and Pliocene suid. Three species have been recognized in the Rudolf basin (Cooke and Ewer 1972), *N. tulotos* at Lothagam (units 1B and 1C), and *N. pattersoni* and *N. jaegeri*[1] at Kanapoi, although the last-named species is also a rare element in units 3 and 1C at Lothagam. Both the Kanapoi species are present, though rare, in the Mursi Formation and in the lower part of the Shungura Formation in the Omo area. *Nyanzachoerus pattersoni* occurs in the Kubi Algi Formation in the East Rudolf region, and also in the Chemeron Formation in the Lake Baringo area. The skulls of *Nyanzachoerus* are as large as those of *Hylochoerus*, or larger, and the genus is characterized by relative enlargement of the third and fourth premolars as well as by laterally expanded zygomatic arches; the cheek teeth are low crowned. The upper canines are moderately small, and the lowers have an almost heart-shaped or U-shaped cross-section toward the base. *Nyanzachoerus* itself is too specialized to have given rise directly to any of the other fossil Suidae, but both *Notochoerus* and *Metridiochoerus* may be descended from the same Miocene parental stock.

Notochoerus

Notochoerus is typically a Pliocene genus but ranges into the Pleistocene. The skull is at least as large as that of *Hylochoerus* and may be substantially larger. Very characteristic are the large, robust canines, whose cross-section in the uppers is roughly an inverted, flattened triangle with rounded corners; in the lowers the usual triangular shape is modified by rounding of the vertex (lower angle) and a groove on the upper face. The zygomatic arch is expanded in the male and may carry a lateral projection or "knob." The columns that form the molars wear to produce folded islands, stellate in some forms but tending toward an H-shape in the more advanced representatives. The crown height is relatively greater than in *Nyanzachoerus*, and there is a tendency for the height to increase in the younger strata, and also for the third molars to increase in length by the addition of extra pairs of pillars at the back of the crown.

The type species, *Notochoerus capensis*, is not very well known, although there exist

---

1. *N. jaegeri* Coppens, 1971, has precedence over *N. plicatus* of Cooke and Ewer (1972).

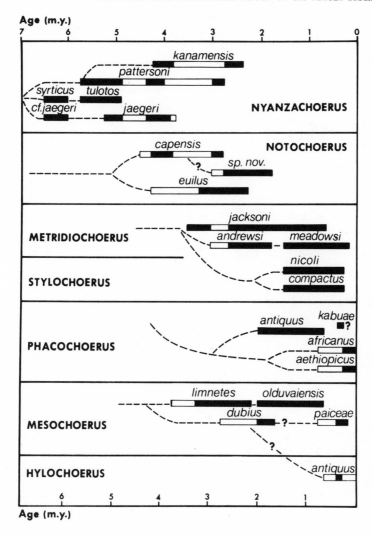

Figure 1. Provisional grouping of the main fossil Suidae from the Plio-Pleistocene of Africa. The black segments indicate known occurrences, the open segments doubtful or in-ferred ranges. *Potamochoerus* is not included since it is not certainly known except in the late Pleistocene; the same is true of *Hylochoerus meinertzhageni*.

much of a skull from the Kubi Algi Formation in the East Rudolf area (Maglio 1972), the back part of a skull from the Usno Formation in the Omo area, and mandibular remains from Kanapoi (Cooke and Ewer 1972). The teeth are stout and large but are only slightly hypso-dont. The zygomatic arches in the male have large thimble-shaped, projecting "knobs" that are very striking and quite unlike those of any other suid.

Notochoerus euilus has third molars of moderate hypsodonty, and the crown has only four or five pairs of lateral pillars, whereas an unnamed new species is distinguished by having more than five pairs of lateral pillars (sometimes as many as nine) and considerably higher crowns. *N. euilus* is the characteristic form at Omo below Tuff C, but rare *euilus*-like specimens occur up to Member G. The unnamed hypsodont species occurs as a very rare element in members B and C, becoming quite abundant in Member D and above. Figure 2 is a

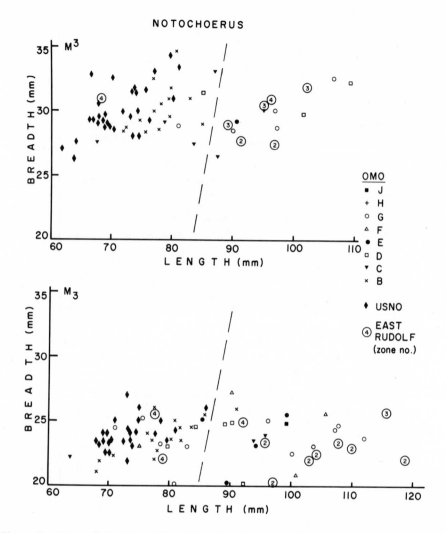

Figure 2. Plots of lengths and breadths of third molars from Omo and East Rudolf referred to *Notochoerus*. The dashed line separates approximately the specimens placed in *N. euilus* (to the left of the line) from the unnamed hypsodont form, but hypsodonty and morphological characters other than length and breadth have to be taken into account.

graph of length-breadth ratios for the measurable third molars in the Shungura Formation; many other specimens are incomplete and cannot be included, and so the graphs do not represent abundances adequately. The dashed line on the graphs represents the approximate boundary between the "*euilus*" form and the unnamed hypsodont form when crown height is taken into account. There is a bimodal distribution at most levels.

Mesochoerus

The skull of *Mesochoerus limnetes*, which is well represented at East Rudolf, is about the size of that of *Hylochoerus* and has structural affinities with it, although the braincase is rounded and the zygomatic arches jut out more abruptly from the maxillae. The males' tusks are like those of *Potamochoerus*, though larger, but the females' are very small. The molars are low crowned and resemble those of *Nyanzachoerus* in a general way, but the premolars are not enlarged and the upper fourth premolar has a distinctively different structure. *Mesochoerus limnetes* is believed to have given rise to the typical Olduvai Bed II species *M. olduvaiensis*, which is also present in the upper levels at East Rudolf and in the Omo area. At Olduvai there is another, smaller *Mesochoerus* in Bed I and in the lower part of Bed II (below the "faunal break"), but it appears to differ specifically from *M. limnetes* and is at present designated *M. dubius* (formerly *Ectopotamochoerus dubius*). *Hylochoerus* may well be descended from some such form.

Coppens was the first to note (in Arambourg, Chavaillon, and Coppens 1969) that there is a progressive increase in length of the third molars of *Mesochoerus* through the Shungura sequence, and a preliminary attempt was made by Cooke and Maglio (1972) to quantify this trend. Figure 3 is a plot of the length-breadth ratios for the measurable third molars now available from the Omo, and although there is a certain amount of overlap in the ranges the general trend is clearly seen. In figure 4 the observed ranges, means, and standard deviations of third-molar length for the samples from each member are plotted against a time

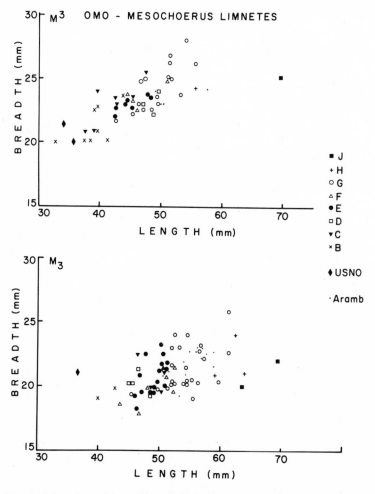

Figure 3. Plots of lengths and breadths of third molars from Omo, assigned to *Mesochoerus limnetes*; the specimens from above Member G are regarded as inseparable from *M. olduvaiensis*.

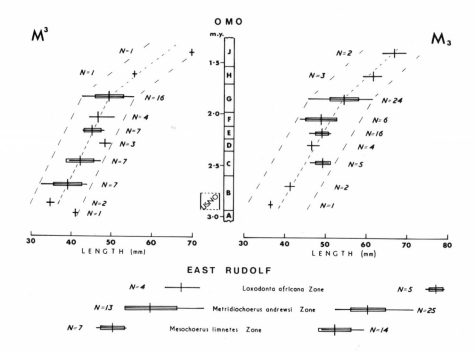

Figure 4. Observed range of length of third molars of *Mesochoerus* from Omo, plotted against the stratigraphic succession with ages controlled by radiometric and paleomagnetic data. The vertical line on the range bar shows the mean, and the boxes represent a range of one standard deviation on either side of the mean; *N* is the sample size. The broken lines show inferred trends and probable limits. Below the scale are the range data for material from East Rudolf in the faunal zones designated; there is no time scale.

scale based on radiometric determinations and the paleomagnetic data (see Brown and Shuey, this symposium). Figure 5 is a plot of the length-breadth ratios for the third molars from East Rudolf, which have been placed in the three appropriate faunal zones defined by Maglio (1972). The observed ranges, means, and standard deviations for the East Rudolf samples have been plotted at the bottom of figure 4, but without a time scale. The possible implications will be discussed below.

Phacochoerus

Although the modern warthog, *Phacochoerus africanus*, is represented abundantly in the upper Pleistocene, most often by the recently extinct variety or species *P. aethiopicus*, its earlier fossil record is obscure. There is also a smaller fossil species *P. antiquus*, first reported from the australopithecine cave breccias in South Africa and more recently identified in Bed I at Olduvai and possibly in Member G at Omo, but it is not itself suitable as an ancestor for *P. africanus*. However, a disturbing number of typical isolated third molars of *P. aethiopicus* type have been found on the surface, all in Member G and above at Omo. This suggests that serious consideration should be given to the probability that a fully developed warthog did exist at that time, although it is possible to "explain away" these finds by assuming that the specimens were derived from the former general cover of the Kibish Formation. Pending discovery of a specimen in situ, it seems best to evade the issue.

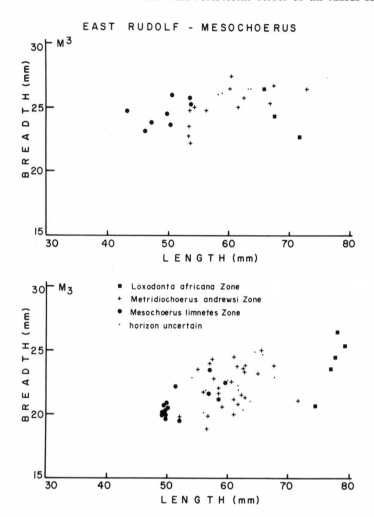

Figure 5. Plots of lengths and breadths of third molars of *Mesochoerus* from East Rudolf, assigned to the three faunal zones of Maglio (1972).

The *Metridiochoerus* Complex

Under this heading are grouped a number of unusual forms whose precise relationships cannot be determined without skull material of some of the members. They share with *Phacochoerus* a tendency toward reduction of the premolars, hypsodonty of the molars, especially the third, and some morphological similarities in the elevation of the braincase and the shape of the mandible. It is extremely improbable that any one of these is closely enough related to the warthog to be ancestral to it.

The most conservative member of this group is *Metridiochoerus jacksoni*, which is small and, as far as can be determined, has a relatively short snout and somewhat elevated braincase. The third molars are of modest size, broad at the base, and have a crown height exceeding the breadth, strong anterior roots, and a characteristic pillar structure and enamel pattern. The first and second molars are reduced rapidly to an expanse of dentine with rings of enamel. The lower jaw is like that of *Phacochoerus*, with a short diastema,

but the front of the symphysis is flatter. The lower canines are smaller, rather less
curved, and narrower than in the warthog; the upper canines are not certainly known.

Metridiochoerus jacksoni is moderately abundant at Omo, and figure 6 is a length-
breadth plot of all the measurable teeth available. Although there is a distinct tendency
for the crown length to increase in Member G, the variation in the earlier units shows no
systematic pattern. The same species occurs at Olduvai in Beds I and II and possibly even
in Bed IV; so it is a stable species with a rather long time range. A few specimens are
recorded at East Rudolf, but it is apparently rare there.

Metridiochoerus andrewsi resembles M. jacksoni in dental characters, but the skull is
much larger and the third molars are both longer and more hypsodont, attaining almost the
proportions of a Phacochoerus molar. The premolars are greatly reduced and are shed with
advancing age. The skull is in some respects hylochoerine, but the braincase is more elevated, though not in quite the same way as in Phacochoerus, since the orbits are not raised

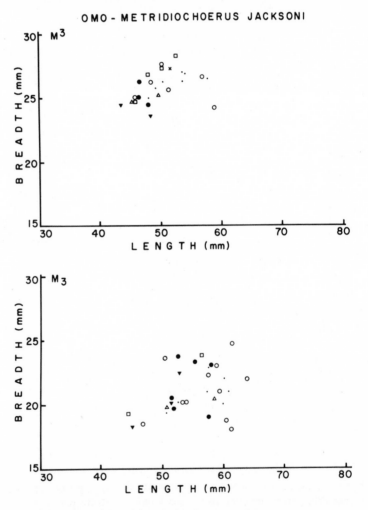

Figure 6. Plots of lengths and breadths of third molars of Metridiochoerus andrewsi from
Omo (symbols as in fig. 3).

substantially from the more normal position. The sockets for the upper canines are extremely large and extend so far back that they incorporate the front edges of the infraor-
bital foramina. The canines are moderately long, sharply curved laterally, and have a
characteristic trefoil cross-section. *Metridiochoerus andrewsi* is characteristic of the
faunal zone above the KBS Tuff in the Koobi Fora Formation at East Rudolf, although it is
not particularly abundant. Figure 7 is a plot of the length-breadth measurements of all
the measurable teeth available. The species is almost unknown at Omo. *Metridiochoerus*
meadowsi (hitherto called *"Tapinochoerus" meadowsi*) occurs at Olduvai and is probably an
evolved form of *M. andrewsi*, but it has not been noted in the Rudolf basin.

Stylochoerus nicoli (formerly *Afrochoerus nicoli*) is part of the *Metridiochoerus* complex, and the molars are generally similar in structure. However, the upper and lower
canines are peculiar, being very elephantlike in form. The lower canines are almost
straight, with a flattened oval cross-section, and they are implanted in the symphysis at

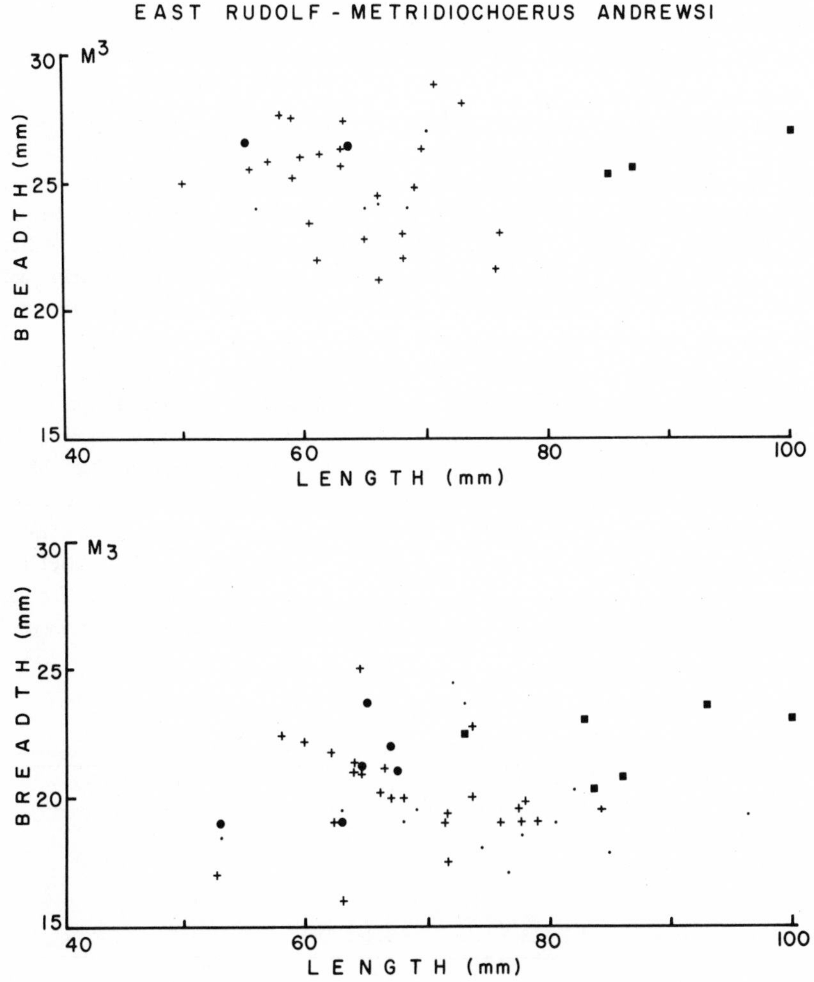

Figure 7. Plots of lengths and breadths of third molars of *Metridiochoerus andrewsi* from
East Rudolf (symbols as in fig. 5).

an angle of about 45° both from the axis of the jaw and from the horizontal plane. They do not meet the upper canines, which are very long, have a gentle curve with a slight twist, and are oval in cross-section. Both upper and lower canines have a core of cellular osteo-dentine extending for about half their length. Two upper canines and a good mandible have been found in the upper part of the Upper Member of the Koobi Fora Formation, and there are a few teeth tentatively assigned to this species from the Kalam area and above Member G in the Shungura Formation of the Omo area. *Stylochoerus compactus* (="*Orthostonyx brachyops*") has not yet been noted in the Rudolf basin.

Inferences

Correlation and Dating

The general similarity of the faunas in the Omo and East Rudolf areas, and their geographical proximity, makes it reasonable to expect good correlation. In the East Rudolf area there are slight discrepancies between the correlations and nomenclature given by Bowen and Vondra (1973) and that presented by Maglio (1972) in which he proposed recognizing four faunal zones. However, the KBS Tuff is a widespread marker horizon above which lie the Upper Member of the Koobi Fora Formation in the Koobi Fora area and the Ileret Member in the Ileret area. The upper part of the Ileret Member of Bowen and Vondra belongs to Maglio's *Loxodonta africana* zone, and between it and the KBS Tuff is the *Metridiochoerus andrewsi* zone; at least the lower part of the Upper Member in the Koobi Fora area also belongs to the latter faunal zone, and it is in this area that the KBS Tuff has been dated as 2.6 ± 0.26 m.y. Below the KBS Tuff is the Lower Member of the Koobi Fora Formation, and this corresponds to Maglio's *Mesochoerus limnetes* zone. The Kubi Algi Formation underlies the Koobi Fora Formation, constituting the *Notochoerus capensis* zone, and a lava at its base is dated as 4.6 ± 0.1 m.y.

In its fauna the *N. capensis* zone corresponds well with the Kanapoi and Ekora assemblages and with the Mursi Formation of the Omo region, and so the date is not unreasonable. Unfortunately the fauna is very limited and a similar assemblage can be found at Omo at least up to the top of Member B, so precise faunal correlation is not yet possible.

The boundary between the *Mesochoerus limnetes* zone and the *Metridiochoerus andrewsi* zone in the East Rudolf area is the KBS Tuff, perhaps involving some kind of stratigraphic break as well. Using the Omo dates then current as a basis for comparison, Maglio (1972) estimated evolutionary rates for both *Mesochoerus limnetes* and *Elephas recki* and assessed the "best fit" and probable limiting ages for the East Rudolf faunal zones as shown in table 1.

Table 1
Maglio's (1972) estimate of Faunal Zones in East Rudolf

Zone	Indicated Age Range (m.y.)		"Best Fit" (m.y.)
	Suidae	*Elephas*	
Loxodonta africana	1.4-0.9	1.7-1.2	1.3
Metrodiochoerus andrewsi	1.8-1.6	2.1-1.4	1.7
Mesochoerus limnetes	2.7-1.8	3.4-2.1	2.3

The recent revision of the Omo time-scale (Brown, this symposium) has the effect of making ages below Member G somewhat younger than they were considered before, and the new

dates would serve to reduce the lower limits now appropriate to Maglio's estimates. Although the number of specimens available is still far from ideal, it is desirable to consider the position once more. There are also obvious dangers in assuming that the ranges
measured in the Omo material truly represent the limits of variation for the whole population of the region, but there are large numbers of broken teeth which, though they cannot
be measured, at least confirm the reality of the general trends.

The few specimens from the Usno Formation are smaller and simpler than those from
Member B, but the sample is too small to be significant. For the upper third molars the
mean values of length show a trend from Member B to Member G which is very close to a
straight line, although the few specimens from D are offset. For the lowers, the means for
C, D, E, and F do not differ significantly, but three of the samples are small, and the
values for the large samples from E and G produce a straight line corresponding to that for
the uppers, so that it is reasonable to regard this as the probable mean trend. The few
measurable specimens available from members H and J are notably larger, as also are several
incomplete specimens, and these are assigned to *Mesochoerus olduvaiensis* rather than to
M. limnetes. Probable limits of size have been sketched in on figure 4.

Considering first the upper third molars, it may be noted that the largest of the
teeth in the *Mesochoerus limnetes* zone at East Rudolf could not be accommodated in strata
older than Member F at Omo, and the "best fit" position would be about at the boundary between members F and G. The *shortest* tooth in the *Metridiochoerus andrewsi* zone is longer
than any Omo specimen below Member F, thus suggesting a probable maximum age for the
M. andrewsi zone. The "best fit" is with Member H at Omo.

Turning now to the lower third molars, similar arguments show that the largest molar
in the *Mesochoerus limnetes* zone cannot be matched at Omo before Member F and that Member
F or Member G would provide the "best fit" position. The *Metridiochoerus andrewsi* zone
would fit best with Member H, but the lower limit is not really clear. The upper third
molars from the *Loxodonta africana* zone correspond to the few specimens from Member J, but
the lower third molars are even larger and are actually longer than all the Olduvai specimens except one from Bed III. From the data on *Mesochoerus*, therefore, it would be inferred that the KBS Tuff should be fairly close in age to the top of Member F at Omo,
which is apparently 2.0 m.y., whereas the radiometric date for the KBS Tuff is 2.6 m.y.
The discrepancy is considerable and cannot be ignored.

One theory is that ecological differences have led to the development of different
races or populations in the East Rudolf area and the Omo basin. This is certainly a possibility, although it is difficult to conceive of a barrier adequate to prevent gene flow
between the two areas. The *Mesochoerus limnetes* zone at East Rudolf would have to be contemporary with Member B at Omo if the dates are correct; yet the probable ranges of size
of the third molars do not even overlap at this apparent time horizon. It is thus necessary to suppose that divergence had taken place long before this, leading to two separate
populations which subsequently converged again to the point of being effectively inseparable.
It might then be assumed that the smaller race was more of a forest dweller (Omo) and the
larger race more adapted to open bush (East Rudolf). It would then be possible for *M.
olduvaiensis* to have evolved in the East Rudolf area and the rather rapid change in size
found in Member G and above at Omo could be attributed to "invasion" of the Omo area by the
larger race following changes in the environment there. However, this fails to account for
the progressive evolution observed in the Omo sequence and involves an improbable amount of
convergence. It is also worth noting that there is a small race of *Potamochoerus* in the
Congo forest, but it cannot be separated dentally from other populations in different

habitats covering most of sub-Saharan Africa. Further study of the problem is clearly desirable, especially since mismatches also occur in other elements of the faunas.

Ecological Inferences

Aside from the issue of correlation, the suids of the Omo and East Rudolf sequences differ in generic representation and in the relative abundance of the various forms. This is almost certainly a reflection of ecological factors. *Mesochoerus* is moderately plentiful in both areas, although not as abundant at East Rudolf as at Omo. *Notochoerus* is fairly common at Omo but relatively rare at East Rudolf. *Metridiochoerus andrewsi* is virtually absent at Omo but moderately common in the East Rudolf area; whereas *M. jacksoni* is precisely the converse.

Mesochoerus limnetes has features which suggest a habitat generally like that of the bush pig, and it is interpreted as ranging rather widely from forest or thick bush country to mixed bush and grassland. The molar crowns in the earlier forms show transverse "ridge and valley" wear, much as in *Hylochoerus*, and perhaps are indicative of a "chomping" action. In the later forms, as in *Mesochoerus olduvaiensis*, the crowns are worn in more planar fashion suggestive of a grinding action. In all probability the earlier forms, with the shorter molars, were more restricted to the bushy environment, whereas the more advanced forms, with the longer molars, might have been able to eat young grasses and extend their range into savanna areas.

Metridiochoerus jacksoni, although possessing hypsodont molars and much reduced premolars, is not as specialized as *Phacochoerus* for dealing with a harsh diet and was probably not primarily a grazer, but a mixed feeder coping with food sources not attractive to the contemporary *Mesochoerus*. The larger and more hypsodont molars of *Metridiochoerus andrewsi*, on the other hand, indicate that its dietary habits were much like those of the warthog, and hence that it was essentially a grass-eating animal. Accordingly, it may be inferred that *M. andrewsi* is associated with fairly open grassland with little bush. *M. meadowsi* and *Stylochoerus* are even more like the warthog in their dentitions and are most probably savanna dwellers. The enormous tusks of *S. nicoli* would be a real handicap in bushy country.

Notochoerus, although it developed large third molars, did not reduce the premolars as drastically as did *Metridiochoerus*. *Notochoerus euilus* molars wear to almost flat occlusal surfaces, but the premolars interlock in adolescent or young adult animals and may have been used for crunching. Clearly the diet was fairly harsh, probably mixed. In the evolved, more hypsodont species of *Notochoerus*, the third molars become narrower and higher crowned, and the columns become more numerous and compacted, so that they resemble those of a giant *Phacochoerus*; there can be little doubt that the animals were essentially grazers. Differential adaptation could have led to the dichotomy, for small *euilus*-like forms persist as contemporaries of the hypsodont species at Omo, although their occurrence is localized. Possibly *euilus* is a browser, and its presence would indicate a more bushy habitat. Its abundance in the Usno Formation is thus probably a reflection of an environment different from that of the contemporary Shungura Formation, where *euilus* is comparatively rare.

The evaluation of environments and habitats necessarily involves an assessment of the total faunas and of their sedimentary settings, toward which Behrensmeyer (this symposium) has already made a notable contribution. Once the associations have been interpreted, there is a good prospect that the Suidae will form useful "indicators" to the various assemblages and thus provide a means for rapid preliminary interpretations of the environments.

This paper is no. 61 in the East Rudolf Project catalogue of publications.

References

Arambourg, C.; Chavaillon, J.; and Coppens, Y. 1969. Résultats de la nouvelle Mission de l'Omo (2e campagne 1968). *C. R. Acad. Sci. (Paris)*, ser. D, 268:759-62.

Bowen, B. E., and Vondra, C. F. 1973. Stratigraphical relationships of the Plio-Pleistocene deposits, East Rudolf, Kenya. *Nature* 242:391-93.

Cooke, H. B. S., and Ewer, R. F. 1972. Fossil Suidae from Kanapoi and Lothagam, north-western Kenya. *Bull. Museum Comp. Zool. Harvard Coll.* 143(3):149-295.

Cooke, H. B. S., and Maglio, V. J. 1972. Plio-Pleistocene stratigraphy in East Africa in relation to proboscidean and suid evolution. In *Calibration of hominoid evolution*, ed. W. W. Bishop and J. A. Miller, pp. 303-29. Edinburgh: Scottish Academic Press; Toronto: University of Toronto Press.

Coppens, Y. 1971. Une nouvelle espèce de Suidé du Villafranchien du Tunisie. *Nyanzachoerus jaegeri* nov. sp. *C. R. Acad. Sci. (Paris)*, ser. D, 272:3264-67.

Howell, F. C. 1972. Pliocene-Pleistocene Hominidae in Eastern Africa: Absolute and relative ages. In *Calibration of hominoid evolution*, ed. W. W. Bishop and J. A. Miller, pp. 331-68. Edinburgh: Scottish Academic Press; Toronto: University of Toronto Press.

Maglio, V. J. 1972. Vertebrate faunas and chronology of hominid-bearing sediments east of Lake Rudolf, Kenya. *Nature* 239:379-85.

24. GIRAFFIDAE FROM THE EAST RUDOLF SUCCESSION

J. M. Harris

Introduction

A summary of the faunal zones that yield mammalian fossils at East Rudolf appears in the introduction to my chapter on the East Rudolf Rhinocerotidae (Harris, this symposium).

Giraffids are uncommon elements of the East Rudolf faunas and have not yet been collected from the Kubi Algi Formation. One species of sivathere and three giraffine species are represented in all three faunal zones of the Koobi Fora Formation. Until recently East Rudolf giraffids were known primarily from cranial and dental material (Harris, in press). A large number of giraffid postcranial elements were, however, collected during the 1973 season, and although this material has not yet been fully investigated it confirms the presence of four distinct giraffid taxa in the Koobi Fora Formation. These taxa exhibit few evolutionary changes other than general increase in size throughout the succession.

Giraffidae

Sivatheriinae

The East Rudolf sivathere is known from a virtually complete cranium (KNM-ER 797A), a maxilla, several mandibles, and a number of isolated teeth. There is no evidence that more than one species was present and, despite some differences in ossicone morphology, the East Rudolf sivathere is identified as *Sivatherium maurusium*--the common African sivathere. It should perhaps be noted here that *S. maurusium* (Pomel) has priority over *S. olduvaiense* (Hopwood).

The East Rudolf sivathere cranium is the most complete yet found in Africa; specimens from elsewhere on the continent are mainly restricted to isolated ossicones, although a few occipital fragments are known from South Africa (Singer and Boné 1960) and Olduvai Gorge in Tanzania. If the East Rudolf cranium is typical of *S. maurusium*, this species apparently differs from *S. giganteum* of Asia in having a longer facial region and a shallower and narrower cranial region. Differences are also seen in the number, form, and orientation of the ossicones. *S. giganteum* possesses four ossicones--an anterior conical pair sited in front of the orbits and a larger, palmate, and vertically aligned pair arising from the frontoparietal region. Anterior ossicones of *S. maurusium* have been reported from South Africa (Singer and Boné 1960), but it seems likely that these specimens really represent fragments of posterior ossicones (Harris 1974). Elongate vertical flanges sited on the lateral edges of the cranial vault behind the orbit are present on the East Rudolf cranium and are indicated on some specimens from Olduvai. These may be more readily interpreted as anterior prolongations of the posterior ossicones than distinct anterior ossicones, as in *S. giganteum*.

Table 1
Distribution of East Rudolf Giraffidae

Taxon	M. limnetes Zone	M. andrewsi Zone	L. africana Zone
Sivatherium maurusium	4	17	4
Giraffa jumae	4	14	2
Giraffa gracilis	5	25	5
Giraffa sp. nov.	3	1	2
Giraffa sp. indet.	2	15	4

The posterior ossicones of the East Rudolf cranium are asymmetrical, and, since paired symmetrical ossicones appear to be the norm for specimens of *S. maurusium* from Olduvai and elsewhere, it is thought that the condition of the East Rudolf specimens is pathological rather than normal. The left posterior ossicone of the East Rudolf cranium is 88 cm long and extends backward and outward, then upward, then inward and forward. The right posterior ossicone is shorter than the left ossicone and is partly atrophied and deformed. The importance of the East Rudolf specimen in enabling other African sivathere ossicones to be correctly oriented has already been described elsewhere (Harris 1974). Available dental and postcranial evidence suggests that only one sivathere species--*S. maurusium*--was common in the African Pleistocene but that males of this species had ossicones that varied greatly in form and alignment.

Other than a general tendency for increase in size through time, little evolutionary evidence is provided by the *Sivatherium* dental material from East Rudolf. The East Rudolf sivathere teeth are slightly smaller than those from sites BK and SHK at Olduvai. This, together with the more slender and less well ornamented ossicones of the East Rudolf cranium, might be taken to suggest that the *M. andrewsi* zone predates the faunal break in Bed II at Olduvai.

Giraffinae

Three giraffine species are present throughout the Koobi Fora Formation. These are separable by size and by shape and orientation of the ossicones. There are some indications that differences between the taxa are also manifest in the postcranial skeleton, and this will probably prove to be the most fruitful source of information on the evolution and behavior of the three taxa. At the moment, however, investigation of the postcranial material is only at a preliminary stage.

The largest giraffine species present at East Rudolf is *Giraffa jumae*. All lateral ossicones referred to this species possess terminal knobs but seem to lack the secondary bone apposition characteristic of male specimens of the extant *Giraffa camelopardalis*. Other than size, the major difference between the ossicones of *G. jumae* and other African giraffines seems to be their orientation, those of *G. jumae* being distinctly more posteriorly inclined. There is no median ossicone above and between the orbits as in male specimens of *G. camelopardalis*.

East Rudolf has yielded the first cranial specimens that may be referred to *Giraffa gracilis*, and the 1973 expedition recovered the first associated cranial, dental, and post-cranial material of this species. There are no terminal knobs on the lateral ossicones of *G. gracilis* from East Rudolf, although they appear to be present on some specimens from Olduvai. Secondary bone apposition occurs in some (male) specimens, as in extant giraffes. The ossicones of *G. gracilis* are shorter than those of *G. jumae* and *G. camelopardalis*. A slight median ossicone appears to have been present.

Teeth of *G. gracilis* are smaller than those of *G. jumae*, although there is no major morphological difference between the dentitions of the two taxa or, indeed, between these taxa and those of *G. camelopardalis*. There appears to have been a gradual increase in size of the teeth of both *G. jumae* and *G. gracilis* between the lower part of the Omo succession and Bed II at Olduvai. At any one level, however, there appears to have been much variation in tooth size in both taxa.

The third giraffine species is also assigned to *Giraffa* but is considerably smaller than the other two East Rudolf giraffines and is known from relatively few specimens. Ossicones from East Rudolf that are assigned to the smallest taxon possess terminal knobs, but secondary bone apposition, when present, is poorly developed. The ossicones assigned to this species are smaller than those of *G. gracilis* and are distinctly slighter. This small taxon is conspecific with the wrongly identified *"Okapia" stillei* from the early part of the succession at Olduvai (Leakey 1965). Teeth of *Giraffa* sp. nov. from the *M. limnetes* zone are smaller than those from Olduvai Bed I, whereas those from the *L. africana* zone are larger.

Discussion

All three giraffine species are represented at the Omo (F. C. Howell, pers. comm.) and at Olduvai and Laetolil in Tanzania. At Laetolil, all three appear to have been included in *"Okapia" stillei* by Dietrich (1942). Reasons for transferring *Okapia stillae* to the Giraffinae are given in a detailed report on the East Rudolf giraffids (Harris, in press) and, since the *"Okapia"* ossicone from Olduvai (Leakey 1965, p. 35) has subsequently proved to be an immature horn core of *Parmularius angusticornis*, the only record of *Okapia* from East African sites appears to be a single ossicone from Kaiso (Cooke and Coryndon 1970, p. 199).

It is likely that some of the fossil giraffines from South Africa assigned to *G. camelopardalis* by Singer and Boné (1960) may prove to belong to at least one of the taxa present at East Rudolf. It is also possible that some of the Rudolf giraffine taxa were present, but misidentified, at certain North African Pleistocene sites (C. S. Churcher, pers. comm.).

Although it is possible to allocate the giraffine dental material to species on the basis of size, the small number of dental specimens and the large amount of size variation at any one level prevent any fruitful comparisons between the Omo and East Rudolf giraffines for the purpose of stratigraphic correlation. On the basis of size and ossicone morphology of *Sivatherium maurusium*, plus the size of the teeth of *Giraffa* sp. nov., it appears that the *M. limnetes* zone should predate Bed I at Olduvai and that the *M. andrewsi* zone should predate Upper Bed II. This is in apparent agreement with currently accepted radiometric dates, even though it is based on relatively few specimens.

The presence of so many giraffine species in the African Plio-Pleistocene may perhaps be partly attributed to rapid evolution on reaching sub-Saharan Africa at the end of the Neogene. Only two giraffine taxa are now known from the Afar region of Ethiopia which may, in part, predate the early Shungura horizons at the Omo. One can be identified as *Giraffa jumae* and the other is intermediate in size between *G. gracilis* and *Giraffa* sp. nov. and may potentially be ancestral to either or both. Difference in size of the three East Rudolf giraffines may reflect adaptation to different ecologies and types of vegetation, with resultant differences in behavior. Some of the postcranial elements of the three taxa exhibit anatomical as well as size differences. I hope that further investigation of the postcranial elements of the African Giraffinae will provide more evidence for functional and behavioral differences between the taxa.

This paper is no. 62 in the East Rudolf Project catalogue of publications.

References

Cooke, H. B. S., and Coryndon, S. C. 1970. Pleistocene mammals from the Kaiso Formation and other related deposits in Uganda. In *Fossil vertebrates of Africa,* ed. L. S. B. Leakey and R. J. Savage, 2:107-224. London: Academic Press

Dietrich, W. O. 1942. Ältestquartäre Säugetiere aus der südlichen Serengeti, Deutsch-Ostafrika. *Palaeontographica,* ser. A, 94:43-133.

Harris, J. M. 1974. Orientation and variability in the ossicones of African Sivatheriinae (Mammalia: Giraffidae). *Ann S. African Mus., Cape Town.*

_____. Pleistocene Giraffidae (Artiodactyla; Mammalia) from East Rudolf, Kenya. In *Fossil vertebrates of Africa.* In press.

Leakey, L. S. B. 1965. *Olduvai Gorge 1951-1961: Fauna and background.* Cambridge: At the University Press.

Singer, R., and Boné, E. L. 1960. Modern giraffes and the fossil giraffids of Africa. *Ann. S. African Mus., Cape Town* 45:357-548.

25. REMAINS OF *CAMELUS* FROM THE SHUNGURA FORMATION LOWER OMO VALLEY

J. -L. Grattard, F. C. Howell, and Y. Coppens

The existence of *Camelus* in the Shungura Formation was first documented in 1968 by the recovery of specimens from members B and F (Howell, Fichter, and Wolff 1969). Since then, more remains have been found, and thus far the genus is represented by nine specimens from seven localities of members B, D, F, and G (table 1). An examination of the collections (in the Muséum national d'histoire naturelle, Paris) of the Mission scientifique de l'Omo, 1932-33, made by the late Prof. C. Arambourg, has afforded another specimen, a right lower molar (probably M_1), whose exact stratigraphic provenance is unknown.

Table 1

Remains of Camelus *from the Shungura Formation*

Provenance	Specimen
Unknown horizon. Collected by C. Arambourg, 1932-33	Right cf. M_1
Member G	
Locality 480	L. 480-7. Left mandible fragment with fractured M_1, M_2, and part of M_3.
Member F	
Locality 52	L. 52-104. Distal right metatarsal
Omo Locality 39	Omo 39-1968-1452. Left calcaneum.
Member D	
Omo Locality 119	Omo 119-1972-14. Posterior phalanx.
Member B	
Locality 1	L. 1-111c. Left cf. M_1
Locality 1	L. 1-36. Proximal right humerus.
Omo Locality 28	Omo 28-1967-577. Anterior phalanx.
Omo Locality 28	Omo 28-1967-494. Right M_3 in mandible fragment.
Locality 382	L. 382-3. Distal portion of metapodial.

Mandible and Dentition

The first element of the dentition recovered (in 1968), and initially recognized as camelid by A. W. and A. Gentry was a worn left lower molar (no. III) from Locality 1, a series of richly fossiliferous levels in the upper sedimentary units of Member B. It is

34.5 mm in length and 21.9 mm in breadth (occlusal surface). The extensive wear has removed most morphological details, but the central cavities show the distinctive external
closure of camelids.

Another right lower molar, an M_3 from locality Omo 28 (1967-494), the same place as
Locality 1, is in a fragment of mandible, lacking the inferior portion of the body, but
preserving the base of the ramus. The tooth is damaged, lacking the internal wall at the
level of the metaconid and entoconid, and the moderate wear has not exposed the base of
the crown. However, it is worn enough to reveal the characteristic swollen form of the
hypoconulid. The internal wall at the level of the hypoconulid is slightly convex and
directed a bit less obliquely distobucally than in the extant species. Its anterior part
is prolonged onto the lingual slope of the entoconid, with a rather marked separation, more
so than in the extant species, in which it is variably, but at most weakly, expressed.
This feature is largely responsible for the slight obliquity of the hypoconulid, which is
directed almost mesiodistally with reference to the axis of the crown. Behind the hypoconulid the marked crest and attendant buccal groove found in extant species are lacking. The
mandibular body has the same overall morphology and massiveness found in extant species.

This Omo 1932-33 lower molar is moderately worn with the crown still rather high (26
mm on the lingual surface at the metastylid level). A comparison of its dimensions with
specimens of *C. dromedarius* and *C. bactrianus domesticus*, in which wear has produced an
equivalent crown height, indicates no noteworthy differences in the breadth to length relationships (the comparison is feasible, since hypsodonty is the same in the fossil and the
recent specimens). The morphology of this tooth does not differ especially from that of
C. bactrianus domesticus, but there are noteworthy differences from *C. dromedarius*. The
internal wall of the metaconid and entoconid are almost flat, a great deal more so than in
both extant species, where a weak convexity is formed, variably expressed according to the
height. The stylids are more strongly expressed than in the extant species, especially
toward the base of the crown. The parastylid and metastylid, respectively mesial and distal to the metaconid, form a well-defined ridge, a great deal detached from the internal
wall of the metaconid in comparison with the extant species. The entostylid is substantially thicker and wider. The separation between the internal walls of the metaconid and
the entoconid, which is displaced bucally, particularly in its mesial part, is unlike the
condition in *C. dromedarius* and more like that of *C. bactrianus domesticus*. The difference
in protoconid and metaconid shape also seems substantial compared with the two extant
species. Thus the buccal wall of the protoconid shows marked angulation between its flat
mesiobuccal and distobuccal portions. The same feature occurs to a lesser extent on the
hypoconid. The shortness of the metaconid compared with the entoconid, the strong separation between the distal part of the metaconid and the mesial part of the entoconid
(stronger on M_1 than on M_2 in *C. b. domesticus*, but practically absent on both molars in
C. dromedarius), the substantial thickness of the metaconid and entoconid, and the crown
length decreasing toward the base suggest an M_1.

This specimen differs from that of Locality 1 (no. III) in the convexity of the internal wall of the metaconid and entoconid, in the absence of separation between the distal
and mesial parts of the metaconid and entoconid internal walls, respectively, and in the
weak development of the stylids (even allowing for its more pronounced wear). In these
respects the Locality 1 (no. III) specimen more closely resembles *C. dromedarius*, whereas
the Omo 1932-33 specimen shows features reminiscent of *C. bactrianus domesticus*.

The partial mandible from Member G (Locality 480, no. 7) is so fragmentary that it is of little use for identification. Only the roots of P_4 are preserved. M_1 lacks much of the lingual portion of the crown, M_2 is badly fractured bucally and lingually, and only the mesiobuccal portion of M_3 is partially preserved. Only the mesiodistal lengths of M_1 and M_2 can be estimated--35.5 mm and about 40 mm, respectively. The former is close in length to the specimen (no. III) from Locality 1 (Member B), and this value is more comparable to *C. dromedarius* than to the larger *C. bactrianus*. However, this specimen is surely too ill-preserved to make other than an assignment to *Camelus* sp. indet.

Postcranial Parts

Fragmentary postcranial parts are known from members B, C, and F.

A proximal humerus from Locality 1 (no. 36) shows features like those of *C. bactrianus domesticus* and unlike those of *C. dromedarius*. This is particularly true for the lower situation of the *tuberculum minus*, the shortened extent of the dorsal margin of the *tuberculum majus*, the orientation of the broadened articular head, the development of the internal groove of the *sulcus intertubercularis*, the higher situation of *tuberculum majus* relative to *tuberculum minus*, and the smaller, more distinct *tuberculum intermedius*. The last four features are all found in *C. bactrianus domesticus*.

The anterior phalanx from Member B closely approaches the form found in extant species. There are, however, certain distinctions in several muscle insertion areas.

Also from Member B (Locality 382) is the internal condyle of a right metacarpal (no. 3). It is too incomplete to identify as other than *Camelus* sp. indet.

The posterior phalanx from Member D (Locality Omo 119) has the same overall morphology found in the extant species but differs in the better defined distal musculature insertion areas and better defined palmar ligament of the proximal end.

The first postcranial part found at Locality 52 was an adult distal right metatarsal. It is broken at the lower end of the diaphysis and preserves the intercondylar notch, a nearly complete internal condyle (mt. III), and, except for small portions of its anterior surface, most of the external condyle (mt. IV). The specimen has the splayed divergence of the condyles, the narrowed intercondylar notch, and posteriorly restricted midcondylar ridges characteristic of *Camelus*. The external condyle is narrower than the internal condyle and projects farther inferiorily. On the basis of measurements provided by Lesbre (1903), and our own observations on other specimens, this metatarsal agrees well in size with *C. bactrianus* and is correspondingly larger than *C. dromedarius*. However, beyond this size resemblance it is only possible to identify it as *Camelus* sp.

A small left calcaneum from Locality Omo 39 evidently represents a young individual; it is no larger than a specimen of a 6-year-old dromedary (Laboratoire de Paléontologie des Vertébrés, Université de Paris, inv. P. 9596). It is well preserved except for the edges of the *tuber calcanei*. Its overall morphology, except for certain details, is not notably different from that of the extant species. There are some slight differences in the form of the *manubrium calcanei*, the *condylus malleolaris*, and the *facies articularis cuboidea*. The latter is well developed, as in the extant species, though its shape is rather different. It is apparently absent in *Paracamelus*.

Discussion

Although fragmentary, the camelid remains from the Shungura Formation are of particular interest because of their persistent occurrence in a well-dated succession. Moreover, remains of these animals are uncommonly rare before the late Pleistocene.

The first demonstration of the unexpectedly ancient arrival of *Camelus* in Africa has been demonstrated by the Shungura Formation occurrences (Howell, Fichter, and Wolff 1969). The first occurrence is at nearly 3 m.y. as attested by the presence of *Camelus* in upper Member B. Remains of *Camelus* have not yet been recovered from lower members of the Shungura Formation or from the Usno and Mursi formations. Elsewhere in eastern Africa *Camelus* has been documented in uppermost Bed II (site BK II, right upper molar), Olduvai Gorge, and (by a left lower molar) at fossiliferous localities northwest of Marsabit mountain, northern Kenya (Gentry and Gentry 1969), in time ranges either younger than (Olduvai) or possibly equivalent to (Marsabit) the uppermost occurrences in the Omo.

One of us (Howell, in Howell, Fichter, and Wolff 1969) has previously discussed the status of Eurasian fossil Camelidae of late Neogene and Quaternary age, including the systematic revisions proposed by Haveson (1950; also 1954*a,b*).

The genus is well represented in the final Neogene or early Quaternary, or both, of China (Schlosser 1903; Zdansky 1926; Teilhard de Chardin and Traessaert 1937), appears in the Pinjor zone of the Upper Siwaliks (Falconer and Cautley 1868; Colbert 1935), is documented in southern Siberia (Orlov 1927, 1929, 1930) and in Kazakstan, around the Black Sea coast and Sea of Azov (esp. summary in Gromova 1965), in Rumania (Stefanescu 1895, 1909; Simionescu 1932), and in the central Danube basin in Hungary (Kretzoi 1954). It is also represented in the hominid occupation sites of 'Ubeidiya (Haas 1966), Israel, and Latamne, Syria (Hooijer 1961). It is generally accepted as an emigrant from the western hemisphere to the eastern hemisphere (Simpson 1947) in the late Neogene or the earliest Quaternary (Repenning 1967).

The classification and the affinities of African fossil Camelidae still pose a number of problems, in large part because of their poor representation in the fossil record and their fragmentary state. Ultimately an adequate basis for comparison will be afforded by the material from Ternifine (Palikao, Algeria) and a late Pleistocene Nile terrace site (1040) in the northern Sudan. The latter occurrence affords several skeletal parts (left hemimandible with heavily worn dentition, right distal tibia, left calcaneum, and three vertebral centra) of the same individual, the remains of which Gautier (1966) attributed to *Camelus thomasi* Pomel. This species was described by Pomel (1883) from collections from Ternifine, including fairly substantial material (maxilla with M^1-M^2, portion of jugal and palate, partial left mandible M_2 and alveoli of M_1 and P_4, two M^3s, a proximal metatarsal, and a metacarpal fragment; Vaufrey (1955) mentions in addition a right distal humerus). In each case these represent *Camelus thomasi*, a species having marked Asiatic affinities. The resemblances between *C. thomasi* and *C. bactrianus domesticus* are particularly evident in cranial morphology and the massiveness of the metapodials, radius, and calcaneum. If the interpretation of these affinities appears to raise certain problems they are nonetheless real. However, their importance and significance can be properly appreciated only through the investigation of specimens from other localities.

The fossil camelid specimens from the Shungura Formation afford little positive evidence of affinities with *C. bactrianus domesticus*. Only the lower molar of uncertain provenance (Omo 1932-33) and the proximal humerus from Member B (Locality 1) show some close resemblances. The other fragmentary specimens are equivocal. On the other hand, the Gentrys (1969) considered that the Olduvai and Marsabit specimens most closely resembled *C. dromedarius*, and this also appears true for the Locality 1 specimen (no. III) from Member B of the Shungura Formation (Howell, Fichter, and Wolff 1969).

Setting morphological considerations aside, simple dimensional comparisons will not

alone resolve the affinities of the Shungura Formation specimens. They do assist in relating fossil specimens to the extant species of *Camelus*. Thus, the proximal humerus appears to represent a moderate-sized, even small individual, as shown by comparisons with
figures given by Haveson (1950) and modern comparative material (Laboratoire d'anatomie
comparée, Muséum national d'histoire naturelle, Paris). On the other hand, the anterior
and posterior phalanges clearly indicate that it was larger than *C. bactrianus* and *C.
dromedarius*, and the differences are rather marked, from the figures given by Haveson (1950).
Additional specimens from Ternifine, collected by R. Hoffstetter and the late C. Arambourg
in 1954-56 and now under study by Grattard, indicate that the Omo phalanges coincide in
size with those of *C. thomasi* from Ternifine. Hence it seems necessary to use both dimensional and morphological criteria. Similarly, if it is difficult to determine affinities
with living *Camelus* species, it is also difficult to link them directly with *C. thomasi*.
For the moment it is necessary to treat the Shungura Formation specimens as *Camelus* sp.,
although more complete fossil material could ultimately permit us to assign at least some
of the material to *C. thomasi*.

It is certainly reasonable to assume affinities with *C. bactrianus* for some African
camelid fossils, including those of Ternifine, north Sudan, certain aforementioned specimens from the Omo, and perhaps a distal metapodial from Bochianga, Chad, collected by
Coppens. This does not permit us to assign these remains to *C. thomasi*, any more than to
consider them as representing a homogeneous group resulting from an early migration from
Asia. These resemblances could well indicate a common origin of *C. bactrianus* and a more
or less homogeneous camelid group which migrated into Africa in ancient times.

There are still greater difficulties in interpreting affinities between *C. dromedarius*
and some of the presumably similar fossil specimens from East Africa (Shungura Member B,
Olduvai Gorge, Marsabit). There is minimal evidence here for inferring direct relationships between these fossil examples and the living African camel *C. dromedarius*, just as
it is difficult to reject their affinities with *C. thomasi*. In fact it is even probable
that these African fossil camelids represent a phylogenetically heterogeneous assemblage,
having substantial geographic (and perhaps also temporal) variations in a number of morphological features. Indeed, they appear to exhibit primitive characters which are found
more or less modified in *C. bactrianus*, specialized characters which parallel those of *C.
bactrianus*, and some features distinctive of the African camel *C. dromedarius*.

Camel remains are also known from other late Pleistocene sites in North Africa in
association with Mousterian industries (Saint-Roch near Oran; Anglade, Sintes, near Algiers),
or Aterian (El Guettar near Gafsa, Tunisia; Chaachas wells, near Tebessa) and Iberomaurusian
(Taza, Morocco) (Arambourg 1938; Gautier 1966; Vaufrey 1955; Zeuner 1963). These particular
fragmentary specimens afford no useful systematic or phyletic information, or evidence
relevant to their relationship with *Camelus dromedarius*, *Camelus thomasi*, or other African
specimens referred to *Camelus* sp.

References

Arambourg, C. 1929. Les mammifères quaternaires de l'Algérie. *Bull. Soc. Hist. Nat.
Afrique du Nord (Alger)* 20:63-84.

———. 1938. Mammifères fossiles du Maroc. *Mém. Soc. Sci. Nat. Maroc (Rabat)* 46:1-74.

Colbert, E. H. 1935. Siwalik mammals in the American Museum of Natural History. *Trans.
Amer. Phil. Soc.*, n. 5. 26, 1:295-301.

Falconer, H., and Cautley, P. T. 1868. On the fossil camel of the Siwalik Hills. In *Falconer's paleont: Notes and memoirs*, 1:227-46. London.

Gautier, A. 1966. *Camelus thomasi* from the northern Sudan and its bearing on the relationship *C. thomasi-C. bactrianus*. *J. Paleont.* 40(6):1368-72.

Gentry, A. W., and Gentry, A. 1969. Fossil camels in Kenya and Tanzania. *Nature* 222:898.

Gromova, V. 1965. Short study of European Quaternary mammalia (in Russian), *Camelidae*. 80. Nauka.

Haas, G. 1966. *On the vertebrate fauna of the Lower Pleistocene site 'Ubeidiya; The Lower Pleistocene of the Central Jordan valley; The excavations at 'Ubeidiya, 1960-1963*. Jerusalem: Israel Academy of Sciences and Humanities.

Haveson, I. I. 1950. Verbludy roda *Paracamelus* [Camels of Genus *Paracamelus*]. *Dokl. AN SSSR* 70(5):917-20.

———. 1954. Tretichnye verbludy Vostochnogo polushariya (rod *Paracamelus*) [Tertiary camels of the eastern hemisphere (genus *Paracamelus*)]. *AN SSSR, Tr. PIN*, 47:100-162.

———. 1954. Dikii odnogorbyi verbludy iz otiozhenii ozera Sevan (Armoniya) [The wild one-humped camel from the deposits of Lake Sevan (Armenia)]. *Dokl. AN SSSR*, 98(3): 475-78.

Hooijer, D. A. 1961. Middle Pleistocene mammals from Latamne, Orontes valley, Syria. *Ann. Archéol. Syrie* 2(117):128-29.

Howell, F. C.; Fichter, L. S. and Wolff, R. 1969. Fossil camels in the Omo Beds, southern Ethiopia. *Nature* 223:150-52.

Joleaud, L. 1910. Sur les faunes de mammifères quaternaires de la Berbérie. *Bull. Soc. Hist. Nat. Afr. du Nord (Alger)* 1:102-4.

Kmomenko, I. P. 1912. *Camelus bessarabiensis* i drugie iskapaemye formy yuzhnoi Bessarabii [*Camelus bessarabiensis* and other fossil forms from southern Bessarabia]. *Tr. Bessarabs. Obshch. Estestvoispy. Lyub. Estestvozn.* 3:92-127.

———. 1914. Otkrytie russil'onskoi fauny i drugie rezul'taty geologicheskikh nablyudenii v yuzhnoi Bessarabii [The discovery of the Roussillon fauna and other results of geological observations in southern Bessarabia]. *Tr. Bessarabs. Obshch. Estestvoispyt. Lyub. Estestvozn.* 6:3-11.

Kretzoi, M. 1954. Ostrich and camel remains from the central Danube basin. *Jahresber. Ungar. Geol. Anstalt, 1953, 213, Acta Geol. Budapest* 2:231-42.

Lesbre, F. 1903. Recherches anatomiques sur les Camélidés. *Arch. Museum Hist. Nat. Lyon* 8:1-195.

Nehring, A. 1901. Ein fossiles Kamel aus Südrussland, nebst Bemerkungen über die Heimat der Kamele. *"Globus," Braunschweig* 80:188-89.

———. 1901. Fossile Kamele in Rumänien. *"Globus," Braunschweig* 79:264-67.

———. 1901. Vorläufige Mitteilung über einen fossilen Kamelschädel (*Camelus knoblochi*) von Sarepta an der Wolga. *Sitzber. Ges. naturf. Freunde Berlin* 1901(5):137-44.

Orlov, J. 1927. Über die Reste eines fossilen Kamels aus dem Gouvernement Akmolinsk (Westsibirien). *Ezhegodnik Zool. Muzeya, AN SSSR* 1927:496-538.

———. 1929. Über die Reste der fossilen Cameliden aus dem Gouvernement Akmolinsk (Westsibirien). *Ezhegodnik Zool. Muzeya, AN SSSR* 1929:549-89.

———. 1930. Über die Reste der fossilen Camelidae aus dem Gouvernement Semipalatinsk (Westsibirien). *Ezhegodnik Russk. Paleontol. Obshch.* 8:99-116.

Pallary, P. 1903. Note sur la girafe et le chameau du Quaternaire algérien. *Bull. Soc. Géol. France*, ser. 4, 3:908-9.

Pavlov, M. V. 1904. *Procamelus* du gouvernement de Kherson. *Mem. Soc. Nat., Nouvelle Russie, Odessa*, 25:113-33.

Pomel, A. 1883. Caméliens et Cervidés. *Carte Géol. Algérie, Paléontol., Mon.,* 1:1-32.

Repenning, C. A. 1967. Palearctic-Nearctic mammalian dispersal in the late Cenozoic. In *The Bering land bridge,* ed. D. M. Hopkins, pp. 288-311. Stanford: Stanford University Press.

Schlosser, M. 1903. Die fossilen Säugetiere Chinas. *Abhandl. Math. Phys. Kl. K. Bayer, Akad. Wiss., München,* II, 22 (fasc. 1):95-97.

Simionescu, I. 1932. Tertiäre et pleistozäne *Camelidae* in Rumänien. *Bull. Sect. Sci. Acad. Roumaine, Bucarest* 15:1-8.

Simpson, G. G. 1947. Holarctic mammalian faunas and continental relationships during the Cenozoic. *Bull. Geol. Soc. Amer.* 58:613-87.

Stefanescu, G. 1895. Le chameau fossile de Roumanie. *Ann. Mus. Geol. Paleont., Bucuresti* 1894:89-123.

_____. 1909. Prima câmilâ fosilâ. *Anal. Acad. Romane* 17:65-71.

Teilhard de Chardin, P., and Piveteau, J. 1930. Les mammifères fossiles de Nihowan, Chine. *Annales Paleont.* 19:1-134.

Teilhard de Chardin, P., and Traessaert, M. 1937. Pliocene *Camelidae, Giraffidae* and *Cervidae* of southeastern Shansi. *Pal. Sin.,* n. s., C, 1.

Vaufrey, R. 1955. Préhistoire de l'Afrique, 1: Magreb. *Inst. Hautes Etudes Tunis (Paris), Pub.,* 4:1-458.

Zdansky, O. 1926. *Paracamelus gigas* Schlosser. *Pal. Sin.,* ser. C, 2(fasc. 4):1-44.

Zeuner, F. E. 1963. *A history of domesticated animals.* New York: Harper and Row.

26. BOVIDAE OF THE OMO GROUP DEPOSITS

A. W. Gentry

Introduction

The following account is based mainly on fossils collected by the Omo Research Expedition, largely those collected under the direction of F. Clark Howell, but also on some of the material collected under the direction of Yves Coppens and the late C. Arambourg. The material comes mostly from the Shungura Formation, with only a small representation from the Mursi and Usno formations. Accounts of the stratigraphy and dating of these formations are given elsewhere in this book.

Specimens are referred to by their catalog numbers, and on their first mention by geological member as well. Thus L36-4 means specimen number 4 from Locality 36 in Member D. The prefixes F or P instead of L indicate some localities collected by F. H. Brown and J. de Heinzelin, respectively. Fossils from the Mursi Formation have the prefix YS. For material collected under the direction of Yves Coppens and C. Arambourg, a number in the form Omo 50 1968-1649 means specimen number 1649 of the year 1968, collected at site number 50, specimens being numbered by field season and not by locality. Measurements are given in millimeters. The authors of Linnaean names are given for fossil species occurring in the Omo deposits; those of living African species may be traced in Allen (1939). The classification of bovids used here is a modified version of that of Simpson (1945), with some improvements from Ansell (1971) and some innovations:

Family Bovidae

Subfamily Bovinae

Tribe Tragelaphini	Kudus, bushbucks, and allied forms, mainly browsers in bush and forest.
Tribe Boselaphini	Now represented only by two tragelaphinelike antelopes in India, but formerly occurring in Africa.
Tribe Bovini	Cattle and buffaloes, the largest bovids.

Subfamily Cephalophinae

Tribe Cephalophini	Duikers, mainly small forest antelopes, rarely fossilized and not present in Omo deposits.

275

Subfamily Hippotraginae

    Tribe Reduncini   Reedbuck, kob, and waterbuck group, very common in the Shungura Formation. Living reduncines are grazing antelopes always found in the vicinity of water.

    Tribe Hippotragini   Roan, sable, oryxes, and addax.

Subfamily Alcelaphinae

    Tribe Alcelaphini   Wildebeest and hartebeest group; grazing, cursorial antelopes of open country. Poorly represented in the Shungura Formation other than by *Aepyceros*, the impala, which I include here.

Subfamily Antilopinae

    Tribe Neotragini   Dik-dik group, including the smallest antelopes.

    Tribe Antilopini   Gazelles, springbok, and blackbuck. Small cursorial antelopes, often adapted to conditions of water shortage (including Saigini).

Subfamily Caprinae

    Tribe "Rupicaprini"   Goral and serow group, but *Rupicapra* itself might be better placed in the Caprini. Not found in Africa.

    Tribe Ovibovini   Musk-ox, takin, and extinct allies.

    Tribe Caprini   Sheep and goats.

Bovids from the Shungura Formation

    The occurrences of fossil bovids in the members of the Shungura Formation are shown in table 1. The following pages offer comments on this table.

Tribe Tragelaphini

Tragelaphus strepsiceros. A single piece of horn core, L627-17 G, appears from its large size to be from a greater kudu. Another fragment of a kudu horn core, P994-45 from Kaalam, is inadequate for determining species level.

Tragelaphus gaudryi (P. Thomas 1884). This species was founded on a right horn core base, figured as a left by Thomas (1884, pl. 1, fig. 7). It came from Ain Jourdel, Algeria, and is thought to be of Villafranchian-equivalent age. Another Algerian frontlet from Mansoura, previously figured by Gervais (1867-69, pl. 19, fig. 4) is of roughly the same age, but no North African kudus are known from later periods. A kudu which I cannot distinguish from *Tragelaphus gaudryi* is found in members E to G of the Shungura Formation, with one additional record, Omo 18 1968-303, from Member C. Appropriately sized tragelaphine teeth may also be referred to this species. It differs from *T. strepsiceros* by its smaller size and by horn cores less mediolaterally compressed, more weakly spiraled, and less uprightly inserted. It is likely that Shungura Formation horn cores become more mediolaterally compressed from Member E to Member G (fig. 1), and this is accompanied by a decline of the lateral keel and accentuation of the anterior keel.

    Tragelaphus gaudryi dies out above Member G. It is unlikely that it is ancestral to *T. strepsiceros*, which occurs in Member G and at a level perhaps contemporary with the

Table 1

Distribution of Bovidae in the Shungura Formation

Taxon	B	C	D	E	F	G	post G
Tragelaphus strepsiceros						0	
*T. gaudryi		0		X	X	X	
T. ?pricei		0					
Tragelaphus sp.		0	0	0			
*Tragelaphus nakuae	X	X	X	X	X	X	
Syncerus sp.	0	0				0	
Pelorovis sp.		0			0	0	
?Hemibos sp.				0		0	
Bovini spp. indet.	X	X	X	X	X	X	X
*Kobus sigmoidalis		0	0	X	X	X	
K. ellipsiprymnus						0	0
K. kob			?	?		?	X
K. ?patulicornis	X						
*Kobus sp.	X	0					
K. ancystrocera	0	X			0	X	
Menelikia sp.		X	0				
*M. lyrocera				X	X	X	X+
Redunca sp.	0	0		0			
Hippotragini sp. indet.		0					
Megalotragus ?kattwinkeli						0	X
Oreonagor/Connochaetes sp.	0						
Beatragus antiquus							0
Parmularius altidens							0
Parmularius/Damaliscus sp.		0					
Alcelaphini spp. indet.	X	X	X	X	X	X	X
*Aepyceros sp.	X	X	X	X	X	X	X
Neotragini spp. indet.				0	0	0	
Antidorcas ?recki	0		?		0	0	0
Gazella praethomsoni						0	
Antilope subtorta		0					
?Tossunnoria sp.			0		0		

NOTE: * = abundant species; 0 = rare; X = common; + = advanced subspecies.

latest T. gaudryi. Also, T. strepsiceros occurs as early as site FLKNN in Bed I, Olduvai Gorge, Tanzania, and radiometric dating (Curtis and Hay 1972, p. 295; Hay 1971, p. 13) indicates that the Bed I fauna would be very nearly contemporary with that of Member G. It is therefore all the more interesting that T. gaudryi was evolving toward T. strepsiceros in its trends to greater mediolateral compression of the horn cores, accentuation of the anterior keel, and loss of the posterolateral keel. Was it cut short in this evolution by the immigration of T. strepsiceros, or could it have evolved into the living lesser kudu, T. imberbis, which it resembles in the poorer divergence and weaker spiraling of its horn cores? However, even the early T. gaudryi from Member E differs from T. imberbis by already possessing a strong anterior keel and poor posterolateral keel.

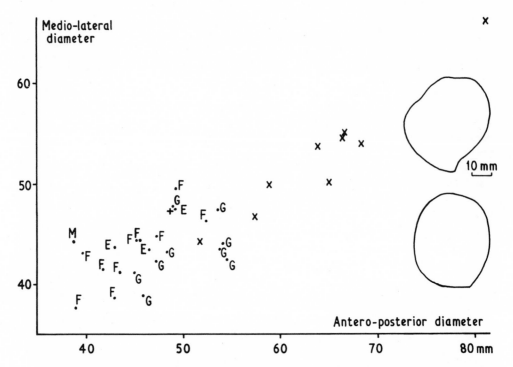

Figure 1. Graph of basal diameters of kudu horn cores. Dots indicate *Tragelaphus gaudryi* from the Shungura Formation, members E, F, and G. M = Mursi Formation; + = *T. gaudryi* holotype; X = Recent *Tragelaphus strepsiceros*.
   On the right are cross sections near the base of right horn cores of *T. gaudryi*: L207-1 E (*above*) and L7-241 G (*below*). The anterior side is toward the base of the diagram and the lateral side toward the left.

Tragelaphus ?pricei (Wells and Cooke 1956). A pair of horn cores, L144-1 and 2 C, are from a small *Tragelaphus* and differ from the living bushbuck, *T. scriptus*, by being less compressed anteroposteriorly and having more upright insertions. They may be provisionally assigned to *T. pricei*, a species founded on dentitions from Makapansgat Limeworks, South Africa.

Tragelaphus sp. indet. A set of tragelaphine right lower molars from Member E and two other individual lower molars from members C and D of the Shungura Formation are too large to match *T. ?pricei* but too small for *T. gaudryi*.

Tragelaphus nakuae Arambourg 1941. This large species is abundant in the Shungura Formation, its type locality. It is not a kudu, and it differs from *T. gaudryi* by its larger size, a transverse ridge across the cranial roof above the occipital, horn cores more anteroposteriorly compressed with a weaker anterior and a stronger posterolateral keel, divergence decreasing instead of increasing from the base upward, and basal pillars (entostyle and ectostylid) present or more frequent on upper and lower molars. The ridge across the top of the occipital is a most striking character and seems to have arisen because the cranial roof in front of it was depressed to make way for the horn cores. It is thus linked with the high setting of the braincase behind the face and the low inclination of the horn cores.

   Tragelaphus nakuae occurs through the Shungura Formation from members B to G, but with

relatively greater rarity in members F and G. The remains from members C to G differ from
the few in Member B by all or most of the following characters: increased size, shorter
horn cores, horn cores with a more curved course overall but less twisting of the keels, a
weaker anterior keel, greater anteroposterior compression, the anterior keel arising from
a more lateral insertion (fig. 2), and wider divergence basally. The Member B *T, nakuae*
is thus morphologically closer to *T. gaudryi*. The available sample does not show a gradual
trend in these characters so much as a relatively sudden change between members B and C.
There may also be a smaller "jump" after Member F in that the advanced characters are most
fully pronounced in Member G.

 T. nakuae from all members retains boselaphinelike cranial characters: the high position of the braincase as seen in profile behind the orbits, the persistence of the temporal
ridges, the large supraorbital pits, the projecting orbital rims, and a large shallow preorbital fossa seen in the only known face. The similarities to a boselaphine like
Selenoportax vexillarius Pilgrim (1937) of the Nagri Formation of the Siwaliks in India and
the contrast with other species of *Tragelaphus* are striking. However, it would be premature
to put *T. nakuae* into *Selenoportax* until more is known about the lineages of boselaphines
and tragelaphines before the time span of the Shungura Formation.

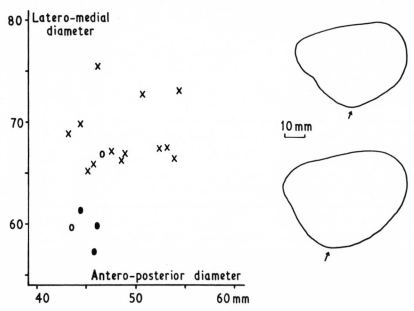

Figure 2. Graph of basal diameters of *Tragelaphus nakuae* horn cores. 0 = Usno Formation;
O = Shungura Formation Member B; X = Shungura Formation C. In Member C the horn cores have
become lateromedially thicker than in the Usno Formation or Member B. Available samples,
not entered on the graph, show that horn cores from Member D are like those of C, those of
E and F revert a little toward the proportions shown in B, and those of G are again like C.
However a horn core with anteroposterior and mediolateral diameters of about 46 and 66 mm
could be found in any member.
 On the right are cross sections near the base of right horn cores of *T. nakuae*:
L1-5 B (*above*) and F165-1 G (*below*, left horn core reversed to appear as of the right side).
The anterior side is toward the base of the diagram and the lateral side toward the left.
The arrows mark the position of the anterior keel.

Tribe Bovini

Syncerus sp. Four partial skulls or fragments thereof from members B, C, and G, and one or two horn cores belong to a species likely to be ancestral to the living African buffalo, *Syncerus caffer*. The braincase is unlike that of the living species by being less short and less low and wide. Temporal ridges are strong but are less so than in the well-known Eurasian Villafranchian *Leptobos*. The horn cores, all from Member C, are markedly short, with dorsoventral compression and a flat dorsal surface. They have a strong concavity on the posteroventral surface near their base. They emerge sideways and slightly upward from the skull, and sinuses extend from the frontals into the bases of the horn cores. Some surface rugosity is beginning to appear on the frontals between the horn bases. *Syncerus* horn cores in Bed II at Olduvai Gorge are larger and relatively longer, which suggests either that the Shungura ones are more primitive or that they are from a woodland-forest subspecies comparable to the living *S. caffer nanus*. The latter hypothesis is interesting for its implication that the difference between *Syncerus* populations in closed and open habitats is a feature of great antiquity.

Pelorovis sp. Parts of some large curved horn cores from Member G belong to this extinct bovine lineage, whose terminal member was the late Pleistocene long-horned buffalo *Pelorovis antiquus*. The Omo horn core pieces belong either to the Olduvai middle and upper Bed II *P. oldowayensis* or to an immediately ancestral species. One or two of the bovine teeth from the Shungura Formation are large enough to be assigned to *Pelorovis* but are not morphologically distinguishable from *Syncerus*.

?Hemibos sp. L16-10 G is the greater part of a massive horn core which may belong to *Hemibos*, a genus related to and perhaps ancestral to *Bubalus*, the southern Asian water buffalo. *Hemibos* occurs in the Pinjor Formation of the Siwaliks and there is a record from Palestine (Pilgrim 1941), but it has not hitherto been recorded from Africa. A distal part of a horn core, L147-48a E, may be conspecific.

Bovini spp. indet. Substantial numbers of isolated bovine teeth are found, particularly in members B and C, most of them probably belonging to the *Syncerus* species. Very similar teeth occur at Olduvai but are somewhat larger (fig. 3). A complete bovine right radius and ulna, L36-12 D, is slightly small in comparison with the larger races of living *S. caffer* and certainly has a small cross section.

Tribe Reduncini

Kobus sigmoidalis Arambourg 1941. This species, originally described from the Shungura Formation, is nearly as large as the living waterbuck. It has long horn cores which are mediolaterally compressed, very divergent, and curve backward at the base. It is abundant in members E to G and also known from members C and D. Frontlets and craniums are rare, and the species is known almost entirely from broken pieces of horn cores. It also occurs in Bed I at Olduvai Gorge but is less common there than at Omo. A small minority of the horn cores from Member G have less mediolateral compression and less of a backward curvature at the base (figs. 4 and 5). These characters resemble those of the living waterbuck, *Kobus ellipsiprymnus*, and suggest that a transition to that species was taking place. *K. sigmoidalis* probably also gave rise to the smaller living Central African lechwe, *K. leche*, which retained the primitive horn core characters of mediolateral compression and backward curvature at the base.

Olduvai Bed III   x   x x   x   x

Olduvai upper Bed II   x x   xx   x   x

Olduvai Bed I   x

Shungura members E to G   ∞   o oo ooo o   ∞ o o

Shungura members B to D   o   o oo o ∞ooo o o   o   oo

| | 30 | 35 | 40 | 45 mm |

Figure 3. Occlusal length of M₃s in Bovini from the Shungura Formation (O) and Olduvai Gorge (X), excluding any thought to be *Pelorovis*.

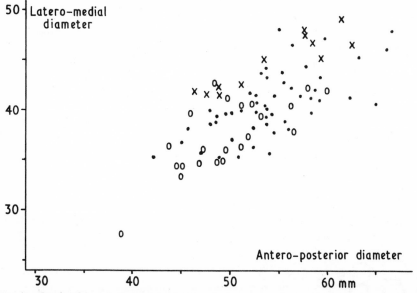

Figure 4. Graph of basal diameters of *Kobus* horn cores. O = *Kobus sigmoidalis* from the Shungura Formation, members E and F; X = Recent *K. ellipsiprymnus*; dots = *K. sigmoidalis* from the Shungura Formation, Member G.

   Most *K. sigmoidalis* from members E and F have horn cores with more mediolateral compression than in *K. ellipsiprymnus* (Os below Xs on the graph). Specimens from Member G begin to have a greater overlap with *K. ellipsiprymnus*.

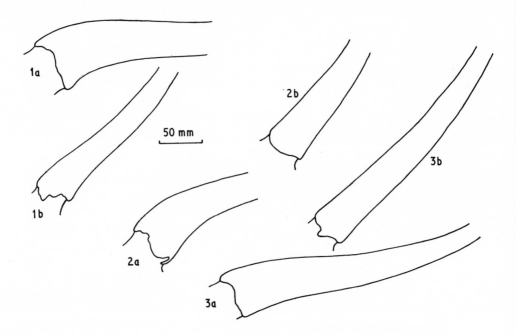

Figure 5.   Selected horn cores of *Kobus sigmoidalis* from Member G of the Shungura Formation, all drawn as if of the left side.   1*a*, 1*b* = lateral and dorsal views of L67-65; 2*a*, 2*b* = lateral and dorsal views of L25-15; 3*a*, 3*b* = lateral and dorsal views of L518-8.
    The first horn core shows the *K. sigmoidalis* characters of basal backward curvature and mediolateral compression, the second shows less compression, and the third shows less curvature and less compression thereby resembling *K. ellipsiprymnus*.

Kobus ellipsiprymnus.   A few horn core pieces from above Member G and one from Member G represent the living waterbuck in the Shungura Formation.

Kobus kob.   A species of kob, presumably the living one, is definitely known from high levels of the Shungura Formation, for example the Kaalam horn cores P995-9, P995-10, and P996-10, and also F203-26 K.   To distinguish individual horn cores from those of *Kobus sigmoidalis-ellipsiprymnus* is difficult.   Smaller size, less divergent horn cores, and closer horn insertions are among the characters one may hope to see in *K. kob*.   Doubtful earlier representatives of kobs are the horn cores L526-1 G, L99-6 E, and L36-1 D.   It is interesting that the evidence for a kob in Member G and earlier should be so feeble.

Kobus ?patulicornis (Lydekker 1878).   A frontlet L1-189 and horn cores L1-24 and L1-25, all from Member B, are very similar to kobs.   It is difficult to know whether they are in fact an early kob, whether they are related to the ancestry of *Kobus sigmoidalis*, or whether they could be conspecific with any Siwaliks reduncine.   For the present they may be taken as comparable to the Pinjor Formation *K. patulicornis*.

Kobus sp.   A partial cranium, L1-53 B, as well as some other horn cores from Member B and one from Member C belong to a reduncine I do not know from anywhere else.   The horn cores are a little compressed anteroposteriorly, without a flattened lateral surface, are inserted at a fairly low angle, and are almost straight in side view.   The braincase is scarcely angled downward at all, the basioccipital has large outwardly splayed anterior tuberosities, and the orbital rims are wide in dorsal view. This very distinctive species is not the *Kobus* sp. of Arambourg (1947, p. 415).

Kobus ancystrocera (Arambourg 1947). This species is known only by its horn cores. They show some mediolateral compression near the base and a flattened lateral surface, are inserted wide apart and at a very low angle, curve upward markedly toward the tips, and are very divergent. The pedicels are set more upright than the lower part of the horn core proper, and there are large supraorbital foramina. *K. ancystrocera* was described from the Shungura Formation and occurs in most members but is never among the most abundant antelopes. Specimens in Member G are larger than those from Member B, but the low numbers of specimens from below G necessitate some caution in accepting or using this conclusion. The species was originally placed in *Redunca*, probably because of the relatively small size of some specimens and the resemblance of the pronounced distal curvature of the horn cores to the horn sheaths of certain living *Redunca* populations. I prefer to retain only the three living reedbuck species and the extinct *R. darti* of Makapansgat Limeworks in *Redunca*. *R. darti* is not at all like *K. ancystrocera* in its smaller size and short horn cores with much less divergence and more upright insertions.

Menelikia lyrocera Arambourg 1941. This species was founded on Shungura Formation fossils and is known from a number of more or less complete skulls and craniums as well as horn core pieces. The frontals are extensively hollowed with internal sinuses anteromedially to the horn insertions. A small preorbital fossa is retained, and the face is deep. It occurs from Member E upward. In members E and F the skull shape tends to be narrow rather than low and wide, and the horn cores are inserted close together, mediolaterally compressed, curving backward near the base, then diverging and finally curving upward toward the tip. In Member G the horn cores begin to be shorter, not mediolaterally compressed, straighter and less uprightly inserted in side view; above Member G and perhaps even in Member G itself the braincase becomes lower and wider, the dorsal parts of the orbital rims project less strongly, there are changes in the basioccipital, and the nuchal crests become less prominent (see figs. 6 and 7). Arambourg (1947) founded a new subfamily for this antelope, but I believe it can be taken as reduncine by the transverse ridges on its horn cores, close approach of the temporal lines posteriorly on the cranial roof, the large maxillary tuberosity, the closeness of the palatal ridges in front of the tooth row, and especially by the characters of the teeth.

Menelikia sp. A group of horn cores from Member C and one from Member D may represent a species ancestral to *Menelikia lyrocera*. They are long and usually mediolaterally compressed in the lower part, show increasing divergence toward their tips, and have very deep irregular longitudinal grooving on the anterior surface. There are internal sinuses in a small part of the frontals. Some *M. lyrocera* retain vestiges of the pronounced grooving (Arambourg 1947, pl. 29, fig. 2), and the frontal sinuses also indicate the suggested relationship.

Redunca sp. A few reduncine teeth are too small for *Kobus* and presumably represent *Redunca*.

Reduncini spp. indet. Medium-sized reduncine teeth are common in the Shungura Formation, but I have been unable to identify them at generic or specific level. Their occlusal structure is a little more primitive than in living reduncines. Many of the larger ones in Member G must presumably belong to *Kobus sigmoidalis*.

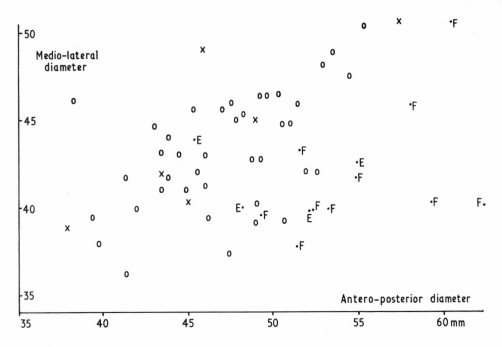

Figure 6. Graph of basal diameters of horn cores of *Menelikia lyrocera* from the Shungura Formation. Those from members E and F are marked by dots. O = Member G, X = members above G. The horn cores are seen to become mediolaterally thicker after Member F.

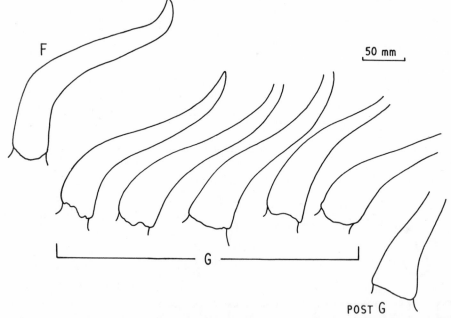

Figure 7. Anterodorsal views of selected horn cores of *Menelikia lyrocera* from the Shungura Formation. All the horn cores have been drawn as if of the left side. *From the left*: L52-3 F, L626-24 G, L48-15a G, L25-135 G, L48-1 G, L7-40 G, P994-42 Kaalam. The series shows a diminishing overall length, curvature becoming less intense, and the base thickening.

Tribe Hippotragini

Part of a right upper molar, L17-30a C, is definitely hippotragine. In size and morphology it matches upper molars of *Hippotragus gigas* L. S. B. Leakey 1965 from Olduvai Gorge, but it would be unwise to take the identification below tribal level. A few other tooth and horn core fragments could also be hippotragine.

Tribe Alcelaphini

Megalotragus ?kattwinkeli (Schwarz 1932). *Megalotragus* is a lineage of extinct alcelaphines, larger than wildebeest and with longer legs and simpler occlusal surfaces of the cheek teeth. The type species is the late Pleistocene *M. priscus* of South Africa, but the earlier *M. kattwinkeli* occurs at Olduvai Gorge. A few horn cores and a frontlet from Member G and above belong to *M. kattwinkeli* or its immediate ancestor. The horn cores are inserted just behind the orbits, sometimes compressed dorsoventrally at the base, and are moderately divergent. They differ from those of Olduvai middle Bed II and later by having a backward curve at the base, and I am uncertain whether this should be taken to indicate membership in a species other than *M. kattwinkeli*. They may also be longer. Large alcelaphine teeth from lower in the Shungura Formation are also likely to belong to *Megalotragus*.

Oreonagor/Connochaetes sp. The somewhat weathered base of a curved horn core, L1-52 B, has a single smooth-walled sinus in its pedicel and is therefore likely to be alcelaphine. It could well be a wildebeest, but its correct generic or specific placing is doubtful. It might belong to *Connochaetes* or to the more primitive *Oreonagor*, a genus based on *O. tournoueri* (P. Thomas 1884) from Ain Jourdel, Algeria.

Parmularius altidens Hopwood 1934. The lower half of a left horn core, F161-37, from above Member G is the sole representative of this species outside Olduvai Gorge, where it is characteristic of Bed I, being especially common at site FLKN near the top of that bed.

Parmularius/Damaliscus sp. L292-29 C is most of a right alcelaphine horn core, which is fairly sharply curved back in the middle of its course. It could be a precursor of *Parmularius altidens* or it could be related to *Damaliscus*.

Beatragus antiquus L. S. B. Leakey 1965. This species differs from the living *Beatragus hunteri*, the herola or Tana River hartebeest, by its larger size, more upright horn core insertions, horn cores diverging from the base and having a less abrupt alteration in course above the initial outward divergence, and wider frontals. The species is known by horn cores alone from Olduvai Gorge Beds I and II, but a subadult cranium with right horn core comes from above Member G of the Shungura Formation.

Alcelaphini spp. indet. Isolated alcelaphine teeth are found in low numbers from Member B upward in the Shungura Formation, and in members E, F, and G they equal or exceed the numbers of bovine teeth. They can be arranged in two size groups, with the larger not attaining the size of the larger teeth at Olduvai. This probably indicates that the *Megalotragus* or *Connochaetes* lineages (or both) at that time were smaller than their descendants. The smallest teeth are smaller than those of living East African hartebeest or topi.

Aepyceros sp. An impala is the most common antelope in members B to G as a whole, in strong contrast to Olduvai, where it is rare. A complete male skull with mandibles, atlas, and axis vertebrae is a notable find from Member B. It differs from skulls of the living impala, *Aepyceros melampus*, by its smaller size, less lyrated horn cores, a shorter face, a trace of a preorbital fossa later to disappear, a relatively longer premolar row, a shorter neck, and shorter and thicker limb bones. Some of these differences are shown on figs. 8 and 9. Nearly all the characters whereby the fossil differs from the living species show a more primitive state in the fossil, and there is no reason to doubt that it is the direct ancestor of the living species. Another skull from Member E is hardly larger, but it has slightly more swollen frontals and possibly a shorter braincase and more anterior tooth row. It also has a narrower basioccipital with longitudinal ridges better developed behind the anterior tuberosities, which is unlike the living impala. It is unfortunate that impala horn cores in the Shungura Formation show no smooth transition from smaller and less lyrated ones to larger and more strongly lyrated ones. Indeed, it is noteworthy that at present adult male impala from the Shaba (formerly Katanga), region of Zaire and adjacent parts of Zambia are small-boned with less lyrated horns than other living populations. They have been named *A. melampus katangae* Lonnberg 1914, and some readings for this subspecies are shown on figure 8.

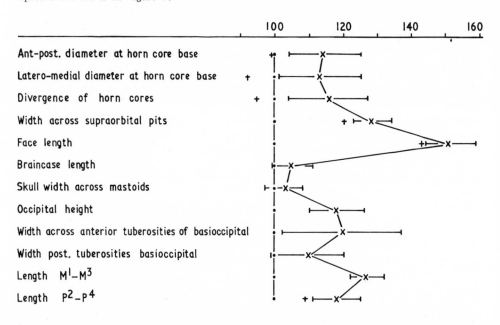

Figure 8. Percentage diagram of some skull measurements in male impala. The readings for the Shungura Formation skull from Member B form the standard line at 100%. The other line is the mean readings and standard deviations of 11 Recent East African *Aepyceros melampus*, expressed as percentages of the standard. + marks the mean readings for 5 *A. melampus katangae* from the N'dola area of Zambia in cases where they lie outside the standard deviations of the other Recent impala. Face length was measured from the front of P2 to the nearest point of the orbital rim, and braincase length was measured from the back of the frontals to the occipital top along the skull midline.

The many small nonreduncine antilopinelike teeth in the Shungura Formation can best be attributed to impala. It is annoying that the teeth are harder to distinguish from those of contemporaneous *Gazella* and *Antidorcas* than they are in the living members of these genera.

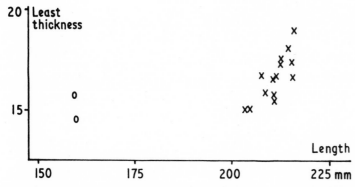

Figure 9. Graph of length and least transverse shaft thickness in *Aepyceros* metacarpals. O = L551-6 D (*above*) and L1-39 B (*below*) from the Shungura Formation; X = Recent *A. melampus*.

Tribe Neotragini

Neotragini spp. indet. A horn core, two mandibular pieces, and a distal metatarsal are the only traces of this tribe in the Shungura Formation. The horn core is rather large, one of the tooth rows shows resemblances to *Raphicerus*, *Dorcatragus*, or *Oreotragus*, and the other tooth row is from a smaller species.

Tribe Antilopini

Antidorcas ?recki (Schwarz 1932). *Antidorcas recki* is an extinct springbok differing from the living *A. marsupialis* by having lived in East Africa as well as or instead of South Africa, by being smaller, and by having horn cores more mediolaterally compressed and more sharply bent backward distally, cheek teeth relatively smaller, and premolar row longer. The species was originally described from Olduvai and shows considerable variation in horn core morphology. It is sparsely represented in the Shungura Formation, but perhaps is less rare in Member G and above. The horn cores are a little smaller than at Olduvai, and the backward bend in the middle of their course is less sharp. If they are not of *A. recki*, they must be its immediate ancestor. The mandible published as *Antidorcas* sp. by Arambourg (1947, p. 390) is from a small alcelaphine.

Gazella praethomsoni Arambourg 1947. The horn core originally described from the Shungura Formation and a second horn core, L35-35 G, are strongly compressed mediolaterally. Two other horn cores are probably from females of this species. Despite its name it may well not be ancestral to the living *G. thomsoni*. The mandibular fragment assigned by Arambourg (1947, pl. 27, figs. 1, 1*a*, *b*) to this species is from a reduncine. Gazelles are also rare at Olduvai Gorge, but there the main species has horn cores with less mediolateral compression.

Antilope subtorta Pilgram 1937. This species was founded on a piece of horn core from the Pinjor Formation of the Siwaliks. It differed from horn cores of the living Indian blackbuck, *Antilope cervicapra*, by its larger size and weaker spiraling. A right and a left horn core from Locality 46 in Member C are the only African record of *Antilope*. They are both poorly spiraled and also differ from the blackbuck by possessing a trace of a postero-lateral keel. They are smaller than the holotype of *A. subtorta* but can be assigned to this species for the present.

Tribe Caprini

?*Tossunnoria* sp. *Tossunnoria* is an extinct genus similar to tahrs, *Hemitragus*, species of
which are still living in Arabia and India and which is known as far back as the earlier
Pleistocene of Austria and Hungary (Daxner 1968). *Tossunnoria* differs from *Hemitragus* by
having horn cores which are not hollowed internally and a basioccipital which is less wide
anteriorly. The type and only species is *T. pseudibex* Bohlin 1937 described from the Tertiary of Tibet. Two or three horn cores from members D and F of the Shungura Formation
are larger than *T. pseudibex* but are very strongly flattened from side to side like
Tossunnoria and some *Hemitragus* and have spongy bone internally.

Bovidae spp. indet.

A fair number of puzzling horn cores are known from the Shungura Formation and suggest
that the above list of species may be distorted or seriously incomplete. As an example,
there are two horn cores, F203-24 and 25 J, which are lyrated and have transverse ridges
like an impala, but which are also large and mediolaterally compressed and have a more
regular oval cross section.

Bovids from the Usno Formation

The Usno Formation has bovids similar to some of those from the Shungura Formation.
There are a frontlet and many horn core pieces of *Tragelaphus nakuae* and many impala horn
cores. There are a few dental remains of Bovini, including a fine mandible, and of Alcelaphini. There is an enigmatic long horn core with strong backward curvature and much mediolateral compression; perhaps this is of *Gazella praethomsoni*. There are no reduncine teeth
or horn cores, which is in strong contrast to the Shungura Formation.

Bovids from the Mursi Formation

Bovid remains from the Mursi Formation are few. The most interesting species is a
kudu apparently ancestral to *Tragelaphus gaudryi*, represented by some pieces of horn core
of which the best is a base of a right horn core YS 1968-2078. This kudu differs from *T.
gaudryi* by its slightly smaller size and by horn cores with greater anteroposterior compression, a stronger posterolateral keel, and a weaker anterior keel, all of which can be
taken as primitive. It is interesting that an earlier kudu should have horn cores with
stronger anteroposterior compression than later kudus, whereas the reverse applies to bush-
bucks. Pieces of kudu horn core from the Mursi Formation can be distinguished from those
of *Tragelaphus nakuae* by having their sharpest (= lateral) keel along the concave edge instead of the convex one. This arises because the horn cores have increasing instead of
decreasing divergence at their bases.

A left upper molar, YS 4-12, shows the presence of a reduncine species.

There are about ten fossil horn cores and parts thereof of an *Aepyceros*. They differ
from those of the Shungura Formation by being more robust for their length, by having poor
transverse ridges, and by having deep longitudinal grooves posterolaterally. They are less
lyrated in their overall course, having a simple backward curvature with increasing then
decreasing divergence.

Discussion

A numerical count of Shungura Formation bovids is given in tables 2 and 3, embracing
only material collected by the American party in 1968-70, only fossils from members B to G,

Table 2

Numbers of Identified Bovid Craniums and Horn Cores in Members B to G, Shungura Formation

Taxon	Members					
	B	C	D	E	F	G
Tragelaphus gaudryi	-	-	-	4 (3%)	25 (18%)	61 (11%)
Tragelaphus nakuae	11 (28%)	65 (54%)	21 (45%)	51 (42%)	16 (11%)	60 (10%)
Syncerus sp.	1 (2%)	2 (2%)	-	-	-	1 (-)
Pelorovis sp.	-	-	-	-	-	5 (1%)
Kobus ?patulicornis	2 (5%)	-	-	-	-	-
Kobus sigmoidalis	-	3 (3%)	3 (6%)	18 (15%)	14 (10%)	172 (30%)
Kobus sp.	10 (25%)	1 (1%)	-	-	-	-
Kobus ancystrocera	2 (5%)	6 (5%)	-	-	1 (1%)	18 (3%)
Menelikia sp.	-	8 (6%)	1 (2%)	-	-	-
Menelikia lyrocera	-	-	-	8 (7%)	16 (11%)	74 (13%)
Aepyceros sp.	14 (35%)	35 (29%)	20 (43%)	40 (33%)	67 (48%)	183 (32%)
?Tossunnoria	-	-	2 (4%)	-	1 (1%)	-
Totals	40	120	47	121	140	574

NOTE: The readings are also given as percentages of the total for each member. Species entirely represented by single finds are omitted.

Table 3

Representation of Major Groups of Bovid Teeth in Members B to G, Shungura Formation (Material collected under the direction of the American party, 1968-1970)

Taxon	Members					
	B	C	D	E	F	G
Tragelaphini	26 (18%)	136 (43%)	62 (43%)	118 (41%)	71 (26%)	272 (24%)
Bovini	20 (13%)	39 (12%)	10 (7%)	12 (4%)	10 (4%)	25 (2%)
Reduncini	59 (40%)	62 (20%)	22 (15%)	62 (21%)	51 (19%)	489 (43%)
Aepyceros sp.	39 (26%)	78 (24%)	44 (31%)	88 (30%)	118 (43%)	336 (29%)
Other Alcelaphini	5 (3%)	3 (1%)	6 (4%)	11 (4%)	21 (8%)	27 (2%)
Totals	149	318	144	291	271	1,149

NOTE: The readings are also given as percentages of the total for each member.

only cranial and dental material, and only species represented by more than one find.

Only *Tragelaphus nakuae* and the impala go through from Member B to Member G, and table 2 shows that *T. nakuae* becomes less abundant in relation to other species in members F and G. The impala never makes up less than a quarter of the identified bovids in any member, and in Member F nearly half the horn cores and teeth are of impala. According to table 2 *Kobus* sp. is the only species which is more common earlier in the Shungura Formation, but table 3 shows that bovine teeth also occur in relatively greater numbers earlier. Table 3 also shows clearly that Reduncini are commonest in members B and G, a conclusion that is supported by the total percentages for their horn cores listed in table 2: B 35%, C 15%, D 8%, E 22%, F 22%, G 46%.

A possible faunal change is indicated in Member E with the regular appearance of *Tragelaphus gaudryi*, *Kobus sigmoidalis*, and *Menelikia lyrocera*. However the sharpness of the change is diminished by a pair of kudu horn cores from Member C (not falling within the criteris for inclusion in table 2), rare records of *K. sigmoidalis* in members C and D, and the *Menelikia* sp. of members C and D. A more definite faunal change takes place in or above Member G, as shown in table 1. *Tragelaphus gaudryi* and *T. nakuae* disappear, *Kobus sigmoidalis* becomes *K. ellipsiprymnus*, and *Menelikia lyrocera* changes subspecifically. The kob appears. Alcelaphines such as *Megalotragus* become more common, and the isolated finds of *Beatragus antiquus* and *Parmularius altidens* both occur above Member G. The single Shungura Formation record of *Tragelaphus strepsiceros* is from Member G. *Antidorcas* may become less rare.

Tables 2 and 3 show continuing changes in the bovid fauna of each member apart from the more marked transitions at the base of Member E and in or above Member G. The changing proportions of the species and tribes represented point to changes in the local environments, but any detailed paleoecological analysis would have to take account of taphonomic factors.

The abundance of tragelaphines, the reduncines, the impala, and in earlier levels the bovines indicates environments with bush or scrub, or areas of grassland close to water. Dry plains of short grass can only have occurred at some distance from the Shungura area, at least until Member G, as shown by the representation of alcelaphines (excluding *Aepyceros*), largely as isolated teeth, and by the scarcity of *Antidorcas* and *Antilope*. The records of *Tossunnoria* open the possibility that a small quota of fossils were contributed from highland or mountainous areas.

The coexistence of so many reduncine species is an interesting problem. Studies in Botswana and Zambia (e.g., Child and Richter 1969; Scheppe and Osborne 1971) suggest the following ecological pattern among living reduncines:

Kobus ellipsiprymnus, the waterbuck, is the largest species. It lives in small herds, sometimes at a greater distance from water than the other reduncines and in areas with trees. It is not found alongside lechwe, even when it goes onto river floodplains.

Kobus leche, the Central African lechwe, is the next largest species and the most gregarious. It is found on the lowest areas of floodplains, adjacent to water, and it sometimes enters the water.

Kobus kob vardoni, the puku--a southern form of kob--is a smaller antelope found in areas spatially between the other two *Kobus*. It is generally seen on the higher parts of floodplains or just beyond them, but not in scrub or bush.

Redunca arundinum, the southern reedbuck, is more lightly built than the puku and is found singly or in pairs. It occurs in open areas of tall grass near water.

The Shungura Formation shows a marginal overlap in time with Olduvai Gorge. The Shungura tuffs G and I have potassium-argon ages of 1.93 m.y. and about 1.84 m.y, and Tuff IB in Bed I at Olduvai has an age of 1.79 m.y. (Curtis and Hay 1972, p. 295). These dates are in accord with the less evolved level of the Shungura bovids from members B to G, as shown by the smaller size and more primitive characters of the kudu, the horn cores of *Tragelaphus ?pricei*, which are anteroposteriorly thicker than comparable *Tragelaphus* horn cores at Olduvai, the absence of the boselaphinelike *T. nakuae* at Olduvai, the smaller bovine teeth (fig. 3), the mediolaterally compressed horn cores of *Kobus sigmoidalis* from Member G downward and at site FLKNN near the base of Olduvai Bed I, and the smaller and more primitive horn cores of the impala and *Antidorcas*. The most notable point of comparison between the bovids of the Shungura Formation and of Olduvai is the abundance of reduncines and the impala and the scarcity of other alcelaphines in members B to G of the Shungura Formation and the reversed proportions of these antelopes at Olduvai. This must reflect a broad difference in the fossil environments of the two areas and is a severe hindrance to studies of bovid evolution. The faunal changes during or above Shungura Member G introduce ecologically different antelopes to the Omo area, which are similar or identical to those at Olduvai: the *Megalotragus, Beatragus antiquus, Parmularius altidens,* the *Antidorcas,* the kob, and the more advanced kudu.

The bovids of the Shungura Formation show interesting signs of affinity with those of the Palaearctic and Indian faunal realms:

1. The similarity of *Tragelaphus nakuae* to boselaphines, which are common in the Siwaliks, although also known from earlier periods in Africa.

2. The horn core which may be of *Hemibos,* otherwise known only from the Siwaliks and Palestine.

3. Some similarities of *Kobus ?patulicornis* and *K. sigmoidalis* to reduncines of the Siwaliks.

4. Living or fossil *Antilope* which is otherwise restricted to India.

The geographical position of the Omo area in Africa as a whole and the resemblances to Siwaliks forms in particular both suggest an earlier connection across Arabia, but it is not known that the connection was still open during the time span of the Shungura Formation. In view of the present aridity of the Arabian peninsula, it is interesting that the link should ever have existed and have involved the reduncines, which must have water nearby. There is still a shortage of clear examples of identical fossil species in Africa and the Siwaliks.

The Shungura Formation bovids provide some slender evidence for intercontinental faunal correlations. Thus as early as Member E *Kobus sigmoidalis* is more advanced than Pinjor Formation reduncines. *Antilope subtorta* of Member C has horn cores at about the same evolutionary level as the same species in the Pinjor Formation. Thus the Pinjor Formation might best correlate with Member C of the Shungura Formation and have an age of about 3 m.y.

References

Allen, G. M. 1939. A checklist of African mammals. *Bull. Museum Comp. Zool. Harv. Coll.* 83:1-763.

Ansell, W. F. H. 1971. Artiodactyla. In *The mammals of Africa: An identification manual,* ed. J. Meester and H. W. Setzer, part 15, pp. 1-93. Washington: Smithsonian Institution Press.

Arambourg, C. 1941. Antilopes nouvelles du Pléistocène ancien de l'Omo (Abyssinie). *Bull. Muséum Nat. Hist. Nat., Paris,* ser. 2, 13:339-47.

———. 1947. Contribution à l'étude géologique et paléontologique du bassin du lac Rudolphe et de la basse vallée de l'Omo. In *Mission scientifique de l'Omo (1932-1933).* Vol. 1. *Géologie-Anthropologie,* fasc. 3, pp. 231-562. Mémoire, Muséum national d'histoire naturelle (Paris).

Bohlin, B. 1937. Eine tertiäre Säugetier-Fauna aus Tsaidam. *Palaeont. Sin. Pekin,* ser. C, 14 (fasc. 1):1-111.

Child, G., and Richter, W. 1969. Observations on ecology and behaviour of lechwe, puku and waterbuck along the Chobe River, Botswana. *Z. Säugetierk., Berlin* 34:275-95.

Curtis, G. H., and Hay, R. L. 1972. Further geological studies and potassium-argon dating at Olduvai Gorge and Ngorongoro Crater. In *Calibration of hominoid evolution*, ed. W. W. Bishop and J. A. Miller, pp. 289-301. Edinburgh: Scottish Academic Press; Toronto: University of Toronto Press.

Daxner, G. 1968. Die Wildziegen (Bovidae, Mammalia) aus der altpleistozänen Karstspalte von Hundsheim in Niederösterreich. *Ber. Deutsch. Ges. Geol. Wiss. Geol. Pal., Berlin* 13:305-34.

Gervais, P. 1867-69. *Zoologie et paléontologie générales*. 1st series. Paris, pp. 1-263.

Hay, R. L. 1971. Geologic background of Beds I and II, stratigraphic summary. In *Olduvai Gorge*, Vol. 3. *Excavations in Beds I and II, 1960-1963*, ed. M. D. Leakey, pp. 9-18. Cambridge: At the University Press.

Hopwood, A. T. 1934. New fossil mammals from Olduvai, Tanganyika Territory. *Ann. Mag. Nat. Hist., London*, ser. 10, 14:546-50.

Leakey, L. S. B. 1965. *Olduvai Gorge 1951-61*. Vol. 1. *Fauna and background*. Cambridge: At the University Press.

Lonnberg, E. 1914. Notes on new and rare mammals from Congo. *Rev. Zool. Afr., Brussels* 3:273-78.

Lydekker, R. 1878. Crania of ruminants from the Indian Tertiaries, and supplement. *Palaeonto. Indica, Calcutta*, ser. 10, 1:88-181.

Pilgrim, G. E. 1937. Siwalik antelopes and oxen in the American Museum of Natural History. *Bull. Am. Mus. Nat. Hist., New York* 72:729-874.

_____. 1941. A fossil skull of *Hemibos* from Palestine. *Ann. Mag. Nat. Hist., London*, ser. 11, 7:347-60.

Scheppe, W., and Osborne, T. 1971. Patterns of use of a flood plain by Zambian mammals. *Ecol. Monogr.* 41:179-205.

Schwarz, E. 1932. Neue diluviale Antilopen aus Ostafrika. *Zentr. Mineral. Geol. Paleontol.* 1-4.

Simpson, G. G. 1945. The principles of classification and a classification of mammals. *Bull. Am. Mus. Nat. Hist., New York* 85:1-350.

Thomas, P. 1884. Recherches stratigraphiques et paléontologiques sur quelques formations d'eau douce de l'Algérie. *Mém. Soc. Géol. France, Paris*, ser. 3, 3 (2):1-51.

Wells, L. H., and Cooke, H. B. S. 1956. Fossil Bovidae from the limeworks quarry, Makapansgat, Potgietersrus. *Palaeontol. Afr., Johannesburg* 4:1-55.

Postscript

Further researches on Omo Bovidae have now (1975) produced additional information on this group. Tragelaphini: *T. nakuae* persists to Member H; the Member C record of *T. gaudryi* appears instead to be a primitive species with similarities to both *T. gaudryi* and *T. strepsiceros;* and *Taurotragus* sp. occurs in Member K. Reduncini: *K. ancystrocera* persists to Member J; *K. ?patulicornis* is now considered to be an early *K. kob*. Hippotragini: *Oryx* sp. occurs in upper Member G. Alcelaphini: *Connochaetes* is definitely documented in upper Member G; members F and G have afforded a new *Aepyceros*-like species. Antilopini: The mandible fragment considered by Arambourg to be *G. praethomsoni* is indeed an antilopine, not a reduncine, but may not be *Gazella*. Caprini: there is no certain evidence for the presence of this tribe in the Omo succession. Ovibovini: this tribe occurs in members C, D, and G.

27. BOVIDAE FROM THE EAST RUDOLF SUCCESSION

J. M. Harris

Introduction

A summary of the faunal zones that yield mammalian fossils at East Rudolf appears in my introduction to the East Rudolf Rhinocerotidae (this symposium).

With the possible exception of the Hippopotamidae, the Bovidae is the largest mammalian family of the East Rudolf fauna. Well over twenty species from seven tribes are represented and the bovids may prove of great value in deciphering the paleoecology of the East Rudolf succession. Many of the taxa are currently represented only by a few individuals. Fewer specimens can be positively identified to species level (table 2) than to tribal rank (table 1). I hope that more intense collecting and further investigation of the less well preserved material will diminish this discrepancy.

Table 1

Distribution of Bovid Tribes in the Koobi Fora Formation

Tribe	M. limnetes Zone	M. andrewsi Zone	L. africana Zone	Indet.	Total
Tragelaphini	17	59	23	-	99
Bovini	1	27	20	1	49
Reduncini	38	144	43	3	228
Hippotragini	-	1	6	-	7
Alcelaphini	26	118	33	2	179
Antilopini	12	41	5	-	58
Neotragini	-	2	-	-	2
Indet.	5	20	26	1	52
Total	99	412	156	7	674

For the sake of uniformity I have followed the bovid classification used by Gentry (this symposium). I believe that the taxa listed here also conform to those described by Gentry, although it is entirely possible that some differences in interpretation may occur. I have had many fruitful discussions with Dr. and Mrs. Gentry, and I gratefully acknowledge their assistance.

Table 2

Distribution of Bovid Taxa in the Koobi Fora Formation

Taxon	M. limnetes Zone	M. andrewsi Zone	L. africana Zone
Tragelaphus strepsiceros	7	37	4
Tragelaphus nakuae	9	2	-
Pelorovis oldowayensis	-	-	5
Pelorovis sp. nov.	1	15	5
Kobus ancystrocera	-	23	-
Kobus ellipsiprymnus	24	26	6
Kobus cf. kob	-	22	18
Kobus cf. leche	-	7	2
Menelikia lyrocera	8	23	3
Redunca sp.	-	1	-
Hippotragus gigas	1	1	-
Oryx sp.	-	2	-
Parmularius angusticornis	-	1	-
Parmularius altidens	-	3	-
Parmularius sp. nov.	-	35	4
Connochaetes sp.	-	20	5
Megalotragus cf. kattwinkeli	4	13	4
?Rabaticeras sp.	-	1	-
Aepyceros sp.	16	21	3
Antidorcas recki	6	24	1
Gazella spp.	8	7	2
Madoqua sp.	-	1	-
Total	84	285	62

Kubi Algi Formation

Fossils of all types are rare in the Kubi Algi Formation, although this unit has received less intense attention than the Koobi Fora Formation. Only a few representatives of two tribes have been collected so far.

Bovini

Two specimens representing this tribe have been collected--a maxilla bearing teeth similar to, but slightly smaller than, those of Pelorovis from later horizons, and a calvaria with horn cores reminiscent of the Asian Bubalus but which may represent an ancestral form of Syncerus. It is possible that both specimens belong to the same taxon.

Reduncini

Two reduncine species appear to be present in the Kubi Algi Formation. One is represented by a partial skeleton with associated horn core fragments. The horn core remnants are very incomplete but are similar in size to Kobus sigmoidalis and exhibit a similar degree of lateral compression.

The other taxon is represented by a virtually complete skull with associated mandible and by a partial skeleton with associated horn core fragments. The cross section of the horn cores is almost circular throughout their length. The horn cores extend backward and upward and diverge uniformly from their base. They are much larger than those of the modern kob and differ in appearance from the horn cores of *Kobus ellipsiprymnus* only in their smaller size, their less flattened proximal portion, and the failure of the distal portions to become subparallel.

Koobi Fora Formation

Well over 600 bovid specimens have been collected from the Koobi Fora Formation. More than 60% of these are from the *M. andrewsi* zone, and this zone also yields the greatest diversity of taxa. Five of the seven tribes are represented in each of the three faunal zones, but only seven species undoubtedly occur throughout the succession. Only specimens that could be positively identified to species level were considered for table 2 and for the following brief account. It is entirely possible that the proportional abundance of certain elements of the fauna may change radically as further and more complete specimens are collected and identified.

The *M. andrewsi* zone has yielded the largest number and greatest variety of bovid species, but the *L. africana* zone has been less intensively collected than either of the other zones. To minimize the disparity caused by uneven collecting, and for purposes of discussion, a distinction is made between actual numerical abundance and proportional abundance (the percentage of each taxon in each zone).

Tragelaphini

Specimens belonging to this tribe occur throughout the succession and are numerically most abundant in the *M. andrewsi* zone. Proportionately, however, tragelaphines fluctuate in importance, making up 17.8% of the *M. limnetes* zone fauna, 14.9% of the *M. andrewsi* zone fauna, and 18.5% of the *L. africana* zone fauna. Only two species have been recognized.

Tragelaphus strepsiceros. This species is represented by calvariae and horn cores in all three faunal zones but is most abundant in the *M. andrewsi* zone. Specimens from the *M. limnetes* zone are smaller and distinctly slighter than those from the *M. andrewsi* zone but are undoubtedly conspecific with the latter. Specimens from the *L. africana* zone are slightly larger and more robust than those from the subjacent zone.

Tragelaphus nakuae. This species is represented by calvariae and horn cores from the *M. limnetes* zone and the lower part of the *M. andrewsi* zone. There is a fair amount of variation in horn core morphology among specimens from the *M. limnetes* zone. Specimens from the *M. andrewsi* zone are more arcuately curved and have a greater span, less torsion, and a weaker anterior keel than earlier representatives. They thus agree with the evolutionary trends exhibited by this species in the Omo succession.

Bovini

Specimens belonging to this tribe have been found throughout the succession but are numerically most abundant in the *M. andrewsi* zone. Proportionately the bovines increase in importance from 1% of the *M. limnetes* zone fauna to 6.8% of the *M. andrewsi* zone fauna and 16% of the *L. africana* zone fauna. Two species are recognized, but they clearly are closely related and can be regarded as part of a single evolutionary lineage.

Pelorovis oldowayensis. The incomplete calvariae and horn cores assigned to this species are restricted to the *L. africana* zone. The specimens are similar in morphology to representatives of this species from Olduvai Gorge but are slightly smaller.

Pelorovis sp. nov. A number of craniums and horn cores similar in morphology to *P. oldowayensis* but distinctly smaller are known from the *M. andrewsi* and *L. africana* zones.

It seems unlikely that the size difference can be explained solely by sexual dimorphism, and the presence of both forms in the *L. africana* zone appears to warrant allocating the smaller form to a different species.

A single specimen comprising an incomplete facial region and proximal right horn core has been collected from the *M. limnetes* zone. This specimen is distinctly smaller than the specimens from the *M. andrewsi* zone, and the horn core is greatly compressed dorsoventrally, but it has obvious close affinities with the representatives from the *M. andrewsi* zone.

Reduncini

This is the most numerous of the East Rudolf bovid tribes. Specimens belonging to this tribe occur throughout the succession but are numerically most abundant in the *M. andrewsi* zone, in which the most species are represented. Proportionately, reduncines decrease slightly through the sequence, making up 40% of the *M. limnetes* zone fauna, 36.3% of the *M. andrewsi* zone fauna, and 34.6% of the *L. africana* zone fauna. Only two species (*Kobus ellipsiprymnus* and *Menelikia lyrocera*) occur in the *M. limnetes* zone, and these continue, with evolutionary modifications, throughout the succession. In all, six reduncine species are recognized.

Kobus ancystrocera. This species is known from several calvariae and a number of isolated horn cores. Although *K. ancystrocera* occurs intermittently in the Omo Shungura sequence from Member B through Member G, at East Rudolf this species is apparently restricted to the *M. andrewsi* zone.

Kobus ellipsiprymnus. This is the most numerous species of the East Rudolf bovid fauna and is represented by numerous craniums, calvariae, and horn cores throughout the sequence of the Koobi Fora Formation. The proportional abundance of this species, however, decreases above the *M. limnetes* zone. Specimens from the *M. limnetes* zone tend to be smaller and to have more laterally compressed horn cores than those from the *M. andrewsi* zone. A tendency for proportionate increase in size and in degree of rounding of horn core bases is also seen between specimens from the *M. andrewsi* and *L. africana* zones, but the change is much less pronounced than it is between specimens from below and above the KBS Tuff. The precise degree of horn core compression varies from specimen to specimen within each faunal zone.

Some explanation of the assigned species name is needed here. *Kobus ellipsiprymnus* is believed to have evolved from *Kobus sigmoidalis* (see Gentry, this symposium). In the Omo sequence the transition from one species to another occurs in Member G. The horn cores of *K. ellipsiprymnus* from the *M. limnetes* zone, although more compressed than those from the *M. andrewsi* zone, are nevertheless wider and larger than horn cores of *Kobus sigmoidalis* from below Shungura Member G in the Omo sequence. Some of the East Rudolf horn cores from the *M. limnetes* and *M. andrewsi* zones which are here assigned to *Kobus ellipsiprymnus* show similarities in horn core compression to specimens from Omo and Olduvai which are assigned to *K. sigmoidalis* (A. W. Gentry, pers. comm.). However, so many specimens from the *M. limnetes* and *M. andrewsi* zones exhibit characters intermediate between *K. sigmoidalis* and *K. ellipsiprymnus* that they cannot readily be precisely allocated to either taxon. Similar but lesser variation in horn core morphology is also shown in specimens from the *L. africana* zone.

It is evident that at East Rudolf the gradual transition between the two species has been accomplished within and throughout the sequence of the Koobi Fora Formation. Because of the difficulty of arbitrarily dividing *K. sigmoidalis* from *K. ellipsiprymnus*, because of the gradual nature of the transition, and because of the greater overall similarity of the East Rudolf specimens to *Kobus ellipsiprymnus*, all the East Rudolf examples are assigned to the latter taxon. However other faunal evidence suggests that the *M. limnetes* and *M. andrewsi* zones cannot both be matched exactly with Member G at the Omo. Consequently, caution must be exercised in inferring stratigraphic correlation on the basis of species names without reference to individual specimens.

Kobus cf. *kob*. A number of craniums and horn cores of a species of *Kobus* closely allied to the extant kob but slightly larger are known from the *M. andrewsi* zone. This species is also present in the *L. africana* zone, where it is the most common reduncine. Despite careful collecting it has not been found in the *M. limnetes* zone.

Kobus cf. *leche*. A number of small horn cores of a fourth species of *Kobus* have been re-covered from the *M. andrewsi* and *L. africana* zones, but none from the *M. limnetes* zone. These horn cores are smaller, more slender, and more laterally compressed than specimens assigned to *K. ellipsiprymnus* and are, in fact, closer in overall morphology to *K. sigmoidalis* than to other species of *Kobus* at East Rudolf. The horn cores agree closely with the configuration of those of the extant lechwe and are compared with this species. Gentry (this symposium) suggests that *Kobus leche* evolved from *K. sigmoidalis*, and the East Rudolf specimens in question appear to support this hypothesis.

Redunca sp. A single horn core from the *M. andrewsi* zone bears a close resemblance to those of *Redunca redunca* in the osteological collections of the National Museum of Kenya.

Menelikia lyrocera. This species is represented by a number of craniums and isolated horn cores and, like *Kobus ellipsiprymnus*, occurs throughout the succession of the Koobi Fora Formation. As in the Omo sequence, two morphological forms are represented. Specimens from the *M. limnetes* zone resemble the "typical" form of *M. lyrocera* that occurs in and below Shungura Member G. Specimens from the *M. andrewsi* zone and *L. africana* zone have shorter, straighter, horn cores which are less laterally compressed and inserted less up-rightly. Like *K. ellipsiprymnus*, *M. lyrocera* is most numerous in the *M. andrewsi* zone but decreases in relative abundance after the *M. limnetes* zone.

Hippotragini

The few East Rudolf specimens assigned to this tribe are restricted to the *M. limnetes* zone (where they form 1% of the fauna) and to the *M. andrewsi* zone (1.5%). Only two species are recognized.

Hippotragus gigas. This species is known from an isolated right horn core from the *M. limnetes* zone and a partial calvaria with an incomplete right horn core from the *M. andrewsi* zone. The latter specimen is the larger and, in comparison with specimens from Olduvai (Leakey 1965), appears to be male rather than female. It is a little smaller than male members of this species recorded from Olduvai.

Oryx sp. Two partial craniums with incomplete horn cores of an as yet undetermined species of *Oryx* are known from the *M. andrewsi* zone.

Alcelaphini

This is the second largest tribe of the East Rudolf fauna. Numerically the alcela-phines are most abundant in the *M. andrewsi* zone where they are represented by seven species and form 29.7% of the fauna. Only two alcelaphine species (*Megalotragus* cf. *kattwinkeli* and *Aepyceros* sp.) are recognized in the *M. limnetes* zone, but they form 27.4%

of the fauna at this level, and both species continue throughout the sequence. Four species, making up 18.4% of the fauna, are known from the *L. africana* zone.

Parmularius angusticornis. A single horn core belonging to this species has been recovered from the *M. andrewsi* zone.

Parmularius altidens. This species is represented by two mandibles and an incomplete cranium with basal horn cores, all of which were collected from the *M. andrewsi* zone. It is the smallest alcelaphine from East Rudolf, and the cranium is smaller than typical examples of *P. altidens* from Bed I at Olduvai. In many features the cranium is reminiscent of the species of *Damaliscus* which makes up the Olduvai VFK herd (and which is also known from Bed I).

Parmularius sp. nov. This species is known from calvariae and isolated horn cores and is the most abundant alcelaphine taxon at East Rudolf, where it is confined to the *M. andrewsi* and *L. africana* zones. The horn cores of specimens attributed to this species are shorter and less stout than those of *P. angusticornis* and are shorter, less straight, and less divergent than those of *P. altidens*. They taper rapidly from the base, extend upward and slightly outward, then curve backward only to recurve upward at the tip. The anterior surface of the horn cores is marked by well-defined transverse ridges. Similar horn cores are found in the collections of Olduvai bovids at the National Museum of Kenya, where they have been tentatively identified as *Damaliscus niro*. The latter do not, however, have typical *D. niro* morphology (laterally compressed and curving gently backward as they taper upward). It is possible that *Parmularius* sp. nov. represents a pre-*Damaliscus niro* stage.

Connochaetes sp. This species is currently recorded only from the *M. andrewsi* and *L. africana* zones. Specimens include a nearly complete skull, incomplete horn cores, and isolated dentitions. The East Rudolf *Connochaetes* differs from the extant *C. taurinus* by the slenderness of its horn cores and by its backward-protruding cranial region. It also differs from the Olduvai *C. africanus* by a number of features including less widely inserted horn cores (A. W. Gentry, pers. comm.).

Megalotragus cf. *kattwinkeli*. This species is known from craniums, horn cores, and dentitions and is the largest of the East Rudolf alcelaphines. Remains are found throughout the Koobi Fora Formation and, unlike most of the taxa represented throughout the sequence, are proportionately more abundant in the *L. africana* zone than in the *M. limnetes* zone. Horn cores of this species appear to vary greatly in size at any one level. Both craniums and horn cores are slightly different in morphology from those of *M. kattwinkeli* found at other sites.

Aepyceros sp. A species of impala is represented by craniums, horn cores, and dentitions from all three faunal zones. Specimens from the *M. limnetes* zone are distinctly smaller and slighter than those from the *M. andrewsi* zone. The contrast between specimens from the latter zone and those from the *L. africana* zone is less striking. This taxon is most numerous in the *M. andrewsi* zone but gradually declines in proportionate abundance from the *M. limnetes* zone. This species is probably conspecific with that from the Omo and is somewhat smaller than the extant *A. melampus*.

?Rabaticeras sp. A single incomplete cranium with badly eroded horn core bases is known from the *M. andrewsi* zone and has a number of features in common with *Rabaticeras*. It is provisionally allocated to this genus.

Antilopini

Members of this tribe occur throughout the succession of the Koobi Fora Formation. They are most abundant in the *M. andrewsi* zone, where they make up 10.3% of the fauna. Proportionately, they decline in importance after the *M. limnetes* zone.

Antidorcas recki. Specimens assigned to this species occur throughout the Koobi Fora Formation but are proportionately and numerically most abundant in the *M. andrewsi* zone and least abundant in the *L. africana* zone. Several incomplete craniums, numerous horn cores, and some isolated dentitions have been recovered to date. The horn core morphology is extremely variable, and, though at this stage all specimens are tentatively assigned to *A. recki*, some of the material shows distinct affinity with *Antidorcas bondi* from Swartkrans (Vrba 1973, p. 308).

Gazella spp. Three species of *Gazella* appear to be present in the Koobi Fora Formation. One taxon (species A), with severely laterally compressed horn cores, is represented by three specimens in the *M. limnetes* zone, one in the *M. andrewsi* zone, and two in the *L. africana* zone. The last two specimens are appreciably larger than specimens from earlier horizons but exhibit the same degree of lateral flattening of the horn cores.

A second species (species B) is known from male and female horn cores from the *M. limnetes* and *M. andrewsi* zones. This taxon has shorter and more rounded horn cores than species A. Five specimens are known from each of the two zones.

A single incomplete horn core (species C) from the *M. andrewsi* zone is similar to species E but larger.

Neotragini

This tribe is represented by only two specimens and is currently restricted to the *M. andrewsi* zone. One specimen is a maxilla with teeth that are attributed to a species of *Madoqua*. The other is an as yet unidentified horn core.

Summary

There are no taxa restricted solely to the *M. limnetes* zone, and no taxa are shared by the *M. limnetes* zone and the *N. capensis* zone. Five species are present in the *M. limnetes* zone and are as abundant or more abundant in the *M. andrewsi* zone (*Tragelaphus strepsiceros, Pelorovis* sp. nov., *Kobus ellipsiprymnus, Megalotragus kattwinkelli* and *Antidorcas recki*). Six taxa are present in the *M. limnetes* zone but decline in importance in the superjacent zone (*Tragelaphus nakuae, Menelikia lyrocera, Hippotragus gigas, Aepyceros* sp. and *Gazella* spp. A and B).

Eight taxa are restricted to the *M. andrewsi* zone (*Kobus ancystrocera, Redunca* sp., *Oryx* sp., *Parmularius angusticornis, Parmularius altidens, ?Rabaticeras* sp., *Gazella* sp. C and *Madoqua* sp.). Seven taxa are present and are as abundant or more abundant in the *L. africana* zone (*Pelorovis* sp. nov., *Kobus* cf. *kob, Kobus* cf. *leche, Lobus ellipsiprymnus, Connochaetes* sp., *Megalotragus* cf. *kattwinkeli*, and *Gazella* sp. A). Nine taxa are present in the *M. andrewsi* zone but thereafter decline in importance (*Tragelaphus strepsiceros, T. nakuae, Menelikia lyrocera, Hippotragus gigas, Parmularius* sp. nov., *Aepyceros* sp., *Antidorcas recki*, and *Gazella* spp. B and C).

Only one taxon, *Pelorovis oldowayensis*, is restricted to the *L. africana* zone.

Guomde Formation

Very few fossils have been collected so far from the Guomde Formation. The only bovid specimen from this unit is a fragment of a left horn core of an impala (probably *A.*

melampus). Associated faunal remains include fragmentary giraffid, equid, and hippo specimens, a hominid femur (KNM-ER 999), and *Struthio* eggshell fragments.

Discussion

The bovid fauna from the Koobi Fora Formation appears to be quite different from those of the Kubi Algi and Guomde formations insofar as they are known. Changing ecological conditions within the Koobi Fora Formation resulted in changes of faunal composition in each of the three faunal zones. The abrupt change in faunal composition between the *M. limnetes* and *M. andrewsi* zones, with the influx of new (to East Rudolf) alcelaphines and reduncines, together with marked evolutionary advances seen in *Tragelaphus strepsiceros*, *Tragelaphus nakuae*, *Pelorovis* sp. nov., *Kobus ellipsiprymnus*, *Menelikia lyrocera*, and *Aepyceros* sp., also suggest that there may have been a considerable hiatus between the two zones. Evolutionary advances of species of the *L. africana* zone fauna over those common to the *M. andrewsi* zone are much less dramatic.

Correlation with the Omo Sequence

Twelve of the East Rudolf bovid species are also found in the Omo sequence. It is perhaps too much to expect that the faunal units of the two regions should coincide exactly and consistently; but some measure of correlation can be achieved, taking into account evolutionary trends within the East Rudolf and Omo sequences together with the timing of the arrival of taxa new to each region and the extinction of existing elements of the faunas.

Seven species appear to have evolved in situ in both regions. Some are better represented and consequently more important than others. *Pelorovis* , for example, is poorly represented at Omo. *Megalotragus kattwinkeli*, or a very similar form, is present throughout the Koobi Fora Formation but is sparsely represented in the Omo succession before Member G. A small species of *Aepyceros*, probably ancestral to the extant *A. melampus*, is represented throughout the sequence of both regions by the same or a similar form but is not currently of much use in correlation. Similarly, *Antidorcas recki* is believed to be present in both regions, and further investigation and comparison of the east and south African specimens may enhance the use of this species as a tool for correlation.

The three most useful taxa are *Tragelaphus nakuae*, *Kobus sigmoidalis-ellipsiprymnus*, and *Menelikia lyrocera*. *T. nakuae* is common in members B through G at the Omo. At East Rudolf the *M. limnetes* zone representatives exhibit features found in the earlier parts of the Shungura sequence, whereas the specimens from the *M. andrewsi* zone agree with the more advanced Omo examples. The evolutionary development and mutual extinction of this species in both regions suggests that the *M. andrewsi* zone be equated with Member G. The apparent transition of *K. sigmoidalis* to *K. ellipsiprymnus* at both Omo and East Rudolf suggests that parts of the *M. limnetes* and *M. andrewsi* zones be equated with Member G. The advanced subspecies of *M. lyrocera* occurs in the *M. andrewsi* zone at East Rudolf but not until after Member G at Omo.

The onset of conditions suitable for support of a more open habitat fauna than exemplified in the early part of the East Rudolf and Omo sequences begins in the *M. andrewsi* zone and at or after Member G. Whether this ecological change was synchronous in both regions is a matter for conjecture. There is some slight evidence for intermigration of faunal elements between the two regions at about this time, which in turn suggests that the early portions of the East Rudolf and Omo sequences were sufficiently different to support species not present in the other region. *Tragelaphus strepsiceros*, common at East Rudolf, makes a brief appearance in Member G, heralding the extinction of the common Omo kudu, *Tragelaphus gaudreyi*. It is not inconceivable that East Rudolf provided emigrant examples of the evolving *Kobus ellipsiprymnus* population to the Omo region during the accumulation of Member G. *Kobus ancystrocera*, a typical but uncommon Omo species, does not appear at East Rudolf until the *M. andrewsi* zone and becomes extinct in both regions in the latter zone and in Member G.

The onset of changing ecological conditions at both Omo and East Rudolf is accompanied by the arrival of forms apparently new to both regions. *Kobus kob* and *Parmularius altidens* are present in the *M. andrewsi* zone and at horizons above G, although there is some evidence of kobs earlier in the Omo sequence. *Kobus leche* and a different species of *Parmularius* also appear suddenly in the *M. andrewsi* zone but fail to reach the Omo region.

In conclusion, we must remember that the bovid faunas from both East Rudolf and Omo include many specimens currently identified only to tribal level. If the identifications of such specimens can be resolved more fully, the stratigraphic ranges and apparent proportions of species already identified may well have to be modified.

Correlation with Olduvai Gorge

The East Rudolf fauna has eleven taxa in common with that from Olduvai. Specimens of *Tragelaphus strepsiceros*, *Kobus ellipsiprymnus* (sensu lato), *Hippotragus gigas*, *Parmularius altidens*, and *P. angusticornis* from the *M. andrewsi* zone appear to agree reasonably well with similar specimens from Olduvai Bed I. Specimens from the *L. africana* zone attributed to *Pelorovis oldowayensis* are slightly smaller than their counterparts from middle and upper Bed II. In view of the geographic separation of the two regions, some discrepancies in the fauna might be expected, but on the whole it appears reasonable to equate the *M. andrewsi* zone broadly with Bed I at Olduvai.

Conclusions

Unlike some of the more stable groups, such as the Rhinocerotidae and Giraffidae, some elements of the East Rudolf Bovidae exhibit pronounced evolutionary changes. Differences in the nature of the assemblage in each faunal unit are, however, primarily due to climatic and ecological changes. The degree of change seen in the taxa from the *M. limnetes* and *M. andrewsi* zones appears greater than that between the *M. andrewsi* and *L. africana* zones, suggesting a greater time interval in addition to ecological changes between the earlier two zones. The *M. andrewsi* zone is richer in number and variety of bovid taxa than the other two zones. This may be partly the result of more intensive collecting at this level, but it could also indicate fairly rapid climatic fluctuations which thereby artificially enhanced the richness of the fauna in this part of the sequence.

I suggest that the *M. andrewsi* zone equates with the upper part of Member G or Member H at the Omo and with Bed I at Olduvai.

This paper is no. 63 in the East Rudolf Project catalogue of publications.

References

Leakey, L. S. B. 1965. *Olduvai Gorge 1951-1961*. Vol. 1. *Fauna and background*. Cambridge: At the University Press.

Vrba, E. S. 1973. Two species of *Antidorcas* Sundevall at Swartkrans (Mammalia: Bovidae). *Ann. Transvaal Mus.* 28:287-352.

28. CARNIVORA OF THE EAST RUDOLF SUCCESSION

M. G. Leakey

Introduction

The Carnivora recovered from East Rudolf between 1968 and 1973 include five families: the Felidae, the Hyaenidae, the Canidae, the Mustelidae, and the Viverridae. The carnivores are a relatively rare element of the fossil fauna; although five families are represented, the number of specimens collected during these five years is equivalent to that of the single family Hominidae (a group which has been collected with equal intensity). Thus the number of specimens representing each carnivore taxon is in most cases small.

A faunal list is given in table 1, together with the number of specimens recovered for each taxon, the areas of recovery, and the faunal zones (after Maglio 1972). Each taxon represented at East Rudolf is discussed briefly below.

Order Carnivora

Family Felidae

Subfamily Machairodontinae

Genus *Homotherium* Fabrini

Homotherium sp.

Material: 2 cranial and 10 postcranial specimens.

Horizon: Various horizons throughout the Koobi Fora Formation and two specimens from the Kubi Algi Formation.

Discussion: *Homotherium* is a large saber-tooth cat (the size of a lion) characterized by large upper canines crenulated on at least one border, very long carnassials, and relatively long, gracile limb bones. Arambourg (1947) records *Homotherium ethiopicus* from the Omo, based on a partial mandible with broken teeth, and Howell and Petter (this symposium) record *Homotherium* sp. from the Usno and Shungura formations of the Omo. The genus is also present in South Africa; the Pleistocene cave breccias of Makapansgat have yielded a specimen of a crushed cranium and mandible, recently described as *Megantereon problematicus* (Collings 1972) which is almost certainly *Homotherium*. The mandibular morphology and measurements of the lower dentition of this specimen and a mandible from East Rudolf, KNM-ER 931, are very close. In table 2 measurements of the lower dentition of the Makapansgat and East Rudolf specimens are compared with the European *H. crenatidens*. It is probable that the East

302

Table 1

Faunal List, with Areas of Occurrence and Faunal Zones (after Maglio 1972) for Each Taxon

Taxon	Faunal Zone	1	2	6	7	7A	8	10	12	102	103	104	105	121	123	125	130	131	204	Number of Specimens
												Area of Occurrence								
Felidae																				
Homotherium sp.	1, 2, 3, 4	X						X			X	X	X	X					X	16
Megantereon eurynodon	1, 2							X												2
Cf. *Megantereon*	1, 2, 3	X	X	X					X		X		X			X				10
Dinofelis barlowi	3					X											X			1
Dinofelis cf. *piveteaui*	1	X																		1
Cf. *Dinofelis*	1			X																6
Panthera cf. *leo*	1	X		X																2
Panthera cf. *crassidens*	1, 3										X						X			2
Hyaenidae																				
Crocuta crocuta	1, 2, 3			X	X		X	X	X	X	X	X	X	X	X			X		29
Hyaena hyaena	1, 2, 3			X			X	X	X	X								X		6
Canidae																				
Canis mesomelas	2											X	X							3
Gen. et sp. indet.	2									X										1
Mustelidae																				
Cf. *Aonyx* sp.	2, 3											X	X				X	X		6
Viverridae																				
Genetta cf. *genetta*	1						X													1
Pseudocivetta ingens	3												X		X		X			4

NOTE: 1 = *Loxodonta africana* zone;

     2 = *Metridiochoerus andrewsi* zone;

     3 = *Mesochoerus limnetes* zone;

     4 = *Notochoerus capensis* zone.

Table 2

Measurements of the Lower Dentition of Homotherium

Specimen	P_3		P_4		M_2	
	L	B	L	B	L	B
H. crenatidens	8.0	5.5	22.0	11.0	32.0	13.0
H. problematicus	13.0	7.0	22.6	9.0	34.0	12.0
KNM-ER 931	11.0	6.8	22.4	9.5	36.2	14.0

SOURCE: *H. crenatidens* from Ballesio 1963; *H. problematicus* from Collings 1972.

Rudolf, Makapansgat, and Omo specimens all represent one species, which should then be referred to *Homotherium ethiopicus* Arambourg.

The East Rudolf postcranial elements are similar to those of *H. crenatidens* in most
respects but do show some morphological differences.

Genus *Megantereon* Croizet and Jobert

Megantereon eurynodon Ewer

Material. 2 cranial specimens.

Horizon. The Ileret Member of the Koobi Fora Formation.

Discussion. *Megantereon* is a saber-tooth cat smaller than *Homotherium* (the size of a
leopard), with slender, dagger-shaped upper canines lacking crenulations on the borders and
with short, stocky limb bones. This species was first described from Kromdraai (Ewer 1955),
where a squashed skull and partial mandible, Ka 64, were recovered. Two other species are
known from South Africa from two very fragmentary pieces of mandible, *M. gracile* and *M.
whitei*. The variability shown by the two East Rudolf specimens suggests that the three
South African species may be conspecific.

The two East Rudolf specimens show slight morphological differences. The most complete specimen, a cranium and half mandible, shows a cranial morphology close to the South
African specimen Ka 64, but the dentition is relatively small compared with the skull and
mandible size and the protocone on the upper carnassial is more reduced. The second specimen, which includes a juvenile mandible and isolated teeth, has a dentition closer in size
to the type specimen, and there is a distinct protocone on the upper carnassial similar to
that of Ka 64. Features seen in this specimen which differ from both Ka 64 and KNM-ER 793
include an additional medial cuspule on the medial lingual surface of I^3 and the relatively
small dimensions of all the incisors compared with the cheek teeth. Measurements of the
dentition of the two specimens are given in table 3, where they are compared with the South
African type specimen. It appears that these three specimens all represent the same lineage; the variability shown does not appear to justify specific separation.

This genus also appears to be present in Bed I at Olduvai. A fragment of mandible
from FLK NN1, described by Ewer (1965) as *Machairodontinae*, is very similar to the mandible
from East Rudolf and could reasonably be referred to *Megantereon*. The genus is recorded
from the Usno and Shungura formations of the Omo (Howell and Petter, this symposium).

cf. *Megantereon*

Ten postcranial specimens are referred to *Megantereon*, but until associated cranial
and postcranial specimens are found this assignation must remain tentative.

Table 3

Measurements of the Dentition of Megantereon eurynodon (in mm)

Specimen	I_1		I_2		I_3		C		P_3		P_4		M_1	
	L	B	L	B	L	B	L	B	L	B	L	B	L	B
Upper dentition														
Ka 64	(4)	-	4.9	-	8.5	9.0	(25.5)	(12.8)	12.0	5.4	30.2	10.6	4.2	7.8
KNM-ER 793	4.6	-	5.3	-	8.1	9.0	-	-	9.0	5.5	24.7	13.3	4.1	6.2
KNM-ER 701	-	-	-	-	-	-	-	-	-	-	(27.0)	(12.5)	-	-
Lower dentition														
Ka 64[a]	-	-	-	-	(5)	-	8.2	(12.1)	6.3	-	(17)	-	19.8	-
KNM-ER 793	-	-	-	-	5.0	6.7	7.2	15.5	4.9	4.3	14.8	7.0	17.2	8.6
KNM-ER 701	2.6	3.7	4.2	4.5	5.0	5.1	-	-	-	-	-	-	(20.0)	(8.8)

NOTE: Parentheses indicate estimated measurements.

[a] Ka 64 = type specimen, from Ewer 1955.

Subfamily Felinae

Genus *Dinofelis* Zdansky

Dinofelis barlowi (Broom)

Material. 1 mandibular specimen.

Horizon. The Lower Member of the Koobi Fora Formation.

Discussion. *Dinofelis* belongs to a group of felids known as the "false sabertooths," which have not developed the long, daggerlike upper canines or the mandibular mental process of the true sabertooth but have relatively large upper and lower canines compared with *Panthera*, sharp cutting carnassials, and a mandibular symphysis which is roughly square or quadrangular.

Hemmer (1965) has shown that three species previously referred to *Therailurus* should be included within *Dinofelis*, and these species represent different stages of evolutionary development of one lineage; *D. diastemata* from France the most primitive, *D. barlowi* from South Africa intermediate, and *D. piveteaui* from South Africa the most advanced of the evolutionary series.

One mandibular specimen from East Rudolf, KNM-ER 1549, which was recovered from deposits several meters below the KBS Tuff, shows morphological features typical of *Dinofelis barlowi*, although the incisors are significantly more elevated above the level of the cheek teeth and P_3 is relatively small compared with M_1. Table 4 gives some comparative measurements.

Dinofelis is recorded from the Shungura Formation of the Omo (Howell and Petter, this symposium) but is not recorded from Olduvai Gorge.

Table 4

Measurements of the Mandible and Lower dentition of Dinofelis *(in mm)*

	Postcanine Diastema	P_3 Length	P_4 Length	M_1 Length
D. diastemata	27	16	23	24
D. barlowi	21	12.2	21.4	25.9
STS 131	-	16.1	24.7	(26.0)
KNM-ER 1549	(16.2)	12.5	21.3	28.7
KNM-ER 666	10.5	10.3	-	-

SOURCE: *D. diastemata* and *D. barlowi* from Hemmer 1965.
NOTE: Parentheses indicate estimated measurements.

Dinofelis cf. *piveteaui* (Ewer)

Material. 1 mandibular specimen.

Horizon. The Ileret Member of the Koobi Fora Formation

Discussion. A mandibular specimen, KNM-ER 666, which was recovered from the Ileret Beds of the Koobi Fora Formation is probably more than a million years later than the mandible referred above to *Dinofelis barlowi*. This second mandible shows morphological differences from KNM-ER 1549, which Hemmer (1965) has shown indicate evolutionary development. These are as follows:

    1. Decrease in the size of the incisors.

2. Less elevation of the incisors above the level of the cheek teeth.

3. Reduction in the length of the postcanine diastema.

4. Reduction in the relative size of P_3.

Unfortunately, only two very fragmentary pieces of mandible of *D. piveteaui* are known, and so the East Rudolf mandible cannot be compared directly with *D. piveteaui*; but it seems most likely that it should be referred to this species.

Cf. *Dinofelis*

One fragment of mandible and 5 postcranial specimens are tentatively referred to *Dinofelis*. More certain taxonomic assignation of the postcranial elements will depend on the recovery of associated cranial and postcranial material.

Genus *Panthera* Oken

Panthera cf. *leo* Linné

Material. 2 postcranial specimens.

Horizon. The Ileret Member of the Koobi Fora Formation.

Discussion. These 2 specimens are too fragmentary to provide much information other than to confirm the presence of this species in the fauna. *P. leo* is recorded from the Omo (Howell and Petter, this symposium) and from Olduvai Gorge (Petter 1973).

Panthera cf. *crassidens* (Broom)

Material. 2 specimens including only postcranial elements.

Horizon. The Lower and Upper members of the Koobi Fora Formation.

Discussion. *Panthera crassidens* was first described from 2 maxillary specimens and 1 mandibular specimen from Kromdraae. Broom (1948) considered the species to be the size of a leopard and similar in many respects to the cheetah (*Acinonyx*). However, it had a number of distinctive features. Since 1948 there has been little additional evidence of this species. A mandible from Bed II at Olduvai has been tentatively referred to *P. crassidens* (Ewer 1965), and several postcranial specimens from Olduvai which are from an animal considerably larger than a leopard have more recently been referred to *P. crassidens* (Petter 1973). Since no associated cranial and postcranial elements of this species are known, the assignation of the East Rudolf specimens must remain tentative.

The two East Rudolf specimens, one of which includes several associated postcranial bones and the other a single ulna, are from an animal slightly smaller than a leopard but showing several features characteristic of *Acinonyx*, although it is clearly distinguishable from this species. The taxonomic assignation to *P. crassidens* thus seems the most reasonable on the present evidence.

Family Hyaenidae

Subfamily Hyaeninae

Genus *Crocuta* Kaup

Crocuta crocuta Erxleben

Material. 29 specimens, including cranial and postcranial fragments.

Horizon. The Lower, Upper, and Ileret members of the Koobi Fora Formation.

Discussion. *Crocuta crocuta* occurs quite commonly at East Rudolf, but the specimens show little morphological change with time, and when compared with the living subspecies of spotted Hyaena, *C. c. crocuta*, they are almost indistinguishable.

Ewer (1967) distinguished two subspecies in the Transvaal cave breccias, *C. c. ultra* and *C. c. venestula*; Ewer considered that the latter, which is the smaller, was probably ancestral. Petter (1973) finds that the evidence from Olduvai suggests the presence of only one valid subspecies, *C. c. ultra*, which is distinguished from *C. c. crocuta* by a shorter tooth row resulting from relatively shorter premolars, and the lower carnassial with a relatively long talonid.

The East Rudolf mandibular specimens have been compared with ten specimens of extant *C. c. crocuta* from East Africa and with specimens of *C. c. ultra* from Olduvai Gorge (table 5). Some measurements of the dentition are illustrated graphically in figure 1. A specimen, KNM-ER 721, from just above the KBS Tuff and a specimen, KNM-ER 723, from the upper part of the Ileret Beds of the Upper Member of the Koobi Fora Formation have measurements close to the modern range. The premolars are not significantly smaller, nor is the talonid relatively large, in any of the East Rudolf specimens. There does not seem to be any evidence which favors subspecific identification of these specimens to *C. c. ultra* rather than *C. c. crocuta*. For the present they are referred to *C. crocuta*.

One maxillary specimen, KNM-ER 121, has a relatively long upper carnassial with an elongated metacone compared with that of a second maxillary specimen, KNM-ER 1541. Kurtén (1956), however, has shown that the length of the metacone relative to the overall length of the tooth increases with size. The size of the metacone relative to the crown length of the carnassial in both these specimens is that expected from measurements taken on large and small carnassials of *C. c. crocuta* by Kurtén (1956).

The present evidence from East Rudolf, both cranial and postcranial, suggests that there was little morphological change in *C. crocuta* during the last 2.0 m.y. More specimens are required to confirm this.

Genus *Hyaena* Brisson

Hyaena hyaena Linné

Material. 6 specimens including cranial and postcranial fragments.

Horizon. The Lower, Upper, and Ileret members of the Koobi Fora Formation.

Discussion. The fossil *H. hyaena*, known from Olduvai and from the Transvaal cave breccias, is small compared with the living striped hyena. The specimens from East Rudolf also show this trend.

A new species of hyena, *H. abronia* (Hendey 1974), which appears to be ancestral to *H. hyaena*, has been recovered from the Pliocene deposits (4-4.5 m.y.) of Langebaanweg in South Africa. This species still retains the lower P_1, M_2, and usually the upper M^2. A skull from several meters below the KBS Tuff at East Rudolf has the dental series of extant *H. hyaena* but shows many features in its cranial morphology which resemble *H. abronia*, suggesting it is a primitive form of *H. hyaena*.

A small hyena from Makapansgat, originally described as *H. makapani* (Torien 1952), shows small differences in the dentition when compared with *H. hyaena* which Ewer (1967) considered only sufficient to warrant subspecific separation. These features, which among others are seen in the lack of development of the anterior cusps of the premolars (excluding the upper carnassial), are also characteristic of *H. abronia*, which suggests they should be considered primitive. Specimens from the Upper Member of the Koobi Fora Formation at East Rudolf and from Bed I at Olduvai also have small anterior cusps, suggesting that these

Table 5

Measurements of the Lower Dentition of Crocuta crocuta *(in mm)*

Specimen	P_2		P_3		P_4		M_1	
	L	B	L	B	L	B	L	B
C. c. crocuta								
Mean	14.4	9.9	20.1	13.9	21.3	12.0	26.2	11.0
Range	13.8-15.5	8.9-10.8	19.2-21.3	12.9-14.5	20.0-23.8	11.1-13.1	24.4-28.0	10.0-11.8
C. c. ultra								
7577	14	10	19.6	13.5	20	12.9	25.4	11.7
7642	-	-	19.5	13.3	19.7	12.3	26.6	11.2
263	12.9	8.8	18.5	12.8	19.7	12.2	26.6	-
1510	-	-	19	13.8	21.2	12.7	-	-
C. crocuta (East Rudolf)								
KNM-ER 721 (Area 131)	14.4	9.4	19.1	13.5	20.0	12.3	26.6	11.8
KNM-ER 896 (Area 104)	-	-	21.0	(14.8)	22.8	13.7	-	-
KNM-ER 358 (Area 105)	13.8	11.1	20.2	14.4	22.0	14.0	-	-
KNM-ER 667 (Area 103)	-	-	20.5	13.9	-	-	-	-
KNM-ER 723 (Area 8)	14.0	10.2	20.5	12.9	21.2	11.8	27.1	12.0
KNM-ER 360 (Area ?)	13.4	9.0	19.4	14.5	-	-	-	-

SOURCE: *C. c. ultra* from Bed I at Olduvai from Petter 1973. Ten individuals of the extant *C. c. crocuta* were used for comparison.

NOTE: Parentheses indicate estimated measurements.

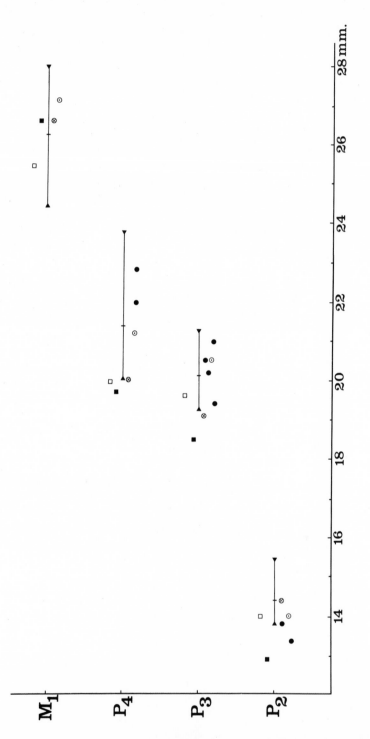

Figure 1. *Crocuta crocuta*: Graphic illustration of the measurements of the length of P_2-M_1 shown in table 5. *C. c. crocuta*: *vertical line*, mean; *horizontal line*, range. *C. c. ultra* from Olduvai: *open square*, 7577; *solid square*, 263. *C. crocuta* from East Rudolf: *crossed circle*, 721 (Area 131); *dotted circle*, 723 (Area 8).

"primitive" dental characters are retained for a relatively long time. Features of the cranial morphology appear to provide a better indicator of the stage of evolutionary development of *H. hyaena*.

Family Canidae

Subfamily Caninae

Genus *Canis* Linné

Canis mesomelas Schreber

Material. 3 mandibular specimens.

Horizon. The Upper Member of the Koobi Fora Formation.

Discussion. These specimens are too fragmentary to show much morphology. Measurements of the dentition are close to those of the jackal from Bed I Olduvai, *C. m. latirostris*.

Genus indet.

Gen. et sp. indet.

Material. 1 mandibular fragment lacking teeth.

Horizon. The Upper Member of the Koobi Fora Formation.

Discussion. This specimen is approximately the size of the extant wild dog *Lycaon*. A large canid is recorded from Olduvai, *Canis africanus*, whereas *Lycaon* is absent. The East Rudolf specimen probably represents one or other of these genera, but the dentition is necessary to determine which taxon is represented.

Family Mustelidae

Subfamily Lutrinae

Genus *Aonyx* Lesson

Cf. *Aonyx* sp.

Material. 2 cranial and 4 postcranial specimens.

Horizon. The Lower and Upper members of the Koobi Fora Formation.

Discussion. These specimens are only tentatively referred to *Aonyx*. With the exception of one specimen, the East Rudolf material appears to be from a relatively large animal compared with the extant clawless otter, *Aonyx capensis*. Petter (1973) refers three specimens from Olduvai Gorge to *Aonyx*, and Howell and Petter (this symposium) refer a relatively large M_2 from the Omo to cf. *Lutra* sp.

Family Viverridae

Subfamily Viverrinae

Genus *Genetta* Oken

Genetta cf. *genetta* Linnaeus

Material. 1 specimen of a palate with dentition.

Horizon. The Ileret Member of the Koobi Fora Formation.

Discussion. This specimen shows close affinities with *G. genetta*, but in view of the very similar dentition of the two living East African species of genets it is only given tentative specific designation. *Genetta* is not recorded from Olduvai but is recorded from the Omo (Howell and Petter, this symposium).

Genus *Pseudocivetta* Petter

Pseudocivetta ingens Petter

Material. 3 cranial and 1 postcranial specimen.

Horizon. The Lower and Upper members of the Koobi Fora Formation.

Discussion. *Pseudocivetta ingens* was first described by Petter (1967) from two specimens from Olduvai Gorge, a juvenile mandible with deciduous dentition and an isolated M^1. Subsequently an upper and a lower second molar were recovered from Olduvai Gorge. Thus nothing is yet known of the permanent anterior dentition, the cranium, or the postcranial skeleton. *Pseudocivetta ingens* appears to have similarities with the African civet *Viverra civetta* but to be considerably larger and to have a specialized dentition.

Two upper molars from East Rudolf, M^1 and M^2 (KNM-ER 2011) closely match the M^1 and M^2 described by Petter (1967, 1973), both in size and in morphology. Associated with the East Rudolf molars is an I^3 which is relatively larger and more complex than the very simple incisors of *V. civetta*. The remaining three specimens from East Rudolf referred to *P. ingens* represent parts of the skeleton not previously recorded for this species; these assignations must therefore be considered tentative. These remaining specimens, which include a cranium lacking the face and dentition, an M_1, and a humerus, show similarities with *V. civetta* but are larger and show a number of morphological characters not seen in *V. civetta*. The cranium in particular shows many interesting features, such as the very enlarged nuchal and sagittal crests, the enlarged pterygoid bone, and the marked extension of the jugular process, which are in accord with Petter's suggestion (1973) that *P. ingens* was an unusual, specialized predator.

Conclusions

The study of the fossil fauna of any locality provides evidence on two important aspects: the paleoenvironment and the age of the deposits. The carnivores, particularly the large predators, are not very useful indicators of paleoenvironment. With the exception of *Aonyx*, all the extant taxa represented in the fossil fauna of East Rudolf are today widely distributed. The carnivores may well prove useful for faunal correlation, but because specimens are rare their usefulness in this respect is somewhat limited. Among the more commonly represented groups, the Felidae show the most obvious evolutionary changes, since certain significant features of the dentition can be quantified. With the recovery of more material, *Megantereon* and *Dinofelis* should be found useful for internal correlation as well as for correlation with other sites. The Hyaenidae are less useful; the dentition appears to have changed very little in the last three million years. *Hyaena hyaena* shows some morphological changes of the skull, but *Crocuta crocuta* appears to change very little. However no skulls of *C. crocuta* have yet been recovered from East Rudolf.

Comparison of the carnivore fossil fauna of East Rudolf and the Omo Valley shows much similarity. The most noticeable difference is the greater number of taxa at the Omo representing small individuals. This probably reflects the nature of the deposits rather than the actual situation in the paleoenvironment.

Acknowledgments

I am grateful to the museum trustees of Kenya for making the study of the East Rudolf material possible and to the sponsors of the East Rudolf Research Project; as well as the National Geographic Society, the National Science Foundation, and the Donner Foundation. I should also like to thank Professor F. Clark Howell and Germaine Petter, who have examined the carnivore material and provided helpful suggestions.

This paper is no. 64 in the East Rudolf Project catalogue of publications.

References

Arambourg, C. 1947. *Mission scientifique de l'Omo (1932-1933)*. Vol. 1. *Géologie-Anthropologie*, fasc. 3, pp. 231-562. Mémoires, Muséum national d'histoire naturelle (Paris).

Ballesio, R. 1963. Monographie d'un Machairodus du gisement villafranchien de Senèze: *Homotherium crenatidens* Fabrini. *Trav. Lab. Geol. Lyon*, n.s., 9:1-129.

Broom, R. 1948. Some South African Pliocene and Pleistocene mammals. *Ann. Transvaal Museum, Pretoria* 21:1-38.

Collings, G. E. 1972. A new species of Machaerodont from Makapansgat. *Palaeontol. Africana* 14:87-92.

Ewer, R. F. 1955. The fossil carnivores of the Transvaal caves: Machairodontinae. *Proc. Zool. Soc. London* 125:587-615.

_____. 1965. Large Carnivora. In *Olduvai Gorge*, 1959-1961, ed. L. S. B. Leakey, 1:19-22. Cambridge: At the University Press.

_____. 1967. The fossil hyaenids of Africa: A reappraisal. In *Background to Evolution in Africa*, ed. W. W. Bishop and J. D. Clark, pp. 109-23. Chicago: University of Chicago Press.

Hemmer, H. 1965. Zur Nomenklatur und Verbreitung des Genus *Dinofelis* Zdansky 1924 (*Therailurus* Piveteau, 1948). *Palaeontol. Africana* 9:75-89.

Hendey, Q.B. 1974. The late Cenozoic Carnivora of the south-western Cape Province. *Ann. South African Museum* 63:1-369.

Kurtén, B. 1956. The status and affinities of *Hyaena sinensis* Owen and *Hyaena ultima* Matsumoto. *Am. Museum Novitates* 1764:1-48.

Maglio, V. J. 1972. Vertebrate fauna and chronology of hominid bearing sediments east of Lake Rudolf, Kenya. *Nature* 239:379-85.

Petter, G. 1967. Petits carnivores Villafranchiens du Bed I d'Oldoway (Tanzanie). *Colloq. Intern. Centre Natl. Rech. Sci. (Paris)*, 163(1966):529-38.

_____. 1973. Carnivores Pléistocènes du Ravin d'Olduvai (Tanzanie). In *Fossil vertebrates of Africa*, ed. L. S. B. Leakey, R. J. Savage, and S. C. Caryndon, 3:43-100. London: Academic Press.

Torien, M. J. 1952. The fossil hyaenas of the Makapansgat Valley. *S. African J. Sci.* 48:293-300.

F. C. Howell and G. Petter

Carnivora are among the less common of the mammalian orders represented in the richly fossiliferous formations of the Omo Group in southern Ethiopia. However, representatives of the Viverridae, Mustelidae, Hyaenidae, and Felidae are found in the Usno and Shungura formations. Unfortunately the remains are usually fragmentary and represent for the most part isolated or associated teeth, jaw parts, and postcranial elements, usually incomplete. Precise identification to species, and sometimes even to genus, is correspondingly difficult.

This chapter is a brief summary of each taxon identified thus far (through 1973) among the Carnivora, with comments on their temporal distribution in the Omo succession (table 1). The material will be fully described and figured by the authors elsewhere.

Family Viverridae

This family of small, primitive carnivores is represented by seven or eight taxa. The smallest species are still the least well known.

Helogale sp.

Material. 6 teeth (2 deciduous, 4 permanent); an edentulous mandible, and a P^4.

Stratigraphic Occurrence. Shungura Formation, members B (Unit B 10) and F (Unit F-1).

Discussion. *Helogale*, the living dwarf mongoose, is represented only by isolated teeth recovered in the course of microvertebrate washing of sediments by H. B. Wesselman in 1972 and 1973. This is the first record of this genus in the African Plio-Pleistocene. Two species appear to be represented (see H. B. Wesselman, this symposium). A very small, probably more primitive form from upper Member B perhaps has affinities with the more equatorial and forest-loving species *H. varia*. A larger species from Member F probably has affinities with *H. hirtula* or *H. parvula*, apparently more characteristic of more open and semiarid to arid habitats. The taxonomy of these viverrids is greatly in need of revision.

Mungos sp.

Material. A single partial left P_3 (L. 819).

Stratigraphic Occurrence. Shungura Formation, Member C.

Discussion. The single specimen is of a size and morphology appropriate to this genus. Petter (1963) has reported two species, including *M. dietrichi*, from Laetolil. The latter

Table 1

Distribution of Carnivore Taxa in the Omo Succession

Taxon	Mursi Fm.	Basal Mb.	Mb. A	Mb. B	Usno Fm.	Mb. C	Mb. D	Mb. E	Mb. F	Mb. G	Mb. H	Mbs. K & L
Helogale				sm.					lg.			
Mungos						X						
Herpestes						X						
Viverra (Civettictis)						X	X			X		
Viverra sp.					cf.							
Viverra leakeyi						X	X			X		
Pseudocivetta ingens										X		
Genetta						X	X	X				
Genetta sp. nov.				X								
Mellivorinae (large sp.)										+		
Lutra					X							
Emhydriodon				X	X	X	X	X				
Lutrinae indet.								X				
Euryboas									cf.			
Perorocuta					cf.	X						
Hyaena aff. *makapani*				X	X	X						
Hyaena hyaena (lg.)					X	X	X	X		X		
Crocuta crocuta										X		
Hyaenidae indet.					X	X						
Homotherium				X		X	X	X		X		
Megantereon				?		X	X	X		X		
Dinofelis			X	X	X	X	+	X		X		

Table 1 (continued)

Taxon	Mursi Fm.	Basal Mb.	Mb. A	Mb. B	Usno Fm.	Mb. C	Mb. D	Mb. E	Mb. F	Mb. G	Mb. H	Mbs. K & L
Panthera leo												X
Panthera pardus				X	X	X		X	X	X		
Panthera crassidens						X		X	X	X		
Acinonyx	?					+						
Felinae indet. (lg.)					X	X	X	X	X		X	
Felix (Lynx) caracal				X			X	X				
Felinae indet. (small)					X	X			X			
Total species recorded	?1	--	1	9	13	16	4	7	12	11	1	2

NOTE: Several additional records are indicated by + in table 1. The *Genetta* sp. nov. may represent *V.* (*Civettictis*), and *Viverra* sp. is probably conspecific with *V. leakeyi*.

and another new species, *M. minutus*, are represented in Olduvai Bed I (Petter 1973).

Herpestes sp.

Material. Left M^1.

Stratigraphic Occurrence. Shungura Formation, Member C (1 locality).

Discussion. The single tooth is unidentifiable as to species. The genus has also been re-corded in eastern Africa at Laetolil (2 species) (Petter 1963) and Olduvai, Bed I (1 spe-cies) (Hendey 1974),[1] at Kromdraai site A (Ewer 1956c), and perhaps at Klein Zee (Stromer 1931).

Viverra (Civettictis) sp.

Material. 3 isolated teeth, a partial right hemimandible; right distal humerus; and cal-caneum.

Stratigraphic Occurrence. Shungura Formation, members C (2 localities), D (2 localities, E (1 locality), and G (1 locality).

Discussion. These fragmentary remains are comparable in size and morphology to the living African civet. This species is practically unrecorded in the later Cenozoic of Africa. Its occurrence is otherwise certainly documented, to our knowledge, only at Kromdraai, site A (Q. B. Hendey, pers. comm.).

Viverra sp.

Material. Distal right tibia.

Stratigraphic Occurrence. Shungura Formation, Member E (1 locality).

Discussion. Comparable in proportions and morphology, but notably larger than *Viverra zibetha*.

Viverra leakeyi Petter (1963).

Material. 4 isolated teeth (left P^3, right P^4, left M_1; left probably dp^3); possibly a phalanx.

Stratigraphic Occurrence. Usno Formation (Brown Sands locality) and Shungura Formation, members C (1 locality) and G (1 locality).

Discussion. The type of this extinct species was established by Petter (1963) on the basis of jaws and teeth from Laetolil (Tanzania). Much of the upper dentition and several lower teeth of this form are now also known from Langebaanweg (South Africa) (Hendey 1974). It is probable that the large form *Viverra durandi* Lydekker (1884), which Pilgrim (1932) as-signed to a new genus *Vishnuictis*, from the Upper Siwaliks of India, is a closely related species. The P^3 and P^4 from the Omo have the basic morphology of the type, and of those from Langebaanweg, but are larger. In this respect there is a closer approach to *Viverra (Vishnuictis) durandi*. No deciduous teeth of *V. leakeyi* have been otherwise reported, and the dp^3 from the Brown Sands locality is therefore only tentatively referred to this species.

Pseudocivetta ingens Petter (1967; also 1973).

Material. A right P^4, and a left humerus lacking the distal epiphysis.

---

1. The well-preserved and varied carnivore fauna at Langebaanweg (cf. Hendey, 1970, 1973) is largely in course of publication by Hendey (in press). Both of us have seen those collections, Howell in 1970 and Petter in 1973. He has kindly made available to us his doctoral dissertation on this group of mammals from that important site (published as Hendey 1974).

Stratigraphic Occurrence. Shungura Formation, Member G (2 localities).

Discussion. The type of this large, extinct genus of civet was established by Petter (1967) on the basis of elements of the dentition from Olduvai Gorge Bed I. It is now also known from several elements of the dentition and a partial cranium from the Lower Member of the Koobi Fora Formation (M. G. Leakey, this symposium). The Omo P^4 essentially duplicates the morphology of the living African civet but is substantially larger and particularly longer. The Omo humerus has all the morphological features of the living African civet but is vastly larger. It is comparable in size with a distal humerus (KNM-ER-2009) from East Rudolf also attributed now to this species. The postcranial skeleton of *Pseudocivetta* has been hitherto unknown.

Genetta sp.

Material. A right M^2 (Locality 1); a right P^4 (Locality 32); and a left mandible with alveoli of $\overline{C}$ to M_2 (1 locality).

Stratigraphic Occurrence. Shungura Formation, members B (1 locality), and C (1 locality), and E (1 locality).

Discussion. The P^4 from Locality 32 is comparable in size and morphology to that of the living genet cat, *Genetta genetta*. The M^2 from Locality 1 is larger than and morphologically distinct from the living species and might well represent a new species. The taxonomy of the modern genets is extremely confused, doubtless greatly oversplit, and surely in need of revision. *Genetta* is rarely recorded otherwise in the African Plio-Pleistocene, except at Langebaanweg (Hendey 1974), Ileret Member of the Koobi Fora Formation (M. G. Leakey, this symposium), and perhaps, Klein Zee (Stromer 1931).

Family Mustelidae

Both Lutrinae and Mellivorinae are known from the Omo succession. There are two representatives of the Lutrinae, one clearly representing a new species, considered here as attributable to the extinct genus *Enhydriodon*. A single specimen is referred to Mellivorinae. This family is in need of revision in spite of its thorough treatment many years ago by Pohle (1919).

Mellivorinae

Mellivorinae indet.

Material. A left $\underline{C}$ and a right P^4.

Stratigraphic Occurrence. Shungura Formation, Member E (Locality 338y).

Discussion. The morphology of both teeth is clearly mellivorine, with basic resemblances to the African ratel, *Mellivora capensis*. However, they are exceptionally large. This is the first documentation of this subfamily in the Plio-Pleistocene of the Rudolf basin. Its evolutionary history in eastern Africa is otherwise unknown except for documentation now in the Kabarsero Beds of the Ngorora Formation (Baringo area, Kenya) in the Upper Miocene. Hendey (1973, 1974) has reported an occurrence at Langebaanweg (South Africa) attributed by him to *Mellivora* aff. *punjabiensis*, previously recorded only from the Middle Siwaliks of India (and raised to the rank of *Promellivora* by Pilgrim 1932). The latter species is smaller than *Eomellivora wimani* of the "Pontian" of northern China (Zdansky 1924). It is known only from the mandible and dentition. *Mellivora sivalensis*, from the Pinjor zone of the Upper

Siwaliks, is a smaller species, slightly larger than the Omo specimens.

Lutrinae

Lutra sp.

Material. Most of a right M_1 and a portion of a left P^4.

Stratigraphic Occurrence. Usno Formation (Brown Sands locality).

Discussion. These fragments clearly represent *Lutra*, but further identification is impossible.

Lutrinae indet.

Material. A right M_2, with root.

Stratigraphic Occurrence. Shungura Formation, Member F (Locality 41).

Discussion. This tooth is of lutrine morphology and is most like *Lutra*, though it is very large (about twice the size of the extant *Lutra maculicollis*). No M_2 is known of *Enhydriodon africanus*, but this specimen is the same length as the alveolus in the Klein Zee (South Africa) specimen (Stromer 1931).

Enhydriodon sp. nov.

Material. Referred elements of the deciduous (incomplete left dp^4, right and left dp_4, incomplete dp_4) and permanent (left P_2, left M_1, left M_2; right P^4) dentition. Referred postcranial parts include proximal two-thirds of a left ulna, a complete right femur, and, perhaps, the diaphysis of a fibula.

Stratigraphic Occurrence. Usno Formation (White Sands, Brown Sands localities); Shungura Formation, members B (2 localities), C (3 localities), E (1 locality), and F (1 locality).

Discussion. Six species of the extinct lutrine genus *Enhydriodon* have been recognized. The smallest, and probably the most primitive, species is *E. lluecai*, from the Vallesian of Teruel (Spain) (Villalta and Crusafont 1945). The oldest species is *E. meneghini* of the Maremmian/Turolian of Monte Bamboli (Tuscany, Italy) (Meneghini 1862; Weithofer 1889). Two species have been recognized in southern Asia: *E. falconeri* (known only from two teeth) from the Indian Siwaliks (probably the Dhok Pathan zone), and *E. sivalensis*, a still larger species, probably from the Upper Siwaliks (Pilgrim 1932; Lydekker 1884). Mathew (1929) made some useful comparative observations on these several taxa and their possible affinities. Two species have been recognized in Africa: *E. africanus* is reported from Klein Zee (Stromer 1931) and Langebaanweg (Hendey 1973, 1974), South Africa, and from Wadi Natrun, Egypt (Stromer 1905, 1913, 1920), and *E.* sp. nov. is reported from Kanapoi, southwest Rudolf basin (Kenya) (B. Patterson, pers. comm.).

The form of *Enhydriodon* from the Omo succession, which is far larger than previously recorded species of this genus, will be described and figured elsewhere.

The deciduous dentition is unknown in the genus, but these several upper and lower deciduous teeth seem referrable to such a lutrine on morphology and size.

P_2, preserved only in *E. lluecai*, is substantially smaller than in the specimen from the Usno Formation (Brown Sands locality). On the basis of M_1 the Omo species is nearly a third again as large as the largest Siwaliks form, *E. sivalensis*. M_2 is known only in *E. lluecai*, in which it was substantially smaller and had a simpler crown pattern. P^4 is known in *E.* sp. nov. from Kanapoi, in *E. sivalensis*, and in *E. falconeri* from the Indian Siwaliks.

In all instances it is substantially smaller overall, though its morphology is not dissimilar to the Omo species.

The postcranial skeleton of this genus has previously been known only from associated bones of the pes and some portions of the manus from Pikermi (Greece), attributed to this genus by Pilgrim (1931). The femur and ulna of the Omo species indicate a very much larger animal, but the lack of comparable skeletal parts evidently hinders comparisons.

Family Canidae

There are still no certain records of this family in Omo group formations. The family is documented at a number of Pliocene and earlier Pleistocene localities in eastern Africa (including the Upper Member of the Koobi Fora Formation and at Olduvai Gorge and Laetolil, in northern Tanzania). In southern Africa it is represented in the Transvaal australopithecine-bearing cave breccias at Makapansgat Limeworks (3 spp.), Taung (2 spp.), Sterkfontein (2 spp., 1 numerous), Swartkrans (2 sp., 1 numerous) and Kromdraai, Site A (3 spp.) (Ewer 1956b). Canidae are exceptionally rare at Langebaanweg; on the basis of size a small species and a much larger species seem to be represented (Hendey 1974).

Family Hyaenidae

Hyaenidae are more common than most other Carnivora, except for Felidae, in Omo Group formations. The family shows relatively little diversity and most specimens are referrable to *Hyaena* or to *Crocuta*. It is still unclear whether one or more species of the former genus are represented. *Percrocuta* may be represented in the Usno Formation.

General discussions of hyaenid phylogeny and of relationships of the principal taxa of the later Cenozoic are to be found in Thenius (1966) and Ficcarelli and Torre (1970).

Percrocuta sp.

Material. Right P_2 and left M_1.

Stratigraphic Occurrence. Usno Formation (White Sands locality).

Discussion. These two specimens are tentatively referred to *Percrocuta*. The P_2 shows the morphology distinctive of this taxon (Kurtén 1954a). It is smaller, and especially shorter, than its homologue from the species reported from Langebaanweg (Hendey 1974). It is larger than, but otherwise very similar to, a species of Vindobonian age from Yugoslavia (Pavlović and Thenius 1965). In Africa earlier occurrences are those from Wadi el-Hammen (Algeria) (Arambourg 1959), a very large species, and the still older Ngorora Formation (Kabarsero Beds), Baringo area (Kenya) (Crusafont and Aguirre 1971b) where a very small species is represented. The M_1 has the morphology characteristic of *Percrocuta* and is slightly smaller than its Langebaanweg homologue (Hendey 1974).

Euryboas sp.

Material. Right M_1.

Stratigraphic Occurrence. Shungura Formation, Member F (1 locality).

Discussion. In size comparable to *Euryboas* of Pardines (France) (Schaub 1941) and Langebaanweg (South Africa) (Hendey 1974). A unique occurrence of teeth, cranial parts, and postcraniums of this unusual hyaenid has recently been reported from Layna, Soria province, Spain, by Crusafont and Aguirre (1971a). This hyaenid genus is well documented in the Sterkfontein and Swartkrans faunal assemblages (Ewer 1955b) and has recently been found at

Langebaanweg as well (Q. B. Hendey 1974). It preserves a vestigial metaconid and a well-formed talonid with posterior cingular margin incised by wear, but has a crestlike, elongated hypoconid.

Hyaena sp.

Material. 2 calcanea, a left metatarsal 3, and a right P_2 (Usno Formation); isolated upper teeth (I^3, M^1, P^4) and lower teeth (P_3, M_1); distal tibia; associated mandibular fragments with dentition, and phalanges of the pes and manus (Shungura Formation).

Stratigraphic Occurrence. Usno Formation (Brown Sands and White Sands localities) and Shungura Formation, members B, C, D, E, G, K (and also a specimen of uncertain stratigraphic provenience) (10 localities).

Discussion. Although these specimens are referrable to genus *Hyaena*, it is impossible with such fragmentary material to determine more precise affinities. Some of the earlier specimens, from the Usno Formation and from Member B of the Shungura Formation, are of a size and morphology which suggest affinity to the small hyena *H. h. makapani*, from Makapansgat Limeworks (Toerien 1955, and Ewer 1954, 1955*a*, 1956*d*). Other specimens from the Shungura Formation are comparatively larger, with different proportions of the cheek teeth. It is unclear whether Hendey's (1974) new species from Langebaanweg, *H. abronia*, which may also be represented at Kanapoi (Kenya) and Sahabi (Libya), is represented. It probably cannot be distinguished on such fragmentary material. A cranium from the Lower Member of the Koobi Fora Formation shows some features reminiscent of this ancient species (cf. M. G. Leakey, this symposium). The affinities of *H. striata* [*sic*] *praecursor* of Ain Brimba (Tunisia) (Arambourg 1970) remains uncertain. Two species of *Hyaena* are apparently represented in the Upper Miocene Beglia Formation (Tunisia) (Robinson and Black 1969).

Crocuta sp.

Material. Right P_3; right P_2; mandible fragment with P_2, P_3, P_4; and a left proximal ulna.

Stratigraphic Occurrence. Shungura Formation, Member G (3 localities).

Discussion. All specimens are comparable in size and morphology to *Crocuta crocuta*. This species is quite commonly represented in the Ileret Member and in the Upper and Lower members of the Koobi Fora Formation, East Rudolf (M. G. Leakey, this symposium). It is also recorded at Laetolil (Dietrich 1942) and Olduvai Gorge Bed I (Tanzania) (Ewer 1965; Petter 1973) and at Kanam (Kenya). The earliest record of this genus in North Africa is at Ain Hanech (Algeria). In southern Africa its earliest recorded occurrence is at Swartkrans and at Kromdraai (site A), Transvaal, where Ewer (1954; 1955*a*; 1967) distinguished the subspecies *C. c. ultra*. One of us (Petter) considers that the specimens from Olduvai should be ascribed to this same subspecies.

Family Felidae

Representatives of this family of Carnivora are the most common in Omo Group formations. Both Machairodontinae and Felinae are represented, with a substantial diversity recorded in each. However, smaller species of Felinae are still very poorly known. Since Matthew's (1910) classic paper on felid relationships there continue to be different interpretations of the relationships of the higher taxonomic categories as evidenced in the discussions of the group by de Beaumont (1964) and Thenius (1967).

Machairodontinae

Two distinctive sabertooths, *Homotherium* and *Megantereon* (Fabrini 1890), are represented in the Omo succession. The cranial and dental morphology of these taxa are well established (cf. Boule 1901) on the basis of some well-preserved specimens from Europe and from southern and northern Asia. Associated cranial and postcranial parts of *Homotherium* are well documented and described from Senèze, France (Ballesio 1963), and from Hundsheim, Austria (Freudenberg 1914), as well as from North America (Meade 1961). The associations of postcranial parts with recognizable cranial and dental parts of *Megantereon* has long been a problem; it was only partially clarified by Schaub's (1925) evaluation of certain specimens from western Europe. The postcranial skeleton of *Megantereon* is still inadequately known and poorly described, and its association with identifiable cranial and dental parts is poorly documented. The complete skeleton of this genus from Senèze, which Schaub planned to publish in monographic form, still remains undescribed. Consequently identification of postcranial parts of the latter genus is still very difficult.

Homotherium sp.

Material. 1_2; P^3; incomplete $\underline{C}$; P_3; P_4; distal humerus and right and left proximal ulnae; left metatarsal 3; left metacarpal 5; right distal femur; right distal radius; femoral condyle; portions of a femur; proximal metatarsal 3; distal metacarpal 3; complete left femur and nearly complete tibia; complete right humerus; right proximal radius and proximal ulna.

Stratigraphic Occurrence. Usno Formation (White Sands locality), and Shungura Formation, members B (1 locality), C (4 localities), D (1 locality), E (1 locality) and G (6 localities).

Discussion. Arambourg (1947) first recorded this genus from the Shungura Formation on the basis of a proximal humerus and a fragment of mandible, attributed by him to *Homotherium aethiopicus*. On the basis of his description and figures it is evident that the humerus is indeed *Homotherium*. However, the mandible fragment probably represents *Dinofelis*.

The specimens from the Usno Formation and the 13 localities of the Shungura Formation are either smaller than, or within the range of, *Homotherium crenatidens* of Europe, considering the variability in size reported for specimens from Senèze (Ballesio 1963) and Hundsheim (Freudenberg 1914) and the fragmentary material from Perrier (Pomel 1842) and Etouaires (Croizet and Jobert 1928), all attributed to this genus by Schaub (1925). A larger species, *Homotherium crenatidens*, and a rather smaller species, *H. latidens*, are generally recognized (cf. Kurtén 1968). Postcranials are not reported in association with a damaged cranium and mandible of *Homotherium*, which was mistakenly attributed by Collings (1972) to *Megantereon problematicus* from Makapansgat Limeworks. It is the only occurrence in southern Africa of *Homotherium* in association with australopithecines. This species was evidently larger than its European counterpart *H. crenatidens*. The same, or at least a closely related form, is present at Langebaanweg (Hendey 1974). The species which occurs in the Kubi Algi Formation and the various members of the Koobi Fora Formation of East Rudolf is also quite large (M. G. Leakey, this symposium). A specimen very similar in size and morphology to that from Langebaanweg, and also large, is recorded in the Rudolf basin at Lothagam (specimens in National Museum of Kenya) from still older deposits.

In northern Africa the first recorded appearance of the genus is in the (upper) Beglia Formation, Bled Douarah (Tunisia) of Upper Miocene age (Robinson and Black 1969). It is also represented at the younger, uppermost Miocene localities of Sahabi (Libya) (cf.

Petrocchi 1943; specimen in Institute di Geologia, Città Universitaria, Rome) and, perhaps, at Wadi Natrun (Egypt) where Stromer (1905, 1913) assigned a mandible fragment to *Machaerodus* aff. *aphanistus*. It is also apparently present at Ain Brimba (Tunisia), from which Arambourg (1970) has listed *Machairodus africanus* n. sp.

Megantereon sp.

Material. Only isolated upper teeth, 4 P^3 and 2 P^4; perhaps a distal humeral epiphysis.

Stratigraphic Occurrence. Usno Formation, White Sands locality; and Shungura Formation, members B (1 locality), C (3 localities), E (3 localities, F (1 locality), and G (1 locality).

Discussion. This small sabertooth is indeed rare in the Omo succession. It is present and seemingly more common in the upper part of the East Rudolf succession (M. G. Leakey, this symposium). It is also documented at Olduvai Gorge in Bed I (cf. Ewer 1965). Except for three records of its occurrence in southern Africa, in association with australopithecines (at Sterkfontein, Swartkrans, and Kromdraai Site A) (Broom 1937; Ewer 1955c), this genus appears to be unrecorded in the Cenozoic of Africa. This is in marked contrast to its common occurrence, frequently in direct association with *Homotherium*, in the Pliocene and earlier Quaternary of Europe (cf. Kurtén 1968).

Felinae

Dinofelis sp.

Material. ? Right proximal metacarpal; proximal half of left femur; crushed cranium with posterior dentition preserved; left proximal femur and lateral condyle; proximal radius; left M_1; right P_4; incomplete left M_1; and crown of right upper $\underline{C}$. Referred tentatively are an associated incomplete distal femur, a largely complete tibia, a patella, both calcanea, an astragalus, 2 tarsals, and a metatarsal 3.

Stratigraphic Occurrence. Usno Formation (? White Sands locality), and Shungura Formation, members A (1 locality) B (1 locality), C (2 localities), D (1 locality), F (3 localities), and G (1 locality).

Discussion. Four species of the "false sabertooth" *Dinofelis* have been distinguished (cf. Hemmer 1965). The type and largest species is *D. abeli* from the (?) "Pontian" of North China (Zdansky 1924). The only record from Europe is *D. diastemata* (Astre 1929; cf. Schaub 1934) designated *Therailurus* by Piveteau (1948), from the Ruscinian fauna of Roussillon (France). Two species have been previously recognized in southern Africa from australopithecine-bearing cave deposits: *D. barlowi* (from Makapansgat Limeworks and Sterkfontein) and *D. piveteaui* (from Swartkrans and Kromdraai Site A) (Ewer 1956a; Ewer 1956d; cf. Toerien, 1955). Hendey (1974, and in press) has now recognized a primitive form of *Dinofelis*, with affinities to *D. diastemata*, at Langebaanweg. M. G. Leakey (this symposium) has suggested that earlier and later species of *Dinofelis* may be represented in material of that genus from East Rudolf, *D.* cf. *barlowi* from the Lower Member of the Koobi Fora Formation, and perhaps *D.* aff. *piveteaui* from the Ileret Member.

The most complete specimen, an almost whole but distorted cranium from the upper part of Member B of the Shungura Formation, shares a number of features with *D. barlowi* and surely differs from *D. abeli* as well as the type of *D. diastemata* (and its related form at Langebaanweg). The several isolated teeth are generally smaller than those of *D. barlowi*. Limb bones associated with cranial and jaw parts of *Dinofelis* have still to be reported, although they do occur at Langebaanweg (Hendey 1974). The femoral attributions to this genus are made here on the basis of a complete femur (and some other skeletal parts) considered to be associated with a largely complete skull, with dentition, from Bolt's Farm (Transvaal, South Africa), in the collections of the Museum of Paleontology, University of California, Berkeley.

The associated lower leg parts from Member G, Shungura Formation, are here only tentatively attributed to *Dinofelis*.

Panthera leo

Material. Right palate fragment with $\underline{C}$ alveolus and roots of P^2 and P^3; and associated right P^4.

Stratigraphic Occurrence. Shungura Formation, Member L (1 locality).

Discussion. In size and morphology these remains accord with the modern lion, *Panthera leo*. The species also occurs in the Ileret Member of the Koobi Fora succession (M. G. Leakey, this symposium) and at Olduvai Gorge (Petter 1973), and also at Laetolil (Dietrich 1942). It is absent from Langebaanweg (as are other Pantherini) and the older australopithecine localities of Makapansgat Limeworks and Sterkfontein. It is recorded at Swartkrans and at Kromdraai (Ewer 1956*a*).

Panthera crassidens

Material. Left mandibular body with $\overline{C}$, P_3 and P_4 roots, and heavily worn M_1; left proximal femur and partial diaphysis; another left proximal femur; right P_3.

Stratigraphic Occurrence. Shungura Formation, members C (1 locality), F (1 locality), and G (2 localities).

Discussion. This distinctive leopard-sized feline was first recorded (the type) from Kromdraai (Broom 1948) and subsequently recognized by Ewer (1965) in Olduvai Gorge Bed I (Petter 1973). Until recently no postcranial remains of the species had been recognized; however, several specimens from Olduvai, attributed by Petter (1973) to *Dinofelis*, must represent *P. crassidens*. The Omo mandible and isolated tooth, though slightly smaller, accord with the type of this species, including the characteristically shortened snout with $\overline{C}$ approximated to P_3. The femora are about the size of *P. pardus*, but like those from Olduvai show some distinctive features which suggest that attribution to *P. crassidens* is reasonable. Several postcranials from the Upper and Lower members of the Koobi Fora Formation also suggest the presence of the species in the East Rudolf succession (M. G. Leakey, this symposium).

This extinct feline is evidently close to, if not actually conspecific with, the Upper Siwaliks form referred by Pilgrim (1932) to *Sivafelis*. He distinguished three species: *S. potens* (smaller) and *S. brachygnathus* (larger) from the Siwaliks, and *S. pleistocaenicus* Zdansky (from the earlier Quaternary of China). The specimens from the Omo are approximately the size of *S. potens*. The East Rudolf specimens are also rather small, whereas those from Olduvai are larger than *P. pardus*. Hendey (1973, 1974) records the occurrence at Langebaanweg of a form similar in size to *S. potens*, but dentally rather more primitive. The species is otherwise unrecorded in Africa.

Panthera aff. *pardus*

Material. P^4; associated upper premolars; incomplete P_4; mandible fragment with 3 teeth;

partial right proximal femur; proximal phalanx, pes; proximal tibia; femur head, metacarpal 2; proximal humerus; ulna; proximal and distal radius fragments; associated radius, ulna, distal humerus, carpal; associated innominate fragment, proximal radius, proximal ulna; proximal phalanx, manus.

Stratigraphic Occurrence. Usno Formation (Brown Sands locality) and Shungura Formation, members B (1 locality), C (7 localities), F (1 locality), G (3 localities).

Discussion. All specimens are similar in size and morphology to *Panthera pardus*. However, they are only tentatively referred to that species, since, particularly in the case of many postcranial parts, it is uncertain whether these can always be distinguished from *P. crassidens*.

P. pardus has a curious distribution in the African Plio-Pleistocene. It is wholly unrecorded in northern Africa. In eastern Africa it appears to be absent from the East Rudolf succession. It is recorded in Olduvai Bed I (Petter 1973) and at Laetolil (Dietrich 1942). In southern Africa it is abundant at Swartkrans, where the subspecies *P. p. incurva* has been distinguished (Ewer 1956a), and is perhaps represented by a single specimen at Sterkfontein. It is unrecorded at Kromdraai and Makapansgat Limeworks, and also at Lange-baanweg.

Acinonyx sp.

Material. Mandible fragment with worn P_3; P_4 and root of M_1.

Stratigraphic Occurrence. Shungura Formation, Member G (1 locality).[2]

Discussion. So far as can be ascertained the cheetah is otherwise unrecorded in Plio-Pleistocene formations in Africa.

Pantherini indet.

Material. Metacarpal 2; partial P^4, damaged proximal ulna and glenoid of scapula; distal metatarsal 3; left P^3; cf. d$\overline{c}$, and 1_2; proximal phalanx, pes.

Stratigraphic Occurrence. Usno Formation (White Sands locality), and Shungura Formation, members C (3 localities), D (1 locality), F (1 locality), and H (1 locality).

Discussion: These specimens are broadly comparable in size to either *Panthera pardus* or *Acinonyx* or are rather larger. They are smaller than *Panthera leo*. At the moment it is impossible to determine affinities more precisely.

Felis (Lynx) caracal

Material. Left M_1; left $\overline{C}$ and right astragalus.

Stratigraphic Occurrence. Usno Formation (Brown Sands locality), and Shungura Formation, members C (1 locality) and F (1 locality).

Discussion. The identity of these specimens is still indeterminate. The alveolar fragment with P^3, and lacking P^2, is about serval-size, but is morphologically distinct from that species.

---

2. R. E. F. Leakey (pers. comm.) has informed one of us (Howell) that a femur shaft of *Acinonyx* was recovered in the course of paleontological survey in the Yellow Sands area in 1967. However, we do not know whether it derived from the Mursi Formation or from the Kibish Formation, which crops out extensively in this area of the basin, with exposures which are locally fossiliferous.

Paleoenvironmental Implications

The most convincing evidence for paleoenvironments derives from the sedimentary record of the Omo succession. It is of course supplemented and enhanced by palynological data of past plant communities and associations, and by microvertebrates which in many cases closely reflect particular habitats.

Carnivores are in general much less indicative of particular paleoenvironments than are many other mammalian taxa. This is particularly true of the larger taxa, which often have wide and varied distributions. The smaller species, and perhaps especially the Viverridae, could afford more direct and precise indications. However, they are still the least well known taxa and, because of their small size and fragmentary preservation, the most difficult to identify precisely. One viverrid does tend to support other evidence (sedimentary and palynological) for substantially forested or wooded situations in (upper) Member B times. However, these small carnivores are still largely undiscovered in other parts of the Omo succession.

A number of the taxa recognized thus far have records of substantial duration in the Omo succession. These presumably reflect continuity in habitats and in their diversity. They include riverine situations (Lutrinae) and forest, woodland, and more open tree or grass savanna habitats within the basin. Unfortunately, it is difficult to evaluate negative evidence--the absence of particular taxa--particularly in a fossil record in which a group is relatively poorly represented, and then generally in fragmentary condition. However, there is some scant suggestion from the Carnivora that conditions may have been more "closed" in the earlier part of the succession, represented by Shungura Formation Member B and the Usno Formation localities, and perhaps in some (or all?) of Member C, than in the middle and upper part of the Shungura Formation. There is corroborative evidence, from soil profiles, from palynology, from microvertebrates, and from some other large vertebrates for the presence in much of Member B of well-developed forest situations associated with wooded savanna conditions. However, the overall stability of a diversity of habitats is perhaps the principal conclusion to be drawn.

Species Diversity

Species diversity is a subject of central concern in modern evolutionary biology. Situations of the present gain substantially from the documentation of the past afforded by the fossil record.

Every major group of Carnivora which is documented in the Omo succession affords some evidence of enhanced species diversity in Plio-Pleistocene times. This is the case in the Viverridae (2-3 extinct species), Mellivorinae, Lutrinae, Hyaenidae, Machairodontinae, and Felinae. However, the documentation is very imperfect because of general deficiency of small species and the overall fragmentary nature of the fossils. Unquestionably the diversity was higher, even substantially so, in some groups we do not yet know well. Diversity among Plio-Pleistocene and earlier Pleistocene carnivores has already been well documented at Olduvai (Petter 1973) and Laetolil (Dietrich 1942; Petter 1963) in the Serengeti area, and in southern Africa in the Transvaal cave breccias (Ewer 1956c) and, especially, at Langebaanweg (Hendey 1973), in a totally different paleoenvironmental situation.

Extra-African Affinities

The Omo fossil record, like some other Plio-Pleistocene occurrences elsewhere in Africa, reveals some instances of faunistic affinities with other continents. This is reflected in the carnivore fauna.

Viverridae are still poorly known. However, *Viverra leakeyi* certainly has affinities with southern Asiatic species, both modern and from the Siwaliks sequence.

Mustelidae also reflect Asiatic relationships. This is the case with *Enhydriodon*, which was more anciently also European. It is probably also the case with the Omo mellivorine.

The affinities of the hyaenids are complex. There is now some justification for considering *Hyaena* as essentially African in origin. *Euryboas* and *Percrocuta*, if indeed they are represented in the Omo, have broad Eurasiatic representations in the Mio-Pliocene, with the former persisting well into the Plio-Pleistocene. *Crocuta*, which now has a provocative pattern of occurrence in the African Plio-Pleistocene, probably indeed immigrated to that continent, as Kurtén (1957b) maintained, but substantially earlier than he estimated.

The machairodontines, *Homotherium* and *Megantereon*, were both widespread in Eurasia. Their center of origin is still unclear, as is the history of their subsequent distribution.

Dinofelis was first recorded in Asia, then in Europe, and in more recent years has been found to have a broad sub-Saharan distribution over a substantial range of time. Its origin and initial distribution are still wholly unknown, but could have been either Asiatic or African.

Hemmer (1973) has convincingly demonstrated that "*Felis*" *cristata* (Falconer and Cautley 1836), from the Pinjor zone of the Upper Siwaliks, is in fact a *Dinofelis* (*D. cristata*), intermediate in certain cranial and dental features between *D. diastemata* and *D. piveteaui*. The genus was almost certainly also present in North America since "*Panthera*" *palaeoonca* (Meade 1961) from the Blancan fauna (Blanco, Texas) should almost certainly also be attributed to this taxon.

The other Pantherini seem to appear rather abruptly in the African fossil record. On available evidence, *P. pardus* clearly antedates *P. leo*. Their origin and initial distribution remains enigmatic. However, both appear earlier in Africa than in Europe, where *P. leo* is first documented in the Cromerian (Hemmer 1967; Dietrich 1968). *P. pardus* appears about the same time or just slightly earlier in Europe (Hemmer 1971). *P. crassidens* shows Asiatic affinities, but its evolutionary history is still unclear. *Acinonyx* was widespread in the Plio-Pleistocene. The European species *A. pardinensis* was a giant form which was probably also distributed into southern and northern Asia. The fossil record of *Acinonyx* in Africa is perhaps suggestive of its immigrant status on that continent. The small felines are still so imperfectly known in Africa, including the Omo, that little of their evolutionary history can be made out.

Kurtén (1968) has suggested that the lynx may have originated in North America and "perhaps entered the Old World at the same time as the genus *Equus*." *Felis* (*Lynx*) *caracal* initially appears low in the Omo succession, probably at a time when *Felis issiodorensis*, the Issoire lynx, was already represented in Europe, as was perhaps its East Asian counterpart, *F. shansius*.

Carnivora at Other Localities about the Rudolf Basin

Lothagam is still the oldest of the late Neogene fossiliferous localities in the Rudolf basin. The preliminary report by Patterson, Behrensmeyer, and Sill (1970) mentions four Carnivora in the Lothagam--1 assemblage, none of which have yet been fully described.[3]

___

3. Carnivora from Lothagam and from Kanapoi have been examined by Howell at Harvard University and the National Museum of Kenya (Nairobi).

With the possible exception of *?Civettictis*, these Carnivora (which include a primitive hyaenid and a *Machairodus*, the latter like that recorded at Langebaanweg) are unlike those known from other Rudolf basin localities.

Three carnivore taxa have been reported from the Kanapoi locality (Patterson 1966) but have still to be described. Only the species of hyaenid found there may prove to have affinities with a species from the Omo and East Rudolf successions.

Some more fruitful comparisons can be made between taxa recorded in the Omo and East Rudolf successions. There are similarities as well as some interesting differences.

Common to the two successions are nine taxa of the eleven recorded thus far in East Rudolf (M. G. Leakey, this symposium). Unlike East Rudolf, the Omo has still to yield Canidae or the lutrine *Aonyx*. Of the taxa in common there are similarities between the two successions in respect to: (*a*) the persistent presence and coexistence of *Homotherium* and *Megantereon*; (*b*) the persistence of *Dinofelis*; (*c*) the long record of *Hyaena hyaena*; and (*d*) the apparent late appearance of *Panthera leo*. On the other hand, there are some important differences, if the correlations afforded by the radiometric dating in the two successions are accepted--notably: (*a*) belated appearance of *Pseudocivetta ingens* in the Omo; (*b*) rarity and belated appearance of *Crocuta* in the Omo succession; and (*c*) absence of *Viverra (Civettictis)*, and especially *Panthera pardus* and *Acinonyx*, in the East Rudolf succession. It is difficult to regard these distinctions as merely a reflection of different paleoenvironments.

Acknowledgments

The governments of Ethiopia and of Kenya have cooperated with the Omo Research Expedition in its field activities in the lower Omo basin. Financial assistance for this work has been provided principally by the Centre national de la recherche scientifique, the National Science Foundation, and the Wenner-Gren Foundation for Anthropological Research.

References

Arambourg, C. 1947. Contribution à l'étude géologique et paléontologique du bassin du lac Rodolphe et de la basse vallée de l'Omo. In *Mission scientifique de l'Omo (1932-1933)*. Vol. 1. *Géologie-Anthropologie*, fasc. 3, pp. 231-562. Mémoire, Muséum national d'histoire naturelle (Paris).

_____. 1959. Vertébrés continentaux du Miocène supérieur de l'Afrique du Nord. *Mém. Publ. Serv. Carte Géol. Algérie*, 4:1-159.

_____. 1970. Les vertébrés du Pléistocène de l'Afrique du Nord. *Arch. Mus. Nat. Hist. Nat.* (Paris), ser. F, 10:1-126.

Astre, G. 1929. Sur un felin á particularités ursoides des limons pliocènes du Roussillon. *Bull. Soc. Géol. France*, ser. 4, 29:199-204.

Ballesio, R. 1963. Monographie d'un *Machairodus* du gisement villafranchien de Senèze: *Homotherium crenatidens* Fabrini. *Trav. Lab. Géol. Lyon*, n.s., 9:1-129.

Beaumont, G. de. 1964. Remarques sur la classification des Felidae. *Ecl. Géol. Helv.* 57: 837-45.

Boule, M. 1901. Revision des éspèces européennes de *Machairodus*. *Bull. Soc. Geol. France*, ser. 4, 1:551-73.

Broom, R. 1937. On some new Pleistocene mammals from limestone caves of the Transvaal. *S. African J. Sci.* 33:750-68.

_____. 1939. A preliminary account of the Pleistocene carnivores of the Transvaal caves. *Ann. Transvaal Museum, Pretoria* 19:331-38.

Broom, R. 1948. Some South African Pliocene and Pleistocene mammals. *Ann. Transvaal Museum, Pretoria* 21:1-38.

Collings, G. E. 1972. A new species of machaerodont from Makapansgat. *Palaeontol. Africana* 14:87-92.

Croizet, J.-B., and Jobert, A.-G. 1928. *Recherches sur les ossements fossiles du départment du Puy-de-Dôme.* Paris.

Crusafont Pairó, M., and Aguirre, E. 1971*a*. *Euryboas lunnensis et Hyaena donnezani* associées, en Espagne, dans le gisement d'age pliocène terminal de Layna (Soria). *C. R. Acad. Sci. (Paris),* ser. D, 273:2476-78.

———. 1971*b*. A new species of *Percrocuta* from the Middle Miocene of Kenya. *Abhandl. Hess Landesamtes Bodenforsch.* 60:51-58.

Dietrich, W. O. 1942. Ältestquartäre Säugetiere aus der südlichen Serengeti, Deutsch-Ostafrika. *Palaeontographica,* ser. A, 94:43-133.

———. 1968. Fossile Löwen im europäischen und africanischen Pleistozän. *Palaeontologische Abhandl., Abt. A, Palaeozoologie* 3(2):323-66.

Ewer, R. F. 1954. The fossil carnivores of the Transvaal caves: The Hyaenidae of Kromdraai. *Proc. Zool. Soc. London* 124:565-85.

——— 1955*a*. The Hyaenidae, other than *Lycyaena*, of Swartkrans and Sterkfontein. *Proc. Zool. Soc. London* 124:815-47.

———. 1955*b*. The fossil carnivores of the Transvaal caves: The Lycyaenas of Sterkfontein and Swartkrans, together with some general considerations of the Transvaal fossil hyaenids. *Proc. Zool. Soc. London* 124:839-57.

———. 1955*c*. The fossil carnivores of the Transvaal caves: Machairodontinae. *Proc. Zool. Soc. London* 125:587-615.

———. 1956*a*. The fossil carnivores of the Transvaal caves: Felinae. *Proc. Zool. Soc. London* 126:83-95.

———. 1956*b*. The fossil carnivores of the Transvaal caves: Canidae. *Proc. Zool. Soc. London* 126:97-119.

———. 1956*c*. The fossil carnivores of the Transvaal caves: Two new viverrids, together with some general considerations. *Proc. Zool. Soc. London* 126:259-74.

———. 1956*d*. Some fossil carnivores from the Makapansgat valley. *Palaeontologia Africana* 4:57-67.

———. 1965. Large Carnivora. *Olduvai Gorge, 1959-1961,* ed. L. S. B. Leakey, Vol. 1. *A preliminary report on the geology and fauna,* pp. 19-22. Cambridge: At the University Press.

———. 1967. The fossil hyaenids of Africa: A reappraisal. In *Background to evolution in Africa,* ed. W. W. Bishop and J. D. Clark, pp. 109-23. Chicago: University of Chicago Press.

Fabrini, E. 1890. I *Machairodus (Megantereon)* del Valdarno superiore. *Bol. R. Comitato Geologica Italia,* ser. 3, 1:121-44, 161-77.

Ficcarelli, G., and Torre, D. 1970. Remarks on the taxonomy of hyaenids. *Palaeontographia Italica* 66:13-33.

Freudenberg, W. 1914. Die Säugetiere des alteren Quartärs von Mitteleuropa (mit besonderer Berücksichtigung der Fauna von Hundsheim und Deutschaltenburg in Niederösterreich). *Geologische Palaeontologische Abhandl.,* n.s. 12 (A/S):455-671.

Hemmer, H. 1965. Zur Nomenklatur und Verbreitung des genus *Dinofelis* Zdansky, 1924 (*Therailurus* Piveteau, 1948). *Palaeontol. Africana* 9:75-89.

———. 1967. Fossilbelege zur Verbreitung und Artsgeschichte des Löwen, *Panthera leo* (Linne, 1758). *Säugetierkl. Mitt.* 15:289-300.

Hemmer, H. 1971.   Zur Kenntnis Pleistozäner mitteleuropaischer Leoparden (*Panthera pardus*). *Neues Jahrb. Geol. Palaeontol. Abhandl* 138:15-36.

—————. 1973. Neue Befunde zur Verbreitung und Evolution der pliozän-pleistozänen Gattung *Dinofelis* (Mammalia, Carnivora, Felidae). *Neues Jahrb. Geol. Palaont. Monatsh.*, Jg. 1973, H.3:157-169.

Hendey, Q. B. 1970. A review of the geology and palaeontology of the Plio/Pleistocene deposits at Langebaanweg, Cape Province. *Ann. South. Africana Museum* 56:75-117.

—————. 1973. Fossil occurrences at Langebaanweg, Cape Province. *Nature* 244:13-14.

—————. 1974. The late Cenozoic Carnivora of the south-western Cape Province. *Ann. South African Museum* 63:1-369.

Kurtén, B. 1957a. *Percrocuta* Kretzoi (Mammalia, Carnivora), a group of Neogene hyenas. *Acta Zool. Cracoviensia., Krakow* 2(16):375-404.

—————. 1957b. Mammal migrations, Cenozoic stratigraphy, and the age of Peking man and the australopithecines. *J. Paleontol.* 31:215-27.

—————. 1968. *Pleistocene mammals of Europe*. London: Weidenfeld and Nicholson.

Lydekker, R. B. A. 1884. Siwalik and Narbada Carnivora. *Palaeontol. Indica,* ser. 10, Z: 178-351.

Matthew, W. D. 1910. The phylogeny of the Felidae. *Bull. Am. Museum Nat. Hist.* 28:289-316.

—————. 1929. Critical observations upon Siwalik Mammals (Exclusive of Proboscidea). *Bull. Am. Museum Nat. Hist.* 56:437-560.

Meade, G. E. 1961. The saber-toothed cat *Dinobastis serus*. *Bull. Texas Memor. Museum,* no. 2, pp. 25-60.

Meneghini, G. 1862. Descrizione dei resti di due fiere trovati nelli ligniti Mioceniche de Monte Bamboli. *Atti Soc. ital. sci. naturali* 4:17-58.

Patterson, B. 1966. A new locality for early Pleistocene fossils in north-western Kenya. 212:577-78.

Patterson, B.; Behrensmeyer, A. K. and Sill, W. D. 1970. Geology and fauna of a new Pliocene locality in northwest Kenya. *Nature* 226:918-21.

Pavlović, M., and Thenius, E. 1965. Eine neue Hyane (Carnivora, Mammalia) aus Miozän Jugoslaviens und ihre phylogenetische Stellung. *Sitzber. Österr. Akad. Wiss. Wien,* no. 9, pp. 177-85.

Petrocchi, C. 1943. Il giacimento fossilifero di Sahabi. *Collezione Sci. Document. Africa Italiana* 12:1-167.

Petter, G. 1963. Etude de quelques Viverridés (Mammifères, Carnivores) du Pléistocène inférieur du Tanganiyika (Afrique Orientale). *Bull. Soc. Geol. France,* ser. 7, 5:265-74.

—————. 1967. Petits carnivores villafranchiens du Bed I d'Oldoway (Tanzanie): Problemes actuels de paléontologie (évolution des vertébrés). *Colloq. Intern. Centre Natl. Rech. Sci. (Paris),* 163(1966):529-38.

—————. 1973. Carnivores Pléistocènes du ravin d'Olduvai (Tanzanie). In *Fossil vertebrates of Africa,* ed. L. S. B. Leakey, R. J. Savage, and S. C. Coryndon, 3:43-100. London: Academic Press.

Pilgrim, G. E. 1931. *Catalogue of the Pontian Carnivora of Europe*. London: British Museum (Natural History).

—————. 1932. The fossil Carnivora of India. *Palaeontol. Indica,* n.s., 18:1-232.

Piveteau, J. 1948. Un félide du Pliocène du Roussillon. *Ann. Paleontol.* 34:99-124.

Pohle, H. 1919. Die Unterfamilie der Lutrinae (eine systematischer-geographische Studie an dem Material der Berliner Museen). *Arch. Naturgesch.,* ser. A, 85:1-247.

Pomel, A. 1842. Notice sur les carnassiers à canines comprimées et tranchantes, trouvées dans les alluvions du Val d'Arno et de l'Auvergne. *Bull. Soc. Géol. France* 14:29-38.

Robinson, P., and Black, C. C. 1969. Note préliminaire sur les vertébrés fossiles du Vindobonien, (formation Beglia), du Bled Douarah, Gouvernorat de Gafsa, Tunisie. *Notes Serv. Géol. Tunisie* 31:67-70.

Schaub, S. 1925. Über die Osteologie von *Machairodus cultridens* Cuvier. *Eclogae Geol. Helv.* 19:255-66.

———. 1934. Observations critiques sur quelques Machairondontines. *Eclogae Geol. Helv.* 27:399-406.

———. 1941. Eines neues Hyaenidengenus von der Montagne de Perrier. *Eclogae Geol. Helv.* 34:279-86.

Stromer, E. 1905. Fossile Wirbeltierreste aus dem Uadi Faregh und Uadi Natrun in Ägypten. *Senckenberg. Naturforsch. Ges.* 29:99-132.

———. 1913. Mitteilungen über Wirbeltierreste aus dem Mittelpliocän des Natrontales (Ägypten). 2. Raubtiere. *Z. Deut. Geol. Ges.*, ser. A, 65:362-72.

———. 1920. Mitteilungen über Wirbeltierreste aus dem Mittelpliocän des Natrontales (Ägypten). 6. Nachtrag zu 2. Raubtiere. *Sitzber. Bayer. Akad. Wiss., Math-Naturw. Kl., Bayer, Akad. Wiss., Muenchen* 1920:361-70.

———. 1931. Reste Süsswasser und Landbewohnender Wirbeltiere aus den Diamantfeldern Klein-Namaqualandes (Südwestafrika). *Sitzber. Bayer. Akad. Wiss., Math.-Naturw. Kl., Bayer, Akad. Wiss., Muenchen* 1931:17-47.

Thenius, E. 1966. Zur Stammesgeschichte der Hyaenen (Carnivora, Mammalia) *Z. Säugetierkunde* 31:293-300.

———. 1967. Zur Phylogenie der Feliden (Carnivora, Mammalia) *Z. zool. Syst. Evolutionsforsch.* 5:129-143.

Toerien, M. I. 1952. The fossil hyaenas of the Makapansgat Valley. *S. African J. Sci.* 48:293-99.

———. 1955. A sabretooth cat from the Makapansgat Valley. *Palaeontol. Africana* 3:43-46.

Villalta Comella, J. F. de, and Crusafont Pairó, M. 1945. *Enhydriodon lluecai* nova sp. el primer lútrido del Pontiense español. Bol. *Real Soc. Españ. Hist. Nat.* 43:383-96.

Weithofer, A. 1889. Über die tertiaren Landsäugethiere Italiens. *Jahrb. K. K. Geol. Reichsan., Wien*, 39:55-82.

Zdansky, O. 1924. Jüngtertiäre Carnivoren Chinas. *Palaeontol. Sinica*, ser. C, Z, fasc. 1, pp. 1-149.

Postscript

Since this was written, additional carnivore specimens have been recovered. The specific and even several of the generic attributions of a few specimens given here require, following our more recent studies, some reconsideration, but that affects hardly at all the distributions given in table 1. The principal taxa concerned are *Genetta*, *Lutra*, *Panthera*, and *Acinonyx*. (The form present in the Omo is unlike recent *A. jubatus*, and is different from *P. crassidens*, which itself has definite *Acinonyx* affinities.) The various forms of hyaenids also require further comparative study and the attributions of some specimens need to be reexamined.

G. G. Eck

The sample of fossil cercopithecoid specimens from the Omo Group deposits, south-western Ethiopia, consists of 3,460 specimens. These were recovered from the Usno Forma-tion at both the White Sands and Brown Sands localities and from all members of the Shun-gura Formation during the 1967-72 field seasons of the international Omo Research Expedi-tion. Deposits of the Mursi Formation have to date yielded no cercopithecoid specimens. A discussion of the ages and stratigraphy of the formations will be found in Brown (1971, and this symposium), Brown and Lajoie (1971), Brown and Nash (this symposium), Brown and Shuey (this symposium), de Heinzelin, Brown, and Howell (1970), and de Heinzelin and Haesaerts (this symposium).

Most of the cercopithecoid specimens are fragmentary. Complete or nearly complete craniums and mandibles are rare. Likewise, most postcranial specimens are fragmentary, al-though a small number of complete specimens have been recovered. Complete isolated teeth are found in large numbers, although the sample of fragmentary specimens is somewhat larger. Table 1 presents the numbers of specimens recovered from the Usno Formation and from each member of the Shungura Formation. The numbers of specimens from the Usno Formation have been placed between those from members A and B of the Shungura Formation in their approxi-mate stratigraphic positions. The table also presents the specimens according to five body-part categories.

Table 1 indicates that 42% of the total sample of cercopithecoid specimens consists of fragmentary teeth; approximately one-third of these have been taxonomically identified to date. Thirty-eight percent of the sample consists of complete isolated teeth; approximately two-thirds of these have been taxonomically identified. The unidentified portion of this part of the sample consists of incisors, canines, deciduous teeth, and heavily worn teeth of other types. Two percent of the sample consists of cranial fragments ranging from a complete cranium to small fragments of calvaria; two-thirds of these specimens have been taxonomically identified. Five percent of the sample consists of mandible fragments, again ranging from nearly complete specimens to small pieces of the horizontal ramus without teeth; two-thirds of these specimens have been taxonomically identified. Thirteen percent of the sample consists of various postcranial specimens, mostly fragmentary long bones; al-though all of these have been identified as to body part, an attempt to identify them to taxon has not yet been made. Thus, of the 3,460 recovered specimens, the vast majority have been identified to body part and approximately 50% of them have been identified taxo-nomically.

Table 1

Numbers of Recovered Specimens by Body Part and by Formation and Member

Body Part	Higher Mbs.	Mb. H	Mb. G	Mb. F	Mb. E	Mb. D	Mb. C	Mb. B	Usno Fm.	Mb. A	Basal Mb.	Mb. Unknown	Total
Total tooth fragments	1	5	188	196	129	103	510	150	137	2	-	31	1,452 (42%)
Unidentified	-	2	107	143	99	82	296	79	84	1	-	27	920
Identified	1	3	81	53	30	21	214	71	53	1	-	4	532
Total complete teeth	3	10	175	108	97	66	412	163	201	7	1	60	1,303 (38%)
Unidentified	-	2	64	35	34	17	115	40	20	2	-	59	388
Identified	3	8	111	73	63	49	295	125	181	5	1	1	915
Cranial fragments	-	-	5	8	6	8	32	2	-	-	-	5	66 (2%)
Unidentified	-	-	3	2	4	1	7	1	-	-	-	2	20
Identified	-	-	2	6	2	7	25	1	-	-	-	3	46
Mandible fragments	-	2	46	28	18	9	70	5	1	-	-	3	182 (5%)
Unidentified	-	-	13	11	13	1	14	2	1	-	-	1	56
Identified	-	2	33	17	5	8	56	3	-	-	-	2	126
Postcranial elements	-	4	54	45	33	30	205	21	33	-	-	32	457 (13%)
Total	4	21	468	385	283	216	1,229	341	372	9	1	131	3,460

The total number of specimens found in each member of the Shungura Formation and in the Usno Formation varies considerably, from 1 specimen in the Basal Member to 1,229 specimens in Member C of the Shungura Formation. Factors that might have contributed to this variability are discussed below.

Specimens assigned to both subfamilies of the Cercopithecidae have been recovered from the Omo Group deposits. Recognized so far are three or four groups of Colobinae specimens, of which one is assigned at the genus level, and four or five groups of Cercopithecinae specimens, of which three or four are assigned at the genus level. Table 2 presents the numbers of identified specimens by formation and member and by specimen group or taxon.

Colobinae

Fossil colobines from Pliocene and Pleistocene sites in East Africa are relatively rare and usually fragmentary. For this reason, the taxonomic relationships between the various fossil specimens and between the fossil specimens and modern taxa of the subfamily are not well understood. Because the colobine specimens of the Omo Group deposits are in general very fragmentary and rare (7% of the taxonomically identified cercopithecoid sample), taxonomic problems are especially acute; consequently the discussion below should be considered very provisional.

Colobus sp.

This taxon is represented by two sets of specimens; remains of two individuals. F8-14 and F8-15 were found near the top of the Shungura Formation in the Namuruputh area near a tuff dated at 1.54 m.y. and thus probably come from Member J or Member K. Specimen F8-14 is a complete RLM3, and specimen F8-15 is a fragment of RLM1 or RLM2. The specimens are similar in size to the teeth of a right maxillary fragment (KNM ER-150) from East Rudolf. All these specimens are considerably smaller than modern *Colobus polykomos*, although they may fall within the size range of some of the smaller modern African colobines. Specimens P997-15a-d and P997-17 are RLC, RLP4, RLM2, RLM3, and LLM3 of a single individual recovered from Member L and thus date from about 0.9 m.y. These specimens are about the same size as modern *Colobus polykomos*. The specimens from P997 were recovered during the 1973 field season and have not been studied in enough detail to determine their taxonomic relationship to those from F8. The specimens from P997 are not included in the tables.

Colobinae gen. et sp. indet. (A)

This group of specimens consists of 8 isolated teeth recovered from localities in members B and C of the Shungura Formation. They thus date from between 2.70 m.y. and 2.4 m.y. All of these specimens are slightly larger than equivalent teeth in modern *Colobus polykomos* and are about the same size as the teeth in a specimen (L2-86) recently recovered from the Awash valley of northeastern Ethiopia (I wish to thank D. C. Johanson for permission to see and refer to this specimen). The Awash specimen, although relatively small, seems to have affinities with *Ceropithecoides williamsi* from South Africa (see Freedman 1957, 1960, 1965; Maier 1970 for a discussion of *C. williamsi*). Taxonomic assignment at the generic level, however, will have to await the recovery of more complete specimens. Specimens similar to these have not yet been recovered at East Rudolf.

Colobinae gen. et sp. nov. (B)

This group of specimens consists of a nearly complete cranium (Omo 75-1012), a mandible lacking the left ascending ramus, right gonial region and anterior teeth (L412-1), a mandible lacking both ascending rami and incisors (Omo 75s-C68), a right mandibular horizontal

Table 2

Numbers of Taxonomically Identified Specimens by Specimen Group or Taxon and by Formation and Member

Group	Higher Mbs.	Mb. H	Mb. G	Mb. F	Mb. E	Mb. D	Mb. C	Mb. B	Usno Fm.	Mb. A	Basal Mb.	Mb. Unknown	Total
Colobus sp.	1	-	-	-	-	-	-	-	-	-	-	-	1
Colobinae gen. et sp. indet. (A)	-	-	-	-	-	-	6	2	-	-	-	-	8
Colobinae gen. et sp. nov.	-	1	17	1	1	1	6	19	33	1	1	2	83
Colobinae gen. et sp. indet. (C)	-	-	10	1	1	1	4	-	-	-	-	-	17
Cercopithecus sp.	-	-	2	-	-	-	-	2	2	-	-	-	6
Small Papionini gen. et sp. indet. (A)	-	-	-	-	-	-	1	3	18	-	-	2	24
Small Papionini gen. et sp. indet. (B)	1	6	1	4	3	-	6	18	16	-	-	-	55
Papio sp.	2	-	22	6	18	6	13	8	6	1	-	-	82
Theropithecus sp.	-	6	175	137	77	77	554	148	159	4	-	6	1,343
Theropithecus[1] *brumpti*	-	-	1	1	1	1	15	-	-	-	-	1	20
Total	4	13	227	149	100	85	590	200	234	6	1	10	1,619

[1]These specimens are included in the counts for *Theropithecus* sp. and thus should not be added in the total count.

ramus with P3-M2 (L627-238), and 79 isolated teeth. The specimens were recovered from the
Usno Formation and from localities in the Basal Member and members A through H of the Shungura Formation. The specimens thus range in age from slightly more than 3.0 m.y. to
slightly less than 1.6 m.y. They are about the same size as those of *Paracolobus chemeroni*
(R. E. F. Leakey 1969) and *Cercopithecoides molletti* (Freedman 1957). However, Meave
Leakey (Leakey and Leakey 1973*b* and pers. comm.) thinks the Omo Group cranium and mandibles
differ significantly from both genera and should therefore be placed in a new genus. Similar specimens have been found in East Rudolf.

Colobinae gen. et sp. indet. (C)

    This group of specimens consists of a left mandibular ascending ramus and horizontal
ramus broken at about M1 with M2 and M3 (L35-59), a left maxillary fragment with M2 and M3
(L9-14), and 15 isolated teeth. The specimens were found in localities in members C through
G of the Shungura Formation and thus date from 2.7 m.y. to 1.8 m.y. The teeth of this taxon
are similar in size to those of the East African anubis baboon. Specimens like these have
not been recovered at East Rudolf. Their taxonomic assignment at the generic level will
have to await the recovery of more complete specimens.

Cercopithecinae

    Cercopithecine specimens are generally found in much larger numbers in Pliocene and
Pleistocene sites of East Africa than are specimens of colobines; however, the numbers and
completeness of recovered specimens vary considerably from genus to genus. Since specimens
of the genus *Theropithecus* (=*Simopithecus*) are commonly found and are in some cases nearly
complete, the genus is the best known of all cercopithecoid genera found in these sites.
The relationship of the fossil specimens at the generic level to modern *T. gelada* is fairly
evident (Jolly 1972); but relationships between groups of fossils at the species level are
not completely understood. Specimens of the genus *Papio* are less regularly found at fossiliferous sites in this region than those of the genus *Theropithecus* and are far less
common and most often very fragmentary. The relationship of these specimens to the modern
members of the genus *Papio* is generally agreed upon, although relationships at the species
level are as yet obscure. A small number of specimens with affinities to members of the
tribe Papionini have been recovered from a number of East African sites. The specimens are
generally small, rare, and fragmentary, usually consisting of isolated teeth. Because of
their fragmentary state and their rarity, the relationships of these specimens to the existing genera of this tribe have not yet been worked out. The genus *Cercopithecus* is rarely
found in East African sites, and the few specimens that are known are not very complete.
The relationship of these specimens at the generic level to the modern members of the genus
is obvious, but the relationships at the species level are very obscure. Ninety-three
percent of the taxonomically identified cercopithecoid specimens from the Omo Group deposits
belong to the subfamily Cercopithecinae.

Cercopithecus sp.

    This taxon consists of the crushed horizontal rami of a mandible with LI1-LC, LP4-LM3
and RP3-PM1 (L621-4a,b), the horizontal ramus of a mandible with LLM1 and part of the maxilla lacking teeth (P994-8a,b), and 5 isolated teeth. These specimens were recovered from
localities in the Usno Formation and in members B, G, and J of the Shungura Formation. The
specimens thus date at about 2.9, 2.7, 1.9, and 1.45 m.y. The specimens from the Usno Formation and from Member G have been discussed in detail by Eck and Howell (1972). The

specimens from members B and J have only recently been found and have not been fully
studied (those from Member J are not included in the tables). The mandible specimens certainly belong to the genus *Cercopithecus*, and the isolated teeth probably do; however, the
relationship of these specimens at the species level to modern representatives of the genus
is essentially indeterminant. The specimens are similar in size and morphology to specimens of at least four species of *Cercopithecus* living in East Africa today. M. G. Leakey
(this symposium, table 2) refers to this taxon as "*Cercopithecus* sp. (B)," indicating that
it may be different from *C.* cf. *aethiops* recovered at East Rudolf. Only a larger number
of specimens from both areas will demonstrate whether this is so.

Small Papionini gen. et sp. indet. (A)

   This group of specimens consists of 24 isolated teeth that were recovered from the
Usno Formation and from members B and C of the Shungura Formation. They seem to be restricted to the lower part of the Omo sequence and date from 2.9 m.y. to 2.5 m.y. They
have affinities to specimens found at East Rudolf and Olduvai and to specimens of the genus
Cercocebus. They are generally smaller than the teeth of specimens assigned to *Parapapio
jonesi* from South Africa (see Broom 1940; Freedman 1957; Freedman and Stenhouse 1972; and
Maier 1970 for a discussion of *P. jonesi*). Their assignment to a taxon at the generic level
must await the recovery of more complete material.

Small Papionini gen. et sp. indet. (B)

   This group of specimens consists of a right mandible fragment with 1/2P4-M3 (Omo K-6-
C146) and 54 isolated teeth. The specimens were recovered from localities in the Usno Formation and members B, C, E-H, and J of the Shungura Formation and thus date from 2.9 m.y.
to about 1.45 m.y. They are similar in size and morphology to specimens found at East
Rudolf and to specimens assigned to *Parapapio jonesi* and *P. broomi* from South Africa. Because the teeth of the smaller Papionini are similar in morphology, the assignment of these
specimens to a taxon at the generic level must await the recovery of more complete material.

   The division of the sample of small Papionini specimens into two groups (small, A; and
large, B) seems to be warranted by slight differences in morphology, although these two
groups could represent sexual dimorphism within a single species. The reference to
Parapapio sp. in Howell, Fichter, and Eck (1969) is based on some of these specimens; it is
now the opinion of Howell and Eck that the identification of *Parapapio* in the Usno Formation
should be withdrawn.

Papio sp.

   This taxon consists of a fragmentary cranium with RP3-RM3 and LM2-LM3 (L185-6), a
maxillary fragment with RP3-RM3 (L4-13), a left mandible fragment with LP3-LM2 (L310-1a),
a right mandible fragment with 1/2RM2-RM3 (L7-160), and 78 isolated teeth. The specimens
were recovered from localities in the Usno Formation and from members A through G, J, and
K of the Shungura Formation. They thus date from slightly earlier than 2.9 m.y. to about
1.2 m.y. The specimens of teeth and mandibles are on the whole similar in size and shape
to both fossil and modern representatives of the genus. The muzzle (L185-16) is broader
and more robust than those of males of the modern anubis baboon, *Papio robinsoni* (Freedman
1957) from South Africa and *P. baringensis* (R. E. F. Leakey 1969) from the Chemeron deposits.
The assignment of these specimens at the species level must await general agreement on the
number of species represented by the modern savannah baboons and the relationship of these
to the fossil specimens.

Theropithecus sp.

This taxon consists of 1,343 taxonomically identified specimens: 83% of all cercopithecoid specimens and 89% of all cercopithecine specimens. Although most of these specimens are complete or fragmentary isolated teeth, the number of relatively complete cranial and mandible remains is too great to list in this report. It is also suspected, for probabilistic reasons, that most of the postcranial elements also belong to this genus. The first specimens of the genus were found by Arambourg during the 1932-33 French expedition to the lower Omo basin and were named *Dinopithecus brumpti* in the 1947 report of the expedition (Arambourg 1947). Although Arambourg noted the similarity between the Omo specimens and modern *Theropithecus gelada*, he seemingly underplayed the similarity of *D. ingens* to modern *Papio* and the differences between modern *Papio* and *Theropithecus*. The type specimens of *Dinopithecus* (Broom 1937; Freedman 1957) from South Africa have obvious affinities to the genus *Papio*, whereas all of Arambourg's specimens from the Shungura Formation belong to the genus *Theropithecus*. The name for these specimens should thus be changed from *Dinopithecus* to *Theropithecus*.

Arambourg's separation of the Omo specimens from specimens of *Theropithecus* (=*Simopithecus*) *oswaldi*, although based on little evidence at the time, has subsequently proved correct (see Andrews 1916; Hopwood 1936; Jolly 1972; Leakey and Whitworth 1958; and Leakey and Leakey 1973a for a discussion of *T. oswaldi*, and Broom and Jensen 1946; Freedman 1957; Maier 1970; and Singer 1962 for a discussion of a closely related if not identical form from South Africa). The present expedition has recovered a number of cranial specimens that preserve the facial region, and these show striking differences from both *T. gelada* and *T. oswaldi*. Both males and females of *T. brumpti* show well-developed maxillary ridges that are not seen in either of these species. Furthermore, the anterior part of the zygomatic arch has a morphology different from all other cercopithecoids. Whereas in other cercopithecoids the inferior margin of the zygomatic arch runs slightly superiorly, laterally, and smoothly posteriorly from its attachment on the maxilla, that of *T. brumpti* runs strongly superiorly, anteriorly, and laterally before it swings medially to join the temporal portion of the zygomatic arch in the normal way. This produces a "winged" anterior zygomatic with very large areas of attachment for the masseter muscle that is situated far more anteriorly and laterally than that of *T. gelada* or *T. oswaldi*, or of any other cercopithecoid, for that matter. This zygomatic arch structure is seen on both males and females of *T. brumpti*, although it is less strongly developed in the females. In other aspects of the skull morphology, however, *T. brumpti* strongly resembles the genus *Theropithecus*. The dental morphology is very similar to both of the other species of the genus, although there is no evidence of reduction in the anterior teeth as seen in later *T. oswaldi*. The mandibles have the basic *Theropithecus* structure, and the relationship of the calvarium to the face is essentially the same as it is in both *T. gelada* and *T. oswaldi*. The separation of the Omo species at the species level from these species is certainly warranted. Their inclusion in the genus *Theropithecus* is based on important similarities of dental, cranial, and mandibular morphology to the two other species of the genus.

Although it is easy to separate specimens of *Theropithecus brumpti* and *T. oswaldi* when they preserve the superior parts of the maxillae or the zygomatic arches, there are no obvious differences between the morphologies of the teeth of these two species. Preliminary quantitative analysis of the isolated teeth indicates that there may very well be two populations of *Theropithecus* present in the Shungura Formation which exhibit slight morphological differences that cannot be explained by sexual dimorphism. It would be surprising if

T. oswaldi did not regularly occur in the Shungura Formation, since it is the dominant baboon at East Rudolf, which is only 90 air miles away, and one of the above populations may in fact represent *T. oswaldi*. Until further quantitative analysis has been completed to determine if there are consistent morphological differences between *T. brumpti* and *T. oswaldi* in dental morphology, only cranial specimens (20 specimens thus far) exhibiting the above-mentioned maxillary and zygomatic structures will be assigned to *T. brumpti*. To date only one partial cranium has been recovered from Omo Group deposits that can be definitely assigned to *T. oswaldi*. This specimen, only recently found, is from Member G and is not included in the tables.

Specimens of the genus *Theropithecus* have been found at both localities in the Usno Formation and at localities in all members of the Shungura Formation except the Basal Member and Member K. They thus range in age from slightly more than 2.9 m.y. to about 0.9 m.y. Cranial fragments that can definitely be assigned to *T. brumpti* have been recovered from localities in members C through G of the Shungura Formation and thus range in age from 2.6 m.y. to slightly less than 1.8 m.y. *T. oswaldi* has been recovered from many Pliocene and Pleistocene sites in East and South Africa and very probably from Ternifine in North Africa. In contrast to this widespread distribution, *T. brumpti* seems to have been restricted to the Rudolf basin for all of its existence. The only other identifiable specimens of this species, four cranial fragments that have been recovered from deposits other than those of the Omo Group, are from the Kubi Algi Formation at East Rudolf.

Variability in Numbers of Specimens Recovered from Each Member

As noted above, there is a wide range in the numbers of specimens recovered from each of the members of the Shungura Formation. The amount of exposure of each of the members varies considerably. One may therefore ask if the variability by member in the numbers of recovered specimens merely reflects the amount of exposure of each of the members or if other factors have contributed to the variability in these numbers. If the variability in numbers of recovered specimens is caused only by the variability in the amount of exposure of the members, then the division of the number of specimens from each member by the total area of exposure of each member will produce a number that is independent of area of exposure. In other words, if the variability by member in numbers of recovered specimens is determined only by the variability in the area of exposure, then the densities of recovered specimens should be the same for all members.

De Heinzelin has mapped, at a scale of 1:10,000, all the exposures of each of the members in the "Type Area" of the Shungura Formation. It is possible, with the aid of a planimeter, to determine the areas of these exposures for each of the members. The Basal Member and Member A are exposed only in the southern part of the "Type Area," and their total areas were determined. Members B through G are exposed in both the northern and southern parts of the "Type Area"; the areas of exposure were determined only for the portion of these members exposed in the northern part of this area. At the time the areas of exposure were measured, mapping information on members H through L was not complete; thus the areas of these three members were not determined. The first row of figures in table 3 presents the areas of exposure in square inches on the map for each of the members as qualified above. The second row of figures presents the transformation of square inches on the map to square kilometers on the ground.

Because of the qualifications in the area of exposure determinations mentioned above,

only taxonomically identified specimens found in the measured areas are used in the following discussion. These factors explain the differences in numbers of specimens listed in
table 2 and table 3. A quick inspection of the figures in the fourth row of table 3 indicates that cercopithecoid specimens are not found in equal densities from member to member.
The densities for the Basal Member and Member A should be treated with caution because the
small areas of exposure of these members probably do not allow the collection of a representative sample; the figures for members B through G are probably far more reliable.

Table 3
Numbers and Densities of Taxonomically Identified Specimens by Member

	Mb. G	Mb. F	Mb. E	Mb. D	Mb. C	Mb. B	Mb. A	Basal Mb.	Total
Area on map (in^2)	68.19	22.29	23.09	28.47	38.86	4.61	1.27	.42	187.20
Area on ground (km^2)	4.40	1.44	1.49	1.84	2.51	.30	.08	.03	12.09
Total no. of specimens	174	93	84	72	409	110	6	1	949
Density	2.55	4.17	3.64	2.53	10.52	23.86	4.72	2.38	--
Colobinae specimens	23	2	1	2	7	12	1	1	49
Density	.34	.09	.04	.07	.18	2.60	.79	2.38	--
Cercopithecinae specimens	151	91	83	70	402	98	5	--	900
Density	2.21	4.08	3.59	2.46	10.34	21.26	3.93	--	--
Papio specimens	17	6	16	3	10	4	1	--	57
Density	.25	.27	.69	.11	.26	.86	.79	--	--
Theropithecus specimens	133	81	65	67	384	76	4	--	810
Density	1.95	3.63	2.82	2.35	9.88	16.49	3.15	--	--

Member B obviously has the highest density of cercopithecoids. The density decreases
rapidly in members C and D, recovers slightly in members E and F, and declines again in
Member G. Since Member G contains lacustrine deposits (units G-14 to G-22) that are generally poor in mammalian fauna and do not occur in members B through F, the density figures
for Member G are probably slightly underestimated. This underestimation is probably not
greater than 10%, however, and thus does not significantly alter the results.

If the cercopithecoid sample is divided into colobines and cercopithecines, the distribution of densities between these two subfamilies seems to behave in slightly different
ways. Beyond the obvious fact that cercopithecines are found in higher densities than
colobines and that in both cases Member B has the highest densities of remains, the colobine density falls off much more rapidly from Member B to Member C, hits its low point in
Member E, and makes a rather strong recovery in Member G. In contrast, the cercopithecine
density declines more slowly from its high point in Member B to its low point in Member D,
recovers slightly to a second high point in Member F, and declines again in Member G.

Unfortunately, the small sample size of the colobines makes the significance of these differences hard to determine. It is possible to look at the differences in densities between the genera *Papio* and *Theropithecus* (the samples of "small Papionini" and *Cercopithecus* are hopelessly small). Specimens of genus *Papio* are obviously found in lower densities than specimens of genus *Theropithecus*, and again both are found in highest densities in Member B. The change in densities through members B through G seems to follow a similar pattern in the two genera; however, *Papio* reaches its second high point in Member E, whereas *Theropithecus* reaches it in Member F. Again, as in the comparison of colobines and cercopithecines, the small sample size of *Papio* makes it difficult to interpret the significance of the differences between *Papio* and *Theropithecus*. It is interesting that of the 17 cranial specimens identified as *T. brumpti* from the northern part of the Shungura Formation, 13 are from Member C and only one each from members D, E, F, and G.

By inspecting table 3, it is possible to answer the question posed at the beginning of this section with a confident no. The observed variability in numbers of specimens recovered from the different members is not caused only by variation in the size of the area of exposure. Although it is fairly easy to answer this, the question of what "other factors" have contributed to this variability is more difficult. Three immediately come to mind. First, the observed variation may be caused by differences in sampling technique from member to member. An attempt was made from the beginning of the expedition to collect all exposures of each member that occur in the northern part of the Shungura Formation (members B through G) with equal intensity, and all cercopithecoid specimens that were found were collected. Certain areas of exposure of each of the members have subsequently been resurveyed, and in most cases far fewer specimens were found on the second survey. This indicates that the first survey was relatively thorough and probably recovered a representative sample of specimens from all exposed members. Sampling vagaries undoubtedly contribute to the observed variability of specimen numbers, but it is unlikely that this is of major significance.

A second factor to be considered is the rate of preservation of specimens both at their deposition and at their subsequent erosion onto the modern land surface. No attempt has yet been made to investigate this problem, but in the future the analysis of specimens recovered from localities which differ in sedimentary structure may help solve it. Since most of the numbers of specimens in table 3 are based on teeth and since teeth seem to be well preserved in most sedimentary situations in the Omo Group deposits, this factor may not contribute significantly to variability as long as teeth are the basis of analysis. This is definitely not true for other skeletal parts, and their analysis will have to consider this problem in some detail.

The third factor that may have contributed to the variability in numbers of cercopithecoid specimens recovered is past environmental conditions. If the environmental conditions changed during the deposition of the Shungura Formation, this should be reflected in the numbers and proportions of cercopithecoid specimens recovered from different members. This would be especially true if changing environmental conditions caused either a change in the absolute number of cercopithecoids living in the region or a change in relationships of the river to the distribution of habitats favorable to cercopithecoid adaptation so that rates of preservation at the time of deposition were changed. Three types of information independent of the cercopithecoid specimens themselves do tend to indicate that such a climatic change did take place. First, there is evidence from sedimentary studies (de Heinzelin and Haesaerts, this symposium) that depositional processes changed significantly

between members B and D. The most developed soils are found in Member B, and the degree of
soil development decreases rather continuously into Member D. De Heinzelin and Haesaerts
have interpreted this change as being due in part to a reduction in local precipitation.
Second, Bonnefille (1972, and pers. comm.) has found a change in pollen spectra between
early members (B and C) and a later member (F) that tends to indicate a reduction in the
numbers and frequency of woody species in the region. This may also indicate a reduction
in local precipitation. Third, a brief analysis of the numbers of genera of bovid specimens recovered from members C and G (members with the largest samples) indicates an increase of 2 or 3 times the numbers of genera found in large numbers in Member G over Member
C. Although the task of environmental reconstruction by analyzing sedimentary structures
and the distribution of floral and faunal remains between members has just begun and much
more work is needed, there seems to be evidence of important environmental change in the
lower Omo basin during the deposition of the Shungura Formation. If this environmental
change can be documented, it may prove to be one of the major factors contributing to the
variation in numbers of cercopithecoid specimens recovered from each member.

Summary

A large number of cercopithecoid fossil specimens have been recovered from the Usno
and Shungura formations of the Omo Group deposits during the 1967 to 1972 field seasons of
the international Omo Research Expedition. These specimens range in age from slightly
greater than 3.0 m.y. to about 0.9 m.y.

Specimens of both subfamilies of the Cercopithecoidea have been recovered, the Cercopithecinae forming a much larger part of the sample than do the Colobinae. The colobines
are represented by at least 3 and probably 4 different groups of specimens. Since most of
these specimens are isolated teeth, the groups are determined by size. The smallest size
group, recovered from the top of the Shungura Formation, consists of two specimens which
are about the size of the smaller members of modern genus *Colobus* and probably belong to
this genus. The second size group consists of a small number of isolated teeth from the
lower part of the Shungura Formation. These teeth are slightly larger than those of the
largest members of the modern genus *Colobus*; the taxonomic affinities at the genus level of
this group are as yet undetermined. The third size group consists of a nearly complete
cranium, several mandible fragments, and a series of isolated teeth recovered from the Usno
Formation and most members of the Shungura Formation. These specimens are considerably
larger than modern genus *Colobus* and probably represent a new genus of colobine. The
largest size group of specimens consists of a mandible fragment, a maxilla fragment, and a
number of isolated teeth recovered from members C through G of the Shungura Formation.
These specimens are similar in size to the modern anubis baboon of East Africa; their affinities at the genus level have not yet been determined.

The cercopithecine specimens represent 4 and possibly 5 genera. Seven specimens of
the genus *Cercopithecus* have been recovered from the Usno Formation and members B, G, and
J of the Shungura Formation. These specimens are similar in size and morphology to several
species of the genus living in East Africa today. Small Papionini of undetermined generic
affinities seem to be represented by two size groups. The smaller of these size groups consists of a small number of isolated teeth recovered from the Usno Formation and members B
and C of the Shungura Formation. These specimens may have affinities to genus *Cercocebus*.
The larger size group consists of a mandible fragment and a series of isolated teeth recovered from the Usno Formation and most members of the Shungura Formation. These specimens

may have affinities to the genus *Parapapio* or perhaps to genus *Papio*. The recovery of more complete specimens of small Papionini will be necessary in order to determine their taxonomic affinities at the genus level. The genus *Papio* is represented by two maxillary fragments, two mandible fragments, and a series of isolated teeth recovered from the Usno Formation and most members of the Shungura Formation. The affinities of these specimens to the genus *Papio* are clear; but their affinities at the species level are still obscure. The genus *Theropithecus* is represented by a large number of specimens from the Usno Formation and most members of the Shungura Formation. Most of the specimens are isolated teeth, although a fair number of relatively complete cranial and mandibular specimens have been found. At present, only specimens that preserve the superior portion of the maxilla or the zygomatic arch have been assigned to *T. brumpti* (=*Dinopithecus brumpti* of Arambourg). The majority of the specimens that can be assigned to *T. brumpti* have been recovered from Member C of the Shungura Formation. Specimens assignable to *T. oswaldi* also occur in the Shungura Formation. The identification of this species is based on the size and morphology of some of the isolated teeth recovered from members F and G and a partial cranium from Member G.

The numbers of specimens recovered from the members of the Shungura Formation vary over a wide range. Analysis of the densities of the specimens from members B through G indicates that this is probably not due to variation in the size of the areas of exposure of the members. Analysis of sedimentary data and preliminary analysis of the distribution of floral and faunal remains from the Shungura Formation indicates that significant environmental changes may have taken place in the lower Omo basin during the deposition of the Omo Group deposits. Thus, environmental change may be an important factor contributing to the variation in numbers of cercopithecoid specimens recovered from each member.

Acknowledgments

The cooperation of the governments of Ethiopia and Kenya in making possible research in the lower Omo basin is gratefully acknowledged. Similar thanks are due to the National Science Foundation and the Wenner-Gren Foundation for Anthropological Research, who gave financial assistance. I thank Professor P. V. Tobias and the Department of Anatomy, the University of Witswatersrand, South Africa; Dr. C. K. Brain and the Transvaal Museum, South Africa; and Dr. Meave Leakey and the National Museums of Kenya for their cooperation when I compared the Omo specimens with specimens from other sites housed in these institutions.

References

Andrews, C. W. 1916. Note on a new baboon (*Simopithecus oswaldi, gen. et sp. nov.*) from the (?) Pliocene of British East Africa. *Ann. Mag. Nat. Hist.*, ser. 8, 18:410-19.

Arambourg, C. 1947. *Mission Scientifique de l'Omo 1932-33.* Vol. 1. *Géologie-Anthropologie,* fasc. 3, Mémoire, Muséum national d'histoire naturelle (Paris).

Bonnefille, R. 1972. Associations polliniques actuelles et quarternaires en Ethiopie (vallées de l'Awash et de l'Omo). Thesis, Paris.

Broom, R. 1937. On some new Pleistocene mammals from limestone caves of the Transvaal. *S. African J. Sci.* 33:750-68.

————. 1940. The South African Pleistocene cercopithecid apes. *Ann. Transvaal Museum* 20:89-100.

Broom, R., and Jensen, J. S. 1946. A new fossil baboon from the caves at Potgietersrust. *Ann. Transvaal Museum* 20:337-40.

Brown, F. H. 1971. Radiometric dating of sedimentary formations in the lower Omo valley, wouthern Ethiopia. In *Calibration of hominoid evolution*, ed. W. W. Bishop and J. A. Miller, pp. 273-87. Toronto: University of Toronto Press.

Brown, F., and Lajoie, K. R. 1971. Radiometric age determinations on Pliocene/Pleistocene formations in the lower Omo basin, southern Ethiopia. *Nature* 229:483-85.

Eck, G. G., and Howell, F. C. 1972. New fossil *Cercopithecus* material from lower Omo basin, Ethiopia. *Folia Primatol.* 18(5-6):325-55.

Freedman, L. 1957. The fossil Cercopithecoidea of South Africa. *Ann. Transvaal Museum* 23(2):121-262.

_____. 1960. Some new cercopithecoid specimens from Makapansgat, South Africa. *Palaeontol. Africana* 7:7-46.

_____. 1965. Fossil and subfossil primates from the limestone deposits at Taung, Bolt's farm and Witkrans, South Africa. *Palaeontol. Africana* 9:19-48.

Freedman, L, and Stenhouse, N. S. 1972. The *Parapapio* species of Sterkfontein, Transvaal, South Africa. *Palaeontol. Africana* 14:93-111.

Heinzelin, J. de; Brown, F. H.; and Howell, F. C. 1970. Pliocene/Pleistocene formations in the lower Omo basin, southern Ethiopia. *Quarternaria* 13:247-68.

Hopwood, A. T. 1936. New and little-known fossil mammals from the Pleistocene of Kenya Colony and Tanganyika Territory. *Ann. Mag. Nat. Hist.*, ser. 10, 17:636-41.

Howell, F. C.; Fichter, L. S.; and Eck, G. G. 1969. Vertebrate assemblages from the Usno Formation, White Sands and Brown Sands localities, lower Omo basin, Ethiopia. *Quarternaria* 11:65-88.

Jolly, C. J. 1972. The classification and natural history of *Theropithecus (Simopithecus)* (Andrews, 1916), baboons of the African Plio-Pleistocene. *Bull. Brit. Museum Geol.* 22(1);1-123.

Leakey, L. S. B., and Whitworth, T. 1958. Notes on the genus *Simopithecus*, with a description of a new species from Olduvai. *Coryndon Mem. Museum Occasional Papers*, no. 6.

Leakey, M. G., and Leakey, R. E. F. 1973*a*. Further evidence of *Simopithecus* (Mammalia, Primates) from Olduvai and Olorgesailie. In *Fossil vertebrates of Africa*, ed. L. S. B. Leakey, R. J. Savage, and S. C. Coryndon, 3:101-20. London: Academic Press.

_____. 1973 . New **large** Pleistocene Colobinae (Mammalia, Primates) from East Africa. In *Fossil vertebrates of Africa*, ed. L. S. B. Leakey, R. J. Savage, and S. C. Coryndon, 3:121-38. London: Academic Press.

Leakey, R. E. F. 1969. New Cercopithecidae from the Chemeron beds of Lake Baringo, Kenya. In *Fossil vertebrates of Africa*, ed. L. S. B. Leakey and R. J. Savage, 1:53-69. London: Academic Press.

Maier, W. 1970. New fossil Cercopithecoidea from the lower Pleistocene cave deposits of the Makapansgat Limeworks, South Africa. *Palaeontol. Africana* 3:69-107.

Singer, R. 1962. *Simopithecus* from Hopefield, South Africa. *Bibliotheca Primatol.*1:43-70.

Postscript

Since the above was written, more than 2,500 additional cercopithecoid specimens from Omo Group deposits have become available for study. Some were recovered during the 1974 field season; the rest were collected during previous field seasons by the French contingent of the expedition and have only recently been unpacked. The number of cercopithecoid specimens recovered from Omo Group deposits now totals just over 6,000.

All of the additional specimens have been identified as to body part and taxon. No new taxa were discovered among these. Unfortunately, I have not yet had the opportunity either to collate this new information with that of the sample described above or to produce new counts and frequency tabulations. However, the impression is that when this is done the absolute counts of body parts and specimens assigned to the various taxa will increase substantially, whereas the relative frequencies between taxa and through time will change very little.

31. CERCOPITHECOIDEA OF THE EAST RUDOLF SUCCESSION

M. G. Leakey

Introduction

The Cercopithecoidea generally inhabit a forested environment. Reconstruction of the paleoenvironment at East Rudolf suggests that the forest was limited and probably always riverine (see Behrensmeyer, this symposium); so it is not surprising that with the exception of *Theropithecus oswaldi*, representatives of the Cercopithecoidea are rare elements of the fossil fauna. *Theropithecus oswaldi* appears to have adapted to a lakeshore, savanna type of environment and is commonly represented in the faunal assemblages of Pleistocene lake-shores.

A faunal list is given in table 1, together with the number of specimens recovered for each taxon, the areas of recovery, and the faunal zones (after Maglio 1972). Taxa labeled (A), (B), etc. correspond to taxa labeled the same way from the Omo (Eck, this symposium); a list showing the relative occurrence of the Cercopithecoid taxa at the two localities is given in table 2.

The specimens discussed were all collected by expeditions led by Richard Leakey during 1968-73 inclusive.

Order Primates

Superfamily Cercopithecoidea

Family Cercopithecidae

Subfamily Colobinae

Genus *Cercopithecoides* Mollet

Cercopithecoides sp. nov.

Material. 7 cranial specimens including 2 relatively complete female crania.

Horizon. The Lower Member of the Koobi Fora Formation.

Discussion. This is the first record in East Africa of this previously monotypic genus known from South Africa. The East African species, although showing the characteristics of *Cercopithecoides*, appears to be considerably larger than the South African species *C. williamsi*, which is larger than any living *Colobus*.

345

Table 1

Faunal List with Areas of Occurrence and Faunal Zones (after Maglio 1972) for Each Taxon

Taxon	Faunal Zone	Area of Occurrence									
		1	3	6	6A	7	7A	8	8A	10	11
Colobinae											
Cercopithecoides sp. nov.	3										
Colobinae gen. et sp. nov.	3										
Colobinae gen. et sp. indet. (B)	2, 3										
Colobus sp.	1, 2	X						X	X		
Cercopithecinae											
Cercopithecus cf. *aethiops*	2										
Cercopithecus sp. (A)	?4										
Cercocebus sp.	1, 2, 3	X	X	X	X			X	X		
Small Papionini (B)	?2, 3										
Papio sp.	3										
Theropithecus oswaldi	1, 2, 3	X	X	X	X	X	X	X	X	X	X
Theropithecus brumpti	4										

NOTE: 1 = *Loxodonta africana* zone;

2 = *Metridiochoerus andrewsi* zone;

3 = *Mesochoerus limnetes* zone;

4 = *Notochoerus capensis* zone.

These specimens are all from below the KBS Tuff in areas 105 and 131. *Cercopithecoides* has not been recorded from the Omo.

Genus and Species Nov.

Gen. et sp. nov.

Material. 5 specimens, including a female cranium and mandible and a mandible with associated postcranial elements.

Horizon. The Lower Member of the Koobi Fora Formation.

Discussion. This taxon is also represented at the Omo, where an almost complete male skull and a male mandible from above Tuff G have been described (Leakey and Leakey 1973). The mandibular and cranial morphology contrast significantly with both *Paracolobus* and *Cercopithecoides*. The affinities between these three genera of large colobines remain obscure. As with *Cercopithecoides*, this genus has so far only been recovered from below the KBS Tuff in areas 105 and 131.

Genus and Species Indet.

Gen. et sp. indet. (B)

Material. 2 mandibular fragments.

Horizon. Lower and Upper members of the Koobi Fora Formation.

Discussion. A colobine which is considerably larger than extant *Colobus*, but significantly smaller than the two large colobines described above, also appears to be present. This colobine appears to be absent at the Omo.

Table 1 (Continued)

12	101	102	103	104	105	106	121	123	124	125	130	131	203	204	Number of Specimens
					X			X		X	X	X			7
					X						X	X			5
				X								X			2
			X												4
		X	X												2
													X		1
				X								X			27
						X					X				2
												X			5
X	X	X	X	X	X	X	X	X	X	X	X	X			300
													X	X	4

Genus *Colobus* Illiger

Colobus sp.

Material. 3 cranial specimens and 1 postcranial specimen.

Horizon. The Ileret Member and Upper Member of the Koobi Fora Formation.

Discussion. These specimens are too fragmentary for specific identification. The dentition of the cranial specimens and morphology of the maxillary specimen suggest affinities with the extant red colobus, *C. badius*. A small species of *Colobus* is also present at the Omo.

Subfamily Cercopithecinae

Genus *Cercopithecus* Linnaeus

Cercopithecus cf. *aethiops* Linnaeus

Material. 2 specimens including a femur and a lower molar.

Horizon. The Upper Member of the Koobi Fora Formation.

Discussion. *Cercopithecus* is rarely found in the fossil record; it is absent at Olduvai, but it has been recorded from the Omo (Eck and Howell 1972). The dentition among the various species of *Cercopithecus* is very uniform, whereas the postcranial long bones are somewhat more variable and easier to identify. The vervet monkey, *C. aethiops*, is adapted for a savanna habitat, and this is reflected to a certain extent in the morphology of the femur.

Cercopithecus sp. (A)

Material. Mandibular fragment with M_2, M_3.

Horizon. ? Koobi Algi Formation.

Discussion. This specimen is of a very small monkey, slightly larger than a talapoin. It

Table 2

Comparison of the Occurrence of the Cercopithecoid Taxa at the Omo and East Rudolf

Taxon	Omo Valley	East Rudolf
Colobinae		
Cercopithecoides sp. nov.	-	+
Colobinae gen. et sp. nov.	+	+
Colobinae gen. et sp. indet. (A)	+	-
Colobinae gen. et sp. indet. (B)	-	+
Colobinae gen. et sp. indet. (C)	+	-
Colobus sp.	+	+
Cercopithecinae		
Cercopithecus cf. aethiops	-	+
Cercopithecus sp. (A)	-	+
Cercopithecus sp. (B)[1]	+	-
Small Papionini (A)/Cercocebus	+	+
Small Papionini (B)	+	+
Papio sp.	+	+
Theropithecus oswaldi	?	+
Theropithecus brumpti	+	+

NOTE: This table was compiled with the help of Gerald Eck.

[1] This taxon may be the same as Cercopithecus cf. aethiops from East Rudolf.

is clearly distinct from the Cercopithecus material recovered from higher in the sequence.

Genus Cercocebus Geoffrey

Cercocebus sp.

Material. 11 cranial specimens and 16 specimens of isolated teeth (single and associated).

Horizon. The Lower, Upper and Ileret members of the Koobi Fora Formation

Discussion. Only 1 specimen of a fossil Cercocebus has previously been described, C. ado from a partial mandible from Laetolil. The majority of the specimens from East Rudolf are from closely related areas at Ileret.

The East Rudolf Cercocebus was slightly larger than the largest of the extant mangabeys, C. torquatus. The incisors are characteristically large, although compared with the molar size they are relatively smaller than in C. torquatus.

Genus Indet.

Small Papionini (B)

Material. 2 cranial specimens.

Horizon. The Lower and ? Upper Members of the Koobi Fora Formation.

Discussion. These two specimens suggest the presence of an intermediate-sized species of Papionini. The evidence, however, is very tentative at present.

Genus Papio Erxleben

Papio sp.

Material. 4 mandibular specimens and 1 maxillary specimen.

Horizon. The Lower Member of the Koobi Fora Formation.

Discussion. These specimens, which are all from Area 131, show close affinities with extant *Papio* in size and morphology. The maxillary specimen indicates that the muzzle may have been relatively short. *Papio* sp. has been recorded from the Omo (Eck, this symposium). An unusual cranium showing affinities with *Papio* has been recovered from Olduvai.

Genus *Theropithecus* Geoffrey

Theropithecus oswaldi (Andrews).

Material. More than 300 specimens including cranial and postcranial elements.

Horizon. Various horizons throughout the Koobi Fora Formation.

Discussion. This species, originally described as *Simopithecus* but subsequently included within *Theropithecus* (Jolly 1970), is well known in the Pleistocene fauna of East Africa. The large number of *Theropithecus* specimens recovered at East Rudolf illustrates the predominance of this genus within the Cercopithecoidea at that time. Today, the genus *Theropithecus* is represented by only one species, *T. gelada*, with a habitat restricted to the Ethiopian highlands.

The evidence from East Rudolf and from other sites suggests that *T. oswaldi* shows certain evolutionary trends which should make this species useful for faunal correlation. There is a general increase in size with time, the molars become relatively larger, the anterior teeth relatively smaller, and the cusp pattern on the molars more complex. The cranium shows a reduction in muzzle length and the mandible an increase in height of the ascending ramus. The specimens from East Rudolf are at present too incomplete for these trends to be quantified, although the contrast between specimens from the Lower and the Upper members of the Koobi Fora Formation is obvious.

Theropithecus brumpti (Arambourg)

Material. 4 cranial specimens.

Horizon. The Kubi Algi Formation.

Discussion. This species is the predominant species of *Theropithecus* at the Omo. Although the dentition in *T. brumpti* and *T. oswaldi* appears very similar, the cranial morphology is clearly distinct. Some of the more fragmentary East Rudolf specimens referred to *T. oswaldi* may be misidentified, but *T. brumpti* was clearly not common. On the present evidence it appears that *T. brumpti* occurs only in the Kubi Algi Formation and *T. oswaldi* occurs only in the Koobi Fora Formation.

Conclusion

The Cercopithecoidea (with the exception of *Theropithecus oswaldi*) have not yet been found to be useful for faunal correlation. This is largely because they rarely occur in most fossil assemblages. *Theropithecus oswaldi* shows evolutionary trends which make it useful for correlation both within East Rudolf and with other Pleistocene sites.

The Cercopithecoidea are, however, useful indicators of the paleoenvironment, since they are generally confined to a specific habitat. Among the Cercopithecoidea living today in East Africa, species of *Colobus* are the most fully arboreal; the stomach is adapted for a diet of leaves and the limbs for arboreal locomotion. Extant species of *Cercocebus* are also restricted to a forest environment. Thus the recovery of both *Colobus* and *Cercocebus* from areas 1, 8, and 8A provides good evidence that these areas were forested. The large number of *Cercocebus* recovered from Area 8 reduces the possibility that the bones found there were transported before fossilization.

The habitat of the large colobines is uncertain. Only one specimen which includes postcranial elements has been recovered from East Rudolf; the morphology of these bones indicates arboreal locomotion. *Papio* today is found in both savanna and forest habitats. However, the frequent occurrence of *Theropithecus oswaldi* in the open savanna surrounding lakeshores, and the absence of *Papio* in this habitat, suggests that during the Plio-Pleistocene *Papio* may have been restricted to a forest environment. The occurrence of *Papio* and the large colobine referred to Colobinae gen. et sp. nov., always below the KBS Tuff and only in areas 105, 130, and 131, may reflect the paleoenvironment, but it may also relate to the age of the deposits.

Today *Cercopithecus aethiops* tends to inhabit a savanna environment. But the evidence for this species in areas 102 and 103 is somewhat tentative.

The common occurrence of *Theropithecus oswaldi* throughout the sequence and from almost every collecting area reflects the wide distribution of this species. *T. brumpti*, which appears to be common at the Omo but is certainly represented only by four specimens at East Rudolf (all from the Kubi Algi Formation), was probably more restricted and specialized in its habitat.

Much of the cercopithecoid material is fragmentary, and so it is sometimes hard to make accurate taxonomic assignations. Table 2, which was compiled with the help of Gerald Eck, shows the comparatively different cercopithecoid fauna occurring at the Omo and at East Rudolf. Among the Colobinae only two taxa appear to occur in both localities, whereas among the Cercopithecinae four are common to both localities. The relatively few occurrences of common taxa in a group which in general is habitat-specific appears to emphasize the very different paleoecology of the two sites.

Acknowledgments

I am grateful to the Museum Trustees of Kenya for making the study of the East Rudolf material possible, and to the sponsors of the East Rudolf Research Project: the National Geographic Society, the National Science Foundation, and the Donner Foundation. I should also like to thank Gerald Eck, with whom I have had many useful discussions about the cercopithecoid material.

This is paper no. 65 in the East Rudolf Project catalogue of publications.

References

Eck, G. G., and Howell, F. C. 1972. New fossil *Cercopithecus* material from the Lower Omo Basin, Ethiopia. *Folia Primat.* 18:325-55.

Jolly, C. J. 1970. The large African monkeys as an adaptive array. In *Old World monkeys; Evolution, systematics, and behaviour*, ed. J. R. Napier and P. H. Napier. New York: Academic Press.

Leakey, M. G., and Leakey, R. E. F. 1973. New large Pleistocene Colobinae (Mammalia, Primates) from East Africa. In *Fossil vertebrates of Africa*, ed. L. S. B. Leakey, R. J. Savage, and S. C. Coryndon, 3:121-38. London: Academic Press.

Maglio, V. J. 1972. Vertebrate fauna and chronology of hominid-bearing sediments east of Lake Rudolf, Kenya. *Nature* 239:379-85.

32.   FOSSIL REMAINS OF MICROMAMMALS FROM THE OMO GROUP DEPOSITS

J.-J. Jaeger and H. B. Wesselman

The Lake Rudolf basin has recently become the focal point for a remarkable intensifi-
cation of interdisciplinary studies. This activity was stimulated by the need for fuller
evidence on the origin and evolution of early man in Africa. Large samples of well-
preserved fossil hominids, in association with vertebrate faunas, are being recovered from
the Pliocene/Pleistocene formations within the Lake Rudolf basin which, including Kanapoi
and Lothagam, span a range of time from less than 1 m.y. to more than 5.5 m.y. The work
of those participating in this symposium has shown that this range of time is of critical
importance to understanding the emergence of a modern African fauna as well as the emergence of *Homo*, and considerable emphasis has been placed upon the need for paleoenvironmental reconstruction.

Stimulated by this need, J.-J. Jaeger made an effort to recover microvertebrate fossils from the Shungura Formation in the 1970 and 1973 field seasons. Microfauna is poorly
represented or absent from most of the Pliocene/Pleistocene fossil localities of East
Africa, Olduvai Gorge and Laetolil being notable exceptions.

The search for microfaunal remains was continued by H. B. Wesselman during the 1972
and 1973 field seasons. Working closely with J. de Heinzelin, he had test samples from
fossil localities within the Shungura and Usno Formations screen washed and hand sorted in
the field. The test samples averaged about 250 lb each and were treated with kerosene to
disperse adhering clays and silts, a method found highly successful. After the washing,
dried residues were examined for microfauna. In this manner more than 30 fossil microvertebrates were recovered from 6 members of the Shungura Formation and they are still
being recovered. These members are: Member B (Unit B-2 and B-10-3 from Locality 1 North),
Member C (Omo 18), Member F (L. 398, Omo 33, and L. 28), Member G (Omo 141, Unit G-3 and
P. 939, Unit G-20), Member J (L. P. 994), and Member L (L. F. 197 in the Kalam West exposures). The samples from F. 197, P. 994, and P. 939 are small, represented only by a few
teeth. Concentrated residues from B-2 (L. 793), Omo 18, Omo 33, and Omo 141 are currently
being sorted. L. 28 has just been found to contain microfauna. In all, more than 30 tons
of sediment have been processed.

The scarcity of microfaunal remains in eastern African deposits of Pliocene/
Pleistocene age and the association of the Omo group formations with many tuffs dated by
K-Ar make these fossil assemblages of considerable interest. A series of microvertebrate
assemblages obtained from demonstrably early ranges of time could be critically important

for the solution of a number of biostratigraphic, paleoclimatic, and biogeographic problems, some of which may have direct relevance to the early phases of hominid evolution.

Table 1 reflects our present state of knowledge about the micromammals and demonstrates their distribution within the Omo group deposits. The specific designations include a cf. pending the appearance of the papers dealing with the detailed systematics of the various groups. As can be observed, the most important collections come from Member B and Member F. This chapter will deal with those two assemblages. Most of the specimens consist only of single teeth, although some maxillary and mandible fragments contain tooth rows.

Micromammals from Member B, Shungura Formation

The largest sample from Member B comes from L. 1 North, Unit B-10-3, which has been dated by K-Ar at 2.94 m.y. It consists of a spread of poorly sorted gravel with concentrations of fossil bone, including teeth of primates, hominids, and micromammals. De Heinzelin (pers. comm.) feels that this heterogeneous accumulation may represent material that was washed from the slope of a paleo-land surface composed of Unit B-9. As of September 1973, 9 tons of this deposit have been screen washed. Unless otherwise designated, all of the following fossils come from B-10-3.

Rodentia

Muridae

Mastomys

Eighty-five specimens are known, all of which strongly resemble a new species which has been described by Jaeger (in press) from Olduvai Bed I as *Mastomys minor*. This species is a little smaller than the living multimammate mouse, *Mastomys natalensis*, and shows some archaic features in the molars. The multimammate mouse has a wide habitat tolerance throughout Africa. It is most abundant in the vicinity of water, dense bush, and long grass and is frequently found on cultivated ground. Fossil *Mastomys* are also present at Taung, Sterkfontein, and Makapansgat Limeworks and are known from Tabun. The large representation of this species in the B-10-3 deposit may represent owl pellet accumulations.

Pelomys

Thirteen specimens represent a large murid and are morphologically close to the contemporary genus *Pelomys*, but they show characters which are unknown in any living species of this genus. These characters are present in the contemporary Asiatic genus *Golunda*, indicating a possible phylogenetic link between the two genera. Contemporary species of both are found along the banks of rivers, lakes, and swamps as well as in long grass on the outskirts of forest.

Arvicanthis

The lower molar teeth of *Pelomys* and *Arvicanthis* are very similar. With the recovery of upper teeth, it became clear that most of the material earlier considered to be *Arvicanthis* belongs in the *Pelomys* group. At present only 1 specimen from B-10-3 is assignable to *Arvicanthis*, contemporary species of which are common in grasslands and cultivated areas in Africa and Arabia.

Mus (Leggada)

One fragmentary M_1 shows very evolved characters, demonstrating that the differentiation of the *Mus (Leggada)* species is an old one. The Omo specimen is smaller but much more

Table 1

Micromammals of the Omo Group Deposits, Shungura Formation

Taxon	A	B	C	D	E	F	G	H	I	J	K	L
RODENTIA												
Muridae												
Mastomys cf. *minor*	X					X	X					
Pelomys sp.	X		X									
cf. *Oenomys* sp.			X									
Arvicanthis sp.	X						X					
Aethomys sp.						X						
Thallomys cf. *quadrilobatus*						X						
Grammomys sp.	X											
Mus (Leggada) sp.	X											
Lemniscomys sp.	X											
Muridae indet.	X		X			X	X					
Cricetidae												
Tatera sp.	X					X						X
Gerbillurus sp.						X						
Dendromus sp.						X						
Dipodidae												
Jaculus cf. *orientalis*						X						
Sciuridae												
Xerus cf. *erythropus*	X											
Xerus sp.						X						
Paraxerus cf. *ochraceus*	X					X						
Sciuridae indet.	X											
Bathyergidae												
Heterocephalus sp.						X						
Thryonomyidae												
Thryonomys cf. *swinderianus*	X					X					X	X
Hystricidae												
Xenohystrix cf. *crassidens*	X											
Hystrix cf. *makapanensis*			X		X		X					
Hystrix cf. *cristata*			X		X		X		X	X		X
CHIROPTERA												
Pteropodidae												
Eidolon cf. *helvum*	X											
Emballonuridae												
Taphozous sp.	X					X						
Coleura sp.						X						
Hipposideridae												
Hipposideros sp. A	X											
Hipposideros sp. B						X						
INSECTIVORA												
Soricidae												
Crocidura sp. A	X					X						
Crocidura sp. B	X											
Suncus cf. *infinitesimus*	X											
LAGOMORPHA												
Leporidae												
Lepus sp.						X						

Table 1 (Continued)

Taxon	Member											
	A	B	C	D	E	F	G	H	I	J	K	L
CARNIVORA												
Viverridae												
Helogale		X				X						
PRIMATES												
Lorisidae												
Galago cf. *senegalensis*	X											
Galago cf. *demidovii*	X											
Galago sp.	X											
HYRACOIDEA												
Heterohyrax sp.	X											
Gigantohyrax sp.			X									

differentiated than the new species which Jaeger has described from Olduvai Bed I.

Lemniscomys

A right M^1 represents the murid *Lemniscomys*. In size and morphology it compares well with the extant *Lemnisomys striatus* but is slightly smaller.

Cricetidae

Tatera

Seven specimens represent a small *Tatera* of the size of *Tatera vicina* found in eastern Africa today. Most modern species of *Tatera* are independent of water and are found in both open and wooded grassland and scrub. *Tatera* is also found in tropical Asia. *Tatera* has also been found from L. 793 in Unit B-2, dated at approximately 3.6 m.y.

Sciuridae

Xerus

Three specimens are morphologically very similar to the large ground squirrel *Xerus erythropus*, which is today distributed throughout tropical Africa in savanna and woodlands. The smaller *Xerus rutilus* is found only in eastern Africa today and is the contemporary form in the lower Omo valley. The fossils are considered to be *Xerus* cf. *erythropus*.

Paraxerus

Thirty teeth represent the small bush squirrel *Paraxerus*. There are at least 11 contemporary species including a predominantly savanna form (*P. cepapi*) as well as lowland and montane forest forms. The fossils most closely resemble the living *Paraxerus ochraceus*. A smaller species may also be present, represented by 1 specimen. The higher frequency of *Paraxerus* relative to *Xerus* may reflect forest near the river, with more open country being much farther away.

Thryonomyidae

Thryonomys

So far only a single upper molar has been found in the B-10-3 deposit. The large, partly amphibious cane rat today inhabits reedbeds and tall grass along riverbanks and swamps and is frequently found in areas subject to seasonal flooding.

Lorisidae

Three specimens representing fossil lorisids were recovered in the 1972 and 1973 seasons. L1-378w is a slightly rolled right M_2, as large as that of *Galago crassicaudatus*. In morphology it resembles in a general way the Miocene lorisid *Komba robustus*, comparative material of which was kindly shown to one of us (Wesselman) by A. Walker in 1972. L1-377w is a broken left maxilla with the roots of P^3, broken P^4 and M^1, and the roots of M^2. The anterior edge of the zygoma and the edge of the orbit are preserved dorsally. The specimen is in poor condition. The zygomatic region is quite robust. Enough is preserved of the molariform P^4 and M^1 to say that in size and morphology the specimen represents a *Galago* smaller than L1-378w. A right M_2 (L1-521w) was recovered in 1973 which in size and morphology strongly resembles *Galago demidovii*. Study of this material is in progress. The fossil maxilla and small right M_2 certainly belong to different taxa. L1-521w might perhaps be thought of as *Galago* cf. *demidovii* at this time, and the larger maxillary specimen as *Galago* cf. *senegalensis*. The largest taxon, L1-378w, is perhaps best considered as *Galago* sp. indet. until more material is found.

Viverridae

Helogale

Six specimens, all single teeth, strongly resemble the living dwarf mongoose *Helogale*. The material includes 2 deciduous P_4s, 2 left M_2s, 1 left M^2, and a left P^4 and is now being studied. Contemporary species of *Helogale* are found most frequently in tree savanna and moist woodlands in association with termite mounds, in which they live.

Chiroptera

Eidolon

A single upper molar of a fruitbat (Pteropodidae) has been recovered from the B-10-3 gravels. It strongly resembles the contemporary *Eidolon helvum*, which is distributed in the forested regions of Africa, Madagascar, and southwestern Arabia. The fossil seems typical and could be called *Eidolon* cf. *helvum*.

Taphozous

A right mandible fragment bearing the root of C, P_3, P_4, and M_1 and preserving part of the symphyseal area was recovered in 1972 from B-10-3. It is assignable to the genus *Taphozous* (Emballonuridae) and is slightly smaller than but probably ancestral to the contemporary *Taphozous* (*Saccolaimus*) *peli* which is the only African emballonurid with a habitat restricted to high forest. One of the largest of the Old World microchiroptera, *T. peli* is distributed in the high forest zone from Liberia through the Congo to the Nandi Forest in western Kenya and to northeastern Angola (Hayman 1967). The presence of this taxon in the B-10-3 assemblage strongly argues for a well-developed forest in the lower Omo valley at 3 m.y.

Hipposideros

Two molar teeth from B-10-3 are assignable to the genus *Hipposideros*. One specimen closely resembles the contemporary *H. camerunensis*; the other seems closer in morphology to *H. cyclops*. Where *H. camerunensis* is found (Cameroun mountains, E. Congo), it is sympatric with *H. cyclops*, which is distributed in high forest from Portuguese Guinea, through western and central Africa, to the northern Congo forest extreme eastern limits. *H. cyclops* is also found in outlying forest areas in Uganda, southwestern Kenya, and Rwanda (Hayman 1967). The presence of these fossils with the large *Taphozous* sp. not only argues strongly for a well-developed forest habitat but raises the possibility of biogeographic connection with the forests of central Africa at 3 m.y.

Insectivora (Soricidae)

Two mandible fragments and 1 isolated molar represent a large species of *Crocidura*. These specimens compare well in size and morphology with the contemporary *Crocidura doriana*, the fossil being slightly smaller. Two mandible fragments with teeth represent a medium-sized shrew, each possibly representing a different taxon. One of these may be assignable to another species of *Crocidura*.

Suncus

The other medium-sized mandible may be a member of this genus. It resembles material from Sterkfontein and Swartkrans, designated as *Suncus* sp., kindly shown to one of us (Wesselman) by C. K. Brain. Four mandible fragments with tooth rows strongly resemble the contemporary *Suncus infinitesimus*, a very small shrew. The fossils are somewhat smaller than the contemporary species. The presence of the larger shrews in the B-10-3 assemblage argues for a wet riverbank and swamp-edge habitat, whereas *Suncus* species are mostly found in savannas of various kinds. Their high frequency may also reflect owl pellet concentrations.

Micromammals from Member F, Shungura Formation

The second major concentration of micromammals occurs in Member F, from a gravel in the lower part of unit F-1-2 designated Locality 28. This locality is distinct from Omo Locality 28, a part of Locality 1 South in Upper Member B. The micromammal locality lies just above Tuff F, which is dated at about 2.04 m.y.; L. 28 has also yielded hominid teeth and derived artifacts. 3½ tons of sediment from this locality have been screen washed. Omo 33, in the silty tuffite F', has also begun to yield microfauna.

Rodentia

Muridae

Mastomys

Five isolated teeth from L. 28 represent *Mastomys minor*, and in size and morphology they fall within the range of the fossils from B-10-3 and those from Olduvai Bed I. Omo 33 has also produced specimens of *Mastomys*.

Aethomys

A large species of *Aethomys* is represented by 18 teeth which are similar in size to a large *Aethomys* in Bed I of Olduvai but differ in morphology. The Omo specimens show characters which are more highly evolved and therefore cannot be attributed to the same lineage. They possibly represent a species within the contemporary *Aethomys nyikae* group. The Olduvai *Aethomys lavocati* is the most abundant murid in Bed I. The habitat preferences of contemporary species of *Aethomys* are diverse, but occur in various types of savanna. More *Aethomys* teeth have recently been recovered from Omo 33.

Thallomys

The 6 teeth assignable to this genus strongly resemble *Thallomys quadrilobatus* from Olduvai Bed I, where it is present but not abundant. All contemporary species prefer the same habitat: they live on *Acacia* trees in both wooded and open dry savanna, although there is no information available about which species of *Acacia* they live on.

Cricetidae

Nine specimens of *Tatera* from L. 28 are virtually identical in size and morphology to the *Tatera* sp. from Member B, which speaks for stability within this lineage.

Gerbillurus

A single M^1 indicates the presence of a small gerbil. This tooth shows no indication of longitudinal crests, and so it can be referred to the genus *Gerbillurus*, a characteristic taxon from dry open savanna. The fossil is similar in morphology to the contemporary *Gerbillurus vallinus* but is much smaller.

Dendromus

A single M^2 represents a large species of *Dendromus*. Most contemporary forms of this genus are associated with dry grasslands, although *D. mesomelas* is found in bush, swamp-margin vegetation, and montane woodlands.

Dipodidae

Jaculus

This characteristic genus of the open arid savanna and semidesert is represented by one M_1 from L. 28. The fossil is similar in size and morphology to *Jaculus orientalis*, which is found in the arid open country in northern Africa. The range of the genus *Jaculus* extends across the Sahara to northern and northwestern Africa and also to central Asia. The Dipodidae are primarily an Asiatic group. Two more molars have recently been recovered from Omo 33.

Sciuridae

Xerus

The single specimen of *Xerus* is of a different species from that in Member B and also seems different from the contemporary *Xerus rutilus*. Both this specimen and one from Omo 33, also in Member F, are smaller than *Xerus erythropus*, but the crown height is higher than is found in *X. rutilus*.

Paraxerus

Paraxerus in Member F seems to be the same species as is found in Member B.

Bathyergidae

Heterocephalus

A single tooth undoubtedly belongs to a bathyergid, probably a species of *Heterocephalus*. These fossorial molerats prefer unconsolidated dry substrates in which they can dig easily, and they are usually found in open savanna and arid biotypes.

Lagomorpha

Lepus

A single tooth fragment of a large species of a leporid has been recovered at L. 28. This and a single upper molar from the excavation at L. 398, also in Lower Member F, represent the only leporid specimens from the Omo group deposits. Leporids are never common in the Pliocene/Pleistocene eastern African deposits.

Carnivora

Helogale

P^4 and an edentulous right half-mandible have been found in the L. 28 gravel. The tooth is larger than the specimen in B-10-3 and may represent a different species.

Chiroptera

Coleura

A single lower molar represents the smallest African emballonurid. The contemporary *Coleura afra* is found in varied habitats including wooded savanna, dry savanna, and semi-arid subdesertic steppe throughout Africa. The fossil is smaller than the contemporary species and may be ancestral.

Hipposideros

Three teeth strongly resemble the contemporary *Hipposideros commersoni*, which with *Taphozous peli* achieves maximum size among the Old World microchiroptera in Africa. The fossil material is very close in morphology and size to the modern condition. This species is found in varied habitats in tropical Africa ranging from lowland forest to wooded savanna and more open grassland. The fossils are a bit smaller than the contemporary species.

Discussion

A few preliminary ideas about the micromammals from the Omo group deposits can be brought forward at this time. It is very interesting that all the genera which have been found are also present in eastern Africa today. In contrast, in the northern African upper Pliocene localities, most of the fossil genera are now extinct, and very few are found in common with eastern African Pliocene/Pleistocene localities. *Mastomys*, *Pelomys*, *Grammomys*, *Xerus*, *Paraxerus*, and *Tatera* are among the most successful contemporary genera of African rodents. Their presence in the B-10-3 assemblage surely reflects their ecological success in the communities close to the river at almost 3 m.y. All the fossil rodents are very similar to modern species, although there are some slightly archaic characters in the teeth, and this confirms what has been found in Bed I at Olduvai. It is remarkable that no archaic lineage among the rodents has been found. This could be interpreted in several different ways. The sample is still small and perhaps not yet representative of the fossil communities. The fossils which have been found could be those which were most abundant. The archaic lineage(s) might therefore not be detected because of their rarity. On the other hand, it is possible that the modern rodent fauna was established in tropical Africa considerably earlier than 3 m.y. Misonne (1969) has suggested that the murids dispersed into tropical Africa during the Pontian, and we might suggest that the modern forms are derived from the initial radiation following this invasion. What we know in general about the mid-Miocene rodents from Fort Ternan is that they most closely resemble the lower Miocene rodent fossil assemblage and are very different from modern rodent communities.

The B-10-3 assemblage, the oldest dated Pliocene/Pleistocene rodent community, is essentially modern, indicating very important changes between 14 m.y. and 3 m.y. This could be explained in several ways. Perhaps the most important may have been the immigration of the murids into tropical Africa, which has been recorded for northern Africa (Jaeger and Martin 1971) during the lower Vallesian. There also may have been drastic climatic change comparable to that which occured in the Mediterranean basin (Crusafont and Villalta 1954; Tobien 1970). The interaction of these factors could easily have caused the transition from the Miocene to the modern faunas.

It could be mentioned here that most of the genera of rodents in the southern African australopithecine-bearing deposits are also modern in character. The recovery of microfaunal assemblages from other localities in eastern Africa would greatly increase resolution of these problems.

Micromammals offer unique opportunities for paleoenvironmental reconstruction and are much more local in their resolution than are palynological investigations, since fossil pollen frequently is carried great distances. The extreme rarity of microfossils within the Shungura Formation surely reflects their failure to "survive" postmortem transport of any distance. From this one might infer that fossil micromammals are derived from nearby communities, although some will obviously be transported from more distant biotypes by carnivorous birds. The relative frequency of different taxa within the fossil assemblage should give indications of proximal and distal communities. All the fossil bone from washed residues is kept for taphonomic analysis.

The B-10-3 assemblage at almost 3 m.y. is first of all characterized by an abundance of murids compared with other rodent taxa, but all suggest a wooded savanna. The bats and prosimians strongly suggest the presence within the Omo basin of a well-developed forest which may have been connected with the forests of central Africa.

The situation seems to be quite different in the L. 28 assemblage from Member F, at 2.04 m.y. Compared with 6 species of murids in Member B, only 4 are represented in Member F, of which 3 belong to different genera. By comparison, the nonmurid fauna is more diversified in Member F. The presence of *Gerbillurus*, *Jaculus*, *Heterocephalus*, and the leporid all indicate that this reflects an environmental change rather than a difference caused by field collection. New specimens recovered from Omo 33 support this conclusion. Even the murids, *Thallomys* and *Aethomys*, and the bats reflect this same change. Most of the microfauna from the L. 28 assemblage argues for the spread of open arid conditions sometime before 2 m.y. The association of derived artifacts, in situ assemblages of which have been reported by Chavaillon and by Merrick and Merrick (this symposium) within the same unit makes this evidence for environmental change of more than just passing interest.

The recovery of microfauna from the Omo group deposits has demonstrated that such small and delicate fossils are preserved within horizons of different ages even when they are unusually rare. Extensive sampling of appropriate sediments combined with an expanded processing operation can produce excellent results. The establishment of a microfaunal biostratigraphy from the deposits within the Rudolf basin could, with that of Olduvai, serve as a scale for all of eastern Africa. It might also provide a basis for comparison with the microfaunal assemblages from the australopithecine localities in southern Africa.

Acknowledgments

Appreciation is due to F. Clark Howell and Yves Coppens of the Omo Research Expedition for their continued encouragement and support of this work. Much of the success of this project hinged on the work, enthusiasm, and energy of Jean de Heinzelin, to whom we express special appreciation. Suggestions and comments have come from Raymonde Bonnefille, Frank Brown, Paul Haesaerts, and Bernard Hubert. Special thanks are due to Muthoka Kivingo, Atiko Akiru, John Kaumbulu, and Charles Ndambuki for their assistance and perseverance in hand sorting the residues of 20 tons of sediment and to Claude Guillemot for his undiminished enthusiasm for finding fossils.

References

Crusafont-Pairó, M., and Villalta Comella, J. de. 1954. Características bióticas del Pontiense español. *XIX Congr. Géol. Int.*, Algeria. *C. R. Sess.*, fasc. 8, sect- 8, pp. 119-26.

Hayman, R. W. 1967. *Preliminary identification manual for African mammals.* XI. *Chiroptera.* Washington, D. C.: Smithsonian Institution.

Jaeger, J.-J. Les Rongeurs (Mammalia, Rodentia) du Pléistocène inférieur d'Olduvai (Tanzanie). I. Introduction générale et Muridés. In *Fossil vertebrates of Africa*, vol. 4. In press.

Jaeger, J.-J., and Martin, J. 1971. Découverte au Maroc des premiers micromammifères du Pontien d'Afrique. *C. R. Acad. Sci. (Paris)*, ser. D, 272:2155-58.

Misonne, X. 1968. *Preliminary identification manual for African mammals*. XIX. *Rodentia*, Washington, D. C.: Smithsonian Institution.

_____. 1969. African and Indo-Australian Muridae, evolutionary trends. Musée Royal de l'Afrique Centrale, Tervuren, Belgique. *Ann. Sci. Zool.*, no. 172, p. 219.

Tobien, H. 1970. Subdivision of Pontian mammalian faunas. *Giorn. Geol.*, ser. 2, vol. 25, fasc. 1, pp. 1-5.

Postscript

During the 1974 field season a further screen washing was carried out by Noel Boaz and Atiko Akieu at localities 1 and 28. Most of the fossil postcranial bones from these localities have now also been identified by one of us (Wesselman), providing additional data summarized below. Numbers in parentheses indicate numbers of specimens, which unless otherwise designated represent teeth recovered in 1974.

Locality 1

Muroidea: incisors (372); postcranial bones (21).

Muridae: *Mastomys minor* (2)

Sciuridae: *Xerus* cf. *erythropus* (1); incisors (2).

Viverridae: *Helogale* sp. (2); phalanges (6).

Mammalia indet. long bone fragments (34)

Serpentes: vertebrae (2).

Anura: postcranial bones (45).

Locality 28

Muroidea: incisors (70); postcranial bones (16).

Muridae: *Mastomys minor* (1).

      Aethomys sp. (2).

Cricetidae: *Tatera* sp. (2).

Sciuridae: incisors (2).

Dipodidae: *Jaculus* cf. *orientalis* (2).

Soricidae: *Crocidura* sp. A. (1).

Emballonuridae: *Taphozous* sp. (1).

Serpentes: vertebrae (4).

Anura: postcranial bones (12).

Of interest is the recovery of additional *Jaculus* specimens from L. 28 confirming aridity in Member F times. The presence of the large species of *Taphozous* and the large *Crocidura* at L. 28, both of which are essentially identical to specimens from Member B, seems to indicate the continued support of developed forest by the Omo River despite this aridity, but on a more restricted scale.

33. THE LOTHAGAM 1 FAUNA: ITS PHYLOGENETIC, ECOLOGICAL,
AND BIOGEOGRAPHIC SIGNIFICANCE

C. Smart

Introduction

A paper devoted to the fauna of part of one fossil locality might seem out of place
in this volume, but fossils from the lower fluviodeltaic level (Unit 1) of sediments in
Lothagam Hill, Turkana District, Kenya, have contributed so much information to our knowledge of the construction of the modern African savanna fauna that a summary of progress is
useful at this time. The importance of the fossils stems from their age (5-6 m.y.--Maglio
1970b; D. W. Powers, pers. comm.) and the excellent preservation of large herbivore species.

Before 1965 the evolutionary history of subsaharan Africa for the period between 14
and 4 m.y. was unknown. Since then several important fossil localities have been discovered in the rift valley of northwestern Kenya. In the Lake Baringo area a sequence of
sites was discovered by the East African Geological Research Unit, under the direction of
Professor B. C. King of Bedford College, The University of London (Bishop et al. 1971).
Particularly important are the Ngorora, Mpesida, and Lukeino sites. Together with Lothagam
1, originally worked by Professor B. Patterson of Harvard University (Patterson, Behrensmeyer, and Sill 1970; Behrensmeyer, this symposium), these sites provide a look at the evolution of the rift valley fauna during the period when grasslands were an important vegetation type in Eurasia and India. I refer to the environment of the so-called Pontian
Hipparion fauna of Eurasia and India; this was "the most famous, the most widely distributed
and the best known of all the [fossil] mammalian faunas of the Old World" (Osborn 1910, p.
264). Thenius (1959) gives a review. Since many of the large mammals of this fauna are
related at the family level to living African forms and were clearly adapted for life on
open grasslands, it seemed likely that some might be ancestral to groups now living in
Africa. Thus discussions of the evolution of the modern African savanna fauna were difficult before the discovery of the Lake Baringo and Lothagam sites.

Fauna

By far the greatest contribution of the Lothagam 1 level has been to our understanding
of the evolution of the large herbivores, whose biomass establishes the savanna as the most
productive of mammalian communities (Watson, Graham, and Parker 1969). These animals have
relatively robust skeletons and are sufficiently abundant in life to have a good chance at
preservation. Consequently the bulk of the work thus far completed has been on large herbivores, and I shall restrict myself to advances made through their study. Table 1 lists the

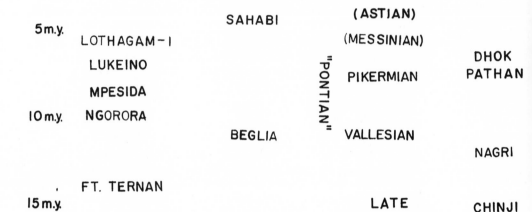

Figure 1. Correlation chart for selected African fossil localities. Subsaharan sites mentioned in this report are compared with important northern African sites, Indian stages, European land mammal ages, and European "standard" stages/ages, the latter in parentheses. Data are taken from Van Couvering (1972) and Maglio (1970b).

fauna of the Lothagam 1 level as it is known at this time. Pollen samples are being studied by Professor D. Livingstone of Duke University.

Progress in Phylogenetic Studies of Large Mammals

Elephants. Maglio (1970a, 1973) studied the Elephantidae from Lothagam 1. Before his investigation the Elephantidae were thought to have arisen from mastodonts such as *Stegodon* and *Stegolophodon* (see Singer and Hooijer 1958). Maglio and Hendey (1970) recognized these genera as members of the family Mammutidae and not related to elephantid ancestry, a very important advance. Maglio (1970a) recognized the genus *Stegotetrabelodon*, present in Lothagam 1, as a primitive genus within the Elephantidae. He points out that *Stegotetrabelodon* was derived from the family Gomphotheriidae. The associated divergence in morphology between the Elephantidae and Gomphotheriidae is related to a shift in the method of chewing (Maglio 1972; 1973, p. 5).

Maglio (1973) considers *Stegotetrabelodon* to be the ancestor of the other Lothagam elephantid genus, *Primelephas*. He further points out that *Primelephas* is ancestral to *Loxodonta*, *Mammuthus*, and *Elephas*, all of which evolved in Africa.

Horses. Hooijer and Maglio (1973, 1974) discuss the *Hipparion* of Lothagam 1; they record three species. *Hipparion primigenium*, the brachydont ancestral Old World *Hipparion* typical of Vallesian sites, is very rare. *Hipparion sitifense*, a widespread pygmy species, is more common. Their study of *H. turkanense*, the most abundant form, has yielded two important results. *H. turkanense* appears to be the descendent of *Hipparion hippidiodium*, a Pikermian

Table 1

The Mammalian Fauna of the B and C Levels from Unit 1 of the Lothagam Hill Fossil Locality

PRIMATES

    Cercopithecidae

        Tribe Papionini cf. *Parapapio* (a small form)
        Cf. *Cercocebus*

    Hominidae

        Australopithecus sp. cf. *africanus*   Patterson (in prep.)

CARNIVORA

    Viverridae
        ??*Civettictis*
    Hyaenidae
        Aff. *Euryboas*
    Felidae
        Subfamily Felinae (a large primitive form)
        Subfamily Machairodontinae

PROBOSCIDEA

    Deinotheriidae
        Deinotherium sp.
    Gomphotheriidae
        Subfamily Anancinae (a primitive form)
    Elephantidae   Maglio 1970*b*, 1973
        Stegotetrabelodon orbus
        Primelephas gomphotheroides

PERISSODACTYLA
    Equidae   Hooijer and Maglio 1973,1974
        Hipparion turkanense
        Hipparion sitifense (a pygmy form)
        Hipparion primigenium (rare)

    Rhinocerotidae   Hooijer and Patterson 1972
        Brachypotherium lewisi
        Ceratotherium praecox

ARTIODACTYLA

    Suidae   Cooke and Ewer 1972
        Nyanzachoerus tulotus
        Nyanzachoerus aff. *jaegeri*

    Hippopotamidae   Coryndon (this symposium)
        Hippopotamus (Hexaprotodon) sp. A
        Hippopotamus (Hexaprotodon) sp. B (a pygmy form)

    Giraffidae
        Giraffa sp. (rare)

    Bovidae   Smart (in prep.)
        *Pachytragus*like aff. Hippotraginae
        Aff. *Kobus*
        Aff. *Redunca*
        Aff. *Aepyceros*
        Aff. *Damaliscus*
        Tribe Hippotragini
        Miotragoceros sp.
        Tragelaphus sp. A
        Tragelaphus sp. B
        Gazella sp. A (large form)
        Gazella sp. B (small form)
        Antilope sp.
        Tribe Neotragini aff. *Rhynocotragus*

TUBILIDENTATA

    Leptorycteropus guilielmi, gen. et sp. nov.   Patterson (1975)

RODENTIA

    Anomaluridae (a nongliding form)   Patterson (in prep.)

NOTE: The nonmammalian portion of the fauna is listed in Patterson, Behrensmeyer, and Sill (1970).

Hipparion from China. Furthermore, *Hipparion turkanense* is probably ancestral to the high-crowned *Hipparion* at Olduvai and other sites generally called "Stylohipparion."

Rhinos. Hooijer and Patterson (1972) found two species of rhinocerotids at Lothagam 1. By far the more abundant is *Brachypotherium lewisi*. The species is large for a *Brachypotherium*, a genus of brachydont, short-limbed rhinos with lineages in the Miocene of both Africa and Europe, where it is an important element of many "Pontian" faunas. Hooijer (in press) will shortly address the question of a European versus African origin for *Brachypotherium lewisi*.

Also present but rare is the earliest known species of *Ceratotherium*, the genus of the living white rhino. *Ceratotherium praecox* not only shows many derived characters unique to *Ceratotherium*, but also shows a number of derived character states which are reminiscent of *Diceros*, the black rhino, and are not present in living *Ceratotherium*. *Ceratotherium praecox* is thus recognizable as an early member of the white rhino lineage, visible "shortly" after divergence from the black rhino *Diceros*.

A greater number of shared derived characters among representatives of an ancestral-descendant group is, of course, to be expected early in the evolution of the descendant form. The Lothagam 1 fauna seems to have been preserved at the right time to see this phenomenon in the rhinos and in the antelopes. Many shared characters are later obliterated by further morphological specialization--in *Ceratotherium*, specializations associated with grazing.

Hooijer and Patterson reason that the presence of *Paradiceros* at Fort Ternan, although it was not the ancestor of *Diceros*, suggests an African origin for the ancestor of *Diceros* and *Ceratotherium*. This is presumably because the European rhinos are well known, and a reasonable ancestor is not available in Europe.

Suids. Cooke and Ewer (1972) described two species of *Nyanzachoerus* from the fossiliferous levels of Lothagam 1. The phylogeny of African suids has long been a source of difficulty; for example, until recently the ancestry of both the diverse groups of Mio-Pliocene African suids (*Nyanzachoerus* and related forms) and of the modern African suids, especially *Potamochoerus* and *Hylochoerus*, was virtually unknown. Recently, however, Cooke (1975) presented evidence for the origins of these groups and Eurasiatic *Bunolistriodon*- and *Sus*like ancestors, respectively. Discovery of the affinities of *Nyanzachoerus* has been greatly aided by the excellent cranial material collected at Lothagam 1.

Hippos. Coryndon (this symposium) has studied the hippopotamids from Lothagam 1. Two forms are known, a large and a pygmy species of *Hippopotamus* (*Hexaprotodon*). The role of the Lothagam 1 collections in the study of hexaprotodont hippopotamids has been to provide well-preserved material for the study of a large part of the skeletal anatomy. As with other large herbivore groups (elephants, horses, rhinos, suids, bovids), earlier material of the same or closely related taxa is available from the Lake Baringo sites, but initial collections from Baringo have often provided only sparse dental material of these animals. From her study of the Lothagam material, Coryndon has been able to show that hexaprotodonts were ancestral to the tetraprotodont hippopotamids common in the Plio-Pleistocene of Africa. Furthermore, a primitive form is known from Rusinga (18 m.y., Van Couvering and Miller 1969); hippopotamids appear to have arisen in Africa (S. C. Coryndon, pers. comm.). Coryndon (1975) will review the evolution and dispersal of the Hippopotamidae.

Giraffes. Thus far, giraffes have proved extremely rare in collections from Lothagam 1. The single dental specimen, an upper molar, is the right size and form for *Giraffa*. The specimen will be studied by C. S. Churcher.

Antelopes. I will describe antelopes elsewhere, but a brief summary may be given here. The antelopes are beginning to show a diversity approaching that found in modern African grasslands. The first eight antelope entries in table 1 are of special interest for phylogenetic studies. The first four are known from excellent skull and dental material as well as some postcranial remains. The first antelope listed, *Pachytragus*like aff. Hippotraginae, refers to a *Pachytragus* which shows a number of derived characters typical of the Hippotraginae. *Pachytragus* encompasses several typical Eurasian and North African Pikermian antelopes. The *Redunca*, *Kobus*, *Aepyceros*, and *Damaliscus* and the hippotragine antelope share derived characters with the *Pachytragus*like antelope which suggest close relationships, and I am now working with the hypothesis that a *Pachytragus*like bovid initiated a radiation of antelopes which resulted in the groups mentioned above.

Whether the *Pachytragus*like antelope is a descendant of some Eurasian or North African *Pachytragus* or a subsaharan form like *?Pseudotragus potwaricus* Gentry seen in the Fort Ternan and Ngorora faunas is not clear. Evidence exists to favor either alternative, and since *Pachytragus* and *Pseudotragus* are probably closely related, the biogeographic question may be difficult to answer.

The Lothagam 1 *Miotragoceros* species is the first record of that genus in subsaharan Africa, and its presence further breaks down earlier impressions of the antiquity of antelope faunule regionality (Gentry 1968). *Miotragoceros* is a typical Eurasian Pikerm antelope. The dental configuration of *Tragelaphus* sp. A suggests that the *Miotragoceros* group is the source of the *Tragelaphus* complex. In our laboratory in Princeton we are currently studying the ear, suborbital, and braincase regions of living and fossil antelopes, including *Miotragoceros* and *Pachytragus*, in an attempt to rigorously demonstrate the distribution of derived character states in the Bovidae by using a frequently fossilized region that can provide a check on dental data.

Environment

Palynological studies of the Lothagam 1 environment are not yet available. Studies of the sedimentology of Lothagam 1 by Behrensmeyer (in Patterson, Behrensmeyer, and Sill 1970; this symposium; and unpublished) and by Powers (pers. comm.) have recognized fluvial and fluviodeltaic environments near a lake. The nonmammalian portion of the faunal list (Patterson, Behrensmeyer, and Sill 1970) reflects the environment of the depositional site. New discoveries include geese (Aves: Anseriformes) and abundant, well-preserved remains of the fish *Polypterus*, which today lives in the waters of the Omo delta.

An examination of those mammals whose modern counterparts show habitat preferences is the primary basis for interpretation of the Lothagam 1 environment at this time. These studies show two main habitat types in the vicinity. There appears to have been a gallery forest fauna near the depositional sites grading through marginal bush into savanna. The *Cercocebus* and the small baboon, the deinothere, the anancine gomphothere, and the anomalurid are probably all forest forms. Much of the rest of the fauna probably lived on the savanna. *Ceratotherium praecox*, *Hipparion turkanense*, *Hippopotamus (Hexaprotodon)* sp. A, *Kobus*, *Redunca*, the hippotragine, *Damaliscus*, *Aepyceros*, and *Gazella* sp. A were probably using grasses as a large part of their diet. In living African elephantids (*Loxodonta*) grasses can form the bulk of the diet (Laws and Parker 1968), but both of the Lothagam elephants have relatively low crowned teeth (Maglio 1973), and it is not clear to what extent they were eating grasses. Thornton (1971) has emphasized the importance of *Hippopotamus* as grazers, especially during a wet season. Moir (1965) discusses the ruminantlike stomach of hippos.

Much of the structure of the Lothagam 1 type fauna was established by Mpesida time (Hooijer and Maglio 1973; see table 2). The origin of conditions necessary for the establishment of extensive grasslands in Eurasia during the Pikermian is not clear. In Africa the development of the rift valley may have contributed to the initial establishment of extensive grasslands. Where the escarpment was high enough, a rain shadow would have formed, causing drought at least part of the year. Many of the grasses are drought-tolerant (Mooney 1972). Grasses are usually thought of as rapidly reproducing, early successional plants (R-selected--Southwood et al. 1974) which have a root-storage strategy (Mooney 1972). Grazing and fires are thought to be important in destroying later successional plants to the advantage of the grasses. Went and Stark (1968) point out that a major consequence of fire is the destruction of symbiotic fungal mycorhiza in the roots which seem to be essential for the growth of trees. Perhaps equally important for grasses living in the Eastern Rift is tolerance to salts and to alkaline soil (Western and Van Praet 1973), which are likely in a closed basin with a history of Miocene alkaline volcanic activity (Williams 1972; Baker, Mohr, and Williams 1972). Presumably grasses became an important food resource there before Ngorora deposition.

Faunal Exchanges

Lothagam 1 probably predates the shift in Eurasia to a cooler, wetter climate during the Astian deduced by Kurten (1972), but it may have been coincident with supposed desiccation in the Messinian of the Mediterranean basin postulated by Hsu, Ryan, and Cita (1973). We have already noted that subsaharan Africa, at least in the Eastern Rift valley, seems to have had a fauna including much of the Lothagam 1 large herbivore faunule during the period corresponding to the Pikermian age of Eurasia (see table 2). It appears that the effects of these climatic and geographic changes, although important in Europe, did not have a strong influence on the established Lothagam 1 fauna. Studies of slightly younger faunas may turn up important Eurasian elements which extended into Africa as the grasslands receded in the north.

At least three herbivores, the ancestor of *Hipparion turkanense*, *Miotragoceros*, *Nyanzachoerus = Sivachoerus*, and possibly also *Hipparion sitifense* and *Pachytragus* appear to have invaded subsaharan Africa from Eurasia or North Africa at some time after the deposition of the Ngorora sediments and before the deposition of the Lukeino sediments. Since the hexaprotodont hippopotamids appear to have arisen in Africa, their presence in the Pikermian of Greece and Spain (S. C. Coryndon, pers. comm.), but not sooner, indicates that the hippopotamids invaded Europe from Africa. Cooke (1975) comments on the relations of *Nyanzachoerus* to North African, Eurasian, and Indian Suidae.

That exchanges between faunas of Eurasia and Africa should have occurred during the Pikermian is not surprising. The work of Crusafont-Pairó (1958), Swartz and Arden (1960), Coryndon and Savage (1973), and Thenius (1959) have all pointed to the absence of important geographical obstacles to mammalian dispersal at that time.

It seems likely that more faunal exchanges will be recognized by other workers. Of course, we see only successful invasions in the fossil record. Since many of the ancestral Pikermian herbivores were distributed all over the Old World by the late Vindobonian, successful invasions must have been rare. Large herbivores reproduce slowly but have evolved elaborate parental care, defense against predators, and optimum feeding strategies to maintain their population levels near the maximum possible for available resources (K-selected, Southwood et al. 1974). This makes them poor invaders but efficient at resisting the

Table 2

Comparison of the Large Herbivore Faunule from Lothagam 1, Showing the Presence or Absence of Selected Taxa in Some Sites from the Lake Baringo Area.

Lothagam 1 (~5.5 m.y.)	"Kaperyon"=Lukeino (~7 m.y.)	Mpesida (~8 m.y.)	Ngorora (~10 m.y.)
Stegotetrabelodon orbus	+	+	
Primelephas gomphotheroides	+		
Hipparion turkanense	+	+	
Hipparion primigenium			+
Brachypotherium lewisi		+	
Ceratotherium praecox		+	
Nyanzachoerus tulotus	+		
Hippopotamus (Hexaprotodon) sp.	X	X	X
Miotragoceros	X		
*Pachytragus*like aff. Hippotraginae	X	X	?

NOTE: The fauna previously listed for the Kaperyon site were actually collected from the underlying Lukeino (M. Pickford, pers. comm.). This confirms the impression that the Lothagam 1 level is older than 5 m.y., the radiometric age obtained for the Kaperyon sediments (Bishop et al. 1971). The symbol + indicates that the same species is present as occurs at Lothagam 1. The symbol X indicates identity at the generic level.

invasions of competing forms. For a small invading population to become established in a new area in the face of similar animals with large populations, the invader must be able to exploit a resource or occupy a habitat which its relatives have failed to use efficiently. Thus *Hipparion turkanense* has teeth much better adapted to eating grasses than the Vallesian *Hipparion primigenium* already present at Ngorora, hexaprotodont hippopotamids had evolved away from the niche of their anthracothere ancestors, and the antelopes *Kobus*, *Redunca*, *Aepyceros*, *Damaliscus*, and the hippotragine probably had different feeding strategies from late Vindobonian open woodland antelopes present at Ngorora.

Whether we shall be able to consider similar questions about rarer elements of the fauna (e.g., Rodentia, Carnivora, Primates) depends on our ability to obtain better material. The trenching methods used so successfully at Fort Ternan (Gentry 1970) should be fruitful at Lothagam 1 and would be particularly valuable if coupled with sieving operations for small specimens. It would be very instructive to compare the faunal exchanges of large herbivores with those of the rodents, which are less mobile and more susceptible to local environmental fluctuations but are able to increase their numbers much more rapidly.

Acknowledgments

I thank the following for discussion: Drs. H. B. S. Cooke (suids), S. C. Coryndon (hippos), D. A. Hooijer (rhinos and horses), V. J. Maglio (elephants and horses), B. Patterson (carnivores, rodents, and aardvark), and R. J. G. Savage (biogeography).

Professor B. Patterson has permitted me to study the Lothagam antelopes. Professor W. Bishop kindly allowed me to examine the collections from the Lake Baringo area. Dr. V. J. Maglio critically read the manuscript.

Mr. W. Selden prepared figure 1 and my wife Susan assisted with the final draft.

References

Baker, B. H.; Mohr, P. A.; and Williams, L. A. J. 1972. Geology of the Eastern Rift System of Africa. *Geol. Soc. Am. Spec. Paper*, no. 136.

Bishop, W. W. 1972. Stratigraphic succession "versus" calibration in East Africa. In *Calibration of hominoid evolution*, ed. W. W. Bishop and J. A. Miller, pp. 219-46. Edinburgh: Scottish Academic Press; Toronto: University of Toronto Press.

Bishop, W. W.; Chapman, G. R.; Hill, A.; and Miller, J. A. 1971. Succession of Cainozoic vertebrate assemblages from the northern Kenya Rift valley. *Nature* 233:389-94.

Colbert, E. H. 1935. Siwalik mammals in the American Museum of Natural History. *Trans. Amer. Phil. Soc.*, n.s., 26:1-401.

Cooke, H. B. S. 1975. Plio-Pleistocene Suidae. In *Evolution of mammals in Africa*, ed. V. J. Maglio. Princeton: Princeton University Press.

Cooke, H. B. S., and Ewer, R. F. 1972. Fossil Suidae from Kanapoi and Lothagam, northwestern Kenya. *Bull. Mus. Comp. Zool. Harvard Coll.* 143:149-296.

Cooke, H. B. S., and Maglio, V. J. 1972. Plio-Pleistocene stratigraphy in East Africa in relation to proboscidean and suid evolution. In *Calibration of hominoid evolution*, ed. W. W. Bishop and J. A. Miller, pp. 303-29. Edinburgh: Scottish Academic Press; Toronto: University of Toronto Press.

Coryndon, S. C. 1975. Hippopotamidae. In *Evolution of mammals in Africa*, ed. V. J. Maglio. Princeton: Princeton University Press.

Coryndon, S. C., and Savage, R. J. G. 1973. The origin and affinities of African mammal faunas. *Spec. Papers Paleontol.* 12:121-35.

Crusafont-Pairó, M. 1958. Endemism and Paneuropeanism in Spanish fossil faunas, with special regard to the Miocene. *Commentat. Biol. Helsingfors* 18:1-30.

Gentry, A. W. 1968. Historical zoogeography of antelopes. *Nature* 217:874-75.

_____. 1970. The Bovidae (Mammalia) of the Fort Ternan fossil fauna. In *Fossil vertebrates of Africa*, ed. L. S. B. Leakey and R. J. Savage, 2:243-323. London: Academic Press.

_____. 1971. The earliest goats and other antelopes from the Samos *Hipparion* fauna. *Bull. Brit. Mus. Geol.* 20:229-96.

Hooijer, D. A. 1975. Rhinocerotidae. In *Evolution of mammals in Africa*, ed. V. J. Maglio. Princeton Press.

Hooijer, D. A., and Maglio, V. J. 1973. The earliest *Hipparion* south of the Sahara in the late Miocene of Kenya. *Koninkl. Ned. Akad. Wetenschap. Proc.*, ser. B, 76:311-15.

_____. 1974. *Hipparion* from the late Miocene and Pliocene of northwestern Kenya. *Zool. Verhandel.* 143:1-34.

Hooijer, D. A., and Patterson, B. 1972. Rhinoceroses from the Pliocene of northwestern Kenya. *Bull. Mus. Comp. Zool. Harvard Coll.* 144:1-26.

Hsü, K. J.; Ryan, W. B. F. and Cita, M. B. 1973. Late Miocene desiccation of the Mediterranean. *Nature* 242:240-44.

Kurtén, B. 1972. *The age of mammals*. New York: Columbia University Press.

Laws, R. M., and Parker, I. S. C. 1968. Recent studies on elephant populations in East Africa. *Symp. Zool. Soc. Lond.* 21:319-59.

Maglio, V. J. 1970a. Four new species of Elephantidae from the Plio-Pleistocene of northwestern Kenya. *Brevoria*, no. 341, pp. 1-43.

Maglio, V. J. 1970*b*. Early Elephantidae of Africa and a tentative correlation of African Plio-Pleistocene deposits. *Nature* 225:328-32.

_____. 1972. Evolution of mastication in the Elephantidae. *Evolution* 26:638-58.

_____. 1973. Origin and evolution of the Elephantidae, *Trans. Amer. Phil. Soc.* n.s., 63(3):1-149.

_____., ed. 1975. *Evolution of mammals in Africa.* Princeton: Princeton University Press.

Maglio, V. J., and Q. B. Hendey, 1970. New evidence relating to the supposed stegolophodont ancestry of the Elephantidae. *S. Afr. Archaeol. Bull.* 25:85-87.

Moir, R. J. 1965. The comparative physiology of ruminant-like animals. In *Physiology of digestion in the ruminant,* ed. R. W. Dougherty, pp. 1-14. London: Butterworth.

Mooney, H. A. 1972. The carbon balance of plants. *Ann. Rev. Ecol. Syst.* 3:315-46.

Osborn, H. F. 1910. *The age of mammals in Europe, Asia and North America.* New York: Macmillan.

Patterson, B. 1975. The fossil aardvarks (Mammalia: Tubilidentata), *Bull. Mus. Comp. Zool. Harvard Coll.* 147(5):185-237.

Patterson, B.; Behrensmeyer, A. K.; and Sill, W. D. 1970. Geology and fauna of a new Pliocene locality in northwestern Kenya. *Nature* 226:918-21.

Singer, R., and Hooijer, D. A. 1958. A *Stegolophodon* from South Africa. *Nature* 182:101-2.

Southwood, T. R. E.; May, R. M.; Hassell, M. P. and Conway, G. R. 1974. Ecological strategies and population parameters. *Am. Nat.* 108:791-804.

Swartz, D. H., and Arden, D. D. 1960. Geologic history of the Red Sea Area. *Bull. Am. Assoc. Pet. Geol.* 44:1621-37.

Thenius, E. 1959. *Handbuch der stratigraphischen Geologie.* Vol. 3. *Tertiär.* Part 2. *Wirbeltierfaunen.* Stuttgart: F. Enke Verlag.

Thornton, D. D. 1971. The effect of complete removal of *Hippopotamus* on grassland in the Queen Elizabeth National Park, Uganda. *E. Afr. Wildl. J.* 9:47-55.

Van Couvering, J. A. 1972. Radiometric calibration of the European Neogene. In *Calibration of hominoid evolution,* ed. W. W. Bishop and J. A. Miller, pp. 247-71. Edinburgh: Scottish Academic Press; Toronto: University of Toronto Press.

Van Couvering, J. A., and Miller, J. A. 1969. Miocene stratigraphy and age determinations, Rusinga Island, Kenya. *Nature* 221:628-32.

Watson, R. M.; Graham, A. D.; and Parker, I. S. C. 1969. A census of the large mammals of Loliondo controlled area, northern Tanzania. *E. Afr. Wildl. J.* 3:95-98.

Went, F. W., and Stark, N. 1968. Mycorhiza. *BioScience* 18:1035-39.

Western, D., and Van Praet, C. 1973. Cyclical changes in the habitat and climate of an East African ecosystem. *Nature* 241:104-6.

Williams, L. A. J. 1972. The Kenya Rift volcanics: A note on volumes and chemical composition. In *East African rifts,* ed. R. W. Girdler, *Tectonophysics,* 15:83-96.

E. Tchernov

It is surprising to find, among a conservative group like the crocodiles, evidences of rapid evolutionary change and faunal discontinuities, as is demonstrated among Neogene and Quaternary taxa in eastern Africa.

Four species of crocodiles occupied the greater Rudolf basin during Pliocene/Pleistocene times. A single species, *Crocodylus niloticus*, is found now in eastern Africa, except for a population of *Crocodylus cataphractus* in the Ujiji River, Lake Tanganyika. This crocodilian fauna is particularly interesting because these four species represent a broad adaptive and ecological spectrum, from an extreme brevirostrine to a gavialoid structure, as exemplified by: *Crocodylus* sp. nov. (short-snouted African crocodile), *Crocodylus niloticus* (Nile crocodile, *Crocodylus cataphractus* (slender-snouted African crocodile, or Khinh), and *Euthecodon brumpti*.

Two species, *Crocodylus* sp. nov. and *Euthecodon brumpti*, became extinct during the mid-Quaternary. In northern Africa and along the Sudanese and Egyptian Nile the short-snouted crocodile probably survived as late as the Mesolithic! *Euthecodon nitriae*, a probable ancestor of *E. brumpti*, was extinct by the Pliocene. *Crocodylus cataphractus* reduced its range substantially, retreating almost wholly from eastern Africa, leaving only the Nile crocodile to occupy the ever-changing and variable freshwaters of that and adjacent regions.

Fossil crocodilians of eastern Africa have not received the careful study they deserve. Only sporadic collecting has been done, and hence a thorough quantitative study of the group is still not possible. More extensive field collecting and restoration of specimens is required in order to appreciate fully their geographic variation and adaptive radiation in the inland waters of this part of Africa. Here the unique crocodilian fauna of the Rudolf basin is briefly reviewed, along with its paleogeographic relations with other parts of eastern Africa. In the Rudolf and Omo successions no evolutionary trends have been discerned in the course of the Plio-Pleistocene; therefore a detailed discussion of their stratigraphic distribution in these and other situations is not offered here. However, some adaptive radiation of the short-snouted crocodile did occur in the Rudolf basin.

Crocodylidae

Crocodylus niloticus Laurenti, 1768
(Nile Crocodile, or Timsah)

Although this familiar species has been mentioned by various workers as occurring in a few Neogene and Quaternary deposits in eastern Africa, its distribution and evolution are virtually unknown. At least some of the fossil material referred to this species, in fact, shows strong affinities to the short-snouted species *Crocodylus* sp. nov. Thus Swinton's (1926) description of *C. niloticus kaisensis* from the Kaiso Formation accords well with the skull morphology and proportions of the short-snouted species. Some of the specimens described by Arambourg (1947) from the lower Omo basin (Shungura Formation) actually represent the short-snouted species; he noted that "sa symphyse paraît aussi proportionellement plus courte."

C. niloticus is regularly associated in Neogene and Quaternary deposits with the short-snouted species, the latter normally predominates, and the Nile crocodile was a much rarer species than is generally believed. I have identified specimens of the latter from the Shungura Formation, Member E (a partial skull from Unit E-5, Locality 40) in the Omo basin, and from upper Bed II, Olduvai Gorge (partial mandibles from site BK II). No remains of this species are known thus far from the East Rudolf succession or from Kanapoi.

These fossil representatives show certain morphological differences from the modern form, particularly in the proportions of the snout. The slight shortness of the snout in *C. niloticus* is evident from table 1 (Omo, index 1). The short-snouted crocodile is included in this table to show the marked differences between the two species. The mandible of the fossil *Crocodylus niloticus* is robust, high, and broad by comparison with *Crocodylus* sp. nov. and the recent Nile crocodile (table 1, indexes 6, 7), sometimes even more than twice the size of the modern form. The mandible of the short-snouted species is delicate and approaches the proportions of the recent Nile crocodile.

The distributional pattern of *C. niloticus* is far from complete because of uncertain taxonomic affinities of Miocene and Pliocene specimens and its relative rarity during the late Pliocene and the Quaternary. However, in spite of its rarity, its wide distribution over the inland waters of eastern Africa is evidently reflected in its occurrence to the north (Omo) and south (Olduvai) of the eastern rift valley.

Crocodylus sp. nov. (short-snouted African Crocodile)

This unique species predominates among eastern African crocodilians from the base of the Neogene through the earlier Quaternary. It became extinct during the mid-Quaternary; but in some areas, for example the Sudan[1], it probably survived as late as the uppermost Quaternary. The species had a wide distribution over northern Africa, including the Sinai peninsula, and the whole of eastern Africa. Specimens I have examined derive from the Sinai peninsula (Erg-el-Ahmar, Miocene), Egypt (Moghara, Miocene), Sudan (Abu Huggar, uppermost Quaternary), Libya (Zelten, Lower Miocene), Ethiopia (Omo Group formations), Kenya (East Rudolf succession, Plio-Pleistocene; Lothagam, uppermost Miocene; Kanapoi, early Pliocene; Lukeino, Baringo, upper Miocene), and Tanzania (Olduvai Gorge, early and mid-Quaternary).

Some populations represent an extreme brevirostrine condition, exceeding that of most recent species. It is well known that the crocodilian rostrum is a "highly variable factor" (Steel 1973) which has enabled these reptiles to adapt readily to ever-changing habitats through sheer elongation of the rostral region, a phenomenon which occurred many times in the history of this group. However, once rostral elongation occurred the ancestral

---

1. Personal communication from K. P. Oakley in respect to a specimen from Abu Huggar, Sudan (housed in the British Museum [Natural History], London).

Table 1

Comparison between Living and Fossil Crocodylus niloticus and the Short-snouted Crocodylus sp. nov.

Index	Crocodylus niloticus			Crocodylus sp. nov. (Short-snouted)	
	Omo (L-5, E-5) (1 fragment of skull)	Olduvai (BK II) (lower jaw)	Lake Rudolf (Recent) (N=42)[a]	Olduvai (BK II, 63) (N=3)[a]	East Rudolf (N=5)[a]
1. Width of skull (across premaxillaries) / Length of premaxillary (along the median ventral suture)	0.837	---	0.748	1.409[b]	1.353
2. Width of skull (across premaxillaries) / Length of premaxillary (along tooth row)	0.335	---	0.271	---	0.483
3. Length of premaxillary (along the median ventral suture) / Width of skull (across 5th maxillary teeth)	0.717	---	0.780	---	0.455
4. Width of skull (across 5th maxillary teeth) / Length of maxillary (along tooth row)	0.558	---	0.464	0.696	0.795
5. Width of skull (across 5th maxillary teeth) / Distance between premax.-max. suture and mid-9th max. tooth	0.692	---	0.710	1.063	1.228
6. Height of mandible (at ant. end of ext. mandible, foramen level) / Distance between 4th and 15th mandibular teeth	---	0.656	0.339	0.348	0.483
7. Height of mandible (at ant. end of ext. mandible, foramen level) / Length of mandible (along tooth row)	---	1.044	0.548	0.537	0.752
8. Height of mandible (at post. end of ext. mandible, foramen level) / Distance between 4th and 15th mandibular teeth	---	0.507	0.331	0.377	0.472

[a]Figure shown is the mean of the specimens.

[b]One fragment of skull.

condition was never regained; reshortening of the snout is never observed (in accordance with Dollo's law). The cranium and the postcranial skeleton are more constant in size and morphology.

The persistance of the brevirostrine condition of this crocodilian group is evident throughout the Miocene. Short-snouted crocodilian fossils from the Miocene of northern and eastern Africa are all rather similar in skull proportions. It is only during the Pliocene and the earlier Quaternary, especially in the Rudolf basin, that local adaptive radiation occurred in eastern Africa. In fact four significantly different, readily distinguishable populations are represented around the several parts of the Rudolf basin--in the north (Omo), in the northeast (East Rudolf), in the southwest (Lothagam), and in the south (Kanapoi).

The basic differences in skull proportions between these four groups of short-snouted crocodiles, and between them and the recent Nile crocodile, are set out in table 2. The stability of the cranial region (index 1) is apparent by comparison with the rostral area (indexes 2-7). The East Rudolf and Lothagam populations maintain the shortest snouts (indexes 3, 4, 5), the Omo population is intermediate, and the Kanapoi population has the most elongate snouts. The single Lothagam specimen has the broadest symphysial area (index 7), although the East Rudolf population is in this respect quite similar. Indexes 2 and 5 clearly reveal that the Kanapoi population is closely related to that of the Omo, whereas the Lothagam example is very similar to that of East Rudolf. This condition could very well represent an example of microconvergent evolution. Could these Rudolf basin populations have formed a continuous topocline with only local differentiation, or were these differences a consequence of short- or long-term barriers attendant upon fragmentation of the ancient widespread lake? The answer is still unknown, of course, but both explanations appear doubtful to me.

The differences in rostral width and length (indexes 2-7) between the Nile crocodile and the short-snouted species are especially impressive. Proportions of the postcranial skeleton are rather constant and are scarcely different from *C. niloticus* or other crocodilids. Evidently the rostrum was the main focus of selective pressures in this group.

Crocodylus cataphractus Cuvier, 1824
(slender-snouted African Crocodile)

This piscivorous reptile, occupying rivers and swamps, is now distributed principally through the drainage of the Congo basin. An isolated population of the species occurs in the Ujiji River, Lake Tanganyika. However, during Pliocene/Pleistocene times *C. cataphractus* was a part of the Rudolf basin fauna.

Remains of this species were first recorded from the Omo basin by Joleaud (1930) and subsequently by Arambourg (1947). Additional representatives of the species have since been recovered from Kanapoi and from East Rudolf. Fossil representatives of this species are still known only from the Rudolf basin. The absence of this species from the Baringo area and from Olduvai could be of paleolimnological significance. However, its historical distribution is surely difficult to appreciate in view of its past and present disjunctive distributions.

A single complete skull, but no mandibles, is known from East Rudolf. Many rostral elements are known from the Omo Group formations, and the Kanapoi sample includes some cranial parts as well.

The fossil form of this species differs in some skull proportions (table 3) from the recent species (based on samples of the Ujiji population in the National Museum of Kenya,

Table 2

Adaptive Radiation in the Short-snouted Crocodile around the Rudolf Basin

Index	Crocodylus niloticus (Recent)	Crocodylus sp. nov. (Short-snouted)			
	Lake Rudolf (N=42)[a]	Omo (N=5)[a]	East Rudolf (N=9)[a]	Kanapoi (N=4)[a]	Lothagam (N=1)
1. Height of skull (base of pterygoid to top at supraoccipital) / Width of skull (across quadratojugals)	0.464	0.405	0.402	0.381	0.397
2. Height of skull (base of pterygoid to top of supraoccipital) / Width of skull (across 5th maxillary teeth)	0.868	0.773	0.5782	0.775	0.592
3. Width of skull (across quadratojugals) / Length of maxillary (along tooth row)	0.871	1.179	1.150	1.044	1.294
4. Width of skull (across 5th maxillary teeth) / Length of maxillary (along tooth row)	0.464	0.617	0.796	0.564	0.868
5. Width of skull (across 5th maxillary teeth) / Distance between premax.-max. suture to mid-9th max. tooth	0.710	0.883	1.227	0.868	1.239
6. Length of symphysis / Width of mandible (across post. end of symphysis)	0.980	0.652	0.806	0.584	---
7. Width of mandible (across post. end of symphysis) / Distance between 4th and 11th mandibular teeth	0.603	0.756	0.970	---	1.160

[a]Figure shown is the mean of the specimens.

Table 3

Comparison between Recent and Fossil Crocodylus cataphractus, Showing a Certain Elongation of Skull and Rostrum in the Present Form

Index	Crocodylus cataphractus (Recent) [Ujiji River] (N=5)[a]	Crocodylus cataphractus (East Rudolf) (N=1)[a]
1. Width of skull (across 5th maxillary teeth) / Length of skull (supraoccipital to tip of snout)	0.118	0.180
2. Width of skull (across ant. end of palatines) / Length of skull (supraoccipital to tip of snout)	0.140	0.187
3. Width of skull (across premaxillaries) / Length of skull (supraoccipital to tip of snout)	0.064	0.101
4. Width of skull (across quadratojugals) / Length of skull (supraoccipital to tip of snout)	0.395	0.514
5. Width of skull (across ant. end of orbits) / Length of skull (supraoccipital to tip of snout)	0.248	0.314
6. Width of skull (across columna postorbitalis) / Length of skull (supraoccipital to tip of snout)	0.317	0.415
7. Width of skull (across premaxillaries) / Width of skull (across ant. end of orbits)	0.260	0.321
8. Height of skull (base of pterygoid to top of supraoccipital) / Length of skull (supraoccipital to tip of snout)	0.185	0.216

[a]Figure shown is the mean of the specimens.

Nairobi, and the British Museum [Natural History], London). The fossil form had a broader rostrum (indexes 1-3) and a wider skull (indexes 4-7). Apparently rostral narrowing occurred through time in relation to skull elongation. Again, it is apparent that in crocodilian morphology change first affects the rostral area toward a longirostrine condition (never the reverse), sometimes (as in this case) through elongation of the skull, or (as in gavials and tomistomids) through flattening of the skull. To some extent flattening of the skull could also have occurred in *C. cataphractus* (index 8).

This slender-snouted crocodile must at least to some extent have had a competitive relationship with the extinct longirostrine tomistomid, *Euthecodon brumpti*, the latter possibly an obligatory piscivorous form. The further elongation of the snout in *C. cataphractus* might thus be accounted for as correlative with the extinction of *E. brumpti*, and hence the occupation of that species' habitat and the assumption of a more wholly piscivorine mode of life. It is worth noting that some elongation of the rostrum occurred in *C. niloticus*, probably during this same range of time when all other species of crocodilians became extinct in eastern Africa during the mid-Quaternary.

Tomistomidae

Euthecodon brumpti Joleaud, 1920

This extinct genus nearly attained, through convergent evolution, the gavial level of organization through occupation of the gavialoid adaptive zone. *Euthecodon* shares cranial characters in common with *Tomistoma schlegeli*--now distributed through peninsular and insular southeast Asia (Malay peninsula, Sumatra, and Borneo)--and is generally considered a tomistomid.

Euthecodon nitriae Fourtau, 1920, has been recovered from Neogene formations in Libya (Savage and Hamilton 1973)[2] and the Wadi Natron, Egypt (Fourtau 1920). The *Euthecodon* of the greater Rudolf basin differs from the older species largely in its longer postorbital region, and in the approximation of the fenestra temporalis superior to the occipital region and that of the supraoccipital to the foramen magnum. *E. nitriae* possessed 24 pairs of mandibular teeth, and *E. brumpti* had 27 pairs. The older form, *E. nitriae*, is of Miocene and Pliocene age and, so far as is known, is restricted to North Africa, whereas *E. brumpti* is recorded only from the Rudolf basin.

It is assumed that the most extreme tomistomid longirostrine condition was attained during invasion of the Rudolf basin. If *C. cataphractus* already occupied the basin, or reached it shortly thereafter, competition between these species should have been severe and perhaps forced *Euthecodon* into a full-fledged gavialoid adaptive zone.

Whether this genus originated from a post-Oligocene *Tomistoma* stock is still unclear. Hecht and Malone (1972), in fact, dispute the possibility that the Fayum species of *Tomistoma* actually are members of the Tomistomidae. Since *Euthecodon* had a typical piscivorous habit, preying on fish in the open lake, it is not too surprising to find that all the populations of the Rudolf basin are very similar. Specimens from Kanapoi, the Omo, and East Rudolf are indistinguishable. Hence, unlike the situation for the short-snouted crocodile, there appear to have been no barriers between *Euthecodon brumpti* populations. If this was indeed so it controverts any suggestion that the ancient Lake Rudolf was previously fragmented and disjunctive. *Euthecodon brumpti*, fundamentally adapted to an

---

2. Dr. R. J. G. Savage (University of Bristol) very kindly afforded me the opportunity to examine the crocodilid collections resulting from his work in Libya.

aquatic medium, has never been found to occur south of the Rudolf basin; hence there were evidently no hydrographic links with the Baringo area.

Concluding Remarks

The coexistence of four crocodylid species around one basin is unusual since there probably was severe interspecific competition within this group. However, it is most likely that this could only have occurred through the occupation of quite different adaptive zones within and about the lake. Thus, there appear to have been four principal adaptations: (1) an almost terrestrial life exemplified by the very broad and short-snouted *Crocodylus* sp. nov.; (2) a semiaquatic type, with a "normal" snout, able to prey upon both terrestrial and aquatic animals, exemplified by *C. niloticus*; (3) a nonobligatory piscivorous longirostrine, exemplified by *C. cataphractus*; and (4) an extreme longirostrine, with a typical gavialoid mode of life, exemplified by *Euthecodon brumpti*.

Neither longirostrine species has ever been found in eastern Africa south of the Rudolf basin. As they were primarily piscivorous and dependent on permanent water, a permanent barrier must have existed between the Rudolf basin and the Baringo area. On the other hand since the ancestor of *Euthecodon brumpti* appears to have been dispersed southward from northern Africa, and as the short-snouted *Crocodylus* sp. nov. was common to both northern and eastern Africa, hydrographic links must have persisted between the Neogene Nile system (the Eonile of Said 1973) and the Rudolf basin.

None of the many species of the genus *Tomistoma*, which underwent adaptive radiation in northern Africa and Egypt during late Oligocene and Miocene times, are known to have invaded the inland waters of eastern Africa. This suggests that hydrographic connections between these realms were opened in the late Neogene, when the genus *Tomistoma* evidently became extinct in the African continent (leaving aside the question, recently raised by Hecht and Malone [1972], of whether the Fayum *Tomistoma* indeed belongs to the Tomistomidae or the Gavialidae).

Whereas most of the North African Neogene freshwater tomistomids are Tethyan refugees, the genus *Crocodylus* is an ancient inhabitant of Africa. This suggests another possible origin for *C. cataphractus*. The history of this species in Africa is still vague, since thus far its fossil record is restricted to the Rudolf basin. Its present distribution in the western part of the continent ranges from Senegal to Gabon and the Congo basin and thus suggests a western African origin. Exchanges of this species between the Rudolf and Congo basins probably persisted until the late Tertiary or early Quaternary. The species never penetrated into other inland waters of eastern Africa.

The coexistence of both brevirostrine crocodilian species at Olduvai, unlike the longirostrine species, testifies to their great potentialities for dispersal across land masses. In some places, such as the Wadi Del (Sudan), these two creatures survived into Mesolithic times. What brought about the impressive subspeciation of the short-snouted crocodile within the Rudolf basin? The fragmentation of the greater Rudolf basin into a series of smaller basins is not an adequate explanation, since it would not create barriers sufficient for the dispersal of this terrestrial animal and would instead encourage speciation among piscivorous crocodilians--which never occurred. The populations of *Euthecodon brumpti* and of *C. cataphractus* are similar all around the basin as well as through time.

It is strange and seemingly inexplicable that *C. niloticus* does not occur in the East Rudolf succession. This species was widespread, though probably not as common as has generally been believed. The short-snouted species clearly appears to have predominated.

In the mid-Quaternary only *C. niloticus* persisted in eastern Africa. Because its competitors, the short-snouted species on the terrestrial side and the slender-snouted species on the aquatic side, no longer existed, the Nile species underwent a certain radiation, as is shown in its wide range of variability and the varied modes of life of recent populations.

The Rudolf basin must have afforded a wide range and diversity of habitats to support these four different species of crocodilians, each of which must have occupied, with a certain amount of overlap, separate adaptive zones. This group certainly testifies to the irreversibility of the evolutionary process. Many genera of crocodilians stem from a brevirostrine ancestral condition and evolved into a more or less marked longirostrine condition without any indication of a return to the ancestral structure. Study of the Rudolf crocodilians illustrates that once the snout elongation was (differentially) achieved in *C. niloticus*, *C. cataphractus*, and some representatives of *C.* sp. nov. the ancestral condition was never regained, an affirmation of Dollo's law.

This paper is no. 66 in the East Rudolf Project catalogue of publications.

References

Arambourg, C. 1947. Contribution à l'étude géologique et paléontologique du bassin du lac Rodolphe et de la basse vallée de l'Omo. In *Mission scientifique de l'Omo (1932-33)*. Vol. 1. *Paléontologie*, fasc. 3, pp. 231-562. Mémoire, Muséum national d'histoire naturelle (Paris).

Fourtau, R. 1920. Contribution à l'étude de vertèbres Miocènes de l'Egypte. Cairo: Géol. Surv. Egypte.

Hecht, M. K., and Malone, B. 1972. On the early history of the gavialid crocodilians. *Herpetologica* 28:281-84.

Joleaud, L. 1930. Les crocodiliens du Pliocène d'eau douce de l'Omo (Ethiopie). *Soc. Géol. France, Livre Jubilaire* 1830-1930:411-23.

Said, R. 1973. The geological evolution of the river Nile. Parts I, II, III. International Conference on Northeast African and Levantine Pleistocene Prehistory. Southern Methodist University, Dallas, Texas.

Savage, R. J. G., and Hamilton, W. R. 1973. Introduction to the Miocene mammal faunas of Gebel Zelten, Libya. *Bull. Brit. Mus. Geol.* 22:515-27.

Steel, R. 1973. *Encyclopedia of paleoherpetology*. Part 16. *Crocodylia*. Ed. O. Kuhn, pp. 1-115. Stuttgart: Gustav Fischer Verlag.

Swinton, W. E. 1926. The geology and palaeontology of the Kaiso bone beds. Part 2. Fossil Reptilia. Uganda Protectorate, Geol. Surv. Dept., Occasional paper, no. 2, pp. 37-44.

35. ASSEMBLAGES OF FOSSIL FRESHWATER MOLLUSKS FROM THE OMO GROUP
AND RELATED DEPOSITS IN THE LAKE RUDOLF BASIN

A. Gautier

Preliminary results of the study of the fossil nonmarine mollusks from deposits in
the Lake Rudolf basin have been summarized in Van Damme and Gautier (1972). No important
new samples from the younger deposits (Bourille Formation, Kibish Formation, subrecent
and recent deposits) have been added to the collections, and basically the results published for these deposits are still acceptable. In the older deposits (Omo Group), however, several exposures yielded new and better-preserved material. As a result our views
concerning the systematic position of several forms have changed. Table 1 gives the tentative sequence of molluscan assemblages in the Omo Group as understood now, but further
changes in nomenclature may be necessary if more material from the basin is presented for
study. The major reason for this state of indecision lies within the material itself.
Since their extant descendants the fossil freshwater mollusks of Africa are very polymor-
phous and subject to marked ecophenotypical variation and parallel evolution, it is often
very difficult to evaluate the affinities and the taxonomic status of specimens, especially
when samples are small and are discontinuous in space and time.

The assemblages listed in table 1 indicate that no marked changes in the molluscan
fauna occurred in the course of time. There is only one major break dividing the sequence
in two local zones. The upper zone contains the shellbeds of the upper Shungura Formation
(members H to L) and the fossiliferous deposits of the Nayiena Epul Formation. The lower
zone contains the Mursi Formation, the Usno Formation, and the basal Shungura Formation.
The Loruth Kaado Formation appears to occupy a transitional position.

The upper zone corresponds to the Upper Shungura grouping (Van Damme and Gautier 1972),
and the lower comprises the Mursi and the Usno grouping of the same authors. In the publication cited, the Mursi and Usno groupings were distinguished by the presence of nyassunionid bivalves, which are now thought to be representatives of one very variable chronospecies. This chronospecies is still present in the upper Shungura grouping. Morphologically
it appears to be related to *Pseudobovaria* of the Kaiso Formation and comparable deposits.
The foregoing does not have chronostratigraphic implications, nor does it mean that migration of *Pseudobovaria* occurred as formerly accepted by Gautier (1966). Possibly both
Pseudobovaria forms (Kaiso Formation; Omo Group) are derived from separate nyassunionid
ancestors, preceding them in their respective hydrographic basins and subject to parallel
evolution. Today the nyassunionid group is restricted to Lake Tanganyika and Lake Malawi.
Hence it is probably a relict of a group much more widely distributed in the past.

The upper zone in the Omo Group is characterized by *Cleopatra arambourgi* nov. subsp.
X, *Melanoides* nov. sp. H, *Mutela* nov. sp. H, and *Corbicula consobrina*. Both *C. arambourgi*
nov. subsp. X and *Melanoides* nov. sp. H are probably endemic forms descending respectively
from *Cl. a. arambourgi* and *M. tuberculata*. *Corbicula* is probably a late addition to the
molluscan fauna of Africa. It does not occur in the lower zone of the Omo Group and has
not yet been found in deposits older than the Omo Group deposits of the lower zone, although
it is recently a very common species.

379

Table 1

Tentative Sequence of Molluscan Assemblages in the Omo Group and Related Deposits

Species	MF[1]	UF	SB	LK	SU	KA	NE
Bellamya unicolor		+					
B. unicolor rudolfianus	+						
B. unicolor nov. subsp. S					+		+
Pila ovata					+		
Gabbiella nov. sp. A						+	
Gabbiella sp.	+						
Melanoides tuberculata	+	+	+	+		?	
Melanoides nov. sp. H					+	+	+
Gastropoda gen. et sp. indet.[2]	+						
Cleopatra arambourgi arambourgi	(+)	+	+				
C. arambourgi nov. subsp. X					+	+	+
Cleopatra sp.				+			
Anisus natalensis						+	
Bulinus truncatus cf. *sericinus*						+	
Caelatura rothschildi				+	+		
C. rothschildi rothschildi			+		+	+	+
C. rothschildi nov. subsp. R					+		
C. rothschildi nov. subsp. K						+	
C. cf. *aegyptiaca*			+				
Caelatura sp.	+	+					
C. (Nitia) chefneuxi					+	+	
C. (Nitia) sp.	+	+	+				
Pseudobovaria nov. sp. P[3]	+	+	+	+	+	+	
Mutela nov. sp. Y					+	?	
Pleiodon nov. sp. B?						+	
Pleiodon sp.		+	+				
Etheria elliptica[4]					+	+	
Corbicula consobrina				+			+
Pisidium (cf.) *pirothi*	+					+	
Eupera parasitica						+	
Eupera sp.	+						

[1]MF: Mursi Formation; UF: Usno Formation; SB: Shungura Formation, Basal Member; LK: Loruth Kaado Formation; SU: Shungura Formation, Member H; KA: Shungura Formation in Kalam area, members J to L; NE: Nayiena Epul Formation.

[2]Form described as *Mysorelloides* sp. (Van Damme and Gautier 1972).

[3]Form described as *Nyassunio* (Van Damme and Gautier 1972).

[4]The several river oyster banks in the lower and middle part of the Shungura Formation are not listed.

In the upper zone *Mutela* replaces *Pleiodon*, typical for the lower zone. Pleiodonto-
form naiads have been found in various Tertiary deposits in Africa (Cox 1955; Verdcourt
1963; Gautier 1966, 1970). Today the taxon is represented only by relicts in Lake Tanganyika and in western Africa. In the deposits of the Kalam area a small naiad with a plei-
odontoform hinge (*Pleiodon* sp. B?) is encountered, whose taxonomic status is not yet clear.
It may be a *Pleiodon* related to the large (and normal) *Pleiodon* of the lower zone. In
this case a transitional zone exists in which *Mutela* and *Pleiodon* occur together. It
should be noted that the *Pleiodon* specimens are all small, a fact which may perhaps be interpreted as dwarfing before final extinction. It is less likely that these small pleio-
dontiform specimens represent a marked ecophenotypical variation of *Mutela*. Such pleio-
dontiform mutelids occur in the Kibish Formation and are thought to be reactive forms of
high-energy sectors in the paleo-lake during Kibish times.

It should be stressed that the boundary between the upper and lower zones cannot yet
be traced precisely in the lithostratigraphic sequence, since samples of the middle Omo
Group with diversified fauna are lacking. The deposits between the upper Shungura Formation (members H to L) and the basal Shungura Formation contain almost no mollusks except
for banks of the river oyster *Etheria elliptica*. These are indicative of a swiftly running
large stream, probably very much comparable with the actual Omo River.

Collections from the Turkana District, Kenya, along the southwestern edge of Lake
Rudolf (Kanapoi, Lothagam, Loperot) are also being studied. The older deposits contain
forms comparable to those found in the "Miocene" of East Africa (Verdcourt 1963). The
younger deposits contain a fauna identical to the one collected in the Kibish Formation.
The deposits known as Lothagam 1, 2, and 3 (Patterson, Behrensmeyer, and Sill 1970) are
characterized by a molluscan assemblage which resembles that of the lower zone in the Omo
Group. The molluscan fauna found in the Plio-Pleistocene deposits of Kanapoi resembles
the assemblage of the upper zone in the Omo Group and appears to be later than the basal
Shungura Formation. As far as we know, this does not fit in with the published correlations. However, radiometric dates and paleomammological zonation also do not agree entirely, as is shown by Maglio (1970).

No systematic collections of the East Rudolf region (Galana Boi Beds, Koobi Fora Formation) have been submitted for study. The few samples examined and some preliminary observations I have made in the field indicate that the lowest part of the Koobi Fora Formation (approximately up to the Tulu Bor Tuff) falls within the lower zone of the Omo Group;
the deposits higher in the sequence are characterized by an assemblage which appears to be
comparable to that of the upper zone in the Omo Group. Since the Koobi Fora Formation contains molluscan assemblages at all levels, it will perhaps be possible to trace a sharper
boundary between the molluscan zones, as defined in the Omo Group, in this formation. Samples of complete stratigraphical columns would hence be very welcome for study.

As was already pointed out, no marked changes in fauna are recorded in table 1. In
the molluscan fauna of the Kaiso Formation (Lake Albert and Lake Edward), striking evolutionary changes have been related to progressive changes in the basin to which it was confined. This basin would have become more and more marshy as time progressed, and the molluscan fauna thus developed adaptive devices ("decurvation," spines, bloated forms) to
counter the deleterious effects of a very soft and oozy substrate (Gautier 1966). In Lake
Tanganyika the older endemic molluscan fauna has been called "thalassoid" because it exhibits features which recall marine mollusks. These features probably develop in response
to strong water movement in the littoral zone, related to the great size and depth of the

lake. Comparable selective mechanisms are probably responsible for the special development of naiads, unionids, vivaparids, and other mollusks in the Kaiso Formation. In my
opinion it is hence more likely that the limnic environment of the Kaiso Formation became
more extensive and deeper in the course of time than that it progressively acquired a more
marshy character. The argument can probably be reversed, and the absence of pronounced
endemism in a limnic molluscan fauna can be considered to indicate the absence of such
changes. This would be the case of the Plio-Pleistocene lake which most of the time may
have closely resembled the present-day lake in general setting.

The question has been asked whether mollusks can give indications about salinity and
its changes in the paleo-lake. Mollusks may be confined to lake sectors with regular influx of freshwater and hence survive locally in an environment otherwise too saline. However, if sectors are found with littoral shelf lacustrine sediments which are devoid of
mollusks, or contain assemblages with stunted forms, they may indicate a salinity too high
for normal molluscan life. The fossil material from the Lake Rudolf basin does not yield
evidence of such situations, but all of it was collected in areas, where in the past a
regular influx of freshwater may have occurred. However, when we look at the general
changes of fauna in the Lake Rudolf basin, a trend is visible. The Omo Group and related
deposits contain a fauna with large forms. In the Bourille and Kibish formations the
fauna contains more smaller forms. In the present-day fauna, special biotopes (Ferguson's
Gulf) contain fluviatile and marshy faunal assemblages whereas the lake itself, as far as
we have been able to ascertain until now, seems to yield only a stunted and poor lacustrine
fauna. The foregoing may indicate a general and progressive increase of salinity mainly
related to the aging of the Lake Rudolf basin.

I would like to stress once more that the foregoing statements are preliminary and
tentative. Sampling of several areas is unsystematic or has not been completed; hence new
collections may bring (un)pleasant surprises involving changes of nomenclature, biozonation,
and paleoecological interpretations.

References

Cox, L. R. 1955. Lamellibranchia from the Nubian Sandstone Series of Egypt. In Topography,
    geology and iron ore deposits of the district east of Aswan, ed. M. Attia. *Geol.
    Surv. Egypt*, App., p. 37.

Gautier, A. 1966. Geschiedenis en evolutie van de zoetwater-molluskenfauna in de Albert-
    en Edwardmeren-slenk (with English summary: History and evolution of the fauna of
    freshwater molluscs in the Lake Albert-Edward Rift). *Natuurwet. Tijdschr.* 48:3-24.

_____. 1970. Fossil fresh water Mollusca of the Lake Albert-Edward Rift (Uganda). *Ann.
    Mus. Roy. Afriq. Centr.*, ser. 8, Sci. Géol., no. 67, Tervuren.

Maglio, V. J. 1970. Early Elephantidae of Africa and a tentative correlation of African
    Plio-Pleistocene deposits. *Nature* 225:328-32.

Patterson, B.; Behrensmeyer, A. K.; and Sill, W. D. 1970. Geology and fauna of a new
    Pliocene locality in northwestern Kenya. *Nature* 226:918-21.

Van Damme, D., and Gautier, A. 1972. Molluscan assemblages from the Late Cenozoic of the
    lower Omo basin, Ethiopia. *Quat. Res.* 2:25-37.

Verdcourt, B. 1963. The Miocene nonmarine Mollusca of Rusinga Island, Lake Victoria and
    other localities in Kenya. *Palaeontograph. Abt.*, A121, 1-3:1-37.

36. FOSSIL ASSEMBLAGES IN RELATION TO SEDIMENTARY ENVIRONMENTS
IN THE EAST RUDOLF SUCCESSION

A. K. Behrensmeyer

The primary goal in this study of the East Rudolf fossil assemblages was to determine whether paleoecologic factors are present in faunas from different sedimentary environments. In order to do this, it was first necessary to establish taphonomic histories for bone assemblages from the East Rudolf succession. Taphonomic analysis included consideration of: (1) evidence for hydrodynamic sorting of the bones; (2) degree of hydraulic equivalence between bones and associated sedimentary grains; and (3) surface textures and completeness of individual bones. Such evidence was used to show whether the bone assemblages were autochthonous or allochthonous with respect to their environment of burial. With this information, the faunal compositions of different assemblages could be examined for meaningful paleoecologic similarities or differences.

The fossil assemblages of East Rudolf consist primarily of surface concentrations of bones of large vertebrates. Most of these bones were disarticulated, fragmented, and transported to some extent before burial. Fossil material is abundant in a wide range of lithologies (silty clays to gravels) deposited in channel, floodplain, and delta-margin to lacustrine environments. Seven sampling localities were used to provide data on the East Rudolf bone-sediment associations. These were selected in areas where there was a clear association between the surface fossils and deposits representing particular sedimentary environments. The deposits were assigned to sedimentary environments on the basis of geologic evidence, independent of evidence from the vertebrate faunas. The deposits sampled for bones included 1 floodplain, 2 channel, and 4 delta-margin environments. Sampling localities fall stratigraphically within the Ileret Member, the Upper Member, and the upper part of the Lower Member of the Koobi Fora Formation. Each locality is coded by a two-part number, for example, "103-0256"; "103" indicating that the locality is in Area 103, and "0256" indicating a stratigraphic section (02) and a bed or horizon in this section (56). The localities cover a time span of about 1.5 m.y. (2.8-1.3 m.y.) and do not represent laterally related environments on a single time plane (see figs. 1 and 2).

Method of Sampling

Bones from the seven sampling localities were collected using grid squares laid out over the chosen area of outcrop. The first square was positioned using an arbitrary spot on an aerial photograph or simply by selecting a local landmark, without specific reference to areas with heavy concentrations of bones. Subsequent squares were measured off from the

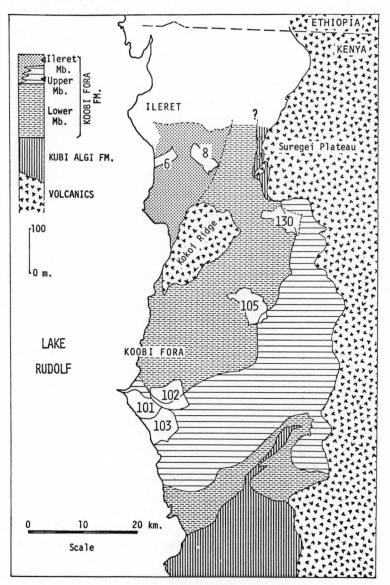

Figure 1. Generalized geologic map and stratigraphic section of East Rudolf, based on Bowen and Vondra (1973) plus unpublished work by Bowen. Numbered areas are those used for controlled sampling of the vertebrate assemblages.

first, with a minimum of 20 m between squares. On horizontal strata, the squares were laid out on an orthogonal 30 x 30 m grid. On dipping strata, the squares were positioned along the strike of the units being sampled. The grid system was adjusted, where necessary, to avoid patches of recent sediment and vegetation. Collecting was done by systematically traversing a square first east-west, then north-south (for a square oriented NSEW). All the surface bones larger than 5 cm (maximum length) were collected in addition to those smaller bones that could be identified to class (fish, mammal, reptile, bird). During the first field season (1971) all samples were removed for identification and study. During the second season, after workers were familiar with the vertebrate taxa and skeletal parts,

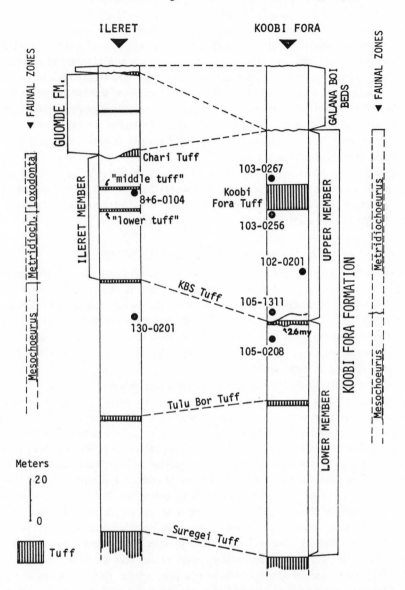

Figure 2. The stratigraphy of East Rudolf, after Bowen and Vondra (1973). Faunal zones as determined by Maglio (1972) are given for the Koobi Fora Formation. The Ileret Member is only in part the time equivalent of the Upper Member (see figure 1). The two-part numbers (e.g., 130-0201) designate the fossil sampling localities used for this study and show their relative stratigraphic positions.

it was possible to do most of the identification in the field. This greatly simplified the logistics of the sampling, enabling workers to leave the field with a card for each square recording taxa and skeletal parts plus the geologic data.

Sampling was designed to give a general picture of the characteristics of bone assemblages preserved in rather broadly defined sedimentary environments. In some localities the bones were derived from a wide range of genetically related lithologies (e.g., sands, silts, and clays, all deposited on a delta margin). The samples thus represent bone accumulations resulting from a wide range of processes associated with channel, floodplain,

and delta-margin environments, in contrast to samples from single beds (e.g., quarry deposits), which are more likely to result from rather localized conditions. The "squares"
sampling method also allows coverage of extensive areas (square kilometers) of outcrops,
on a scale comparable to the habitat sizes of many of the larger East African vertebrates.

The abundance of fossil material in the sample localities was sufficient to provide
an average of 34 identifiable fragments per square and to give a good representation of
the most common skeletal parts and animals in each assemblage. A total of over 9,000 fragments was collected from 213 squares. Collecting was aimed at obtaining the largest possible comparative samples from all localities. Since the surface concentrations of bones
varied from locality to locality, the number of squares collected in each varied as well.
Thus it was necessary to collect more than 60 squares for 8+6-0104 (the floodplain), which
had a low surface concentration, but only 20 for 105-0208 (delta margin). At least 20
squares (=2,000 m^2) were collected in each locality (table 1).

Method of Representing Fossil Abundance

The object in sampling the bone assemblages was to establish the relative abundance
of different skeletal parts and of different animals in a variety of sedimentary environments. The samples could then be compared to determine whether similar environments had
similar proportions of, for example, teeth, vertebrae, and so on and similar numbers of
hippos, crocodiles, and such. The proportions of bones with different original densities,
such as vertebrae and teeth, was particularly important as an indication of the degree of
hydrodynamic sorting in each sample.

It was necessary to devise a method of representing relative bone abundance which
would truly reflect the composition of the original burial assemblages rather than the
numbers of identifiable parts of bones in the surface fossil concentrations. The most
satisfactory method of representing bone abundance is to use the number of squares with a
particular skeletal part or animal. This is done as follows: if one vertebra, or several,
or dozens of pieces of the same one, occur in a sample square, this is counted as 1 occurrence. If one tooth of the same animal occurs in each of 5 squares, this is counted as
5 occurrences. The number of occurrences of each bone or animal is then converted to a
"square frequency" by dividing by the total number of squares in the locality. Thus, 5
occurrences out of a sample of 20 squares gives a frequency of 0.25 (or 25%).

The "square frequency" measure of relative abundance has several advantages that make
it useful in the broadly defined sedimentary units of interest for this study:

1. It gives a measure of the *dispersed* abundance of the different bones or animals
    in space and time, which should be a result of the *overall* conditions of each
    sedimentary environment.

2. Problems encountered in using simple totals of fragments identifiable to a par-
    ticular bone or animal are essentially eliminated, since using presence or absence
    in a square greatly reduces the effects of differential identifiability. Also,
    since the squares are widely spaced, the probability of sampling parts of the
    same bone or even the same animal more than once is very low.

The square frequencies of vertebrate skeletal parts and taxa in the seven sample
assemblages serve as the basis for taphonomic and faunal analysis to be discussed in the
following sections.

Table 1

Stratigraphic Data and Sample Size of the Seven Fossil Sampling Localities

Sampling Locality	No. Sample Squares	Stratigraphic Interval Sampled (m)	Basic Lithology	General Depositional Environment	Koobi Fora Fm. Faunal Unit	Stratigraphic Unit
130-0201	21	7.0	Sand, silt, and clay	Delta margin	*Mesochoerus*	Lower Mb., Koobi Fora Fm.
105-0208	20	2.5	Sand, silt, and clay	Delta margin and lagoon	*Mesochoerus*	Lower Mb., Koobi Fora Fm.
103-0267	20	3.0	Sand and gravel	Distributary-beach complex	*Metridiochoerus*	Upper Mb., Koobi Fora Fm.
103-0256	27	.75	Sand	Transgression over deltaic mud flats	*Metridiochoerus*	Upper Mb., Koobi Fora Fm.
102-0201	34	5.0	Sand and gravel	Channel	*Metridiochoerus*	Upper Mb., Koobi Fora Fm.
105-1311	25	3.0	Sand and gravel	Channel	*Metridiochoerus*	Upper Mb., Koobi Fora Fm.
8+6-0104	66	4.5	Silt	Floodplain	*Locodonta*	Ileret Mb., Koobi Fora Fm.

NOTE: Sample squares are 10 x 10 m, representing 100 m^2 each.

Sorting in Bone Assemblages of the Koobi Fora Formation

Square frequencies for mammalian and reptilian skeletal parts are given in table 2. The different bone assemblages show considerable variation in the relative abundance of skeletal parts. In order to determine whether consistent patterns of variation are present in the different sedimentary environments, the data were analyzed quantitatively using multiple regression and factor analysis.

Correlation coefficients[1] between the different assemblages, based on the relative abundances of mammal bones only, were generated using a program for multiple regression developed for the Wang 600 computer. Correlations based on the relative abundances of the five most common bones--teeth, vertebrae, phalanges, scapulae, and radii/ulnae--are shown in figure 3. An obvious feature of all the correlations is that they are high (>.5). This shows a basic similarity in the proportions of the five skeletal elements in all the sample assemblages. This similarity probably reflects the relative numbers of the different bones most likely to survive carnivore activity and surface weathering and become sedimentary particles available to all the depositional environments.

Many of the correlations shown in figure 3 are significantly different in spite of the overall similarity. The highest and lowest coefficients differ with a probability of significance ≥.95, according to the "z test" (Simpson, Roe, and Lewontin 1960, p. 246). Other coefficients are indicative of trends even when their differences are not within the acceptable limits of significance (p>.95). Channel assemblages are closely correlated with each other and with the floodplain. The delta-margin assemblages have relatively low correlations with the floodplain, variable degrees of correlation with the channels, and high correlations among themselves. From this it is clear that similar sedimentary environments are similar in the compositions of their bone assemblages.

The next step in the analysis was to determine which skeletal parts were most important in causing the observed correlations. This was done using a Q-Mode factor analysis, "CABFAC," which was run on the frequency data from all the mammalian skeletal parts. A solution of three varimax factors (axes placed within the data array) explained 97% of the total variance in the assemblages. The projection of the data for each locality on these axes is plotted on the triangle diagram shown in figure 4. The three factors consist of: (1) vertebrae and phalanges; (2) teeth; and (3) limb parts such as tibiae, metapodials, and astragali. Factors 1 and 2 are most effective in separating the samples. Three of the deltaic localities have a relatively high proportion of vertebrae and phalanges, and the channels and the floodplain have high proportions of teeth. One deltaic locality (103-0267), a distributary-beach complex) falls between the two groupings.

The three factors shown in figure 4 are closely comparable to bone groups that have been shown to have different dispersal potentials under hydrodynamic stress. These can be referred to as "Voorhies groups," after Voorhies (1969), who did the original flume studies on disarticulated skeletons of sheep and coyote. The dispersal groups apply to larger animals as well, since the densities of different skeletal parts vary consistently regardless of size. Voorhies Group I includes vertebrae and phalanges and is the most easily transported bone group. This is due primarily to the low density of these bones, plus a relatively high surface area to volume ratio for the vertebrae. Voorhies Group II includes limb parts and the denser or larger elements that are less easily transported and tend to move as part of the bed load. Voorhies Group III, which includes skulls, half mandibles, and high-density parts such as teeth, forms a lag group of relatively low dispersal

---

1. Pearson's product moment correlation.

Table 2

Square Frequencies of Reptile and Mammal Skeletal Parts in the Seven Sample Localities

Body Part	Delta				Channel		Floodplain
	130- 0201	105- 0208	103- 0267	103- 0256	102- 0201	105- 1311	8+6- 0104
Reptile							
Tooth	.86	.85	.50	.33	.26	.68	.12
Skull/jaw	.10	.05	.30	.07	.15	.08	.00
Vertebra	.19	.05	.15	.19	.18	.00	.02
Limb	.14	.05	.05	.15	.09	.00	.00
Scute	.24	.40	.50	.30	.24	.40	.02
Phalanx	.10	.15	.00	.04	.00	.04	.00
Carapace/ plastron	.24	1.00	.70	.81	.24	.32	.12
No. of occurrences per square (average)	1.9	2.5	2.2	1.9	1.1	1.1	.3
Mammal and Reptile							
Tooth	.95	1.00	.80	.59	.76	1.00	.67
Rib	.76	.90	.85	.63	.53	.64	.32
Pelvis	.14	.25	.25	.04	.06	.16	.05
Diaphysis	.57	1.00	.95	.89	.71	.92	.55
Phalanx	.52	.55	.35	.30	.15	.32	.12
Vertebra	.57	.85	.55	.59,	.29	.48	.15
Mammal							
Tooth	.67	.85	.70	.56	.62	1.00	.52
Jaw part	.24	*.10*	*.10*	*.04*	.21	*.08*	*.09*
Maxilla	*.05*	*.00*	*.00*	*.00*	*.00*	*.00*	*.02*
Cranial part	*.05*	.25	.15	*.07*	.12	*.08*	*.08*
Horn core	.19	.25	.35	.15	.18	.36	*.03*
Vertebra	.48	.75	.50	.59	.15	.36	.15
Sacrum	*.00*	*.00*	*.05*	*.04*	*.00*	*.00*	*.00*
Scapula	.14	.45	*.15*	.15	.12	.20	*.09*
Pelvis	*.10*	*.20*	.20	*.04*	*.03*	*.12*	*.05*
Humerus	.19	.50	.30	.11	*.06*	.20	.14
Radius/ulna	.14	.40	.20	.11	.15	.20	.15
Femur	.14	.40	*.05*	*.07*	.18	.16	*.08*
Tibia	*.10*	.30	.25	*.07*	*.06*	.28	.14
Patella	*.05*	*.05*	*.00*	*.00*	*.00*	*.04*	*.00*
Metapodial	*.10*	.40	.40	.22	.18	.32	.14
Astragalus	*.10*	*.20*	.25	.11	*.03*	*.08*	.14
Calcaneum	*.10*	*.15*	.15	.15	*.00*	*.12*	*.08*
Podial	*.10*	.45	*.10*	.19	.24	.20	.18
Phalanx	.48	.65	.35	.26	.15	.28	.12
Total no. of squares	21	20	20	27	34	25	66
No. of occurrences per square (average)	3.4	6.4	4.2	2.9	2.4	4.1	2.2
Associated parts	.04	.20	.05	.04	.00	.00	.06
Juveniles	.14	.30	.05	.04	.06	.12	.00
% hippo bones	18%	16%	21%	6%	12%	7%	2%

Total no. of squares for all localities: 213

Average occurrences per square: 690/213 = 3.2

NOTE: Frequencies are calculated as the number of squares with a particular element divided by the total number of squares in each locality. The frequencies of associated partial skeletons and juvenile bones are calculated in the same manner. Italic frequencies indicate the elements which would occur in each locality if the total number of bone occurrences were equal to 30 (see text). Mammal and reptile bones are combined in the second listing to include those which could not be definitely assigned to one or the other class. This shows the relatively high proportion of rib and diaphysis fragments in the total bone sample.

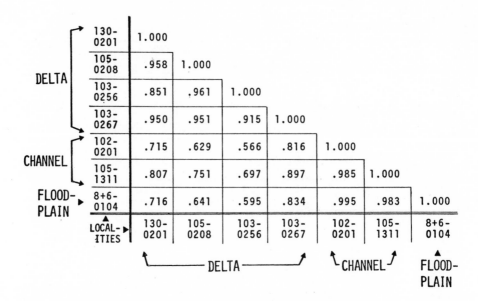

Figure 3. Correlation coefficients between sampling localities according to the proportions of the five most common skeletal parts; teeth, vertebrae, phalanges, radii/ulnae, and scapulae. Highest correlations show strong similarities between channel and floodplain environments in terms of the proportions of the different skeletal parts.

potential. Thus the three factors for the fossil bone assemblages indicate that hydrodynamic sorting is important in creating the observed similarities between assemblages from similar sedimentary environments.

One possible interpretation of the patterns of bone occurrence is that the channels and floodplain retained the lag component of the local thanatocoenose while the more transportable bones were carried out to the delta margins. This implies that the original thanatocoenoses were divided into two major groups by the processes of hydrodynamic sorting, and that all of the assemblages are more or less allochthonous with respect to the original habitats of the mammalian faunas. However, this interpretation is not in agreement with the total composition of the bone assemblages from the delta margin deposits, which include many bones belonging to Voorhies groups II and III as well as to the more easily dispersed Group I.

Comparisons of the square frequency data with the relative proportions of different bones in a single whole skeleton can be used to show how greatly the assemblages have been altered from their original states. Average proportions of bones in a single skeleton were calculated, combining the most common mammal groups in the fossil assemblages--bovids, hippos, suids, and equids. Figure 5 shows the comparison of the fossil and single skeleton bone proportions for the five most common parts. The assemblages fall into two obvious groups, with the delta-margin samples closely correlated with the single skeleton whereas the channel and floodplain samples show considerable alteration of bone proportions from those of the single skeleton. This clearly indicates that the delta-margin assemblages are not composed primarily of allochthonous Group I material but represent thanatocoenoses that were preserved with a minimum of selective sorting. It seems highly unlikely that these assemblages could have resulted from the fortuitous combination of transported material. The taphocoenoses are therefore basically autochthonous with respect to the delta-margin

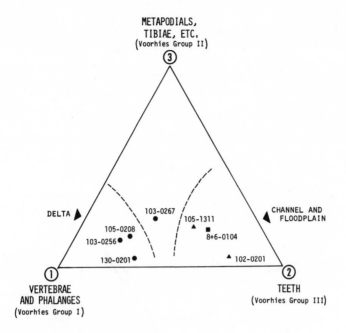

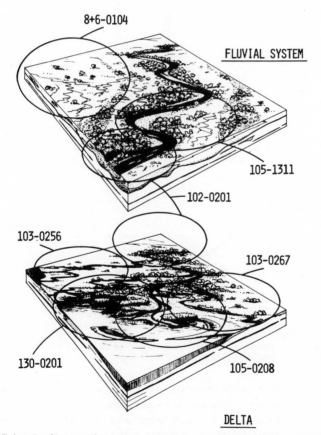

Figure 4. Triangle diagram showing the results of a three-factor analysis of the frequency data for all mammalian bones. Block diagrams indicate the sedimentary environments of each of the fossil sample localities, as determined by geologic evidence.

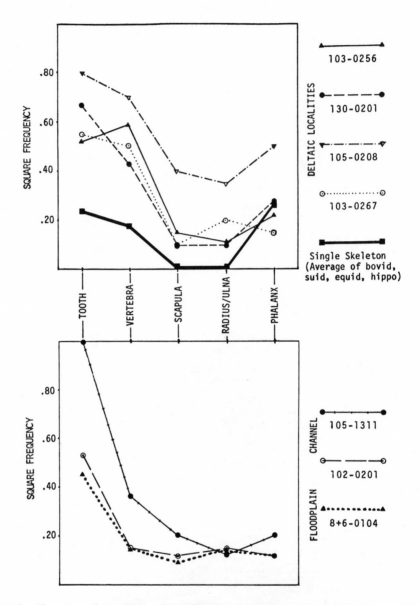

Figure 5. The square frequencies of the five most common mammalian skeletal parts in each locality compared with the relative abundance of the same elements in a single, average skeleton. The localities separated by the factor analysis (fig. 4) are distinct in their degree of alteration from single skeleton proportions.

habitats. Other evidence such as the generally good condition of the fossil bones, indicating minimal transport abrasion, supports this conclusion.

The channel assemblages show the high concentration of teeth which has often been observed in such deposits. There is also considerable evidence for bone abrasion. The channel assemblages were clearly transported and lost most of the lighter and smaller bones either through winnowing and abrasion, through weathering, or through both. Therefore, most of the vertebrates preserved in the channel assemblages are allochthonous with respect to their original habitats. However, the bones were derived from upstream floodplains and channel banks and can be associated with a fluvial environment which is distinct from the delta-margin environments. The floodplain assemblage, 8+6-0104, is similar to the channels in having large numbers of teeth and relatively few low-density bones. However, it differs from the channels in that there is little evidence for abrasion on the bone surfaces. Also, the bones are preserved in silts that are much finer grained than the hydraulically equivalent grain sizes of the bones (=coarse sand to pebbles). In the channels, the bones occur in association with gravels of similar equivalent grain sizes. The floodplain assemblage appears to be autochthonous but altered, with the lighter elements removed through winnowing or selective weathering or both.

Thus, the most useful samples for paleoecologic interpretation of the vertebrate faunas will be those from the delta-margin and floodplain deposits. For the mammal assemblages of the Koobi Fora Formation, these samples represent autochthonous thanatocoenoses. The channel assemblages should provide interesting faunal comparisons, since they represent thanatocoenoses that were probably similar to that of the floodplain but that are environmentally distinct from those of the delta margin.

Patterns of Faunal Abundance in the Sample Assemblages

The fossil assemblages consist of material that can be identified at a number of different taxonomic levels. Groups of vertebrates used for faunal comparisons among the sample localities were designated according to two criteria: (1) each group should be represented by a large enough square frequency sample to permit statistically meaningful comparisons between assemblages; (2) the numbers of each group should have approximately equal numbers of identifiable parts. The groups that allowed the most satisfactory faunal comparisons between the sample assemblages are shown in figure 6, along with their square frequencies in each locality. The fauna from the squares sample as a whole includes 14 out of the 20 major vertebrate groups listed by Maglio (1972) for the Koobi Fora Formation. Square frequencies are not directly comparable for mammals and reptiles because of the differential identifiability of their bones, and these appear on separate graphs in figure 6. Several mammalian tribes and genera were abundant enough in the samples to allow comparisons at lower taxonomic levels. These include the suids *Mesochoerus*, *Metridiochoerus*, and *Notochoerus*, *Hippopotamus* cf. *ethiopicus*, and bovids of the groups Reduncinae, Tragelaphini, and Alcelaphinae.

For the mammals, the graph in figure 6 shows that there is an overall similarity in the relative abundance of the different groups in the seven sample assemblages. In general, the delta-margin environments are less diverse in terms of terrestrial mammals, although these environments preserve as many or more bones of terrestrial animals as do the channels or floodplain. For the autochthonous delta-margin and floodplain assemblages, the relative abundances of the larger animals, particularly the suids, bovids, hippos, and equids, should in part reflect the original relative abundances of these animals in their ecosystems over the time spans sampled. However, there is a definite taphonomic bias against the smaller animals due to the greater destructability and dispersal potential of their bones, and the square frequencies of rodents, carnivores, and primates do not necessarily reflect their relative abundance in the original ecosystems.

The reptilian groups show more variable patterns of relative abundance which may

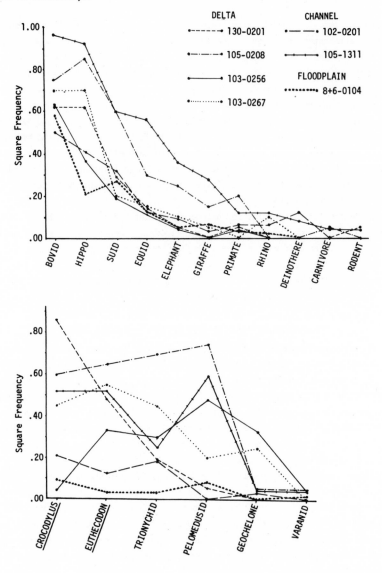

Figure 6. Comparisons of the square frequencies of mammal and reptile groups in the seven sample localities.

reflect, to a certain extent, their ecological preferences (excepting varanids and *Geochelone*) for aquatic habitats with characteristics that are not preserved in the sedimentary record. Such characteristics could include vegetation and water turbidity. The two crocodilians, *Euthecodon* and *Crocodylus*, were recorded only on the basis of teeth, which should have essentially equivalent hydraulic properties and not be subject to differential transport sorting. On the basis of the comparable square frequencies of the two forms in most of the localities, it is valid to conclude that they occupied overlapping ranges; that is, both were present in the deltaic and channel environments. Specific habitat preferences of *Euthecodon* may be reflected in its relative abundance in the delta-margin deposit, 103-0256, compared with *Crocodylus*. The sediments of 103-0256 were deposited during a relatively rapid transgression of beach sands over a deltaic mud flat, and the open and evidently nonturbid water apparently was favored by *Euthecodon*, as well as a pelomedusid, which is also relatively abundant in 103-0256.

The low frequencies of the aquatic reptiles and also of *Hippopotamus* in the floodplain assemblage is consistent with the environmental interpretation based on geologic evidence. In the more aquatic sedimentary environments of the channels and delta margins, the aquatic and semiaquatic vertebrates are abundant, but purely terrestrial animals are nearly as abundant as aquatic ones in these environments. This leads to the rather interesting conclusion that the aquatic or nonaquatic habits of the fossil vertebrates could not be validly inferred from their relative abundances in the channel or delta-margin environments of deposition.

Patterns of Occurrence of Specific Mammalian Groups

Suids.

Three genera of suids are common in the sample assemblages and occur in variable frequencies from locality to locality. Square frequencies (based only on molars) are indicated in figure 7. *Notochoerus* and *Metridiochoerus* are combined since molar fragments of the two are difficult to distinguish. They are similar in having high-crowned, elongate third molars adapted for grazing, and both are thought to belong to the same group as the modern *Phacochoerus* (Cooke and Maglio 1972, p. 312). *Mesochoerus* is easily distinguished from the other suids by its low-crowned molars, which are apparently adapted for softer vegetation. *Mesochoerus* is believed to be close to the ancestral stock of the recent

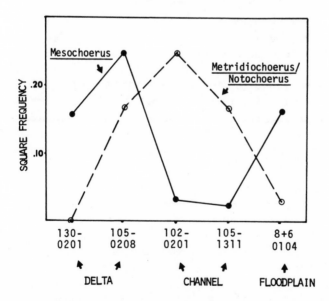

Figure 7. A comparison of the square frequencies of the two suid groups, *Mesochoerus* and *Metridiochoerus/Notochoerus*. The latter two genera are combined because the molar fragments used in determining the square frequencies are often not identifiable as one or the other. Localities 103-0256 and 103-0267 are omitted because of their low frequencies of suids identifiable to genus.

Hylochoerus (Cooke and Maglio 1972, p. 311), a dense bush or forest animal.

The pattern of occurrences of the two suid groups as shown in figure 7 suggests that in some cases they are almost mutually exclusive in the fossil assemblages. *Notochoerus/ Metridiochoerus* is more common in the channel assemblages, and *Mesochoerus* is more typical of the floodplain and two of the delta-margin assemblages (103-0256 and 103-0267 were excluded because of their low frequencies of both suid groups). The separation of the two groups is best explained by paleoecologic factors, since there is little cause to suspect selective sorting or preservation of the molar fragments in the different environments. If *Mesochoerus* can be associated with more densely vegetated habitats, then its pattern of occurrence indicates that the delta margins and the floodplain were more densely vegetated than the areas that provided vertebrate remains to the channel deposits. This suggests a lack of extensive gallery forests bordering the channels away from the lake.

Bovids.

The three most abundant bovid groups, Alcelaphinae, Tragelaphini, and Reduncinae, are well known in terms of the habitat preferences of modern species. Alcelaphines generally prefer open grasslands, tragelaphines mixed grassland, bush, and gallery forest environments, and reduncines dense bush to open woodland environments (Dorst and Dandelot 1970; Bigalke 1972; Estes 1974). Table 3 gives the square frequencies of the different bovid groups in the fossil assemblages from the Koobi Fora Formation. The patterns of occurrence are not as well defined as for the suids, but bush forms are generally more common in the deltaic environments, whereas the grassland form is associated with the channels. The mud flats assemblage of 103-0256 shows a high frequency of alcelaphines, which is notably comparable to the present abundance of these bovids on the deltaic mud flats bordering the east side of Lake Rudolf.

Hippos.

The habitat of the extinct small hippo, *Hippopotamus* cf. *ethiopicus*, can be generally inferred from its frequency in the bone assemblages (table 3). It occurs in all localities except 105-1311 and is most abundant in 103-0256, the deltaic mud flats environment. In general, it is associated with both bush and grassland faunas. Relatively greater abundance and better skeletal representation of the small hippo in the autochtonous delta-margin assemblages indicate that it was probably a lake-margin form, preferring deltaic flats with mixed bush and grassland environments. It may have been less aquatic than the larger hippos, but this can be validly inferred only from morphological data, not from the taphonomic evidence now available.

Open and Closed Habitat Mammalian Faunas

The most common terrestrial mammals from the sample assemblages can be separated into two ecological groups based on morphology and on the habitat preferences of recent analogues. These groups include *Mesochoerus*, reduncines, and tragelaphines as representatives of the bush-preferring or "closed"-habitat fauna and alcelaphines, and *Notochoerus/ Metridiochoerus* and *Equus* as representatives of the grassland or "open"-habitat fauna. The relative proportions of these groups in two of the most sedimentologically distinct localities, 130-0201 (delta margin) and 105-1311 (channel) are compared in figure 8. There is a significant faunal difference between the two assemblages which correlates with the difference in sedimentary environment and indicates more closed habitats associated with the delta. The temporal difference between the two faunas (see fig. 2) should not have a

Table 3

Frequencies of Fossil Bovids and the Small Hippopotamus in the East Rudolf Assemblages

Taxon	Delta				Channel		Floodplain
	130-0201	105-0208	103-0267	103-0256	102-0201	105-1311	8+6-0104
Tragelaphini	.24	.10	.20	.00	.12	.16	.02
Reduncinae	.24	.25	.15	.11	.15	.12	.15
Alcelaphinae (*Damaliscus*-size)	.14	.15	.05	.33	.00	.40	.12
Alcelaphinae (*Megalotragus*)	.00	.00	.15	.04	.00	.48	.03
Hippopotamus cf. *ethiopicus*	.03	.20	.10	.26	.09	.00	.06

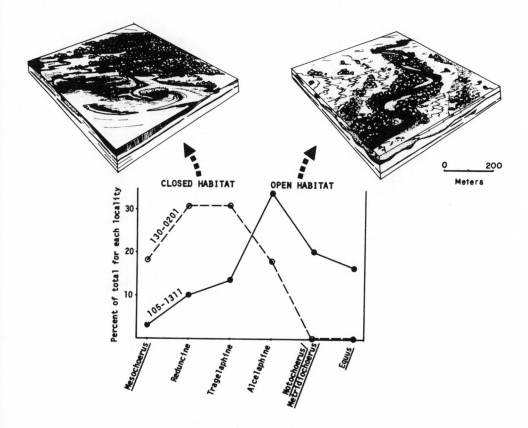

Figure 8. A comparison of the relative abundances of the six mammal groups chosen to represent open- and closed-habitat faunas for two localities that are very different in terms of sedimentary environment. Percentages were calculated on the basis of the cumulative totals of square frequencies of the six animals in each locality. The reconstructions represent the general sedimentary contexts of each fossil assemblage.

significant effect on the faunal differences, since the six taxa are present at both time
horizons in the East Rudolf deposits.

If the square frequencies for the three closed- and three open-habitat forms are combined and recalculated in terms of percentage for each locality, this gives a general indication of the vertebrate communities that were most heavily sampled in the taphocoenoses
of each sedimentary environment. Figure 9 shows that in general the channel environments
include more open habitat forms and the deltaic environments more closed habitat forms,
with the exception of 103-0256, which was evidently free of extensive vegetation other than
grass (deltaic mud flats). The floodplain shows a mixed fauna, as might be expected from
analogies with recent faunas such as that of the Kafue Floodplain in Zambia (Sheppe and
Osborne 1971).

The patterns of faunal occurrence in the fossil assemblages of the Koobi Fora Formation show that the different sedimentary environments preserve different faunal assemblages
which can be related to ecologically distinct vertebrate communities comparable to those of
the modern East African ecosystems.

<u>Comparison of Koobi Fora Formation Faunas
and Recent Terrestrial Faunas</u>

Bovids, suids, and equids are the most abundant large terrestrial mammals in all seven
of the fossil assemblages and also in many of the recent undisturbed East African

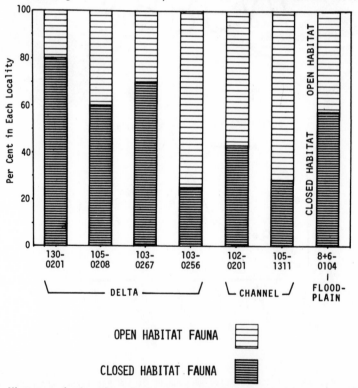

Figure 9. Histogram showing the relative percentages of closed- and open-habitat mammals
in each of the sample localities. Closed-habitat forms include *Mesochoerus*, reduncines,
and tragelaphines; open-habitat forms include *Damaliscus*-size alcelaphines, *Notochoerus/
Metridiochoerus* and *Equus*. Percentages were calculated on the basis of the total square
frequencies for the closed- and open-habitat groups.

ecosystems (e.g., Foster 1967; Sheppe and Osborne 1971). The relative abundance of these mammals in the fossil faunas is compared with their abundance (based on game census) in recent faunas in figure 10. Bovids are most common in all cases. However, equids are less common than suids in all of the fossil samples, and the faunal proportions are most comparable to those of the recent Kafue Park fauna. Taphonomic causes do not satisfactorily explain the greater frequency of suids in the fossil assemblages. It is possible that higher productivity in suids, resulting in a more rapid rate of population turnover, may be in part responsible for their greater fossil abundance. However, this abundance also correlates with the greater diversity of the Suidae in the Plio-Pleistocene of East Rudolf, with at least five contemporaneous species recognized from the total fauna (Maglio 1972). Equids may have relatively lower fossil representation because they were more ecologically separated from the sedimentary environments or because they were generally less abundant in the East Rudolf region during the time period represented by the fossil deposits.

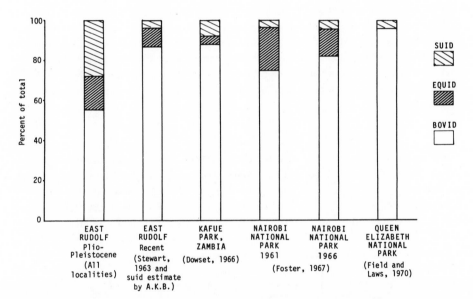

Figure 10. Comparisons of the relative percentages of bovids, suids, and equids in the seven Plio-Pleistocene localities used for this study (averaged) and in Recent ecosystems. All relative abundances for the recent examples are based on numbers of individuals (game counts).

Hominid Paleoecology

The hominid fossils that occur in the Koobi Fora Formation should reflect the same taphonomic processes as the remains of other vertebrates. Therefore, they can be examined in the context of the rest of the fauna for possible paleoecologic factors. The abundance of hominids in the East Rudolf collections is due to an intensive program of hominid collecting and does not reflect their true relative abundance in the total fauna. In reality they are fairly rare, as is indicated by occurrences in only 2 out of the 213 sample squares used for this study. This is comparable to the relative abundance of rodent fossils. It would be necessary to sample hundreds or thousands of squares to provide enough hominid material for valid quantitative comparisons of frequencies in different sedimentary environments. This is not feasible, but it is possible to relate the hominids (and other rare taxa) to the different environments and to the closed- or open-habitat faunas using the sedimentary and faunal context of each specimen. Based on the patterns of occurrence of other mammals, it seems possible that two lineages of hominids, *Australopithecus* and *Homo* (after R. Leakey), from East Rudolf were associated with different habitats.

As of April 1973 the East Rudolf hominid collection consisted of 50 specimens assigned to *Australopithecus*, 34 assigned to *Homo*, and 10 unassigned (Meave Leakey, pers. comm.). Both taxa are represented by a wide variety of skeletal parts. The greater abundance of *Australopithecus* specimens is due primarily to a larger number of partial mandibles of this form. This may reflect taphonomic processes (e.g., carnivore activity, surface weathering) that operated to selectively destroy the less robust *Homo* mandibles, rather than a greater original abundance of *Australopithecus*.

There is as yet no clear pattern indicating occurrences of the two forms in different sedimentary environments. Both occur in deltaic and floodplain deposits. *Australopithecus* is possibly the only hominid occurring in the 105-1311 channel, where it is relatively common (at least 7 separate specimens plus 2 occurrences in squares). This is interesting in that it correlates with other faunal peculiarities of 105-1311, which has a high proportion of open-habitat mammals plus forms (deinotheres, rhinos) that are rare in the deltaic assemblages. However, since a variety of habitats were evidently sampled in the 105-1311 assemblage, it would be premature to draw any conclusions on the habitat preferences of *Australopithecus*.

Fossil Assemblages in Relation to Archeological Sites

The sample assemblage from 105-0208 (delta margin) occurs in deposits several meters below the KBS Tuff, which is the horizon bearing a number of hominid "campsites" dated at about 2.6 m.y. (Isaac, Leakey, and Behrensmeyer 1972). The relative abundance of the different vertebrate groups (fig. 6) is probably broadly representative of the fauna that was extant on the deltaic plain at the time of the hominid habitation sites in Area 105. At this time, however, the delta margin had changed in position, probably receding farther to the southwest. The deposits directly associated with the KBS Tuff (primarily a channel fill in Area 105) are fine-grained silty clays with some sand lenses. The sediments indicate extensive interdistributary marshes and mud flats that were probably seasonally dry. Such environments do not seem to be conducive to fossil preservation on the recent Omo Delta (Butzer 1971, p. 103), and fossils are indeed rare in the silty clays associated with the habitation sites. Thus evidence for the faunal context of the tool-manufacturing hominids must come indirectly from the older 105-0208 fauna. This provides at least regional, if not local, evidence for the ecological context of the hominid campsites.

This is paper no. 67 in the East Rudolf Project catalogue of publications.

References

Bigalke, R. C. 1972. The contemporary mammalian fauna of Africa. In *Evolution, mammals and southern continents*, ed. A. Keast, B. Glass, and F. C. Erk, pp. 141-94. Albany: State University of New York Press.

Bowen, B. E., and Vondra, C. F. 1973. Stratigraphical relationships of the Plio-Pleistocene deposits, East Rudolf, Kenya. *Nature* 242:391-93.

Butzer, K. W. 1971. Recent history of an Ethiopian delta: The Omo River and the level of Lake Rudolf. University of Chicago Dept. of Geography, Research Paper no. 136.

Cooke, H. B. S., and Maglio, V. J. 1972. Plio-Pleistocene stratigraphy in East Africa in relation to proboscidean and suid evolution. In *Calibration of hominoid evolution,* ed. W. W. Bishop and J. Miller, pp. 303-29. Edinburgh: Scottish Academic Press; Toronto: University of Toronto Press.

Dorst, J., and Dandelot, P. 1970. *Larger mammals of Africa.* London: Collins Press.

Dowsett, R. J. 1966. Wet season game population and biomass in the Ngoma area of the Kafue National Park. *Puku,* no. 4, pp. 135-45.

Estes, R. D. 1974. *Social organization of the African Bovidae.* In *The behaviour of ungulates and its relation to management,* ed. V. Geist and F. Walther. Morges, Switzerland: I.U.C.N.

Field, C. R., and Laws, R. M. 1970. The distribution of the larger herbivores in the Queen Elizabeth National Park, Uganda. *J. Appl. Ecol.* 7:273-94.

Foster, J. B. 1967. Nairobi National Park game census, 1966. *E. Afr. Wildl. J.* 5:112-20.

Isaac, G. L.; Leakey, R. E. F.; and Behrensmeyer, A. K. 1971. Archeological traces of early hominid activities east of Lake Rudolf, Kenya. *Science* 173:1129-34.

Maglio, V. J. 1972. Vertebrate faunas and chronology of hominid-bearing sediments east of Lake Rudolf, Kenya. *Nature* 239:379-85.

Sheppe, W., and Osborne, T. 1971. Patterns of use of a floodplain by Zambian mammals. *Ecol. Monogr.* 41:181-205.

Simpson, G. G.; Roe, A.; and Lewontin, R. C. 1960. *Quantitative zoology.* New York: Harcourt, Brace and World.

Stewart, D. R. M. 1963. Wildlife census, Lake Rudolf. *E. Afr. Wildl. J.* 1:121.

Voorhies, M. 1969. Taphonomy and population dynamics of an early Pliocene vertebrate fauna, Knox County, Nebraska. *Contrib. Geol. Spec. Paper* no. 1. Laramie: University of Wyoming Press.

D. C. Johanson, M. Splingaer, and N. T. Boaz

Paleontological excavation in the deposits of the Shungura Formation, lower Omo basin, has been carried out each year since 1969 by a variety of workers. The sites investigated range in age from approximately 2.8 m.y. in Member B to 1.9 m.y. in Member G. The purpose of this chapter is to report and summarize the findings of these excavations.

By providing data in the form of fossil finds in a known sedimentary regime, excavation (with taphonomic analysis) can answer questions relating to the phylogeny, autecology, and morphology of a species. Second, it can provide indications of the paleoenvironment and synecology of the biotic community at one time level. Third, through these first two aspects, excavation supplies essential data for the reconstruction of the total way of life and evolution of early hominids.

Four major excavations, at localities 345, 338y, 398, and 626, have been carried out. These four sites are diagramed and their age, geology, areal extent, faunal composition, and taphonomy are discussed. A number of minor localities have been investigated, and these are summarized by member.

Excavations

Locality 345

The fossiliferous horizon at Locality 345 occurs on a dark brown sand-silt interface in Member C some 10 to 15 m below Tuff D, dated by potassium-argon at 2.35 ± 0.12 m.y. (Brown, de Heinzelin, and Howell, 1970, p. 256; Brown and Nash, this symposium). The bone-bearing horizon dips toward the southeast corner of the excavated area (fig. 1). The sediments at Locality 345 are interbedded sands and silts.

The excavation was made on a tongue between two erosion gullies. An immense overburden was present varying from 2 m in the front of the excavation to 8 m in thickness at the back wall. This was removed with picks in 1970 and with the use of a gasoline-powered jackhammer in 1973, to a level approximately 1/2 m above the bone-bearing layer.

Investigation of this locality was first suggested by finds of cercopithecine remains and a hominid parietal fragment by Gerald Eck in 1969. Excavation was carried out in 1970 by D. Cramer and Johanson and in 1973 by Boaz. A total area of 65 m^2 has been exposed and mapped (fig. 1).

The orientations of long bones with a discernable long axis were plotted from maps of the excavation (fig. 2). Surprisingly, a definite east-west orientation was preferred.

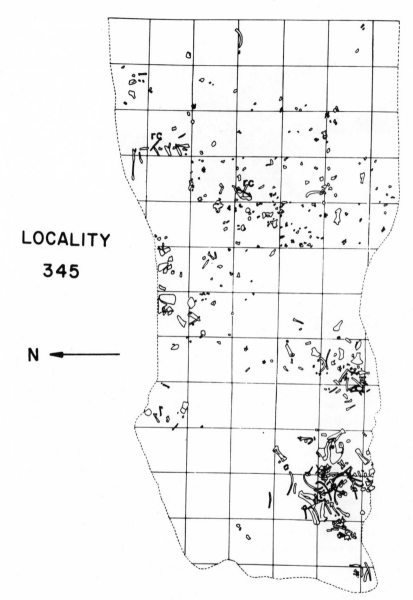

LOCALITY

345

N ←———

Figure 1. Map of 1970 and 1973 excavations at Locality 345, Member C.

L. 345 has previously been thought to represent a pond or similar low-energy depositional
situation with little or no current activity. This conclusion derived from the relative
completeness and unrolled nature of the skeletal remains. Two disarticulated but nearly
complete *Hippopotamus protamphibius* skeletons were excavated in 1970 (southwest quadrant
of the excavation). However, as can be seen from figure 2 and from figure 3, in which
bones within 20° of the east-west axis are shaded, a predominant orientation is present and
is not confined to one area of the site or to one type of bone.

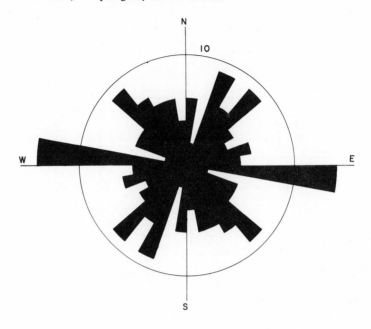

Figure 2. Orientations of long axes of bones excavated at Locality 345 in 10° intervals. Circle indicates magnitude at 10 bones.

The most probable hypothesis concerning the taphonomy at L. 345 is that the site represents a backswamp or near-channel "slough" subjected perhaps several times to flowing water which oriented the bones but effected minimum transport.[1] Preliminary results on flume experiments with recent bones by one of us (Boaz) and A. K. Behrensmeyer indicate that human hemimandibles orient with the medial border up and the condylar end pointing upstream. A similar *Theropithecus brumpti* hemimandible, excavated in 1970, had its condylar end pointing east and lay with its medial side up. Of the specimens shaded in figure 3 the larger ends point east (therefore indicating east-to-west current flow, after Voorhies 1969, p. 66), except for the *Hippopotamus* pelvis, which seems to be partially articulated. These are tentative indications of an east-to-west flow of water that oriented the bones. Root casts (labeled "rc" in fig. 1) were excavated 5 to 15 cm above the main bone layer and indicate subaerial conditions after deposition.

Cercopithecines are common in the faunal assemblage and account for 32% of the excavated fauna (fig. 4). Parts of at least four *T. brumpti* individuals occur, as well as the two *Hippopotamus* individuals. Table 1 summarizes percentages of identified specimens. These percentages have been only partially corrected to represent the probable number of individuals present, since field identifications were necessarily employed in the calculations because some materials had not been studied. No specimens, however, were assumed to show the presence of more than one animal when they could be determined to belong to the same individual. Because of the probable sedimentary conditions and the complete and relatively untransported nature of the remains, it is possible to hypothesize that this was an autochthonous fauna. In comparison with other excavated occurrences, the preponderance of

1. The authors are indebted to A. K. Behrensmeyer and Bruce Hanson, University of California, Berkeley, Department of Paleontology, for this suggestion.

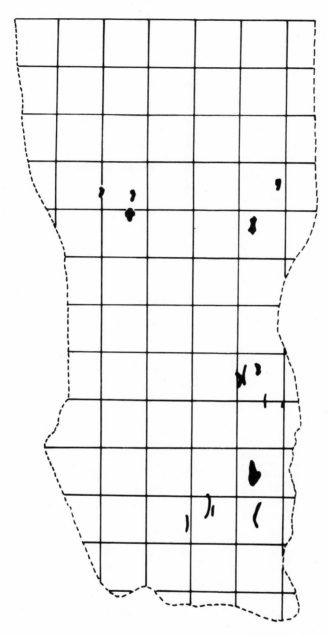

Figure 3. Bones at Locality 345 whose long axes lie within 20° of the east-west axis. Bones in this orientation are not confined to one area of the site and may indicate east-to-west current flow.

reptiles and fish (51%) and the small percentage of bovids (8%) is noteworthy.

In 1973 L. 345 yielded one of the most complete and well-preserved crania of *Theropithecus brumpti* yet discovered. The dentition was complete except for canines and incisors (one canine found eroding from the fossiliferous horizon in 1971 later proved to be from the same individual and fits perfectly into the upper left alveolus). The

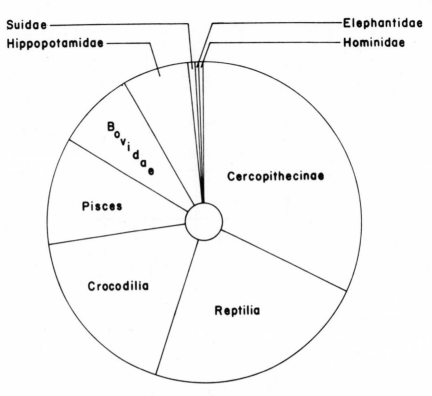

Figure 4. Pie diagram illustrating percentages of identified taxa present at Locality 345 (see table 1).

Table 1

Locality 345, Composition of Fauna

Taxon	Number of Specimens	Percentage
Bovidae	17	07.94
Cercopithecinae	69	32.24
Elephantidae	1	00.47 (1)
Hippopotamidae	14	06.54
Hominidae	1	00.47 (1)
Suidae	2	00.93
Reptilia	49	22.90
Crocodilia	38	17.76
Pisces	23	10.75

$$\frac{214 \text{ specimens identified}}{390 \text{ total specimens}} = 54.87\% \text{ of total identified}$$

NOTE: Tables 1 through 4 include faunal specimens from both surface survey and excavation.

supraorbital ridges were broken but were found close to the cranium and were reconstructed in the laboratory.

Unfortunately, no further hominid remains came to light in the excavation. The original hominid parietal fragment was somewhat darker than most of the excavated bone at L. 345 and may have derived from a higher level in the sedimentary sequence.

Locality 338y

L. 338y occurs in Member E below Tuff F, which has been dated at 2.04 ± 0.10 m.y. (Brown, de Heinzelin, and Howell 1970, p. 256; Brown and Nash, this symposium). The fossiliferous horizons occur in Unit E-3, lying below secondary Tuff S. Unit E-3 has been divided into four subunits which indicate: (1) an initial phase of minor erosion and alluvial deposition followed by silty deposits, perhaps due to over-bank flooding (E-3-1); (2) a later episode of minor alluviation with formation of sandbanks and silt lenses, followed by terminal floodplain alluviation and attendant subaerial emergence (E-3-2); (3) a major alluvial episode followed by development of soil (E-3-3); and (4) a terminal minor alluvial phase with silt deposition. A few rolled fossils occur in Subunit E-3-1, but the richest accumulation of fossils is present in the basal sand of Subunit E-3-2, indicating that the hominid and other vertebrate remains present here were washed in during the period of minor alluviation. Animal tracks are found in both E-3-2 and E-3-3 (shaded in fig. 5) during the subaerial stage.

Investigation of this locality was first begun late in the 1969 field season when G. Eck put in a test excavation after J. de Heinzelin first recognized a juvenile hominid cranial bone exposed by erosion. Splingaer continued excavation at this locality during the 1970, 1971, and 1972 field seasons and exposed a total of 158 m^2 (fig. 5).

Some 7,327 fossil specimens have been recovered from L. 338y, 1,103 of which have been assigned to taxa (table 2). *Hippopotamus* (11.5%) and cercopithecines (9%) are the most common mammalian groups present, and crocodilians (38.5%) and fish (18.7%) are predominant (fig. 6). The presence of one gastropod specimen is interesting, but there is a possibility that this is a surface contamination derived from the more recent lacustrine Kibish exposures nearby.

The orientations of long bones were plotted from the map of the excavation and no significant orientation was seen to be present (fig. 7). Since measurements of bones excavated in Subunits E-3-1 and E-3-2 were not separately graphed, it is possible that orientation by two alluviation episodes is being simultaneously measured.

L. 338y yielded three more portions of skull (marked by circles in fig. 5) which matched the original hominid cranial fragment, so that an essentially complete juvenile calvaria, consisting of two parietals, an occipital, and a basioccipital, was eventually pieced together.

Locality 398

L. 398, in Member F, represents sediments that date from approximately 2.03 m.y. (Brown and Nash, this symposium). The site consists of channel deposits of sands and interbedded tuffaceous sediments, derived from Tuff F and therefore termed Tuff F'.

The fossiliferous horizon is concentrated below current-bedded fluviatile sands and overlies a sterile silt. Clay balls reaching 3 cm in diameter are associated with the fossils but are at times separated from them by a layer of silt. The surface on which the fossils were deposited exhibits a number of shallow depressions which sometimes contain concentrations of bone.

Figure 5. Map of Locality 338y, Member E. Animal tracks in northwest area of excavation are shaded. Hominid cranial fragments in 1969 excavation are marked by darkened circles.

1969
1970
1971
1972

Table 2

Locality 338y, Composition of Fauna

Taxon	Number of Specimens	Percentage
Bovidae	89	08.07
Cercopithecinae	104	09.43
Felidae	1	00.09 (1)
Deinotheriidae	1	00.09 (1)
Elephantidae	6	00.54
Hippopotamidae	127	11.51
Giraffidae	4	00.36
Hominidae	9	00.82
Mustelidae	2	00.18
Suidae	39	03.54
Crocodilia	425	38.53
Pisces	206	18.68
Gastropoda	1	00.09 (1)
Rodentia	3	00.27
Unidentified Carnivora	4	00.36
Aves	1	00.09 (1)
Reptilia	81	07.34

$$\frac{1,103 \text{ specimens identified}}{7,327 \text{ total specimens}} = 15.05\% \text{ of total identified}$$

L. 398 (fig. 8) is the largest area excavated so far in the Omo succession. A total of 178 m^2 has been exposed by Johanson and R. Ciochon in 1971, Johanson in 1972, and Boaz in 1973. To date, 2,717 fossil specimens have been recovered. The site is of the same age and sedimentological context as Omo Locality 33, several km to the south, excavated under the direction of Claude Guillemot.

The presence of abundant surface fossils and the identification of a well-delineated fossiliferous horizon strongly recommended excavation at this locality. In the 1972 and 1973 excavations it was necessary to remove a large overburden (5.5 m and more thick) using a jackhammer. The overburden becomes progressively thicker from east to west owing to the 14° dip of the fossiliferous bed.

The depositional environment of the fossiliferous bed seems to have been a fast-flowing stream or river heavily laden with sediment. Occasional bones occur as much as a meter above the main bone bed, possibly indicating a high-water density with a large amount of suspended sediment. High angles of inclination of many bones indicate turbidity and a rapid current. The presence of a large *Hippopotamus* humerus and *Crocodilus* cranium also suggests a rapid current. Many small fragments of bone approximately 1 cm long are present and have been considerably rolled. A few of these are polished, which may indicate secondary fossil deposition.

The trends and plunges of all long bones were measured in situ in 1972 and 1973 by F. H. Brown, Johanson, and Boaz and later plotted in stereographic projection. The plot was then rotated to remove the component of inclination due to the dip of the deposits. Clusters of points in the northeast and southwest quadrants indicate that the axis of the current was in this direction. The slightly higher plunge toward the northeast suggests a northeast-to-southwest current direction (after Voorhies 1969). The smaller clusters

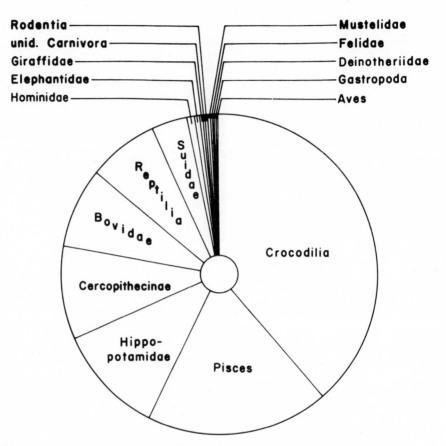

Figure 6. Percentages of identified taxa present at Locality 338y (see table 2).

oriented southwest and northeast are interpreted as bones that oriented by rolling transversely to the current. Figure 9 presents these data in a polar diagram.

Table 3 summarizes the percentages of taxa present at L. 398, which have been corrected, as far as is possible, to represent the number of individual animals present. It has been pointed out by several workers, for example, Clark, Beerbower, and Kietzke (1967, p. 115), that such percentages of forms in an obviously derived taphonomic situation bear little or no relationship to actual numbers of living animals. However, when the taphonomic factors that affect the composition of the assemblage--such as transport, sorting, and differential loss of bones of small animals--are taken into account, such tabulations may prove useful.

L. 398 provided the only excavated specimen of a leporid and an example of a colobine. Bovids (26%), hippopotamids (20%), and cercopithecines (15.8%) are the most common mammals. Unlike localities 345 and 338y, reptiles, crocodilids, and fish are much less numerous and do not individually exceed 10% of the fauna. The only hominid remains are 14 isolated teeth, some of which are incomplete (fig. 10).

Locality 626

L. 626, or "Bovid Hill," occurs in Member G and consists of exposures of units G-12 and lower G-13. The deposits lie above Tuff G and date from approximately 1.9 m.y.

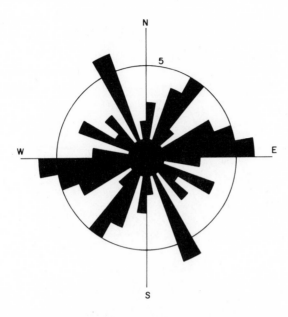

Figure 7. Orientations of long bones at Locality 338y as measured from the map of the excavation (fig. 5). No preferred orientation seems to be present.

In 1971 Johanson excavated an area of approximately 55 m^2 at the base of Unit G-12 (fig. 11). L. 626 is stratigraphically composed of lower silt and sand levels yielding many fossils and overlain by limonite-stained clays, followed by less fossiliferous sands and pebbly clay horizons and succeeded by silts which yielded only remains of *Hippopotamus*.

The taphocoenosis at L. 626 seems to have been a backswamp with little or no current orientation of bone. As figure 12 illustrates, no predominant current direction was observable in the long bone orientations plotted from the excavation map. Nevertheless, the fossil remains are disarticulated and unassociated and seem to indicate some degree of transport.

Table 4 presents the percentages of taxa identified from L. 626. The large proportion of bovids (52.5%) is at once apparent. Only one other group, hippopotamids (15%), accounts for more than 10% of the excavated fauna (fig. 13). Three tribes of bovids are represented. Reduncines *(Kobus, Menelikia*--19 specimens), Tragelaphines *(Tragelaphus*--20 specimens), and Alcelaphines (16 specimens) are present in similar numbers.

The exact nature of the taphonomy of L. 626 is not fully understood. The backswamp depositional conditions, the lack of current orientation, and the very large preponderance of one form (bovids) argue for an autochthonous fauna. However the widely spread and disarticulated remains of many animals uncovered in the excavation (fig. 11) seem to contravene this conclusion.

Minor Excavations

Test pits and excavations of limited scope, in conjunction with sieving operations, have been carried out since 1969 at several localities. These methods augment surface finds and indicate whether more extensive excavation at a locality is warranted.

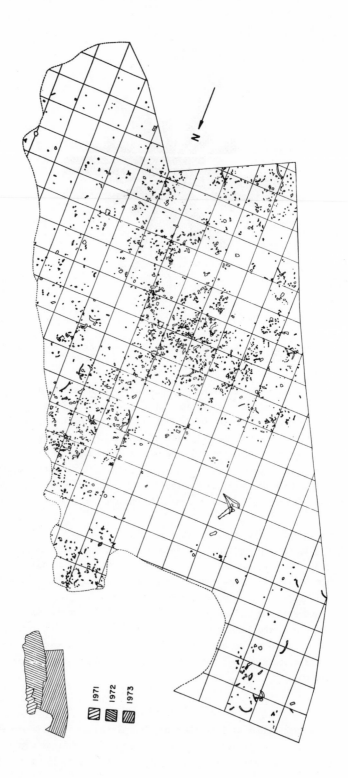

Figure 8. Map of the excavation at Locality 398, Member F.

1971
1972
1973

N

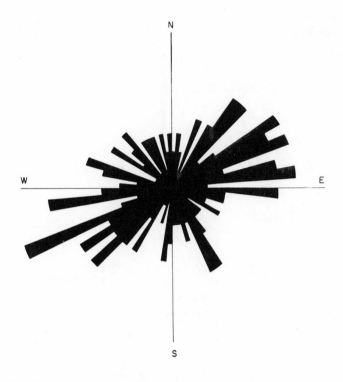

Figure 9. Polar diagram of orientations of long axes of bones at Locality 398 in 5° intervals. Based on field measurements of trends and dips of excavated bones in situ in 1972 and 1973.

Table 3

Locality 398, Composition of Fauna

Taxon	Number of Specimens	Percentage
Bovidae	265	26.24
Cercopithecinae	160	15.84
Colobinae	1	00.10 (1)
Deinotheriidae	2	00.20
Elephantidae	35	03.46
Equidae	10	01.00
Felidae	5	00.50
Giraffidae	27	02.67
Hippopotamidae	203	20.10
Hominidae	14	01.39
Rhinocerotidae	2	00.20
Suidae	101	10.00
Leporidae	1	00.10
Reptilia	42	04.16
Crocodilia	78	07.72
Pisces	64	06.34

$$\frac{1{,}010 \text{ specimens identified}}{2{,}744 \text{ total specimens}} = 36.77\% \text{ of total identified}$$

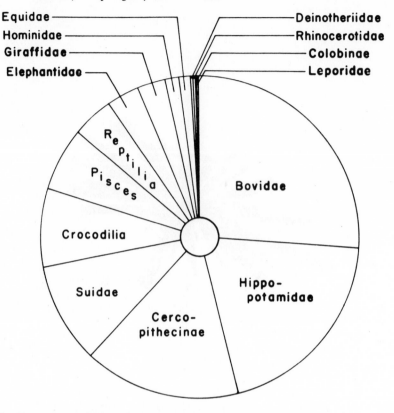

Figure 10.   Percentages of identified taxa at Locality 398 (see table 3).

Member B

L. 1, along with Omo Locality 28, is the oldest site tested by excavation in the Omo deposits. It dates to approximately 2.8 m.y. and consists of fossiliferous exposures of units B-9, B-10, B-11, and B-12. The locality covers an extensive area, and six fossiliferous horizons have been identified.

Excavation 1 was carried out by H. B. Wesselman in 1971 in Unit B-12. The excavated fossil bone occurs with numerous clay balls and hematite pebbles and cobbles which rest on a silt layer. The fossiliferous layer dips to the west 10°. Two areas representing the same stratigraphic level but separated by an erosion gully were exposed.

The fossil concentration was very low and in a total of some 25 m^2 only 12 specimens were recovered. These included fairly complete but rolled bovine and *Giraffa jumae* skulls, 2 proboscidean long bones, and *Euthecodon* and fish fragments.

The depositional environment seems to have been fluviatile with a rather rapid current. This conclusion is indicated by the presence of clay balls, large-diameter sediment particles, and large, dense angular bones and small, dense fragments that would remain in a lag deposit even in strong currents (Behrensmeyer 1975).

A small excavation and sieving operation carried out in Unit B-10 in 1971 and termed Excavation 2 yielded a more diverse fauna and numerous cercopithecine remains. The specimens consist exclusively of isolated teeth and bone fragments. The deposits are composed of a coarse, poorly sorted gravel that is thought to represent a point-bar deposit. The initial results here indicate that further excavation would be profitable.

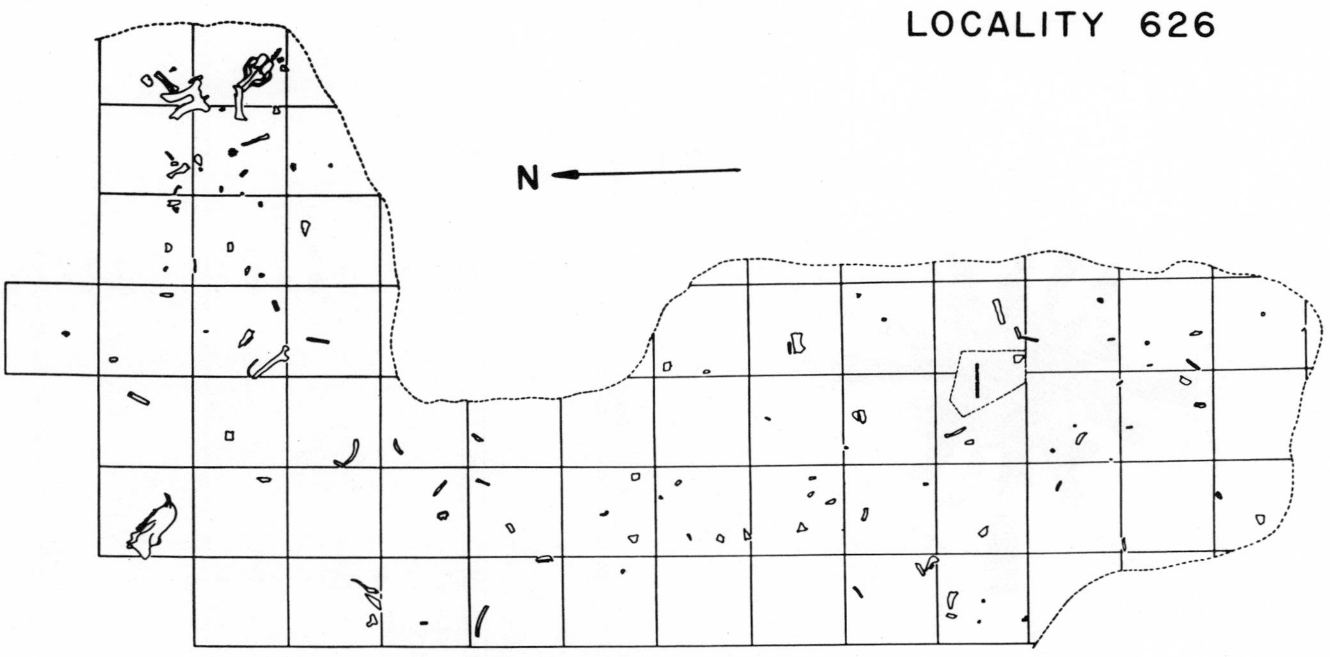

LOCALITY 626

N

Figure 11. Map of the excavation at Locality 626, Member G.

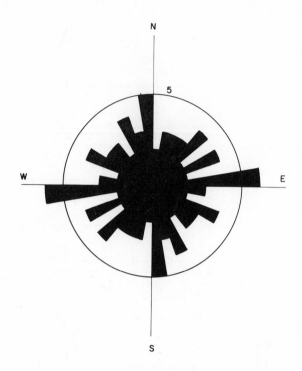

Figure 12. Orientations of long axes of bones excavated from Locality 626. Measured from excavation map (fig. 11) and diagramed in 10° intervals.

Table 4

Locality 626, Composition of Fauna

Taxon	Number of Specimens	Percentage
Bovidae	93	**52.54**
Cercopithecinae	13	07.34
Deinotheriidae	1	00.56 (1)
Equidae	6	03.39
Felidae	1	00.56 (1)
Giraffidae	1	00.56 (1)
Hippopotamidae	27	15.25
Hominidae	1	00.56 (1)
Suidae	10	05.65
Reptilia	4	02.26
Crocodilia	5	02.82
Pisces	15	08.47

$$\frac{177 \text{ specimens identified}}{281 \text{ total specimens}} = 62.99\% \text{ of total identified}$$

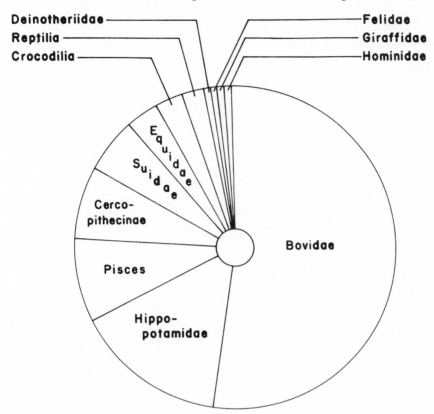

Figure 13.   Percentages of identified taxa at Locality 626 (see table 4).

Excavation 3, also in Unit B-10, was the site tested by Wesselman in 1972 and 1973 for microfaunal analysis (see Jaeger and Wesselman, this symposium). In addition to a diverse microfauna, a hominid upper premolar fragment and a right lower second molar were recovered.

Member C

In addition to the major excavation at L. 345, three other localities have been tested in Member C. A concentration of bovid, *Hippopotamus*, carnivore, and cercopithecoid specimens on a knoll in L. 32 indicated that excavation might prove worthwhile. Eck and Wesselman excavated an area of approximately 10 m^2 in 1971 but were unable to find an in situ concentration of fossils. A bed of poorly preserved mollusks was discovered, however--the only ones known between the Basal Member and Member H. The deposits consist of a medium sand, stained and partially indurated by manganese oxides.

The discovery of 7 hominid teeth and several stone artifacts on the surface of L. 51 prompted excavation at this locality. Approximately 10 m^2 were excavated by Cramer in 1970 and an additional 15 m^2 by Eck, Johanson, and Wesselman in 1971. Only isolated teeth of crocodilids were recovered. The stratigraphy of the excavation seemed to indicate that the hominids were derived from sediments that had been removed by erosion, just above those excavated. The deposits consisted of a well-sorted medium sand underlain by a silt.

The recovery of several relatively complete bovid and *Hippopotamus* specimens and several nearly complete cercopithecoid limb bones stimulated excavation at L. 292. Eck and Wesselman excavated approximately 10 m^2 in 1971, but as in the other tests in Member C,

no in situ concentration of fossils was located from which the surface specimens might
have derived. The sediments consisted of a homogeneous clayey silt.

Member D

Fossil occurrences in Member D are relatively sparse, and for this reason no excavations have yet been conducted at localities in this member. These deposits are characterized by extensive development of channels. The sediments are occasionally fossiliferous
but seldom present bone concentrations that merit excavation.

Member E

Of the five excavations in this member, L. 338y has already been discussed.

L. 146 is large, and numerous surface finds of bovids, suids, and hippopotamids plus
a few giraffid and cercopithecine finds indicated excavation. Johanson tested this locality in 1972 and located several in situ specimens. The bone found proved to be well preserved but of quite low concentration. The fossiliferous layer occurred in a sand overlain by a sterile silt.

After the 1971 surface find of a hominid right ulna at L. 40, at the base of Unit E-5,
cleaning, sieving, and finally limited excavation were carried out there. Excavation
proved largely unproductive; only a few *Hippopotamus* fragments were found. A total of 35
surface specimens including bovids, hippopotamids, a deinothere, a femur of *Panthera
crassidens*, crocodilids, and the hominid ulna are known. The deposits consist of a massive
medium sand, probably a channel deposit, in which no concentration of fossils could be
found.

L. 865 was investigated in 1973 by D. E. Dechant, D. Hamburger, and M. Steiner, and
is remarkable in that all excavated bones belong to one individual of *Theropithecus
brumpti*. The surface find of a *T. brumpti* cranium with limb fragments and vertebrae in
1972 prompted excavation. A mandible and articulated hand of this same individual were
uncovered in an excavation covering approximately 14 m^2. Deposition must have been in an
undisturbed sedimentary situation which caused minimum disarticulation of the remains.
The sediments here consist of fine-grained silts.

Member F

Two major excavations and two tests have been carried out in Member F. L. 398 and
Omo Locality 33 have been mentioned previously. A small test of approximately 5 m^2 was
put in at the base of Tuff F' just east of L. 28 by Wesselman and Eck in 1971. The presence on the surface of several complete *Hippopotamus* limb bones, probably from the same
individual, indicated that excavation might prove fruitful. The deposits excavated were
completely sterile. This locality is of interest because the test is located only several
hundred meters south of the excavation at L. 98 and exactly the same stratigraphic
level. The sediments and type of fossilization at L. 28 are also comparable. The dearth
of fossil remains at this site is thus in marked contrast to the extreme abundance of fossils at L. 398.

L. 238 represents exposures of units F-3 and F-4, and a rich assemblage is known
through surface survey; 297 specimens are known from this locality, most of which are
identifiable. The known fauna includes three species of bovids, cercopithecines, and rare
colobines, and somewhat less abundant specimens of suids, hippopotamids, proboscideans,
and aquatic reptiles. One hominid molar is known.

A test excavation made at L. 238 by Johanson in 1971 failed to expose the fossiliferous horizon. As at other localities the fossil occurrence may have been a lens deposit

and was essentially removed by erosion. The tested sediments consisted of a thin bed of well-sorted medium sand underlain by silts and overlain by silts and clays.

In 1973 P. Mulumbi and J. Kithumbi discovered a hominid mandible with partial lower dentition at L. 860 in Unit F-1 (dating approximately 2 m.y.). Very limited screening by Howell and Boaz failed to reveal any additional hominid fragments, but the locality, which is rich in surface bone, remains a prime candidate for future excavation. Small quartz artifacts have been recovered in situ in tests (by H. V. Merrick, Jr.) at the same level a few meters to the east. The mandible appears to have been derived from a tuffaceous silt.

Member G

The major excavation in Member G is L. 626, discussed above. The only other excavation in this member was a small test made by Boaz during the last two weeks of the 1973 field season at L. 894 in Unit G-28. This is the highest unit of Member G known to yield vertebrate fossils in any quantity. Extensive sieving of the surface at this locality revealed several additional teeth and cranial fragments of a hominid skull, discovered by Mathias and J. Kithumbi while surveying with Howell. The cranium seems to have weathered out of the deposit occipital end first, judging from the progressive sequence of weathering in which the fragments can be arranged.[2] The fossiliferous horizon at L. 894 has not yet been located, and the microstratigraphy here is not completely understood. Future work should help to elucidate the exact nature of this deposit.

Concluding Remarks

Most excavated localities in the Shungura Formation indicate some type of fluviatile deposition of bone. However, there exists a wide spectrum of depositional environments ranging from very quiet situations, with intact and occasionally articulated remains, to rapid current situations. L. 865 is the best example of an undisturbed depositional situation, in which one adult *Papio* individual is preserved and the bones semiarticulated. L. 345 also represents essentially a low-energy depositional environment, such as a back-swamp, but the orientation of long bones indicates that flowing water did transport the bones to some extent. Localities 338y and 626 suggest a stronger depositional current and unlike L. 345 probably contain an allochthonous fauna. L. 398, L. 1, and most other localities indicate rapid-current bone accumulation. Fluviatile deposition by fast-flowing currents is the most common situation in which bones are found fossilized in the Shungura Formation. This accounts for the fragmentary and disarticulated nature of the remains recovered from Omo excavations and contrasts with the relatively complete state of preservation of fossils in the lower-energy depositional situations found at the East Lake Rudolf Plio-Pleistocene deposits.

Further careful taphonomic studies should help to determine what relationships exist between the excavated fauna in various depositional situations and actual populations of living animals.

Acknowledgments

Appreciation is expressed to all members of the international Omo Expedition for their encouragement, assistance, and friendship. Special thanks are due to F. Clark Howell, who has been continually understanding and helpful.

2. We are indebted to Dr. Alan Walker for this observation.

We are grateful to Frank Brown for his numerous suggestions in the field and for his contributions in the analysis of the Locality 398 excavation.

Excavation is a tedious and painstaking venture, and without the dedicated assistance of our excavation crews, none of this would have been possible; we express our sincere appreciation for their perseverance.

Thanks are also due to Tom Gray, Gerald Eck, and Dorothy Dechant for their helpful discussions and editorial help.

References

Behrensmeyer, A. K. 1975. The taphonomy and paleoecology of Plio-Pleistocene vertebrate assemblages east of Lake Rudolf, Kenya. *Bull. Mus. Comp. Zool. Harvard. Coll.* 146:473-578.

Brown, F. H.; Heinzelin, J. de; and Howell, F. C. 1970. Pliocene/Pleistocene formations in the lower Omo basin, southern Ethiopia. *Quaternaria* 13:247-68.

Clark, J.; Beerbower, J. R.; and Kietzke, K. K. 1967. Oligocene sedimentation stratigraphy, paleoecology, and paleoclimatology in the Big Badlands of South Dakota. *Fieldiana Geol., Mem.* 5:1-158.

Voorhies, M. R. 1969. Taphonomy and population dynamics of an early Pliocene vertebrate fauna, Knox County, Nebraska. *Contrib. Geol. Spec. Paper* no. 1. Laramie: University of Wyoming Press.

38. PALYNOLOGICAL EVIDENCE FOR AN IMPORTANT CHANGE IN THE VEGETATION
OF THE OMO BASIN BETWEEN 2.5 AND 2 MILLION YEARS AGO

R. Bonnefille

Palynological studies in the Omo basin started with the discovery of fossil pollen in a coprolite recovered from the fossiliferous sands containing hominid remains at Omo 18 (Bonnefille, Chavaillon, and Coppens 1970; Bonnefille 1970). Because pollen offers unique opportunities for paleoenvironmental reconstruction, further investigations have been made in the Shungura Formation. Our researches have been closely connected with the detailed stratigraphy established by J. de Heinzelin and P. Haesaerts. We sampled different types of sediments and obtained good results for four stratigraphic levels.

Stratigraphic Position of the Fossil Pollen Spectra

The oldest pollen record comes from the fossiliferous sands of Unit B-10 at hominid locality 1 (Omo 28). Potassium-argon dates on Tuff B-10 give an age of 2.95 ± 0.1 m.y. (Brown, this symposium). Among the 55 pollen grains extracted, the pollen from herbaceous taxa (nonarboreal pollen = NAP) are predominant. They are represented by: grasses (45 grains), Chenopodiaceae (1) Crucifereae (1), sedges (Cyperaceae):(4), and *Typha* (3). The pollen from tree taxa (arboreal pollen = AP) is represented by a single grain of *Podocarpus*, a species from the montane forest. Reconstruction of the past vegetation for this level is impossible because the total number of pollen grains is inadequate.

More adequate data have been obtained for three stratigraphic levels in Member C and Member E of the Shungura Formation: a coprolite from the fossiliferous sands from Unit C-7 or C-8 at hominid locality Omo 18, a reduced clay with calcareous concretions on the top of Unit C-9 at the same locality, and a sandstone from Unit E-4 at hominid locality Omo 57. The first two units, C-7/8 and C-9, were deposited slightly before Tuff D, for which the age of 2.39 ± 0.15 m.y. can be adopted (Brown, this symposium). The third one, E-4 is slightly below Tuff F', dated 2.06 and 1.99 m.y.

Pollen Analysis

Sediment samples were prepared by standard methods, but the quantity of sediment treated has been increased. Identification of pollen types was aided by a reference collection of three thousand slides of the Ethiopian and East African flora. Detailed results of the pollen analysis are given in tables 1 and 2.

To facilitate the interpretation of the pollen analysis, pollen taxa have been arranged in three categories which reflect three different plant associations. These

421

Table 1

Pollen Analysis of Plio-Pleistocene Sediments of the Shungura Formation: Trees and Shrubs

| Trees and Shrubs | 2.5 m.y. | | | | 2 m.y. | |
| | C-7/C-8 | | C-9 | | E-4 | |
	N	%	N	%	N	%
Montane forest: Long-distance element						
Podocarpus cf. *Podocarpus gracilior*	185	62.2	22	24	13	42
Juniperus cf. *Juniperus procera*	20	6.7	16	17.4	-	-
Olea africana	2	0.6	3	3.3	-	-
Olea sp. (cf. type *O. hochstetteri*)	5	1.7	8	8.7	1	3.2
Hagenia abyssinica	3	1.0	1	1.1	-	-
Myrsine africana	-	-	1	1.1	-	-
Myrica sp.	-	-	-	-	2	6.5
Rosaceae	-	-	-	-	1	3.2
Buddleya sp.	-	-	1	1.1	-	-
Hypericum	-	-	3	3.3	-	-
Erica arborea	3	1.0	-	-	-	-
Dodonaea viscosa	4	1.3	7	7.6	2	6.4
Macaranga	-	-	1	1.1	-	-
cf. Sapotaceae	1	0.3	-	-	-	-
Total	223	75.1	63	68.5	19	61.3
Riverine community: Local element						
Myrtaceae (*Syzygium* type)	-	-	-	-	1	3.2
Ricinus communis	2	0.6	-	-	-	-
Celtis sp.	6	2.0	5	5.4	-	-
Rhamnaceae (cf. *Ziziphus*)	2	0.6	-	-	-	-
Combretum and *Terminalia*	3	1	1	1.1	-	-
Ebenaceae	-	-	1	1.1	-	-
Moraceae	-	-	1	1.1	-	-
Apocynaceae (climber type)	8	2.6	-		-	-
Total	21	7.1	8	8.7	1	3.2
Steppe or savanna: Regional element						
Acacia sp.	3	1	3	3.3	1	3.2
Capparaceae (including *Cadaba* and *Crateva*)	24	8.1	4	4.3	2	6.4
Maerua sp.	4	1.3	1	1.1	-	-
Commiphora cf. *boiviniana*	-	-	2	2.2	-	-
Commiphora sp.	3	1	1	1.1	3	9.7
Salvadoraceae (*Salvadora* and *Dobera*)	6	2	6	6.5	-	-
Cordia	1	0.3	-		-	-
Hymenocardia acida	4	1.3	4		-	-
Euphorbia sp.	-	-	1	1.1	-	-
Euphorbia triaculeata	-	-	1	1.1	-	-
Monadenium	-	-	1	1.1	-	-
Apocynaceae	5	1.7	-	-	-	-
Loranthaceae	-	-	-	-	1	3.2
Boerhavia	3	1	-		4	13
Total	53	17.8	21	22.8	11	35.5
Total arboreal pollen (AP)	297	100	92	100	31	100
Total spores and pollens	1,072		693		1,062	

NOTE: The basis of calculation for the percentages is the total sum of arboreal pollen.

Table 2

Pollen Analysis of Plio-Pleistocene Sediments of the Shungura Formation: Herbaceous Plants

Herbs	2.5 m.y.				2 m.y.	
	C-7/C-8		C-9		E-4	
	N	%	N	%	N	%
Compositae tubuliflorae	–		1	0.1	2	0.2
Compositae liguliflorae	2	0.2	–	–	–	–
Plantago	–	–	3	0.5	–	–
Paronychieae	1	0.1	–	–	–	–
Heliotropium	1	0.1	–	–	–	–
Acalypha sp.	14	1.9	24	4.0	–	–
Typha	114	15.6	86	14.5	15	1.6
Cyperaceae	31	–	52	8.7	–	–
Gramineae	489	66.8	413	69.4	766	75
Chenopodiaceae/Amaranthaceae	27	3.7	–	–	1	0.09
Digera muricata	23	3.1	3	0.5	2	0.2
Dasysphaera prostrata	6	0.8	–	–	163	16
Celosia	–	–	1	0.1	–	–
Papilionaceae	2	0.2	–	–	–	–
Indigofera	1	0.1	2	0.3	–	–
Crotalaria	–	–	1	0.1	–	–
Solaneae	2	0.2	2	0.3	–	–
Polygala	–	–	–	–	71	6.9
Cucurbitaceae	1	0.1	–	–	–	–
Resedaceae	2	0.2	–	–	–	–
Caylusea	5	0.7	–	–	–	–
Blepharis	5	0.7	1	–	–	–
Justicia	1	0.1	–	–	–	–
Tribulus	3	0.4	–	–	2	0.2
Euphorbiaceae	2	0.2	1	0.1	–	–
Vitaceae	–	–	1	0.1	–	–
Zygophyllaceae	–	–	4	0.7	–	–
Total nonarboreal pollen (NAP)	732	100	595	100	1,022	100
Pteridophytes	6		2		3	
Total spores and pollens	1,072		693		1,062	

NOTE: The basis of calculation for the percentages is the total of nonarboreal pollen.

categories derive from plants growing in different ecological settings relative to the site where the pollen has been deposited, the Omo basin (fig. 1).

Montane Forest

This first group includes *Podocarpus*, *Juniperus* (Cedar), *Olea* (Olive), *Hagenia abyssinica*, and so forth, the more important species of the forest on the Ethiopian highlands at 2,500 m. Pollen from those species has been dispersed by wind and carried by wind or by river down to the lower Omo valley where it has been deposited. Derived from plants growing outside the neighborhood of the basin, these pollens are considered a *"long-distance element."*

Riverine Communities

Celtis, *Ziziphus*, *Syzygium*, *Combretum*, *Terminalia*, and *Ricinus* are common trees or shrubs in the closed woodland or the riverine forest on the edges and meanders of the Omo River (Carr 1976). Pollens produced by plants growing on the margins of rivers or lakes near the place where sediments are deposited belong to the *"local element."* The most characteristic species of the riverine vegetation, *Ficus* and *Trichilia roka*, have not been found in the fossil pollen spectra. Those plants are pollinated by insects and produce little pollen. It should also be noted that they are not present in the samples of contemporary Omo River deposits taken near the Shungura village (Bonnefille 1972).

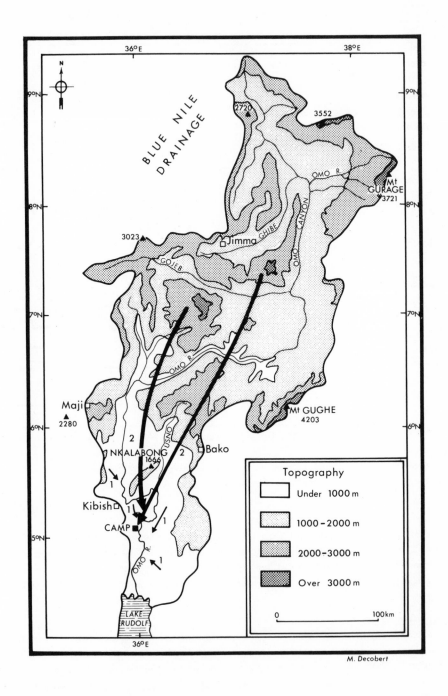

Figure 1. Model of pollen deposition in the Omo basin: (1) local and regional pollen;
(2) long-distance-transported pollen. Redrawn after K. W. Butzer, *Recent History of an
Ethiopian Delta*, University of Chicago, Department of Geography, Research Paper 136 (1971),
Fig. 1-2.

Savanna and Steppe

The third category of pollen includes *Acacia*, *Commiphora*, *Cadaba*, and all other Capparidaceae. These plants are abundant in the tree shrub savanna, shrub thicket, and grassland which occur in the lower Omo valley and around Lake Rudolf. Euphorbiaceae and Salvadoraceae could be added to this group as well as *Cordia*. Their pollen, produced by plants growing in the neighborhood of the basin, is considered a *"regional element."*

It was not possible, however, to differentiate the "long distance," "regional," and "local" elements among the pollen of herbaceous plants because of the difficulty of making reliable generic or specific determination on the pollen grains of such large families as Compositeae, Chenopodiaceae, and Gramineae.

Interpretation of the Palynological Data

Despite some recent investigations (Grichuk 1967; Muller 1959; Maley 1972), more information on the deposition of pollen in river sediments and on pollen productivity of the African species is needed before an accurate interpretation of the fossil pollen record is possible. However, a number of useful remarks can be made, especially with respect to the results of the pollen analysis of surface samples and modern sediments.

General Considerations

Modern Character of the Pollen Taxa. All the fossil pollen grains which have been found in the Plio-Pleistocene sediments are also present in the contemporary East African flora. In northern Europe, deposits of the same age, Praetiglian and Tiglian (van der Hammen, Wijmstra, and Zagwijn 1971), still contain Tertiary relic forms. The modern character of the types of pollen grains characterizes Plio-Pleistocene pollen analysis in the tropical lower Omo valley. It is interesting to note that similar remarks have been made by H. Wesselman and J.-J. Jaeger (this symposium) for their studies of fossil remains of micromammals. The outlines of tropical environmental conditions may have been established earlier than 2 m.y. ago.

Reconstruction of the Plio-Pleistocene Landscape. The fossil pollen spectra of the Shungura Formation (Omo Group) show the same three categories of pollen that have been recognized in the pollen analysis of modern deposits of the Omo River (Bonnefille 1972). It may be considered that the past vegetation of the whole Omo basin was roughly similar to what it is today. There was a forest on the highlands and a tree shrub savanna on the lowlands. Near the river a wooded vegetation was present, but it appears to have been less developed than the existing riverine forest along the Omo. The palynological data are in complete agreement with geological and faunal evidence, which reflect the deltaic and fluviodeltaic character of the sedimentation.

It is not unreasonable to assume that during the period between 2.5 and 2 m.y. the landscape was not occupied by a real forest. It was an open vegetation with grassland areas. The mosaic character of the vegetation was already established. However, the density of the trees has changed through time.

Changes in the Fossil Pollen Spectra

Tree Taxa. The number of arboreal pollen grains in the spectra of units C-9 and E-4 is lower than in the present-day spectrum of the Omo river deposit (see table 3), whereas in unit C7/8 the number is slightly higher. These results are difficult to interpret because the different spectra contain pollen which is a mixture from three types of vegetation.

Table 3

Distribution of Arboreal (AP) and Nonarboreal Pollen (NAP) in the Fossil and Modern Spectra

Pollen	C-7/C-8 N	%	C-9 N	%	E-4 N	%	Modern N	%
AP	297	27.7	92	13.2	31	2.9	228	22.8
AP (excluding Podocarpus)	112	10.4	70	10.1	18	1.6	168	16.8
AP/NAP	0.4	--	0.15	--	0.01	--	0.3	--
Number of AP taxa	22	--	24	--	11	--	59	--

However, the extremely low frequency of the "arboreal taxa" (2.9% or 1.6%) in the spectrum of the unit E-4 should be noted. About 2 m.y., the vegetation of the Omo basin was a savanna with very few trees, which may reflect much drier conditions than those which prevailed both before and today.

The ratio of arboreal pollen to nonarboreal pollen is very low in spectrum E-4. Simultaneously, we register a considerable decrease in the number of tree taxa (table 3). L. R. Holdrige's (1967) work on tropical vegetation suggests that a decrease in the number of tree species may be correlated with a decrease in temperature and rainfall.

Long-Distance Element. In the fossil pollen spectra from units C-7/8, C-9, and E-4, the percentages of montane forest taxa are 75.1, 68.5, 61.1, respectively, higher than in the present Omo River deposit (48.2%; see table 4). This is also true when the same percentages are calculated with *Podocarpus* excluded from the total pollen sum, as is seen in table 5. Such an increase in the "long-distance element" might be the result of greater transport from the highlands, with the Omo River carrying more water. Alternatively, during the Pleistocene the forest may have been situated at lower altitude on the Ethiopian highlands, closer to the site where the pollen were deposited. As a consequence of a slightly more humid climate, the montane forest may have been more extensive than now. Whatever explanation is adopted, it seems to imply a wetter climate for the period between 2.5 and 2 m.y.

Table 4

Distribution of the Arboreal Taxa in the Pollen Spectra of Plio-Pleistocene Sediments from the Shungura Formation and of a Modern Deposit of the Omo River

Element	2.5 m.y. C-7/C-8 N	%	C-9 N	%	2 m.y. E-4 N	%	Modern Omo River Deposits N	%
Long-distance element (montane forest)	223	75.1	63	68.5	19	61.1	110	48.2
Local element (riverine communities)	21	7.1	8	8.7	1	3.2	77	33.7
Regional element (steppe, savanna)	53	17.8	21	22.8	11	35.5	41	17.9
Total AP	297		92		31		228	

NOTE: Percentages are calculated with respect to the total of arboreal pollen: AP.

When the data of table 4 are considered in more detail we can see that, although the percentage of "long-distance" element in spectrum E-4 is almost the same as in spectrum C-9, the total number of pollen types from this group is very low. This is a consequence of the decrease of arboreal pollen in this spectrum. An important vegetation change is registered in Unit E-4, 2 m.y. ago.

Table 5

Distribution of the Arboreal Taxa in the Pollen Spectra of Plio-Pleistocene Sediments from the Shungura Formation and of a Modern Deposit of the Omo River

Element	2.5 m.y. C-7/C-8 N	2.5 m.y. C-7/C-8 %	C-9 N	C-9 %	2 m.y. E-4 N	2 m.y. E-4 %	Modern Omo River Deposit N	Modern Omo River Deposit %
Long-distance element	38	33.9	41	58.5	6	33.3	50	29.7
Local element	21	18.7	8	11.4	1	5.5	77	45.8
Regional element	53	47.3	21	30	11	61.1	41	24.4
Total (AP *Podocarpus*)	112		70		18		168	

NOTE: *Podocarpus* is excluded in these calculations.

<u>Indicative Value of *Celtis*, *Acalypha*, and *Myrica*</u>. It has been demonstrated in Uganda that the pollen grains of *Celtis* and *Acalypha* are well dispersed. "Their abundance gives a good indication of regional moisture conditions" (Hamilton 1972, p. 99). The greater percentages of those pollen in the fossil pollen spectra of the Omo sediments are matched in units C-7/8 and C-9, dated 2.5 m.y. (fig. 2). The attested presence of a pollen of *Macaranga*, a euphorbiaceous tree common in "wetter highland forests," involves moister conditions for spectrum C-9. The lack of *Acalypha* and *Celtis* pollen in the spectrum of Unit E-4 is interpreted as reflecting drier conditions for the period at 2 m.y.

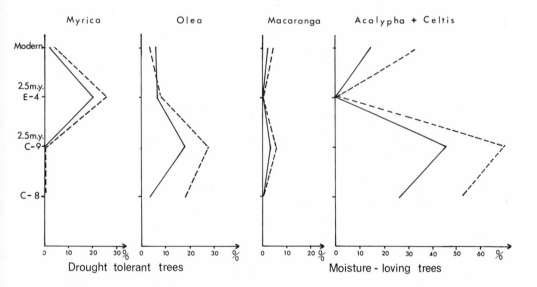

Figure 2. Frequencies of drought-tolerant trees and moisture-loving trees in the fossil pollen spectra from the Shungura Formation and in modern deposit of the Omo River. Percent-arboreal pollen. *Broken line, Podocarpus* excluded from tne sum; *solid line, Podocarpus* included.

At the present time in East Africa, *Olea*, the olive tree, is a component of the *Podocarpus* forest which occurs in areas where the mean annual rainfall is 1,000 mm. It is also common in the juniper forest, on dry slopes, and in areas where the mean annual rainfall varies between 750 and 1,200 mm. In his studies of surface samples on the highlands in Uganda, Hamilton considers *Olea* a drought-tolerant species like *Dodonaea viscosa* and *Myrica salicifolia*.[1] The rise of *Myrica* in the pollen spectrum E-4 of 2 m.y. is matched by a decrease of *Olea* and the virtual absence of small porate grains of *Acalypha* and *Celtis* (fig. 2).

The "long-distance element" suggests that in the highlands of the upper Omo valley somewhat more arid conditions at 2 m.y. succeeded the humid conditions which prevailed at 2.5 m.y.

Increase of Steppe-Savanna Taxa 2 M.Y. The group of arboreal pollen which belongs to steppe or savanna vegetation types is much more abundant in spectrum E-4 than in the two preceding spectra (tables 4 and 5). Simple tests such as the chi-square statistic suggest that the number of savanna taxa in spectra C-7/8 and C-9 are significantly different from those found in spectrum E-4. An important change in the vegetation of the lower valley appeared at 2 m.y. The development of extensive grasslands which replaced a wooded savanna implies drier conditions at that time.

Grasses become rather abundant in spectrum E-4, where they constitute 75% of the total of the nonarboreal pollen (see table 2). Among grass pollen, size can be a useful means of separating the different families (Bonnefille 1972). The histogram of figure 3 represents measurements of 100 grass pollen grains in the two spectra E-4 and C-9. The increase in the amount of pollen in the classes over 30 microns can be correlated with a higher proportion of Andropogoneae, the most frequent grass family in the savanna. At 2 m.y., extensive grasslands replaced the wooded savanna which occurred earlier in the lower Omo valley. A considerable amount of Chenopodiaceae, together with the rise of grasses and the four pollen grains of *Boerhavia* (Nyctaginaceae) in spectrum E-4, are indicative of more xerophytic vegetation. Clearly then, the interpretation of the lowlands vegetation provides strong indications of a drier climate 2 m.y.

Decrease of *Typha* and Cyperaceae. *Typha* and Cyperaceae are common plants on riverbanks or lakeshores. Their pollen has been considered poorly dispersed or "local pollen" (Hamilton 1972). If a poorly dispersed pollen type is abundant in the pollen sum, its parent species were very likely to be growing in the adjacent vegetation. A high percentage of pollen from those aquatic plants is recorded in the two pollen spectra from C-7/8 (19.8%) and C-9 (23.1%). But in spectrum E-4 *Typha* and Cyperaceae represent only 1.4% of the nonarboreal pollen. This is a strong indication of a decrease in aquatic vegetation under the more arid conditions which prevailed 2 m.y. ago in the lower Omo valley.

Conclusions

The palynological data confirm the mosaic character of the vegetation in the lower Omo valley between 2.5 and 2 m.y. ago. The environment of the hominid sites was occupied by more or less wooded savanna with some riverine woodland. The montane forest on the highlands was more developed than it is today. Strong evidence for a change in vegetation has been demonstrated by the reduction of arboreal species and a considerable extension of

---

1. However, the presence of *Myrica* with no specific determination is not indicative only of dry conditions; some species in central Africa (Albert Park; Shaba, Zaïre) grow in swamps.

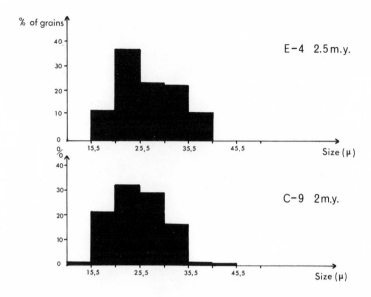

Figure 3. Size distribution of grass pollen (100 measurements) in two fossil pollen spectra from the Shungura Formation.

grasslands which occurred sometime between the deposition of Tuff D and Tuff F', that is, between 2.5 and 2 m.y. ago. The change has affected both the montane forest and the vegetation of the lowlands. This most probably reflects a climatic change toward drier conditions.

Paleoecological indications have also been suggested by macrofaunal studies. A possible faunal change among the bovids is noticed in Member E by Gentry (this symposium). The considerable increase in horn cores of impala (*Aepyceros*), a grazing antelope from open country, in Member F would be consistent with the development of grasslands as is suggested by the palynological data.

Among the two forms of *Mesochoerus limnetes* (Cooke, this symposium), the first one having a bush-pig-like habitat is situated about 2.3 m.y. ago, whereas the more advanced grass-eating form occurs after Tuff F, 2 m.y. ago.

The different forms of micromammals from Unit B-10 and Member F seem to confirm the palynological conclusions (Jaeger and Wesselman, this symposium). So does the variability in numbers of colobines and cercopithecines reported by Eck (this symposium) before and after Tuff D.

Hence paleoecological information suggested by the faunal pictures fits well with the palynological data. However, we need more information before correlating the vegetation changes in the Omo with the floristic changes shown in Europe during the cooler phase of the Praetiglian at 2.3 m.y. ago (van der Hammen, Wijmstra, and Zagwijn 1971) or with the general temperature shift of the Pliocene/Pleistocene transition.

Acknowledgments

Thanks are expressed to Professor F. Clark Howell and Yves Coppens for their continued encouragement and support during the Omo Research Expeditions. I would like to express

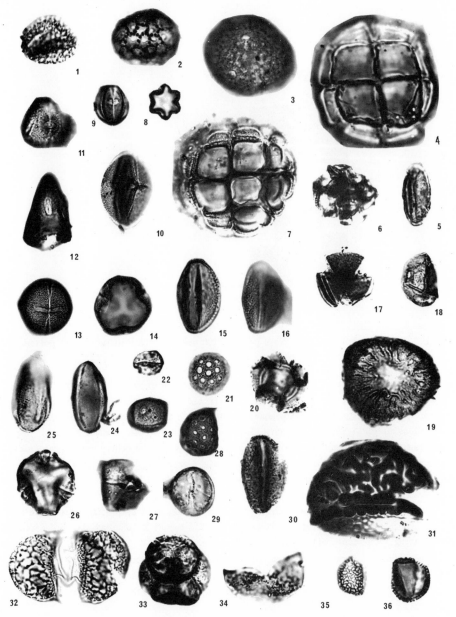

Figure 4. Photomicrographs of fossil pollen from Unit C-7/8 (Shungura Formation, Omo Valley) (x 455): *1, Commiphora* sp.; *2, Tribulus; 3, Boerhavia; 4, Acacia* cf. *mellifera; 5,* Capparidaceae; *6, Acacia* sp.; *7, Acacia* other sp.; *8-9,* cf. *Terminalia brevipes; 10,* unknown; *11, Dodonaea viscosa; 12, Cyperus* sp.; *13-14, Ricinus communis; 15-16, Maerua; 17,* unknown; *18,* triporate grain; *19,* pteridophyte; *20, Compositae liguliflorae; 21, Achyranthes; 22, Acalypha; 23, Celtis; 24-25, Blepharis; 26, Hagenia abyssinica; 28,* Amaranthaceae; *29,* unknown; *30, Cadaba* sp.; *31,* pteridophyte *32, Podocarpus; 33, Erica arborea; 34, Juniperus procera; 35-36, Olea* cf. *africana.*

gratitude to J. de Heinzelin and P. Haesaerts for their constant help in the field and their useful suggestions which have added greatly to the success of this work. Special appreciation is due to Dr. J. B. Gillett and Miss C. Kabuye from the East African Herbarium in Nairobi for their assistance in the establishment of our reference collection. Thanks are given to J. Chavaillon, J.-J. Jaeger, H. Wesselman, F. Brown, and G. Eck for their field aid. Special thanks are due D. A. Livingstone and D. Johanson for their valuable comments on the manuscript.

References

Bonnefille, R. 1970. Premiers résultats concernant l'analyse pollinique du Pléistocène inférieur de l'Omo (Ethiopie). *C. R. Acad. Sci. (Paris)*, ser. D, 270:2430-33.

_____. 1972. Associations polliniques actuelles et quaternaires en Ethiopie (vallées de l'Awash et de l'Omo). Thesis, Paris.

Bonnefille, R.; Chavaillon, J.; and Coppens, Y. 1970. Résultats de la nouvelle mission de l'Omo (1969). *C. R. Acad. Sci. (Paris)*, ser. D, 270:924-27.

Carr, C. J. 1976. Riverine ecological studies in the lower Omo basin, Ethiopia. *J. Biogeogr.* vol. 2, no. 4. In press.

Grichuk, M. P. 1967. The study of pollen spectra from recent and ancient alluvium. *Rev. Palaebot. Palynol.* 4:107-12.

Hamilton, A. C. 1972. The interpretation of pollen diagrams from highlands of Uganda. In *Paleoecology of Africa*, ed. E. M. Van Zinderen Bakker, 7:46-149. Bloemfontein.

Hammen, T. van der; Wijmstra, T. A.; and Zagwijn, W. H. 1971. The floral record of the late Cenozoic of Europe. In *Late Cenozoic Glacial Ages*, ed. K. K. Turekian, pp. 392-424. New Haven: Yale University Press.

Holdrige, L. R. 1967. *Life zone ecology*. San Jose, Costa Rica: Tropical Sciences Center.

Maley, J. 1972. La sédimentation pollinique actuelle dans la zone du lac Tchad (Afrique centrale). *Pollen et Spores* 14:263-306.

Muller, J. 1959. Palynology of recent Orinoco delta and shelf sediment: Report of the Orinoco shelf expedition. *Micropaleontology* 5:1-30.

Postscript

Since this was written the author has processed other sediment samples from Omo Group formations and pollen, sufficient to produce spectra, have been recovered from five additional horizons--High Cliffs North, Usno Formation (equivalent to Basal Mb., Shungura Fm.), Shungura Fm., members F-1, G (Tuff G), J-2, and L-9. Thus, there are now nine horizons which afford pollen spectra in the Omo succession.

C. J. Carr

Introduction

In addition to contributing to the general understanding of the semiarid tropical environments, an ecological analysis of contemporary plant life in the lower Omo basin is useful for reconstructing Plio-Pleistocene environments. According to palynological studies of the Shungura Formation (Bonnefille, this symposium), a significant shift toward a more xerophytic flora is suggested for the lower basin between 2.5 and 2 m.y. This shift toward more xeric conditions is supported by the faunal studies of Jaeger and Wesselman (this symposium) and Eck (pers. comm.) as well as the sedimentological research by de Heinzelin and Haesaerts (this symposium). Bonnefille further concludes that the vegetation of the Plio-Pleistocene very possibly was of the same general character as that which exists today. In support of this hypothesis, although fossil pollen analyses are incomplete, by my calculation 86% of the woody plant pollen taxa identified to date from Plio-Pleistocene sediments are present in the contemporary flora. A detailed though necessarily preliminary comparison of the pollen data and existing plant taxa for the lower Omo basin is presented in the last section of this paper. This comparison clearly substantiates the similarity between the two periods, showing that a description of present vegetation is relevant to the interpretation of the Plio-Pleistocene environments.

This chapter is an overview of the major forms of vegetation within the lower Omo basin, with particular emphasis on the (Omo) riverine-associated and plains[1] environments. Special attention is given to the geographical distribution of woody as opposed to herbaceous taxa, since woody plants are of greater value in palynological interpretation for this region of the tropics (Bonnefille, pers. comm.). On the basis of the present plant community types discussed, the concluding section reexamines the palynological data made available by Bonnefille, with some variations from her conclusions in this symposium.

Physical Conditions for Plant Growth

Climatic, depositional, and other geomorphic aspects of the lower Omo basin are described in detail by Butzer (1970, 1971) and are therefore only summarized here. Semiarid to arid conditions (Koppen BShw to BWhw regimes) prevail throughout the lower basin, and

---

1. "Plains" are here defined as the relatively dry, undulating lands making up most of the lower Omo basin, including sands, silts, and clays of various origins and supporting relatively xerophytic types of vegetation (see fig. 1).

conditions for plant growth are harsh, primarily because of the wide fluctuations in available moisture. Two rainy seasons are characteristic, a larger one between March and May and a smaller one between late August and October. Both are extremely irregular in occurrence and intensity and in some years do not exist at all. Although no systematic climatic data exist for any substantial period of time,[2] annual precipitation between 320 and 380 mm is likely. Temperature data also have been only sporadically collected, but daily maximum ranges of 22-39° C have been recorded (see Carr and Butzer in Appendix A of Butzer 1971).

The Omo River is the only perennial watercourse in the lower basin and, along with Lake Rudolf, provides the vast majority of mesic habitats within the region. Information on the periodicity and flow of the Omo is lacking. No systematic study of surface sediments associated with the river's natural levee has been undertaken, but scattered samples taken by Carr and by Butzer indicate that these soils are predominantly silty clays and silts (see Appendix B in Butzer 1971). These are, as analyzed by Butzer, of mixed deltaic, alluvial, and littoral origin. The previous floodplain of the Omo River (including the "delta flats" as described by Butzer 1971) exhibits old meander belts, point bar ridges, abandoned channels, a few oxbow lakes, and large-scale cracking phenomena, and in combination these provide significant habitat variation for plant growth. Of the several ephemeral streams which exist within the lower Omo basin, the largest in the zone studied (west of the Omo River) is the Kibish River (see fig. 1), where a heavy flow during several months of the year is reduced to only subterranean water during the long drought periods.

The relatively dry plains which make up most of the land surface of the lower Omo basin exhibit sediment variation which is primarily the result of facies changes or surface drainage (Butzer 1970). Drainage within the plains is internal, with essentially unintegrated shallow streams and washes (Carr 1975). Several types of contemporary topography/ soil units which are associated with particular depositional forms recur throughout most of the plains. These typically correspond to distinctive plant community types and may be briefly characterized as follows: (1) Ridges of predominantly medium- to coarse-grained sand which have been identified by Butzer (1971) as fossil beach ridges (often remodeled). Drainage within the ridges is rapid and good, and topographic relief between the ridges and the surrounding lands is variable, with 6-10 m relief frequently recorded in transects. (2) Inter-ridges, commonly of sandy silt or silty sand, with fair to good drainage and generally greater moisture available for plant growth than is generally present within the ridges. (3) Mud flats of dark, margallitic clays (also termed vertisols and black cotton soils), which characteristically are waterlogged during rainy periods and develop deep cracking patterns during the drought months. These mud flats usually are situated lower than the other two units.

There is a general correlation between plant community type (as defined first by physiognomy and second by dominant taxa) and habitat type within the lower basin which makes possible a grouping according to the main habitats of plains environments, riverine-associated environments, and anomalous habitats of peripheral or geographically restricted occurrence. The last of these categories includes volcanic highlands (e.g., Koras and Nkalabong; see fig. 1) and outcrops, catchment streams (e.g., Kolon channel; fig. 1), Sanderson's Gulf mud flats, the Omo Group exposures, and a hot springs locality.

General Character of Vegetation

Floristic affinities of the lower Omo basin are predominantly East African. Even the

---

2. See Butzer (1971) for a description of all climatic data available for the region.

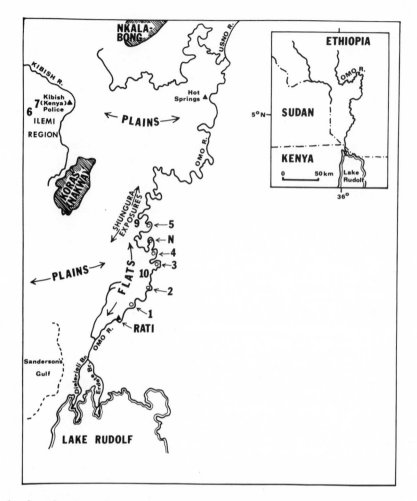

Figure 1. Locational map for ecological studies in the lower Omo basin.

species of the riverine forest, geographically linked to the more mesophytic vegetation to the north by an almost continuous band of riverine vegetation, are most aligned with the East African flora. Both Hedberg (1962) and Gillett (1955) describe southern Ethiopian highland taxa as more closely related to East African highland vegetation than to that of northern Ethiopia. Floristic variability in the lower Omo valley is low, a fact largely attributable to the arid character of the region and to recent large-scale geomorphic changes (uplifting of the Shungura Formation and superficial sediments with subsequent erosion, shifts in the Omo River channel, lake-level changes, etc.). So far my collections have yielded 76 families, 193 genera, and 321 species.[3]

The only relevant sources of vegetation classification available are for the region defined much more broadly in geographic terms. The lower basin is included in Naveh's

---

3. Plant collections have been contributed to the East African Herbarium in Nairobi. These counts do not include any additional species collected by Bonnefille, which require additional information regarding collection locations.

(1966) xerophyllous *Acacia* savanna[4] belt, Pichi-Sermolli's (1957) undifferentiated savanna and xerophile scrub, Keay's (1959) wooded steppe with abundant *Acacia* and *Commiphora* and subdesert steppe, and Good's (1964) Sudanese park steppe. Although these terms suggest one of the predominant vegetation types of the plains environments, there exists a wide range of community types, ranging from semiaquatic grasslands through forests and wooded grasslands to nearly desertlike open scrub. Rather than forming broad geographic zones which may be correlated with gradients of precipitation or other climatic variables, plant community types in the lower Omo basin form mosaiclike patterns, whether examined in small or large scale. This mosaic quality is explained by the complex interaction of such factors as moisture availability, soil type variation, topographic changes, faunal activity, and the impact of indigenous peoples. In the context of harsh conditions for plant growth caused by the prevalent semiarid conditions, even small variations in microtopography (e. g., soil cracking, small earth hummocks), often produce striking vegetation differences and thus increase the mosaic character of plant community types. The schematic profile shown in figure 2 is a typical sequence from the relatively xerophytic community types of the plains (at site 7; see fig. 1) to the more mesophytic ones near the Omo River. These are discussed in more detail below.

Plant forms of the lower basin include: (1) perennials, especially dense in wetter environments where drainage conditions permit, but also scattered throughout the plains: (2) ephemerals), in virtually all habitats; and (3) accidentals (often considered to be ephemerals), especially in such localities as silt berms along the Omo River and where low plant cover exists, such as in the mud flats near the river. The life form (Raunkiaer 1934) of some species exhibits notable plasticity, as is common for plants of arid zones. Examples from the lower basin are species which are variably evergreen and deciduous, those which

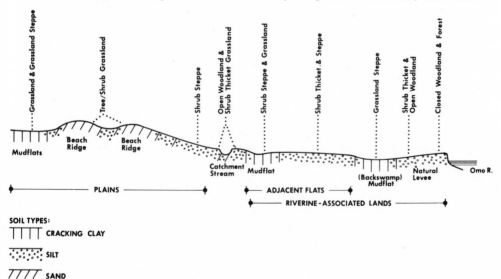

Figure 2. Schematic profile of vegetation types in the lower Omo valley.

---

4. Because the term "savanna" has been employed in so many different contexts and with such widely divergent meanings, I have avoided it here. The physiognomic category "tree/shrub grassland" which is used in this chapter, however, is basically analogous to the "savannah" described by Walter (1963), where he follows Schimper's definition of the term.

vary markedly in stature when mature (e.g., from dwarf shrubs to tall trees), and those
which grow as erect plants or as climbers and trailers.

Vegetation of the Plains

Introduction

Much of the lower basin plains vegetation (exclusive of environments closely associated with the Omo River, Lake Rudolf, or the anomalous localities mentioned above) is some
form of grassland.[5] Major plant community types recurrent within the plains are recognizable on the basis of structure, floristic composition, and various ecological relationships; these are briefly summarized in table 1. The classification presented in the table
is based on physiognomic character, with more precise categorization based on conspicuous
plant species.

The complex distribution of community types within the plains is indicated by the
vegetation map (fig. 3) of a 3 km^2 selected locality within the Ilemi lands of Sudan (see
fig. 1), and these community types basically correspond to changes in topography and soil
type.

Several types of transecting methods were used for studying plains vegetation, depending on the particular objectives. The studies summarized in table 2 were based on a total
of 60 circular plots (radius 15 m), selected in a stratified random manner during the dry
season in the Ilemi lands of Sudan (site 6; see fig. 1). These lands represent the least-
disturbed area from the standpoint of human activities and of grazing by domestic stock and
burning.[6] All species were rated on the cover-abundance scale as used by the Zurich-
Montpellier school of phytosociology, and on the sociability scale (Ellenberg 1956; Braun-
Blanquet 1964). Only woody species are included in the summary table. Geomorphic and
edaphic character were noted. Some soil samples were taken and angle of slope and aspect
were measured on sloping sites. Total vegetation cover, woody versus herbaceous cover,
the presence and character of termite mounds, and land use were also recorded.

Plant Community Types on Sands and Silts.

Plant Community Types on Sands and Silts. This vegetation complex covers significantly
more plains area within the lower Omo basin than does that of the cracking clay mud flats.
Unless otherwise specified, the following description applies to vegetation undisturbed by
human activities.[7] Plant community types on sands and silts within the plains generally
vary among grassland, tree shrub grassland, shrub grassland, and shrub steppe.

The highest ridges within this complex, exemplified by those in the Ilemi region
(plots 19, 20, and 21 in table 2), are of very high sand content (commonly 60-75% medium-
and coarse-grain sand).[8] These ridges are in strong relief with nearby clay mud flats;
I have recorded a maximum of 11 m in topographic variation. Ridge tops are nearly devoid
of woody plants except for a few *Acacia tortilis* shrubs. This absence of woody growth is
correlated with rapid drainage conditions and the high capacity of fibrous-rooted grasses

---

5. "Grassland" is here intended to include plant community types of predominantly
grasses and/or forbs, characterized by essentially continuous ground cover. The presence
of woody plants is specified as "shrub grassland," etc. "Grassland steppe" is here defined
as grassland with discontinuous cover, and "shrub steppe" as grassland with discontinuous
cover and scattered or clumped shrubs.

6. Studies of natural versus disturbed plant community types of the plains are described in Carr (1976).

7. The whole southern sector of the lower Omo valley, for instance, is severely disturbed by domestic stock overgrazing, and so is excluded from this description.

8. See textural analyses of soils sampled by Carr and Butzer in table B-2 of Butzer
(1971).

Table 1

Major Plant Community Types of the Plains within the Lower Omo Basin

Plant Community Type	Soil Type/ Topography	Conspicuous Plant Species	Land Use	Termite Mounds
Grassland	Sandy soil; high beach ridges	*Sporobolus marginatus, Cenchrus setigerus, Dactyloctenum* sp. nov., *Indigofera spinosa, I. ciferrii, Heliotropium*	Undisturbed or only light grazing[a]	Present
Grassland and grassland steppe	Cracking clay; mud flats	*Abutilon fruticosum, A. hirtum, A. pannosum, Cyathula orthacantha, Ocimum hadiense, Eriochloa nubica, Sporobolus helvolus, Panicum poaoides, Digeria muricata, Portulaca quadrifida*	Undisturbed or only light grazing	Absent
Tree/Shrub Grassland	Silty sand and sand; beach ridges and inter-ridges	*Sporobolus marginatus, Cenchrus setigerus, Dactyloctenium* sp. nov., *Chloris roxburghiana, Aristida mutabilis, Indigofera hochstetteri, Tribulus cistoides, Cordia sinensis, Acacia tortilis, Grewia tenax, Ziziphus mucronata, Maerua crassifolia, M. subcordata*	Undisturbed or only light grazing	Present
Shrub steppe	Silty; relatively flat	*Cenchrus ciliaris, Tetrapogon cenchriformis, Sporobolus marginatus, Aristida mutabilis, Cenchrus roxburghiana, Sericocomopsis pallida, Grewia tenax, Cadaba rotundifolia, C. glandulosa, Cordia sinensis, Acacia reficiens, A. mellifera*	Undisturbed or only light grazing	Present
Shrub thicket and steppe	Silty sand and sand; possible poor drainage	*Acacia nubica, A. mellifera, A. refinciens, Cadaba rotundifolia, C. glandulosa, C. farinosa, Grewia tenax, Cordia sinensis, Barleria acanthoides, Indigofera* spp., *Solanum*	Disturbed	Present
Shrub thicket and steppe	Cracking and noncracking clays, mud flats and depressions	*Acacia horrida, A. paolii, A. mellifera, A. reficiens, Cadaba rotundifolia, Cyathula orthacantha, Ocimum* spp., *Tetrapogon tenellus*	Disturbed	Absent

[a]Grazing by domestic stock.

Table 2
Woody Plant Cover-Abundance Data from Transects in the Plains

Community Type	Plot Number	Soil (S=sandy; s=silty; C=clayey)	Total Plant Cover (%)	Woody Plant Cover (%)	Acacia horrida	A. mellifera	A. nubica	A. paolii	A. reficiens	A. tortilis	Boscia coriacea *	Cadaba farinosa	C. gillettii	C. glandulosa	C. rotundifolia *	Commiphora boiviniana	C. sp. *	Cordia sinensis *	Grewia bicolor	G. tenax	G. villosa	Maerua crassifolia	M. oblongifolia *	M. subcordata	Ziziphus mucronata
Tree/Shrub Grassland **	6	sS	65	10							*+				*+		*+	*+					*+		
	7	sS	70	5																+		+			
	8	sS	75	0						2															
	13	S	80	12						+								+			+				
	14	sS	70	0																					
	15	Cs	75	10																					
	22	sS	85	15							+			*+					*+				*+		2
	26	sS	70	5		*+			+					*+	*+		*+	*+		*+		+			+
	27	sS	75	10																					
	28	sS	70	0																					
	44	sS	65	<3						+															
	45	sS	80	5						2									+						
Tree Grassland	19	S	75	5						2															
	20	S	70	<3						+															
	21	S	75	0																					
Grassland	9	S	75	0																					
	10	S	70	0																					
	11	S	80	0																					
	12	S	75	0																					

Grassland	42	S	75	0																					
	43	S	70	0																					
	1	C	80	0																					
	16	C	85	0																					
	17	C	80	0																					
	18	C	90	0																					
Shrub Grassland	3	S	70	0																					
	4	S	75	<3																					+
	5	S	70	10							+		+*			+*		+*							
	23	sS	80	0																					
	24	sS	85	15						+										2	+		+		
	30	s	75	<3						+															
	31	sS	70	0																					
	32	S	75	5												+*								+*	
	33	S	70	<3						+															
	35	sS	65	<3					+																
	40	s	70	8								+			2			+							
	41	sS	85	0																					
	46	sS	80	10																			+		2
	47	sS	75	0																					
	48	S	80	12																		2	+*		+
	49	sS	75	5			+				+													+	
	50	S	80	<3																					
	51	S	70	1											+										
	55	sS	80	5		+																			2
	56	sS	75	0																					
	57	sS	65	<3								+*						+*						+	
	58	sS	70	0																					
	59	s	75	10		+	+											2		+					
	60	s	65	0																					

Table 2 (Continued)

Community Type	Plot Number	Soil (S=sandy; s=silty; C=clayey)	Total Plant Cover(%)	Woody Plant Cover(%)	Acacia horrida	A. mellifera	A. nubica	A. paolii	A. reficiens	A. tortilis	Boscia coriacea	Cadaba farinosa	C. gilletii	C. glandulosa	C. rotundifolia	Commiphora boiviniana	C. sp.	Cordia sinensis	Grewia bicolor	G. tenax	G. villosa	Maerua crassifolia	M. oblongifolia	M. subcordata	Ziziphus mucronata
Shrub Steppe	25	sC	50	20		2			+			+			2			+							
Shrub Steppe	29	s	45	10		+									+		+	+					+		
Shrub Steppe	36	s	60	15				+	2			+						+							
Shrub Steppe	39	Cs	50	15											2			2							
Shrub Thicket and Steppe	2	C	55	30	+			2	+				+		2			+							
Shrub Thicket and Steppe	37	C	60	20		+		+	2						+										
Shrub Thicket and Steppe	38	C	55	10	+	+		2	2						+		+								
Shrub Thicket and Steppe	52	sC	45	20		2									+										
Shrub Thicket and Steppe	53	sC	50	15		+		+							+	2			+						
Shrub Thicket and Steppe	54	C	55	25	2	+		2						+	+										

* Occurring on termite mound.

** Physiognomic type is noted for the locality, more broadly defined than individual plot.

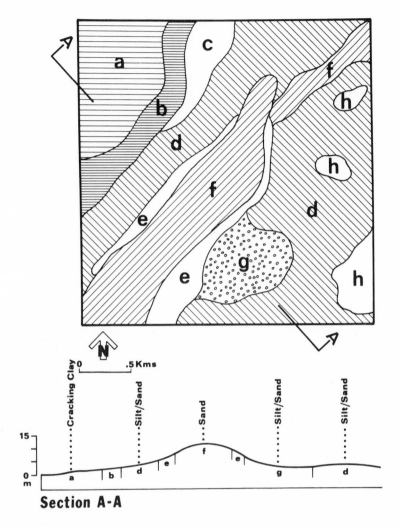

Section A-A

Figure 3.   Physiognomic variation of the plains vegetation; transect at site 7 in Ilemi region (compare fig. 1): *a*, grassland steppe; *b*, grassland (clay); *c*, tree/shrub steppe; *d*, tree/shrub grassland; *e*, shrub steppe (sand); *f*, grassland (sand); *g*, shrub thicket and steppe; *h*, shrub steppe (clay).

to absorb rainfall quickly. *A. tortilis* is somewhat adapted to such conditions because of its deeply penetrating root system. Grasses usually predominate over forbs on the high ridges, with *Sporobolus marginatus*, *Cenchrus setigerus*, *Eragrostis cilianensis*, and *Dactyloctenium* sp. nov. of high cover abundance. Forbs of significant cover abundance include *Indigofera spinosa*, *I. ciferrii*, *I. volkensii*, and *Heliotropium* spp. Termite mounds are more numerous here than in any other part of the lower Omo basin plains, and although the mounds generally do not support the clumps of woody vegetation so characteristic elsewhere, they nevertheless do contribute to vegetation patterning. This occurs in at least two ways: relatively more luxuriant (taller and greener in the dry season) growth of grass and forb species in and around the antbear holes associated with the mounds, and monospecific rings of vegetation (frequently *Dactyloctenium* sp. nov.) immediately adjacent to the mounds, or at least rings of grass species to the exclusion of forbs.

The more widespread sandy and sand/silt habitats of the lower ridges and inter-ridges (e.g., plots 8, 14, and 22 in table 2) have a high component of shrub grassland and tree/shrub grassland with very little grassland devoid of woody growth. Herbaceous ground cover is similar to that described above but with greater variation in the forb/grass ratio and with more species present. Other herbaceous species that occur frequently include *Aerva persica*, *Barleria acanthoides*, *Commelina forskalaei*, *Indigofera hochstetteri*, *Pupalia lappacea*, *Sericocomopsis pallida*, *Tribulus cistoides*, *Aristida mutabilis*, *Cenchrus ciliaris*, *Chloris roxburghiana*, and *Tetrapogon cenchriformis*. The overall greater species diversity on the lower ridges and inter-ridges may be correlated with the clumping of woody plants on the older termite mounds as well as their scattered distribution throughout, greater moisture availability, and changed soil properties (e.g., higher silt and clay content). Common tree and shrub species scattered within these grasslands are *Grewia tenax*, *Cordia sinensis*,[9] *Maerua oblongifolia*, *M. crassifolia*, *M. subcordata*, *Ziziphus mucronata*, and *Acacia tortilis*. In addition, *Grewia villosa*, *G. bicolor*, *Cadaba rotundifolia*, *Acacia mellifera*, and *A. reficiens* are present, with the latter three essentially limited to areas where ground cover is reduced. *Acacia tortilis* is particularly abundant throughout this part of the Ilemi and grows both in shrub and tree form. All these woody species are apparently fire-sensitive except for *Maerua crassifolia*.[10]

A brief note concerning the nature of disturbed (by human activities) plant communities in the sand/silt plains is relevant to an overall ecological interpretation of palynological data, especially since human-induced vegetational disturbance is often convergent in structure and floristics with vegetation resulting from geomorphic change (e.g., stratigraphic uplift and subsequent partial erosion). Disturbance of grassland (without woody growth) on sandy ridges through burning and domestic stock grazing gives rise to a reduction of overall cover, a rise in the proportion of forbs relative to grasses, a reduction in grass height, and a shift in graminaceous species in favor of *Cenchrus ciliaris*, *Chloris roxburghiana*, *Tetrapogon cenchriformis*, and, less frequently, *Aristida mutabilis*. When tree/shrub grassland on lower ridges and inter-ridges is disturbed, however, a different plant growth results. Overall cover is reduced and the proportion of forbs is increased, but the lessened ground cover permits the invasion of certain shrubs such as *Cadaba rotundifolia*, *C. glandulosa*, *Acacia reficiens*, *A. mellifera*, and especially *A. nubica*. This may result in a range of community types from shrub thicket with a very sparse understory of predominantly forbs to open shrub steppe or nearly barren land if disturbance is severe enough.

Deltaic and littoral sediments which are predominantly silty are distributed throughout the lower Omo basin and support a vegetation somewhat in contrast to that described above for the lower ridges and inter-ridges. Total cover is greatly reduced (15-45%), and the characteristic shrub steppe or shrub thicket and steppe has a significantly higher proportion of woody plants than was described for the beach ridges and inter-ridges. Woody species most common to these habitats include a high component of *Acacia reficiens*, *A. mellifera*, *Cadaba rotundifolia*, *C. glandulosa*, and *C. farinosa*.

---

9. *Cordia sinensis* has two very distinct growth forms within the lower Omo basin, as is noted below.

10. It is significant that even in localities where fires have been known to occur, the woody species diversity remains much the same owing to the presence of trees and shrubs on termite mounds, which offer considerable protection from fires.

<u>Community Types of the Cracking Clays</u>. The mud flats of intrazonal, margallitic clays are habitats with extreme conditions for plant growth owing to alternate waterlogging and desiccation. In addition to radical changes in moisture and aeration, the alternate swelling and contracting processes of the soil and the development of cracking (to a maximum of ca. 1 m deep) tend to break the roots of perennial plants. Consequently, plants which inhabit the mud flats must either be adapted to such extremes or else complete their life cycles very rapidly (e.g., ephemerals which germinate during the rains and mature before the drought months). Topographic relief within the mud flats is very limited, with depressions of 5-10 cm sufficient to create significant alterations in plant growth.

Vegetation in the mud flats varies widely according to drainage conditions and precipitation patterns in particular. In the larger mud flats of the Ilemi region a roughly concentric vegetation zonation of at least two recognizable units occurs.[11] In the center, where waterlogging and desiccation of the surface layers are most pronounced, woody growth is entirely absent and plant cover is a highly discontinuous grassland steppe composed mostly of forbs, where total cover is as low as 5-15% during the dry months (Fosberg's 3C2: seasonal desert herb vegetation). Herbs of highest cover abundance in this central zone include *Abutilon fruticosum*, *A. hirtum*, *A. pannosum*, *Cyathula orthacantha*, *Barleria acanthoides*, *Ocimum hadiense*, *Hibiscus* sp. (=Carr 938), and *Ipomoea sinensis* subsp. *blepharosepala*. The outer zone of these large mud flats, by contrast, has less pronounced moisture extremes, although it is also subject to seasonal waterlogging alternating with desiccation and cracking. Vegetation in this zone (e.g., plots 1, 16, and 17) is usually grassland (Fosberg's 1M2: seasonal short grass) of high total cover ranging up to 80-90%. On a cover-abundance scale, this outer zone is dominated by the grasses *Eriochloa nubica*, *Sporobolus helvolus*, *Panicum poaoides*, and *P. coloratum*. The following forbs occur in varying proportion: *Acalypha indica*, *Digeria muricata*, *Justicia anselliana*, *Corchorus trilocularis*, *Ruellia patula*, *Portulaca quadrifida*, and *Abelmoschus esculentus*. Woody plants are not present except at the outer periphery of this zone where the mud flat forms a transition to the surrounding sand/silt habitats. This vegetation type is also characteristic of numerous small (relatively undisturbed by humans) cracking clay mud flats which receive high amounts of moisture from surrounding lands, such as those between sandy ridges.

Mud flats receiving less water and, correspondingly, less depressed relative to surrounding lands frequently support a shrub steppe with varying cover values. The shrubs most commonly encountered in the mud flats include *Acacia horrida*, *A. paolii*, *Cadaba rotundifolia*, and to a lesser degree *Acacia reficiens* and *A. mellifera*. Whereas *Cadaba rotundifolia* is present throughout all major types of habitats in the lower Omo basin, and *Acacia reficiens* and *A. mellifera* also grow in sand/silt habitats, *Acacia horrida* and *A. paolii* are essentially specific to cracking (and a few noncracking) clays within the region.[12] It is unknown to what degree the shrubs listed above are able to establish themselves in the mud flats under natural conditions (i.e., without being preceded by overgrazing or other forms of human disturbance).[13] Further research on soil character, water

---

11. This condition obtains mainly because these large flats in the Ilemi receive considerable drainage from adjacent sandy ridges as well as runoff moisture from nearby highlands.

12. One exception to this is the occurrence of *A. horrida* in the Shungura Formation exposures.

13. The disturbance sequence of plant community types within both clays and the sand/silt environments is discussed in detail by Carr (1975).

properties, and cracking as well as on the root system and requirements of plant species inhabiting the mud flats remains to be undertaken.

Human-induced disturbance of the clay mud flats results either in grassland steppe where woody growth is prohibited by drainage conditions or in shrub steppe which may progress to shrub thicket and steppe where drainage is more favorable. If overgrazing is particularly severe or prolonged, even shrub seedlings may be destroyed, and bare ground surface results. Total ground cover, particularly the proportion of grasses, is reduced, and soil tends to be compacted and the cracking obliterated because of trampling.

Vegetation of Mesic Environments

Introduction

Mesic environments in the lower Omo basin include those associated with the Omo River --the modern delta, silt berms, natural levees, and adjacent flats;[14] the lands immediately adjacent to the Kibish and Usno rivers (fig. 1) and the Lake Rudolf shoreline; the mud flats of Sanderson's Gulf; and the Kolon channel (syn. Kalaam River in Butzer 1971). Since the Omo River is responsible for most of the mesic environments in the lower basin, its associated vegetation is the major subject of this section.[15]

With the possible exception of ephemerals, flora is more diverse in the mesic environments than in the plains. This is attributable to greater overall habitat variation among the mesic environments as defined above, to less extreme conditions for plant growth in the mesic environments, and to reduced ecological disturbance by human beings in the mesic habitats (with the exception of the modern delta region and Kolon channel). Physiognomically there is some convergence between plant community types characteristic of the plains and those of the riverine zone (see table 1).

The Omo River provides enough year-round groundwater to maintain tall forest and dense woodland on large portions of the natural levees adjacent to the river. There is, however, a wide range of variation in plant life along the natural levees, notably from the modern delta region northward to about 5° N, in the form of a gradient of increasing age of natural levee vegetation development (at least woody vegetation) and increasing river sinuosity. This gradient is primarily due to recent changes in the lake level.[16]

Vegetation of the Modern Delta and Silt Berms

Plant life bordering the relatively straight Omo channels in the modern delta region (see fig. 1)[17] occupies the most newly exposed and relatively poorly drained natural levees of the river. The modern delta consists of nonfunctional interdistributary basins, lagoonal mud flats, and networks of distributary channels (Butzer 1971). The southernmost river margins are thickly vegetated with the aquatics *Ceratophyllum dermersum, Pistia stratioides,*

---

14. "Adjacent flats" is used here to refer to the monotonous silty and clayey mud flats occurring lateral to the Omo River (see fig. 1). They include much of what Butzer (1971) terms "delta flats."

15. Plant communities adjacent to the Omo River are described in detail in Carr (1976). Descriptions of Sanderson's Gulf and Kolon channel vegetation are included in Carr (1976).

16. See Butzer (1971) for a detailed discussion of these changes. Their importance for plant growth is dealt with in Carr (1975).

17. The modern delta is here considered to include both the lands between the two major branches of the Omo River, the Dielerhiele and Erdete (fig. 1), and the lands adjacent to this region which are of similar mesic character.

Nymphae lotus and the tall semiaquatics *Phragmites australis, P. ?karka, Loudetia phragma-toides,* and *Typha latifolia*. Slightly removed from the water's edge are a variety of grasses and sedges of high cover abundance, including *Cyperus* spp., *Echinochloa haploclada, Eriochloa nubica, Eragrostis namaquensis,* and *Cynodon dactylon*. Numerous forbs appear, especially where grass cover is removed and where there is some protection from grazing by domestic stock. These species of forbs overlap strongly with those occurring on the silt berms (see below). Still farther removed from the water on the nearby natural levee back-slopes are several plant community types: tree/shrub grassland and steppe, shrub thicket and steppe, and grassland.[18] *Ficus sycomorus, Cordia sinensis, Salvadora persica, Ziziphus mauritiana,* and *Racinis communis* are among the most common woody species. A mosaiclike pattern of plant community types occurs within the rest of the modern delta, especially toward the lake. This complex pattern is due to intricate variation in sediment type and depositional pattern, microtopography, and cracking phenomena (see Butzer 1971). It is composed of tree/shrub steppe, shrub grassland, shrub steppe, grassland, shrub thicket and steppe, and aquatic and semiaquatic grassland.

Silt berms are particularly well developed loci of recent channel deposits along the convex (inside) bends of the Omo River, and they are most developed in the sections of the river with high sinuosity. Periodic flooding and inundation render the silt berms and much of the delta quite similar in conditions for plant growth, and ephemerals are the dominant life form in both. Woody growth on the silty and sandy berms is limited to fast-growing species which generally survive for only a year (e.g., *Racinis communis*), except for the slightly higher deposits along the bankside edge of the berms, which support well-established shrub and small tree growth, including *Combretum aculeatum, Cordia sinensis, Securinega virosa, Grewia fallax, Acacia sieberana, Phyllanthus reticulatus,* and *Harrisonia abyssinica*. Among the most common herbaceous species on the berms, almost all of which I have also seen in the modern delta, are: *Abutilon fruticosum, Cassia occidentalis, Cayratia ibuensis, Celosia argentea, Cynodon dactylon, Cyperus alopeduroides, C. articulatus, Eragrostis namaquensis, Eriochloa nubica, Euphorbia hypericifolia, Hyptis pectinata, Heliotropium steudneri, H. ovalifolium, Indigofera tinctoria, I. oblongifolia, Ipomoea* sp. (=Carr 728), *Justicia flava, Peristrophe bicalyculata, Polygonum senegalense, Ruellia patula, Sesamum latifolium, Sesbania sesban, S. sericea, Sorghum verticilliflorum, Sphaeranthus ukambensis, Vigna radiata,* and *Withania somnifera*.[19]

Riverine Woodland

Systematic recording of natural levee backslope gradient, bank elevation, water table, and edaphic character has not yet been undertaken for the lower basin, and these data would contribute significantly to an understanding of plant life along the natural levees. Groundwater conditions adjacent to the river, for instance, cannot be surmised beyond postulating a general decrease in available moisture with distance from the river, which is apparent from basic changes in vegetation throughout the lower basin riverine zone (see also Morgan 1971). Levee overspill does not occur along the Omo River, except in portions of the modern delta.[20] Although drainage within the study area of the riverine zone from

---

18. Most of this land is highly disturbed by local settlement, making it impossible to ascertain its natural vegetation.

19. Many of these species are also occasionally present in the riverine transition zone.

20. There are, however, several breaches in the natural levee through which flood-waters periodically enter the lands behind the levee crests (e.g., backswamps in highly sinuous portions of the river).

the north shore of Lake Rudolf to about 5°N may be assumed to have generally improved after the recent lake retreat southward, this has no doubt been greatly complicated by micro- and macrotopographic features and variations in river morphology.

The term "woodland" (most closely corresponding to Fosberg's category 1A1 4: evergreen hardwood orthophyll forest) refers to the plant community type in the lower Omo basin which is characterized by large (5 m tall) multitrunked and spreading shrubs forming a closed or open canopy cover and by an irregular ground cover. Open woodland (with large shrubs not touching or infrequently touching) or closed woodland is defined here as vegetation with a closed canopy cover of large (15 m tall) single-trunked trees, understory trees and shrubs of varying heights, and sparse ground cover.

Riverine vegetation along the levees shows a progressive development toward forest from the Omo terminus at Lake Rudolf northward to about site 4 (see fig. 1), and this development may possibly be considered to represent riverine vegetational succession.[21] The south-to-north gradient of riverine vegetation development includes the following phases: shrub thicket and grassland (or steppe), shrub thicket and open woodland, open woodland, closed woodland, and forest. This sequence is most characteristic of the natural levees on convex (inside) bends of the Omo, though it is also somewhat applicable to concave (outside) bends.[22] In the more sinuous portions of the river, woodland and forest community types are only part of a whole range of vegetation, which reflects differences in soil character, moisture properties, topographic variation, and land use by indigenous peoples.

The riverine woodland community type described here refers to that occupying the levee crest and immediate backslope. It is, however, similar to some open woodland occurring in the transition zone--that is, between the closed woodland/forest along the river and the adjacent flats (see below). Distribution of woodland in the riverine zone is such that, although woodland is replaced by forest along the natural levee in the more sinuous parts of the study zone (see fig. 4), the southernmost woodland along the natural levees (e.g., site 2) is somewhat continuous with natural levee woodland in the northern sector of the region, through the relatively continuous transitional zone woodland.

At each riverine woodland or forest study site along the south-to-north gradient belt, profile transects using line intercept and Braun-Blanquet cover-abundance measures were used for physiognomic characterization. Point-center quarter transects, modified slightly from Cottam and Curtis (1956), were utilized for more precise description of floristic and structural variations. A small number of soil samples were taken, both from pits to 60 cm and from holes to 3 m, but systematic soil studies were not undertaken. (Details of these methodologies and their results are given in Carr (1976).

Riverine woodland canopy is composed mostly of large *Ficus sycomorus* trees near the riverbank and two species of spreading shrubs, *Cordia sinensis* and *Maytenus senegalensis*. The two types of shrubs commonly grow to about 15 m, and their spreading habit makes the overall density of woody plants relatively low (see table 3). They are often draped with

---

21. The term succession must be used with reservation, however, since the south-to-north gradient of increasing woodland/forest development may represent differential plant community development based on a corresponding gradient of habitat conditions such as increasing soil development and natural levee drainage, period of development, migration of woodland and forest species southward along the natural levees, or all three.

22. The question arises whether existing riverine woodland along the natural levees may be viewed as transitional to forest, given sufficient additional time for development, or whether drainage conditions must improve before forest can be established. This can only be resolved with the aid of systematic studies of soil and moisture properties of the levees.

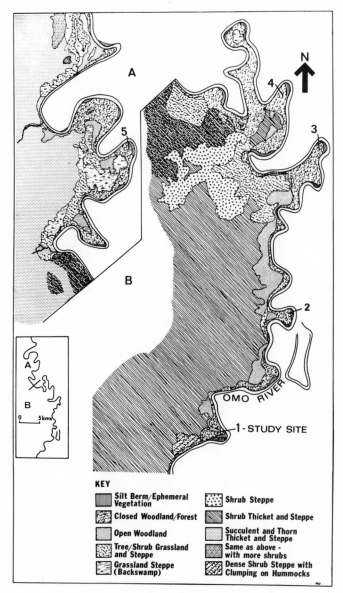

Figure 4. Riverine vegetation zones along the lower Omo river.

huge masses of the succulent *Cissus quadrangularis*, and climbing shrubs and vines are also characteristically associated with them. In addition to *Cordia*, *Maytenus*, and *Ficus*, other woody species include (table 4): *Ximenia caffra*, *Grewia fallax*, *Securinega virosa*, *Ziziphus mauritiana*, *Harrisonia abyssinica*, *Allophylus macrobotrys*, *Acacia tortilis*, and *A. sieberana*. Understory shrubs and herbaceous ground cover are both highly irregular. Nearly impenetrable thickets, for example, are often contiguous with expanses of woodland floor having almost no herbaceous or small shrub cover at all. Leaf litter is also relatively thin and unevenly distributed.

Table 3

A Comparison of Structural Characteristics of Riverine Woodland and Forest

Measurement	Site R	Site 1	Site 2	Site 3	Site 4	Site 5
Total number of woody species	13	15	11	15	12	14
Number of woody plants per acre[a]	810.5	964.8	1,119.1	1,770.6	1,889.5	1,472.1
Number of woody plants ($\leq$7m:7-13m:>13m)	211:22:0	182:55:3	146:85:9	123:79:38	127:89:24	115:99:25
Total basal area (m^2)	55.3	60.6	119.1	134.3	101.7	69.6

[a]Woody plants $\geq$ 2 m are included in the data.

Riverine woodland also occurs along the seasonal Kibish River (fig. 1). Here ground is much reduced, resulting in a more limited woodland development, both in terms of its structure and its lateral extent from the river. Except for the land between the Kibish River and Koras Mountain (syn. Nakwa, Nakua; see fig. 1)--where runoff from Koras contributes significantly to the available soil moisture to produce an extensive *Acacia tortilis* woodland--the Kibish woodland is limited to a narrow fringe along both banks of the river, varying between open and closed woodland.[23] The predominant woody species are *Acacia tortilis*, *A. sieberana*, *Terminalia brevipes*, *Combretum aculeatum*, *Cadaba rotundifolia*, *Salvadora persica*, *Ziziphus mauritiana*, and *Z. mucronata*. The large spreading shrubs *Cordia sinensis* and *Maytenus senegalensis* which are so characteristic along the Omo are less common here, though their growth form is clearly paralleled by that of *Terminalia* and *Combretum*.

Riverine Forest

Riverine forest[24] in the lower basin is present only along the Omo River on natural levees where there is sufficient year-round groundwater, drainage, and period of vegetational development. Unlike the riverine woodland, riverine forest is characterized by woody species for the most part specific to that habitat, and this is significant in the interpretation of palynological data. A possible successional sequence was suggested in the last section. As was pointed out earlier, forest development is generally more advanced on the convex bends of the river, though limited forest development also occurs on concave bends in some older, highly sinuous sections of the river (see fig. 4). Along approximately the lower 40 km of the Omo River, the natural levees generally become increasingly sinuous from south to north. North of the latitude of about site 9 (fig. 1), forest development becomes markedly less extensive within the convex bends. These highly sinuous bends are instead dominated by woodland or, rather, a vegetation type intermediate between woodland and forest. Furthermore, within the most concave bends, xerophytic vegetation of the adjacent flats may extend clear to the river's edge, breaking the continuity of the riverine

---

23. Unlike the woodlands along the Omo River, which are only modified to a limited degree by local tribespeople, those bordering the Kibish River are highly disturbed, making an accurate account of natural woodland conditions here difficult for all but the canopy species.

24. None of the forest subdivisions of Fosberg's 1A1 category (evergreen forest) are satisfactory for describing the riverine forests along the Omo, and so no precise equivalent is offered here.

Table 4

Importance Values for Woody Species of Riverine Woodland and Forest

Species	Site 1	Site 2	Site 3	Site 4	Site 5
Acacia mellifera	0.6	--	--	--	--
A. tortilis	5.8	--	--	--	--
A. sieberana	12.3	1.0	--	--	--
Acalypha fruticosa	--	--	--	--	0.2
Allophylus macrobotrys	8.7	3.8	7.4	0.2	4.7
Cadaba rotundifolia	1.1	--	--	--	--
Capparis fascicularis	1.1	--	--	--	--
Celtis integrifolia	--	--	1.8	1.7	6.9
Cordia sinensis	41.5	42.2	1.7	1.7	19.8
Cretaeva adansonii	--	--	1.3	0.2	--
Ficus sycomorus	--	23.0	36.5	39.6	9.7
Grewia fallax	2.3	1.0	0.2	--	--
G. villosa	--	--	--	--	0.2
Harrisonia abyssinica	--	3.1	1.1	--	1.6
Maerua subcordata	2.1	--	--	--	--
Maytenus senegalensis	4.5	12.8	4.4	0.2	1.9
Melanodiscus oblongus	--	--	1.0	6.7	6.2
Salvadora persica	2.7	0.2	--	--	--
Securinega virosa	5.9	15.3	--	--	--
Tamarindus indica	--	--	2.7	13.6	2.3
Tapura fischeri	--	--	2.7	13.6	2.3
Terminalia brevipes	--	--	--	0.4	--
Trichilia roka	--	--	36.7	20.3	22.2
Uvaria sp.	--	--	4.0	6.6	2.1
Ximenia caffra	10.6	7.0	0.2	--	1.6
Ziziphus mauritiana	0.2	--	--	--	--
Z. pubescens	0.4	1.1	0.2	8.5	19.3

NOTE: Importance values (I.V.) are calculated from point-center quarter transect data as the sum of the relative density and relative basal area for each woody species, divided by 2. Density and basal area data are given in Carr (1975).

woodland and forest. This is a reversal from the trend toward increased continuousness of woodland and forest between convex and concave bends to a point slightly north of site 4, a trend which corresponds to increasing river sinuosity (see fig. 4). Such a reversal may be related to increased evaporation from the steep banks of strongly concave bends, lessened infiltration from the river, and burning by indigenous peoples.

Riverine forests grow to a height of 25-30 m, with a canopy cover resulting from columnar-trunked (and often buttressed) trees. A limited ground cover, mostly herbs and shrubs, is characteristic except in clearings and along the bank, where shrub and herbaceous cover is thick. On the basis of importance values calculated from point-center quarter transects (table 4), those woody species of greatest significance are: *Ficus sycomorus, Trichilia roka, Celtis integrifolia, Ziziphus pubescens, Tapura fischeri, Melanodiscus oblongus, Uvaria* sp. (=Carr 543), and *Capparis fascicularis*. Of these, *Tapura fischeri, Melanodiscus oblongus, Capparis fascicularis,* and *Uvaria* sp. are understory plants, whereas the others are major components of the canopy. In addition, the larger bankside woody species include

Acacia sieberana, A. tortilis, A. mellifera, and *Cordia sinensis.* A few *Tamarindus indica, Crateva adansonii,* and *Allophylus macrobotrys* are scattered in the forest interior. Leaf litter in the forest is essentially continuous, with a thickness of 3-6 cm. Lianas are common in the forest canopy, and where trees serving as support are removed, these form large loops nearly to the ground. *Capparis fascicularis* and *Saba florida* are among the most frequently identified liana species, though both also grow as erect or trailing shrubs.

Clearings within the forest result from the removal of canopy trees and they are usually shrub thicket with high ground cover surrounding the thicket. Other than those understory plants named above, the most common species include *Ziziphus mauritiana, Grewia fallax, Cissampelos mucronata, Talinum portulacifolium, Abutilon fruticosa, A. figareanum, Ocimum kilimandscharicum, Cadaba farinosa, C. rotundifolia, Maerua oblongifolia, Ximenia caffra,* and *Urochloa setigera.* Thus clearings within the forest constitute small islands for species otherwise occupying the natural levees far to the south which are occupied by shrub thicket and woodland, or alternatively, the transition zone and the adjacent flats.

Maximum forest development in the study area was at site 4 (fig. 1), where density of woody plants and tree height is greatest (see table 3) and where the large spreading shrubs *Cordia* and *Maytenus* are nearly absent. Although there is no greater woody species diversity within the riverine forest compared with woodland (table 3), there is greater species patchiness in the forest. This patchiness is due in particular to the contagious distribution of *Ficus* and *Trichilia,* and it may in part be a result of their dissemination by *Colobus* and baboon, which I have often seen feed on them.

The northernmost forest which was studied in detail was at site 5 (fig. 1), and the vegetation here is intermediate between woodland and forest in several respects: density of trees and shrubs, woody plant height, tree versus shrub density, and floristics (tables 3 and 4). This intermediate character between woodland and forest recurs at other convex bend natural levee sites to the north, and such localities are likewise within highly sinuous segments of the river. It is possible to speculate that the lessened forest development may be related to poorer drainage conditions within the levee--that is, moisture conditions more similar to those farther south along the river where woodland is predominant. This explanation is supported by the occurrence of backswamps in the interior of a number of such bends. Data on natural levee elevations and infiltration rates will be necessary to confirm this hypothesis.

Observations of forests in the northern lower Omo basin were very limited, and no detailed floristic account may be offered here. *Trichilia roka, Celtis integrifolia, Ficus sycomorus,* and *Ziziphus pubescens* apparently continue to be important within the forest, and the spreading shrubs *Cordia, Maytenus,* and *Terminalia* are widely evident members of the woodland community type. In addition, *Commiphora boiviniana* (a common species on and around the Nkalabong Range and scattered in the relatively mesophytic grasslands of the plains) and the tree succulent *Euphorbia tirucalli* are conspicuous along the Omo River and also on small lava outcrops near the river. The doum palm (*Hyphaene*) is another addition to the northern sector riverine flora. It is most commonly encountered in small glades within the forest and woodland, at the hot springs (fig. 1), and on small sandy islands within the Omo River.

Riverine Transitional and Adjacent Flats Vegetation

Transitional vegetation is defined here as that between riverine closed woodland and forest on the one hand and the drier vegetation of the adjacent flats on the other. It

occurs where closed woodland or forest occupies the immediate backslope--that is, not
along the southernmost levees and most concave bends to the north. Where it is present on
concave bends, it usually forms only a narrow zone roughly parallel to the river's edge,
whereas on convex bends it is more variable in distribution and often forms a complicated
mosaic of different physiognomies (see fig. 4). The transition zone includes a wide variety of topographic, drainage, and soil conditions which produce considerable heterogeneity
in plant life. Surface sediments are predominantly silty alluvium except for some clay
localities. Topographic variations from piping phenomena, small- and large-scale cracking,
and hummocks of earth[25] are important in increasing both structural and floristic variation
within both the transition zone and adjacent flats zone.

Plant life within the transition zone varies among the following community types: open
woodland, tree/shrub grassland, tree/shrub steppe, shrub thicket and steppe, grassland, and
grassland steppe. Woody species growing within the transition zone include most of those
present in both the natural levee woodland and the adjacent flats, so that the diversity
of woody species is greatest here. Large spreading *Cordia sinensis* shrubs of the riverine
form[26] are common throughout the transition zone, and other woody species include *Maytenus
senegalensis* (relatively few), *Ximenia caffra* (few), *Salvadora persica*, *Cadaba rotundifolia*, *Acacia tortilis*, *A. sieberana*, *A. mellifera*, *A. reficiens*, *Ziziphus mauritiana*,
Dichrostachys cinerea, *Terminalia brevipes*, and *Combretum aculeatum* (the latter two are
relatively localized in distribution along the Omo).

Of the community types listed above, the grassland steppe of backswamps within the
interior of some very sinuous bends is highly distinct (e.g., near site 5; see figs. 1 and
4). The origin of this community type may be linked to seasonal inundation of the dark
clays there during the Omo River's flooding period. Woody growth is essentially excluded
(except for a few *Mimosa pigra*, *Acacia mellifera*, etc.) owing to the degree of waterlogging
and the swelling and contracting of the soil. The remaining herbaceous cover is limited
and irregular and includes many ephemeral species listed for the clay mud flats of the
plains.

Where topography decreases gradually perpendicular to the river and where no significant edaphic changes or burning occur, the decrease in available moisture away from the
river results in a relatively smooth rise in xerophytic components of the vegetation so
that the boundary with the adjacent flats is indistinct. There are, however, examples of
abrupt shifts in plant community types, such as: (1) where fires produce sharp interfaces
between burned grassland and fire-resistant thickets or woodlands which have insufficient
ground cover to carry the fire (see Carr 1975); or (2) where a significant topographic break
occurs so as to cause a marked shift in plant life or where substantial localized inundation occurs, or both. An example of the latter situation is the sharp boundary between
open woodland and thicket on the natural levee and backswamp in the interior of some river
bends (e.g., site 5).

Abundant examples of both physiognomic and floristic patchiness occur within the

---

25. These hummocks very likely form or are enlarged by windblown deposits which are
trapped by vegetation. Most such hummocks are thickly vegetated with small shrubs, some
succulents (especially *Cissus quadrangularis*), and herbs.

26. *Cordia sinensis* occurs in two markedly distinct forms within the lower Omo basin.
One is that typical of the plains: a low shrub (to 1.5 m) with irregular branching and
with roughened and somewhat thickened leaves. The other is typical of riverine and large
ephemeral stream zones: a large spreading shrub (to 15 m) with secondaries forming a vertical branching pattern and with relatively thin, smooth, and elongated leaves. Both types
occur within the adjacent flats.

transition, including nearly monospecific patches of *Ecbolium revolutum*, *Salvadora persica*, *Cadaba rotundifolia*, *Panicum meyerianum*, *Acalypha indica*, and *Cissus quadrangularis*. The overall irregularity of plant cover is contributed to not only by the strong variations in ground cover but also by the high level of contagious distribution among these species.

Adjacent flats may be defined as extensive silty and clayey mud flats lateral to the Omo River which have little topographic relief and support a relatively xerophytic plant life.[27] Drainage within the adjacent flats is internal, and there are numerous incomplete distributary channels throughout the zone (Butzer 1971). Moisture conditions in the surface layers are extreme from wet to dry seasons, with drainage largely impeded (sometimes forming sheets of standing water) during the rainy seasons, followed by desiccation during the drought months. Even topographic variations of a few centimeters are significant for plant growth under these conditions. The large intersecting patterns of cracking throughout much of the flats provide mesic microhabitats which are strongly reflected by the vegetation; cracks and pits associated with those patterns are usually less than 1 m deep (though they may reach 3 m) and often support a more luxuriant growth of the same species as are present elsewhere in the flats. Furrows, swales, and pits from piping and so forth also provide increased mesicity for plant growth. An inverse situation is widespread in the adjacent flats, where slight rises associated with shrub growth result in richer plant growth than is present in the intervening flats or slight depressions (see Mott and McComb 1974 for a discussion of similar patterning in Australia). Together, these features contribute to what is the most striking characteristic of vegetation within the adjacent flats: irregularity of cover.

Reduced plant cover within the adjacent flats, giving them a disturbed appearance, cannot be attributed to microtopographic variations alone, however. Nor is it attributable to human activities, which, except for very limited localities, are negligible in this zone. Instead, poor drainage caused by the low topographic gradient, low permeability of the soil, high seasonal fluctuation in soil moisture, and soil salinity may help cause the low total plant cover. Seasonal oscillation between extreme drought with high evaporation from upper soil levels and waterlogging with reduced aeration, for instance, inhibits the growth of shallow-rooted plants. The possible significance of salinity in the reduction of plant cover can be interpreted only after systematic soil studies, but some accumulation of soluble salts may be expected on the basis of the flats' exposure to prolonged arid conditions and periodic lake advances.[28] It is important to note that even though these forces may be helpful in explaining the reduced total plant cover of the adjacent flats, they cannot explain its irregularity. For this, the reproductive behavior and competitive abilities of individual plant species must also be considered (see below). Transecting methods employed in the adjacent flats included circular plots (radius 15 m) located in a stratified random manner, for recording of community type, Braun-Blanquet cover-abundance values for woody species, herbaceous and woody cover, microtopographic feature, and herbaceous species observations (see table 5).

27. These mud flats correspond essentially to Butzer's (1971) "delta flats" and "eastern flood basin."

28. Inhibition of vegetation resulting from salinity has been described for the soils of the arid Turkana district of Kenya, and in the South Turkana area it is associated with large amounts of bare area and abundant *Salvadora persica* (Morgan 1971), which is also extremely abundant throughout the adjacent flats of the Omo region. Inhibition of woody growth in areas near water but not immediately adjacent occurs elsewhere in East Africa, for example, the Mbugas of Zambia (J. B. Gillett, pers. comm.).

Table 5

Woody Species Cover Abundance and Plant Cover Data from Transects in Riverine Adjacent Plats

Plot Number	Total Cover (%)	Total Woody Cover (%)	Total Number of Species	Total Number of Woody Spp.	Acacia mellifera	A. reficiens	Cadaba rotundifolia	C. farinosa	Commiphora sp.	Cordia sinensis	Grewia tenax	Maerua oblongifolia	M. sub-cordata	Salvadora persica
1	35	8	15	4			+				+	+		2
2	20	5	12	3		+	1				+			
3	40	12	18	5			2	1		+	+			+
4	15	3	10	2			1				+			
5	40	15	14	4	+				+	+	+			+
6	25	10	11	4			1							1
7	5	<1	4	1										1
8	30	8	19	5		+		1		+	+			1
9	20	5	13	3			2	1			1			+
10	30	8	11	3			1	+			1			1
11	15	<3	10	3			1				+		+	
12	25	5	8	5			1		+		1		+	+
13	10	5	9	2	+		1				1			
14	15	10	11	3			1				+			+
15	20	10	13	4			2				1			
16	25	8	12	4		+	2		+		+			+
17	18	10	21	6			1	+		+	+	+		
18	50	12	9	2			2	+	+		+	+		2
19	20	3	11	4				+			+			+
20	25	15	17	4	+	+	2			+				1
21	30	15	8	3			1				+			1
22	15	5	14	4			1						+	+
23	20	10	13	3			2				+		1	+
24	12	5	7	2			1	+			+			+
25	10	5	11	4			1				1			
26	35	20	12	2			2					+	+	2
27	20	5	16	5			+							+
28	30	20	4	1	+		1			+		+		2
29	5	<1	9	3	+									+
30	25	5	9	3			+		+		1			1

Plant community types of the adjacent flats form a somewhat variegated pattern but represent a narrower spectrum of variation than is true for either the transition zone or the plains. These types range primarily among shrub thicket and steppe, shrub steppe, shrub grassland, and grassland steppe. Viewed on a large enough scale (e.g., 1 km^2), shrub thicket and steppe is clearly prevalent. The flats also have relatively homogeneous flora, with the same factors likely responsible for the limited species diversity as were suggested above for the irregular cover. From table 5 it can be seen that woody species of significance are few and include *Cadaba rotundifolia*, *C. farinosa*, *Cordia sinensis*, *Grewis fallax*, *Acacia mellifera*, *A. reficiens*, and *Salvadora persica*. *Acacis sieberana* and *A. tortilis* are also present, though only sparsely, along old distributary channels (they are more common along Kolon channel; see fig. 1). Strong patterning occurs on a floristic as well as a physiognomic level within the flats. This is most notable in the case of *Cadaba rotundifolia*. A nearly ubiquitous shrub in the lower Omo basin, *Cadaba* exhibits a somewhat regular pattern of almost monospecific clusters and of individual shrubs within the flats, much like that described by Beals (1969). Such patterning suggests negative interaction between the plants, likely in the form of competition for water.[29] The problem of pattern in the adjacent flats is the subject of a separate study, the results of which will be published elsewhere.

Vegetation of Selected Anomalous Environments

Lava Highlands. Although Nkalabong Mountain may be considered part of the lower Omo valley (fig. 1), floristically it is more closely related to the Ethiopian highlands to the north than to the surrounding plains and mesic environments. A short characterization of its vegetational structure as well as its floristic character is offered here on the basis of two sites studied at the altitude of approximately 900 and 1,100 m.

The lithosolic character of the soil and the large volcanic rocks forming much of the surface of the slopes of Nkalabong are strong limiting factors on plant growth in spite of the relatively high rainfall compared with the lowland plains described avove. Plant community types on the slopes are predominantly tree/shrub grassland and tree/shrub steppe (Fosberg's 2D1: evergreen shrub steppe savanna). Grasses are tussocklike in form and predominate over forbs in all localities investigated. Grass heights range up to 1 m. The open character of the vegetation is partially maintained by the high frequency of fires, and most woody species which survive are morphologically adapted for fire resistance. By contrast, draws are heavily wooded and apparently escape most fires. Species overlap between plants of Nkalabong and those of the lowland plains is limited, the most notable species common to both being *Grewia villosa*, *Commiphora boiviana*, *Maerua subcordata*, and *Cadaba farinosa*.

The following is a list of common species on the Nkalabong slopes (the most important from the standpoint of cover abundance are marked with an asterisk). Woody species include *Acacia drepanolobium**, *A. seyal**, *Boscia* sp. cf. *angustifolia*, *Boswellia hildebrandtii**, *Commiphora* sp., *Cordia crenata*, *Cyphostemma* sp., *Fagara chalybea*, *Grewia bicolor*, *G. villosa*, *Heeria reticulata*, *Lannea floccosa*, *Rhoicissus* sp., and *Rhus natalensis**. Herbaceous species include *Cassia nigricans*, *Crotalaria polysperma*, *Heteropogon contortus**, *Indigofera arrecta*, *Justicia striata*, *Ormocarpum trichocarpum*, *Panicum maximum**, *Sehima nervosum**,

---

29. *Cadaba rotundifolia* has two types of root systems (Glover 1951), both a deep one and a lateral one. As such it is well adapted to the alternating surface moisture collection (rainy periods) and deep-water source (drought months).

Sporobolus fimbriatus var. *latifolius**, *Tarenna graveolus*, *Tephrosia purpurea* var. *pubescens*, and *Vernonia* sp.

Koras Mountain, although highly xeric in character, offers a habitat for plant growth markedly different from the plains surrounding it. The mineralogical character of the volcanics which form much of the surface, the irregularly developed lithosol, and the limited amount of moisture available for plants due to rapid runoff and low surface absorption combine to produce specialized and harsh conditions for vegetation. The lower slopes of Koras are predominantly tree/shrub steppe and tree/shrub thicket and steppe (Fosberg's 3A1: evergreen desert forest). Total plant cover has a maximum value of about 40% and is frequently as low as 10% where the slope is steep or where the surface is almost entirely rock. Grasses are primarily tussocklike and less than 0.5 m high. Some termite mounds occur, but these are usually small compared with those in the surrounding plains. The most frequent woody species recorded in representative belt transects on the lower slopes were *Acacia reficiens*, *A. mellifera*, *Adenium obesum*, *Cadaba rotundifolia*, *Cadaba glandulosa*, *Commiphora* spp., and *Grewia tenax*. A variety of succulent plants, including *Euphorbia heterochroma*, *Adenium obesum*, *Cissus quadrangularis*, and others are sparsely scattered throughout the slopes.

The middle and upper slopes of Koras exhibit significant floristic and physiognomic differences from the lower slopes. A shift toward denser tree growth occurs at least locally, with some limited open woodland with trees to 8-10 m tall. Herbaceous growth is discontinuous except for small sheltered localities, where grass cover may be nearly continuous and up to 1 m high. Woody species of highest cover abundance include *Acacia mellifera*, *A. reficiens*, *A. senegal*, *Adenium obesum*, *Boswellia hildebrandtii*, *Delonix elata*, *Grewia tenax*, and *Terminalia brevipes*. Although many of the herbaceous taxa found here overlap with those of the surrounding plains, some do not, and these include *Helichrysum glumaceum* and *Enneapogon brachystachys*, both of high cover value in some localities of the higher slopes. There is considerable species overlap between plants of the Omo Bed exposures and those present on Koras, including taxa specific to these habitats only within the lower basin.

<u>Shungura Formation Exposures</u>. These are of silt, sand, and clay sediments with relatively flat topography and tilted tuffaceous ridges, supporting plant life highly differentiated from the rest of the lower Omo basin. A large part of the exposures is nearly barren of plants, with only scattered forbs or tussocks of grasses. But the predominant plant community types are tree/shrub steppe and shrub thicket with steppe. These most closely correspond to Fosberg's category 3B1: evergreen desert scrub. Succulents make up a significant proportion of the flora of the exposures, a characteristic distinguishing the plant life here from all the environments described above, with the partial exception of Koras Mountain. The low amount of available moisture together with low organic content in the sediments may be correlated with the abundance of succulents. Large colonies of *Sarcostemma viminale*, *Kleinia kleinioides*, and *Cissus quadrangularis* are common, and these often include individual plants of *Euphorbia grandicornis* (a dominant species in the exposures which grows to heights of 4 m) and *Sansevieria* spp., as well as numerous other shrubs and herbs.

Although the flora of the Shungura Formation exposures is not at all indicative of the lower basin's ecology as a whole, some floristic characterization is appropriate here since some of the taxa present there have been recovered in Plio-Pleistocene pollen samples by Bonnefille (see next section). Woody species common within the Omo Bed exposures include

Acacia horrida,[30] *A. mellifera, A. reficiens, Adenium obesum, Boerhavia erecta, Cadaba gillettii, C. glandulosa, C. rotundifolia, Commiphora africana, C. madagascariensis, Commiphora* sp. (=Carr 227), *Delonix elata, Grewia tenax, Maerua oblongifolia,* and *M. subcordata.* Herbaceous plants and succulents which are common include *Aerva persica, Aristida adscensionia, A. mutabilis, Caralluma russelliana, C. somaliea, Cissus quadrangularis, C. rotundifolia, Cleome brachycarpa, Dactyloctenium* sp. nov., *Dasysphaera prostrata, Euphorbia grandicornis, E. heterochroma, E. triaculeata, Kedrostis gijef, Kleinia kleinioides, Plicosepalus sagittifolius, Polygala erioptera, Sansevieria ehrenbergii, Sarcostemma viminale, Schoenefeldia transiens,* and *Senra incana.*

Notes on the Interpretation of Plio-Pleistocene Pollen

The following is a preliminary attempt to interpret the types of habitats likely to correspond to the hominid-bearing sediments of 2.5 m.y. and 2 m.y., using palynological data presented by Bonnefille (1972; and this symposium) and the contemporary plant ecological studies summarized above. More definitive paleoenvironmental reconstruction must await further pollen data for the region as a whole, but on the basis of the evidence available to date certain generalizations may already be suggested. The results of contemporary plant ecological studies in the lower Omo basin, when considered alongside Bonnefille's data, support her fundamental conclusions regarding Plio-Pleistocene plant life while offering some points of contrasting perspective.

On the basis of the pollen identified from the 2.5 m.y. (units C-7/8 and C-9) and 2 m.y. (unit E-4) sediments, Bonnefille considers three basic categories: montane forest, or long-distance element; riverine communities, or local element; and savanna and steppe, or regional element. If one accepts Bonnefille's assertion that the montane forest element of Plio-Pleistocene pollen recovered is in fact derived (via wind and river transport) from outside the lower Omo valley, then the remaining pollen taxa overlap sufficiently with the taxa of contemporary plant communities within the region to justify a detailed interpretation which attempts to specify the most likely habitats and plant community types with which these taxa were associated.

For those Plio-Pleistocene pollen taxa already identified which are present within contemporary plant communities of the lower Omo valley (or contiguous areas of Ethiopia, Kenya, and Sudan), a system of classification different from Bonnefille's has been selected for use here. Specifically, Bonnefille's "riverine" and "savanna and steppe" categories are here broken into three categories: (1) mesic community types, (2) plains[31] community types, and (3) both plains and mesic community types. This is desirable for at least two reasons. First, a number of taxa assigned to one or the other of Bonnefille's categories actually occur in both. Since much of the pollen recovered is only identifiable to family or genus as opposed to species, it is not possible to assign a substantial amount of this pollen to one or the other habitat. Consequently, efforts toward ecological interpretation of the fossil pollen are well served by separating out those taxa specific to wetter versus drier contemporary environments from those which are affiliated with both.[32] Second, some of the fossil pollen taxa occur in contemporary vegetation types other than "riverine" or

---

30. *Acacia paolii,* which usually accompanies *A. horrida* in the clay mud flats of the plains, is virtually absent in the Shungura Formation exposures.

31. Both "plains" and "mesic" environments are defined in earlier sections of this paper.

32. Those taxa which are not present in the lower Omo valley or in contiguous regions are excluded from this interpretation.

"savanna and steppe," so that broader categories are helpful. The different classification for pollen taxa affiliation with habitat and plant community type is significant in producing some of the conclusions offered below. It is desirable to correlate the Plio-Pleistocene pollen being considered (i.e., all but the "long-distance element") with more specific contemporary plant community types within the mesic and plains categories, and this is attempted in the last section below.

Table 6 indicates the classification of Plio-Pleistocene pollen within the generalized habitat categories of "mesic" and "plains" within the lower Omo basin. Based on Bonnefille's data for individual taxa, percentage abundance of each taxon is recalculated on the basis of the proposed classification system. These data are selectively summarized in table 7. In general the data support the generalization offered by Bonnefille that the environment at 2 m.y. was significantly drier than that at 2.5 m.y. The proportion of graminaceous vegetation is high for both periods (i.e., 63% and 67% for 2.5 m.y. and 74% for 2 m.y.), suggesting the presence of significant open vegetation (shrub grassland, grassland, etc.) for both time ranges. But there are striking contrasts between the two periods. Pollen identified as of mesic habitat affiliation decreases markedly, from 22.3% and 27.8% for the 2.5 m.y. samples to only 1.4% at 2 m.y. This is in contrast to the large increase in the proportion of pollen with a plains habitat affiliation--that is, from 4.4% and 0.8% at 2.5 m.y. to 23.4% at 2 m.y. Together these facts indicate a striking change toward a more xerophytic vegetation. It must be pointed out, however, that a large percentage (96%) of the E-4 (2 m.y.) plains pollen is composed of only two genera, *Polygala* and *Dasysphaera*, and may therefore be attributable to dispersal patterns or other phenomena not indicative of their actual importance in the flora. Similarly, a disproportionately large percentage (65%) of the C-7/8 and C-9 (2.5 m.y.) pollen is *Typha*. These qualifications notwithstanding, the indication of more xeric conditions at 2 m.y. than at 2.5 m.y. is further supported by the much lower percentage abundance of pollen from woody plants. Specifically, the percentage of pollen from woody plants decreases from 10.7% (C-7/8) and 3.9% (C-9) to 0.9% (E-4). Also, the total diversity of plant taxa is reduced from 27 and 24 taxa (C-7/8 and C-9, respectively) to 12 taxa (E-4), a change which may be correlated with drier and more extreme conditions at 2 m.y. According to the classification of taxa into mesic and plains habitats which is offered in table 6, although the number of mesic taxa does decrease over this 0.5 m.y. period, there is no corresponding increase in the number of plains taxa over the same period. Some clearer pattern of floristic diversity may emerge as we collect more pollen data.

Because the categories mesic and plains actually include numerous plant community types, more detailed correlation of Plio/Pleistocene pollen with these community types is necessary. Selected major plant community types are correlated with the Plio-Pleistocene pollen taxa in tables 8 and 9 for 2.5 m.y. and 2 m.y., respectively. The distribution of of 2.5 m.y. fossil pollen taxa among contemporary community types (table 8) indicates a significant presence of riverine forest and riverine woodland, especially the latter. Because the only riverine-forest-associated taxon not also present in riverine woodland is *Celtis*, and there are at least two taxa (*Combretum/Terminalia* and *Ziziphus*) which are associated with woodland but not forest, woodland is suggested as the more likely affiliation of the pollen taxa. Of the other indicator taxa for forest and woodland, Moraceae (e.g., *Ficus sycomorus* in contemporary communities), is the clearest, and it occurs in both community types. Other taxa which indicate either woodland or forest are less useful for this since they require more specific pollen identification to correlate them with specific plant

Table 6

Correlation of Plio-Pleistocene Pollen Taxa with Contemporary Mesic versus Plains Environment

| Taxon | 2.5 m.y. | | | | 2 m.y. | |
| | C-7/8 | | C-9 | | E-4 | |
	No. of pollen	%	No. of pollen	%	No. of pollen	%
Mesic Environment Taxa						
Racinis communis	2	1.2	--	--	--	--
Crotalaria			1	0.6	--	--
Celtis	6	3.5	5	3.0	--	--
Rhamnaceae(*?Ziziphus*)	2	1.2	--	--	--	--
Combretum/Terminalia	3	1.7	1	0.6	--	--
Moraceae			1	0.6	--	--
Acalypha	14	8.1	24	14.2	--	--
Typha	114	66.4	86	50.9	15	100.0
Cyperaceae	31	18.0	52	30.8	--	--
Total mesic pollen	172		170		15	
Plains Environment Taxa						
Apocynaceae	13	38.3	--	--	--	--
Maerua	4	11.8	1	20.0	--	--
Ebenaceae	--	--	1	20.0	--	--
Euphorbia triaculeata	--	--	1	20.0	--	--
Commiphora	3	8.8	1	20.0	3	1.2
Polygala	--	--	--	--	71	29.4
Loranthaceae	--	--	--	--	1	0.4
Dasysphaera	6	17.7	--	--	163	67.5
Blepharis	5	14.7	1	20.0	--	--
Boerhavia	3	8.8	--	--	4	1.7
Total plains pollen	34		5		242	
Taxa of Mesic and Plains Environment						
Commiphora boiviniana	--		2		--	
Capparaceae	24		4		2	
Solaneae	2		2		--	
Acacia sp	3		3		1	
Salvadoraceae	6		6		--	
Chenopodiaceae/ Amaranthaceae	27		--		--	
Cordia	1		--		--	
Cucurbitaceae	1		--		--	
Gramineae	489		413		766	
Papilionaceae	3		2		--	
Heliotropium	1		--		--	
Vitidaceae	--		1		--	
Justicia	1		--		--	
Tribulus/Zygophyllaceae	3		4		2	
Celosia	--		1		--	
Euphorbiaceae	2		2		--	
Compositae	2		1		2	

Table 7

Summary of Pollen Data for 2.5 and 2 M.Y.

| | 2.5 m.y. | | 2.0 m.y. |
	Unit C-7/8	Unit C-9	Unit E-4
No. of plains pollen taxa[a]	34	5	242
% (of total) plains pollen taxa	4.4	0.8	23.4
No. of mesic pollen taxa	172	169	15
% (of total) mesic pollen taxa	22.3	27.8	1.4
Total no. of pollen taxa	27	24[b]	12
Total no. of woody pollen taxa	72	24	10
% woody pollen taxa	10.7	3.9	0.9
Total no. of graminaceous pollen taxa	489	413	766
% graminaceous pollen taxa	63.4	67.1	74.3
Total no. of pollen taxa	771	615	1031

[a]Long-distance pollen taxa are omitted from all calculations in this table.

[b]The combined number of pollen taxa for C-7/8 and C-9 is 34.

community types. A specification at least to genus is needed for Capparaceae and to species for *Acacia*. Other taxa such as Salvadoraceae and *Cordia* are nearly ubiquitous among community types of the lower Omo valley, so that in the absence of larger pollen samples they are not very useful indicators beyond providing evidence for the character of vegetation at the region level.

Table 8 also indicates that a substantial number of fossil pollen taxa are associated with lava exposures or tuffaceous sediments. The taxa Apocynaceae and *Boerhavia* are most indicative of these habitat types.

The importance of plains vegetation at 2.5 m.y. is highly unclear from the data in table 8, since most of the pollen taxa associated with the plains (*Cordia*, Capparaceae, *Acacia*) correspond to a wide range of other environments as well. But it may be tentatively suggested that what plains plant community types did exist at 2.5 m.y. likely had a substantial amount of woody growth. This may have been of the order of the tree/shrub grasslands of the lower beach ridges or much like the riverine-associated adjacent flats (though possibly with a higher component of graminaceous cover). In summary, then, vegetation of the 2.5 m.y. period may be hypothesized to have included closed and/or open woodland, tree/shrub grassland, grassland, and some shrub thicket and shrub steppe. We cannot yet surmise whether this variation in community types formed a mosaic pattern or a more homogeneous plant life. This seems more likely to be resolved by analyses of Plio-Pleistocene sediments than by fossil pollen data.

Since only a few taxa are represented by the pollen of 2 m.y. (12 taxa in all), interpretation of specific plant community types can be only most tentative. The drier conditions of 2 m.y. compared with 2.5 m.y. have already been suggested as likely on the basis of the decrease in woody taxa, increase in graminaceous taxa (table 7), and general pattern mesic versus plains taxa affiliation (table 6), as well as more specific quantitative data for certain taxa (e.g., decrease of *Typha* and Cyperaceae). The absence of taxa specific to

Table 8

Contemporary Plant Community Type Correlation with Fossil Pollen Taxa of 2.5 M.Y.

Fossil Pollen Taxa	Riverine Aquatic and Semiaquatic Grassland	Riverine Woodland	Riverine Forest	Riverine Transitional Vegetation	Adjacent flats; shrub thicket and Steppe	Plains: Tree/Shrub Grassland and Grassland	Plains: Shrub Steppe	Lowland Volcanics and Omo Bed Exposures: Shrub/Succulent Thicket and Steppe	Silt Berms: Ephemeral Vegetation
Racinis communis	(x)*								x
Crotalaria	(x)								x
Celtis			x						
Rhamnaceae (*Ziziphus*)		x		x		(x)			
Combretum/Terminalia		x		x					
Moraceae		x	x						
Acalypha		x	x						
Typha	x					(x)			(x)
Cyperaceae	x								x
Apocynaceae									
Maerua		(x)		x		x		x	
Ebenaceae									
Euphorbia triaculeata/Euphorbiaceae								x	
Commiphora/*C. boiviniana*			(x)			(x)		x	
Dasysphaera							x	x	
Blepharis							x	x	
Capparaceae		x	x	x	(x)	x	x	x	
Solanaceae				x	x	x	x	x	
Acacia sp.		x	(x)	x	x	x	x	(x)	
Salvadoraceae					(x)	(x)	x	(x)	
Chenopodiaceae/Amaranthaceae			(x)	(x)	(x)	x		x	
Cordia		(x)	(x)		x	x	x	x	
Cucurbitaceae		x	x		(x)	x	x	(x)	
Papilionaceae				x	x	x	x		x
Heliotropium				x	x	x	x		x
Vitidaceae							(x)		
Justicia		x		(x)	(x)	(x)			x
Tribulus				x	x	x	x	x	
Zygophyllaceae							x	(x)	x
Compositae	(x)					(x)	x	(x)	x

Table 9

Contemporary Plant Community Type Correlation with Fossil Pollen Taxa 2 M.Y.

Fossil Pollen Taxa	Riverine Aquatic and Semiaquatic Grassland	Riverine Woodland	Riverine Forest	Riverine Transitional Vegetation	Adjacent flats; shrub thicket and Steppe	Plains: Tree/ Shrub Grass- land and Grassland	Plains: Shrub Steppe	Lowland Volcanics and Omo Bed Exposures: Shrub/Succulent Thicket and Steppe	Silt Berms: Ephemeral Vegetation
Typha	x								(x)
Commiphora			(x)			(x)		x	
Polygala						x		x	x
Loranthaceae					(x)	(x)		x	
Dasysphaera							x	x	
Boerhavia								x	
Capparaceae		x	x	x	(x)	x			
Acacia sp.		x		x	x	x	x	x	
Chenopodiaceae/ Amaranthaceae				(x)	(x)	x		x	
Tribulus/ Zygophyllaceae				x	x		x	(x)	x
Compositae	(x)					(x)		(x)	x

riverine forest is notable (see table 9), and those taxa which are associated with the contemporary riverine woodland are also present in plains community types. Affiliation of
this age pollen with the plains plant community types is suggested both by the absence of
mesic taxa and by the high grass component (table 7). Fossil pollen taxa which may be associated exclusively with the plains, however, are absent. As with the 2.5 m.y. data,
there is some indication of plant community types associated with either lava outcrops or
tuffaceous deposits. In general, then, the character of plant life suggested by the 2 m.y.
data now available suggests the somewhat more xerophytic plant community types of grassland, tree/shrub grassland, shrub thicket, and shrub steppe.

Appendix: Species Collected in the Lower Omo River Basin by C. J. Carr

PTERIDOPHYTA

Polypodiaceae

Actiniopteris radiata (Swartz) Link

ANGIOSPERMAE: DICOTYLEDONES

Acanthaceae

Barleria acanthoides Vahl
B. eranthemoides R. Br. ex C. B. Cl.
Blepharis linariifolius Pers.
B. persica (Burm. f.) Kuntze
Ecbolium anisacanthus (Schweinf.) C. B. Cl.
E. revolutum (L.) C. B. Cl.
Hypoestes verticillaris R. Br.
Justicia anselliana T. Anders.
J. caerulea Forsk.
J. flava Vahl
J. odora (Forsk.) Vahl
J. striata (Flotsch.) Bullock
J. sp. (=Padwa 275)
Peristrophe bicalyculata (Retz.) Nees
Ruellia patula Jacq.

Aizoaceae

Corbichonia decumbens (Forsk.) Exell
Trianthema triquetra Willd. var. *sanguinea*
T. triquetra Willd. intermed. betw. var.
  triquetra and var. *sanguinea* (Volk. and
  Irmsch.) Jeffrey
Zaleya pentandra (L.) Jeffrey

Amaranthaceae

Aerva persica (Burm. f.) Merrill
Achyranthes aspera L.
Celosia argentea L.
C. schweinfurthiana Schinz
Cyathula orthacantha (Hochst.) Schinz
Dasysphaera prostrata (Gilg.) Cavaco
Digeria muricata L.
Psilotrichum eliottii Bak.
P. ghaphalobryum (Hochst.) Schinz
Pupalia lappacea (L.) Juss.
P. lappacea (L.) Juss. Vergens var.
  orbiculata Schinz
Sericocomopsis pallida (C. B. Cl.) Schinz

Anacardiaceae

Heeria reticulata (Bak. f.) Engl.
Rhus natalensis Bernh. ex Krauss

Annonaceae

Uvaria sp. (=Carr 543)

Apocynaceae

Adenium obesum (Forsk.) Roem. and Schult.
Saba florida (Benth.) Bullock

Asclepiadaceae

Caralluma russelliana (Brongn.) Cuf.
C. somaliea N. E. Br.
Curroria volubilis (Schtr.) Bullock
Gomphocarpus fruticosus (L.) Ait
Leptadenia hastata (Pers.) Decne
Pergularia daemia (Forsk.) Chiov.
Sarcostemma viminale R. Br.
Tacazzea galactogoga Bullock

Balanitaceae

Balanites aegyptiaca (L.) Del.
B. zeylanicum (Burm.) R. Br.
B. sp. (=Carr 859)

Boraginaceae

Cordia crenata Delile
C. sinensis Lam.
Heliotropium indicum L.
H. ovalifolium Forsk.
H. somalense Vatke
H. steudneri Vatke
H. supinum
Trichodesma zeylanicum

Burseraceae

Boswellia hildebrandtii Engl.
Commiphora africana (A. Rich.) Engl.
C. boiviniana Engl.
C. madagascariensis Jacq.

Capparaceae

Boscis coriacea Pax
B. angustifolia A. Rich. var.
    angustifolia
Cadaba farinosa Forsk. spp. *farinosa*
C. gillettii R. A. Graham
C. glandulosa Forsk.
C. rotundifolia Forsk.
Capparis fascicularis DC. var.
    elaeagnoides (Gilg.) De Wolf
C. fascicularis DC. var. *fascicularis*
C. tomentosa Lam.
Cleome parvipetala
C. brachycarpa DC
Crateva adansonii DC.
Maerua crassifolia Forsk.
M. oblongifolia (Forsk.) A. Rich.
M. subcordata (Gilg.) De Wolf

Celastraceae

Hippocratea africana (Willd.) Loes.
Maytenus senegalensis (Lam.) Exell

Ceratophyllaceae

Ceratophyllum demersum L.

Chenopodiaceae

Suaeda monoica Forsk. ex Gmel.

Combretaceae

Combretum aculeatum Vent.
Terminalia brevipes Pampan.

Compositae

Delamerea procumbens S. Moore
Helichrysum glumaceum DC.
Kleinia kleinioides (Sch. Bip.) M. R. F. Taylor
K. longiflora DC.
Pluchea dioscoridis DC.
P. ovalis (Pers.) DC.
Sphaeranthus ukambensis Vatke and O. Hoffm.
Vernonia cinerascens Sch. Cip.
V. sp. (=Newbould 6823)

Convolvulaceae

Hildebrandtia obcordata S. Moore
Ipomoea aquatica Forsk.
I. sinensis (Desr.) Choisy subsp.
    blepharosepala (A. Rich.) Meeuse
I. sp. (=Carr 728)
Seddera hirsuta Hall. f. var. *hirsuta*

Cucurbitaceae

Coccinia grandis (L.) Voigt
C. sp. (=Carr 618)
Cucumis dipsaceus Spach
C. figarei Naud.
Kedrostis gijef (Gmel.) Jeffr.
K. foetidissima (Jacq.) Cogn.
Luffa ?echinata Roxb.
Momordica rostrata A. Zimm.

Dichapetalaceae

Tapura fischeri Engl.
Tapiera sp.

Ebenaceae

Diospyros sp. (=Carr 578)
D. scabra

Elatinaceae

Bergia suffruticosa (Del.) Fanzl

Euphorbiaceae

Acalypha fruticosa Forsk.
A. indica L.
Euphorbia grandicornis Goebel
E. heterochroma Pax
E. hypericifolia L.
E. tirucalli L.
E. triaculeata Forsk.
Jatropha fissispina Pax
Phyllanthus amarus Schumach. and Thonn.
P. maderaspatensis L.
P. reticulatus Poir.
P. sp. (=Carr 411)
Ricinus communis L.
Securinega virosa (Willd.) Pax and
    K. Hoffm.
Tragia hildebrandtii Muell. Arg.

Gentianaceae

Enicostema hyssopifolium (Willd.)
    Verdoor

Labiatae

Basilicum polystachion (L.) Moench
Hyptis pectinata (L.) Poit
Leucas ?glabrata R. Br.
L. nubica Benth.
Leonotis nepetifolia R. Br.
Ocimum americanum L.
O. hadiense Forsk.
O. kilimandscharicum Guerke
Orthosiphon somalensis Vatke
Plectranthus sp. (=Carr 739)

Leguminosae: Caesalpinioideae

Cassia didymobotrya Fres.
C. italica (Mill.) F. W. Andr. var
    micrantha Brenan
C. nigricans Vahl
C. occidentalis L.
Delonis elata
Tamarindus indica L.

Leguminosae: Mimosoideae

Acacia brevispica Harms
A. drepanolobium Sjodtedt
A. horrida (L.) Willd.
A. mellifera (Vahl) Benth.
A. mellifera (Vahl) Benth. subsp.
    mellifera
A. nubica Benth.
A. paolii Chiov.
A. reficiens Wawra spp. *misera* (Vatke)
    Brenan
A. senegal (L.) Willd.
A. seyal Del.
A. sieberana DC.
A. tortilis (Forsk.) Hayne subsp.
    spirocarpa (Hochst. ex A. Rich.) Brenan
Dichrostachys cinerea (L.) W. and A.
Mimosa pigra L.

Leguminosae: Papilionoideae

Canavalia cathartica Thou.
C. virosa Wight and Arn.
Crotalaria polysperma Kotschy
C. pycnostachya Benth.
Indigofera arrecta Hochst. ex A. Rich.
I. ciferrii Chiov.
I. coerulea Roxb. var. *occidentalis* Gill. and Ali
I. hochstetteri Bak
I. oblongifolia Forsk.
I. schimperi Jaub. and Spach.
I. spicata Forsk.
I. spinosa Forsk.
I. tinctoria L.
I. volkensii Taub. forma
Ormocarpum trichocarpum (Taub.) Engl.
Rhynchosia minima (L.) DC. var. *prostrata* (Harv.) Meikle
R. pulverulenta Stocks
Sesbania sesban (L.) Merrill
S. sesban (L.) Merr. var. *nubica* Chiov.
S. sericea (Willd.) Link
S. somalensis Gillett
Tephrosia purpurea (L.) Pers. var. *pubescens* Bak
T. uniflora Pers.
T. uniflora Pers. subsp. *uniflora*
Vigna luteola (Jacq.) Benth.
V. radiata (L.) Wilczck. var. *sublobata* (Roxb.) Verdc.
V. unguiculata (L.) Walp.

Loranthaceae

Loranthus sp. (=Carr 880)
Plicosepalus sagittifolius (Sprague) Danser
Tapinanthus aurantiacus (Engl.) Danser

Malvaceae

Abelmoschus esculentus (L.) Medic.
Abutilon figarianum Webb
A. fruticosum Guill. and Perr.
A. graveolens W. and A.
A. hirtum (Lam.) Sweet
A. pannosum (Forsk. f.) Schlecht.
Hibiscus micranthus L. f.
H. sp. (=Carr 857)
Pavonia patens (Andr.) Chiov.
P. zeylonica (L.) Cav.
Senra incana Cav.
Sida rhombifolia L.

Meliaceae

Trichilia roka (Forsk.) Chiov.

Menispermaceae

Cissampelos mucronata A. Rich.

Moraceae

Ficus sycomorus L.

Nyctaginaceae

Boerhavia erecta L.
Commicarpus plumbagineus (Cav.) Standl.
C. stellatus (Wight) Berhaut

Nymphaeceae

Nymphae lotus L.

Olacaceae

Ximenia americana L.
X. caffra Sond.

Onagraceae

Ludwigia leptocarpa (Nutt.) Hara

Passifloraceae

Adenia venenata

Pedaliaceae

Sesamothamnus busseanus
Sesamum latifolium

Pistaceae

Pistia stratiotes L.

Polygalaceae

Polygala eroptera

Portulacaceae

Portulaca foliosa
P. oleracea
P. quadrifida
Talinum portulacifolium

Rhamnaceae

Ziziphus mauritiana
Z. mucronata
Z. pubescens

Rubiaceae

Kohautia caespitosa
Tarenna graveolens

Rutaceae

Fagara chalybea

Salvadoraceae

Dobera glabra
Salvadora persica

Sapindaceae

Allophylus macrobotrys
Lepisanthes senegalensis
Cardiospermum macrobotrys
Haplocoelum foliolosum
Melanodiscus oblongus

Scrophulariaceae

Stemodia ?serrata
Striga hermontheca

Simaroubaceae

Harrisonia abyssinica

Solanaceae

Nicotiana tabacum
Solanum hastifolium
S. incanum
S. nigrum
S. sepicula
S. sp. aff. *longestamineum*
Withania somnifera

Sterculiaceae

Melochia corchorifolia
Sterculia sp.

Tiliaceae

Corchorus olitorius L.
C. trilocularis L.
Grewia bicolor Juss.
G. fallax K. Schum.
G. tenax (Forsk.) Fiori
G. villosa Willd.

Ulmaceae

Celtis integrifolia Lam.

Vahliaceae

Vahlia goddingii E. A. Bruce

Verbenaceae

Phyla nodiflora (L.) Greene
Premna resinosa (Hochst.) Schauer
Priva adhaerens (Forsk.) Chiov.
Svensonia laeta (Fanzl. ex Walp.) Moldenke

Vitaceae

Cayratia ibuensis (Hook. f.) Suesseng.
Cissus cactiformis Gilg.
C. quadrangularis L.
C. rotundifolia (Forsk.) Vahl
Cyphostemma sp.

Zygophyllaceae

Tribulus cistoides L. s. lat.
T. terrestris L.
Zygophyllum simplex L.

ANGIOSPERMAE: MONOCOTYLEDONES

Agavaceae

Sansevieria ehrenbergii Bak.

Commelinaceae

Commelina benghalensis L.
C. forskalaei Vahl

Cyperaceae

Cyperus alopeceroides Rottb.
C. articulatus (Cav.) Steud.
C. laevigatus L.
C. longus L.
C. maritimus L.
C. rotundus L.
C. teneriffae Poir.
Scirpus maritimus L.

Gramineae

Aristida adscensionia L.
A. keniensis Henr.
A. mutabilis Trin. and Rupr.
Cenchrus ciliaris L.
C. setigerus Vahl
Chloris roxburghiana Schult.
C. virgata Sw.
Chrysopogon aucheri (Boiss.) Stapf
  var. *aucheri*
Cymbopogon schoenanthus (L.) Spreng.
  var. *proximus*
Cynodon dactylon (L.) Pers.
Dactyloctenium giganteum Fischer and
  Schweickt.
D. sp. nov.
Digitaria macroblephara (Hack.) Stapf

Gramineae, cont'd

Dinebra retroflexa (Vahl) Panzer
Echinochloa haploclada (Stapf) Stapf
Enneapogon brachystachyus (Jaub. and Spach) Stapf
E. cenchroides (Roem. and Schult.) C. E. Hubb
Enteropogon macrostachyus (A. Rich.) Benth.
Eragrostis cilianensis (All.) Lutati
E. namaquensis Nees
E. namaquensis Schrad. var.
    diplachnoides (Steud.) Clayton
Eriochloa nubica (Steud.) Thell.
Heteropogon contortus (L.) Roem. and Schult.
Lintonia nutans Stapf
Loudetia phragmitoides
Panicum coloratum L.
P. maximum Jacq.
P. meyeranum Nees
P. poaeoides Stapf
Perotis patens Gand. var. *parvispicula*
    Robyns
Phragmites australis (Cav.) Steud.
P. ?karka (Retz) Steud.
Schoenefeldia transiens (Pilger) Chiov.
Sehima nervosum (Willd.) Stapf
Setaria acromelaena (Hochst.) Dur. and Schinz
Sorghum verticilliflorum (Steuf.) Stapf
S. virgatum Stapf
Sporobolus consimilis Fresen.
S. fimbriatus Nees var. *latifolius*
S. helvolus Trin.) Dur. and Schinz
S. marginatus A. Rich.
S. pellucidus Hochst.
S. pyramidalis Beauv.
S. spicatus (Vahl) Kunth
Stipagrostis hirtigluma (Trin. and Rupr.) De Winter
Tetrapogon cenchriformis (A. Rich.) Clayton
T. tenellus (Roxb.) Chiov.
Tragus berteronianus Schult.
Urochloa setigera (Retz.) Stapf
Vossia cuspidata (Roxb.) Griff.

Liliaceae

Urginea indica Kunth
Asparagus sp.

Palmae

Hyphaene ?thebaica

Typhaceae

Typha sp.

References

Beals, E. W. 1969. Spatial pattern of shrubs on a desert plain in Ethiopia. *Ecology* 59: 744-46.

Braun-Blanquet, J. 1964. *Pflanzensoziologie*. Vol. 3. New York: Springer.

Butzer, K. W. 1970. Contemporary depositional environments of the Omo Delta. *Nature* 226: 425-30.

_____. 1971. Recent history of an Ethiopian delta. University of Chicago Dept. of Geography Research Paper no. 136.

Carr, C. J. 1976. Riverine ecological studies in the lower Omo basin, Ethiopia. *J. Biogeogr.* Vol. 2, no. 4. In press.

_____. 1975. The Dasenitch of southwest Ethiopia: A system of societal/environmental change. University of Chicago, Dept. of Geography, Research Paper.

Cottam, G., and Curtis, J. T. 1956. The use of distance measures in phytosociological
    sampling. *Ecology* 37:451-60.

Ellenberg, H. 1956. Aufgaben und Methoden der Vegetationskunde. In *Einführung in die
    Phytologie,* ed. H. Walter. Stuttgart: E. Ulmer.

Fosberg, F. R. 1967. A classification of vegetation for general purposes. In *Guide to
    the check sheet for IBP areas,* ed. G. F. Peterken. International Biological Pro-
    gramme Handbook no. 4.

Gillett, J. B. 1955. The relation between the highland floras of Ethiopia and British
    East Africa. *Webbia* 9:459-66.

Glover, P. E. 1951. The root systems of some British Somaliland plants. IV. *E. Afr. Agr.
    J.* 17:38-50.

Good, R. 1964. *The geography of the flowering plants.* New York: Wiley.

Hedberg, O. 1962. Mountain plants from southern Ethiopia, collected by Dr. John Eriksson.
    Arkiv. Botanik. 4:421-35.

Keay, R. W. J. 1959. *Vegetation map of Africa south of the Tropic of Cancer.* Unesco.
    London: Oxford University Press.

Morgan, W. T. W. 1971. The South Turkana Expedition scientific papers. IV. Land units
    of the Lorori Area. *Geogr. J.* 137:14-28.

Mott, J. J., and McComb, A. J. 1974. Patterns in annual vegetation and soil microrelief
    in an arid region of western Australia. *J. Ecol.* 62:115-26.

Naveh, Z. 1966. The need for integrated range research in East Africa. *Trop. Agr. Trin.*
    43:124-36.

Pichi-Sermolli, R. E. G. 1957. Una carta geobotanica dell'Africa Orientale (Eritrea,
    Ethiopia, Somalia). *Webbia* 13:115-32.

Raunkiaer, C. 1934. *The life forms of plants and statistical plant geography: Being the
    collected papers of C. Raunkiaer.* Oxford: Clarendon Press.

Walter, H. 1963. The water supply of desert plants. In *The water relations of plants,* ed.
    A. J. Rutter and F. H. Whitehead. Oxford: Blackwell Sci.

Part 3

PALEOANTHROPOLOGY

Edited by F. C. Howell and G. Ll. Isaac

F. C. Howell and G. Ll. Isaac

The contributions which follow do not and indeed cannot at this juncture represent a complete overview of the nature, diversity, and significance of paleoanthropological discoveries in the Rudolf basin during the past decade. There is simply too much data available from associated researches in the physical and natural sciences, and too many fossil specimens, which are required for analysis and appropriate comparison, are still waiting to be prepared and restored.

However, the papers present a sampling of what contributors now think about this material. Evidently each may not necessarily feel the same another day, as additional data--their own and others'--is analyzed. Each paper is, rather, a measure of current individual responses to a new wealth of paleobiological and paleocultural information on the nature, diversity, and behavior of ancient Hominidae.

Several aspects of hominid paleobiological and paleocultural investigations merit consideration in view of the conference discussion and symposium papers.

Depositional Paleoenvironments and the Preservation of Hominidae and Other Vertebrate Fossils

Evidently paleosedimentary conditions affect in a primary way the nature, associations, preservation, and completeness of fossiliferous occurrences. The diversity of such occurrences, as exemplified in a few tested or more extensively excavated Omo samples, is shown briefly by Johanson, Boaz, and Splingaer (this symposium). The seeming differences in hominid preservation and recovery in the East Rudolf and Omo situations have been alluded to by several participants (cf. A. K. Behrensmeyer, and W. W. Bishop, this symposium). These differences have been attributed, at least in part, to contrasting environments of deposition. In particular, lake margin and deltaic plain situations in East Rudolf have been compared with situations which prevailed on the floodplain of a major perennial river in the Omo basin. It has been suggested that differing depositional regimes have been largely, perhaps even wholly, responsible for differences in vertebrate fossil frequencies, and in particular the number and preservation of hominid fossils (see lists in R. E. F. Leakey, and in Howell and Coppens, this symposium).

However, without all the requisite vertebrate fossil and contextual data at hand, we may well overlook other relevant factors. More remains of Hominidae have been recovered from fluviatile than from other contexts in the East Rudolf situation (A. K. Behrensmeyer, pers. comm.). However, these contexts are not exactly analogous to those of the Omo, since the fluvial environments at East Rudolf seem to have involved a series of small, and in most cases seasonal, channels rather than a major perennial river. A number of the Omo occurrences are associated with deltaic plain as well as with fluviatile situations. A major difference between the two areas, which may be of primary importance to in situ and subsequent surface preservation, is geochemical--notably, abundant sodium carbonate in the East Rudolf sediments. Such carbonates are nearly or wholly absent in the Omo sediments (J. de Heinzelin and P. Haesaerts, pers. comm.). Consequently, although vertebrate fossils may be exquisitely preserved in situ in fine sediments (especially silts), upon exposure by erosion such occurrences are rapidly dispersed and fragmented. In coarser sediments (sands), mineralization is extensive and surface-exposed fossils are consequently less liable to be destroyed. However, in many such situations the partial or fragmentary nature of specimens reflects fluvial transport.

The areas of fossiliferous sediment exposure, regardless of age, in the surveyed East Rudolf area (Vondra and Bowen, this symposium) are about ten times as great as those of the Omo Group formations (de Heinzelin, Haesaerts, and Howell, this symposium). Proximity, and the logistics of the East Rudolf operation, has enabled the expedition staff to work there for many months of the year. In fact, the permanent organization and logistics of the East Rudolf operation are now a model for such interdisciplinary researches in remote field situations. By contrast, the Omo field activities have been restricted to a few summer months each year, since there is no permanent field establishment and all participants have their principal institutional responsibilities thousands of miles away.

Analytical Procedures

In recent years there has been extensive application of multivariate statistics to comparative primate morphological studies in general and to those of hominid paleontology in particular, as well as much discussion of the subject. Although the symposium contributions by Day and by Wood refer to and employ such analyses on some hominid postcranial parts, at the symposium there was no open discussion of the nature and appropriateness of such comparative/analytical procedures. In view of the increasingly widespread use of such analyses to determine sample heterogeneity and degrees of resemblance and affinity, this is an important and unfortunate omission. The necessity of combined morphological and multivariate statistical analyses was repeatedly stressed, and the dearth of biomechanical analyses of critical portions of postcranial anatomy was clearly recognized.

The bases for recognizing and comparing phena (phenotypically reasonably uniform samples, in the usage of G. G. Simpson) were considered with particular reference to the greatly enhanced representation of early hominid postcrania, especially the large sample now known from East Rudolf. The significance of associated individual skeletal parts has been stressed by Day (this symposium)--the most important occurrences of which (for the present) are ER-803 (from the upper part of the Ileret Member), considered to represent *Homo* aff. *erectus*, and ER-1500 (from the Lower Member of the Koobi Fora Formation), attributed to *Australopithecus*. Day has also set out important criteria for evaluating such associations, real or presumed. In view of the disparate and often incomplete postcranial specimens previously known, which came largely from the South African cave infillings but also from some hominid occupation situations at Olduvai Gorge, these new additions to the hominid fossil record offer both splendid opportunities and difficult challenges. Efforts are now being made to elucidate their taxonomic affinities and their functional implications.

Systematics of Early Hominidae

A decade ago the classification of Cenozoic Hominidae seemed to be fairly straight-forward, although the affinities of a few specimens were particularly in dispute. As a consequence of the greatly accelerated pace of hominid fossil recovery in recent years there is now increasingly widespread concern over classification. Although deliberate efforts were made at the symposium to circumvent inevitably acrimonious discussion of such matters, it was frankly impossible to sidestep such issues.

Most of the principal participants (Day, Howell, R. E. F. Leakey, Walker, and Wood) were familiar with the extensive East Rudolf hominid collections, and these remains were a focal point for much of the symposium discussion. It was generally agreed that a substantial corpus of hominid fossils throughout the Koobi Fora Formation represented cranial, mandibular, and diagnostic postcranial remains attributable to the same taxon as is represented by hypodigms from Swartkrans and from Olduvai Gorge (e.g., Old. H-5, 28, etc.) and by some more complete and published specimens from the Omo sequence (e.g., L. 7 and L. 74 mandibles, L. 40 ulna, etc.). Howell (cf. Howell and Coppens, this symposium) maintained that this taxon, a lineage (paleospecies) of substantial documented duration, could also, following criteria set out by J. T. Robinson (*Transvaal Mus. Memoir, Pretoria,* vol. 9 [1956]), be distinguished on some (*not all*) features of dental morphology. Specimens representing this taxon have been recovered from at least Member E upward in the Shungura Formation. Others, especially, R. E. F. Leakey and A. Walker, candidly disavowed taxonomic assessments based on isolated teeth or even on the basis of tooth rows.

That taxon was unanimously agreed to have coexisted with, and in some situations probably to have been sympatric with, at least one other hominid taxon. This is the case in both the East Rudolf and the Omo situations. In the latter, Howell (in Howell and Coppens, this symposium) has tentatively suggested that in the Usno Formation and the earlier hominid-bearing members (members B through D) of the Shungura Formation probably only one hominid taxon, with affinities to *Australopithecus africanus*, is represented. From members E through G (at least), that taxon and a robust australopithecine are both represented. The material with affinities to *A. africanus* was thought by some to be more similar to *Homo* than to the robust australopithecine in some morphological features. However, agreement was not reached either on whether assignment to *Homo* was indeed always appropriate (cf. Walker, this symposium) or on which of several similar or distinctive, related or unrelated lower taxonomic categories might be represented. Thus, Day mentioned some resemblance to *Homo erectus* of ER-1481 and ER-1472 (femora), both recovered some distance below the KBS Tuff in the Lower Member of the Koobi Fora Formation, and of ER-741 (tibia),[1] recovered on outcrops of the upper part of the Ileret Member. However, the leg of *Homo erectus* is in fact unknown, and so the comparison of ER-741 to the latter is made indirectly through the ER-803 postcranial remains, which include various lower limb elements, including both tibia and femur. The femur is of course represented in the Choukoutien sample of that taxon. Attention is drawn to the resemblance of some specimens, including ER-992 and ER-820 mandibles, to *H. erectus* (B. A. Wood) or perhaps even a more evolved form of *Homo* (F. C. Howell). Also noteworthy is the similarity of some femora, such as ER-999 (from the base of the Guomde Formation) and ER-736 and ER-737 (from the

---

1. Day noted that the tibia of Olduvai H-35 (FLK. 1. site), attributed to *Homo habilis*, in fact resembles its counterpart in the ER-1500 partial skeleton (attributed to *Australopithecus*). And Wood regards the talus in the Olduvai H-8 foot (FLK. NN. 1 site) as unlike *Homo* (for example that of the ER-803 skeleton).

Upper Member, Koobi Fora Formation), to *Homo* and even in some respects (in the case of ER-736) to the structure found in modern *Homo sapiens* (M. H. Day). R. E. F. Leakey noted, however, that no cranial parts attributable to *Homo erectus* are known from these sediments.

In another instance discussion focused on the extent to which the cranium ER-1470, also from the Lower Member of the Koobi Fora Formation, approximated *Homo* (contributions of Leakey and of Wood, this symposium) or diverged in important ways from that taxon and in those respects approximated *Australopithecus* sensu lato (Walker, this symposium). Wood and Leakey considered that the ER-1590 (cranial and dental remains) might well represent the same hominid phenon. Several participants, especially Howell and R. E. F. Leakey, considered that ER-1482, a hominid mandible (also from the Lower Member), diverged significantly from the several aforementioned phena.

Although divergent opinions were expressed there was little resolution of some such differences, at least in part because a number of specimens, including these, have still to be studied analytically and comparatively. Moreover, the recovery of additional, well-preserved hominid cranial and mandibular remains during the 1973 field season in East Rudolf has raised an unexpected new set of problems (see R. E. F. Leakey, this symposium). It was also apparent that evidence afforded by associated cranial-dental-postcranial elements of Hominidae will ultimately assist immeasurably in resolving such problems.

Although the composition and nature of hominid phena was discussed and resemblances to other early hominid samples were sometimes noted, the classification of early Hominidae was not directly considered. This and other aspects of hominid paleobiology are discussed in another recent symposium volume, *African Hominidae of the Plio/Pleistocene* (edited by C. J. Jolly), that built in part on the foundations laid at this symposium.

Human origins are distinguished more by changes in behavior than by changes in gross anatomy, so that archeological traces of characteristic human activities are a crucial complement to the fossils in reconstructing the trajectory of evolution. The Shungura Formation and the Koobi Fora Formation are yielding artifacts that seem to rank as the oldest securely dated ones yet known. They certainly date from at least 2 m.y. ago. If the KBS Tuff date of 2.5 m.y. is confirmed, the record extends back that far. In the Omo, artifacts are now documented in situ in the upper sediments of Member C (J. Chavaillon, pers. comm.); the overlying Tuff D has a conventional K-Ar age of ~2.4 m.y. (Brown and Nash, this symposium).

Four papers provide a summary of archeological researches up to the 1973 season. The papers reflect a healthy diversity of interests and emphases in research. Jean Chavaillon gives a thorough account of the artifacts he has recovered from several sites, mainly in Member F of the Shungura Formation. He uses these to raise important questions about stages in the development of tool use and manufacture. Harry and Joan Merrick report on their investigations at essentially the same horizons as those of Chavaillon. Their account, although comprehensive, pays particular attention to the paleogeographic setting of the artifacts and its implications for understanding site preference and land use. In treating the East Rudolf material Isaac, Harris, and Crader are also able to discuss the implication of bone food refuse found associated with the artifacts. This evidence, linked with that from Olduvai, shows that the distinctively human practices of hunting and of sharing food were getting under way back in the Pliocene.

Two phases of stone craft appear to be represented at East Rudolf. An early one in the KBS Tuff and Lower Member involves untrimmed flakes with fortuitously diverse forms and a small series of core tools--that is, pebbles and chunks from which useful flakes have been removed and which thereby become sharp and serviceable themselves. The varied forms of the assemblage were produced by fairly simple application of percussion to pebbles, and this has prompted Isaac to suggest, in contradistinction to Chavaillon's model, that the beginnings of stone-tool making may have involved thresholds rather than long gradualistic evolution. The younger, "Karari" assemblages of the Koobi Fora Upper Member show clearly that by 1.5 m.y. ago some hominids had become habitual, deft, and fairly muscular stone-tool makers.

There were only three or four practicing archeologists at the conference, and elaborate technical discussions would not have been possible or appropriate. However, the general implications of the archeological data did not escape the meeting. The fossil evidence shows clearly the existence of bipedal primates from the 2 to 3 m.y. time range-- perhaps two or three taxa, perhaps with partly contrasting locomotor habits. As a complementary indicator the archeological evidence shows that at least some of the hominids found their mobility made hunting or scavenging easier and were using their freed forelimbs to make tools and to carry stone and meat.

Several questions naturally arise. Did all the early hominids do these things? If not, can we tell which forms did? The conference treated these questions in part jokingly, because there are no objective answers. Most hominid-find spots do not have artifacts, and most archeological sites do not have hominids--and when they do, as with Hominid 5 at Olduvai, it is questionable whether the particular fossilized hominid "owned" the site. Until we find a number of hominids preserved with their tools in their hands, our response to these questions will remain largely subjective or speculative. What we can tell is that at least one lineage of beings had undergone critical behavioral transformations in the direction of humanity--there *were* toolmaking, meat-eating, food-sharing primates around operating out of "campsites." Whether they could "talk" in any degree goes beyond the present powers of archeologists to determine.

The hominid fossils of the Rudolf basin now form an impressive series comprising several hundred specimens spanning a time range of 4 or 5 m.y. The record promises to form both an important complement to the Olduvai series, which was previously the richest and most diverse in East Africa, and a valuable extension back in time. But the significance of the Rudolf basin hominid finds does not lie merely in their number or time span. Between the Omo and East Rudolf, large sectors of ancient landscapes can be explored. Once the time equivalences have been established we can plot the occurrences of hominid taxa and of archeological relics against a background of varied habitats and topographies (see especially Behrensmeyer, this symposium). The papers in this volume seem to hold out promise that patient researches will eventually be rewarded by vivid factual reconstructions both of the bodily forms of early men and of how they used the varied world in which they lived.

41. AN OVERVIEW OF THE HOMINIDAE FROM EAST RUDOLF, KENYA

R. E. F. Leakey

By September 1973, the East Rudolf locality had produced 110 fossil hominid specimens, listed in table 1. All the specimens were collected following natural exposure rather than discovered through formal excavation. A majority of specimens can be considered surface material, but with a few exceptions the stratigraphic provenance can be documented to within a few meters, if not precisely.

The absolute age of the various fossils has been determined within the framework of K-Ar dates, paleomagnetic chronology, and faunal correlation. The stratigraphy of the basin provides control for relative ages, and there is a substantial time succession over a large geographical area (ca. 1,000 km) which offers potential for paleoecological studies. Dating of the East Rudolf deposits relative to other East African sites is clearly important; the East Rudolf succession overlaps in part with Olduvai Gorge and in part with the Shungura Formation of the Omo valley. The possibility of noting changes through time in the hominid collection is of considerable interest and can be attempted on the more complete specimens, but the hominids are unlikely to prove useful for dating in the same way as has been proposed for some faunal elements such as the suids and proboscideans.

The East Rudolf collection includes specimens representing most elements of the skeleton (table 2). The material has been provisionally listed within three groups, *Australopithecus*, *Homo*, and indeterminate. The last includes fragments that are either too incomplete for more positive attribution or specimens that show morphological features which lead me to feel uncertain about attributing them to either *Homo* or *Australopithecus*. The present classification of the East Rudolf material has been made in advance of comprehensive study in an attempt to provide a basis for reference and discussion. The criterion for generic attribution has been morphological similarity within the collection, and no detailed comparisons with other African material have been attempted. The ultimate taxonomic status of any specimen will be subject to the conclusion of current studies, but in the meantime some preliminary comments might be useful.

Australopithecus

The East Rudolf collection that has been attributed to *Australopithecus* (Leakey 1970, 1971, 1972, 1973*a,b*) includes large and small individuals and a number that are intermediate in size. These specimens probably represent the single species recorded at Olduvai Gorge, *Australopithecus boisei*, where it is best represented by OH 5 (Zinjanthropus). There is a

Table 1

East Rudolf Hominids Collected 1968-73

KNM-ER No.	Year	Area	Specimen Detail
164a	1969	104	Parietal fragment
164b-c	1971	104	Two phalanges, two vertebrae
403	1968	103	Right mandible
404	1968	7A	Right mandible M_2, M_3
405	1968	105	Palate lacking teeth
406	1969	10	Cranium lacking teeth
407	1969	10	Cranium lacking face
417	1968	129	Parietal fragment
725	1970	1	Left mandible
726	1970	11	Left mandible
727	1970	6A	Right mandible
728	1970	1	Right mandible
729	1970	8	Mandible with dentition
730	1970	103	Left mandible with symphysis, left M_1-M_3
731	1970	6A	Left mandible
732	1970	10	Demicranium, parietal P^4
733	1970	8	Right mandible, left maxilla, and cranial fragments M^1, M_3
734	1970	103	Parietal fragment
736	1970	103	Left femur shaft
737	1970	103	Left femur shaft
738	1970	105	Proximal left femur
739	1970	1	Right humerus
740	1970	1	Distal left humerus fragment
741	1970	1	Proximal right tibia
801	1971	6A	Right mandible, M_3, M_2, and associated isolated teeth
802	1971	6A	Isolated teeth
803	1971	8	Associated skeletal elements
805	1971	1	Left mandible
806	1971	8	Isolated teeth
807A	1971	8A	Right maxilla fragment M^3, partial M^2
807B	1973	8A	Right maxilla fragment M^1
808	1971	8	Isolated juvenile teeth
809	1971	8	Isolated teeth
810	1971	104	Left mandible, M_3
811	1971	104	Parietal fragment
812	1971	104	Juvenile left mandible fragment
813	1971	104	Right talus and tibia fragment
814	1971	104	Cranial fragments
815	1971	10	Proximal left femur
816	1971	104	Canine and molar fragment
817	1971	124	Left mandible fragment
818	1971	6A	Left mandible P_3-M_3
819	1971	1	Left mandible

Table 1 (Continued)

KNM-ER No.	Year	Area	Specimen Detail
820	1971	1	Juvenile mandible with dentition
992	1971	1	Mandible with dentition
993	1971	1	Distal right femur
997	1971	104	Left metatarsal III
998	1971	104	Isolated incisor
999	1971	6A	Left femur
1170	1971	6A	Cranial fragments
1171	1971	6A	Isolated juvenile teeth
1462	1972	130	Isolated M_3
1463	1972	1A	Right femur shaft
1464	1972	6A	Right talus
1465	1972	11	Proximal left femur fragment
1466	1972	6	Parietal fragment
1467	1972	3	Isolated M_3
1468	1972	11	Right mandible
1469	1972	131	Left mandible, M_3
1470	1972	131	Cranium
1471	1972	131	Proximal right tibia
1472	1972	131	Right femur
1473	1972	131	Proximal right humerus
1474	1972	131	Parietal fragment
1475	1972	131	Proximal left femur
1476	1972	105	Left talus and proximal left tibia
1477	1972	105	Juvenile mandible with dentition
1478	1972	105	Cranial fragments
1479	1972	105	Isolated molar fragments
1480	1972	105	Isolated molar
1481	1972	131	Left femur, proximal and distal left tibia, distal left fibula
1482	1972	131	Mandible, right P_4, left P_3-M_3
1483	1972	131	Left mandible, fragment M_2
1500	1972	130	Associated skeletal elements
1501	1972	123	Right mandible
1502	1972	123	Right mandible fragment with M_1
1503	1972	123	Proximal right femur
1504	1972	123	Distal right humerus
1505	1972	123	Proximal left femur
1506	1972	121	Right mandible, M_1, M_2, isolated P^3, P^4
1507	1972	127	Juvenile left mandible with dentition
1508	1972	127	Isolated molar
1509	1972	119	Isolated teeth C-M_3
1515	1972	103	Isolated incisor
1590	1972	12	Partial cranium with juvenile dentition
1591	1972	12	Right humerus lacking head
1592	1972	12	Distal right femur

Table 1 (Continued)

KNM-ER No.	Year	Area	Specimen Detail
1593	1972	12	Cranial and mandibular fragments
1648	1972	105	Parietal fragment
1686	1972	123	Cranial fragment
1800	1973	130	Cranial fragment
1801	1973	131	Left mandible, P_4, M_1, M_3
1802	1973	131	Mandible, left P_4-M_2, right P_3-M_2
1803	1973	131	Fragment right mandible
1804	1973	104	Right maxilla, P^3-M^2
1805	1973	130	Cranium and mandible with dentition
1806	1973	130	Mandible lacking teeth
1807	1973	103	Shaft right femur
1808	1973	103	Associated skeletal and cranial elements
1809	1973	121	Shaft right femur
1810	1973	123	Proximal left tibia
1811	1973	123	Left mandible fragment
1812	1973	123	Fragment right mandible, isolated left I_1, M_1
1813	1973	123	Cranium
1814	1973	127	Maxillary fragments
1815	1973	1	Right talus
1816	1973	6A	Immature mandible with dentition
1817	1973	1	Right mandible
1818	1973	6A	Isolated I^1
1819	1973	3	Isolated M_3
1820	1973	103	Left mandible, M_1
1821	1972	123	Parietal fragment

Table 2

Number of Pieces Representing Each Body Part in the East Rudolf Collection (1968-73).

Skeletal Element			Number	Total
Cranium		a	6	
	Parietal	b1	13	24
	Maxillary	b2	5	
Mandible		a	9	35
		b	26	
Clavicle		a	--	--
		b	--	
Scapula		a	--	1
		b	1	
Humerus		a	2	7
		b	5	
Radius		a	--	2
		b	2	
Ulna		a	--	2
		b	2	
Pelvis		a	--	--
		b	--	
Femur		a	2	16
		b	14	
Tibia		a	--	7
		b	7	
Fibula		a	--	2
		b	2	
Talus		a	3	5
		b	2	
Calcaneum		a	--	1
		b	1	
Phalanges		a	2	3
		b	1	
Metapodials		a	--	4
		b	4	
Isolated teeth				16

NOTE: Where a body part from one individual is represented by more than one fragment or by both the left and right side it has been assessed as one piece only; a = relatively complete, b = half or less.

marked paucity of dental evidence from East Rudolf; most cranial specimens are mandibular, lacking the crowns of the teeth. Some attempts have been made to estimate crown dimensions from the roots and alveoli, but this evidence cannot be adequately tested until a larger sample is available.

In previous publications I have proposed the existence of a single species of *Australopithecus* at various levels in the Koobi Fora Formation at East Rudolf, thus suggesting a species that changed little for more than 1.5 m.y. The large variation in size, demonstrated by craniums, mandibles, and some postcranial elements, has been attributed to sexual dimorphism. Three craniums, KNM-ER 406, 407, and 732, demonstrate the apparent sexual dimorphism in this alleged single species; KNM-ER 406 is a large robust cranium with sagittal and nuchal crests, and KNM-ER 407 and 732 are more gracile craniums lacking any trace of cresting. Postcranial specimens appear to support the single species concept insofar as this evidence can be used. The femur shows a wide size range while retaining the characteristics of this form: small head, long flattened neck, and short shaft.

Homo

The sample of specimens currently attributed to *Homo* is not as large as that attributed to *Australopithecus*. Certain specimens show morphological features that contrast markedly with the *Australopithecus* material from the same localities at East Rudolf.

A number of mandibular specimens from the Upper Member in both the Koobi Fora and Ileret localities have been assigned to *Homo*. The best examples of this form of *Homo* are mandibles KNM-ER 992 and KNM-ER 820. These specimens have been compared with *Homo erectus*, but in the absence of cranial material some caution seems necessary. At present there is only one specimen of a parietal fragment that can be assigned to *H. erectus*.

The Lower Member of the Koobi Fora Formation has also yielded evidence for *Homo*. The situation appears more complex owing to the apparent existence of both a "small" and a "large" form, both of which are distinct from the typical *Australopithecus* from the same levels. Perhaps further examples will establish the range of individual variation in early *Homo* and permit a final conclusion on the validity of two apparent models of *Homo*.

The alleged Lower Member "small" form of *Homo* can best be demonstrated by mandibles KNM-ER 1501 and 1503. The mandibles are small and lightly built and have a correspondingly small dentition. No cranial evidence of this form is yet known.

The alleged "large" form of *Homo* can best be represented by the craniums KNM-ER 1470 and 1590 and by some mandibular material such as KNM-ER 1802. The cranium KNM-ER 1470 has a relatively large capacity, estimated at approximately 775 cc and KNM-ER 1590, which appears to have had an even larger cranium, shows a dentition with relatively small cheek teeth compared with specimens referred to *Australopithecus*. The mandibular material shows features generally typical of *Homo*. This material seems to contrast markedly with other known models of *Homo* except with respect to certain specimens from Olduvai Gorge that have been assigned to *Homo habilis*; the type of *Homo habilis*, OH 7, and the skull OH 16 are specific examples.

Indeterminate

A number of specimens which are too fragmentary to show a diagnostic morphology have been referred to this category, but these do not require further discussion. Several specimens which show morphological features which are not entirely consistent with specimens previously referred to either *Homo* or *Australopithecus* are for the moment assigned to genus indet., and these are of particular interest.

A skull, KNM-ER 1805, recovered in situ from the BBS Tuff, has both sagittal and nuchal crests, but relatively small cheek teeth and a small mandible. This contrasts with the expected situation in which sagittal and nuchal crests are associated with large teeth and a large mandible. It also appears to have a relatively large cranial capacity compared with the craniums from East Rudolf previously referred to *Australopithecus*. Do the small molars and premolars indicate that this specimen should not be included within *Australopithecus*, or can the specimen be included within the acceptable limits of morphological variation of *Australopithecus* but perhaps represent a separate species?

A second cranium, KNM-ER 1813, also recovered in situ, but from deposits close in age to the KBS Tuff, has a cranial morphology quite similar to KNM-ER 407 and 732 (the craniums considered to represent female *Australopithecus*) but has a maxillary dentition which is relatively very small. The cranial capacity of this specimen is probably less than 500 cc. Thus the maxillary dentition suggests attribution to the "small" *Homo*, a model which has previously been represented only by mandibular specimens, whereas a number of morphological features of the cranium, including the small cranial capacity, suggest attribution to *Australopithecus*. Should dental evidence outweigh other characters in generic attribution?

Finally a well-preserved, relatively large mandibular specimen, KNM-ER 1482, from below the KBS Tuff suggests that there may be evidence for a third hominid genus in the Lower Member at East Rudolf. The mandible shows significant differences from either *Australopithecus* or *Homo*. In the absence of additional material the importance of this single specimen cannot be confirmed, but there are specimens from the Shungura Formation that may relate, and detailed comparative studies should be done.

Conclusions

Plio-Pleistocene hominid evolution is complex, and there is a significant lack of data available for the final interpretation of sexual dimorphism, individual variation, and speciation. The existing collection from East Rudolf has shown areas for future research and underlined the need for caution when considering phylogenetic models.

The large robust form of *Australopithecus* is well represented. This species may be sexually dimorphic, and it seems to change little over the time succession represented at East Rudolf.

Contemporary occurrence of a larger-brained hominid has been shown, and the material has been assigned to *Homo*. Dental, cranial, and postcranial evidence presents a reasonable argument for this attribution, although final comparative studies are yet to be concluded.

There has been little or no evidence for a gracile species of *Australopithecus* at East Rudolf, but the new cranium KNM-ER 1813 should be a critical specimen in this respect.

A small-brained *Homo* has been proposed by others (Robinson 1972) and should perhaps be given careful consideration. The clear fact is that the "large" form of *Homo* was a contemporary of both the "small hominid" and the robust *Australopithecus*. There is as yet no clear evidence for antecedent relationships in any of the fossil forms now known.

The past five years of fieldwork at East Rudolf have established that hominid fossils are comparatively rare, but further work should add to the sample. The total number of hominid finds has been compared with collections of Carnivora and Cercopithecidae (excluding *Theropithecus*) in table 3. All these groups have been collected with equal intensity.

I should like to thank members of the East Rudolf Research Project for their assistance, especially A. K. Behrensmeyer, B. Bowen, and I. Findlater. Thanks are also due to the National Geographic Society, the National Science Foundation, the W. H. Donner Foundation, the National Museums of Kenya, and others for sponsoring the five years' research at East Rudolf.

This is paper no. 68 in the East Rudolf Research Project catalogue of publications.

Table 3

Relative Numbers of Specimens of Hominidae, Carnivora, and Cercopithecidae in the East Rudolf Collection, and Relative Numbers of Hominid Specimens Attributed to Homo, Australopithecus, and Indeterminate

Group	Number of Specimens	Percentage
Hominidae	89	33.3
Australopithecus	*49*	*55.0*
Homo	*29*	*32.6*
Genus Indeterminate	*11*	*12.4*
Carnivora	92	34.5
Cercopithecidae (excluding *Theropithecus*)	86	32.2

References

Leakey, R. E. F. 1970. Fauna and artifacts from a new Plio-Pleistocene locality near Lake Rudolf in Kenya. *Nature* 226:223-24.

_____. 1971. Further evidence of Lower Pleistocene hominids from East Rudolf, North Kenya. *Nature* 231:241-45.

_____. 1972. Further evidence of Lower Pleistocene hominids from East Rudolf, North Kenya. 1971. *Nature* 237:264-69.

_____. 1973*a*. Further evidence of Lower Pleistocene hominids from East Rudolf, North Kenya. 1972. *Nature* 242:170-73.

_____. 1973*b*. Evidence for an advanced Plio-Pleistocene hominid from East Rudolf, Kenya. *Nature* 242:447-50.

Robinson, J. T. 1972. *Early hominid posture and locomotion.* Chicago: University of Chicago Press.

42.   REMAINS ATTRIBUTABLE TO *AUSTRALOPITHECUS*

IN THE EAST RUDOLF SUCCESSION

A. Walker

> It is a common illusion to believe that what we know today is all we
> can ever know. Nothing is more vulnerable than scientific theory, which
> is an ephemeral attempt to explain facts and not an everlasting truth in
> itself.
>
> C. G. Jung

Having been asked to report on remains of *Australopithecus* from East Rudolf, I am
faced with several basic problems. Some of these are purely nomenclatural, others are related to the fact that there is no uniform viewpoint among authorities, and yet others are
related to more basic matters such as the possibility that the genus *Australopithecus* may
not, in fact, be separable from the genus *Homo*. In previous descriptive papers dealing
with the East Rudolf material (Leakey, Mungai, and Walker 1971, 1972: Leakey and Walker
1973), we have implied that there are good grounds for keeping the subfamily Australopithecinae. Simpson (1961*b*) has dealt with this point and shows that if there are only two
genera in the family Hominidae then the need for subfamily distinctions falls away. However, other genera that might be included in the Hominidae are *Ramapithecus*, *Paranthropus*,
and *Gigantopithecus*, and others including *Oreopithecus* have also been suggested. *Ramapithecus* may be a hominid, but I feel that at present the paucity of material only allows us
to place it as hominoid. *Gigantopithecus* has been amply demonstrated to be a pongid and
hence has no place in this scheme. Robinson (1972) has recently placed *Paranthropus*
(+ *Gigantopithecus*) in the Paranthropinae and placed *Australopithecus africanus*, together
with *H. erectus* and *H. sapiens*, in the genus *Homo*. Thus, according to Robinson, *Australopithecus* is no longer available as a generic term. With due respect, I am not able to
follow Robinson's scheme, which, *Gigantopithecus* apart, splits into two subfamilies, let
alone genera, some specimens that are close enough to be thought of (with a reasonable case)
as being sampled from one sexually dimorphic species lineage. The similarities of cranial
and dental morphology seem to be easily accommodated by generic cover and possibly could be
accounted for by placement in an evolving single species. The postcranial remains I find
to be so similar that I think generic separation on postcranial elements also is unjustified.

It seems that except for Robinson there is a general consensus that most, if not all,
the South African fossil hominids belong in the genus *Australopithecus*. There has been
general agreement over most of the early hominid fossils from East Africa, with the exception of certain individuals from Olduvai Gorge and East Rudolf.

It can be argued that until the species have been sorted out we cannot sort the genera.

484

However, one has only to glance through the paleontological literature to see that most paleontologists use genera in preference to species. Simpson, in several papers, has pointed out why this is so, and the following quotation summarizes his viewpoint. "As regards fossils genera are at present usually not only better defined, but also more indicative of the status of taxonomic sampling. Comparisons of relative completeness of knowledge are reasonably reliable and most significant in terms of genera, if the genera have been reviewed by one researcher using comparable criteria throughout" (Simpson 1961*b*). Genera are monophyletic units of one or more species which differ in some ways from other such units. The species that make up the genus have many features in common but do not necessarily always have any particular feature; in other words, the genus is based on the total spectrum of characters among its species (Michenor 1957). The genus is a sufficiently small taxonomic unit to have some practical use and also has a recognizable duration in the fossil record (Simpson 1961*a*). It is extremely unlikely that we shall be able to easily sort out the species of fossil hominids. Taking the example of the sexual dimorphism theory that has been put forward to accommodate big and small individuals in one *Australopithecus* species, it might seem highly likely that this is so, but proving it definitely probably will be impossible. We shall probably never be able to safely say that one sexually dimorphic species is present rather than two less-dimorphic ones. It seems, on the other hand, that general agreement might be reached over whether two species belong to the same genus.

The fundamental reason for indulging in paleontological taxonomy is to elucidate the evolutionary processes in the group being studied. There are two theoretical types of evolutionary change, anagenesis and cladogenesis. Anagenesis involves change in time without diversification, and cladogenesis involves branching and splitting of an ancestral form into two or more derived ones. It is quite clear that until the lineages are sorted out no meaningful evolutionary statements can be made, and it is the purpose of taxonomy to sort specimens by criteria that can be recognized by all workers in populations on the same time horizons and also through time. For generic classification I am advocating here a frankly "grade classification," that is, in effect, a classification that places similar-looking animals in close categories. The alternative approach, classification by "clade," stresses the importance of a group at the beginning of a new lineage by incorporating the group in the taxon of the new lineage. This is essentially what Leakey, Tobias, and Napier (1964) did when they included a group of specimens called *H. habilis* in the genus *Homo*, since in their view they were part of the ancestral population leading to modern man. They were emphasizing the new adaptive plateau being approached rather than the similarities of the specimens to other known early hominids. Reed (1967) argued that as more material is found a classification will automatically change from "grade" to "clade" and that all our difficulties will resolve themselves. As things stand at present I have no confidence that general agreement will soon be reached on lineages of fossil hominids; the magnificent new collections from East Rudolf have only led to more questions rather than giving us any answers. For this reason I prefer to classify things on the basis of what they look like, rather than on what they might evolve into if, by any chance, we happen to have our lineages correctly documented. I admit that "grade" classification has its drawbacks, since there will come a point where, if the logic is followed to its conclusions, one generation will be in one taxon and the next in another, but if the logic of the "clade" classification is followed to its conclusion, part of a single population will be in one taxon and another part of the same population will be in the next. At present workers are more likely to reach agreement over whether a specimen could be part of one of the known populations than over whether a specimen did or did not give rise to a later population.

If we are to play the game safely and use genera, in the long-term hope that the species situation will sort itself out with better sampling, then the question arises, Can we
form a clear differential diagnosis, however informally, between the two currently recognized hominid genera? If the answer is no, the logical conclusion is that all the early
hominids should be brought into the genus *Homo*. I believe that the diagnoses so far put
forward are inadequate and do not stand up to close scrutiny. This is largely a matter of
history and the purposes for which those early diagnoses were compiled. Our sample is now
much greater, and if differential diagnoses are attempted now, we should be in a better
situation to arrive at a meaningful answer to the basic question. Below are a few guidelines for the sorts of criteria that ought to be used. Before stating them, however, I
must emphasize that the purpose of a differential diagnosis, even an informal one, is communication, and that even if it proves unsatisfactory at present this is no bar to our
making better efforts as new samples and more accurate observations are made. If we want
to get our ideas of hominid evolution across clearly and without ambiguity, we must define
what it is we are talking about. This is not an academic exercise, but an attempt to pull
together all the vague hunches and known facts so that other workers understand our viewpoint, even though they might disagree with it.

In order to make a differential diagnosis, the following points should be taken into
account.

1. The diagnosis should be based on all available parts that are known *in common* for
both genera.

2. The diagnosis should be based on material that can be shown to be (*a*) definitely
associated or (*b*) *reasonably* attributed, and resort should not be made to parts that are
doubtfully associated unless this is clearly stated. Where cranial remains of two genera
are known and postcranial remains of one can be definitely associated, it is reasonable to
attribute a second series of limb bones to the other genus, provided that what has been
done is stated and provided that the bones can be distinguished.

3. The diagnosis should be made *on the morphology alone* and not upon inferences from
the morphology. Presumed diet, locomotion, and such should *not* be used, since these are,
after all, only inferences from the morphology and can easily be erroneous. The morphology
upon which the inferences are based should be sufficient and has the virtue of being available for checking.

4. Cultural "associations" are not to be recommended, since the proof of such an association is not likely to be forthcoming.

5. The geological age of the specimen and the geographical location should play no
part in the diagnosis. The *known* ranges of the genus in time and space can be given as information after the diagnosis.

6. Specimens showing gross pathological features or artificial distortion should not
be taken into account without due caution.

7. If the information is available, not only should the maximum number of skeletal
parts be used to differentiate genera, but infant and senile material should be treated
separately.

8. If the species of the genera are sexually dimorphic and this can be demonstrated,
the nature of the dimorphism should be stated.

9. Wherever possible, statistical evidence should be presented to substantiate or
amplify statements; for, since taxonomy is a science that deals only with samples, it is
by definition a statistical science.

10. Great care should be taken when making statements about taphonomically altered specimens, and especially when measuring them. If distorted specimens have been used, the limits of the distortion should be measured and all factors related to this taken into consideration.

11. Care should be taken not to give weight to the same distinguishing features twice or more, but fragmentary material could be more easily assigned if the various correlates of a single functional whole are stated.

I am not at this stage giving differential diagnoses for *Australopithecus* and *Homo*, but I have indicated some features that might be used in such diagnoses. I have not concerned myself here either with juvenile or senile members of the two taxa or with postcranial material (for which see M. H. Day, this symposium), but in another paper (Walker 1973) I have given differences between the femora of the two genera. I am *not* concerned with the number of species in the genera. The features I am pointing out here are based on specimens that most authorities except Robinson agree belong to one or other of the genera. For *Homo* this includes *H. sapiens sapiens*, *H. sapiens neanderthalensis*, *H. erectus* from Java and China, *H. erectus* from Olduvai (OH 9), and *H.* cf *erectus* from Ileret (KNM-ER 992). For *Australopithecus* I have included the Makapansgat, Kromdraai, and Sterkfontein material as well as nearly all the Swartkrans material, together with some material from Olduvai (OH 5), East Rudolf (e.g., KNM-ER 406, 732, 407, 733 and a collection of mandibles), Omo (several mandibles), Chesowanja, and Peninj. I have *not* considered specimens such as the *habilis* material from Olduvai, the composite cranium from Swartkrans, and cranium KNM-ER 1470. I shall take the last specimen as an example of how these features might help in deciding a specimen's affinities.

The overriding difference between skulls of *Australopithecus* and *Homo* is that in the former the neurocranium is small and the splanchnocranium large, whereas the opposite is true for *Homo*. This one major difference is responsible for most of the morphological differences that various authorities have given as distinctive characters. An index that shows the relationships between the two parts of the cranium is facial height (nasion to alveolare) x 100/total cranial length (glabella to opisthocranium). The range in *Australopithecus* is 51.0 to 64.5 (Sts 5 to OH 5) and the range in *Homo* is from 30.0 to 45.0 (the greatest value is for the big-faced Broken Hill cranium). Because of facial-skeleton predominance, postorbital constriction is greater in *Australopithecus* than in *Homo*. An index that shows this is minimum frontal width x 100/maximum width of the cranium, where the range for *Australopithecus* is 45.0 to 56.0 and for *Homo* 59.0 to 90.0. The known range of *Australopithecus* cranial capacities is 440 to 530 cc. (Holloway 1971), while the *Homo* range is from about 750 to more than 2,000 cc. The calvaria in *Australopithecus* is globular and thin-walled, whether or not there are ectocranial superstructures built upon it. In *Homo* the cranium is expanded laterally at various levels, according to species and population, and the vault varies from very thick to very thin, but mean thicknesses are greater than in *Australopithecus*. In posterior view, the *Australopithecus* calvaria has a characteristic bell-shaped outline, with the maximum width of the calvaria at the mastoid or supramastoid crest. In *Homo* the outline is a rounded pentagon with the widest point higher or lower depending upon the species. Associated with the small neurocranium and the greatly developed facial skeleton in *Australopithecus* is the laterally placed mandibular fossa, and a great part of the fossa may be overhung by the root of the zygomatic process of the temporal. Typically in *Homo*, the joint is tucked under the calvaria so that the mandibular fossa is roofed by the bones of the middle cranial fossa. The mandibular fossa in

Australopithecus is transversely elongated to accept a large, wide condyle, whereas in *Homo* it varies from a transversely elongated to a roundish depression; but even in specimens with large condyles the width of the larger *Australopithecus* specimens is never reached. This feature is expressed in the same way with the mastoid processes, which form the "corners" of the back of the cranium in *Australopithecus* but are tucked under in *Homo*. The "forehead" region in *Australopithecus* varies from flat or actually dished behind the supraorbital tori to rising gently toward bregma with sometimes a shallow groove behind the tori. Massive tori, such as those seen in *H. erectus* or *H. sapiens neanderthalensis*, are never found in *Australopithecus*, nor is the condition as in *H. sapiens sapiens*, where the tori are incorporated into steeply rising frontal bones. The nasal bones in *Australopithecus* reach upward in an inverted V toward glabella, whereas in *Homo* they do not V-upward, and the frontonasal suture is usually nearly horizontal. The occipital condyles (or porion, since these usually lie on the same coronal plane) are well behind the anteroposterior midpoint of the cranial length in *Australopithecus* and placed farther forward in *Homo*. The mandible in *Australopithecus* is usually fairly massively built, and the internal mandibular contour is either V-shaped or pointed U-shaped as opposed to the less strongly built mandible and open U-shaped internal mandibular contour in *Homo*. In *Australopithecus* there are usually strongly developed inferior and superior mandibular tori, with the inferior normally projecting more posteriorly. In *Homo* there is a tendency for the buttresses to be built upon the mental surface, but internal ones are also found, though never to the same degree as in *Australopithecus*. There is a tendency in *Australopithecus* for the greatest depth of the body to be far forward, and a postincisive planum is always present and usually fairly extensive. In *Homo* the depth of the mandibular body is more constant along its length and the postincisive planum is very reduced. The ramus in *Australopithecus* is usually tall and in *Homo* it is usually relatively short.

I have had great difficulty in finding any definite morphological differences in the dentition, and to my mind the problem of relative proportions of the various parts of the dentition is still, except in certain extreme cases, unresolved. On the whole, though, in *Homo* the teeth are small relative to the size of the cranium, and in *Australopithecus* they are large. Absolute dimensions, except at the high and low ends of the ranges, do not appear to differentiate them.

These few characters may serve to distinguish the two genera, and it is instructive to look at KNM-ER 1470 to see how this specimen can be allocated. As regards the major indexes, the following are the values for this cranium: The face/cranium index is 59.0 and lies at about the middle of the range of *Australopithecus*. The postorbital constriction index is 58.0, between the ranges for *Australopithecus* and *Homo*. The cranial capacity has yet to be fully determined by Professor Holloway, but is likely to be between 770 and 775 cc, a value that is in the very low part of the range of *Homo*. The posterior profile has the characteristic bell-shaped profile of *Australopithecus* and is thin-walled. The widest part of the cranium is at the supramastoid ridges as in *Australopithecus*. The mandibular fossae are transversely elongated and are partly overhung by the zygomatic processes of the temporals, although it is difficult to determine by how much, since the processes are broken. The "forehead" region in 1470 is of the type that rises gently to bregma from not very salient tori. The frontonasal suture is seen to peak up toward glabella. The position of porion is within the *H. sapiens* range for the right side, but the left side is very close to the recorded position for *Australopithecus*. This difference is clearly due to distortion, and it remains to be determined which is the correct position, but one just cannot take the average until the manner of distortion has been measured.

Leakey (1973) has said that "there does not seem to be any basis for attribution (of this specimen) to *Australopithecus*," but on the criteria given here it can be seen that several features that seem to be constantly found in *Australopithecus* are found in this cranium, not the least of which is the relative proportion of the facial skeleton to the neurocranium. I am not suggesting that on this evidence 1470 is an *Australopithecus*, but I am arguing for caution, even when wanting to avoid keeping specimens in "suspense account," when we may be dealing with an extremely complex evolutionary problem.

Finally, I would like to remind people of the statement by Mayr (1963) which suggested that not even *Australopithecus* has unequivocal claims for generic separation. He was dissuaded from this view later by some authors who pointed out that the upright locomotion of *Australopithecus* was still incomplete and inefficient. Mayr also noted, however, that the tremendous evolution of the brain since *Australopithecus* permitted man to enter a new niche so completely different that generic separation is fully justified. Here, he said, it is important not merely to count characters but to weight them. We now know enough about *Australopithecus* limbbones to know that in these species upright locomotion might have been fully developed, although possibly not in the way that *Homo* has developed it. Since we also now know that some sort of *Australopithecus* (if we can separate them) was contemporary with *Homo* cf. *erectus*, and since 1470 is the oldest cranium known, the statement concerning brain development since *Australopithecus* stands as an anachronism. Or does it?

This is paper no. 69 in the East Rudolf Research Project catalogue of publications.

References

Holloway, R. H. 1971. Australopithecine endocasts, brain evolution in the Hominoidea, and a model of hominid evolution. In *Evolutionary biology of Primates*, ed. R. Tuttle. Chicago: Aldine.

Leakey, L. S. B.; Tobias, P. V.; and Napier, J. R. 1964. A new species of the genus *Homo* from Olduvai Gorge. *Nature* 202:7-9.

Leakey, R. E. F. 1973. Evidence for an advanced Plio-Pleistocene hominid from East Rudolf, Kenya. *Nature* 242:447-50.

Leakey, R. E. F.; Mungai, J. M.; and Walker, A. C. 1971. New australopithecines from East Rudolf, Kenya. *Am. J. Phys. Anthropol.* 35:175-86.

————. 1972. New australopithecines from East Rudolf, Kenya (II). *Am. J. Phys. Anthropol.* 36:235-52.

Leakey, R. E. F., and Walker, A. C. 1973. New australopithecines from East Rudolf, Kenya (III). *Am. J. Phys. Anthropol.* 39:205-22.

Mayr, E. 1963. The taxonomic evaluation of fossil hominids. In *Classification and human evolution*, ed. S. L. Washburn. Chicago: Aldine.

Michenor, C. D. 1957. Some bases for higher categories in classification. *Syst. Zool.* 6: 160-73.

Reed, C. A. 1967. The generic allocation of the hominid species *habilis* as a problem in systematics. *S. African J. Sci.* 63:3-5.

Robinson, J. R. 1972. *Early hominid posture and locomotion*. Chicago: University of Chicago Press.

Simpson, G. G. 1961a. *Primate taxonomy*. In *The relatives of man*, ed. J. Buettner-Janusch. *Ann. N.Y. Acad. Sci.* 102:497-514.

————. 1961b. *Principles of animal taxonomy*. New York: Columbia University Press.

Walker, A. 1973. New *Australopithecus* femora from E. Rudolf, Kenya. *J. Human Evol.* 2: 545-55.

B. Wood

Before attempting the classification of hominid fossils from East Rudolf, it must be made clear what is meant by any classificatory scheme. In the past (and we will no doubt go on doing this in the future) paleoanthropologists have not adhered strictly to the Code of Zoological Nomenclature when classifying fossil hominids. The reasons have been understandable, but the result has been the introduction of ambiguity into a system that was designed to be a common and unambiguous language to describe biological material.

The fragmentary nature of many of the fossils makes it difficult to apply a system designed for classifying samples adequate enough to characterize a population. Also, dealing with fossils, however complete, causes added difficulty because the basic and most meaningful unit in classification, the species, can be determined with reasonable certainty only in living populations.

Thus, in classifying fossil material into neontological species one has to identify, from a small sample, populations that are genetically isolated and relate these to other fossil populations and to any extant breeding populations. But, dealing with fossils means that the only evidence available is indirect, and morphological similarity has to be relied on as a guide to genetic affinity. The pitfalls of such an exercise have been pointed out (Mayr 1950) and include problems of parallel evolution and also convergence, owing either to allometrically related features or similarity of adaptive pressures. It must be decided whether the population under study is evolving as a single polytypic species or as a number of species, because the latter situation is of course unequivocally excluded under the neontological species definition. The distinction is most important, for although species attribution may be made on scanty evidence it does not change its far-reaching implications. For example, to say that there were three contemporary species of hominids in the Pleistocene means a priori that modern human populations inherited their gene pool exclusively from one of these species. To decide whether a fossil hominid population is made up of one or a number of neontological species probably demands more evidence than can be mustered at present.

A second, more pragmatic, approach to fossil classification is to say it is only possible to identify a paleospecies (Cain 1954) or chronospecies (George 1956). Unfortunately, there is some confusion about whether these synonymous terms should apply to a whole lineage taxon (George 1956) or a segment of a lineage (Pilbeam 1972). However, let us accept, for the sake of argument, that a paleospecies is a morphological stage or grade within an evolving lineage: the latter Mayr (1963) has described as a "progressively developing anatomical

and adaptive complex." The identification of such grades is an exercise in assessing similarity, which can be made easier by using techniques developed by numerical taxonomists.
But because evolution is a dynamic process, if no attempt is made to place these grades
into an evolutionary scheme, it is just a sterile exercise.

How then, can we identify fossils that represent successive populations of an evolving
lineage and how do we describe that lineage? To answer the latter question first, because
we are dealing with a sequence of paleospecies (which, furthermore, are probably exploiting
a similar ecological niche), it seems reasonable to use the generic category to describe
the whole sequence. As to recognizing its membership, we must seek evidence of adaptive
trends that appear to unite the various stages. And it is surely among functional complexes
such as mastication, locomotion and posture, and brain size and shape (where the pressures
of natural selection are operating) that we should expect to be able to identify these
trends.

It is important also to appreciate the consequences of dealing with taxa that have a
temporal as well as a geographical range. First, early and late members of the same taxon
may be dissimilar. Second, if two taxa are derived from a common population, early members
of both taxa may retain shared features as well as their own distinctive morphology. Third,
because of mosaic evolution not all morphological features are going to show changes between
grades; for example, there may be marked differences in the dental apparatus between temporally separated populations that justify a grade separation while postcranially the populations may be indistinguishable. Fourth, until we know the evolutionary history of any
proposed hominid taxon more completely than we do now, it may be unwise to label features
as basic to one taxon or another. There may indeed be features within a taxon that are
characteristic of one or more of the paleospecies within it. But there is no guarantee
that the same features will be found in earlier members of the taxon. For example, *Homo*
sapiens and *Homo erectus* differ morphologically, but these differences are no longer considered a bar to the inclusion of the species *H. erectus* in the genus *Homo* as they once
were. Is it any less logical to accept that even earlier members of *Homo* may differ from
both *H. sapiens* and *H. erectus* yet can still belong to *Homo*? In order to trace the progress
of any lineage, a prerequisite is adequate dating information. It is apparent that the
sites in the Lake Rudolf basin, like those at Olduvai, offer a better chronological framework in which to assess affinities and trace developments between fossil samples than do
sites in South Africa. Since the latter were discovered first, the South African fossil
hominids have precedence in the literature, but it is important not to perpetuate any confusion that may exist about the affinities of these fossils to the East African fossils,
where with present dating technology the prospects seem better for a more completely documented and dated sequence.

The sample of fossil hominids from East Rudolf, though all sharing some morphological
similarities with modern man, may not all belong to the evolutionary unit that includes
Homo sapiens with his large brain, characteristic upright and bipedal gait and considerable
conceptual and manipulative ability and extensive cultural associations. There is evidence,
as set out below, of at least one other population evolving broadly parallel with the
taxon but with different morphology and by inference a different behavior pattern. Any
such population would have been genetically isolated from the *Homo* population and as such
would have no modern representative. This will make the functional interpretation of morphology in these other taxa more difficult, for we lack the modern data we have for *Homo*.

That part of the fossil sample from East Rudolf that is reasonable to assign to the

genus *Homo*, as defined above, will be presented along with evidence of the kind outlined.
Only the more complete fossils will be discussed. Fragmentary remains can be more satisfactorily classified after lineages are identified using the better-preserved fossils.

Cranial Evidence

Craniums (excluding mandibles)

Cranial remains from East Rudolf, excluding mandibles and isolated teeth, numbered 19
specimens at the end of the 1972 season. Many are too fragmentary to provide adequate
data for classification into any one evolving population unit. Two specimens will be described. The first, KNM-ER 1470, is complete enough to provide good evidence about brain
size and shape and more limited evidence about the masticatory complex. The second, KNM-ER
1590, is more fragmentary but shows similarities to KNM-ER 1470.

KNM-ER 1470. This specimen has been described briefly and illustrated (Leakey 1973). It
comes from a horizon 35 m below the KBS Tuff, which has been dated at 2.61 ± 0.26 m.y.
(Fitch and Miller 1970) in Area 131. Preliminary paleomagnetic evidence points to an age
of about 3 m.y. The skull is adult. The overall skull shape has not been seen in any
other fossil hominid. Superficial similarities to the cranium of Sts 5 are not supported
on closer examination. The sagittal profile of 1470 is more tightly curved in the region
of the lambda, with a rounded occipital region and a reduction in the area devoted to the
nuchal musculature. A coronal profile in the plane of the external auditory meati shows
pronounced parietal eminences. These features of the shape of the vault also contrast with
the specimens of *Homo erectus* from China and Java. The capacity of the cranial cavity has
been estimated by Dr. R. Holloway (pers. comm.) to be 775 cc. Rightly or wrongly, it has
been the absolute volume of the cranial cavity rather than any consistent changes in vault
shape that has chiefly influenced decisions about inclusion of specimens in the genus *Homo*,
and until detailed investigations of the endocranial cast have been made, the cranial capacity of the vault of KNM-ER 1470 will have to be used as a guide to its affinities.

Few workers would now disagree that the fossil hominid material from Java and China,
assigned by most workers to the species *H. erectus*, should be included in the genus *Homo*.
However, the dating of both sites is uncertain. Estimations on the underlying Putjangan
beds in Java, where some of the fossils are said to come from, have given one date of
1.9 ± 0.4 m.y.(Jacob 1972), but otherwise the vast majority of *Homo erectus* material can,
in the light of present knowledge,be said to be less than 1 m.y. old. The mean cranial
capacity of six specimens from Java is 859 cc, with a range of 750-975 cc, and for the five
specimens from Choukoutien the mean is 1,043 cc with a range of 915-1,225 cc. (Tobias 1971);
the skull from Lantian has an estimated capacity of 780 cc (Woo 1965). Thus, KNM-ER 1470
has a cranial capacity within one standard deviation of the Java hominid sample mean and
is likely to have come from a population with a capacity similar in range to *Homo erectus*.
However, it has a differently shaped cranial vault and is nearly 2 m.y. older. Other well-
dated cranial material of anything like this antiquity comes only from Olduvai Gorge,
Tanzania. Hominid 9, first attributed to *Homo leakeyi* (Heberer 1963) but later to *Homo
erectus*, was found in situ in Upper Bed II and is broadly contemporaneous with the sites in
Java. Its cranial capacity is estimated at about 1,000 cc (Holloway 1973). Estimates of
cranial capacity are available for other fossil hominids found in Bed I and in Bed II below
the Aeolian Tuff member, with a date of approximately 1.8 m.y. (Curtis and Hay 1972).
Leaving aside for the moment comments about the validity of these cranial capacity estimates, the mean for hominids 7, 13, 16, and 24 is 637 cc (Holloway 1973). The finding of a

cranium with a significantly larger capacity than this, some 1 m.y. older, must weigh heavily in any discussion of the affinities of the Olduvai material.

Of the robust australopithecine cranial material, two specimens from East Rudolf, KNM-ER 406 and KNM-ER 732, have cranial capacities of 510 and 506 cc respectively (Holloway 1973). These compare favorably with an average for measurable robust australopithecine craniums of 517 cc. Assuming a coefficient of variation of about 10, the value for 1470 is significantly different from the robust australopithecine population.

As for those features of the cranium that may relate to posture, there is no marked nuchal crest, and quite a small area is available for nuchal muscle attachment in the East Rudolf specimen. In the provisional reconstruction--with the cranium oriented in the Frankfurt Horizontal--the plane of the foramen magnum is nearly horizontal. The position of the external auditory meatus on the right side in relation to the maximum length of the vault, as demonstrated by a simple index (fig. 1), shows affinities with samples drawn from the *Homo* taxon, but the distortion of the skull reduces the value of this evidence.

Evidence from the cranium relating to the masticatory complex is less complete. There are no surviving tooth crowns. The broken roots of the premolars and parts of the M^1 and M^2 roots are preserved, as are the partly matrix-filled alveoli of the anterior teeth. There are no marked temporal lines, the loss of the zygomatic arches means there is no information about the origin of the masseter muscles, and the surviving bone can only indicate that the infratemporal fossae were not very deep.

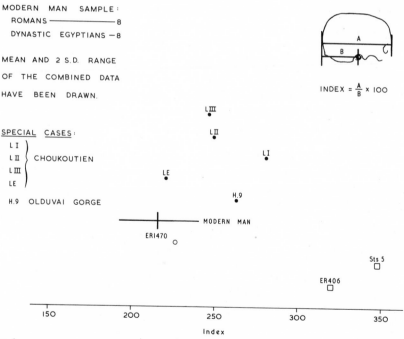

Figure 1.

The palate is incomplete, and although one can see that the labial border is straight and the remaining roots of the teeth indicate a parabola-shaped dental arcade, the broken posterior border makes remarks about the total shape of the palate only speculative.

The alveoli and broken roots of the teeth give an indication of the dental proportions. The available space for the two premolar teeth between the canine alveolus and the broken mesial M^1 root is 16.5 mm: this compares with a value of 17.5 mm from the maxilla of Sangiran IV, the *Homo erectus* from the Putjangan beds in Java, and with 22.5 mm, the equivalent distance in OH 5. These measurements, together with the appearance of the broken roots, indicate that the premolars were probably unlike those of *A. robustus* and *A. boisei*. The palate is remarkably broad, which is a feature of other early *Homo* palates and differs from the narrower palates of the robust australopithecines.

In summary, the cranial capacity, as much as it reflects brain size, indicates that this specimen belongs to a population with a brain larger than that of other contemporaneous East African hominids. The morphology of the palatal region seems to corroborate the evidence of the vault that this specimen probably represents the earliest cranial evidence of *Homo*.

KNM-ER 1590. This specimen was recovered from a horizon below the KBS Tuff in Area 12 at Ileret. It has been illustrated (Leakey 1973) but not described. The shape of this reconstructed juvenile cranial vault is very similar to that of KNM-ER 1470. This specimen probably represents additional evidence of *Homo* at this early age.

More cranial material was discovered during the 1973 field season. These specimens are still being prepared and will not be considered here.

Mandibles and Isolated Teeth

Up to the close of the 1972 season, the number of hominid mandibles collected was 28; 13 of these have one or more preserved tooth crowns. Fifteen individuals are represented by isolated teeth alone; all but one of these are specimens of permanent teeth. The specimens discussed below are three mandibles: two adult and one juvenile, KNM-ER 730 (Leakey 1971), KNM-ER 992 and 820 (Leakey 1972). Specimen KNM-ER 730 was found in Area 103 on the Koobi Fora ridge, from a horizon just below the Koobi Fora Tuff which has been dated at 1.57 m.y. (Fitch and Miller, this symposium). The two other specimens were found in the Ileret area, KNM-ER 992 from a horizon between the Chari Tuff and the Lower/Middle tuff complex and KNM-ER 820 from a horizon between the Lower/Middle tuff complex and the KBS Tuff. Their probable ages are about 1.3 m.y. and between 1.6 and 2.6 m.y., respectively.

KNM-ER 730. This specimen consists of most of the left side, the symphyseal region, and the anterior part of the right side of a mandibular body. The worn crowns of the left molar teeth are retained, as are the broken roots of the anterior and premolar teeth of both sides. The body of the mandible is heavily constructed compared with modern *Homo sapiens* mandibles, and when it is related to the crown area of the M_1, the estimated cross-sectional area of the mandibular body at the M_1 is similar to that of other fossil *Homo* mandibles (fig. 2). There is a distinct depression between the alveolar margin and the mental trigon at the symphysis; this, Weidenreich (1934) claimed, indicated the presence of a true chin, and KNM-ER 730 resembles in this respect the mandibles described from Choukoutien. The molar teeth show considerable interstitial wear, but despite this the mesiodistal diameter of M_3 is similar to that of M_1, the inference being that when dentition was unworn it was certainly not longer than M_1.

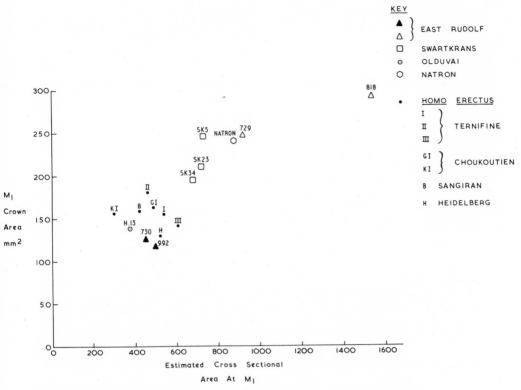

KEY

▲ } EAST RUDOLF
△ }
☐ SWARTKRANS
⊙ OLDUVAI
○ NATRON

• HOMO ERECTUS
I }
II } TERNIFINE
III }

GI }
KI } CHOUKOUTIEN

B SANGIRAN
H HEIDELBERG

CROSS SECTIONAL AREA ESTIMATED USING FORMULA FOR AN ELLIPSE.

Figure 2.

KNM-ER 992. This is an adult mandible with well-preserved dentition, complete except for three incisors. The two sides are separate; the line of fracture is irregular in the region of the symphysis. The teeth show much less wear than KNM-ER 730 and, as far as it can be reconstructed, are arranged in a parabola-shaped arcade. There is no true chin. The premolars have a distinct distal shelf but do not have the accessory cusp development on this shelf that is seen in KNM-ER 729 and specimens of *A. robustus* from Swartkrans, a tendency that is exemplified in SK 9. Figure 3 shows that mandibles of *A. robustus* have large premolars because they have large molars; the change in morphology of P_4 is thus related to a proportional increase in crown area. None of these tooth measurements takes account of the effect of interstitial wear on the shape of the tooth crown; the small size of the sample renders it impractical to match worn with worn and unworn with unworn teeth. The molar size order is $M_2 > M_3 > M_1$. The canines are reduced in size compared with fossil and recent hominoids, but the size reduction related to the crown area of the M_1 is less than that seen in the samples of *A. robustus* from Swartkrans and robust australopithecines from East Rudolf (fig. 4). This shows that despite large differences in overall size of the mandibles, the size of the canine teeth does not vary between *Homo* and robust australopithecines.

The robustness of the mandibular body has been proposed as a distinguishing factor

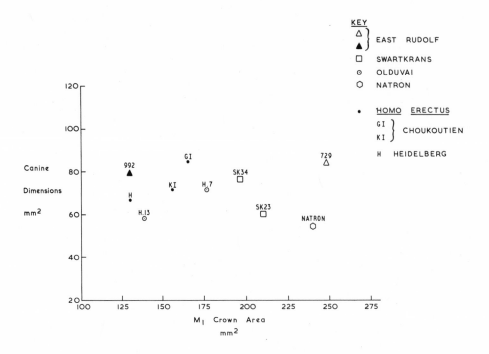

Figure 3.

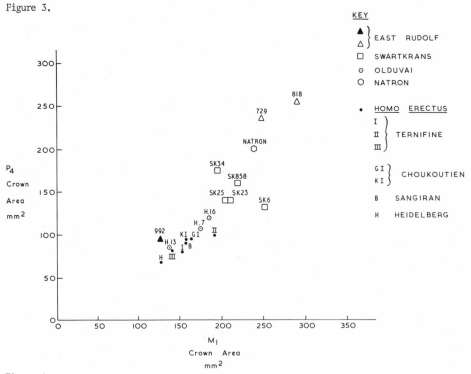

Figure 4.

between the mandibles of the known samples of *Homo* and robust australopithecines. No satisfactory index of mandibular robusticity is widely used; Martin and Saller used an index
of mandibular body thickness and height taken at the mental foramen, and Morant (1936) in
his studies made no attempt to assess the cross-sectional profile of the body. To assess
robusticity the maximum thickness and height at the middle of the site of M_1 has been taken
and an index calculated (table 1). Eleven specimens of *Homo erectus* have been used (including Heidelberg, whose inclusion in the taxon is by no means agreed [Campbell 1963],
and H 13 and H 22 from Olduvai Gorge) and eighteen specimens of robust australopithecines;
the parameters of the samples are given in table 1.

Table 1
Index of Mandibular Robusticity

	Homo erectus	A. robustus/A. sp. indet.
Number	11	18
Mean	56	70
Range	47≈66	55≈84
s	6.7	7.1
SE	2.0	1.7

$t = 5.2$, $p = <.01$

NOTE: Robusticity index $= \dfrac{\text{Max. thickness}}{\text{Max. height}}$ X 100 of the mandibular body at M_1.

The results of a t test show that such a robusticity index serves to distinguish the
two samples. However, the ranges overlap and it may be (see above) that the index will be
a less useful discriminator between samples of earlier representatives of both lineages.
The indexes for KNM-ER 992 and KNM-ER 730, 63, and 59 place them within the *Homo erectus*
range; their allocation to *Homo* is also confirmed by numerous morphological resemblances,
but space limitations prevent their presentation here.

A plot of robusticity index against the estimated cross-sectional area of the body at
M_1 (fig. 5) shows two interesting features. The *Homo* mandibles cluster, with low values in
both axes. Second, the robusticity index of the australopithecine mandibles is remarkably
constant over a large overall size range--the shape of the mandibular body in small robust
australopithecine mandibles is still distinctive, but they nevertheless overlap with the
Homo mandibles in terms of overall size.

KNM-ER 820. This specimen is a juvenile mandible with a very well preserved body and dentition. The permanent dentition is represented by the incisors and first molars and the
deciduous dentition by the canines and molars. The form of the dental arch and the shape
of the mandibular body contrast with juvenile mandibles from Swartkrans and a juvenile
mandible KNM-ER 1477 from East Rudolf, but the limited use of parameters taken in specimens
at different stages of development, and the paucity of specimens, make this difficult to
demonstrate. The deciduous molars are worn enough to obscure the details of the cusp pattern. Robinson (1956) admits that dm_2 is not a good discriminator, but a plot of the diameters of the dm_2 of both *Homo erectus* and *A. robustus* shows a well-marked size difference;
KNM-ER 820 lies in the *Homo* group. The incisor teeth in the two taxa are similar in size
even though the M_1 crown areas differ significantly; the values for KNM-ER 820 and KNM-ER
992 place them within the range of *Homo erectus* mandibles.

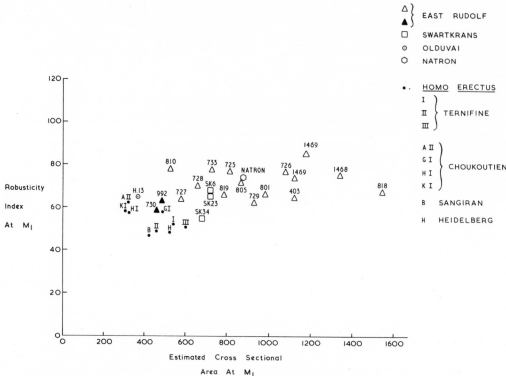

Figure 5.

What this brief discussion of the morphological and metrical characters of these three mandibles has shown is that in East Rudolf there is evidence of at least two populations of hominid. The evidence for this is the apparently bimodal distribution of the fossils, both in relation to dental proportions and in relation to mandibular body size and shape. The parameters of one population sample, which I shall call *Australopithecus* sp. indet. (sensu Leakey 1971), appear to be well matched by the majority population that is sampled at Swartkrans and classified as *Australopithecus* or *Paranthropus robustus*; these two populations, separated by thousands of miles, show a homogeneity that indicates a very similar ecological adaptation. A feature of this population sample is the remarkably consistent mandibular morphology extending over a time span that encompasses horizons from just below the Chari Tuff at Ileret to beneath the KBS Tuff--probably more than 1.5 m.y. Because so few mandibles belonging to this population have intact tooth crowns, and these happen to represent the larger end of the range, on tooth size alone it appears that there is little or no overlap in absolute size between this and the second population sampled at East Rudolf. That this is not the case is seen in figure 5. It is postulated that the other part of the bimodal distribution is sampling a *second* population. This, unlike the *Australopithecus* one, shows no metrical affinity to the majority population at Swartkrans, but instead shows similarities to specimens which, though geographically widely dispersed, are all considered to belong to the *H. erectus* grade of the *Homo* lineage. This is not to say that the East Rudolf specimens necessarily belong to the paleospecies *H. erectus*, for in some features they are more closely similar to early European mandibles, but they certainly belong to the same lineage and thus are properly included in the genus *Homo*.

Postcranial Evidence

It is now apparent that in parts of the postcranial skeleton of fossil hominids there is evidence of significant morphological differences between the robust australopithecines and the *Homo* lineage.

Fossil limb material described by Weidenreich (1941) from Choukoutien and by Day (1971) from Olduvai Gorge shows some differences from selected samples of modern human bones; but these variations are relatively minor, and this material, along with the femora from Trinil, can be confidently considered early examples of the same morphological pattern as modern man.

In 1950 Broom reported two proximal femoral fragments from Swartkrans, and in 1952 Broom and Robinson wrote about a pelvic fragment. Although the pelvic fragment, SK 50, is crushed and distorted, Le Gros Clark (1955) and Napier (1964) saw enough evidence to convince them that the specimen belonged to a biped. But there were features such as the elongated ischial segment and the orientation of the iliac crest that suggested a different morphological pattern from that seen in *Homo*; Napier (1964) made essentially the same judgment about the two proximal femoral fragments SK 82 and SK 97. Since then, new discoveries at Olduvai Gorge and East Rudolf have confirmed the morphology of this type of femur, such as the small head, rather elongated and flattened neck, and more acute neck angle. Other characters have been claimed to be characteristic of this group. One, the posterior position of the lesser trochanter, is difficult to measure and variable even in modern human femora. The second, the absence of a bony ridge for the iliofemoral ligament, must allow for the fact that young adult and female femurs are occasionally unmarked in dissecting-room bones even though the ligament is present (pers. obs.).

Thus, because bone shape is known to reflect mechanical stresses, the morphological distinctiveness of the proximal end of the femoral shaft indicates a difference in mechanical arrangement, and along with data on talar morphology (Day and Wood 1968; Wood 1973*b*), is the chief evidence for a *second* bipedal locomotor adaptation in early hominids. Some workers (Lovejoy, Heiple, and Burstein 1973) would claim that this is insufficient evidence. Although I agree with their admonition that the exact mechanical meaning of these differences in femoral anatomy must await a proper biomechanical analysis of the pelvic-femoral complex, nevertheless they are probably functionally significant.

Indirect evidence associates this pelvic and femoral material from East Rudolf and South Africa with the robust australopithecine skull material, and because it has been seen that this form evolved parallel with *Homo* in East Africa, the clear inference is that its locomotor pattern was also evolving independently of *Homo* and that the two locomotor forms were not sequential, as has been suggested. If this hypothesis is correct, there should be quite early fossil evidence of this locomotor dichotomy.

At the close of the 1972 season, 24 postcranial bones and 4 sets of associated limb bones had been collected from the East Rudolf region. Specimens that are considered to belong to the first of the two proposed locomotor complexes, the one we associate with *Homo*, are KNM-ER 737 (Leakey 1971); KNM-ER 803 and 813 (Leakey 1972); and KNM-ER 1472 and 1481 (Leakey 1973). The first two will be considered in detail by Day (this symposium), and only specimens 813, 1472, and 1481 will be discussed here.

A talus, with an associated tibial fragment, KNM-ER 813, was found in Area 104 from a horizon that lies between the Koobi Fora and the KBS tuffs, and is broadly contemporary with KNM-ER 730. KNM-ER 1472 and 1481 are femurs, the latter associated with fragments of a tibia and fibula, that were recovered from horizons respectively 13 and 31 meters beneath the KBS Tuff and are more than 2.6 m.y. old.

KNM-ER 813. This material consists of a nearly complete right talus and an uninformative fragment of right tibial shaft. The good preservation of the talus enables comparisons with modern and fossil samples to be made.

There are many features of the bone, such as the torsion of the head, the relatively high angle of inclination, the low horizontal angle of the neck, and the compactness of the body that indicate it belonged to the foot of a creature that was habitually bipedal. Using measurements detailed in Day and Wood (1968), a comparison has been made in figure 6 with samples drawn from knuckle-walking apes and modern human populations. The means of the comparative groups have been plotted, enclosed by lines corresponding to 2 SD either side of the mean. In such a plot, KNM-ER 813 follows the trend of the modern human bones, and in only one variable does it fall outside the 2 SD range. Canonical analysis of the data has been performed using seven comparative groups as outlined in Day and Wood (1968) and Wood (1973b). A plot of the first two canonical axes (fig. 7), which represent 97% of the total dispersion, shows that the groups cluster according to their locomotor mode. The fossil talus KNM-ER 813 falls within the "modern human walking" group (two Neanderthal tali have been included to verify the technique). Results of Mahalanobis D^2 distance tests

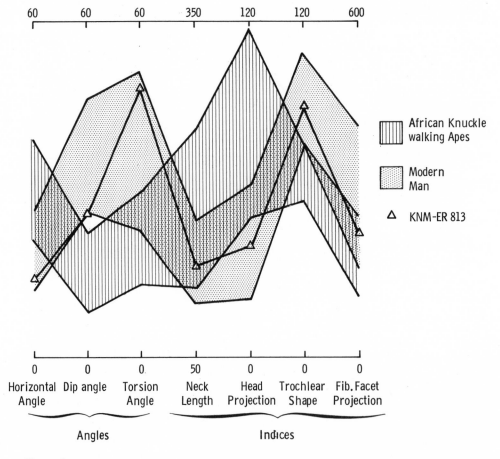

Figure 6.

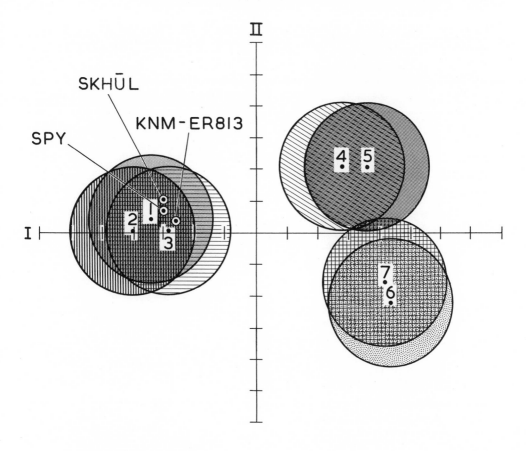

COMPARATIVE GROUPS :

1
2 } MODERN HOMO
3 } SAMPLES

4 GORILLA

5 PAN

6 PAPIO

7 CERCOPITHECUS

   mona and nictitans

Circles have radius of
2 eigenvalues.

Figure 7.

(table 2), which assess total morphological affinity, confirm the similarity of KNM-ER 813 with modern human bones, and indeed probability levels show it to be not significantly different from tali of modern bushmen.

KNM-ER 1472 and KNM-ER 1481. These specimens will be considered together. Detailed anatomical descriptions of them are being prepared, and only morphological characters relevant

Table 2

Mahalanobis D^2 Distances and Probability Levels between Groups and Special Cases

Specimen	Homo sapiens Dissecting Room	Homo sapiens Anglo-Saxon/ Romano-British	Homo sapiens Bushmen	Gorilla	Pan	Papio	Cercopithecus
KNM-ER 813	15.1 (2.5%)	22.6 (<0.5%)	11.7 (25-10%)	53.9 (<0.5%)	54.7 (<0.5%)	72.2 (<0.5%)	64.0 (<0.5%)
Spy	12.3 (10.0%)	19.4 (0.5%)	11.1 (25-10%)	52.4 (<0.5%)	54.1 (<0.5%)	75.2 (<0.5%)	66.7 (<0.5%)
Skhūl	11.6 (25-10%)	15.7 (2.5%)	13.2 (10-5%)	50.7 (<0.5%)	52.9 (<0.5%)	75.0 (<0.5%)	70.0 (<0.5%)

to a decision about their locomotor affinities will be considered here. KNM-1472 is a complete right femur. The bone is long and slender, the width of the shaft tapering distally as it tends to do in femora of *Homo erectus* (Weidenreich 1941; Day 1971): the convex medial border is another feature it shares with *Homo erectus*. The angle of obliquity is near the mean for English femurs (Parsons 1914), and this, together with the raised lateral femoral condyle, indicates a habitual upright stance. The neck is rounded in cross section and anteverted, bearing a damaged but quite large head. The femur KNM-ER 1481 is better preserved. The shaft shows marked distal tapering and is bowed anteroposteriorly. The rounded neck bears a well-preserved and large head.

To establish whether these specimens belong to *Homo* and thus the "modern human walking" locomotor category, attention has been concentrated on the proximal femoral anatomy. Three indexes have been calculated: those relating to neck length and head size are after Napier (1964), and a third is used to describe the shape of the femoral neck. A diverse modern human sample has been used, as detailed in the legend of figure 8. The mean and the 2 SD ranges of this modern sample have been plotted, along with fossil femora of *Homo sapiens* and a *Homo erectus* femur from Trinil. In all these indexes, figures 8 to 10 and table 3, there is a clear separation between samples belonging to the two proposed locomotor groups and, moreover, the femurs of *A. robustus* and *A. sp. indet.* form, with one exception, a homogeneous cluster. The proposed *Homo* femurs from East Rudolf always fall within a single standard deviation. (When the neck indexes are combined in figure 11 the same locomotor separation is seen.)

The data not only confirm the dichotomy in proximal femoral anatomy but also clearly show that femurs 1472 and 1481 from East Rudolf belong to the "modern human walking" locomotor group.

Conclusions

I have attempted to demonstrate the existence of a second hominid lineage at East Rudolf, in addition to the well-recognized *Australopithecus* (sensu Leakey) population. Evidence has been provided of dichotomies in functional complexes such as brain size, mastication, and locomotion between *Australopithecus* and the second population, *Homo*.

This scheme is probably an oversimplification since a cranium from the 1973 collection, KNM-ER 1813, and some rather fragmentary lower jaws indicate a morphological heterogeneity within the *Homo* material that may be significant. Also, a mandible, KNM-ER 1482, shows features which cannot easily be accommodated in either population. However, it is the hypothesis that best fits the current facts. But like all hypotheses it is mortal and should be kept under review.

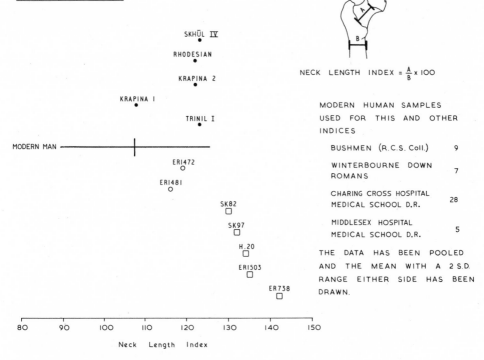

FEMUR NECK LENGTH

SKHŪL IV

RHODESIAN

KRAPINA 2

KRAPINA I

TRINIL I

MODERN MAN

ERI472

ERI481

SK82

SK97

H.20

ERI503

ER738

NECK LENGTH INDEX = $\frac{A}{B}$ x 100

MODERN HUMAN SAMPLES
USED FOR THIS AND OTHER
INDICES

BUSHMEN (R.C.S. Coll.)	9
WINTERBOURNE DOWN ROMANS	7
CHARING CROSS HOSPITAL MEDICAL SCHOOL D.R.	28
MIDDLESEX HOSPITAL MEDICAL SCHOOL D.R.	5

THE DATA HAS BEEN POOLED
AND THE MEAN WITH A 2 S.D.
RANGE EITHER SIDE HAS BEEN
DRAWN.

```
80    90   IOO   IIO   I20   I30   I40   I50
```

Neck   Length   Index

Figure 8.

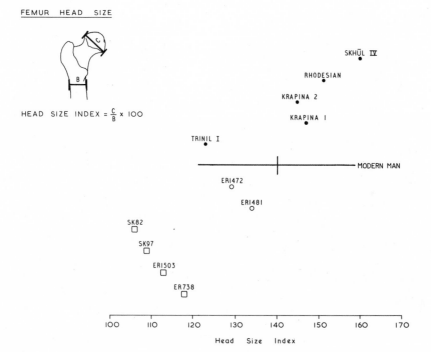

FEMUR HEAD SIZE

HEAD SIZE INDEX = $\frac{C}{B}$ x 100

SKHŪL IV

RHODESIAN

KRAPINA 2

KRAPINA I

TRINIL I

MODERN MAN

ERI472

ERI481

SK82

SK97

ERI503

ER738

```
IOO   IIO   I20   I30   I40   I50   I60   I70
```

Head   Size   Index

Figure 9.

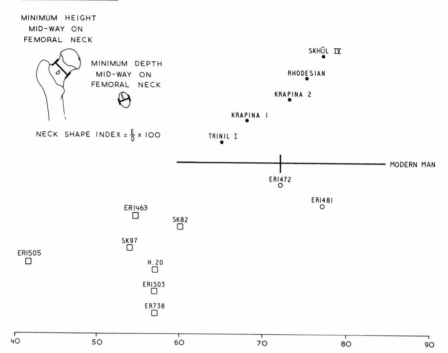

Figure 10.

Table 3

Indexes of Proximal Femoral Anatomy

	Modern Man	*A. robustus/A.* sp. indet.
Neck length index		
Number	49	5
Mean	107	135
Range	89-126	130-142
s	8.9	4.6
Head size index		
Number	49	4
Mean	140	112
Range	124-167	106-118
s	8.7	5.2
Neck shape index		
Number	49	7
Mean	72	55
Range	61-90	41-60
s	6.5	6.3

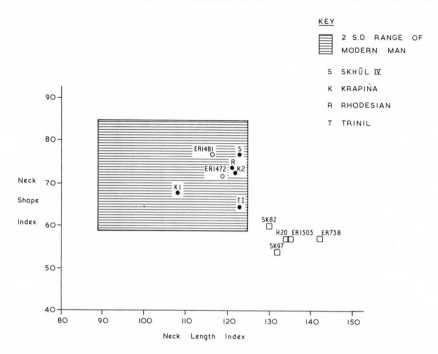

Figure 11.

Acknowledgments

I would like to thank Richard Leakey and Glynn Isaac for inviting me to take part in the East Rudolf Project and for their companionship and guidance, both in and out of the field. Richard and Meave Leakey have provided generous hospitality and rendered many kindnesses to my family and myself during visits to Nairobi.

This work has been supported by the National Science Foundation and the National Geographic Society.

Measurements were made on original specimens where possible, and I thank the people who take care of the specimens for their ready cooperation. Casts were used for measurements of material from the following sites: Choukoutien, Heidelberg, Ternifine, Trinil, Skhūl, and Krapina.

This is paper no. 70 in the East Rudolf Research Project catalogue of publications.

References

Broom, R., and Robinson, J. T. 1950. Notes on the pelves of fossil ape-men. *Am. J. Phys. Anthropol.* 8:489.

_____. 1952. Swarkrans ape-man. *Transvaal Museum Mem.*, no. 6.

Cain, A. J. 1954. *Animal species and their evolution.* London: Hutchinson.

Campbell, B. 1963. Quantitative taxonomy and human evolution. In *Classification and human evolution,* ed. S. L. Washburn. Chicago: Aldine.

Le Gros Clark, W. E. 1955. *The fossil evidence for human evolution.* Chicago: University of Chicago Press.

Curtis, G. H., and Hay, R. L. 1972. Further geological studies and potassium-argon dating at Olduvai Gorge and Ngorongoro Crater. In *Calibration of hominoid evolution,* ed. W. W. Bishop and J. A. Miller, pp. 289-301. Toronto: University of Toronto Press, Edinburgh: Scottish Academic Press.

Day, M. H. 1971. Postcranial remains of *Homo* erectus from Bed IV, Olduvai Gorge, Tanzania. *Nature* 232:383-87.

Day, M. H., and Molleson, T. 1973. The Trinil femora. In *Human evolution*, ed. M. H. Day, pp. 127-54. London: Taylor and Francis.

Day, M. H., and Wood, B. A. 1968. Functional affinities of the Olduvai Hominid 8 talus. *Man* 3:440-55.

Fitch, F. J., and Miller, J. A. 1970. Radioisotopic age determinations of Lake Rudolf artefact site. *Nature* 226:226-28.

_____. 1973. Internal report of rock dating group.

George, T. N. 1956. Biospecies, chronospecies and morphospecies. In *The species concept in paleontology*, ed. R. C. Sylvester-Bradley, pp. 123-37. Systematics Association Publication no. 2.

Heberer, G. 1963. Ueber einen neuen archanthropien Typus aus der Oldoway-Schlucht. *Z. Morph. Anthropol.* 53:171-77.

Holloway, R. L. 1973. New endocranial values for the East African early hominids. *Nature* 243:97-99.

Jacob, T. 1972. The absolute date of the Djetis beds at Modjokerto. *Antiquity* 47:148.

Leakey, R. E. F. 1971. Further evidence of Lower Pleistocene hominids from East Rudolf, North Kenya. *Nature* 231:241-45.

_____. 1972. Further evidence of Lower Pleistocene hominids from East Rudolf, North Kenya, 1971. *Nature* 237:264-69.

_____. 1973. Evidence for an advanced Plio-Pleistocene hominid from East Rudolf, Kenya. *Nature* 242:447-50.

Lovejoy, C. O.; Heiple, K. G.; Burstein, A. H. 1973. The gait of *Australopithecus*. *Am. J. Phys. Anthropol.* 38:757-80.

Mayr, E. 1950. Taxonomic categories in fossil hominids. *Cold Spring Harbor Symp. Quant. Biol.* 15:109-18.

_____. 1963. *Animal species and evolution*. Cambridge: Belknap Press of Harvard University Press.

Morant, G. M. 1936. Study of the human mandible. *Biometrika* 28 (I,II):84-122.

Napier, J. R. 1964. The evolution of bipedal walking in the hominids. *Arch. Biol. (Liège)* 75(suppl.):673-708.

Parsons, F. G. 1914. The characters of the English thigh-bone. *J. Anat. Physiol.* 48:238-67.

Pilbeam, D. 1972. *The ascent of man: An introduction to human evolution*. New York: MacMillan.

Robinson, J. T. 1956. The dentition of the Australopithecinae. *Transvaal Museum. Mem.*, 9.

Tobias, P. V. 1971. *The brain in hominid evolution*. New York: Columbia University Press.

Weidenreich, F. 1934. Das Menschenkinn und seine Entstehung: Eine Studie und Kritik. *Ergeb. Anat. Ent.* 31:1-124.

_____. 1941. The extremity bones of *Sinanthropus pekinensis*. *Paleontol. Sinica*, n.s. D, no. 5, pp. 1-82.

Woo, J. K. 1965. Preliminary report on the skull of *Sinanthropus lantianensis* of Lantian, Shensi. *Scientia Sinica* 14:1032-35.

Wood, B. A. 1973*a*. Locomotor affinities of Hominoid tali from Kenya. *Nature* 246:45-46.

_____. 1973*b*. A *Homo* talus from East Rudolf, Kenya. *J. Anat.* 117:203-4.

44. HOMINID POSTCRANIAL REMAINS FROM THE EAST RUDOLF SUCCESSION
A REVIEW

M. H. Day

Introduction

One of the most exciting aspects of the East Rudolf explorations and excavations in recent years has been the recovery of postcranial skeletal material attributable to the Hominidae. Seventy-four postcranial bones, or parts of bones, have been identified as hominid,
and these remains occupy 29 separate Kenya National Museum numbers allocated during the
seasons 1970, 1971, and 1972.

The purpose of this chapter is to provide a brief review of the material and of the
provisional identifications and attributions made in the initial publications. Second, it
will highlight the range and extent of the postcranial bones and their anatomical distribution, and, third, it will outline any functional and taxonomic inferences that we may
fairly draw from their examination at this stage.

The Postcranial Bones

The rapid buildup of postcranial finds over the past three years can be seen from
table 1, where all the finds are listed with their provisional identifications, provisional
attributions, localities, areas, and references. It is of interest, however, to group the
material into anatomical categories (tables 2 and 3) in order to see the differential preservation of the various parts of the hominid skeleton from this area and the sample sizes
of the material available from the limbs and functional complexes that we wish to examine.

It is immediately apparent that the lower limbs are better represented than the upper
limbs and that the skeleton of the trunk of the East Rudolf hominids is virtually unknown
(table 2). Similarly, although something is known of the upper and lower limbs of these
forms, nothing at all is known of how they were attached to the trunk through the limb
girdles (table 3).

Finally, in assessing a group of fossil limb bones that almost certainly derive from
more than one taxon, the greatest possible assistance is obtained from clear and unequivocal knowledge of anatomical association--that is, the certainty that a given group of bones
belonged to one individual, one limb, or one functional complex such as a hand or a foot.
From material of this kind convincing evidence of locomotor capability can be derived. Locomotor capability may also be of taxonomic value if a recognizable locomotor pattern is
agreed as a taxonomic criterion; on the other hand it may not, since locomotion may be almost identical in two species that only differ dentally or cranially.

Seven groups of associated hominid postcranial remains are known from East Rudolf,

Table 1

Postcranial Bones of East Rudolf Hominids

Museum No.	Provisional Identification	Locality	Area	Provisional Attribution	References
1970					
KNM-ER 736	Left femoral shaft	Koobi Fora	103	*Australopithecus* sp. (now? *Homo* sp.)	Leakey 1971; Leakey, Mungai, and Walker 1972; Walker 1973
KNM-ER 737	Left femoral shaft	Koobi Fora	103	*Homo* sp.	Leakey 1971; Day and Leakey 1973
KNM-ER 738	Left femur (proximal end and shaft)	Koobi Fora	105	*Australopithecus* sp.	Leakey 1971; Leakey, Mungai, and Walker 1972; Walker 1973
KNM-ER 739	Right humerus (shaft and distal end)	Ileret	1	*Australopithecus* sp.	Leakey 1971; Leakey, Mungai, and Walker 1972; McHenry 1973
KNM-ER 740	Left humerus (fragment of distal end)	Ileret	3	*Australopithecus* sp.	Leakey 1971; Leakey, Mungai, and Walker 1972
KNM-ER 741	Left tibia (proximal end and part of shaft)	Ileret	1	*Australopithecus* sp. (now? *Homo* sp.)	Leakey 1971; Leakey, Mungai, and Walker 1972
1971					
KNM-ER 164	2 proximal hand phalanges 1 cervical vertebra,C_7 1 thoracic vertebra,T_1	Koobi Fora	104	*Homo* sp.	Leakey 1972; Day and Leakey 1974
KNM-ER 803	Partial skeleton (listed separately)	Ileret	8A	*Homo* sp.	Leakey 1972; Day and Leakey 1974
KNM-ER 813	Right talus and tibial fragment (?femoral fragment)	Koobi Fora	104	*Homo* sp.	Leakey 1972; Leakey and Wood 1973
KNM-ER 815	Left femur neck	Ileret	10	*Australopithecus* sp.	Leakey 1972; Leakey and Walker 1973; Wood 1973
KNM-ER 993	Right femur (part of shaft and distal end)	Ileret	1	*Australopithecus* sp.	Leakey 1972; Leakey and Walker 1973; Walker 1973
KNM-ER 997	Metatarsal(? II or III)	Koobi Fora	104	*Australopithecus* sp.	Leakey 1972; Leakey and Walker 1973;
KNM-ER 999	Femur	Ileret	6A		Unreported

Table 1 (Continued)

Museum No.	Provisional Identification	Locality	Area	Provisional Attribution	References
1972					
KNM-ER 1463	Right femoral shaft	Ileret	1A	*Australopithecus* sp.	Leakey 1973a
KNM-ER 1464	Right talus	Ileret	6A	*Australopithecus* sp. (now? *Homo* sp.)	Leakey 1973a
KNM-ER 1465	Left femur (proximal end)	Ileret	8	*Australopithecus* sp.	Leakey 1973a
KNM-ER 1471	Right tibia (proximal half)	Ileret	131	*Australopithecus* sp. (now? *Homo* sp.)	Leakey, 1973a
KNM-ER 1472	Right femur (complete)	Ileret	131	*Homo* sp.	Leakey 1973a,b
KNM-ER 1473	Head of right humerus	Ileret	131		Leakey 1973a
KNM-ER 1475	Right femur (proximal end (+ shaft fragment)	Ileret	131	*Homo* sp.	Leakey 1973a
KNM-ER 1476	Tibia (proximal end) Left talus and part of shaft	Koobi Fora	105	*Australopithecus* sp.	Leakey 1973a
KNM-ER 1481	Lower-limb partial skeleton	Ileret	131	*Homo* sp.	Leakey 1973a,b
KNM-ER 1500	Fragmented skeleton	Ileret	130	*Australopithecus* sp.	Leakey 1973a
KNM-ER 1503	Right femoral fragment	Kubi Algi	123	*Australopithecus* sp.	Leakey 1973a
KNM-ER 1504	Right humeral fragment	Kubi Algi	123	*Australopithecus* sp.	Leakey 1973a
KNM-ER 1505	Left proximal femoral fragment	Kubi Algi	123	*Australopithecus* sp.	Leakey 1973a
KNM-ER 1591	Humerus lacking a head	Ileret	12	*Homo* sp.	Leakey 1973a
KNM-ER 1592	Distal half of femur	Ileret	12	*Australopithecus* sp.	Leakey 1973a

Table 2

KNM-ER Specimens by Anatomical Category

Upper Limb		Lower Limb					Trunk	Partial Skeletons
164	1473	736	815	1463	1475	1592	164	803
739	1504	737	993	1464	1476			1500
740	1591	738	997	1465	1481			
		741	999	1471	1503			
		813	1181	1472	1505			

Table 3

KNM-ER Specimens by Anatomical Category

Upper Limb			Lower Limb			Limb Girdles		Axial Skeleton
Arm	Forearm	Hand	Thigh	Leg	Foot	Upper	Lower	
739	803	164	736	741	803	1500	none	164
740	1500	803	737	803	813			
1473			738	?813	997			
1500			803	1471	1464			
1504			?813	1476	1476			
1591			815	1481	1500			
			993	1500				
			999					
			1463					
			1465					
			1472					
			1475					
			1481					
			1500					
			1503					
			1505					
			1592					

including two partial skeletons and one partial lower limb skeleton. These groups of bones, each from a single individual, can be expected to provide valuable evidence unobtainable in other ways: perhaps evidence of body size, body proportion, limb length, and limb proportion, in addition to evidence of the locomotor capabilities of the limb or the individual as a whole (table 4).

The question of the association of fossil remains in a deposit is of such particular importance that it seems worthwhile to suggest a number of criteria that may be used to test whether fossil bones simply found together in a deposit are indeed truly associated-- that is to say, anatomically associated paleontological skeletal material derived from one individual. Evidence for this form of association may be anatomical or geological and has been set out as a series of guidelines with explanations and comments on the way that these guidelines may be applied (see Appendix).

The Upper Limb

The hominid upper limb remains from East Rudolf are fewer than those from the lower limb, and upper limb girdle remains are confined to a fragment of scapula (KNM-ER 1500). In effect nothing is known of how the upper limb is attached to the trunk in this group of hominids.

The skeleton of the arm (table 3) is represented by 6 humeral fragments of which by far the most important is KNM-ER 739. This robust right humerus has a gently medially curved shaft, marked muscular impressions, and a deep intertubercular groove. The head of the bone is missing. The lower one-third features a brachioradialis flange, a ridge of the

Table 4

Partial Skeletons and Other Associated Remains

KNM No.	Upper Limb			Lower Limb			Limb Girdles		Axial Skeleton
	Arm	Forearm	Hand	Thigh	Leg	Foot	Upper	Lower	
164 b			2 proximal phalanges						
164 c									1 cervical vertebra C_7; 1 thoracic vertebra T_1
803 a-t (see table 5)		c,d,p	t	a	b,g,n,o	e,f,j,k, l,m,q,r			
813 a,b				? Right femoral fragment (b)	? Right tibial shaft fragment (b)	Right talus (a)			
1476					Proximal tibia and part of shaft	Left talus			
1481				Left femur	Proximal tibia and distal tibia, distal fibula				
1500 A-T (see table 6)	L	E,F,I,K		B,D	A,C,G,H,J,R	M	O		

medial intermuscular septum, and a keeled lower articular surface divided into trochlear and capitular portions. The olecranon fossa is shallow and lacks the steep lateral wall typical of knuckle-walkers. It has been attributed to the genus *Australopithecus*. In a multivariate study of this bone (McHenry 1973) it has been suggested that it is morphologically unique in relation to *Homo sapiens, Gorilla, Pongo, Pan troglodytes,* and *Pan paniscus.* However, the question of the use of the forelimb has been left open to the extent that no "knuckle-walking" affinities were found. The remaining humeral fragments are not very helpful in terms of either attribution or function, since they are in the main fragmentary.

The only forearm bones known from East Rudolf come from KNM-ER 803 and KNM-ER 1500, partial skeletons that will be separately described.

The few hand bones from this site come from KNM-ER 164, a composite specimen still partly embedded in matrix. It seems to consist of two proximal phalanges, a fragment of the third phalanx, and the head of a metacarpal in articulation with the shorter of the two phalanges. From what can be seen of these phalanges they appear to be relatively modern in form and will be attributed to the genus *Homo* sp. (Day and Leakey 1974).

The Lower Limb

Of the lower limb remains none are known from the girdle. Once again we have no knowledge of how the limb was attached to the trunk in the East Rudolf hominids.

The femur, however, is the best-represented bone in the whole of the postcranial collection, perhaps reflecting its durability in the face of the vicissitudes of scavenging and fossilization. From the 16 or 17 examples recovered, two main patterns of femoral morphology seem to emerge, one attributed to *Australopithecus* and the other to the genus *Homo*.

The best summary of the australopithecine type of femur has been given recently (Walker 1973). It is described as being more robust than that of *Homo sapiens*, having a rather small head and a long neck, with a low neck-shaft angle, an anteroposteriorly compressed neck, a greater trochanter that does not flare out from the shaft, a rather high femorocondylar angle, and a rather short overall length.

Previously one of the earliest australopithecine femora described was that of Sts 14 (Broom, Robinson, and Schepers 1950). However, this specimen is so poor that it is of little value (Walker 1973; Day 1973). The 2 femoral necks from Swartkrans were first recognized as australopithecine by Napier (1964), and this diagnosis was vindicated by the discovery of Olduvai Hominid 20 (Day 1969, 1973). Now there are 10 femoral necks from South Africa, Olduvai, and East Rudolf (KNM-ER 738, 815, 1465, 1500, 1503, and 1505), all showing the most characteristic combination of features yet recognized in the australopithecine postcranium and underlining the view held here that it is the combination of morphological characters that is most important in both taxonomic and functional terms.

Similarly, the recovery of the OH 28 (Day 1971) drew attention to a combination of features first described by Weidenreich (1941) for the Peking femora (*Homo erectus*). These features include a general platymeria, a low position of the minimum breadth, an acute medial border, a longitudinally convex medial border, a gluteal bulge, and a low linea aspera, but no pilaster. In none of his writings did Le Gros Clark accept this combination as distinctive, since he found that each feature independently fell within the range of modern man.

This pattern of femoral morphology is now recognized from East Rudolf in KNM-ER 737 (Day and Leakey 1973; Day 1973) and confirmed on metrical grounds in relation to shaft dimensions and cortical thicknesses (Kennedy 1973). Two other East Rudolf femora are of interest: KNM-ER 736, a massive femoral shaft; and KNM-ER 999, a massive, almost complete femur. Both of these femora show necks, medially placed lesser trochanters, similar gluteal markings, gradually widening shaft contours, and anterior convexities. The KNM-ER 736 shaft has a low minimum breadth and external and internal shaft diameters that multivariate analysis shows to have affinities with *Homo* (Kennedy 1973). I would attribute both of these specimens to the genus *Homo*.

Of the remaining lower-limb material, that from the tibia is confusing in that taxonomically distinctive morphological features are not readily identifiable at present. It seems likely that some of the provisional attributions already made may have to be changed.

The foot material from East Rudolf includes several important tali, such as KNM-ER 813a, 1464, and 1476a.

The KNM-ER 813a talus is well-preserved and shows many features well known to be characteristic of a nonprehensile propulsive bipedal foot. In particular, the low horizontal neck angle and the high torsion angle of the neck are familiar from the examination of modern human series (Day and Wood 1968). Detailed consideration of this talus, using the same techniques as in the publication cited above, have now been reported by Wood (1973). His results support the anatomical opinion expressed earlier that this bone should be assigned to *Homo* sp. (Leakey 1972) (fig. 1). Of the remaining tali, KNM-ER 1464 has mixed features but seems likely to be allocated to the genus *Homo*, whereas KNM-ER 1476a is similar to the OH 8 talus.

The two sets of truly associated remains are KNM-ER 803 and KNM-ER 1500. Both of these partial skeletons satisfy enough of the anatomical and geological criteria that I believe are essential for true association (see appendix to this chapter).

KNM-ER 803a-t (Leakey 1972; Day and Leakey, in press)

Table 5 gives the full list of remains recognized from this skeleton. The only cranial remains of this individual consist of a left upper canine tooth and a right upper central incisor (h and i).

a. Left femoral shaft. This specimen lacks both proximal and distal ends. Above, it is broken across just below the lesser trochanter but above the gluteal tuberosity; below, it is broken 23 mm below the point of divergence of the supracondylar lines. The shaft is gently curved anteroposteriorly but is straight from the front, having a slight medial convexity. In a number of respects it resembles the shaft of KNM-ER 737 both anatomically and metrically. In its flatness and lack of pilaster it also resembles the OH 28 and Peking *Homo erectus* femora (Day 1973) (figs. 2 and 3).

b. Left tibial shaft. This specimen is broken and lacks both its upper and its lower ends. The shaft is straight with a rounded anterior border throughout; in section the shaft is oval above and triangular below. The posterior border is rounded and separates the medial and posterolateral surfaces. It is interrupted by a heavy oblique line that demarcates the popliteal surface above. From the center of this line a well-marked "vertical line" runs inferiorly, separating the attachment areas of flexor digitorum longus and tibialis posterior.

c. Left ulnar shaft. Built of four fragments from the coronoid process above to the junction of the lower one-third/upper two-thirds below. The shaft is straight in anteroposterior view. The subcutaneous posterior border is sigmoid and the interosseous border is rounded above but sharp and prominent below.

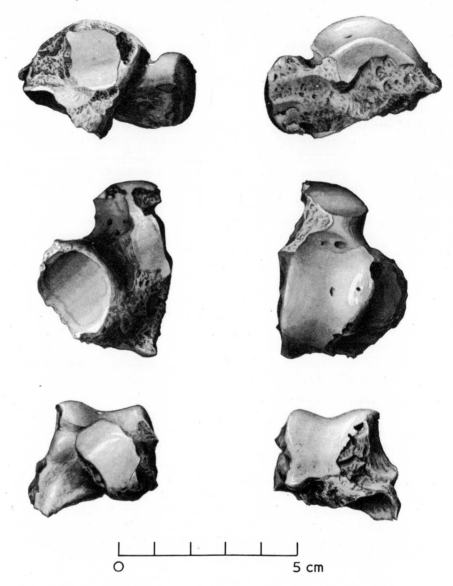

Figure 1. KNM-ER 813a. A right talus--six views.

d.   Section of the midshaft of a left radius, oval in section. Pronator teres insertion well marked on the lateral aspect of the bone.

The femoral, tibial, ulnar, and radial fragments all show features well known in modern human skeletons. The femur shows a combination of features that is unusual for modern man. Comparison of ER 803 with ER 737, OH 28, and the Peking femora has revealed morphological and metrical similarities with these fossils. In a multivariate analysis of shaft dimensions and cortical thicknesses it has been shown to have marked similarities to an *"erectus"* group made up of Trinil I-IV, Peking I and IV, and OH 28 (Kennedy 1973).

Table 5

KNM-ER 803 Partial Skeleton

Letter	Identification	Side
a	Femoral shaft	Left
b	Tibial shaft	Left
c	Ulnar shaft	Left
d	Section of midshaft of radius	Left
e	Fragment of talus	Left
f	Base of 5th metatarsal	Left
g	Fragment of medial condyle of tibia	Left
h	Upper canine tooth	Left
i	Upper central incisor tooth	Right
j	Third metatarsal	Left
k	Intermediate phalanx of toe (? III)	?
l	Intermediate phalanx of toe (? II)	?
m	Terminal phalanx of toe (? IV or V) (specimen osteoarthritic)	?
n	Fragment of fibular shaft, lower one-third to one-half	Left
o	Fragment of fibular shaft, upper one-third to one-half	Right
p	? very short segment of radius	?
q	Proximal phalanx of great toe (shaft only)	Left
r	Proximal phalanx II or III toe (distal half only)	? Right
s	Unidentified fragment	--
t	Metacarpal base IV ?	Right

The most important bone of the remainder is:

j.   A third left metatarsal missing only its head. The shaft is intact, and the base is
a little eroded. The bone is gently curved, concave ventrally, and the shaft is
flattened from side to side in typical human metatarsal fashion. The shaft is buttressed proximally to withstand propulsive forces, and the shaft is markedly torsed
so as to bring the head into contact with the ground. It is very similar in its
general form to a modern human nonprehensile, bipedal third metatarsal.

From the examination of this partial skeleton there seems to be nothing to contradict
the original attribution of the specimen to the genus *Homo* sp. Comparison of the individual
bones with those of modern man indicates an individual of moderate stature; detailed reconstructions may disclose more information on limb proportions. The femur shows some clear
similarities to the OH 28 femur, the Trinil femora, the Peking femora, and the ER 737 femur.

KNM-ER 1500a-t (Leakey 1973*a*)

Table 6 gives the detailed list of remains recognized from this assemblage. No cranial
remains are known.

A.   A gracile upper end of a left tibia with a rounded anterior border and a laterally
compressed shaft. A prominent soleal line is present (cf. OH 35).

B.   A gracile lower end of a left femur with eroded condyles and a flat popliteal surface
(cf. Sts 34 and TM 1513).

Figure 2. A comparison of hominid femora in anterior view. *From left to right:* Peking IV, Olduvai Hominid 28, KNM-ER 803, KNM-ER 737, Peking I.

C.   A gracile lower end of a left tibia with a prominent medial malleolus bearing an oblique facet to articulate with a "dorsiflexion stop" on the comma surface of the corresponding talus (cf. OH 35).

D.   A gracile neck of a left femur. Typical australopithecine pattern; anteroposteriorly compressed neck, little or no intertrochanteric line, posteriorly placed lesser trochanter, well-buttressed neck.

E.   Small head and slender neck of a radius, rounded head with capitular depression.

F.   Small proximal end of a right ulna, olecranon process, coronoid process, and trochlear notch present.

G.   Lower end of a right fibula with part of talar facet (cf. OH 35).

Figure 3. A comparison of hominid femora in posterior view. *From left to right:* Peking IV, Olduvai Hominid 28, KNM-ER 803, KNM-ER 737, Peking I.

From the examination of this partial skeleton there seems to be nothing to contradict the original attribution of this specimen to the genus *Australopithecus* sp. (Leakey 1973a). The general size and relationship of the bones indicate an individual of gracile form, and the femoral neck is distinctive. The bones are similar in several respects to their counterparts from Olduvai and thus must provoke a serious consideration of the former attribution of some of the Olduvai postcranial bones to the genus *Homo*.

The two partial skeletons (KNM-ER 803 and KNM-ER 1500) appear to typify the two main morphological patterns of the lower limb referred to previously (Day 1973) in terms of the Lower and Middle Pleistocene. At the same time it was suggested that these patterns may tend to blur at earlier levels. Some confirmation of this suggestion has come from the recovery of a femur, KNM-ER 1472, and a lower-limb partial skeleton KNM-ER 1481a-d (Leakey 1973a,b). Although these remains are not yet fully described it seems that they come from

Table 6

KNM-ER 1500 Partial Skeleton

Letter	Identification	Side
A	Tibia; upper end	Left
B	Femur; lower end	Left
C	Tibia; lower end	Left
D	Femur; neck	Left
E	Radius, head, neck, and some shaft	Right
F	Ulna; proximal end	Right
G	Fibula; lower end	Right
H	Tibia; lower end	Right
I	Ulna; fragment of proximal shaft	Right
J	Tibia; short section of shaft	Right
K	Radius; short segment of shaft	Right
L	Humerus, supracondylar fragment	?Left
M	Metatarsal base; III	Right
N	Unidentified; short section of slender long bone shaft	?
O	Scapula; glenoid fragment	Left
P	Unidentified; short section of slender long bone shaft	?
Q	Unidentified fragment	--
R	Tibia; short segment, crushed	?
S	Unidentified fragment	--
T	Unidentified fragment	--

an early stratum of the East Rudolf deposits (probably greater than 2.6 m.y.) and that they have mixed features, a few of which recall *Australopithecus*, some *Homo erectus*, and others even *Homo sapiens*. Detailed studies of KNM-ER 1481a-d may well result in both taxonomic and functional information, since this lower-limb skeleton can be reconstructed.

Summary

The hominid postcranial bones from East Rudolf are now sufficient in number to allow a review of their taxonomic and functional characters. This review suggests that two patterns of hominid limb morphology can be distinguished, one attributable to *Australopithecus*, the other to *Homo* cf. *erectus*. Although both forms are regarded as upright bipeds, there is not yet enough evidence to determine fine differences in stance and gait between these two forms.

Appendix

I. Anatomical Evidence

    A.   1. *The anatomical restoration of fossil bone fragments shall form larger fragments or complete bones.*

                  The restoration of fragments should show an interlocking fit; there should be surface congruity both internal and external; there should be continuity of anatomical, radiological, and artifactual features across fracture lines.

2. *The articulation of related fossil bones to form parts of the limbs, trunk, or skull shall form recognizable anatomical complexes.*
   There should be congruity of joint surfaces after due allowance for the absence of nonosseous intra-articular tissues. There should be congruity of dental occlusal surfaces.

3. *The articulation of skeletal complexes shall form a single skeleton.*
   The assembly of skeletal complexes to form a complete skeleton should be by congruity of joint surfaces after due allowance for the absence of nonosseous intra-articular tissues.

B. *There shall be no duplication of midline structures or parts of midline structures or of bilateral structures that can be assigned to their correct sides.*
   Midline structures should be single, bilateral structures may be single, or double and opposite in side. In the case of phalanges, sesamoid bones, or other structures whose side may not readily be determined, there should not be more than the total complement expected for a single individual.

C. *There shall be internal consistency in the remains in terms of taxonomic allocation, identity, morphology, age, sex, size, and metrical characteristics.*
   The taxonomic allocation of the individual parts should not preclude association; the identity of the individual parts should be established; the morphology of symmetrical parts should be similar; the degree of skeletal maturity of the parts should be harmonious; the sexual characteristics of the parts should not conflict; the size of the parts should be comparable and bilaterally symmetrical; the metrical characteristics of the parts should be within normal limits.

II. Geological Evidence

A. *The circumstances of the find shall be such that the material is recovered from: (1) a restricted area of one site, or (2) one stratigraphic level.*

1. This criterion must be viewed in the light of the legal concept of the "reasonable man." It would be unwise and unworkable to attempt to lay down rules dependent upon measured distances between parts or areas containing parts. It is possible that reworking can separate fragments that clearly fit together into widely different areas. In this event the anatomical criteria must prevail.

2. The same attitude must apply to this criterion. It is possible that reworking can separate parts that clearly fit together into widely different areas. In this event the anatomical criteria must prevail.

B. *The relative dating of the find shall be consistent in its constituent parts.*
   The results of relative dating methods such as fluorine analysis, radiometric assay, nitrogen analysis, amino-acid spectrum, or other relative dating and analytical techniques should be consistent and performed on the fossils themselves. If it is not possible to demonstrate consistency for technical or other reasons, it may be sufficient that the analytical evidence does not show disparate dating of the parts.

C. *The chronometric dating of the find shall be consistent in its constituent parts.*
The results of radiocarbon analysis, uranium-thorium analysis, uranium series
dating, or other chronometric evidence should be consistent and performed on the
fossils themselves. If it is not possible to demonstrate consistency of chronometric dating by analytical methods for technical or other reasons, it may be
sufficient that the chronometric evidence does not demonstrate disparate dating
of the parts.

In applying the criteria the following guidelines should be adopted.

1. Anatomical criteria shall always take precedence over geological criteria in establishing association.
2. Anatomical criteria (A) 1, 2, and 3 must be satisfied if they are applicable.
3. Anatomical criteria (B) and (C) shall be satisfied in every case.
4. Geological criteria (A) 1 and 2 may support the anatomical criteria if all are satisfied *or* if only (B) and (C) are satisfied, (A) being inapplicable.
5. Geological criteria (B) and (C) may support the anatomical criteria if all are satisfied or if only (B) and (C) are satisfied, (A) being inapplicable.

Ideally, all the criteria should be satisfied before an assemblage can be generally
accepted as the remains of one individual, but clearly not every one will be applicable in
all circumstances. However, reference to this code should help reinforce valid claims put
forward in respect to multiple finds possibly relating to one individual.

This is paper no. 71 in the East Rudolf Research Project catalogue of publications.

References

Broom, R.; Robinson, J. T.; and Schepers, G. W. H. 1950. Sterkfontein ape-man, *Plesianthro-
pus*. *Transvaal Museum Mem.*, no. 4, pp. 1-117.

Day, M. H. 1969. Femoral fragment of a robust australopithecine from Olduvai Gorge, Tanzania. *Nature* 221:230-33.

_____. 1971. Postcranial remains of *Homo erectus* from Bed IV, Olduvai Gorge, Tanzania.
Nature 232:383-87.

_____. 1973. Locomotor features of the lower limb in hominids. In *Concepts of human
evolution*, ed. S. Zuckerman. *Symp. Zool. Soc. Lond.* 33:29-51.

Day, M. H., and Leakey, R. E. F. 1973. New evidence for the genus *Homo* from East Rudolf,
Kenya (I). *Am. J. Phys. Anthropol.* 39:341-54.

_____. 1974. New evidence of the genus *Homo* from East Rudolf, Kenya (III). *Am. J.
Phys. Anthropol.* 41:367-80.

Day, M. H., and Wood, B. A. 1968. Functional affinities of the Olduvai Hominid 8 talus.
Man 3:440-55.

Kennedy, G. E. 1973. The anatomy of the middle and lower Pleistocene hominid femora. Ph.D.
thesis, University of London.

Leakey, R. E. F. 1971. Further evidence of Lower Pleistocene hominids from East Rudolf,
North Kenya. *Nature* 231:241-45.

_____. 1972. Further evidence of Lower Pleistocene hominids from East Rudolf, North
Kenya. *Nature* 237:264-69.

_____. 1973*a*. Further evidence of Lower Pleistocene hominids from East Rudolf, North
Kenya, 1972. *Nature* 242:170-73.

Leakey, R. E. F. 1973*b*. Australopithecines and hominines: A summary on the evidence from the early Pleistocene of eastern Africa. In *Concepts of human evolution*, ed. S. Zuckerman, *Symp. Zool. Soc. Lond.* 33:53-69.

Leakey, R. E. F.; Mungai, J. M.; and Walker, A. C. 1972. New Australopithecines from East Rudolf, Kenya (II). *Am. J. Phys. Anthropol.* 36:235-52.

Leakey, R. E. F., and Walker, A. C. 1973. New Australopithecines from East Rudolf, Kenya (III). *Am. J. Phys. Anthropol.* 39:205-22.

Leakey, R. E. F. and Wood, B. A. 1973. New evidence for the genus *Homo* from East Rudolf, Kenya (II). *Am. J. Phys. Anthropol.* 39:355-68.

McHenry, H. H. 1973. Early hominid humerus from East Rudolf, Kenya. *Science* 180:739-41.

Napier, J. R. 1964. The evolution of bipedal walking in hominids. *Arch. Biol. (Liège)* 75:673-708.

Walker, A. 1973. New *Australopithecus* femora from East Rudolf, Kenya. *J. Human Evolution* 2:545-55.

Weidenreich, F. 1941. The extremity bones of *Sinanthropus pekinensis*. *Palaeontol. Sinica*, n.s., D, no. 5, pp. 1-150.

Wood, B. A. 1973. A *Homo* talus from East Rudolf, Kenya. *J. Anat.* 117:203-4.

45. AN OVERVIEW OF HOMINIDAE FROM THE OMO SUCCESSION, ETHIOPIA

F. C. Howell and Y. Coppens

The Omo succession, as represented by the several formations of the Omo Group, spans a time range from the early Pliocene well into the early Pleistocene (Howell 1975).[1] Remains of Hominidae (table 1), usually fragmentary, have been recovered from two of the several fossiliferous localities which compose the Usno Formation and from 92 localities in 9 (of 12) members of the Shungura Formation (Howell, Coppens, and de Heinzelin 1974). No hominid remains, or remains of other primates, for that matter, have yet been recovered from the Mursi Formation, which comprises the oldest fossiliferous deposits in the basin, or from the lowest member of the Shungura Formation. On the basis of conventional K-Ar age determinations (Brown and Nash, this symposium) and geomagnetic polarity measurements (Brown and Shuey, this symposium) from very intensive sampling the hominid remains range in age from 2.9 to ~1.0 m.y.

Here we present a brief overview of the available Omo hominid sample, with particular reference to questions of taxonomic affinity, diversity, and biological organization. These samples have been compared (by Howell in East and South Africa, Coppens in East Africa) with appropriate hominid samples from a number of localities elsewhere in Africa. Only the general results are reported here; we will publish the details elsewhere. Assignment to recognized hominid taxa has been attempted when feasible, admittedly a bold procedure considering the now prevalent complexities, ambiguities, and argumentations in regard to the taxonomy of early Hominidae. Some brief remarks on nomenclature are presented at the end of the chapter.

Usno Formation

Five of the eight named exposures of the Usno Formation yield vertebrate fossils. The richest localities, and the only two to afford remains of Hominidae, are exposures designated Brown Sands and White Sands (de Heinzelin and Brown 1969). These remains and rich, diverse associated vertebrate assemblages occur in Unit 12 of the Usno succession, which has been considered by Coppens (in Arambourg, Coppens, and Chavaillon 1969) on paleontological grounds as equivalent to Basal Member, members A and B of the Shungura Formation and which has now been demonstrated on comparative stratigraphic, paleontological, radiometric,

---

1. The Miocene/Pliocene boundary is here drawn at 5 m.y., and the Pliocene/Pleistocene (Tertiary/Quaternary) boundary at 1.8 m.y., following the most current biostratigraphic conclusions (and correlations) from marine micropaleontology (see Berggren 1973; also 1969, 1971, 1972; compare Funnell 1964).

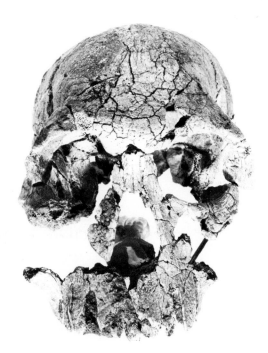

1.   *ER-1470.* Largely complete adult cranium, lacking dentition; right lateral and facial views. *Homo* sp. indet. East Rudolf, Area 131, Karari, below KBS Tuff.

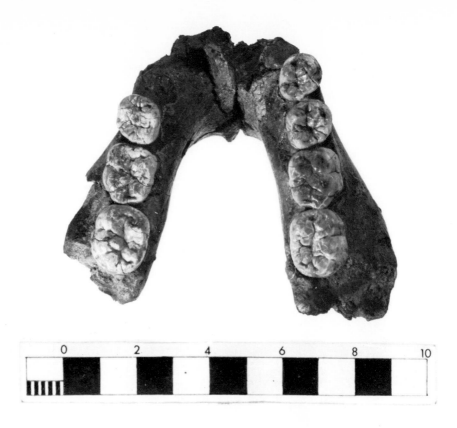

2. *ER-1802*. Mandible with partial premolar-molar dentition; superior and right lateral views. *Homo* sp. indet. East Rudolf, Area 131, Karari, below KBS Tuff.

3. *ER-1482.* Partial adult mandible; superior view.
Hominidae sp. indet. East Rudolf, Area 131, Karari, below
KBS Tuff.

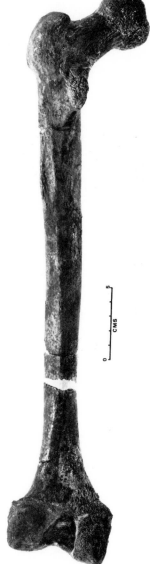

4. *ER-1481.* Complete left femur; posterior view. *Homo* sp.
indet. East Rudolf, Area 131, Karari, below KBS Tuff.

5. *ER-406*. Complete adult cranium, lacking tooth crowns. Left lateral and facial views. *Australopithecus* cf. *boisei*. East Rudolf, Area 10, Ileret, above KBS Tuff.

6.   *ER-732.* Partial right cranium; right lateral and facial views. *Australopithecus* cf. *boisei.* East Rudolf, Area 10, Ileret, above KBS Tuff.

7. *ER-729*. Adult mandible with permanent dentition; superior and right lateral views. *Australopithecus* cf. *boisei*. East Rudolf, Area 8, Ileret, above Lower Tuff.

8.   *ER-1477*. Juvenile mandible with deciduous dentition; superior view. **Australopithecus** cf. *boisei*. East Rudolf, Area 105, Koobi Fora ridge, above KBS Tuff.

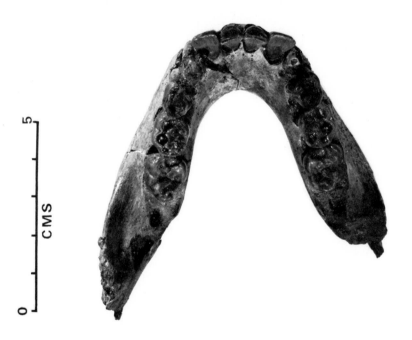

9.   *ER-820*. Juvenile mandible with deciduous molars, canines, and partial permanent dentition; superior view. Hominidae sp. indet. East Rudolf, Area 1, Ileret, above KBS Tuff and below Lower Tuff.

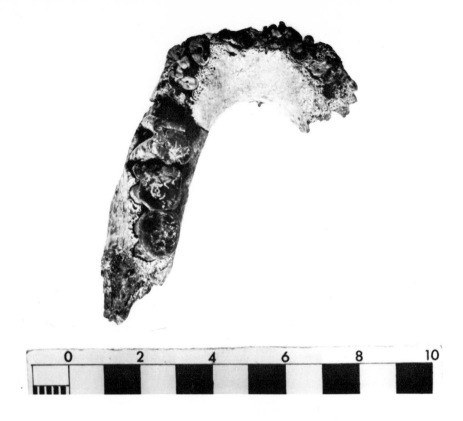

10.   *ER-730.* Incomplete adult mandible with worn dentition; superior view. *Homo* sp. indet. East Rudolf, Area 103, Koobi Fora, above KBS Tuff and below Koobi Fora Tuff.

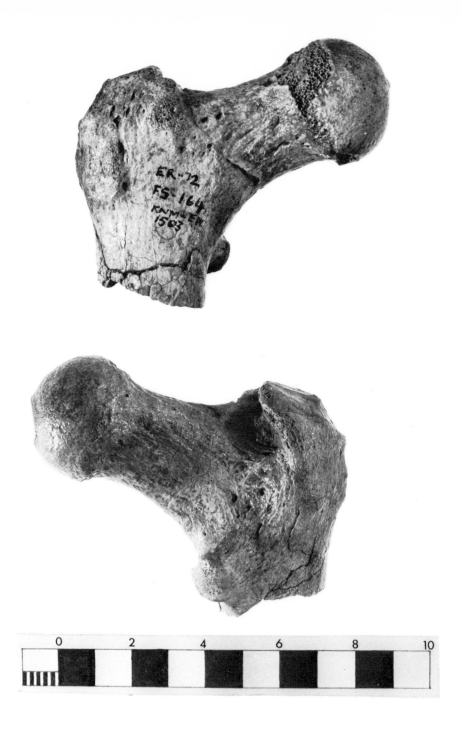

11. ER-1503. Right proximal femur; anterior and posterior views. *Australopithecus* cf. *boisei.* East Rudolf, Area 123, Koobi Fora, above KBS Tuff.

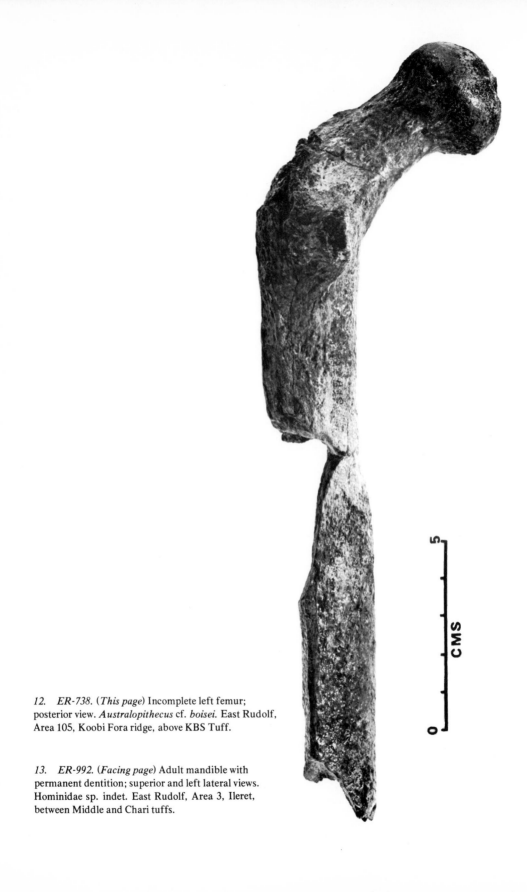

12. *ER-738.* (*This page*) Incomplete left femur; posterior view. *Australopithecus* cf. *boisei.* East Rudolf, Area 105, Koobi Fora ridge, above KBS Tuff.

13. *ER-992.* (*Facing page*) Adult mandible with permanent dentition; superior and left lateral views. Hominidae sp. indet. East Rudolf, Area 3, Ileret, between Middle and Chari tuffs.

14. *ER-739.* Adult right humerus, lacking proximal
end; anterior view. *Australopithecus* cf. *boisei.* East
Rudolf, Area 1, Ileret, just above Middle Tuff.

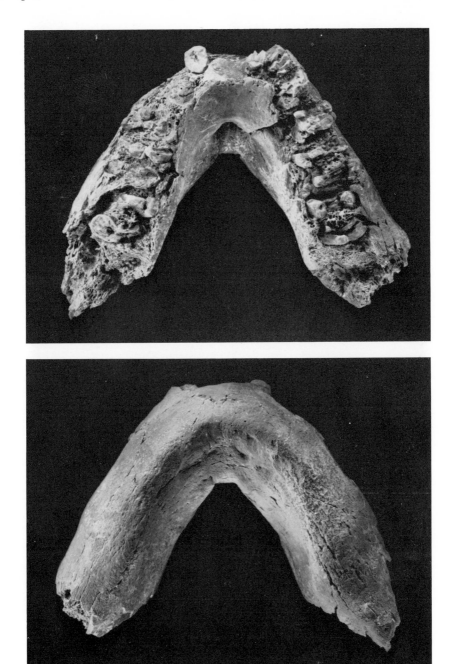

15.   *Omo 18 (1967-18).* Adult mandible, lacking tooth crowns; superior and inferior views. *Australo-pithecus* cf. *africanus.* Shungura Formation, Member C.

16. Omo 119 (1973-2718). Left proximal humerus; anterior and medial views. *Australopithecus* cf. *africanus.* Shungura Formation, Member D.

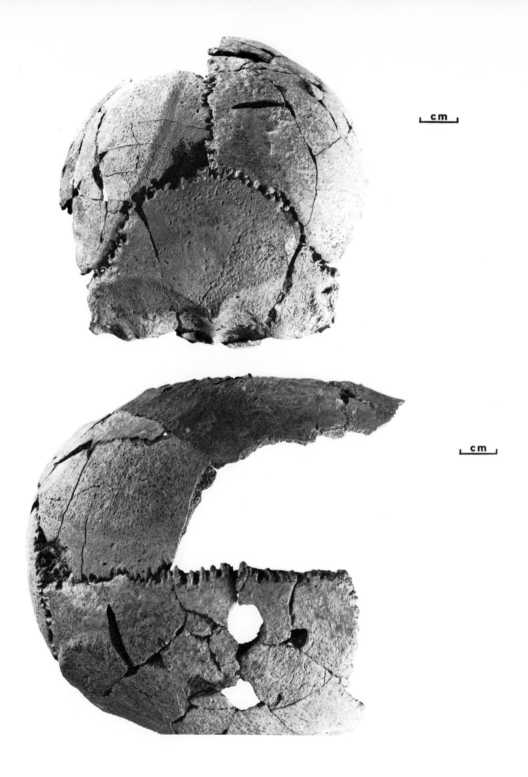

17.   *Locality 338y* (6.). Parieto-occipital portion of immature cranium, posterior and superior views. *Australopithecus* cf. *boisei.* Shungura Formation, Member E.

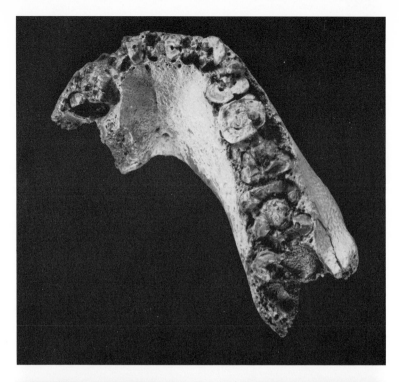

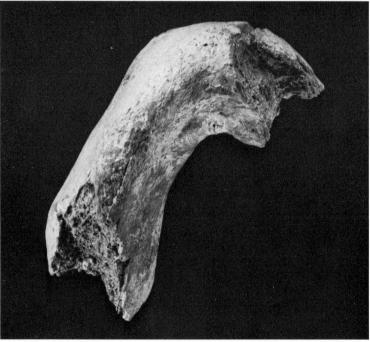

18.   *Omo 57 (1968-41)*. Partial adult mandible, largely lacking tooth crowns; superior and inferior views. *Australopithecus boisei*. Shungura Formation, Member E.

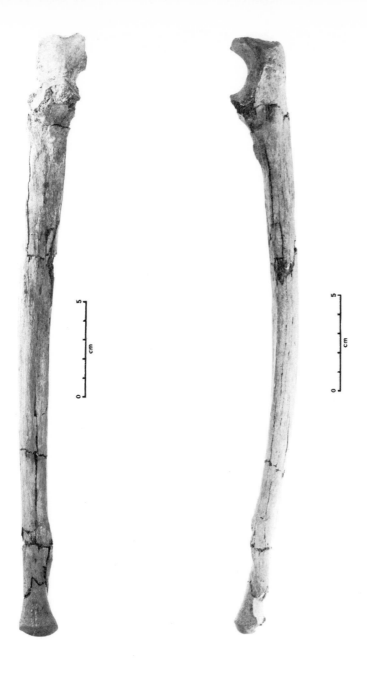

19. *Locality 40 (19).* Complete right ulna; anterior and lateral views. *Australopithecus boisei.* Shungura Formation, Member E.

cm

cm

20. *Locality 860 (2.)*. (*This page*) Eroded mandible with premolars and molar; superior and lateral views. *Australopithecus* cf. *africanus*. Shungura Formation, Member F.

21. *Locality 7A (125)*. (*Facing page*) Adult mandible with permanent dentition; superior and inferior views. *Australopithecus boisei*. Shungura Formation, Member G (lower).

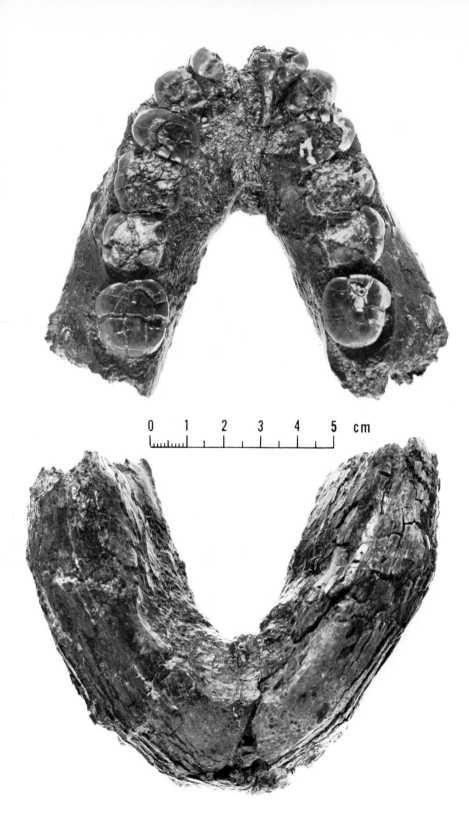

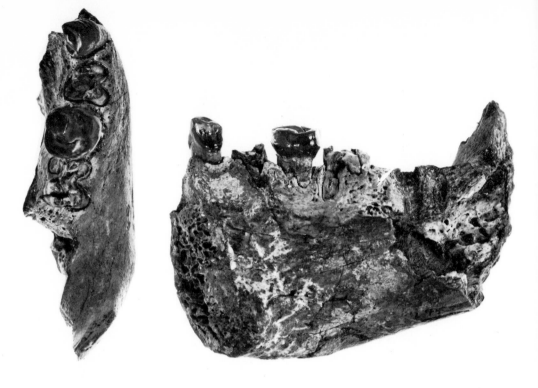

22.   *Locality 74A (21)*. Adult partial right mandible; superior and lingual views. *Australopithecus boisei.* Shungura Formation, Member G (lower).

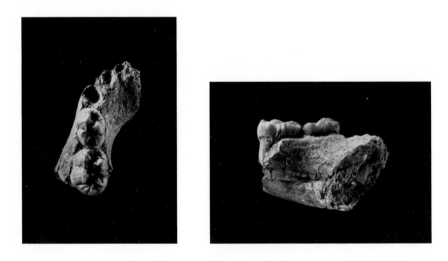

23.   *Omo 222 (1973-2744)*. Juvenile left mandible, with deciduous molars; superior and lingual views. *Australopithecus* cf. *africanus.* Shungura Formation, Member G (lower).

Table 1

Inventory by Geological Formation and Member of Skeletal Parts of Hominidae, Omo Succession

Source	Localities	Craniums	Mandibles	Teeth	Postcranials
Shungura Formation					
Mb. L	2	--	--	2	--
Mb. K	2	1i	--	1	--
Mb. H	2	--	--	1	1
Mb. G	25	1i;f	5	58	2
Mb. F	16	--	1	44	--
Mb. E	12	1i	2	16	1
Mb. D	10	--	--	12	1
Mb. C	18	f	1	39	2
Mb. B	5	--	--	13	1
Mb. A	1			1	
Usno Formation	2	--	--	21	--
Totals	94	4i;2f	9	208	8

NOTE: i = incomplete; f = fragment. Total specimens = 231.

and paleomagnetic grounds to equate with the base (Unit B-2) of Shungura Formation Member B (de Heinzelin, Haesaerts, and Howell, this symposium) and to correspond in age with the earlier part of the Kaena Event of the Gauss Normal Epoch (Shuey, Brown, and Croes 1974). These remains thus represent the oldest Hominidae recovered so far from the Omo succession.

Only elements of the dentition are represented, comprising 21 teeth, some of which were found associated. Except for an I^1 the anterior dentition is unknown. The remainder are permanent upper and lower premolars and molars and 3 second deciduous molars. On the basis of absolute size, crown proportions (shape indexes, modules), proportions between adjacent premolars or between P_4 and M_1, and crown morphology these specimens most closely resemble specimens from South African localities (Sterkfontein and Makapansgat Limeworks) referred to *Australopithecus africanus*. They are, however, unusually small. The occlusal morphologies of I^1, P^3, P^4, dm^2, M^1, and M^2 in the upper dentition and that of P_3, P_4, dm_2, and M_1 in the lower dentition reveal numerous features particularly characteristic of *A. africanus* (cf. Robinson 1956). Hence all specimens[2] from the Usno Formation are considered to represent *Australopithecus* and are attributed to *A. (Australopithecus)* aff. *africanus*.

Shungura Formation

Member B

The earliest hominid remains from the Shungura Formation have been recovered from the upper sedimentary units (B-9, B-10, B-11) of Member B, from five localities, four of which are essentially coterminous (Howell, Coppens, and de Heinzelin 1974). They correspond in age to the middle of the Gauss Normal Epoch (Brown and Shuey, this symposium). Only elements of the dentition are known, 7 lower molars and portions of an upper premolar and an upper molar.

2. It has been previously suggested (Howell 1969a,b; Howell and Coppens 1973) that 2 or all of the deciduous molars from these localities might be another taxon (with affinities to that represented by the Swartkrans sample). In fact, in size and several morphological features they are not unlike Taung and Sterkfontein homologues and hence there is scant justification for assigning them to another taxon.

Four specimens from Unit B-10 and 1 from Unit B-11 resemble Usno Formation homologues (in the case of M_1) or (in the case of M_1, M_2, and M_3) cannot be separated on the basis of size, proportions, and crown morphology from *Australopithecus africanus* samples from Sterkfontein and Makapansgat Limeworks. This is also the case for a partial upper premolar. An M_3 from Unit B-9 is on the large side and within the range of robust australopithecines (="*Paranthropus*"), as is perhaps a partial M_3 from Unit B-10. However, a series of morphological features of the crown of the former are like Sterkfontein homologues (rather than robust australopithecines) and for this reason size alone is an inadequate basis for placing either in another taxon. Previously we (Howell 1969a, Coppens 1970b) had suggested that two hominid taxa might be represented in upper Member B. This view now seems to us to be ill-founded.

Member C

Eighteen localities in this member have yielded hominid remains. Only an isolated lower molar is known from a locality in the very base (Unit C-1) of this member; 8 localities represent the middle units (largely C-4/5, with one locality in C-6); and 9 localities represent the uppermost units (largely C-9). Most of the specimens are isolated teeth (12 localities) or associated permanent teeth, and 4 deciduous molars--all together nearly 30. The largest number are from two localities in the uppermost units (C-8/9) one of which also yielded a mandible (lacking tooth crowns) and a manus phalanx. No other postcranial parts are as yet known, and cranial parts are unknown except for a parietal fragment.

Member C represents the latter half of the Gauss Normal Epoch (Brown and Shuey, this symposium) and is capped by Tuff D, the radiometric age of which is wholly consistent with the age of the base of the Matuyama Reversed Epoch (Brown and Nash, this symposium).

Fragmentary specimens are evidently largely indeterminate. The M_3 from Unit C-1 is larger (especially in breadth) than known *A. africanus* homologues and falls well within the robust australopithecine range (Swartkrans and East Rudolf samples). However, its morphology is characteristic of *A. africanus* and deviates from that of robust australopithecines. Here, as in other instances, there appears to be a notable size increase (dentally) from the Usno Formation specimens. Only 10 specimens, all teeth except for a palate fragment, are known from the middle units (C-4/6); several are fragments. However, elements of the upper dentition (I^1, palate fragment with P^4) and of the lower dentition (M_1, M_2, partial M_3) in their size, proportions, and occlusal morphology all most closely approximate the condition considered characteristic of *Australopithecus africanus*.

There is a more useful sample from localities in the upper sedimentary units. Three localities have yielded upper and lower second deciduous molars, 2 incomplete or poorly preserved (Howell and Coppens 1973). The size and proportions of 2 overlap or exceed the known ranges of South African australopithecine homologues, but in their morphology they most closely approximate the *A. africanus* condition. A finely preserved specimen is the next smallest dm_2 of early hominid known. In its size and proportions it most closely resembles Sterkfontein and Makapansgat Limeworks homologues, and its morphology is most like that of the former sample. This specimen in particular, as well as the others, is most like *A. africanus* homologues, and correspondingly diverges from robust australopithecines.

The permanent dentition is represented by nearly 20 permanent teeth from two localities, both related to Unit C-9 channels, one also having yielded a mandible lacking tooth crowns. The mandible, referred by Arambourg and Coppens (1967, 1968; also Coppens 1970b) to *Paraustralopithecus aethiopicus*, is distinguished by its low and robust body; markedly V-shaped internal mandibular contour, with basal thickening anterior to M_1; low, thick symphysis, with pronounced transverse tori, short, slightly oblique alveolar planum, and large, deep genioglossal fossa; lingual situation of digastic impressions; midheight situation of mental foramen; broad, large-rooted premolar/molar dentition, moderately large rooted canines, and very narrow incisors. Dimensions and proportions contrast with robust australopithecines and are most comparable with homologues (from Sterkfontein) of *A. africanus*.

Incisors (except for I_2) are known from both localities. I^1, especially, to a substantial extent agrees not only in size and proportions, but also in form and surficial morphology with homologues (especially Sterkfontein) of *A. africanus*. Only P^3 and M^1 and M^2 are known of the other upper teeth. P^3 is quite large and shows the surficial and occlusal morphology found in *A. africanus*. M^1 and M^2 are within or at the top of the *A. africanus* range in size and proportions, and their occlusal morphologies are also similar in most respects. I_1 is comparable in size to that taxon and shows some similarities in form and morphology. P_3, P_4, M_1, and partial M_2 are known of the lower dentition. P_3 is within the *A. africanus* range and intimately duplicates the morphology of that taxon. P_4 is below, or at the base of, the known robust australopithecine range and in its occlusal morphology and lack of enlarged talonid closely resembles *A. africanus* homologues. The known lower molars are small (M_1) to moderate (M_2) in size and in their surficial and occlusal morphology closely resemble *A. africanus* homologues. This is apparently so as well for a partial M_3 from another locality.

The manus middle phalanx (Coppens 1973) shows features (including shaft curvature and flexor insertion areas, cf. Napier 1962) recorded in the hand attributed to OH 7 (considered the type of *H. habilis*). However, this portion of any australopithecine skeleton is unknown in any South African early hominid samples and so taxonomic attributions are uncertain. This portion of the skeleton is also thus far unrepresented in the very substantial sample of hominid postcranial parts from East Rudolf.

The small anteromedial portion of right parietal reveals patent coronal and sagittal sutures. There is a faint but distinct trace of the anterior extent of the superior temporal line immediately adjacent to the sagittal suture extending at least to within 1.8 cm of the coronal suture. Hence there is some indication for some development of at least an incipient sagittal crest in a more fully adult individual.

Overall there is no fully convincing evidence for the presence of more than one hominid species in Member C. All the remains are most reasonably assigned to *Australopithecus* aff. *africanus*. However, the midsagittal morphology of a parietal might suggest, if this feature indeed has exclusive taxonomic diagnostic validity among early hominids, that this conclusion may not reveal the whole story.

Member D

Hominid remains are known from 10 localities in this extensively channeled member. Two occurrences are at the base (Unit D-1) of the member and the remainder from the uppermost unit(s) (usually D-5, several perhaps from D-4). Except for a proximal humerus all specimens are isolated teeth--a total of 10, 2 of which are deciduous.

Two (upper and lower) third molars from the basal unit have the morphological features characteristic of *A. africanus*, and, in the case of the M^3, dimensions and proportions outside the range (in width) of robust australopithecine homologues (Swartkrans sample).

Four upper and lower molars from the upper unit(s) are so worn or incomplete as to be of uncertain affinity. An M^3 is large, particularly in breadth, but appears to have several distinctively *A. africanus* features. An I^1 shows specific resemblances to the characteristic *A. africanus* condition.

There are 2 well-preserved lower deciduous molars, dm_1 and dm_2 (Howell and Coppens 1973). The dm_1 is exceptionally large, the longest such specimen known among early hominids. Its overall morphology is most like that characteristic of *A. africanus* (especially Taung and Sterkfontein samples), although there are minor differences in details (and even some resemblances to Swartkrans homologues). The dm_2 is also exceptionally large, at the top of the range of australopithecine homologues for both dimensions. This specimen has no exact parallels in morphology with australopithecine homologues, although a number of features are shared, in one way or another, with homologues from Makapansgat Limeworks and Sterkfontein and that of the Taung infant. Most important, it is very different from its homologue (L. 576) from Unit C-9 in Member C. The significance of this difference is unclear and is not stressed here, but the difference may well be significant.

The proximal humerus (Coppens, in press) has hitherto been one of the lesser known portions of the skeleton of an early hominid.[3] The Omo specimen (from Omo locality 119) is more complete and better preserved than other examples and shows several distinctively hominid features. It is not small and appears to resemble several specimens now referred to *A. africanus*.

Overall the hominid sample from Member D is such that determining taxonomic affinity is extremely difficult. Localities suitable for the recovery of more complete skeletal parts are, so far as is known, indeed difficult to come by in this member. Elements of the deciduous dentition do show some important resemblances to homologues assigned to *A. africanus*, as do several elements of the upper permanent dentition. However, additional and more complete specimens are required to substantiate these attributions and to demonstrate whether another hominid taxon may be represented.

Member E

Remains of Hominidae are known from 12 localities in this member. Four, yielding a few permanent teeth and a mandible fragment, represent the lowest sedimentary units (E-1, E-2). Two, yielding a number of teeth and a partial juvenile cranium, represent the middle unit (E-3). The remainder, yielding teeth, a partial mandible, and a complete ulna, represent the uppermost sedimentary unit(s) (E-4, or especially E-5).

Of the few specimens from low in this member, all are comparable in size, proportions, or dental morphology with *Australopithecus africanus*. This is also the case for an isolated upper molar and an isolated P_3 from two other localities of still undetermined microstratigraphic position.

Some of the few specimens from the middle unit (E-3) suggest the presence of another hominid, a robust australopithecine, *A. boisei*. Several upper and lower premolars and molars and a partial upper deciduous molar (from L. 338x) are distinctively like that taxon in size, proportions, and details of surficial and occlusal morphology.

A juvenile partial cranium, comprising the parieto-occipital region, is known from an adjacent locality (L. 338y) and the same stratigraphic level. The lambdoidal and sagittal sutures are patent and the spheno-occipital synchondrosis unfused, indicating a subadult of mid- to late adolescent age. The estimated (total) cranial capacity is 420 cc, suggesting an adult capacity approaching 440 cc, similar to that projected for the Taung individual (Holloway 1970, 1973). Certain features of the endocranial cast approach the *A. africanus* condition and diverge from that found among robust australopithecines (Howell and Holloway,

---

3. Only 2 other specimens are known--a fragment from Sterkfontein (Sts 7) (Robinson 1972), associated with a glenoid portion of scapula, representing *A. africanus*, and another (ER-1473) from East Rudolf (Area 131, Lower Member, Koobi Fora Formation) of uncertain affinity (pers. obs. of F. C. Howell and M. H. Day, pers. comm.). Most recently the most complete specimens have been recovered from the Afar (Hadar area), eastern Ethiopia.

in preparation). The superior temporal lines are strongly developed and are anteriorly convergent parallel to the sagittal suture (and hence less convergent than the MLD-1 specimen of Makapansgat Limeworks). The form and proportions of the occipital squama and planum are distinctive, however, and seemingly unlike the poorly known *A. africanus* condition (in juvenile or subadult individuals).

The largely fragmentary teeth--partial molars and premolars--from the upper units of this member are essentially unhelpful for taxonomic purposes. However, a partial mandible (from Omo 57-4 locality, Unit E-4) (Coppens 1970*b*) is very robust in body and symphysis, having a high symphysis with strong transverse tori, marked alveolar planum, and narrow intercanine distance for the incisors, a molarized P_4 and extremely large, especially broad molars (the roots of which are preserved). The overall morphological pattern is suggestive of *A. boisei*.

A complete right ulna (L. 40, Unit E-5) is exceptionally well preserved. It reveals interestingly significant divergences from the morphology of *Homo* (Howell and Wood 1974). However, this portion of the skeleton is almost unknown in early Hominidae[4] and so comparisons and morphological interpretations are difficult.

The specimen is distinguished by its substantial length; general attenuation; lack of mediolateral shaft sinuosity; substantial dorsoventral curvature and dorsoventral shaft flattening; lack of accentuated interosseous border; weakly convex ulnar head articular surface; flattened unbuttressed ulnar tuberosity; and poorly developed supinator crest. Its overall size, proportions, and morphology, when compared with other forelimb skeletal elements reasonably assignable to a robust australopithecine, suggest that attribution to *A. boisei* is appropriate.

Member E yields the first tenuous but provocative evidence of the coexistence of two early hominid taxa. Their closest affinities, on available evidence, are with *A. africanus* and *A. boisei*.

Member F

Remains of Hominidae are known from 16 localities in this member. Only 3 of these localities represent the upper sedimentary units (F-3 and/or F-3/4), whereas the remainder (13) represent the lowest units of the member (either the reworked equivalent [F'] of Tuff F, at 4 localities, or the succedent unit, F-1).

There are only 2 hominid lower premolars and an upper molar from the uppermost units of Member F. So far as wear or their in part imperfect state affords observation, all are in size, proportions, and morphology broadly within the *A. africanus* range of variation-- or, *at least*, they diverge from robust australopithecines in these respects.

There is a more substantial sample, especially a number of teeth (13 and 14 each from 2 localities, and each related to Tuff F') isolated or associated, and a mandible with partial dentition (from another locality), from situations representing the basal unit of this member.

On the basis of size, proportions, and occlusal morphology, 2 associated lower molars (from Locality F-22, Kalam area) clearly represent a robust australopithecine. There are 2 other occurrences which yield specimens suggestive of such a taxon--one with a huge,

---

4. Proximal fragments are known only from Kromdraal (KR-1517; cf. Robinson 1972) and from East Rudolf, Lower Member, Koobi Fora Formation (ER-1500, in association with other fragmented postcranial parts). Specimens considered to represent early *Homo* include a largely complete specimen from Olduvai, upper Bed II (Olduvai H-36) and the comparable part of a less well preserved specimen (ER-803), associated with some lower limb parts, from the Ileret Member, Koobi Fora Formation, East Rudolf (Day and Leakey 1974).

isolated M_2, and another with fragmentary specimens including partial P_4s of a compatible morphology.

Elements of the dentition, and a mandible with partial dentition, from at least 4 other localities are indicative of another hominid taxon, unlike a robust australopithecine. A series of upper and lower permanent teeth--upper canine, lower and upper premolars and molars--from 2 excavated localities extremely rich in derived vertebrate fossils (L. 398 and Omo locality 33)--are in terms of size, proportions, and surficial and occlusal morphology broadly similar to *A. africanus*. (However, the former locality also yields a partial M_3 with features suggestive of a robust australopithecine.) Another locality (L. 28) yields several elements of the lower dentition which are divergent from robust australopithecine homologues. A mandible[5] with partial premolar/molar dentition is unlike robust australopithecines in body and symphysial proportions and structure, and is divergent in lower dentition morphology (and size/proportions), so far as these aspects are determinable from a fairly aged individual.

Overall the available evidence for Member F suggests the presence of two hominids, one of which is still very poorly known. Most common is a hominid whose dental and mandibular structure is unlike that of a robust australopithecine and which correspondingly resembles *A. africanus* or an assumedly related form. There is scant but suggestive evidence for the presence of a second hominid taxon, whose dental morphology is robust australopithecine, that is, like *A. boisei*.

Member G

Twenty-five localities in this member have yielded remains of Hominidae. With one exception all the occurrences are in the prelacustrine and fluviatile sedimentary units (Units 1-13) making up the lower half of the member. The sediments are approximately 1.85 to 1.95 m.y. in age and encompass two pre-Olduvai normal events and an antecedent reversed interval (interpreted as that time between the Reunion Events) within the earlier part of the Matuyama Reversed Epoch (Shuey, Brown, and Croes 1974; Brown and Shuey, this symposium). The hominid-bearing localities (as well as those with other vertebrates) are very unequally distributed, however, through these initial 13 units of the member. Four hominid localities are known at the base (in G-1), with only a few teeth, and also only four at the top (units G-12, G-13), the latter yielding much of an adult individual's associated upper and lower dentition. Units G-7/8 have afforded three localities (each yielding 1 to 4 teeth). The richest occurrences are in units G-3 (2 localities), G-4 (2 localities) and, especially, G-5 (7 localities). An adult mandible with dentition is known from G-5, as is a juvenile hemimandible, and isolated teeth have been found at a number of other localities. An adolescent partial mandible (Coppens, in press), a femoral diaphysis, and several teeth are known from Unit G-4 or from G-4/5 localities. A single hominid occurrence, comprising portions of a cranium and upper premolar/molar dentition, is known from the postlacustrine sequence of Member G, in Unit G-28.

The nature of the successive occurrences and their likely affinities so far as determinable are set out briefly below. Two (at least) hominid taxa are represented in the lower units (through G-8), and sometimes in the same unit.

G-1. Of the eight permanent molars known from 3 localities (Omo 136, 76, 35), most, and seemingly all, diverge in occlusal morphology from robust australopithecines. These specimens, and others of similar morphology, size, and

---

5. This specimen reveals a number of resemblances to a recently discovered and better-preserved mandible (with premolar/molar dentition) from East Rudolf (ER-1802, Lower Member, Koobi Fora Formation) (Leakey 1974).

proportions in subsequent units are attributed to *A.* aff. *africanus*.

G-3. The most useful specimens are 9 (of 11) teeth from L. 628. Most, following size, proportions, and morphology (of P^3, P^4, P_4, M_3), represent a robust australopithecine, *A. boisei*. Two other lower molars, a partial upper molar, and two incomplete upper molars from another locality (Omo 141) seemingly diverge from that condition and *could* represent a second hominid taxon. Omo 141 also yields a proximal ulna and cranial fragment.

G-4. An immature hemimandible (from L. 427) diverges in P_3, P_4, and M_2 morphology from the robust australopithecine condition, resembles homologues from G-1 and G-13 (Omo locality 75), and hence resembles *A. africanus*. A femoral diaphysis (L. 754) is poorly preserved, shows a substantial linea aspera, and is for the moment of undetermined affinity.

G-5. Two localities (cf. Howell 1969a) have each yielded a massive adult mandible, with dentition (L. 7-A), and a hemimandible (with lower C, large-rooted and elongate P_3, and heavily molarized P_4) (L. 74-A) which are characteristically robust australopithecine in morphology and are assigned to *A.* aff. *boisei*. Isolated premolars from two other localities (L. 726, 797) resemble the same taxon. An infant hemimandible (with deciduous molars) (Omo locality 222) diverges in dental morphology from the robust australopithecine structure and correspondingly approaches the condition (cf. Robinson 1956) characteristic of *A. africanus* (as well as of *Homo*). Two other localities (Omo 29; 75i) have each yielded an isolated P_3 which diverges from that characteristic of either *A. africanus* or *A. boisei* but is elongate, with altered occlusal morphology comparable to that found in specimens (OH 7 and 13) assigned to *Homo habilis*. Lower molars from two other localities (Omo locality 75 and L. 7) are small and lack some features considered characteristic of *A. boisei*.

G-7/8. Two isolated molars from two localities and 4 at least (of 5) from a third locality are all small and lack characteristically robust australopithecine morphological features. Although the evidence is very poor a hominid taxon other than the latter seems to be represented. A single I^2 is known from a locality in G-10.

G-12. One locality has yielded a damaged single upper central hominid incisor. It appears in size and some morphological features to diverge from a robust australopithecine condition.

G-13. A single locality (Omo 75) has yielded associated, poorly preserved upper and more adequately preserved lower premolars and molars of an adult individual (Coppens 1971). The mandible body is neither robust nor deep, and the size, proportions, and surficial and crown morphology of the lower premolars and molars duplicates that of specimens from Unit G-1 (see above) and a partial mandible from Unit G-4 (see above) which are assigned to *A.* aff. *africanus*.

G-28. The postlacustrine sediments (units G-23 through G-29) reflect the renewal of rhythmic depositional conditions suggestive of delta fringe or prodeltaic situations (de Heinzelin, Haesaerts, and Howell, this symposium). They show normal remnant magnetization and represent the initial part of the Olduvai Normal Event (Shuey, Brown, and Croes 1974). Vertebrate remains other than fish are infrequent. However, unit G-28 yields some occurrences with a number of mammals, including hominid remains at one locality (L. 894). They include the fragmented basilar portion of an adult cranium and the worn upper premolar-molar dentition. The teeth are all small and in their size, proportions, and observable morphology diverge from the robust australopithecine condition. Portions of the vault, base, and facial skeleton suggest affinities with an early species of *Homo*.

Member H

One locality (Omo 74) in this member has yielded a single hominid tooth, a P_4 germ. This poorly fossiliferous locality is situated between two tuffs (H_2 and H_4), and the member represents the middle of the Olduvai Normal Event (Brown and Shuey, this symposium). This single specimen is essentially an exact duplicate, in size, proportions, and occlusal morphology, of its homologue in the mandible of OH 13. An incomplete metatarsal 3 is also known.

Member K

Another locality (F-203), in Member K-4, has yielded a single, substantially worn M_3. Its affinities are indeterminate.

A single fossiliferous occurrence (L. P-996) at the top of this member has yielded a variety of vertebrate fossils, including parts of a hominid. These sediments represent that portion of the Matuyama Reversed Epoch just before the Jaramillo Normal Event (Brown and Shuey, this symposium). A portion of the frontoparietal region and the orbitotemporal region of a cranium are known thus far. The extreme cranial vault thickness and intra-cranial morphology are reminiscent of the structure found in *Homo erectus*.

Member L

Two localities in Member L have each yielded an isolated hominid tooth--an I^2 and one lower molar. These specimens diverge from robust australopithecine structure. An unworn M_3 and I^2 at least are suggestive of *Homo* (in the former case, OH 13, in particular).

Concluding Remarks

The Usno and Shungura formations of the lower Omo basin yield a largely fragmentary fossil record of Hominidae extending, on conventional radiometric and paleomagnetic grounds, from ~3 m.y. to ~1 m.y. ago. The nature of the sedimentary sequence afforded by Omo Group formations is such that a very continuous sampling of this 2 m.y. time range is available.

A necessarily cursory overview of this hominid fossil record, as known thus far, has been offered here. Insofar as is feasible, specimens have been tentatively assigned to extinct hominid taxa on the basis of Howell's comparative study and understanding of sam-ples of early Hominidae from localities elsewhere in eastern and southern Africa. These assignments are evidently subject to revision as further comparative studies, by ourselves and others, are pursued and completed.

One of us (Howell 1975) discusses elsewhere the fossil record of African Hominidae, including recurrently vexatious questions of diversity and taxonomy of samples from the Pliocene and earlier Pleistocene time range. Somewhat similar, as well as markedly diver-gent, viewpoints prevail; we hope that ongoing and future researches and new discoveries will ultimately resolve such controversies.

We suggest that at least four hominid taxa are represented in this time range in the lower Omo basin (for elsewhere, see Howell 1975).

1. Specimens from the Usno Formation, and from Shungura Formation members B, C, D, E, F, and G (lower units), are attributed to *Australopithecus* aff. *africanus*. The oldest (notably Usno Formation) specimens are generally small and morphologically simple and may ultimately prove, with additional material, to represent a distinctive, though related, lower taxonomic category.

2. Some specimens from certain units of Shungura Formation members E, F, and G are attributed to another taxon of *Australopithecus*, a robust australopithecine, designated *A. boisei*.[6]

3. A very few localities in Shungura Formation members (upper) G and H, and perhaps L, have yielded teeth and cranial parts which are remarkably similar to those attributed (Leakey, Tobias, and Napier 1964) to *Homo habilis*. Whatever all the various component parts originally, even provisionally assigned to that taxon may prove to be, it has in our view a validity and differs (as defined elsewhere by one of us) from *A. africanus* as well as *H. erectus*.

4. Some cranial fragments from (uppermost) Member K are suggestive of *Homo erectus*

---

6. This taxon (Howell 1975) is clearly related to *A. crassidens* (Swartkrans sample), which is often considered to be conspecific with *A. robustus* (Kromdraai sample), although the latter is in fact morphologically distinctive in respect to dental as well as cranio-facial morphology.

in several diagnostic features. We hope that additional cranial parts may ultimately be recovered.

If the taxonomic attributions offered here are in essence correct, they may well have some provocative implications for the early diversification and evolution of Hominidae. *A. africanus* or an allied, diminutive hominid species is characteristic of the ~3 to 2.5 m.y. time range. This, or a larger descendent species, is persistent until ~1.9 m.y. A related, though morphologically quite distinctive species, *A.* aff. *boisei*, of unknown origin but presumably distantly related affinity, appears ~2.1 m.y. ago and persists for upward of a million years, presumably (from evidence in East Rudolf) unchanged in cranio-facial morphology. By ~1.85 m.y. another hominid taxon, *H. habilis* (of authors), is sug-gestively present. And by ~1.1 m.y. ago, *at least*, typical *Homo erectus* is present.

It is perhaps not too discouraging that these suggestions are not in conflict with a conservative evaluation of the available evidence of the earlier phases of hominid evolu-tion in Africa. Surely there is much to be found, in places now known and not a few as yet unknown, which may reveal how inadequate, and even provincial at this moment, this overview may be.

References

Arambourg, C., and Coppens, Y. 1967. Sur la découverte dans le Pléistocène inférieur de de la vallée de l'Omo (Ethiopie) d'une mandibule d'australopithécien. *C. R. Acad. Sci. (Paris)*, ser. D, 265:589-90.

———. 1968. Découverte d'un australopithécien nouveau dans les gisements de l'Omo (Ethiopie). *So. Afr. J. Sci.* 64:58-59.

Berggren, W. A. 1969. Cenozoic chronostratigraphy, planktonic foraminiferal zonation and the radiometric time-scale. *Nature* 224:1072-75.

———. 1971. Tertiary boundaries. In *Micropaleontology of oceans*, ed. B. F. Funnell and W. R. Riedel, pp. 693-809. Cambridge: At the University Press.

———. 1972. A Cenozoic time-scale: Some implications for regional geology and paleo-biogeography. *Lethaia* 5:195-215.

———. 1973. The Pliocene time scale: Calibration of planktonic foraminiferal and calcareous nannoplankton zones. *Nature* 243:391-97.

Coppens, Y. 1970*a*. Localisations dans le temps et dans l'espace des restes d'Hominidés des formations plio-pléistocène de l'Omo (Ethiopie). *C. R. Acad. Sci. (Paris)*, ser. D, 271:1968-71.

———. 1970*b*. Les restes d'Hominidés des séries inférieures et moyennes des formations Plio-Villafranchiennes de l'Omo en Ethiopie. *C. R. Acad. Sci. (Paris)*, ser. D, 271: 2286-89.

———. 1971. Les restes d'Hominidés des séries supérieures des formations Plio-Villafranchiennes de l'Omo en Ethiopie. *C. R. Acad. Sci. (Paris)*, ser. D, 272:36-39.

———. 1973. Les restes d'Hominidés des séries inférieures et moyennes des formations Plio-Villafranchiennes de l'Omo en Ethiopie (récoltes 1970, 1971 et 1972). *C. R. Acad. Sci. (Paris)*, ser. D, 276:1823-26.

Day, M. H., and Leakey, R. E. F. 1974. New evidence of the genus *Homo* from East Rudolf, Kenya (3). *Am. J. Phys. Anthropol.* 41:367-80.

Funnell, B. M. 1964. The Tertiary period. In *The Phanerozoic time scale: A symposium. Quart. J. Geol. Soc. London* 120(S):179-91.

Heinzelin, J. de, and Brown, F. H. 1969. Some early Pleistocene deposits of the lower Omo valley: The Usno Formation. *Quaternaria* 11:31-46.

Holloway, R. 1970. Australopithecine endocast (Taung specimen, 1924): A new volumetric determination. *Science* 168:966-68.

_____. 1973. Endocranial volumes of early African hominids, and the role of the brain in human mosaic evolution. *J. Human Evolution* 2:449-59.

Howell, F. C. 1969*a*. Remains of Hominidae from Pliocene/Pleistocene formations in the lower Omo basin, Ethiopia. *Nature* 223:1234-39.

_____. 1969*b*. Hominid teeth from White Sands and Brown Sands localities, lower Omo basin, Ethiopia. *Quaternaria* 11:47-64.

_____. 1975. Hominidae. In *Mammalian evolution in Africa,* ed. V. J. Maglio. Princeton: Princeton University Press.

_____. Overview of the Pliocene and earlier Pleistocene of the lower Omo basin, southern Ethiopia. In *Human origins: Louis Leakey and the East African evidence,* ed. G. Ll. Isaac and E. Mc Cown. Menlo Park, Calif.: W. A. Benjamin.

Howell, F. C., and Coppens, Y. 1973. Deciduous teeth of Hominidae from the Pliocene/ Pleistocene of the lower Omo basin, Ethiopia. *J. Human Evolution* 2:461-72.

Howell, F. C.; Coppens, Y.; and Heinzelin, J. de. 1974. Inventory of remains of Hominidae from Pliocene/Pleistocene formations of the lower Omo basin, Ethiopia (1972-1973). *Am. J. Phys. Anthropol.* 40:1-16.

Howell, F. C., and Wood, B. A. 1974. An early hominid ulna from the Omo basin, Ethiopia. *Nature* 249:174-76.

Leakey, L. S. B.; Tobias, P. V.; and Napier, J. R. 1964. A new species of the genus *Homo* from Olduvai Gorge. *Nature* 202:7-9.

Leakey, R. E. F. 1974. Further evidence of Lower Pleistocene hominids from East Rudolf, North Kenya, 1973. *Nature* 248:653-56.

Napier, J. R. 1962. Fossil hand bones from Olduvai. *Nature* 196:409-11.

Robinson, J. T. 1956. The dentition of the Australopithecinae. *Transvaal Museum, Pretoria, Mem.*, no. 9, pp. 1-179.

_____. 1972. Early hominid posture and locomotion. Chicago: University of Chicago Press.

Shuey, R. T.; Brown, F. H.; and Croes, M. K. 1974. Magnetostratigraphy of the Shungura Formation, southwestern Ethiopia: Fine structure of the lower Matuyama polarity epoch. *Earth Planet. Sci. Letters* 23:249-60.

46. ARCHEOLOGICAL EVIDENCE FROM THE
KOOBI FORA FORMATION

G. Ll. Isaac, J. W. K. Harris, and D. Crader

Archeological finds in the East Rudolf area began with Richard Leakey's portentous helicopter reconnaissance of 1967 and have continued ever since. More than 20 Plio-Pleistocene sites have been discovered, and excavation or testing has been carried out at some 10 localities. Since this work is still in progress, the report presented here is a compilation of notes rather than a balanced, comprehensive account.

Our present sample of artifact assemblages is drawn from two separate segments of the Koobi Fora Formation. The older of the two comes from within the KBS Tuff and from below it and can be provisionally termed the "KBS Industry." The younger is known from the Upper Member along the Karari Escarpment (areas 130 and 131) and from the Ileret Member. This can provisionally be called the "Karari Industry." As is explained subsequently, the KBS Industry appears to be classifiable as an early component of the Oldowan Industrial Complex (M. D. Leakey 1966, 1971). However, the Karari Industry is distinctive, and nothing quite like it has ever been reported before. It seems to include simple bifaces as a very rare ingredient, but has as its most prominent forms a varied suite of thick, heavy-duty scrapers/cores.

The KBS Industry derives from the *Mesochoerus limnetes* zone and the Ileret occurrence of the Karari Industry from the *Loxodonta africana* zone of Maglio (1972). Geophysical data has led us to date the former to the time range between 2.5 and 3 m.y., but some paleontological evidence can be construed as being more consistent with an age close to 2 m.y. The question remains to be resolved by further geophysical research, though we think the balance of evidence favors the earlier date.

A dual system of site reference is in use. Important localities are given three letter labels such as KBS (Kay Behrensmeyer site) or HAS (Hippo-artifact-site), but in addition all sites are being classified by the 1/4 x 1/4 degree squares of the Standard African Site Enumeration System (SASES), for example, FxJj1 (Nelson 1971).

Two reports dealing specifically with the archeology have so far been published: M. D. Leakey (1970) and Isaac, Leakey, and Behrensmeyer (1971). This chapter offers a preliminary summary of the results of the first three field seasons (1970-72) and attempts to portray the state of knowledge with regard to site and assemblage characteristics and their broad behavioral implications.

Table 1

A List of Archeological Occurrences (1969-72)

Guomde Formation	Area 6/4	(GFS) FwJi1
Ileret Member	Area 8	(NAS) FwJj1 + minor scatters
	Area 6	
Upper Member	Areas 130-131	FxJj11, FxJj16, FxJj17, FxJj18, FxJj19, FxJj20, plus numerous other sites
Lower Member--KBS Tuff	Area 105, 118	(KBS) FxJj1, (HAS) FxJj3, (PBS) FxJj4, (NMS) FxJj10, plus minor scatters
	Area 130	FxJj14
Lower Member--below the KBS Tuff	Area 105	(CPH) FxJj13
	Area 130	FxJj15 ?

NOTE: Excavated sites are underlined.

Sites in the Lower Member: The KBS Industry

The KBS site itself was discovered by Kay Behrensmeyer in 1969, and excavations have been conducted there each year since then. Other sites have also been discovered subsequently, generally in association with tuff-filled distributary channels (Isaac, Leakey, and Behrensmeyer 1971). Extensive stratigraphic work has been done on the surrounding area (Area 105) by Behrensmeyer and Isaac, and this leads to the possibility of rather detailed reconstruction of the paleoenvironmental setting of hominid activities. We will prepare a full account of the work, but a brief summary of the findings is presented here because of their relevance to the archeology.

The archeological sites are stratified within the top of the Lower Member, which in Area 105 consists largely of lacustrine and lake-margin sediments. The lower part of the local sequence consists largely of silty claystones deposited under stable lake waters. The shoreline was evidently some distance to the east and northeast. Then follows a sequence indicative of fluctuating conditions, with one or two regressions and transgressions shifting the shoreline backward and forward across Area 105. A ridge of broken shell appears to have been thrown up by wave action at a late stage in the sequence, and lagoon or swamp conditions were established behind it in a zone at least 1 to 1.5 km wide.

The uppermost beds of the Lower Member document the final withdrawal of lake waters, with the shoreline moving several km farther to the west. The "lagoon" filled up with fine silty sands and flood basin clays. Rivers and streams coming from the northeast established winding distributory channels across the newly emergent flats; it was at this stage that archeological traces show that tool-using hominids occupied the area. It was also at this stage that an eruption occurred somewhere in the catchment area, choking the incoming river or rivers with vitric tuff. As a consequence a series of the distributary channels have been fossilized by being filled in with sand-grade ash, while sheets of finer-grained tuff silt also occur as over-bank deposits. This is the KBS Tuff.

Figure 1 presents an idealized reconstruction of the landscape as it appears to have been during the final phases of deposition of the Lower Member. It is within an environment involving these ingredients that tool-making hominids operated.

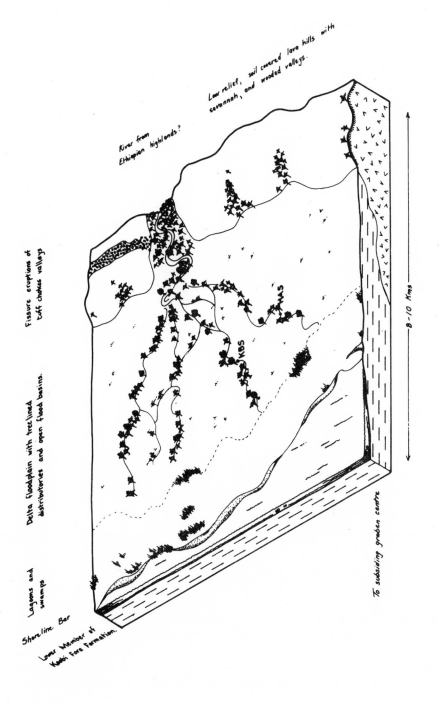

Low relief, soil covered lava hills with savannah, and wooded valleys.

River from Ethiopian highlands?

Fissure eruptions of tuff chokes valleys.

Delta floodplain with tree lined distributaries and open flood basins.

Lagoons and swamps

Shoreline Bar

Lower Member of Koobi Fora Formation.

KBS

8-10 Kms

To subsiding graben centre

Figure 1. An imaginative reconstruction of the original setting of the KBS Tuff archeological sites.

In spite of the widespread presence of artifacts, no hominid fossils have been recovered from the Lower Member in Area 105; but a rich and varied series has been recovered from Area 131, 15 km to the north, from beds that are laterally equivalent. However, in Area 131 only a very few artifacts have been found, all associated with the KBS Tuff.

Following the deposition of the KBS Tuff on the lake margin floodplains, the process of emergence was continued, either through the uplift of the area, through retreat of the lake waters, or both. Deposition ceased and the sediments of the Lower Member were subjected to erosion and weathering. Later, fluviatile sediments with contrasting lithology were laid down over the local disconformity. These deposits make up the local expression of the Upper Member of the Koobi Fora Formation. They have yielded a rich assemblage of mammal fossils and were classified by Maglio (1972) as part of the *Metridiochoerus andrewsi* zone. An important series of hominid fossils has been recovered from these beds, of which all the identifiable examples are robust australopithecines. The only possible artifacts from the fossiliferous part of Upper Member in Area 105 are a series of rare and slightly dubious abraded flakes in the gravels.

The KBS Archeological Sites (FxJj1)

The investigation of this site has involved a total of more than five months' work and has been the largest undertaking to date. Much of the work has been done under the patient day-to-day supervision of J. Barthelme. We have painstakingly uncovered what appears to be a portion of an occupation-site scatter. Excavations have yielded 139 stone artifacts, and 79 more pieces were recovered from the surface in circumstances that strongly indicate a common derivation. Associated with the artifacts is fragmentary bone material identified by John Harris as representing at least 10 taxa (table 2). The site probably has a diameter of 12 to 15 m, with the excavated area estimated at between 25 and 33% of the original area (figs. 2 and 3). Slightly more than half of the scatter had probably been destroyed by erosion before discovery. We have deliberately left portions of the site for excavation in some future research program.

Figures 2 to 4 present some of the specific features of the site. The artifacts and bone occur in beds of KBS Tuff which choked a distributary channel. They are concentrated on and just above an interface where fine-grained unbedded tuff silt (? eolian and colluvial) rests on ripple-drift bedded tuffaceous sand. The mode of occurrence (fig. 4) and the presence of leaf casts in the encasing silts bespeak extremely quiet conditions and minimal disturbance.

It appears that the tool-making hominids occupied the dry, sandy bed of a seasonally active distributary channel in which water flow had effectively ceased. Probably the spot was attractive because of a gallery of larger trees and bushes which had grown up along the watercourse, a vegetation pattern that is conspicuous today on the Omo, the Ileret, and the Turkwell deltas. The presence of impressions of leaves in the sediments encasing the archeological material lends support to this interpretation. The leaf casts have not yet been specifically identified. Inspection of the overall morphology of the best casts led Dr. J. Gillett to suggest that they were *Ficus*-like leaves. Considering the role of fig leaves in the Adam and Eve myth, this possibility is amusing in spite of being unconfirmed!

The scatter of broken-up bones at the site is not spectacular, but the density does appear significantly higher than anything that was encountered in numerous trenches dug for geological purposes into the tuff outside the area of artifact concentration. As table 2 shows, the animals represented include at least one individual each of porcupine, pig,

Table 2

Faunal Remains from KBS: A Summary of Identifications Made by J. M. Harris

Identification	Body Parts Represented and Notes
Fish	
Catfish cranial plates	
Polypterus scale	Not definitely associated with occupation
Reptilia	
Euthecodon	2 teeth not definitely associated with occupation
Crocodile	7 teeth scattered over the floor
Hystricomorpha	
Hystrix sp.	2 tooth fragments
Canidae	Part RM^1, surface, not necessarily associated
Bovidae	
Antidorcas recki	LM_1, LM_3, LP_4--all in SE extension LP^3-M^1 surface (adjacent gully)
Kobus cf. *sigmoidalis*	RP_3, LM^3, LP_4, LM_{2-3}, upper LM--scattered on the floor
Aepyceros sp. ?	RM ? above the floor
Damaliscus sp. cf. *niro*	Upper RM--SE extension
Damaliscus sp. cf. *aegelaius*	RM^1, LM_3
Cephalophini indet.	LM_3--may be above the occupation scatter
Antilopini	Upper M fragment
Alcephalophini	M fragment
Reduncini ?	Tooth fragment--probably below occupation level
Bovidae indet.	More than 30 other tooth fragments
Bovidae indet.	Distal femur, mandible fragment, axis vertical
Giraffidae	
cf. *Giraffa jumae* ?	LP^3
Giraffid indet.	Terminal phalanx
Suidae	
Mesochoerus limnetes	M fragment surface find
Metridiochoerus andrewsi	M^3 surface find
Indet.	Phalanx, 2 tooth fragments
Undetermined	Tusk, M_3, $2M_3$ fragments, phalange
	Scapular head, 3 tooth fragments--from the floor
Hippopotamidae	3 tusks/tusk fragments, 7 tooth fragments Pelvis fragment, mandible fragment Metapodial fragment

gazelle, and waterbuck. In addition, several pig and hippo tusks were present--perhaps introduced for use as tools? The circumstantial evidence of coincidence between a concentration of discarded artifacts and a patch of broken-up bone strongly suggests that this was in some sense the base of operation of flesh-eating, tool-making hominids who brought portions of carcasses back to their "den"--presumably to share them.

The artifact series at KBS consists of a fairly rare series of core tools and a much more numerous series of flakes and flake fragments. The former include some classic choppers, two discoids, a polyhedron, and a scraper on a split pebble. The debitage is morphologically varied; it includes some flakes up to 6 or 7 cm in maximum dimension and one bladelike piece. There are also numerous small flakes and chips that range down to less than 1 cm in length. The representation of pieces which are small enough to be blown away

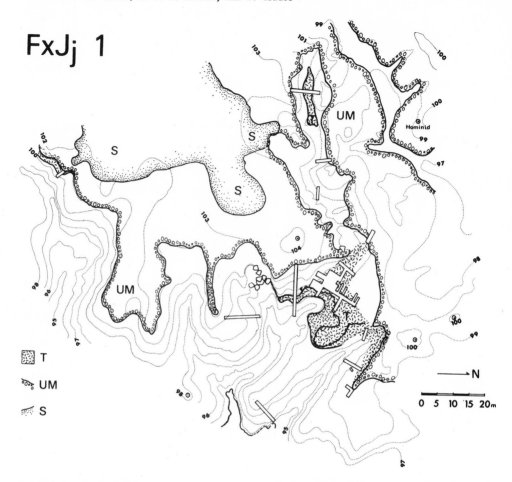

FxJj 1

Figure 2. A contoured plan of the KBS locality: (T) the KBS Tuff; (UM) the "disconformity"; (S) recent eolian sands.

by the wind if not handled with care probably indicates that at least some of the flaking was done at this spot, and that disturbance during the covering of the site by sediment has been minimal.

Tools, in the technical sense of secondarily trimmed, designed objects, are rare (5% of 139), and small flake tools such as scrapers on flakes have not been found at all. However the varied set of edges, spurs, and points seems fully adequate to the range of tasks that one might attribute to these early hominids: cutting up carcasses, trimming staves, digging sticks, and clubs, slitting skin and membranes, and so forth.

Almost all the artifacts were made from lava cobbles and pebbles which must have been carried into Area 105 from at least several km away. Further technical and comparative information on the artifacts is given by Isaac (this symposium).

The HAS Archeological Site (FxJj3).

About 1 km south of KBS a concentrated patch of bones and some artifacts were found on the eroding surface of the KBS Tuff along the course of one of the tuff-filled channels

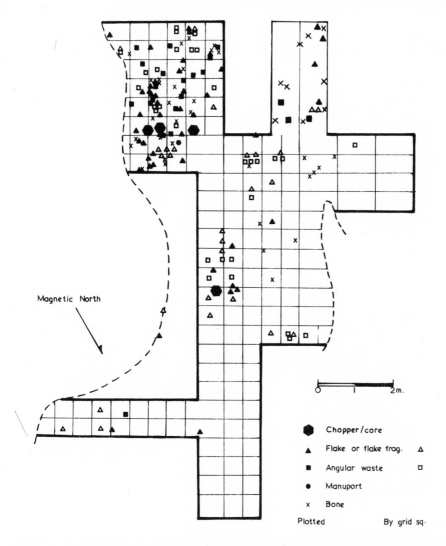

Magnetic North

0   1   2m.

● Chopper/core
▲ Flake or flake frag.   △
■ Angular waste   □
● Manuport
× Bone
Plotted   By grid sq·

Figure 3. The distribution of artifacts recovered from the main excavation at KBS.

(fig. 5). The bones represent a fair proportion of the carcass of a single hippo--an example of the distinctive lower Pleistocene East Rudolf hippo (S. Coryndon-Savage, this symposium). A test trench in 1970 revealed a weak weathering horizon at the top of the fine-
grained facies of the tuff. A few artifacts and badly weathered bones were recovered from
the small area of the paleosol then uncovered. During three months in 1971 a much larger
area was opened under the supervision of J. C. Onyango-Abuje and J. W. K. Harris. This
revealed a patch of about 120 artifacts scattered over about 15-20 m^2. Bone was also
present, especially in the corner of the cutting adjacent to the surface scatter of hippo
bones. However, the bone is very badly preserved and the preservation becomes worse away
from this northwest corner (fig. 6). The fragments of bone include definite pieces of
hippo teeth.
      In 1972 excavations of a month's duration were undertaken under the supervision of

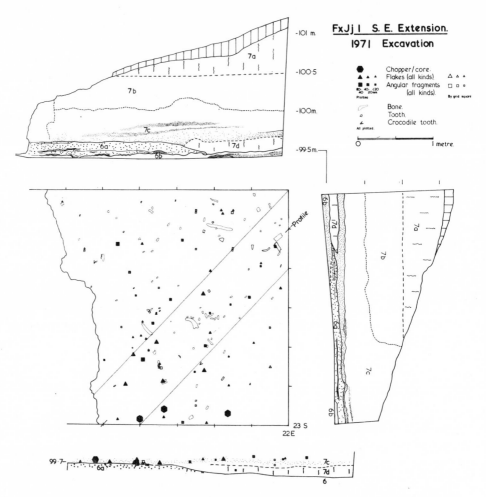

Figure 4. Detail of the plan and sections of FxJj1 SE. The profile shows the vertical relation of finds within the diagonal strip marked on the floor.

J. C. Onyango-Abuje, later assisted by D. Crader, to explore the lateral extent of the artifacts and bone-bearing horizon. An extension was undertaken at the northeast corner and at the western margin. Both these cuttings rapidly ran out of the artifact-bearing zone, thus demonstrating that the material recovered in 1971 *comes from a discrete patch of artifacts and weathered bone*, the outcrop of which is exactly contiguous to the patch of hippo bones previously exposed by erosion.

Since the old ground surface on which the artifacts rested is now known to slope in the direction of the patch of hippo bones, it seems very probable that these formerly lay in a hollow within the choked and largely silted-up channel. Artifacts were used and discarded among these hippo bones and also on the elevated bank adjacent. It seems highly probable that this site does represent an early instance of butchering, although there is no indication of whether the hominids killed the hippo.

The excavated series of artifacts consists largely of small flakes and flake fragments plus 1 polyhedron and 2 unclassifiable sundry pieces, but the surface series includes 3 or

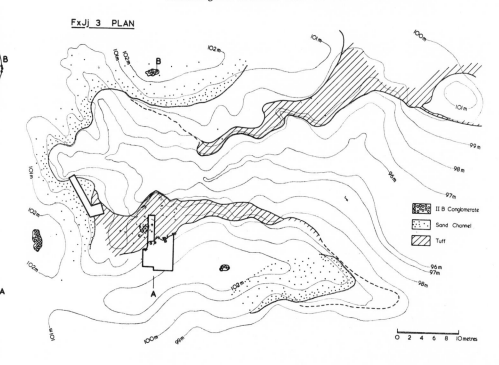

FxJj 3 PLAN

II B Conglomerate

Sand Channel

Tuff

0 2 4 6 8 10 metres

Figure 5. Contoured plan of the "Hippo-site" (HAS). Dots represent surface and outcrop finds.

4 small choppers. The assemblage is less varied than that of KBS, and there is a possibility that this is linked with a more restricted range of activities at a butchering site. The tendency of butchery site assemblages to be dominated by small, simple artifacts has been well documented (Clark and Haynes 1969). Bone remains of animals other than the hippo are present at the site in small quantities that could be fortuitous.

The NMS Archeological Site (FxJj10)

Across the valley and about 3 km to the northeast of KBS, there is a moderately extensive outcrop of the KBS Tuff. This outcrop is in the form of a dissected shelf, truncated in the west by a fault and a sand river. To the east and north, the tuff and laterally equivalent beds pass under sandstones and conglomerates of the Upper Member which are poorly exposed in this vicinity. Artifacts were found on the tuff outcrop in 1970 by a party including N. Mudoga, after whom the site complex was named (NMS). The site is in a portion of Area 118, adjoining Area 105.

During July 1972 G. Ll. Isaac and J. W. K. Harris began investigation of the site by undertaking a survey. A 1:200 map was made and 272 artifacts were pegged, numbered, and registered to the collection. Although densities are nowhere very high, it was found that a persistent scatter of material occurred on and just below the edge of the tuff outcrop. Where pieces appeared to be in situ, they were generally located at the base of a zone of calcification (caliche) which caps the tuff complex.

Three loci of greater concentration of material could be discerned within the general

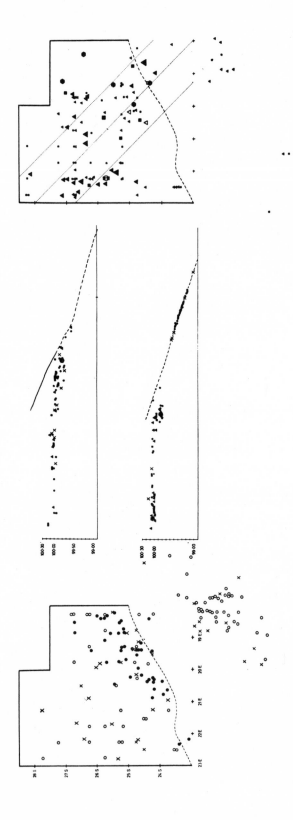

Figure 6. Plans and profiles of finds at HAS.

scatter, and at one of these a test excavation was conducted by D. Stiles and D. Crader during the week before the 105 camp closed for the year. A small step trench yielded artifacts which here proved to be scattered through a thickness of some 50 cm in weathered, redeposited tuffaceous floodplain sediments immediately under the caliche. The series includes a chopper and 4 other core tools.

More extensive excavations in 1973 under the supervision of J. Barthelme have confirmed these preliminary findings and have greatly enlarged the artifact sample. At one level within the artifact-bearing tuffaceous sands, a floor seems to be detectable. The total artifact series recovered from these excavations approaches that recovered from the trenches at both KBS and HAS together, but unfortunately hardly any bone is preserved. The study of the artifacts has not been completed and cannot be reported here, save to say they appear comparable with those of KBS, but that some flakes may show small amounts of secondary retouch.

A. K. Behrensmeyer made a preliminary study of the mode of deposition of the tuff in this vicinity, and it appears that at least three phases are represented: (1) deposition of fine laminated tuff under swampy or ponded conditions with only weak flow; (2) incision of channels into the phase 1 deposits and their subsequent infilling with poorly sorted medium-grade tuff; (3) establishment of a more vigorous channel bed down the eastern margin of the site complex. The channel deposits consist of coarse quartzose sands and lenses of pumice granule gravels which are laterally equivalent to finer-grained over-bank deposits of tuffaceous silts. These mantle deposits of phases 1 and 2 are in turn capped by the caliche. Most of the artifacts derive from tuffaceous sands that are laterally equivalent to the phase 3 channel deposits. This channel has cut into the phase 1 and 2 tuff units and there has been discussion among us on whether it may represent an episode of transport of tuffaceous material that is entirely separate from that documented by the KBS Tuff in its type area (105). Further research is needed to clarify this point.

The CPH Archeological Site (FxJj13)

In the far eastern sector of Area 105, artifacts were discovered apparently eroding out from gravelly sands approximately 8-10 m below the level of the KBS Tuff. The principal locality consists of an isolated pinnacle devoid of all sedimentary units other than beds belonging to the upper part of the Lower Member. Small channel-fill tongues of the KBS Tuff crop out in the escarpment nearby.

A low-density surface scatter of artifacts, which have the characteristic Koobi Fora Formation preservation, was noticed and a collection of 24 pieces was made. We would estimate with 99% certainty that these pieces derive from the gravelly sands below the KBS Tuff.

A small test excavation into the deposits was carried out at the foot of the cliff, and this yielded 10 small but definite artifacts.

The surface series includes a large chopper, a small chopper, and a small discoid plus flakes ranging from about 8 cm in length down to minute chips. The excavated series consists entirely of slightly rolled flaking "waste."

The material falls within the morphological range of the KBS and HAS series, and the site would be trivial were it not the oldest known artifact occurrence. As it is, the principal interest of this locality is the evidence for the movement into Area 105 of tool-making hominids as soon as delta floodplain conditions were established. Once again, hominid tool-making activities are shown to be associated with stream channels.

Sites in the Upper Member: The Karari Industry
(co-authored with J. W. K. Harris*)

These sites were discovered in 1971 by G. Ll. Isaac and R. E. F. Leakey during a brief reconnaissance of areas 130 and 131. Artifacts were found to be eroding from brown tuffaceous silty sediments now known as the "BBS complex," which forms a very distinctive horizon along the Karari escarpment.

The Upper Member of the Koobi Fora Formation in areas 130 and 131 disconformably overlies the KBS Tuff and consists of beds of coarse conglomerates containing boulders, cobbles, and coarse gravels which represent at times quite vigorous cut-and-fill fluvial sedimentation, and which interdigitate with sands and floodplain silts. In the middle of the Upper Member is the BBS complex, containing the archeological occurrences. A scatter of potassium-argon results have been obtained for this complex, among which Fitch and Miller (this symposium) favor a value of 1.57 m.y. This is a zone 8-10 m thick composed of brown tuffaceous silts in which channel deposits interdigitate with lenses of pure tuff. The complex is capped by the Karari Tuff.

From a series of paleomagnetic determinations, the beds of the Upper Member show reversed polarity. This means the beds are certainly older than 700,000 years. In all probability the Karari Tuff and the Chari Tuff are the same, and values of 1.2 to 1.3 m.y. are favored as age estimates for these tuffs (see Brock and Isaac and Fitch and Miller, this symposium).

Although the microstratigraphy is as yet incomplete, a preliminary reconstruction of the paleogeography shows a river floodplain environment with at times quite vigorous fluvial activity. Some sedimentary environments represent streams with traces of hominid activities situated on their sandy banks or on gravel bars. Other archeological sites were on the banks and the floodplains stratified in tuffaceous silty deposits of the BBS complex. These sites have bone preserved in association with stone artifacts in primary context and promise further information on hominid activities related to patterns of economic exploitation and dietary preferences.

The industry, or complex of industries, has a number of distinctive features. We recovered approximately 3,000 artifacts from exploratory trenches at five localities and plotted and collected an additional 700 from two large discrete surface occurrences. This provides us with a fair initial representation of the forms of the Karari Industry and shows an increase in the variety of forms compared with the earlier sites at Lake Rudolf.

Large cobbles and boulders of basalt from the stream beds with evidence of bold flaking were often used as cores. Consequently, one commonly finds well-struck, longish flakes with characteristic small platforms and diffuse bulbs of percussion.

The most distinctive set of tool forms present are heavy-duty core scrapers. The larger specimens have steep edges and high backs with two or three generations of flake scars flaked from flat bases to create a steep-angled planing or scraping edge. Some of these forms may well be cores as well as scrapers.

Some smaller core scraper forms have delicate scalloped edges flaked along two intersecting edges; a few with low backs resemble in appearance the limace forms of the European Middle Paleolithic.

Also present are protobifaces, choppers, polyhedrons, discoids, and light-duty flake scrapers. Another distinctive form is "spindly polyhedrons" with trihedral sections.

---

*J. W. K. Harris is now engaged in an intensive program of research on the Karari Industry and sites.

A few massive picklike forms were recovered, and on the surface were two Acheulianlike hand axes and two cleavers. Although none of these forms have yet been recovered in excavation, their derivation from the same beds is almost certain. Further evidence of this kind has been found in 1973.

A variety of raw materials were used. Basalt is the principal stone used in the manufacture of the artifacts, and cobbles and boulders found in the channel beds provided an excellent source of this raw material. Artifacts made of chert, chalcedony, and quartz also occur. Table 3 provides a tentative summary of the representation of artifact categories at the various sites hitherto tested.

An important aspect of the continuation of this work is understanding the ecological relationships that may have existed by a study of site location in relation to geographical features. Also, by analyzing the patterns of association of stone artifacts with bone debris from occupation sites, we plan to seek recurrent patterns of distinctive tool forms in association with varying economic traces.

The BBS Tuff complex is believed on good evidence to be laterally equivalent to the Lower and Middle Tuff complex, 20 km away at Ileret (see Findlater, this symposium). This is the stratigraphic zone that has yielded the greatest density of hominid fossils, including both robust *Australopithecus* specimens and *Homo* specimens (see R. E. F. Leakey, this symposium). Also, in 1973 two important hominid fossils were found in the Upper Member of Area 130 close to some of the archeological sites (specimens KNM-ER 1805 and 1806, R. E. F. Leakey 1974). The details of the interrelations between archeological and fossil evidence remain to be worked out, but the artifacts do document the presence of very strong hominids who were making a far more abundant, varied, and purposive set of implements than the hominids of KBS Tuff times.

An Archeological Site in the Ileret Member (NAS or FwJj1)
(coauthored with D. Crader)

During the 1971 season Mr. Peter Nzube discovered in Area 8 a surface concentration of artifacts which appeared to have been exposed as a result of the erosion of the Ileret Member. The site is within a local cluster of hominid find spots (see maps in Findlater, this symposium).

Excavation has confirmed that the artifacts derive from low-energy fluvial beds which lie between the "Lower Ileret Tuff" and the "Middle Ileret Tuff." A resistant sandstone capping had to be broken back before the archeological horizon could be properly exposed (fig. 7). It turned out that the material was concentrated entirely at the interface between a sandy mudstone and an overlying sand lens. Both these units form part of the infilling of a small channel, and it appears that the material was discarded on a bar or bank feature. Burial must have occurred with a minimum of transport and disturbance, since the pieces are fresh and unworked--and because we found numerous instances of split pieces which fitted back together (fig. 8).

In 1973 excavations cutting more deeply into the hillock proved that the patch of artifacts was sharply limited in this direction. The scatter and its associated thin sandy lens terminates in the axis of the small channel. We do not yet know whether this configuration is due to occupation pattern, transport mechanisms, or an erosional truncation of a larger scatter.

The evidence of the lithologies, taken together with the results of Kay Behrensmeyer's taphonomic samples, indicates a low-lying floodplain--perhaps close to the lakeshore, and

Table 3

Area 130 (1972): Archeological Sites

Finds	FxJj 11 No.	%	FxJj 16 No.	%	FxJj 17 No.	%	FxJj 18 No.	%	FxJj 20 Main No.	%	FxJj 20 East No.	%
Tools	104	16.4	183	33.2	4	5.8	112	10.6	20	5.4	8	2.5
Utilized	5	0.7	49	8.9	0	0	1	0.1	1	0.3	1	0.4
Waste	527	82.9	320	57.9	65	94.2	941	89.3	349	94.3	306	97.1
Total	636		552		69		1,054		370		315	
Tools												
Choppers		14.4		18.4		--		6.2		--		12.5
Protobifaces		2.9		5.3		--		--		--		--
Bifaces		--		--		--		--		--		--
Polyhedrons		12.5		13.1		--		2.7		5.0		--
Discoids		9.6		12.5		25.0		8.0		--		--
Spheroids		--		--		--		--		--		--
Modified battered nodule		--		--		--		1.8		--		--
Scrapers (heavy-duty)		13.5		30.5		25.0		17.0		25.0		12.5
Scrapers (light-duty)		17.3		12.6		50.0		42.9		25.0		50.0
Burins		--		--		--		--		--		12.5
Awls		--		--		--		--		--		--
Outils écaillés		--		--		--		--		--		--
Laterally trimmed flakes		--		--		--		--		--		--
Sundry tools		29.8		7.6		--		21.4		45.0		12.5
Spindly polyhedron		--		--		--		8.0%		--		--
Split cobbles with opportunistic flaking		15.4%		2.1%		--		--		--		--
Casually trimmed flaked pieces		14.4%		5.5%		--		13.4%		45.0%		12.5%
	N=104		N=183		N=4		N=112		N=20		N=8	

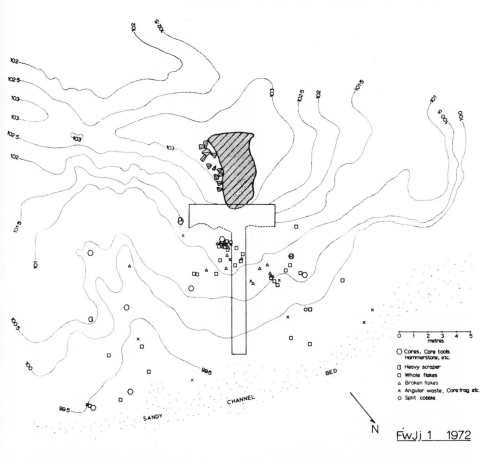

Figure 7.   Contoured plan of site FwJj1 in area 8, Ileret. The stippled and hatched pattern represents a resistant calcified sandstone outcrop period.

perhaps with trees growing along the small channels and distributaries as in the case of KBS. We anticipate that detailed reconstruction will be possible.

The silts immediately underlying the occurrence have reversed polarity (see Brock and Isaac, this symposium).

Ninety-one artifacts were recovered from the surface and 313 from the excavations (table 4). Choppers, polyhedrons, and a heavy-duty scraper are present in the surface series, but no trimmed tools were recovered from the excavations.

The flakes range from one the size of a big handax to minute chippings and broken flakes. The morphology of the flakes indicates forceful flaking from lava cobbles and boulders and is reminiscent of the morphology of the Karari flakes. The presence of a heavy-duty scraper is also consistent with the notion of relationship.

Some bone material was interspersed with the artifacts, but is very sparse and fragmentary.

A few low-density scatters of artifacts that appear to derive from the Ileret Member have been located elsewhere in Area 8 and in Area 6, but no other concentrations have yet been found.

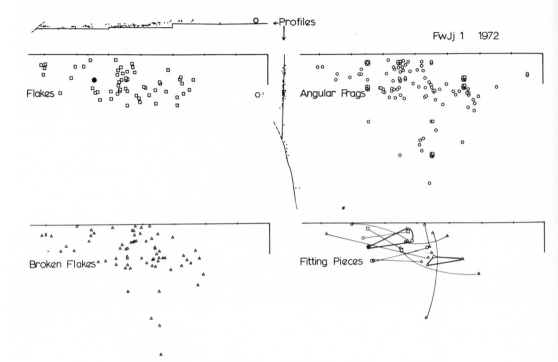

Figure 8.   The distribution of finds within the T-trench at FwJj1, Ileret.

Summary and Conclusions

The archeological findings from the KBS Tuff sites represent a very useful increment to our information on behavior in the Plio-Pleistocene time range. There are only two other sets of sites of this period for which complete assemblages and detailed contextual data have been recovered by excavation. These are the Omo sites (Chavaillon, Merrick, this symposium) and Olduvai Bed I (M. D. Leakey 1971). If the geophysical age estimate of about 2.5 m.y. that we currently favor proves correct, the sites are the oldest known occupation sites. (For discussion of this question including alternative chronologies, see various other contributions to this symposium.)

It is clear that by the time of the KBS Tuff, some hominids were already involved in behavior patterns that were of fundamental importance for the evolutionary differentiation of our species from other living primates, namely: tool manufacture and use; meat eating (and presumably hunting); and operation out of a home base. It seems highly likely that food sharing and some cooperative division of labor would also have been involved. The pattern of behavior and adaptation could have been rather similar to that so well documented for Olduvai Bed I (M. D. Leakey 1971). The archeological evidence is entirely consistent with the indications of hominid fossils from the Lower Member, which show that some hominids at this time were effective bipeds, presumably with hands free to engage in tool use and in carrying food to share. Similarly, some of the hominids had brains that were both absolutely and relatively larger than those of either apes or the Transvaal australopithecines. However, our sample is not yet adequate for us to be sure how constant brain size was as a species (lineage) character. It is possible that selection pressures

Table 4
Artifacts from FwJj1 (NAS) 1972: Ileret

	Surface	Excavated
Assemblage		
Tools	5	?1
Utilized	13	1
Debitage	91	313
Manuport ?	NC	1
Total	109	316
Tools		
Choppers	3	?1 (quartz)
Cf. polyhedron	1	
Large scraper	1	
Total	5	1
Utilized		
Hammerstone	1	1
Broken cobble	1	--
Edge-damaged chert	10	--
Edge-damaged lava	1	--
Total	13	1
Debitage		
Whole flakes	39	58
Broken flakes	23	66
Angular fragments	25	189
Core fragments	2	--
Cores	2	--
Total	91	313

Summary of fitting pieces:

2 x AF onto 1 polyhedron/core (AF = angular fragment)

2 AF onto 2 flakes

11 pairs of split flake halves

1 AF onto a split flake

1 AF onto another AF

3 of these fits involve a combination of excavated and surface pieces.

set up by establishment of the basic behaviors that have just been enumerated served to reduce variability in favor of the large end of the spectrum of brain size.

There is at present no way to ascertain whether more than one hominid species contributed to the formation of the archeological record, or whether the traces derive exclusively
from the activities of the one lineage ancestral to modern man. This question deserves
careful investigation as research proceeds.

We have no significant sites or artifact assemblages from the *Metridiochoerus andrewsi*
zone, and the next set of archeological evidence comes from the *Loxodonta* zone about 1 m.y.
later than the KBS Tuff, if the currently favored chronology is correct. The later set of
occurrences differs conspicuously in the following ways: the abundance of the later artifacts contrasts strongly with the rarity of the early material, and the later material
covers a much wider range of sizes and forms. It appears that hominid skill and purposive-
ness in tool manufacture had developed greatly during the time interval separating the industries. Perhaps the flaking of stone had become a more frequent habit. There are some
specimens that would have required far more strength to make and wield than anything yet
found in the Lower Member. In this connection it is interesting to note the existence of
contemporary hominid fossils such as ER 992, which can be compared in size and morphology
with *Homo erectus* or archaic *H. sapiens*.

A comparable increase in the abundance, typological diversity, and size range of artifacts can be seen in the change from Bed I to Middle and Upper Bed II assemblages at Olduvai (M. D. Leakey 1971, p. 269), though some of the specifics of the change differ between
the two sequences.

In continuing the archeological research at East Rudolf, we will seek to search out
earlier occurrences that may extend the record of behavior patterns back into the Pliocene.
We will also attempt to amplify our information on economic and ecological patterns in the
time range of the known occurrences.

These studies, along with the rest of paleoanthropology, represent endeavors toward an
increasingly detached and well-substantiated scientific replacement of the Adam and Eve
and other origin allegories. The replacement, like the Book of Genesis version, has relevance for our conception of the nature of human nature--and the more sites we can find
where there are tools, food refuse, and, when we are lucky, even "fig-leaf" casts preserved
in patterned associations, the more vivid and the more accurate can be our factual reconstructions of the formative phases of human evolution.

This is paper no. 73 in the East Rudolf Research Project catalogue of publications.

References

Clark, J. D., and Haynes, C. V. 1969. An elephant butchery site at Mwanganda's village,
    Karonga, Malawi, and its relevance for Palaeolithic archaeology. *World Archaeol.*
    1:390-411.

Isaac, G. Ll; Leakey, R. E. F.; and Behrensmeyer, A. K. 1971. Archaeological traces of
    early hominid activities east of Lake Rudolf, Kenya. *Science* 173:1129-34.

Leakey, M. D. 1966. A review of the Oldowan culture from Olduvai Gorge, Tanzania. *Nature*
    210:462-66.

_____. 1970. Early artefacts from the Koobi Fora area. *Nature* 226:228-30.

_____. 1971. *Olduvai Gorge*. Vol. 3. *Excavations in Beds I and II, 1960-1963.*
    Cambridge: At the University Press.

Leakey, R. E. F. 1974. Further evidence of Lower Pleistocene hominids from East Rudolf, North Kenya, 1973. *Nature* 248:653-56.

Maglio, V. J. 1972. Vertebrate faunas and chronology of hominid-bearing sediments east of Lake Rudolf, Kenya. *Nature* 239:379-85.

Nelson, C. M. 1971. Standard African site enumeration system. Bulletin No. 2 of the Panafrican Congress on Prehistory. Berkeley. Mimeographed.

G. Ll. Isaac

Artifact assemblages have been recovered by excavation at two localities, for which geophysical data suggest an age of about 2.5 m.y. The lava flakes and choppers indicate that at least some hominids at this time were competent at stone knapping, and the material is broadly comparable with the Oldowan of Olduvai Gorge. One locality seems to be a "camp," the other a hippopotamus "butchery" site.

Plio-Pleistocene Artifact Assemblages
from East Rudolf, Kenya

During the years 1969-72 excavation at two sites in East Rudolf yielded assemblages of stone artifacts that are of Late Pliocene or basal Pleistocene age. Hitherto, substantial excavated assemblages of this age have been reported only from Olduvai Gorge (M. D. Leakey 1966, 1971) and most recently from the Shungura Formation in the lower Omo Valley (Merrick et al. 1973). Our stock of information on the earliest known stages of hominid involvement with stone technology thus comes from a very limited number of localities, and each new instance has commensurately large importance. A brief account is offered here of the characteristics of the East Rudolf assemblages, which may be the oldest yet known.

The sites in question were discovered in 1969 during the course of an expedition led by R. E. F. Leakey (R. E. F. Leakey 1972), and the small sample of artifacts recovered in that year was described by Dr. Mary Leakey (M. D. Leakey 1970). Subsequently I have directed three seasons of excavations at each of the two sites, and a preliminary report on their stratigraphy and context appeared in 1971 (Isaac, Leakey, and Behrensmeyer 1971). This chapter offers an account of the main features of morphology and technology observed in the excavated assemblages. Some relevant data from the DK I assemblage from Olduvai Gorge, Bed I, is presented as a basis for preliminary comparisons. The DK I data comes partly from Mary Leakey's monograph (M. D. Leakey 1971) and partly from firsthand observations which I made on a systematic subsample of 1 in every 3 items in the DK I collections. The laboratory work was carried out with the benefit of advice from Mary Leakey.

Provenance and Dating

The assemblages reported here were recovered from two neighboring sites in Area 105 of the East Rudolf region, which are referred to either by the three-letter symbols KBS and HAS or by their SASES (Nelson 1971) registration codes--FxJj1 and FxJj3. Both sites consist of outcrops of the KBS Tuff on which A. Kay Behrensmeyer, Richard Leakey, and others found clusters of artifacts which appeared to have been eroded out of the tuff. As was previously reported, this impression has been amply confirmed by the recovery during archeological excavations of assemblages of artifacts embedded in the tuff.

The KBS Tuff forms the capping stratum of the Lower Member of the Koobi Fora Formation as defined by Bowen and Vondra (Bowen and Vondra 1973). A potassium-argon age of 2.61 ± 0.26 m.y. has been determined by Fitch and Miller (Fitch and Miller 1970) on sanidine crystals in pumice cobbles contained within the tuff. This date received partial support from paleontological evidence (Maglio 1972) and most recently has had added support from the results of a paleomagnetic study which indicates a Gauss Normal Epoch age for the tuff (Brock and Isaac 1974). Further K-Ar dating studies have produced wide scatters of apparent ages for which various geophysical explanations are being considered; however, Fitch and Miller conclude from the additional determinations that an age of about 2.5 m.y. is still the best estimate. Differences in the fauna from the Lower Member of the Koobi Fora Formation and that of the allegedly coeval members B and C of the Shungura Formation (Omo) have led to suggestions that the currently accepted time equivalences between the two neighboring formations might be in error. However, the possibility of ecological determinants for the faunal anomalies needs to be more fully assessed. Resolution of this dilemma may be helped by a program of paleomagnetic determinations which is currently in progress and which will provide a check on the potassium-argon chronology of the Shungura Formation tuffs (Brown 1972) and also aid direct correlation with the Koobi Fora Formation. Meanwhile, the date of 2.5 m.y. for the KBS Tuff, depending as it does on both potassium-argon and paleomagnetic determinations, continues to appear as a reliable estimate of the age of the deposit.

A second series of artifacts has been recovered from the upper member of the Koobi Fora Formation in the Karari and Ileret areas. These assemblages derive from beds that are well dated to between 1.6 and 1.3 m.y. (Brock and Isaac 1974). The second industry contrasts markedly with that described in this paper, and since it is still being explored and studied it will not be discussed further. In addition, excavations have been completed in 1973 at an additional site close to the age of the two reported here; however, laboratory studies are not sufficiently complete to allow the results to be included.

The Composition of the KBS
Tuff Artifact Assemblage

At an elementary level, the KBS Tuff assemblages are composed of two clearly distinguishable series of objects; first there are cobbles and chunks of stone that have been sharpened and shaped by deliberate fracture, and second there are thin, sharp-edged flakes and splinters of stone that have been generated from larger lumps of stone by percussion: these are generically termed "debitage." A third series of objects is present in most stone industries, namely flakes whose shape has been adjusted by the secondary removal of small trimming or retouch chips. So far this third series is missing from the KBS assemblage or at best is very poorly represented.

In Bed 1 at Olduvai the Oldowan Industry includes all three series, and a clearly defined typological system has been devised by Mary Leakey (M. D. Leakey 1966) to permit more detailed analysis than would be possible with the rudimentary distinctions that have just been mentioned. In spite of the virtual absence of one series from the KBS Tuff artifact samples, the characteristics of the other two series are similar enough to render Mary

Leakey's system entirely applicable and appropriate, and it has been used for the analysis presented here. Table 1 shows the actual numbers of specimens classified into each relevant category of the system; table 2 shows percentage values for the representation of the categories in the KBS Tuff samples, and in selected comparable Olduvai Bed I samples. Nonspecialist readers should note that archeologists make a technical distinction between "artifacts" and "tools." When flaked stone is under discussion, the term "artifacts" includes all objects believed to have been formed by humanly induced fracture, whether as purposive target forms or as by-products. However, the term "tool" is reserved for objects with a series of trimming scars believed to indicate designed modification for use. Most flakes and other items of debitage have sharp edges and corners which give them high potential for use in cutting, piercing, or whittling. However, in spite of widespread conviction among archeologists that raw flakes and so forth have been extensively used throughout stone age prehistory, the term "tool" in its technical sense is not applied to them, though they can be called "implements." Where "nontools" show clear signs of damage through use they are classified as utilized. Manuports are stones believed to have been introduced by man but not showing signs of modification or use damage (M. D. Leakey 1966).

Table 1

Composition of KBS and HAS Assemblages

Finds	KBS Surface	KBS Excavated	HAS Surface	HAS Excavated
Tools				
Choppers	6	2	3	--
Broken and/or irregular choppers	2	1	--	1
Polyhedrons	--	1	1	1
Discoids	--	2	--	--
Light-duty scrapers[1]	--	1	1?	--
Sundry	--	--	1	1
Total	8	7	6	3
Utilized				
Hammerstones	--	--	--	1
Utilized cobbles/pebbles	3	--	--	--
Light-duty utilized flakes, etc.	1	3	1	--
Total	4	3	1	1
Debitage				
Whole flakes	34	41	15	32
Core resharpening flakes	4	3	1	1
Broken flakes	28	85	23	81
Core fragments	1	--	1	--
Total	67	129	40	114
Total of Artifacts	79	139	47	118
Manuports	2	5	--	3
Raw Materials				
"Basalt"[2]	74	130	43	113
Other volcanics	3	8	3	5
Quartz	1	--	--	1
Chert	1	1	1	--

[1]The excavated "L.D. Scraper" from KBS is a core-tool not a flake tool.

[2]Basalt or trachy-andesite identified by R. L. Hay in M. D. Leakey (1971).

Table 2

Percentage Composition of Assemblages

	KBS (exc.)	HAS (exc.)	KBS + HAS (all)	OLDUVAI I (Selected Sites)			
				DKE	FLK Zinj	FLKN 1-2	FLKN 3
Total assemblage							
Tools	5.0	2.5		12.8	2.4	12.4	16.4
Utilized	2.1	0.8		15.6	5.4	17.7	28.6
Debitage	93.0	96.7		71.5	92.1	69.9	55.0
Number	(139)	(118)		(1,198)	(2,470)	(1,205)	(171)
Tools							
Choppers			45.8	30.4	28.3	57.8	67.8
Broken/irregular choppers			16.9	--	--	3.3	3.6
Polyhedrons			12.5	20.8	15.0	3.4	10.7
Discoids			8.3	17.5	5.0	5.4	7.1
Light-duty scrapers			8.3	13.0	30.0	8.0	--
Sundry tools			8.3	5.2	--	2.0	--
Subspheroids and spheroids			--	4.5	--	8.0	7.1
Heavy-duty scrapers			--	6.5	15.0	8.7	3.6
Burins			--	2.0	6.6	--	--
Protobifaces			--	--	--	3.4	--
Number	(7)	(3)	(24)	(154)	(60)	(149)	(28)
Debitage							
Whole flakes	31.8	28.1		28.2	11.3	21.1	29.8
Core resharpening flakes	2.3	0.9		1.8	--	0.3	--
Broken flakes	65.9	71.0		56.1	81.8	68.3	64.9
Core fragments	--	--		13.8	6.8	10.3	5.3
Number	(129)	(114)		(857)	(2,275)	(842)	(94)
Percentage of lava debitage	99.2	99.1		64.0	3.4	15.0	17.4

The KBS Tuff artifacts are almost exclusively made of lava, though there are a few quartz and chert specimens, as is shown in table 1. Further comment on raw material is made below.

Figure 1a shows the frequency distribution of size in the assemblages as expressed by measurements of the maximum dimension of each piece, without regard to category. Figure 1b provides comparative data for DK I and for two assemblages from the Shungura Formation (Merrick et al. 1973). Each of the assemblages is numerically dominated by small pieces, which are in fact flakes and flake fragments. However, in the case of KBS and DK I the presence of larger pieces skews the curve to the right, and a second mode may be indicated. The larger pieces in these two samples belong predominantly in the classes treated here as "core tools."

Tools

Tools, in the technical sense indicated above, make up only a very small part of the KBS Industry. In the two excavated samples they are 5.0 and 2.5% respectively, and in the aggregate recovered from the excavation and the surface there are only 24 "tools" out of 384 artifacts (i.e., 6.25%). These values are low, but they overlap the range observed at Olduvai Bed I (2.4%-28.3%). In order to obtain a large enough number to compute percentage composition of the subsidiary categories of tools, the surface material has to be combined

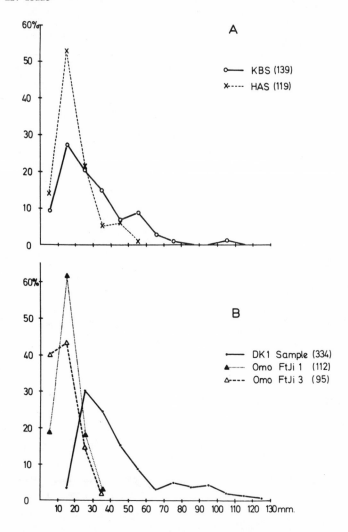

Figure 1. Frequency distribution of the maximum dimension of artifacts in excavated assemblages from the KBS Tuff, Olduvai DK I, and the Shungura Formation at Omo 13. Numbers in
parentheses indicate sample size.

with the excavated sample, and even then the total of 24 items leaves a wide margin of uncertainty in estimates of relative proportion.

The most important tools are a series of forms made on small cobbles. Following Mary
Leakey these can be divided into choppers, polyhedrons, and discoids. All the specimens
of these forms are well within the morphological range of the same categories from Olduvai
Bed I. The choppers are of normal morphology, and a sample of them was illustrated in M.
D. Leakey's (1970) preliminary report on the KBS finds. A discoid and two polyhedrons are
shown in figure 2. With regard to the categories that are not illustrated here, one of
the light-duty scrapers is a chunky little chopperlike specimen, and the "sundry tool" is
a flat, irregularly flaked piece with one burinlike facet.

All these categories can conveniently be grouped together under the old-fashioned

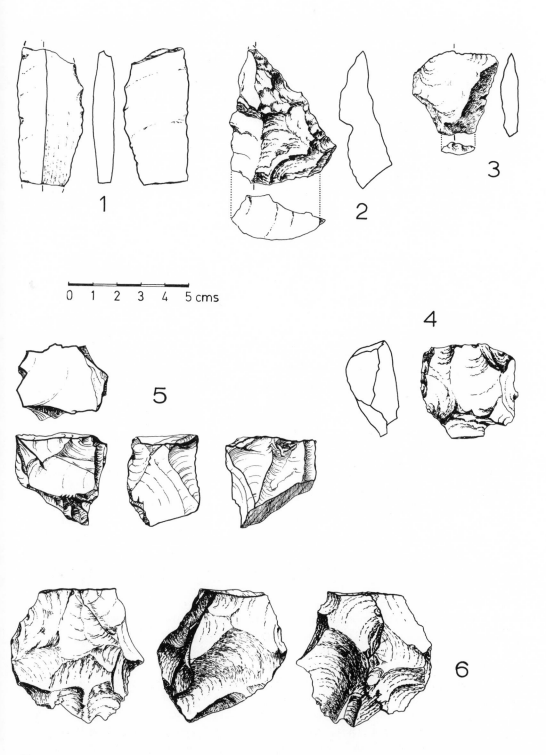

Figure 2. Selected artifacts excavated from the KBS Tuff in Area 105: 1, a bladelike flake fragment with slight utilization damage; 2 and 3, flakes; 4, discoid; 5 and 6, polyhedrons. Classic choppers have been illustrated in M. D. Leakey (1971). Number 5 is from HAS, all others from KBS.

0 1 2 3 4 5 cms

label "core tools." Table 3 lists mean values and standard deviations for these treated as an entity. Figure 3 shows frequency distributions of size as expressed by the maximum dimension and intensity of modification as expressed by the number of trimming scars.

The scraper from the surface series at HAS is a small, weathered piece of flake with what appears to be secondary retouch. Its significance is doubtful.

Table 3

Means and Standard Deviations of Artifact Attributes

	KBS[1]	HAS[1]	DK I Sample
Core Tools	N=15	N=6	N=40
Weight in g	177	43	254
SD	145	14	171
Maximum dimension	63.8	43.8	72.1
SD	16.6	17.0	21.9
B/L ratio	0.84	0.86	0.84
SD	0.11	0.06	0.08
T/B ratio	0.85	0.78	0.81
SD	0.16	0.08	0.13
Number of trimming scars	9.5	10.8	10.1
SD	4.4	2.5	3.6
Whole Flakes	N=46	N=33	N=82
Oriented length	28.2	19.3	34.9
SD	14.3	9.9	12.5
Ratio flake breadth/length	0.98	0.94	0.95
SD	0.32	0.35	0.28
Ratio thickness/breadth	0.42	0.45	0.46
SD	0.12	0.18	0.14
Number of dorsal scars	3.2	2.8	3.4
Number of platform scars	1.4	1.2	1.2

[1]Core tools include excavated and surface specimens of choppers, polyhedrons, discoids, etc. Only the in situ flakes have been included.

Utilized Pieces

Very low overall percentages in the utilized category reflect the fact that traces of utilization in the form of chipped and battered edges or bruised and crushed faces are not particularly conspicuous in the KBS Tuff assemblages. One notable exception is specimen 510 from HAS, which is a typical hammerstone—it is a lava cobble weighing 222 g. and has percussion marks at both ends. A number of cobbles from the surface of KBS appear to show battering, but the stratified specimens do not show this kind of damage. The edges of flakes and flake fragments have occasional fine nicks, but even the few pieces classified as "light-duty utilized flakes, etc." probably have much less edge damage than the corresponding category at Olduvai. The excavated choppers in general have undamaged edges.

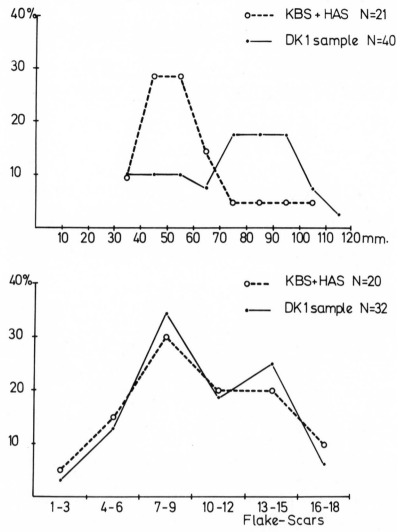

Figure 3. Frequency distributions of attributes of core tools from the KBS Tuff and Oldu-vai DK, compared: *top*, maximum dimension; *bottom*, number of flake scar facets.

Flakes and Technology

Along with the tools, the flakes in the assemblage provide clear evidence of compe-tence in stone knapping; however, in spite of the presence of a few multifaceted core-trimming flakes there is no evidence of involvement with elaborate techniques such as a "prepared-core" or "blade" technique. The frequency distribution data in figure 4a and table 3 summarize some salient aspects of morphology and technology. As can be seen, flake size has a positively skew distribution with modes between 14 mm (HAS) and 25 mm (KBS) and a variable "tail" of larger flakes which rarely reach lengths of 75-85 mm. It is not clear whether the small-size modal class represents by-products from the processes of tool manu-facture and the striking of larger flakes or whether many of the small flakes were also deliberately made for use as implements. End-struck flakes predominate over side-struck

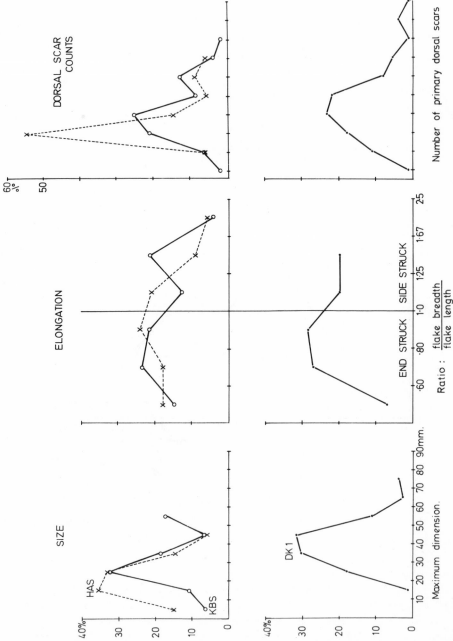

Figure 4. Frequency distribution of attributes of flakes from KBS and HAS compared with a sample from Olduvai DK I.

flakes, but figure 4 shows that, as in many early stone industries, most specimens are not markedly elongated (Isaac and Keller 1968). Scar counts and patterns are similarly of a rather generalized character (fig. 4).

Raw Materials

The incidence of raw material types is shown in table 1, and it can be seen that the great majority of artifacts were made from small basalt cobbles and pebbles, but that some other volcanic rocks such as welded tuff and nephelinite were also used. At each site one or two little flakes of quartz and chert occur. Detailed petrographic studies will be undertaken along with research into the geology of the basin margin which is currently in progress. Meanwhile, all that can be said with certainty is that conglomerates involving clasts of the size being used at the sites do not occur within the Lower Member in Area 105. It is clear that the hominids using the KBS and HAS sites were transporting stone over distances of at least 3 or 4 km and probably much farther. The absence of core pieces of sufficient size to produce the larger flakes strongly suggests that at least some of the artifacts were made elsewhere and carried to the sites.

The Behavioral Implications of the Artifacts

The assemblages from both KBS and HAS come almost entirely from a single horizon at each site and the artifacts in each case form a scatter of limited spatial extent (Isaac, Leakey, and Behrensmeyer 1971). In the case of HAS a patch of artifacts about 7 m in diameter was situated on the margin of a silted distributary channel and exactly coincides with the broken-up remains of a hippopotamus skeleton. The majority of large fossil hippo bones and some artifacts were found eroded out from the site of a depression in the center of the channel. Other artifacts and small fragments of hippo tooth enamel were recovered from the paleosol which developed on the bank. This circumstantial evidence strongly suggests that the artifacts represent implements made and discarded in connection with the butchery of a hippo carcass. We have no means of knowing whether the hominids who made the artifacts killed this animal or found it dead. It is of interest that sites at Olduvai and elsewhere, at which the carcasses of large animals have been butchered, tend, like HAS, to show a preponderance of small implements (M. D. Leakey 1966; Clark and Haynes 1970). The lack of artifact variety by comparison with the home base site of KBS may also be significant.

At KBS the artifacts occurred as a patch with an estimated diameter of some 12 to 15 m. The material accumulated on the sandy bed of a distributary channel, after the cessation of any appreciable water flow and during the initial phases of deposition of a fine-grained tuff silt. Preservation is excellent, and significant quantities of broken-up mammal bones occur among the artifacts. Preliminary identifications by Dr. John Harris indicate 4 or 5 species of antelope, 2 of pig, a giraffe, and a porcupine. Impressions of tree leaves also occur in the encasing silt. This site appears to be an early example of what is generally termed an "occupation site." Presumably the artifacts were made and discarded in the context of a fairly broad spectrum of activities including cutting up animal carcasses. In this connection the paucity of "tools" in the technical sense may be misleading. The comparatively large number of flakes, broken flakes, and splinters includes, as always, many very serviceable-looking pieces of varied sizes and shapes (see fig. 2). Very probably early stone tool use was in part opportunistic, with untrimmed flakes having quite as much adaptive importance as the more elaborate core tools.

Taken together the two sites and their contents document a highly distinctive set of behaviors which at their apparent level of intensity are distinctively hominid: namely, manufacture and use of equipment, organization of behavior around a home base, hunting, and food sharing. Given that the sites may be of the order of 700,000 years older than those of Olduvai Bed I, where these behaviors are even more clearly in evidence, it is of interest to note that the low densities of artifacts and bone refuse may imply lesser intensities for these behaviors. This remains to be tested in further work.

Relationships to Hominid Fossils

No hominid remains have been found in association with the artifacts, or indeed from the KBS Tuff outcrops. However, hominids have been recovered in Area 105 in many other areas from above the KBS Tuff, and in the adjoining areas 130 and 131 from below the KBS Tuff (R. E. F. Leakey 1973). At least two kinds of hominids are represented in both series --large-toothed, "*Zinjanthropus*"-like australopithecines, and forms assigned to the genus *Homo*. Presumably the lineage of the tool-makers themselves is represented among the fossils, but a decision regarding the involvement of either or both taxa is for the moment a matter of intuition. However, the artifacts show very clearly that by 2 to 2.5 m.y. ago, at least one species of hominid was extensively involved in tool-making and had material equipment as a part of its pattern of adaptation.

Comparisons with other Early Assemblages
from East Africa

As was already indicated, the artifact collections from Olduvai Gorge Bed I are the largest and best-studied samples of comparable age, and they have consequently been used as an explicit and implicit standard of reference in reporting the KBS material. The comparison can now be summed up as follows:
1. The morphological and technological characteristics of all specimens recovered from the two KBS Tuff sites can be matched in the much larger collections from Olduvai. However, there are some forms present at Olduvai that are not definitely known from the KBS sites. Most notable among these are "flake scrapers," which are represented at KBS only by a doubtful specimen from the surface. Subspheroids are also lacking.
2. The modal sizes of both tools and debitage in the East Rudolf assemblages are smaller than those of Olduvai. But the difference between the two KBS Tuff samples is as great as the difference between KBS and DK. The possible influence of available raw material on this cannot be assessed.

At the same time that the excavations were carried out in the East Rudolf area other early artifact assemblages were recovered from the north end of Lake Rudolf in the Shungura Formation. I have been privileged to see parts of the unpublished material obtained by J. Chavaillon, and also some of H. V. Merrick's material on which a brief report has been published (Merrick et al. 1973). The main artifact occurrences are in Member F, with an estimated age of 2 m.y., though as explained above, it is possible that this date may need to be revised to a somewhat earlier one.

The Shungura artifacts so far recovered consist almost entirely of small flakes and fragments of "smashed" quartz. For comparison the frequency distribution of artifact size in Merrick's assemblages is shown in figure 1. It seems very probable that the small size and technical simplicity of this material was determined in large measure by the remoteness of larger rock particles. Perhaps the known assemblages from the Shungura area represent very incomplete samples of the total artifact repertoire which may only be represented in areas where the territorial range of the hominids gave them access to larger stones. Presumably the hominids who smashed the little quartz pebbles made effective opportunistic use of the sharp edges and angles generated, but detailed morphological comparison of these with the KBS Tuff artifacts would have no meaning.

Conclusion

We are not yet in a position to choose decisively between various possible models of process in the early stages of the development of hominid stone technology. It was formerly customary to think in terms of sequences showing inexorable progressive change. Subsequently Mary Leakey's Olduvai data and other results from elsewhere have indicated the possibility that over long periods there was fluctuation but little systematic change in technology (M. D. Leakey 1966; Isaac 1972). It is possible that thresholds of innovation may separate static blocks of technological conservatism. If, as seems likely, the 2.5 m.y. age of the KBS Tuff continues to be confirmed, then the assemblages reported here represent a great backward extension of the known record of hominid involvement with tools and equipment. However, the material is not radically different or much more primitive than the 1.9 m.y. old Olduvai Gorge material. The artifacts hitherto recovered show competence at stoneworking but a certain simplicity in their lack of clear-cut designs. They could be seen as being grouped with the Olduvai Bed I industries as representatives of generalized craft practices which had crossed a threshold formed by the discovery of conchoidal fracture, but which had not yet incorporated the more specific design elements which characterize industries after 1.5 m.y. ago: namely the Acheulian and the Developed Oldowan (M. D. Leakey 1966).

Further fieldwork in earlier time ranges will be needed to test the value of the concept of a threshold at the outset of hominid stone craft. At present there is no way of judging from the oldest known artifacts how long a time had elapsed between their manufacture and the striking of the first flakes or the preparation of the first chopper.

The similarity of the KBS Tuff assemblage with the classic Oldowan of Olduvai Bed I seems strong enough to justify incorporating the East Rudolf assemblages as the *KBS Industry* within the *Oldowan Industrial Complex* (Bishop and Clark 1967, esp. p. 893). More detailed reports on the sites, the food refuse, and the artifacts are in preparation for publication elsewhere.

Acknowledgments

This work was done with the help of Richard Leakey and many other members of the East Rudolf Research Group. Co-workers and assistants in the field and laboratory have included J. Barthelme, N. A. Mudoga, J. W. K. Harris, John Onyango-Abuje, D. Stiles, J. Karoma, and D. Crader. Barbara Isaac drew the artifacts and diagrams. The work was done with the encouragment of the Museum's trustees and the government of Kenya. Financial support was received from the Wenner-Gren Foundation; the National Science Foundation of Washington; and the Miller Institute, University of California, Berkeley. H. V. Merrick read and commented on a draft of the paper.

This is paper no. 72 in the East Rudolf Research Project catalogue of publications.

References

Bishop, W. W., and Clark, J. D., eds. 1967. *Background to evolution in Africa.* Chicago: University of Chicago Press.

Bowen, V. E., and Vondra, C. F. 1973. Stratigraphical relationships of the Plio-Pleistocene deposits, East Rudolf, Kenya. *Nature* 242:391-93.

Brock, A., and Isaac, G. Ll. 1974. Paleomagnetic stratigraphy and chronology of hominid-bearing sediments east of Lake Rudolf, Kenya. *Nature* 247:344-48.

Brown, F. H. 1972. Radiometric dating of sedimentary formations in the lower Omo valley, Ethiopia. In *Calibration of hominoid evolution,* ed. W. W. Bishop and J. A. Miller, pp. 273-87. Edinburgh: Scottish Academic Press; Toronto: University of Toronto Press.

Clark, J. D., and Haynes, C. V., Jr. 1970. An elephant butchery site at Mwanganda's village, Karonga, Malawi, and its relevance for Palaeolithic archaeology. *World Archaeol.* 1:390-411.

Fitch, F. J., and Miller, J. A. 1970. Radioisotopic age determinations of Lake Rudolf arte-fact site. *Nature* 226:226-28.

Isaac, G. Ll. 1972. Chronology and the tempo of cultural change during the Pleistocene. In *Calibration of hominoid evolution,* ed. W. W. Bishop and J. A. Miller, pp. 381-430. Edinburgh: Scottish Academic Press; Toronto: University of Toronto Press.

Isaac, G. Ll., and Keller, C. M. 1968. Note on the proportional frequency of side- and end-struck flakes. *So. African Archaeol. Bull.* 23:17-19.

Isaac, G. Ll., Leakey, R. E. F., and Behrensmeyer, A. K. 1971. Archaeological traces of early hominid activities east of Lake Rudolf, Kenya. *Science* 173:1129-34.

Leakey, M. D. 1966. A review of the Oldowan culture from Olduvai Gorge, Tanzania. *Nature* 210:462-66.

————. 1970. Early artifacts from the Koobi Fora area. *Nature* 226:228-30.

————. 1971. *Olduvai Gorge.* Vol. 3. *Excavations in Beds I and II, 1960-1963.* Cambridge: At the University Press.

Leakey, R. E. F. 1972. New fossil evidence for the evolution of man from Kenya. *Social Biol.* 19:99-114.

————. 1973. Evidence for an advanced Plio-Pleistocene hominid from East Rudolf, Kenya. *Nature* 242:447-50.

Maglio, V. J. 1972. Vertebrate faunas and chronology of hominid-bearing sediments east of Lake Rudolf, Kenya. *Nature* 239:379-85.

Merrick, H. V.; Heinzelin, J. de; Haesaerts, P.; and Howell, F. C. 1973. Archaeological occurrences of early Pleistocene age from the Shungura Formation, lower Omo valley, Ethiopia. *Nature* 242:572-75.

Nelson, C. M. 1971. A standardized site enumeration system for the continent of Africa. Commission on Nomenclature and Terminology, bulletin 4. Department of Anthropology, University of California, Berkeley (mimeographed).

48. EVIDENCE FOR THE TECHNICAL PRACTICES OF EARLY PLEISTOCENE HOMINIDS
SHUNGURA FORMATION, LOWER OMO VALLEY, ETHIOPIA

J. Chavaillon

Since 1967, the members of the international expedition to the Omo have been fortunate
enough to find hominid remains in the Plio-Pleistocene formations of the lower valley of
the Omo. However, although it seemed certain that there had indeed been ancient inhabi-
tants, there was still no evidence for the tool kit which it was suspected they were using.
It was only in 1969 that the first elements of a stone and bone tool kit came to light as
a result of the discovery of the site of Omo 71, and its excavation in 1970. Since then,
the excavations carried out by me, and at other sites by H. V. Merrick, have uncovered an
industry made on flakes, together with numerous angular artifacts. This chapter offers a
brief account of the results of my 1972 and 1973 excavations. However, I will first give
a brief resume of the results from the site of Omo 71 so as to provide a better understanding of the whole picture.

Omo 71: Side Chopper and Bone Industry

The archeological horizon is found several dm above Tuff E. It is associated with a
fine gravel: small pellets of limonitic clay and coarse sand. The excavation was made
particularly difficult by the thickness of the overburden it was necessary to remove. Because of this, only 25 m^2 were excavated, of which only 9 were fossiliferous.

The thickness of the layer was irregular and varied from a few centimeters to a maximum of 15 cm. The accumulation of gravel seems to have been controlled in this section by
features of an ancient topography and probably was deposited below lake waters and along a
shoreline. Excavation uncovered a surface which appeared to be marked with weak parallel
undulations, each showing a steep side backed by a gentle slope.

Below the outcrop of this level and less than a meter away, I discovered a pebble tool
of quartz. It proved to be a bifacial side chopper (*chopper latéral biface*). The sinuous
cutting edge is well battered and heavily encrusted with ferruginous concretions like other
pebbles which have their provenance in this tuff (Bonnefille et al. 1970; Chavaillon 1970).
Excavations undertaken in 1969 and 1970 gave little further evidence (Chavaillon 1971).
There were quartz pebbles broken transversely which were sometimes marked by small flakes
on the sharp edge of the fracture. There were also quartz pebbles which simply showed
signs of percussion, marks made by battering, and small flake scars. The bone objects were
more interesting: three fragments had been either utilized or worked. One had been broken
while still fresh, with one of the fractures forming a bevel. Small scratches and chips on

this cutting edge suggested that it had been used. Another piece was a flat fragment of bone; one of its faces appears to have been thinned by a series of flake removals; on one margin a series of small scars form a steep edge, and some very small scaling could be interpreted as traces of utilization. This piece could have been a scraper. Finally a fragment of basicranium from a silurid might have been a serviceable artifact; one end is broken, but it cannot be said that it was intentional. However, the proximal end, also broken, reveals a scar, elongated, flat, and narrow, where a flake was detached from the bevel, thus making it more pointed. On each side of this narrow extremity traces of battering and small flaking scars can be seen. If this bone were used, it could have functioned as a perforator or as a dagger.

Since these finds, the antiquity of the hominids' tool kit has been demonstrated from excavation by H. V. Merrick (Merrick et al. 1973) and by G. Isaac and R. Leakey at the East Rudolf sites (Isaac, Leakey, and Behrensmeyer 1971). Added to the results of these researches are the data from the sites of Omo 57 and Omo 123. The report in the following pages completes our present understanding of the very early prehistory of this region (Coppens, Chavaillon, and Beden 1973).

The Deposits at Omo 57 and Omo 123

The artifact samples were recovered from sedimentary strata that span only a very restricted time range even though the localities are spaced out over several kilometers.

At Omo 57, the artifacts come from two neighboring localities forming part of the gravel layers with silty clay pellets and coarse sands. Silt layers separate the gravel levels. The density of artifacts in situ is about 2 per m^2. Thirty artifacts were recovered.

At Omo 123 a clayey stratum encloses the artifacts, and the thickness of the artifact-bearing units ranges up to 25 or 30 cm. The density is clearly higher than at Omo 57: about 25 pieces per m^2 at Locality J, and as many as 120 at Locality K.

Both of these archeological occurrences belong in the lower sedimentary units of Member F.

Some 223 artifacts were recovered from Omo 57 in 1972, among which 30 came from trenches at two different spots. Surface prospecting at Omo 123 in 1972, and especially in 1973, yielded 1,014 specimens, and almost 900 artifacts were recovered in situ from two cuttings J and K, of which the latter was the most prolific. At Omo 57, if both in situ and surface pieces are counted, the areas of excavation at localities 5 and 7 provide 57% of the objects from this site. Farther away, localities 1 and 2 provide only 9% of the assemblage. At Omo 123, the excavation at Locality J produced only 5% of the total assemblage of artifacts, while localities A, B, H, and M, which are effectively along the same east-west line and very close to each other, yielded 25%. Locality K, elsewhere on the site, proved very rich in stratified and surface material and furnished about 50% of the assemblage. It is clear that there are concentrations in particular parts of the site.

If the two sites are compared, several common traits are noticeable. First, they belong effectively within the same geological strata and the same time period, even though Omo 123 may be very slightly more recent than Omo 57. At both sites the principal raw material is quartz, with rare examples of other rocks such as quartzite, jasper, and chalcedony. These are found more frequently at Omo 57 than at 123. It is interesting to compare the percentage of pieces recovered in excavation with those from surface collections (table 1).

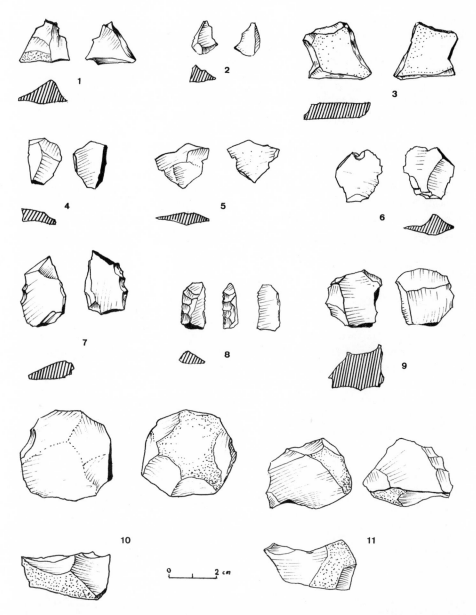

Figure 1. Artifacts from Omo 57 and Omo 123 localities: *1, 2, 3* = Omo 123J, quartz fragments, in situ; *4* = Omo 57-7, broken quartz flake, in situ; *5* = Omo 57-7, quartz flake, in situ; *6* = Omo 123C, quartz flake, surface; *7* = Omo 57-7, utilized quartz flake, in situ; *8* = Omo 57-7, retouched and utilized jasper flake, in situ; *9* = Omo 123C, quartz polyhedral core, surface; *10* = Omo 57-4, quartz discoidal core, surface; *11* = Omo 57-2, quartz polyhedral core, surface.

Table 1

Frequency Distribution of Artifacts by Type (%)

| Artifact Category | OMO 57 | | OMO 123 | |
	Surface 193	Excavation 30	Surface 1014	Excavation 767
Fragment	65.03	70.00	56.31	56.45
Fragment of core	6.14	6.66	6.90	2.35
Core	3.68	0.00	2.37	1.56
Flake	25.15	23.34	34.12	38.86
Piece	9.81	6.66	0.30	0.26

There is an obvious statistical resemblance between surface finds and in situ pieces. It should be noted, for example, that there is a much higher proportion of fragments in the excavated assemblage at Omo 57. This is because in excavation all the artifacts are collected, even the smallest of fragments, whereas on the surface the latter are often hidden in the cracks of the dry clay and consolidated sand. They are also more easily washed away by running water.

Study of the Debitage

Fragments. These are the most numerous artifacts: 56% at Omo 123 and 66% at Omo 57. Except for a few fragments of quartzite, quartz is the only raw material utilized at Omo 123. Size varies from a few mm to 40 mm. For the frequency distribution presented in table 2, the categories of angular fragments and core fragments have been combined. The modal size is 20-30 mm at Omo 57 (surface) and 5-10 mm at Omo 123K (excavation). Collections from the excavations are richer in small fragments than those made on the surface, despite meticulous care. This is particularly evident with Omo 123.

Table 2

Frequency Distribution of Artifacts by Size (%)

Artifact Category and Location	Less than 5 mm	5-10 mm	10-20 mm	20-30 mm	30-40 mm	40-50 mm	50-60 mm
Angular fragments and core fragments							
Omo 57, surface and excavation	--	3.14	33.08	50.40	12.60	0.78	--
Omo 123, surface	--	6.86	58.97	28.08	5.62	0.47	--
Omo 123, excavation K	3.33	51.66	37.25	6.43	1.11	0.22	--
Cores							
Omo 123, surface	--	--	4.17	50.00	37.49	4.17	4.17
Omo 123, excavation K	--	--	25.00	66.67	8.33	--	--
Flakes							
Omo 123, total surface	--	--	23.76	55.25	17.68	2.76	0.55
Omo 123, surface K	--	--	39.13	56.52	4.35	--	--
Omo 123, excavation K	--	8.43	60.24	27.72	3.61	--	--

The fragments are flat, polyhedric, pyramidal, or occasionally elongated. The fractures are steep or vertical, sharp, and angular. Geometrical forms are predominant: most often they are irregular, triangular or with a quadrilateral outline. Some fragments retain a vestige of cortex from the pebble, either on one face or along the edge. The cross section is either a polygon, a quadrilateral, or a triangle. These fragments derive either from deliberate flaking or from violent smashing of quartz pebbles by percussion.

Cores. These are not numerous. The term core is used for each globular piece showing multiple flake scars. There are 36 at Omo 123, of which 12 were found in situ--about 2% of the total assemblage. More than half the total is made up by the pieces in the 20-30 mm class. Note that cores are the largest class of artifacts. The majority are quartz, but there are very occasional specimens of chalcedony and jasper.

Two types of cores are recognizable: (a) Discoidal cores (fig. 1:10) are characterized by bifacial centripetal flake scars which are shallow and fairly large. (b) Polyhedric cores are the most numerous. Some of them are hemispherical with a plain striking platform and one principal flake release. These are rare; it is more common for the cores to be varied examples of cubic (fig. 1:9), pyramidal, or pentagonal forms. They are often small cuboid pieces rather like sugar lumps. The flake scars are not particularly clearly marked because quartz does not lend itself easily to regular flaking. Small, with perpendicular facets, these cores are exhausted; they are waste, with no further use.

It should be noted that several cores retain traces of cortex; one is a quartz pebble which has a fairly large flake release scar. The remainder, including one chalcedony and one quartzite specimen, show several flake scars. Finally, several cores show traces of battering along the edges and ridges. This could be interpreted as indicating utilization: first the piece was a core, then a tool.

Core Fragments. It is uncertain whether these should be included in the category of angular fragments, but they do show flake scars, often concave. They are not flakes, but fragments of quartz lumps or pebbles, making up 6 to 7% of the assemblage. Their modal size is in the 20-30 mm class. Fragments which retain traces of cortex are rare, and they are always irregular in shape, though often pyramidal. Some fragments recall crested blades (lames à crêtes) which are elongated and trihedral in section. These fragments bear primary flake scars and traces of battering. One of them displays signs of bipolar percussion.

Some of these pieces are without doubt core fragments, but others one hesitates to place either among the cores or in the category of angular fragments. The limits are somewhat difficult to define.

Flakes. Largely because of the character of the quartz from which they were made, the flakes are of indifferent quality. They form a high proportion of the total assemblage-- from 34 to 39% at Omo 123, and from 23 to 25% at Omo 57. There are more flakes with the platform broken or entirely missing than with it completely preserved. Furthermore, whole flakes are rare in the entire series. Let me give the example of Omo 123, where whole flakes formed 10.82% of the total assemblage from the excavation, broken flakes without platforms made up 24%, and a further 4.04% were broken flakes still retaining their platforms. In other words, among the flakes alone, whole flakes make up almost a quarter.

The most frequently utilized raw material is quartz, but flakes in quartzite, jasper, and chalcedony are moderately frequent and make up between 5% and 12% depending on the site. The most frequent size range is between 10 and 30 mm (table 2). Small flakes (5-10 mm) and large ones (50-60 mm) are rare.

Some flakes retain traces of cortex--a rare 2% on the dorsal face and some 8% on the platform or distal extremity. The large majority consist of secondary flakes, bearing marks of fracture or flake scars deriving from the worked faces of cores.

Flakes are divided between the categories very broad, broad, and moderately elongate. Long flakes, blades, or bladelets are rare, representing about 6% of the whole flakes recovered by excavation at Omo 123K. Certain bladelets in jasper with a triangular cross section demonstrate the skill with which these hominids could detach flakes from blocks of stone or pebbles. The cross section of these flakes is usually flat, but the upper surface is sometimes convex. The cross section may also be triangular, in which case the flake may display a raised median ridge.

Flakes with a plain platform are most numerous (table 3), making up 62 to 77% of the total flakes of which the platform is preserved. Dihedral platforms are rare. The proportions of cortical flakes, flat or convex--about 20%--indicate a centripetal, radial debitage with the stoneworker using the cortex as a striking platform.

The angle formed by the intersection of the striking platform and the flake release surface is highly variable. However, it is usually between 90° and 120°.

Table 3

Characteristics of Flakes Found at Omo 123

Characteristic	Total Surface	Surface K	Excavation K
Platform			
Plain (with or without cortex)	77.16%	78.26%	62.28%
Dihedral	5.56	4.35	1.75
Punch	17.28	17.39	35.97
Flake Dimension			
Very broad or side flake	34.10	34.78	28.92
Broad flake	31.79	21.74	38.55
Moderately elongate flake	31.21	43.48	26.51
Elongate (length more than twice breadth)	2.90	--	6.02
Angle of platform/ flake release surface			
80° and less	3.66	--	11.76
90°	31.71	4.76	32.25
100°	15.85	38.10	14.71
110°	18.29	23.80	5.88
120°	24.39	19.05	17.65
130° and over	6.10	14.29	17.65

Three-quarters of the flakes are broken, the fractures being of two kinds. One type affects the flake transversely, separating the distal and the proximal end. Occasionally the flake fragment includes only the middle segment. More frequently breaks are longitudinal or radial, and often they affect the platforms. These fractures are steep, sharp, and without subsequent scaling. It must be emphasized that corner-struck flakes are numerous, and there are also hinge flakes, including one of jasper, where the flake release surface is convex at the distal end. Note should be taken of concave-convex flakes.

The flakes are quite large if allowance is made for the character of the raw material, and this presupposes deliberate choice of the largest pebbles available: 60-80 mm. Likewise, the presence of small flakes is in harmony with the presence of small polyhedric cores. Given that the raw material dictated the striking of small flakes, the observed mean size of this assemblage becomes less surprising.

Studies of Chipping and Damage Patterns on Fragments and Flakes

These marks are of two kinds, the first are mechanical, the second could be interpreted as signs of use, or occasionally even as retouch.

Battering is more often found on flake fragments than on whole flakes, which are rare. One end, or exceptionally two, shows crushing and scaling from impacts connected with the flaking process which usually preceded the detaching of the particular flake or fragment. These generally show transverse breaks which cut across one end and which could have happened while the fragment was being detached. Two fragments with small scars defining a kind of bec should be noted. I would equally call attention to battering along the ridges and sharp edges, which has often produced small notches. Finally small, scalelike scars are often visible along the edges or on the extremities.

It might be supposed that these damage patterns relate entirely to the processes of flaking; however, certain fractures and bruising definitely occurred after the artifact was detached. These features could be accidental as a result of trampling by hominids or animals. The sediments of fine sand, pellets of clay, and silt which enclose the artifacts made subsequent mechanical battering unlikely. Meanwhile, none of these marks are proof of definite utilization.

Flake fragments which show signs resulting from use are mainly broken flakes on which two kinds of damage can be observed: traces on the sharp edges are numerous and consist of the nibbling of edges, fine scaling, and irregular denticulation. Notches are less frequent, but one piece has small scars around the interior of the notch; another flake shows fine scalar damage. Among these, several recall utilized pieces. In particular, one flake from the excavations at Omo 57 displays fine scaling along an edge with small scars which affect the flat flake release surface rather than the slightly domed dorsal surface; the edge also shows small denticulations with low relief (fig. 1:7).

In pieces which show small flake scars, the damage suggests retouch rather than marks due to manufacturing processes. For example, in the Omo 123K sample, one jasper flake shows a series of centripetal scars on the ventral face, and a quartz flake has scars on both surfaces. Two pieces show abrupt retouch; one of them is a broken jasper flake which shows a continuous line of abrupt retouch emphasized by scalar chipping and bruising along the junction with the ventral face. This piece, which is from the Omo 57 excavation, resembles a small scraper (*grattoir latéral*).

It might seem reasonable to think that certain pieces, utilized and with some low intensity retouch, derive from an assemblage which is of no great age when the relevant pieces are part of surface collections. I do not feel in a position to impose such an arbitrary sorting, especially since the objects found in situ, notably at Omo 57, are among the most significant, I would even say among the most evolved. These present the most obvious evidence for original utilization. The pieces which show such signs are about 5.6% of the total assemblage at Omo 57. Among these, some are unmistakable. This means there is a very low percentage indeed of definitely utilized and retouched pieces. In the excavation at Omo 57, the proportion of this category is 6.6%. In contrast, at Omo 123 retouched pieces are extremely rare--0.3% among the surface collection of artifacts and 0.26%

of those which come from the excavation at Locality K. One can therefore claim that the surface collections of secondarily chipped pieces are likely to be contemporaneous with those from the excavations, with, however, a certain reserve in recognition of their surface position.

Conclusion

The collections made at Omo 57 and Omo 123 as well as the sites excavated by Merrick (this symposium) indicate the presence of a flake industry struck from chunks and pebbles and show some subsequent utilization damage affecting certain fragments and flakes. The age of the industry would be estimated at about 2 m.y. These discoveries raise various questions:

1. The place of this tool kit in the chronology of stone industries. In previously published papers I have contemplated the following hypothetical developmental lineage: First stage--utilization of a pebble as a hammerstone, necessarily associated with fragments detached during percussion. Second stage--the hominids continued to use pebbles as hammers, but in addition used the scraps, sharp fragments obtained during the course of manufacture. Third stage--the hominids deliberately broke pebbles in order to obtain flakes, the pebble thereby becoming a core, with the flake as one of the aims of the operation. The core could look like a chopper or a polyhedral. Fourth stage--this stage involved two purposes. The flake continued to be sought after, but cores which carried cutting edges could themselves be used as tools. The sites of Omo 57, Omo 71, and Omo 123 belong to this stage. Fifth stage--this leads into the Oldowan industries of Olduvai and Melka Kontouré.

2. The designation of this assemblage. It is certain that the material found in the excavations of the Omo valley is at times clearly different from that found in the deposits of East Rudolf. It seems to me premature, with present knowledge, to classify the artifacts as Oldowan. Pending further information I propose the term "Shungura facies."

3. Chopper, polyhedral, and core. In the Omo valley sites, cores are present. Their shape is varied but is principally polyhedric. Could it be supposed that certain choppers and polyhedrals from the Omo valley and other sites were cores? That would explain the absence of signs of use on certain of these pieces, but would not exclude the possibility that choppers and polyhedrals had been cores before serving as tools.

4. What do these artifacts mean? Whether we are concerned with Omo 57 or Omo 123, the collected industry is principally made up of fragments, flakes, and cores. The rarity of retouched and utilized pieces is particularly significant in these levels. Should we think that we have only the waste from a core or the residue from utilizing a quartz pebble as a hammerstone? Does this tool kit give a true image of the industry prevalent during the time of deposition of the Shungura, or is it rather only a part of the actual tool kit being used away from the occupation floors? It is likely that subsequent excavations will throw more light on this.

One curious fact should be noticed. At Omo 71 we have evidence, disputable but likely, of a bone industry alongside a stone industry. At Omo 57 there is no proof of a bone industry, and at Omo 123 no bone at all. This poses another question: What could be the use of these very small fragments? It cannot be said that they were for butchering animals or cutting up meat. But there is nothing to gainsay the argument that they could have been used to cut up roots, rhizomes, and branches.

It appears that the site at Omo 123K is an undisturbed occupation occurrence in the silts. The abundance of artifacts, which reaches 191 specimens in 1 m^2, confirms this. So does the presence of two fitting fragments of a large quartz blade which were found at the same level 18 cm apart. Thus the excavations of 1973 have brought to light the remains of the actual site where a group of hominids fractured quartz pebbles, on the floodplain of the lower Omo valley, two million years ago.

References

Bonnefille, R.; Chavaillon, J.; and Coppens, Y. 1970. La nouvelle mission de l'Omo (3° campagne). *C. R. Acad. Sci. (Paris)*, ser. D, 270:924-27.

Chavaillon, J. 1970. Découverte d'un niveau oldowayen dans la basse vallée de l'Omo (Ethiopie). *C. R. Séances Mensuelles, Bull. Soc. Préhisto. France, Paris* 67:7-11.

_____. 1971. Etat actuel de la préhistoire ancienne dans la vallée de l'Omo. *Archeologia* no. 38, pp. 34-43.

Coppens, Y.; Chavaillon, J.; and Beden, M. 1973. Résultats de la nouvelle mission de l'Omo (campagne 1972): Découverte de restes d'Hominidés et d'une industrie sur éclats. *C. R. Acad. Sci., Paris)*, ser. D, 276:161-64.

Isaac, G.; Leakey, R. E. F.; and Behrensmeyer, A. K. 1971. Archaeological traces of early hominid activities east of Lake Rudolf, Kenya, *Science* 173:1129-34.

Merrick, H. V.; Heinzelin, J. de, Haesaerts, P.; and Howell, F. C. 1973. Archaeological occurrences of early Pleistocene age from the Shungura Formation, lower Omo valley, Ethiopia. *Nature* 242:572-75.

Postscript

Further archeological survey in 1974 revealed an in situ artifact occurrence in Member C-8 (upper), the oldest yet found in the Omo succession.

H. V. Merrick and J. P. S. Merrick

Introduction

Stone artifacts have been excavated from stratified contexts in the upper members of
the Shungura Formation. One occupation site and several secondarily derived concentrations
of artifacts were found. Potassium-argon age determinations for these occurrences indicate
an age of approximately 2.0 m.y. The artifacts recovered offer a contrast to those known
from Lower Pleistocene deposits at Olduvai Gorge, Tanzania, and from older deposits east
of Lake Rudolf, supposedly Kenya.

Archeological sites have been found stratified in Lower Pleistocene deposits in the
Omo Valley. This is an important addition to the limited number of Plio-Pleistocene localities which have yielded artifacts, fauna, hominid remains, and radiometrically datable materials. The only other notable occurrences in this time range are those of Olduvai Gorge,
Bed I (Leakey 1971), and east of Lake Rudolf, Kenya (Isaac, Leakey, and Behrensmeyer 1971).

Stratified concentrations of artifacts in derived contexts were first located in the
Shungura Formation in 1971 by J. de Heinzelin and F. C. Howell. These occurrences, desig-
nated FtJi1 and FtJi3 (see Nelson 1971), are in fossil localities 204 and 208 within Member
F (previously, localities 204 and 206-208 were assigned to Member E; see Brown and Lajoie
1971). Subsequently a program of excavation and intensive survey undertaken by H. V.
Merrick in 1971 and 1972 led to the location of a possible occupation site (FtJi2) in
Locality 396 in Member F. This chapter summarizes (1) the stratigraphy and geochronology
of known archeological occurrences in the Shungura Formation, (2) the specific features of
the two sites so far excavated, and (3) the characteristics of the artifact assemblages.

Archeological Occurrences in the Shungura Formation

The Shungura Formation has an aggregate thickness of more than 760 m and a surface
area of exposure of about 200 km^2. A series of K-Ar age determinations suggests that the
base of the formation is older than 3.75 m.y. and the top is somewhat younger than 1.0 m.y.
(pers. comm. F. H. Brown). The formation has been divided into twelve members on the basis of
nine widespread volcanic tuffs, designated tuffs A through L. Each member except the Basal
Member is composed of a principal volcanic tuff and the overlying series of sediments up to
the base of the next principal tuff. The sediments of members A through lower G are primarily fluvial, and the sediments of middle Member G and above are generally prodeltaic and
lacustrine.

The lower members, Basal Member through Member E (roughly 4 to 2 m.y.) have not yet yielded stone artifacts or occupational surfaces in situ in completely unambiguous situations. J. Chavaillon has reported the finding of a chopper in an outcrop of Member E, but subsequent excavation did not reveal any associated concentration of other artifacts (Chavaillon 1970). Other occurrences of artifacts, none of which is definitely attributable to an occupational surface, were found between 1968 and 1971 by J. de Heinzelin and F. C. Howell in sediments and tuffs of Member D and in channel situations in Member C (Howell 1972). At these occurrences the artifacts were found on the surface in situations which suggest that they originated from Shungura Formation deposits, but positive proof of this origin is lacking.

Thus far Member F deposits contain the oldest stone artifacts which are definitely in situ and the oldest artifacts associated with occupational surfaces. Occurrences in Member F have been found in two separate areas approximately 2 km apart in the northern outcrops, and two other sites have recently been located in the southern outcrops (J. Chavaillon, this symposium). Isolated in situ artifacts have also been excavated from channel gravels in lower Member G, and other occurrences still to be studied have been found eroded from this member. No archeological occurrences have been located in the uppermost lacustrine members, H, J, K and L, of the Shungura Formation (fig. 1).

Stratigraphy and Geochronology of the
Member F Occurrences

Member F has a measured thickness of some 35 m of fluvial and floodplain sediments. Tuff F, at the base of the member, usually varies between 4.0 and 4.5 m but may attain a maximum thickness of 7 m. The average of two K-Ar age determinations for Tuff F gives an age of 2.04 ± 0.10 m.y. (Brown and Lajoie 1971). Overlying Tuff F are four to five cyclic units of fluvial and floodplain sedimentation. Each unit is usually composed of a graded sequence of coarse sands passing upward through medium and fine sands to silts and clays. Occasional weakly developed paleosols occur on the top of some of the silt and clay subunits within the individual cyclic units. The lowest unit in Member F, F-1, contains a widespread minor tuff, Tuff T. Figure 2 illustrates the nature and variation of the sedimentary sequence near the FtJi2 occurrence and the relative stratigraphical positions of the FtJi1 and FtJi2 occurrences within Member F. Tuff G, which directly overlies Member F, has yielded a K-Ar age determination of 1.93 ± 0.10 m.y. (Brown and Lajoie 1971).

The FtJi2 Occurrence in Locality 396

The FtJi2 occurrence in Locality 396 appears to be a primary context occupation site. The site is now being dissected by the erosion of a small spur of fluviatile sediments. Thus far a small excavation of 2 x 5 m has recovered 95 artifacts in situ. The stratigraphical sequence at this locality is summarized in figure 3. The occurrence is a low-density concentration of small artifacts scattered in a lens 12 to 15 cm thick, situated about 130 cm above the base of subunit F-1(3) (fig. 3). The artifacts, almost entirely small fragments of shattered quartz lumps and pebbles, are the only stone fragments in the entire 2.5 m thickness of clay forming the lower half of subunit F-1(3). The artifact-bearing horizon has not yielded bone at this locality, but fossil pollen is preserved (pers. comm. R. Bonnefille). The excavation has not yet determined the areal extent of the occurrence. The surface scatter of artifacts along the adjacent erosion exposure suggests a maximum north-south extension of about 20 m, but the east-west extent of the occurrence cannot yet be determined.

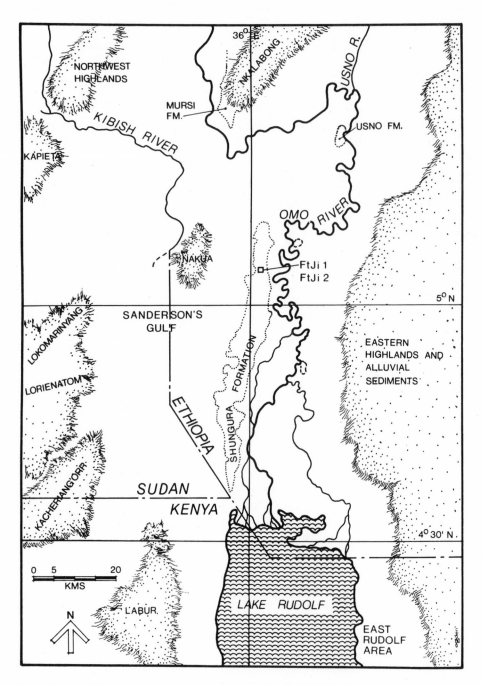

Figure 1. Generalized map of the lower Omo basin, southern Ethiopia, indicating the locations of Plio-Pleistocene exposures. Highlands are stippled.

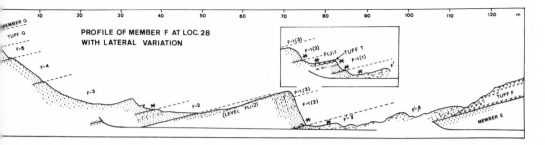

Figure 2. Profile of Member F at Locality 28, near the FtJi2 occurrence, The inset profile indicates the relative stratigraphic position of the FtJi1 occurrence.

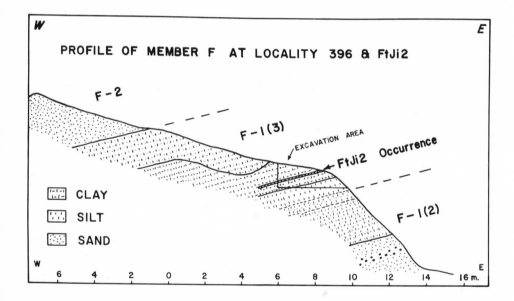

Figure 3. Profile of Member F at Locality 396 and the FtJi2 occurrence.

That the initial concentration of the artifacts was the result of hominid activity and
that the occurrence can be considered an occupation surface is suggested for the following
reasons. First, the artifacts occur in a very localized vertical and horizontal concentration in a clay deposit in which stone fragments and pebbles are otherwise totally lacking.
Their physical condition is invariably fresh; so the possibility that these artifacts could
have been selectively transported, concentrated, and deposited in these sediments can be
eliminated. Second, quartz lumps, small cobbles, and their shattered fragments are generally
extremely rare even in the coarsest gravels of the Member F deposits. This suggests that
quartz is an exotic raw material introduced into the deposits from sources at least several
kilometers distant. Thus only hominid activity can feasibly account for the localized

presence of the quartz artifacts in the fine clay sediments.

It is not yet possible to reconstruct the detailed environmental setting of this occurrence. Stratigraphical studies (by J. de Heinzelin and P. Haesaerts) suggest, however,
that initially the artifacts were scattered on a temporary land surface of silty clay in a
backswamp or in a marginal flood basin situation. Subsequently, continued deposition under
backswamp conditions buried the site. As a result of both the secondary development of a
calcium carbonate concretionary horizon and the location of the site in clays which are
subject to marked swelling and shrinkage with wetting and drying, all traces of the original temporary land surface have been obliterated. Undoubtedly this has slightly disturbed
the scatter of artifacts and may account in part for their vertical dispersion.

<u>The Locality 204-208 Area and the FtJi1 Occurrence</u>

Figure 4 shows the distribution of surface artifacts near fossil localities 204-208
and 215. There are six small (± 25 m^2) patches of densely concentrated artifacts in the
500 x 100 m area included in these localities. Furthermore, the entire Locality 206-207
area is covered by a low-density scatter of artifacts. These surface occurrences are almost entirely small quartz artifacts. The position of the artifacts at the base and on the
steep slopes of freshly eroded exposures makes it almost certain that most of them were
recently eroded from Member F sediments. The absence of exposures of the Kibish Formation
(of late or post-Pleistocene age) overlying the Shungura Formation in this area largely ex-
cludes the possibility that these discrete patches of artifacts could derive from geologically recent sediments. Moreover, each occurrence is associated with eroded exposures of
a small stream channel which has been shown by excavation in Locality 204 (the FtJi1 occurrence) to contain artifacts in situ. It is therefore highly probable that most of the artifacts in these surface scatters are of Member F age.

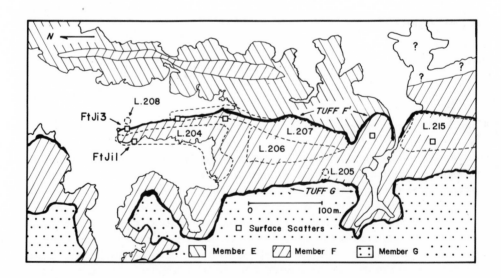

Figure 4. Location of the FtJi1 and FtJi3 occurrences and surface artifact scatters in the
Locality 204-208 and 215 area. Locality boundaries are shown with dashed lines.

The FtJi1 occurrence in Locality 204 was tested by an excavation of 2 x 4 m. A total of 130 artifacts and probable artifacts was recovered in situ from a small lens of sands and gravels, approximately 30 cm thick, filling the base of a small meandering channel. This channel is stratigraphically some 6 to 8 m below the FtJi2 occurrence and is situated at the base of the F-1(2) subunit (fig. 2, inset profile). Mammalian fossils, including elephant, hippopotamus, and several species of bovids, were also found. The artifacts appear to be in a secondarily derived context; most were found in the gravel lenses of the channel fill, and their physical condition varies from fresh to heavily abraded. The fossils also appear to be in a derived context, for they vary in condition from unrolled to heavily rolled. This suggests that both artifacts and fossils were concentrated in and deposited as part of the bed load of the stream. Since numerous channel fills in Member F contain abundant mammalian fossils but lack artifacts, the presence of both artifacts and fossils in this channel may be fortuitous. Any postulated association between the artifacts and fossils due to hominid activity before their incorporation into the channel deposits is problematical.

Stratigraphical studies are inconclusive as to the original surface(s) from which the artifacts are derived. They may have been derived from primary contexts on the channel banks and flood basins adjacent to the small channel. The FtJi2 occurrence would be an example of a primary-context site in a similar situation. It is also possible that the artifacts may have been preferentially discarded on the sandy substratum of the dry stream channel and subsequently reworked into the bed load of the stream. A pattern of preferential tool discard in channel situations such as this has been noted for the early sites east of Lake Rudolf (Isaac, Leakey, and Behrensmeyer 1971).

Artifact Assemblages

The artifacts recovered in the FtJi1 and FtJi2 excavations and from the adjacent surface scatters are recorded in table 1. A selection of the excavated artifacts from FtJi2 is illustrated in figure 5. The artifacts recovered from both sites are predominantly of milky white vein quartz. Most of them are small angular fragments of shattered pebbles and lumps of stone. Large core tools, such as choppers, and large artifically introduced unmodified natural stones (manuports) are not present in any of the excavated or surface samples. The size of the artifacts recovered in both excavations is small (see table 1). The mean maximum length of quartz artifacts from FtJi1 is slightly greater (16 mm to 13.4 mm) than that of those from FtJi2. The frequency distribution of maximum length indicates that there are significantly fewer very small artifacts at FtJi1. This may be attributable in part to size sorting by stream action during deposition at FtJi1.

Most of the quartz artifacts from both occurrences are fragments of shattered quartz lumps. Whole flakes and flake fragments (pieces with a part of the bulb of percussion remaining) are rare. Pieces exhibiting intensive secondary retouch are absent. Several excavated pieces from FtJi2, however, show minor traces of edge damage, perhaps caused by utilization. These quartz artifacts can probably be interpreted best as the debris resulting from the intensive smashing of small quartz lumps and pebbles.

In the FtJi1 excavated samples there are two lava artifacts--one a split flake and the other an angular fragment. There are also six possible chert artifacts. All six are very small angular fragments and are slightly abraded. Small chert pebbles occur with moderate frequency in the stream channel deposits so that it is possible that these were produced naturally.

Table 1

Artifacts Recovered in the FtJi1 and FtJi2 Excavations

| Artifact Category | FtJi1 | | | | | FtJi2-1 | | | |
| | Excavated (1971) | | | Surface (Quartz Only) | | Excavated | | Surface | |
	Quartz	Lava	Chert	1971	1972	1971	1972	1971	1972
Debitage									
Flakes	11	--	--	17	2	1	2	2	3
Flake fragments	4	1	--	29	1	--	2	10	3
Angular fragments	107	1	6	197	11	11	77	52	23
Manuports	--	--	--	--	--	--	2	1	--
Total artifacts	122	2	6	243	14	12	83	65	29

Range of maximum length (mm)	7-39	19-55	9-17	10-64		5-32		8-40	
Mean maximum length (mm)	16.0	--	12.7	24.8		13.4		20.4	

Distribution of maximum length (mm)

1-5	--					1.1%			
6-10	18.9%					38.9			
11-15	36.0					30.5			
16-20	23.7					12.6			
21-25	13.1					10.5			
26-30	4.9					4.2			
31-35	2.5					2.1			
36-40	0.8					--			
41-45	--					--			

The artifact density of 9.5 artifacts per square meter on the FtJi2 occupation surface is low compared with most of the Lower Pleistocene occurrences at Olduvai Gorge (Leakey 1971). It is fairly comparable to the low densities of artifacts recorded from the early sites east of Lake Rudolf (Isaac, Leakey, and Behrensmeyer 1971), particularly because the ideal depositional conditions at the FtJi2 occurrence and the recovery techniques used allow the recovery of minute fragments which increase the apparent density of artifacts.

Comments

By comparison with the early archeological occurrences known from Olduvai Gorge and from east of Lake Rudolf, the most notable features of the Omo occurrences are the absence of large tools, such as choppers, the preponderance of quartz as a raw material, and the generally smaller size of the artifacts. Although part of these differences may relate to different activity facies, at least part may be explained by the nature and proximity of the available raw material. Member F sediments are almost totally lacking in raw material

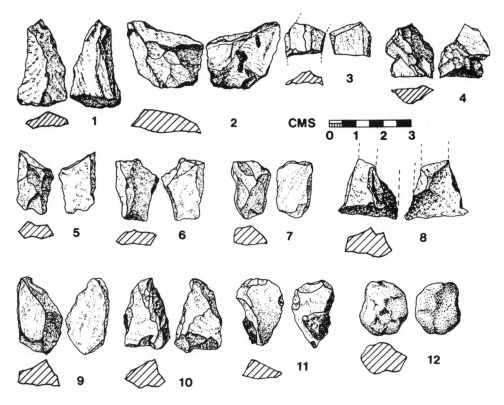

Figure 5. In situ quartz artifacts from the FtJi2 occurrence. Flake fragments (1-2), angular fragments (3-11), and small pebble (manuport) (12).

suitable for tool manufacture. A tentative paleogeographical reconstruction of the lower Omo basin for this time suggests that the principal outcrops of lava and quartz may have been 20 to 30 km distant. The nearest source of raw material probably would have been in stream channels several kilometers distant. These channels, draining the highlands forming the eastern margin of the valley, would have provided only small quartz lumps and pebbles for raw material.

Addendum: Summary of the Archeological Research Conducted during the 1973 Field Season

This chapter summarizes the archeological investigations conducted by H. V. Merrick through the 1972 field season. During the 1973 field season excavations were continued at the FtJi1 and FtJi2 occurrences, and an intensive survey for additional archeological sites was undertaken. Numerous surface scatters of artifacts of probable Shungura Formation origin were located and another Member F artifact occurrence (FtJi5), in situ, but secondarily derived, was tested by excavation.

At the FtJi1 and FtJi2 occurrences continued excavations doubled the total number of artifacts previously recovered in situ at each site. Small quartz artifacts, largely angular fragments, continued to predominate in both excavations. A very small number of chert and lava artifacts and manuports was also recovered. One new class of artifacts was noted in the excavated sample: at FtJi1 a single small casual quartz core was recovered. The total inventory of artifacts recovered to date from the excavated occurrences is summarized in table 2.

Preliminary analysis of the additional data from the FtJi2 excavation indicates that a reassessment of the spatial relationships of the artifacts may be needed. Previously the occurrence was thought to be a single lens of artifacts and tentatively interpreted as the remnant of a single short-term occupation. Now, however, the occurrence is being interpreted tentatively as the results of two short-term occupations. The occurrence appears to be composed of two low-density concentrations of artifacts scattered in two horizontally overlapping lenses. Each lens of artifacts appears to be about 15 cm thick, and they are separated vertically by 10 to 15 cm. However, there is considerable vertical overlap between the two lenses, which makes the positive identification of the occurrence as the result of two distinct occupation horizons less certain.

The surface survey, conducted in the northern third of the Shungura Formation exposures, concentrated on Member C, D, E, F, and G exposures. A few artifact scatters were found on Member C, D, and E exposures, but none of those examined appeared likely to have been derived from those sediments. Artifact scatters were found on Member F and G exposures much more frequently than had been previously reported. Most of these surface scatters were associated with lag deposits of gravel, suggesting derivation from stream channel deposits. A few of the artifact scatters were associated with finer-grained sediments, but the exact locations of the primary sources of these scatters could not be confirmed. Visual inspection in the field indicated that the artifacts in the Member F and G surface scatters were almost entirely small quartz artifacts, similar to the surface and excavated artifacts described in the preceding chapter. Although large tools such as choppers and polyhedrons were absent, small artifacts with secondary modification appeared more frequently than has been observed in the excavated samples.

At a surface scatter on Member F exposures just west of Locality 4, a test excavation located an in situ artifact occurrence. The occurrence, FtJi5, is the earliest Member F site to be tested thus far. The artifacts are in a secondarily derived context. They are concentrated in a thin layer of unsorted gravel, sand, and rolled balls of clay and tuff filling the base of a small channel near the base of the F-1 subunit just below Tuff T. Although the artifacts are in a derived context, their condition is usually fresh, suggesting that they have not been transported a great distance. The artifacts recovered at the site are summarized in table 2. Of special note are three casual cores identified in the surface collection.

These field studies have been supported by grants-in-aid to F. C. Howell from the National Science Foundation. We gratefully acknowledge the continued support and encouragement of the government of Ethiopia and thank the Kenyan government for its continued cooperation.

References

Brown, F. H., and Lajoie, K. R. 1971. Radiometric age determinations on Pliocene/Pleistocene Formations in the lower Omo basin, Ethiopia. *Nature* 229:483-85.

Chavaillon, J. 1970. Découverte d'un niveau oldowayen dans la basse vallée de l'Omo (Ethiopie). *Bull. Soc. Préhist. France* 67:7-11.

Howell, F. C. 1972. Pliocene/Pleistocene Hominidae in Eastern Africa: Absolute and relative ages. In *Calibration of hominoid evolution,* ed. W. W. Bishop and J. A. Miller, pp. 331-68. Edinburgh: Scottish Academic Press; Toronto: University of Toronto Press.

Table 2

Artifacts Recovered from the FtJi1, FtJi2, and FtJi5 Occurrences

Artifact Category	FtJi1				FtJi2			FtJi5	
	Excavated			Surface	Excavated		Surface	Excavated	Surface
	Quartz	Lava	Chert	(Quartz Only)	Quartz	Lava	(Quartz Only)	(Quartz Only)	(Quartz Only)
Debitage									
Flakes	16	--	1	19	3	--	6	1	6
Flake fragments	7	1	--	30	4	--	14	--	1
Angular fragments	344	1	6	221	215	1	110	23	67
Cores	1	--	--	--	--	--	--	--	3
Total artifacts	368	2	7	270	222	1	130	24	77
Manuports	--	--	--	--	7	2	--	--	--
Mean maximum length (mm) of artifacts	16.4		13.8	24.4	13.7	11.0	19.7	16.2	25.2
Range of maximum length (mm) of artifacts	6-49	19-55	9-19	9-64	5-35	--	8-40	6-40	10-65

Isaac, G. Ll.; Leakey, R. E. F.; and Behrensmeyer, A. K. 1971. Archaeological traces of early hominid activities, east of Lake Rudolf, Kenya. *Science* 173:1129-34.

Leakey, M. D. 1971. *Olduvai Gorge*. Vol. 3. *Excavations in Beds I and II, 1960-63.* Cambridge: At the University Press.

Nelson, C. M. 1971. A standardized site enumeration system for the continent of Africa. Pan African Congress on Prehistory and the study of the Quaternary, Commission on Nomenclature and Terminology, bulletin 4, pp. 6-13.

50. THOUGHTS ON THE WORKSHOP: "STRATIGRAPHY, PALEOECOLOGY,
     AND EVOLUTION IN THE LAKE RUDOLF BASIN"

W. W. Bishop

It was a privilege for an "outsider," with experience gained from the Lake Baringo area of the rift valley, some 160 km to the south of Lake Rudolf, to be able to participate in a conference of those working in the Rudolf basin. What follows is not a systematic analysis of the contributions that were made at the workshop. That can be obtained from study of the other chapters in this volume. These "thoughts" represent one person's view of the more lasting impressions gained from the workshop concerning progress made during the last years and of the outstanding problems that emerged from the formal presentations, discussion sessions, and field excursions.

For me the most important revelation at the meeting was the exposition of the fascinating differences encountered in detailed correlation of the Plio-Pleistocene faunas, isotopic dates, and sedimentary sequences of the Omo valley with those of the East Rudolf area. The importance of these may previously have been overlooked in attempts to seek common ground and because of the assumption that correlation between two field study areas, lying in one lake basin and separated by little more than 80 to 100 km, would be a simple exercise.

Contrasting Fluviatile Regimes

One of the principal differences between the two areas appears to be created by the presence of the Omo River itself. This is a large, permanently flowing river controlled by rainfall in the Ethiopian highlands. At present the complex birdsfoot delta and attendant meanders, levees, and over-bank and backswamp localities dominate the northern end of Lake Rudolf. A sharp line in the lake separates water bodies of different color, density, and salinity. This fluctuates with river discharge from wet to dry season but is always present. Similarly, the older sediments of the Omo valley provide evidence of the persistent presence near the midline of the "Rudolf graben" through 2 to 3 m.y. of a major proto-Omo River. They reflect its interplay with ancestral Lake Rudolf, into which it discharged.

By contrast, the East Rudolf area lies to one side of the axial region of the rift on the shoulder of the warp which delimits the eastern margin of Lake Rudolf. In the past as at the present this area was fed by short streams carrying more locally derived sediment loads. The one exception was a river which formerly drained out of the present basin of internal drainage of Lake Stefanie at times of heavier rainfall. This longer river entered the Rudolf basin through the Stefanie gap. The underfit nature of the present stream in the gap and the beveled spurs between its "dry valley" tributaries are indicative of periods

of greater discharge. With this exception the short, 50 km long or less, East Rudolf
rivers, having only intermittent, unpredictable flow regimes, fed small, ψ-shaped deltas.
Their deposits, together with deposition in shallow, marginal areas of the lake, can be
traced in the stratigraphic record which ranges through more than 3 m.y. The sediments,
and the implied regime, contrast with those dominated by the permanently flowing and larger
Omo River. Study of fully lacustrine, lake margin, and fluviatile deposits in both areas
is revealing a complex pattern of facies changes in which allowance must be made for the
different input of the contrasting fluvial systems.

Stratogeometry of Tuffs

A similar contrast, which is probably also in part related to size of catchment and
the style and periodicity of the fluviatile regimes, is seen in the numbers of "tuff" horizons in the two sequences. In the Omo succession there are 120 tuff-capped lithological
units and subunits in the Shungura Formation (an average of 1 tuff every 18,000 years) or
a time range of from 0 to 30,000 years between tuffs. In contrast, only 15 recognizable
tuffs have been mapped in the East Rudolf sequence (an average of 1 tuff every 230,000
years). The Omo units present a unique and almost ideal situation for detailed lithostratigraphic subdivision and mapping. The tuffs can be thought of as virtually instantaneous
sedimentary events which allow synchronous surfaces to be traced throughout the basin and
plotted on maps and sections. The source volcanoes were situated outside the Omo and East
Rudolf study areas, and neither the volcanic centers, nor their flanking primary tephra
have been specifically located. However, the behavior of modern volcanic analogues in New
Zealand suggests that the tuffaceous deposits which clog the Rudolf alluvial channels may
safely be considered geologically as instantaneous events. In New Zealand the tephra that
represent primary volcanic fallout and flow of ash pass laterally into tephra-derived alluvial fills which for a brief span dominate the valley sediments. These have been shown
to accumulate for only short periods after each eruption before normal sedimentation is
resumed.

The detailed mapping carried out by Vondra and Bowen and others in the East Rudolf
area has suffered from a comparative lack of these ideal tephra-derived marker horizons.
This, coupled with change of facies, has made the task of finding and tracing mappable units
more arduous. However, the usefulness of those few tuffaceous horizons that do occur cannot
be overstressed. Findlater has carried out valuable investigation of the microstratigraphy
of the East Rudolf tuff bands in order to assess the reliability of samples from them submitted for K-Ar dating.

Narrow-Mesh Time Sieve

East Rudolf and the Omo offer an unrivaled opportunity to analyze paleontological collections made from within well-defined lithological units. Upon the unique stratigraphic
framework there has been built up an equally unique time control. This is provided by
potassium-argon dating combined with paleomagnetic polarity studies of long sedimentary sequences.

Sequences of potassium-argon dates have been established for both the Omo (Brown and
Nash, this symposium) and East Rudolf areas (Fitch and Miller, this symposium). For the Omo
the eight dated tuff horizons, with ages in agreement with the order of superposition of the
strata and without overlap of the error bars, are most impressive evidence. They have been

further supported by the results of a detailed sampling program to establish paleomagnetic polarity through the sedimentary sequence (Brown and Shuey, this symposium).

Similarly, the sequence of dates for tuffaceous horizons in East Rudolf (Fitch and Miller, this symposium) is further supported by paleomagnetic polarity studies by Brock and Isaac (1974). The Omo and East Rudolf areas together make up a unique sequence for the calibration of a comparatively short time span in a localized part of one drainage basin. And yet there is a clash between geochronometry and mammalian paleontology.

The possibility that there is a small "creeping" error affecting the Omo sequence of ages and yet leaving them in correct age order as established from the Law of Superposition seems difficult to accept. Equally, the hypothesis that *some* of the East Rudolf dates are affected by a low temperature hydrothermal event (or events) which transmitted to the sample no effect visible to the petrologist is equally hard to comprehend. It has the disadvantage that if some areas or samples are selectively affected by this invisible event it becomes difficult to rely on any dates established upon tuffaceous sediments, however rich in potassium.

Large assemblages of mammalian fossils, unique hominid material, and occurrences of artifacts have been studied extensively and collected selectively. They provide an opportunity to observe rates of evolutionary change in particular parameters and also the possibility, for those fossil collections which are large enough to have statistical validity, of seeing pulses of accelerated development and quiescent phases in evolving lineages. Above all, the area offers the possibility of applying paleoecological reconstructions throughout a basin in which strands of the network of isotopic dates are never likely to be far from any individual horizon or locality. Also, the range of variation at one time plane can be investigated for certain well-dated horizons on which fossils or artifacts occur in abundance.

And yet there are the rumblings of controversy rather than excited expectancy over the differences revealed by attempts at "local" correlation within the Rudolf basin. The spatial differences which are the basis for argument are so small that they would be ignored or indeed pass unnoticed in many other deposits yielding mammalian fossils where the stratigraphy is less clear and the calibration less precise.

Problems of Correlating the Omo and East Rudolf Sequences

Behrensmeyer has outlined very clearly the possible reasons for the lack of correlation *over a comparatively short distance within one drainage basin.* I do not propose to repeat them here.

However, I believe that it would be remarkable and perhaps even "suspicious" if such imprecise methods of correlation as those depending upon stage of evolution of mammalian taxa or even statistical analysis of mammalian fossil assemblages yielded results identical with those based upon isotope chronometry. Both paleontological approaches depend ultimately upon correct assignment to particular taxa of bones from assemblages that, although they include more complete skeletal material than in many fossil mammal localities, are still dominated by the chance survival of individual bones from disarticulated skeletons. It is not possible to review the wide range of taphonomic variables which are likely to have affected the various occurrences of mammalian fossils in the Rudolf basin. It must suffice to say that the approach to taphonomy taken by Behrensmeyer (e.g., this symposium), Hill, and others is one of the most exciting developments in the Rudolf basin research.

However, it is still barely through its teething stages, and many more observational data are required before firmly based reconstructions of the paleoecology are possible even in these well-endowed fossil mammal localities.

The differences between the Omo and East Rudolf areas at the present day have already been outlined. The contrasts in morphology of hominid material collected in the two areas serve to show how dangerous it is to assume that neighboring regions even in one basin are likely to have identical forms living in them--or, more correctly, dying in them. Paradoxically, even if they do have identical forms living in them--and this would seem unlikely in view of the way the sedimentary record emphasizes how different the two areas were in the past as well as at present--animals may not meet with equal success in both areas in running the taphonomic gauntlet that is essential to their survival as fossils.

It was interesting to note the overall composition of hominid finds from Omo and East Rudolf (see table 1). Some of the contrasts-- for instance, that in numbers of isolated teeth--may possibly reflect collection differences. However, there seems little doubt that the principal cause is to be sought in the conditions governing preservation in the two areas.

Table 1

Numbers of Specimens of Hominid Fossils

Body Part	Omo (Since 1967)	East Rudolf (Since 1969)
Postcranial specimens	8	50
Craniums, maxillae, and mandibles (whole or part)	15	59
Isolated teeth	208	16
Total	231	125

Geochronological problems arise when correlations between Omo and East Rudolf are attempted using only evidence from mammalian paleontology. At present it seems premature to place too much emphasis upon the paleontological evidence, since the fossil mammal "zones" as defined by Maglio (1972) need to be more vigorously collected. The evidence from rates of morphological evolution of both suid and proboscidean fossils, as summarized by Cooke (this symposium) and Cooke and Maglio (1972) seems to suggest that some of the isotopic dates may be in error either at the Omo or at East Rudolf--or at both. Larger samples of fossils from each area (such as those described by Gentry for the bovids), in combination with detailed stratigraphic mapping akin to that of Vondra or de Heinzelin, are essential in order to resolve the paleontological side of these problems.

Conclusion

The uncertainties in the paleontological and geochronological interpretation of the northern and eastern areas of the Rudolf basin, although minor, are both challenging and exciting. Previously it has not been possible to look at mammalian or hominid (including cultural) evolution in one area yielding a rich bounty of both fossils and early lithic artifacts, set within a clear lithological framework. To this must be added the unique calibration by a combination of isotopic and paleomagnetic methods.

Never before have mammalian fossils been viewed against such a narrowly spaced mesh of time lines. It is small wonder that we do not yet understand the full meaning of the evidence that is being accumulated at the Omo and East Rudolf.

References

Brock, A., and Isaac, G. Ll. 1974. Palaeomagnetic stratigraphy and chronology of hominid-bearing sediments east of Lake Rudolf, Kenya. *Nature* 247:344-48.

Cooke, H. B. S., and Maglio, V. J. 1972. Plio-Pleistocene stratigraphy in East Africa in relation to proboscidean and suid evolution. In *Calibration of hominoid evolution*, ed. W. W. Bishop and J. A. Miller, pp. 303-29. Edinburgh: Scottish Academic Press; Toronto: University of Toronto Press.

Maglio, V. J. 1972. Vertebrate faunas and chronology of hominid-bearing sediments east of Lake Rudolf, Kenya. *Nature* 239:379-85.

GENERAL BIBLIOGRAPHY

1. Selected Published Sources on the Rudolf Basin
Assembled by F. C. Howell

A. Exploration, Geography, and Travelers' Accounts

Archer, G. F. 1913. Recent exploration and survey in the north of British East Africa.
Geograph. J. 42:421-30.

Arkell, H. 1903. *An ivory trader in north Kenya.* London: Longmans.

Athill, L. F. I. 1920. Through south-western Abyssinia to the Nile. *Geograph. J.* 56:347-70.

Austin, H. H. 1899. Journeys to the north of Uganda. II. Lake Rudolf. *Geograph. J.*
14:148-55.

_____. 1902a. A journey from Omdurman to Mombasa via Lake Rudolf. *Geograph. J.* 19:
669-90.

_____. 1902b. *Among swamps and giants in equatorial Africa.* London: Pearson.

Avanchers, Léon des. 1859. Esquisse géographique du pays Oromo ou Galla. *Bull. Soc. Paris,*
no. 8, ser. 4.

Baker, M. J., and Lovenbury, H. T. 1971. The South Turkana Expedition. VII. The 1969
season survey. *Geograph. J.* 137:349-60.

Beke, C. T. 1843. On the countries south of Abyssinia. *J. Roy. Geograph. Soc.* 13:262-64.

Bourg de Bozas, R. 1903. D'Addis Ababa au Nil par le lac Rodolphe. *Géographie* 7:91-112.

_____. 1906. *Mission scientifique du Bourg de Bozas de la Mer Rouge à l'Atlantique à
travers l'Afrique tropicale, Octobre 1900, Mars 1903.* Paris: F. R. de Rudeval.

Brooke, J. W. 1905. A journey west and north of Lake Rudolf. *Geograph. J.* 25:525-31.

Bulatovich, A. K. 1900. Dall'Abissinia al Lago Rodolfo per il Caffa. *Boll. Soc. Geograf.
Ital.* ser. 4, 1:121-42.

Caukwell, R. A. 1971. The South Turkana Expedition. VI. Field survey in South Turkana.
Geograph. J. 137:157-64.

Cavendish, H. S. H. 1898. Through Somaliland and around and south of Lake Rudolf. *Geograph.
J.* 11:372-96.

Champion, A. M. 1935. Teleki's volcano and the lava fields at the southern end of Lake
Rudolf. *Geograph. J.* 85:322-41.

_____. 1937. Physiography of the region to the west and southwest of Lake Rudolf.
Geograph. J. 89:97-118.

Copley, H. 1948. *Lakes and rivers of Kenya.* Nairobi: Longmans, Green.

Escherich, Georg. 1921. *Im Lande des Negus.* Berlin: G. Stilke.

Field, H. 1949. The University of California African Expedition. II. Sudan and Kenya. *Am.
Anthropol.* 51:72-84.

Fuchs, V. E. 1935. The Lake Rudolf rift valley expedition, 1934. *Geograph. J.* 86:114-42.

Graham, A. 1973. *Eyelids of morning: Mingled destinies of crocodiles and men.* New York:
New York Graphic Society.

Gregory, J. W. 1896. *The great rift valley.* London: John Murray.

Gwynn, C. W. 1911. A journey in southern Abyssinia. *Geograph. J.* 38:113-39.

Gwynne, M. D. 1969. The South Turkana Expedition I. Preliminary Report on the 1968 season. *Geograph. J.* 135:331-42.

Harrison, J. J. 1901. A journey from Zeila to Lake Rudolf. *Geograph. J.* 18:258-75.

Hillaby, J. 1964. *Journey to the Jade Sea.* London: Constable.

Hodson, A. 1929. Journeys from Maji, southwest Abyssinia. *Geograph. J.* 73:401-28.

Hoey, A. C. 1911. Lake Rudolf. *J. E. African Nat. Hist. Soc.* 2:47-51.

Höhnel, L. von. 1890. Ostäquatorial-Afrika zwischen Pangani und dem neuentdeckten Rudolf-See. *Petermann's Geograph. Mitt.*, Ergänzungsheft, no. 99.

_____. 1892. *Zum Rudolph-See und Stephanie-See: Die Forschungsreise des Grafen Samuel Teleki in Ost-Äquatorial-Afrika, 1887-1888, geschildert von seinem Begleiter Ludwig Ritter von Höhnel.* Vienna: A. Höhder.

_____. 1894. *Discovery of lakes Rudolf and Stefanie: A narrative of Count Samuel Teleki's exploring and hunting expedition in eastern Equatorial Africa in 1887-1888.* London: Longmans and Green.

_____. 1938a. The Lake Rudolf region: Its discovery and subsequent exploration. *J. Roy. African Soc.* 37:21-45, 206-26.

_____. 1938b. Über Veränderungen im "Teleki-Vulkangebiet." *Petermann's Geograph. Mitt.* 3:84-88.

Leontieff, N. de. 1900. Explorations des Provinces équatoriales d'Abyssinie. *Géographie* 2:105-18.

Lloyd, Jones W. 1925. *Havash: Frontier adventures in Kenya.* Bristol: Arrowsmith.

Maud, P. 1904. Exploration in the southern borderland of Abyssinia. *Geograph. J.* 23:552-79.

Neuman, A. H. 1898. *Elephant hunting in East Equatorial Africa.* London.

Neuman, O. 1904. From the Somali coast through Ethiopia to the Sudan. In *Smithsonian Report for 1903*, pp. 775-92. Washington, D.C.: Smithsonian Institution.

Richards, C. G. 1961. *Some historic journeys in East Africa.* London: Oxford University Press.

Schottenloher, Rudolf. 1938. Bericht über eine Forschungsreise in Südäthiopien. *Sitzber. Math.-Naturw. Abt., Bayer. Akad. Wiss. Muenchen,* pp. 205-10.

Sclater, P. L. 1899. Results of the second Bottegò expedition into Eastern Africa. *Science* 10:951-55.

Scott; Hugh. 1952. Journey to the Gughé Highlands (Southern Ethiopia): 1948-1949. *Proc. Linnean Soc. London* 163:85-189.

Smith, A. D. 1896. Expedition through Somaliland to Lake Rudolf. *Geograph. J.* vol. 8, no. 2, pp. 120-37; no. 3, pp. 221-39.

_____. 1897. *Through unknown African countries.* London: Arnold.

_____. 1900. An expedition between Lake Rudolf and the Nile. *Geograph. J.* 16:600-625.

Stigand, C. H. 1910. *To Abyssinia through an unknown land.* Philadelphia: Lippincott.

Thomson, J. 1881. *To the central African lakes and back.* Boston: Houghton Mifflin.

Vannutelli, L., and Citerni, C. 1897. Relazione preliminare sui risultati geografici della seconda spedizione Bottegò. *Boll. Soc. Geograf. Ital.*, ser. 3, 10:320-30.

Vannutelli, L., and Citerni, C. 1899. *Seconda spedizione Bottegò. L'Omo. Viaggio di Esplorazione nell'Africa orientale.* Milano: U. Hoepii.

Wellby, M. S. 1900. King Menelik's dominions and the country between Lake Gallop (Rudolf) and the Nile valley. *Geograph. J.* 16:292-306.

————. 1901. *Twixt Sirdar and Menelik.* London.

Worthington, E. B. 1932*a*. Scientific results of the Cambridge Expedition to the East African lakes, 1930-1931. I. General introduction and station list. *J. Linnean Soc., London, Zool.,* no. 38, pp. 99-120.

————. 1932*b*. The lakes of Kenya and Uganda. *Geograph. J.* 79:275-97.

Worthington, S. 1932. Surveying on Lake Rudolf. *Empire Surv. Rev.* 1:217-20.

Worthington, S., and Worthington, E. B. 1933. *Inland waters of Africa.* London: Macmillan.

Zavattari, E. 1941. Vom Djuba-Fluss zum Rudolfsee: Geographisch-geologische Reisen und Entdeckungen im südlichen Äthiopien. *Mitt. Geograph. Ges. Wien* 84:86-118.

————. 1942. I laghi Stefania e Rodolfo (A.O.I.) secondo i risultati della Missione Zavattari (1939). *Mem. Ist. Idrobiol. M. de Marchi Verbania* 1:77-83.

B. Geology, Geophysics and Geochemistry: General Accounts Germane to the Geology of the Rudolf Basin

Arambourg, C. 1950. Les limites et les corrélations du Quaternaire africain. *Intern. Geol. Congr., 18th, London, 1948.* Part II, pp. 49-54.

Baker, B. H.; Mohr, P. A.; and Williams, L. A. J. 1972. Geology of the eastern rift system of Africa. *Geol. Soc. Am., Spec. Paper,* no. 136, pp. 1-67.

Baker, B. H.; Williams, L. A. J.; Miller, J. A.; and Fitch, F. J. 1971. Sequence and geo-chronology of the Kenya Rift volcanics. *Tectonophysics* 11:191-215.

Baker, B. H., and Wollenberg, J. 1971. Structure and evolution of the Kenya Rift valley. *Nature* 229:538-42.

Bishop, W. W. 1967*a*. Annotated lexicon of Quaternary stratigraphical nomenclature in East Africa. In *Background to evolution in Africa,* ed. W. W. Bishop and J. D. Clark, pp. 375-95. Chicago: University of Chicago Press.

————. 1967*b*. The later Tertiary in East Africa: Volcanics, sediments and faunal in-ventory. In *Background to evolution in Africa,* ed. W. W. Bishop and J. D. Clark, pp. 31-56. Chicago: University of Chicago Press.

————. 1971. The late Cenozoic history of East Africa in relation to hominid evolution. In *Late Cenozoic glacial ages,* ed. K. K. Turekian, pp. 493-527. New Haven: Yale University Press.

Bullard, E. C. 1936. Gravity measurements in East Africa. *Phil. Trans. Roy. Soc. London,* no. 235, ser. A, pp. 445-531.

Cooke, H. B. S. 1958. Observations relating to Quaternary environments in East and Southern Africa. *Trans. Geol. Soc. S. Africa* 60 (annexure). 73 pp.

Cooke, H. B. S., and Maglio, V. J. 1972. Recent Pliocene-Pleistocene discoveries in East Africa. In *Palaeoecology of Africa, the surrounding islands and Antartica,* ed. E. M. van Zinderen Bakker, 6:163-67. Cape Town: A. A. Balkema.

Dainelli, G. 1943. *Geologia dell'Africa orientale.* 4 vols. Rome: Reale Accademia d'Italia.

Dixey, F. 1946. Erosion and tectonics in the East African rift system. *Quart. J. Geol. Soc. London* 102:339-88.

————. 1956. The East African rift system. *Colonial Geol. Mineral Resources (Gt. Brit.), Bull. Suppl.* no. 1, pp. 1-71.

Dosaj, N. P., and Walsh, J. 1970. Bibliography of the geology of Kenya. *Kenya Geol. Surv. Bull.*, no. 10.

Evernden, J. F., and Curtis, G. H. 1965. Potassium/argon dating of Late Cenozoic rocks in East Africa and Italy. *Current Anthropol.* 6:343-85.

Fuchs, V. E., and Paterson, T. T. 1947. The relation of volcanicity and orogeny to climatic change. *Geol. Mag.* 84:321-33.

Girdler, R. W. 1963. Geophysical studies of rift valleys. *Phys. Chem. Earth* 5:121-56.

_____. 1968. Drifting and rifting of Africa. *Nature* 217:1102-6.

_____. 1972. *East African rifts: Developments in geotectonics.* Amsterdam: Elsevier.

Gregory, J. W. 1919. The geological history of the Rift valley. *J. E. Africa Uganda Nat. Hist. Soc.* 15:429-40.

_____. 1920. The African rift valleys. *Geograph. J.* 56:13-47.

_____. 1921. *The rift valleys and geology of East Africa.* London: Seeley, Service.

Kent, P. E. 1942. Pleistocene climates in Kenya and Abyssinia. *Nature* 149:736-37.

_____. 1944. The age and tectonic relationships of East African volcanic rocks. *Geol. Mag.* 81:15-27.

Khan, M. A., and Mansfield, J. 1971. Gravity measurements in the Gregory Rift. *Nature* 229:72-75.

King, B. C. 1970. Volcanicity and rift tectonics in East Africa. In *African magnetism and tectonics,* ed. T. N. Clifford and I. G. Gass, pp. 263-83. Edinburgh: Oliver and Boyd.

King, B. C., and Chapman, G. R. 1972. Volcanism of the Kenya Rift valley. *Phil. Trans. Roy. Soc. London,* no. 271, ser. A, pp. 185-208.

Leakey, L. S. B. 1950. The lower limit of the Pleistocene in Africa. *Intern. Geol. Cong. 18th, London, 1948,* part 9, pp. 62-65.

Mohr, P. A. 1962. The Ethiopian rift system. *Bull. Geophys. Obs. Addis Ababa* 5:33-62.

_____. 1964. *The geology of Ethiopia.* Asmara: University College Addis Ababa Press.

_____. 1967. The Ethiopian rift system. *Bull. Geophys. Obs. Addis Ababa* 11:1-65.

_____. 1968. The Cainozoic volcanic succession in Ethiopia. *Bull. Volcanol.* 32:5-14.

_____. 1971. Ethiopian rift and plateaus: Some petrochemical differences. *J. Geophys. Res.* 76:1967-84.

Mussett, A. E.; Reilly, T. A.; and Raja, P. K. S. 1964. Palaeomagnetism in East Africa. A progress report on the Tertiary volcanics. *Proc. E. African Acad.* 2:27-35.

Pulfrey, W. 1960. Shape of the sub-Miocene erosion bevel in Kenya. *Geol. Surv. Kenya,* bull. no. 3, pp. 1-18.

Saggerson, E. P., and Baker, B. H. 1965-66. Post-Jurassic erosion surfaces in eastern Kenya and their deformation in relation to rift structure. *Quart. J. Geol. Soc. London* 121 (1965):51-72; 122 (1966):88-90.

Sowerbutts, W. T. C. 1969. Crustal structure of the East African plateau and rift valleys from gravity measurements. *Nature* 223:143-46.

UNESCO. 1965. *East African rift system.* Upper Mantle Committee, UNESCO seminar, Nairobi, April 1965. Nairobi: University College.

Talling, J. F., and Talling, I. B. 1965. The chemical composition of African lake waters. *Intern. Rev. Ges. Hydrobiol.* 50:421-63.

Williams, L. A. J. 1969. Volcanic associations in the Gregory Rift valley, East Africa. *Nature* 224:61-64.

———. 1971. The volcanics of the Gregory Rift valley, East Africa. *Bull. Volcanol.* 34:439-65.

Willis, B. 1936. East African plateaus and rift valleys. *Carnegie Inst. Wash. Publ.*, no. 470.

Wohlenberg, J. 1968. Seismizität der Ostafrikanischen Grabenzonen zwischen 4° N und 12° S sowie 23° E und 40° E. *Bayer. Akad. Wiss., Jahrb.*, Munich, no. 23.

Wright, J. B. 1963. A note on possible differentiation trends in Tertiary to recent lavas in Kenya. *Geol. Mag.* 100:164-80.

———. 1965. Petrographic sub-provinces in the Tertiary to recent volcanics of Kenya. *Geol. Mag.* 102:541-57.

C. Geology, Geophysics, and Geochemistry:
The Rudolf Basin

Angelis d'Ossat, G., and Millosevich, F. 1900. *Studio geologico sul materiale racolto da M. Sacchi: Secondo spedizione Bottegò (Afrique orientale).* Rome: Società Geògrafica Italiana.

Behrensmeyer, A. K. 1975. Late Cenozoic sedimentation in the Lake Rudolf basin, Kenya. *Ann. Geol. Surv. Egypt* 4:287-306.

Champion, A. M., and Smith, W. C. 1937. The volcanic region around the southern end of Lake Rudolf, Kenya Colony. *Z. Vulkanol.* 17:163-72.

Dixey, F. 1944. Miocene sediments in South Turkana. *J. E. Africa Nat. Hist. Soc.* 18:13-14.

———. 1948. Geology of northern Kenya. *Geol. Surv. Kenya, Rept.*, no. 15.

Fuchs, V. E. 1934. The geological work of the Cambridge expedition to the East African lakes, 1930-1931. *Geol. Mag.* 71:97-112.

———. 1939. The geological history of the Lake Rudolf basin, Kenya Colony. *Phil. Trans. Roy. Soc. London*, ser. B, 229:219-74.

Höhnel, L. von; Rosiwal, A.; Toula, F.; and Suess, E. 1891. Beitrage zur geologischen Kenntnis des östlichen Afrika. *Denkschr. Kaiserl. Akad. Wiss. Wien, Math.-Naturwiss. Klasse*, no. 58.

Holland, W. P. 1926. Volcanic action north of Rudolf in 1918. *Geograph. J.* 68:488-91.

Joubert, P. 1966. Geology of the Loperot area. *Geol. Surv. Kenya, Rept.*, no. 74, no. 1.

Merla, G. 1963. Missione geologica nell'Etiopia meridionale del Consiglio nazionale delle ricerche 1959-1960: Notizie geo-morfologiche e geologiche. *Giorn. Geol.*, ser. 2, 31:1-56.

Parkinson, J. 1920. Report on the geology and geography of the northern part of the East Africa Protectorate. *East Africa Protectorate, Col. Rept., Misc.*, no. 91.

Raja, P. K. S.; Reilly, T. A.; and Mussett, A. E. 1966. The paleomagnetism of the Turkana lavas. *J. Geophys. Res.* 71:1217-22.

Reilly, T. A.; Mussett, A. E.; and Raja, P. K. S. 1966. Age and polarity of the Turkana lavas, northwest Kenya. *Nature* 210:1145-46.

Rhemtulla, S. 1970. The South Turkana Expedition. III. A geological reconnaissance of South Turkana. *Geograph. J.* 136:61-73.

Smith, W. C. 1938. Petrographic description of volcanic rocks from Turkana, Kenya Colony, with notes on their field occurrence from the manuscript of Mr. A. M. Champion. *Quart. J. Geol. Soc. London* 94:507-33.

Walsh, J., and Dodson, R. G. 1969. Geology of northern Turkana. *Mines Geol. Dept. Kenya*, rept. no. 82.

Whitworth, T. 1965. The Pleistocene lake beds of Kabua, northern Kenya. *Durham Univ. J.* 57:88-100.

D. Mammalian Paleontology

Arambourg, C. 1933. Mammifères Miocènes du Turkana. *Ann. Paleontol.* 22:121-46.

Cooke, H. B. S. 1972. The fossil mammal fauna of Africa. In *Evolution, mammals and southern continents*, ed. A. Keast, F. C. Erk, and B. Glass, pp. 89-139. Albany: State University of New York Press.

———. 1974. Plio-Pleistocene deposits and mammalian faunas of Eastern and Southern Africa. *Committee on Mediterranean Neogene Stratigraphy, 5th Session*, Lyon, 1971, pp. 99-108. Mém. du B.R.G.M. 78.

Cooke, H. B. S., and Maglio, V. J. 1972. Plio-Pleistocene stratigraphy in East Africa in relation to proboscidean and suid evolution. In *Calibration of hominoid evolution*, ed. W. W. Bishop and J. A. Miller, pp. 303-29. Edinburgh: Scottish Academic Press; Toronto: University of Toronto Press.

Coryndon, S. C. 1970. The extent of variation in fossil *Hippopotamus* from Africa. *Symp. Zool. Soc. London*, no. 26, pp. 135-47.

———. 1972. Hexaprotodont Hippopotamidae of East Africa and the phylogeny of the family. *Cong. Panafr. Prehist., Dakar, 1967, Actes du 6me Session*, pp. 350-52.

Coryndon, S. C., and Savage, J. G. 1973. The origin and affinities of African mammal faunas. *Spec. Papers Palaeontol.* 12:121-35. Systematics Association Publication 9, Palaeontological Association, London.

Deraniyagala, P. E. P. 1948. Some scientific results of two visits to Africa. *Spolia Zeylan.* 25:1-42.

———. 1951. A hornless rhinoceros from the Mio-Pliocene deposits of East Africa. *Spolia Zeylan.* 26:133-35.

Hooijer, D. A. 1968. A note on the mandible of *Aceratherium acutirostratum* (Deraniyagala) from Muruaret Hill, Turkana district, Kenya. *Zool. Mededeel. Rijksmuseum Natuurl. Hist., Leiden* 42(21):231-35.

Leakey, L. S. B. 1943. New fossil Suidae from Shungura, Omo. *J. E. Africa Nat. Hist. Soc.* 17:45-61.

———. 1967. Notes on the mammalian faunas from the Miocene and Pleistocene of East Africa. In *Background to evolution in Africa*, ed. W. W. Bishop and J. D. Clark, pp. 7-29. Chicago: University of Chicago Press.

Madden, C. T. 1972. Miocene mammals, stratigraphy and environment of Muruarot hill, Kenya. *Paleobios* (Museum of Paleontology, University of California, Berkeley), 14:1-12.

Maglio, V. J. 1975. Late Tertiary fossil vertebrate successions in the northern Gregory Rift, East Africa. *Ann. Geol. Surv. Egypt* 4:269-86.

Whitworth, T. 1960. Fossilized human remains from northern Kenya. *Nature* 185:947-48.

———. 1966. A fossil hominid from Rudolf. *S. African Archaeol. Bull.* 21(83):138-50.

E. Biology, Natural History, Soils, and the
     Paleontology of Nonmammalian Organisms

Bate, R. H. 1970. A new species of *Hemicypris* (Ostracoda) from ancient beach sediments of Lake Rudolf, Kenya. *Palaeontology* 13:289-96.

———. 1972. Fossil and living *Hemicypris* (Ostracoda) from Lake Rudolf, Kenya. *Palaeontology* 15:184-85.

Beadle, L. C. 1932. Scientific results of the Cambridge Expedition to the East African lakes 1930-1931: The waters of some East African lakes in relation to their fauna and flora. *J. Linnean Soc. London, Zool.* 38:157-211.

_____. 1962. The evolution of species in the lakes of East Africa. *Uganda J.* 26:44-54.

Beaux, O. de. 1943. *Mammalia: Missione Biologica Sagan-Omo.* Vol. 7. *Zoologia I: Mammalia -Aves-Reptilia-Amphibia-Pisces.* Roma: Reale Accadèmia d'Italia, Centro Studi per l'Africa Orientale Italiana, no. 6.

Boulenger, G. A. 1895. An account of the reptiles and batrachians collected by Dr. A. Donaldson Smith in Western Somaliland and Golla country. *Proc. Zool. Soc. London* 1895:530-40.

_____. 1896. Second report on the reptiles and batrachians collected by Dr. A. Donaldson Smith during his expedition to East Rudolf. *Proc. Zool. Soc. London* 1896:212-17.

_____. 1897-98. Concluding report on the late Captain Bottegò's collections of reptiles and batrachians from Somaliland and British East Africa. *Ann. Museo Civico Storia Nat. Genova,* ser. 2, no. 18, pp. 715-23.

Buxton, D. R. 1936. A natural history of the Turkana fauna. *J. E. Africa Uganda Nat. Hist. Soc.* 13:85-104.

Coe, M. 1972. The South Turkana Expedition. IX. Ecological studies of the small mammals of South Turkana. *Geograph. J.* 138:316-38.

Duff-Mackay, A. 1965. Notes on the biology of the carpet viper, *Echis carinatus pyramidum* (Geoffroy) in the northern Frontier province of Kenya. *J. E. Africa Nat. Hist. Soc.* 25:28-40.

Hemming, C. F. 1972. The South Turkana Expedition. 8. The ecology of South Turkana: A reconnaissance classification. *Geograph. J.* 138:15-40.

Hemming, C. F., and Trapnell, C. G. 1957. A reconnaissance classification of the soils of the South Turkana desert. *J. Soil Sci.* 8:167-83.

Krug, W. 1971. A survey of trypanosomiasis with particular reference to livestock, in the southwest province of Ethiopia. *Bull. Epizoot. Diseases Afr.* 19:243-55.

Lindroth, S. 1956. Taxonomic and zoogeographic studies of the ostracod fauna in the inland waters of East Africa. *Zool. Bidrag Fran Uppsala* 30:43-156.

Lowe-McConnell, R. H. 1969. Speciation in tropical freshwater fishes. *Biol. J. Linnean Soc. London* 1:51-75.

Makin, J. 1969. Soil formation in the Turkana desert. *E. Africa Agr. Forest. J.* 34:493-96.

Missione Biologica Sagan-Omo, 1939-1945. Vol. 1- . Reale Accadèmia d'Italia. Centro Studi per l'Africa Orientale Italiana, no. 6. Rome: Reale Accadèmia d'Italia.

Mission scientifique de l'Omo, Zoologie. 1935. (Published under the direction of R. Jeannel). Mémoires du Muséum national d'histoire naturelle, Paris, n.s. (Zoologie). Vol. 2 (1935) et seq.

Modha, M. L. 1967. The ecology of the Nile crocodile on Central Island, Lake Rudolf. *E. African Wildlife J.* 5:74-95.

Neuville, A. A., and Anthony, R. 1906*a*. Aperçu sur la faune malacologique des lacs Rodolphe, Stéphanie et Marguérite. *C. R. Acad. Sci. (Paris)* 143:66-67.

_____. 1906*b*. Contribution a l'étude de la faune malacologique des lacs Rodolphe, Stéphanie et Marguérite. *Bull. Soc. Philomath., Paris* 8:275-300.

Parker, H. W. 1932. Scientific results of the Cambridge Expedition to the East African lakes, 1930-1931. 5. Reptiles and amphibians. *J. Linnaean Soc. London, Zool.,* no. 38, pp. 213-29.

_____. 1936. Reptiles and amphibians collected by the Lake Rudolf Rift Valley Expedition, 1934. *Ann. Mag. Nat. Hist.,* ser. 10, 18:594-609.

Pichi-Sermoli, R. 1957. Una carta geobotanica dell'Africa orientale (Eritrea, Etiopia, Somalia). *Webbia* 15:15-132.

Rhoads, S. N. 1897. Mammals collected by Dr. A. Donaldson Smith during his expedition to Lake Rudolf, Africa. *Proc. Acad. Nat. Sci., Philadelphia* 1896:517-46.

Rochebrune, A. T. de, and Germain, L. 1904. Mollusques recueillis par la Mission du Bourg de Bozas. *Mém. Soc. Zool. Française* 17:5-29.

St. Leger, T. 1937. Mammals collected by the Lake Rudolf Rift Valley Expedition, 1934. *Ann. Mag. Nat. Hist.* 19:524-31.

Stewart, D. R. M. 1963. Wildlife census: Lake Rudolf. *E. African Wildlife J.* 1:121.

Stewart, D. R. M., and Stewart, J. 1963. The distribution of some large mammals in Kenya. *J. E. Africa Nat. Hist. Soc. Coryndon Museum* 24(3):1-52.

Thomas, O. 1897-98. On the mammals collected during Captain Bottegò's last expedition to Lake Rudolf and the upper Sobat. *Ann. Museo Civico Storia Nat. Genova,* ser. 2, no. 18, pp. 676-79.

Trewavas, E. 1933. Scientific results of the Cambridge Expedition to the East African lakes, 1930-1931. II. The cichlid fishes. *J. Linnaean Soc. London, Zool.,* no. 38, pp. 309-41.

Urban, E. K., and Brown, L. H. 1968. Wildlife in an Ethiopian valley. *Oryx* 9:342-53.

Van Damme, D., and Gautier, A. 1972. Some fossil molluscs from Muruarot hill (Turkana district, Kenya). *J. Conchol.* 27:423-26.

Watson, R. M. 1969. The South Turkana Expedition. II. A survey of the large mammal population in South Turkana. *Geograph. J.* 135:529-46.

Watson, R. M.; Graham, A. D.; Bell, R. H. V.; and Parker, J. S. C. 1971. A comparison of four East African crocodile (*Crocodylus niloticus laurenti*) populations. *E. African Wildlife J.* 9:25-34.

Western, D. 1974. The distribution, density, and biomass density of lizards in a semiarid environment of northern Kenya. *E. African Wildlife J.* 12:49-62.

Worthington, E. B. 1932. Scientific results of the Cambridge Expedition to the East African lakes, 1930-1931. 2. Fishes other than Cichlidae. *J. Linnaean Soc. London, Zool.,* no. 38, pp. 121-34.

————. 1937. On the evolution of fish in the great lakes of Africa. *Int. Rev. Ges. Hydrobiol.* 35:304-17.

————. 1954. The speciation of fishes in African lakes. *Nature* 173:1064-67.

Worthington, E. B., and Ricardo, C. K. 1935. Scientific results of the Cambridge Expedition to the East African lakes, 1930-1931. 15. The fish of Lake Rudolf and Lake Baringo. *J. Linnaean Soc. London, Zool.* 39:353-89.

————. 1936. Scientific results of the Cambridge Expedition to the East African lakes, 1930-1931. 17. The vertical distribution and movements of the plankton in Lakes Rudolf, Naivasha, Edward and Bunyoni. *J. Linnaean Soc. London, Zool.* 40:33-69.

Zavattari, E. 1946. La missione biologica Sagan-Omo. *Riv. Biol. Coloniale (Rome)* 7:97-108.

F. Archeology, Ethnography, and Social Anthropology

Barton, Juxton. 1921. Notes on the Turkana tribe of British East Africa. *J. Roy. African Soc.* 21:204-11.

Beckingham, C. F., and Huntingford, G. W. B. 1954. *Some records of Ethiopia, 1593-1646.* London: Hakluyt Society.

Cerulli, Ernesta. 1956. Peoples of Southwest Ethiopia and its borderlands. In *Ethnographic survey of Africa, Part III, Northeast Africa.* London: International African Institute.

Dyson, W. S., and Fuchs, V. E. 1937. The Elmolo. *J. Roy. Anthropol. Inst.* 67:327-28.

Emley, E. D. 1927. The Turkana of Kolosia district. *J. Roy. Anthropol. Inst.* 57:157-201.

Gulliver, P. H. 1951. *A preliminary survey of the Turkana: A report compiled for the government of Kenya,* no. 26. Capetown: University of Capetown, Rondebosch.

_____. 1952*a*. The Karamajong cluster. *Africa* 22:1:1-22.

_____. 1952*b*. Kinship and property amongst the Jie and Turkana. Ph.D. thesis, University of London.

_____. 1955. *The family herds: A study of two pastoral tribes in East Africa--The Jie and Turkana.* London: Routledge and Kegan Paul.

_____. 1958. The Turkana age organization. *Am. Anthropol.* 60(5):900-922.

Gulliver, P., and Gulliver, P. H. 1953. The central Nilo-Hamites. *Ethnographic Survey of Africa, Part VII, East Central Africa.* London: International African Institute.

Haberland, E. 1963. *Die Galla Süd-Äthiopiens.* Stuttgart: Kohlhammer.

Huntingford, G. W. B. 1950. The hagiolithic cultures of East Africa. *Eastern Anthropol.* 3:119-36.

_____. 1955. The Galla of Ethiopia. *Ethnographic Survey of Africa, Part II, Northeastern Africa.* London: International African Institute.

Jensen, A. E. 1959. *Altvölker Süd-Äthiopiens.* Stuttgart: Kohlhammer.

Morgan, W. T. W. 1971. The South Turkana Expeditions. Scientific Papers IV. Land units of the Lokori area. *Geograph. J.* 137:14-28.

_____. 1974. The South Turkana Expeditions: Scientific Papers X. Sorghum gardens in South Turkana: Cultivation among a nomadic pastoral people. *Geograph. J.* 140:80-93.

Nowack, Ernst. 1954. Land und Volk der Konso. *Bönner Geograph. Abhandl.* 14:1-71.

Pauli, E. 1950. Die Splitterstämme nördlich des Rudolfsees. *Ann. Laterani* 14:61-191.

Prins, A. H. J. 1953. *East African age-class systems.* Groningen, Holland.

Robbins, L. H. 1967. A recent archaeological discovery in the Turkana district of northern Kenya. *Azania* 2:69-73.

_____. 1970. Rock paintings at Napedutt Hill. *Uganda J.* 34:79-80.

_____. 1972. Archaeology in Turkana district, Kenya. *Science* 176:359-66.

Robbins, L. H., and Robbins, M. E. 1971. A note on Turkana dancing. *J. Soc. Ethnomusicol.* 15(2):231-35.

Spencer, P. 1965. *The Samburu: A study of gerontocracy in a nomadic tribe.* Berkeley: University of California Press.

_____. 1973. *Nomads in alliance: Symbiosis and growth among the Rendille and Samburu of Kenya.* London: Oxford University Press.

Torry, W. 1971. Animal husbandry and social organisation among the Gabbra, with notes on the Rendille Tribe. Unpublished manuscript to Range Management Division, Nairobi.

Tucker, A. N., and Bryan, M. A. 1956. The non-Bantu languages of northeastern Africa. In *Handbook of African Languages III.* London: International African Institute.

Turton, E. R. 1970. The pastoral tribes of Northern Kenya: 1800-1916. Ph.D. thesis, University of London.

Vangby, B., and Jacobs, A. H. 1972. Traditional housing of the Elmolo. *J. Architect. Assoc. Kenya,* vol. 3, no. 3.

Whitworth, T. 1966. Artifacts from Turkana, northern Kenya. *S. African Archaeol. Bull.* 20(78):75-78.

2. Mission Scientifique de l'Omo, 1932-33 (Including Paleontological Studies on Bourg de Bozas Collections)

Assembled by F. C. Howell

Arambourg, C. 1933*a*. Découverte d'un gisement de mammifères Burdigaliens dans le bassin du lac Rodolphe (Afrique orientale). *C. R. Somm. Soc. Géol. France*, fasc. 14, pp. 221-22.

_____. 1933*b*. Les formations prétertiares de la bordure occidentale du lac Rodolphe. *C. R. Acad. Sci. (Paris)* 197:1663-65.

_____. 1933*c*. Mammifères miocènes du Turkana (Afrique orientale). *Ann. Paléontol.* 22: 123-47.

_____. 1933*d*. Observations sur la bordure nord du lac Rodolphe. *C. R. Acad. Sci. (Paris)* 197:856-57.

_____. 1934*a*. Le *Dinotherium* des gisements de l'Omo. *C. R. Somm. Soc. Géol. France*, fasc. 6, p. 86.

_____. 1934*b*. Le *Dinotherium* des gisements de l'Omo (Abyssinie). *Bull. Soc. Géol. France*, ser. 5, 4:305-9.

_____. 1934*c*. Les formations éruptives de Turkana (Afrique orientale). *C. R. Acad. Sci. (Paris)* 198:673.

_____. 1934*d*. Les résultats géologiques de la mission de l'Omo (1932-1933). *C. R. Somm. Soc. Géol. France*, no. 4, pp. 63-64.

_____. 1941. Antilopes nouvelles du Pléistocène ancien de l'Omo (Abyssinie). *Bull. Mus. Nat. Hist. Nat., Paris*, ser. 2, 13:339-47.

_____. 1942. L'*Elephas recki* Dietrich: Sa position systématique et ses affinités. *Bull. Soc. Géol. France*, ser. 5, 12:73-89.

_____. 1943. Observations sur les suidés fossiles du Pléistocène d'Afrique. *Bull. Mus. Nat. Hist. Nat., Paris*, ser. 2, 15:471-76.

_____. 1944*a*. Au sujet de l'*Hippopotamus hipponensis* Gaudry. *Bull. Soc. Géol. France*, ser. 5, 14:147-53.

_____. 1944*b*. Les hippopotames fossiles d'Afrique. *C. R. Acad. Sci. (Paris)* 218:602-4.

_____. 1946. Au sujet des variations saisonnières du Lac Rodolphe Pléistocène. *C. R. Somm. Soc. Géol. France*, 16, no. 5:74-75.

_____. 1947. *Mission scientifique de l'Omo (1932-1933)*. Vol. 1. *Paléontologie*, fasc. 3, pp. 231-562. Mémoire, Muséum national d'histoire naturelle, Paris.

_____. 1952. The African Pleistocene mammals. In *Proceedings of the Pan-African Congress on Prehistory, 1947, Nairobi*, pp. 18-25. Oxford: Basil Blackwell.

Arambourg, C.; Chappuis, P. A.; Jeannel, R.; and Jérémine, E. 1935. *Mission scientifique de l'Omo (1932-1933)*. Vol. 1. *Géologie-Anthropologie*, fasc. 1, pp. 1-59. Mémoire, Muséum nationale d'histoire naturelle, Paris.

Arambourg, C., and Jeannel, R. 1933. La mission scientifique de l'Omo. *C. R. Acad. Sci. (Paris)* 196:1902-4.

Arambourg, C.; Lester, P.; and Roger, J. 1943. *Mission scientifique de l'Omo (1932-1933)*. Vol. 1. *Géologie-Anthropologie*, fasc. 2, pp. 60-230. Mémoire, Muséum nationale d'histoire naturelle, Paris.

Bachmann, H. 1938. Mission scientifique de l'Omo: Beiträge zur Kenntnis des Phytoplanktons ostafrikanischen Seen. *Z. Hydrol.* 8:119-40.

Boulenger, G.-A. 1920. Sur le gavial fossile de l'Omo. *C. R. Acad. Sci. (Paris)* 170:913-14.

Breuil, H., and Kelley, H. 1936. Les collections africaines du département de préhistoire exotique du Musée d'ethnographie du Trocadero. V. Documents préhistoriques recueillis par la mission du Bourg de Bozas, en Abyssinie (1901-1902). *J. Soc. Afr.* 6:111-40.

Chappuis, P. A. 1939. Le peuplement du Lac Rodolphe et la répartition des Mormyidae dans la nord-est de l'Afrique. *C. R. Somm. Soc. Biogeograph., Paris* 136:54-57.

Haug, E. 1912. *Traité de géologie*. II. *Les périodes géologiques*. Paris: Armand Colin.

Jeannel, R. 1934. *Un cimetière d'éléphants*. Paris: Société des amis du Muséum national d'histoire naturelle.

Joleaud, L. 1920*a*. Contribution a l'étude des hippopotames fossiles. *Bull. Soc. Géol. France*, ser. 4, 20:13-26.

_____. 1920*b*. Sur la présence d'un gavialidé du genre *Tomistoma* dans le Pliocène d'eau douce de l'Ethiopie. *C. R. Acad. Sci., Paris* 170:816-18.

_____. 1928. Eléphants et Dinotheriums Pliocènes de l'Ethiopie: Contribution a l'étude paléogéographique des proboscidiens africains. *Intern. Geol. Congr. Madris, 14th sess.* 3:1001-7.

_____. 1930. Les crocodilians du Pliocène d'eau douce de l'Omo (Ethiopie). Contribution a l'étude paléobiogéographique des *Tomistoma* et des crocodiles à museau de gavial. *Soc. Geol. France, Livre Jubilaire*, 1830-1930, 2:411-23.

_____. 1933. Un nouveau genre d'Equidé Quaternaire de l'Omo (Abyssinie): *Libyhipparion ethiopicum*. *Bull. Soc. Géol. France*, ser. 5, 3:7-28.

Pottier, G. 1951. L'*Elephas recki* du gisement de l'Omo (Abyssinie). *Bull. Soc. Prehist. France* 48:438-40.

Rochebrune, de, and Germain, L. 1904. Mollusques de la Mission du Bourg de Bozas. *Mem. Soc. Zool. France* 17:5-29.

3. Harvard and Princeton University
Expeditions to Turkana, Kenya

Assembled by F. C. Howell

Cooke, H. B. S., and Ewer, R. F. 1972. Fossil Suidae from Kanapoi and Lothagam, northwestern Kenya. *Bull. Museum Comp. Zool., Harvard Coll.* 143:149-296.

Coon, C. S. 1971. A fossilized human mandibular fragment from Kangatotha, Kenya. *Am. J. Phys. Anthropol.* 34:157-63.

Hooijer, D. A. 1971. A new rhinoceros from the late Miocene of Loperot, Turkana district, Kenya. *Bull. Museum Comp. Zool., Harvard Coll.* 142:339-92.

Hooijer, D. A., and Maglio, V. J. 1973. The earliest *Hipparion* south of the Sahara, in the late Miocene of Kenya. *Koninkl. Ned. Akad. Wetenschap.-Amsterdam, Proc.*, ser. B, 76:311-15.

_____. 1974. Hipparions from the late Miocene and Pliocene of northwestern Kenya. *Zool. Verhandel. Rijksmuseum Nat. Hist. Leiden*, no. 134, pp. 1-34.

Hooijer, D. A., and Patterson, B. 1972. Rhinoceroses from the Pliocene of northwestern Kenya. *Bull. Museum Comp. Zool. Harvard Coll.* 144:1-26.

Leakey, M. D. 1966. Primitive artefacts from Kanapoi valley. *Nature* 212:579-81.

Maglio, V. J. 1969. A shovel-tusked gomphothere from the Miocene of Kenya. *Breviora*, no. 310.

_____. 1970 . Early Elephantidae of Africa and a tentative correlation of African Plio-Pleistocene deposits. *Nature* 225:328-32.

_____. 1970 . Four new species of Elephantidae from the Plio-Pleistocene of northwestern Kenya. *Breviora*, no. 341.

_____. 1973. Origin and evolution of the Elephantidae. *Trans. Am. Phil. Soc.*, n.s., 63:1-149.

Patterson, B. 1966.   A new locality for early Pleistocene fossils in northwestern Kenya. *Nature* 212:577-78.

_____. 1968.   The extinct baboon, *Parapapio jonesi*, in the early Pleistocene of northwestern Kenya. *Breviora*, no. 282.

_____. 1975.   The fossil aardvarks (Mammalia: Tubulidentata). *Bull. Mus. Comp. Zool.*, *Harvard Coll.* 147:185-237.

Patterson, B.; Behrensmeyer, A. K.; and Sill, W. D. 1970.   Geology and fauna of a new Pliocene locality in northwestern Kenya. *Nature* 226:918-21.

Patterson, B., and Howells, W. W. 1967.   Hominid humeral fragment from early Pleistocene of northwestern Kenya. *Science* 156:64-66.

Thomson, K. S. 1966.   Quaternary fish fossils from west of Lake Rudolf, Kenya. *Breviora*, no. 243.

4.   Omo Research Expedition, 1966-74

Assembled by F. C. Howell

Arambourg, C. 1967.   La deuxième mission scientifique de l'Omo. *Anthropologie* 71:562-66.

_____. 1969*a*.   Les corrélations paléontologiques et chronologiques entre le Pléistocène inférieur de l'Europe et celui de l'Afrique. *Bull. Soc. Géol. France*, ser. 7, 11: 106-15.

_____. 1969*b*.   La nouvelle expédition scientifique de l'Omo. *Riv. Sci. Preist.* 24:1-13.

Arambourg, C.; Chavaillon, J.; and Coppens, Y. 1967.   Premiers résultats de la nouvelle mission de l'Omo (1967). *C. R. Acad. Sci. (Paris)*, ser. D, 265:1891-96.

_____. 1969.   Résultats de la nouvelle mission de l'Omo (2e campagne 1968). *C. R. Acad. Sci. (Paris)*, ser. D, 268:759-62.

_____. n.d.   Expédition internationale de recherches paléontologiques dans la vallée de l'Omo (Ethiopie) en 1967. *Actes du 6e Congrès panafricain de préhistoire et d'études du Quaternaire.* Dakar, 2-8 December, 1967:135-40. Chambery, France: Imprimeries Réunies de Chambery.

Arambourg, C.; Chavaillon, J.; Coppens, Y.; and Koeniguer, J. C. 1969.   Sur quelques fossiles hétéroxyles de la série du Lubur (Turkana, Kenya). *C. R. Acad. Sci. (Paris)*, ser. D, 268:2867-69.

Arambourg, C., and Coppens, Y. 1967.   Sur la découverte dans le Pléistocène inférieur de la vallée de l'Omo (Ethiopie) d'une mandibule d'australopithécien. *C. R. Acad. Sci. (Paris)*, ser. D, 265:589-90.

_____. 1968.   Découverte d'un australopithécien nouveau dans les gisements de l'Omo (Ethiopie). *S. African J. Sci.* 64:58-59.

Arambourg, C., and Wolff, R. G. 1969.   Nouvelles données paléontologiques sur l'âge des "grés de Lubur" (Turkana grits) à l'Ouest du lac Rodolphe. *C. R. Somm. Soc. Géol. France*, fasc. 6, pp. 190-91.

Beaucournu, J. C.; Houin, R.; and Rodhain, F. 1970.   *Xenopsylla coppensi* n. sp. (Siphonaptera) puce nouvelle du groupe nilotica en provenance d'Ethiopie. *Ann. Parasitol.* 45: 111-14.

Beaucournu, J. C.; Rodhain, F.; and Houin, R. 1972.   Sur quelques insectes (Siphonaptera, Anopiura) ectoparasites des mammifères dans la basse vallée de l'Omo. *Bull. Soc. Pathol. Exotique* 65:867-80.

Bonnefille, R. 1970.   Premiers résultats concernant l'analyse pollinique d'échantillons du Pléistocène inférieur de l'Omo (Ethiopie). *C. R. Acad. Sci. (Paris)*, ser. D, 270: 2430-33.

_____. 1971*a*.   Atlas des pollens d'Ethiopie: Pollens actuels de la basse vallée de l'Omo. Récoltes botaniques 1968. *Adansonia*, ser. 2, 11(3):463-518.

_____. 1971*b*.   Atlas des pollens d'Ethiopie: Principals espèces des fôrets de Montagne. *Pollen et Spores* 13(1):15-72.

Bonnefille, R. 1972. Associations polliniques actuelles et Quaternaires en Ethiopie (vallée de l'Awash et de l'Omo). Thèse de doctorat d'état, Université de Paris.

_____. 1972. Considération sur la composition de'une microflore pollinque des formations plio-pléistocènes de la basse vallée de l'Omo (Ethiopie). In *Palaeoecology of Africa*, ed. E. M. Van Zinderen Bakker, 7:22-27. Cape Town: A. A. Balkema.

_____. Mise au point sur l'état actuel des recherches palynologiques du gisement de l'Omo (Ethiopie). *Actes du 7ᵉ Congrès panafricain de Préhistoire et d'Etude du Quaternaire.* Addis Ababa, 6-12 décembre 1971. In press.

Bonnefille, R.; Brown, F. H.; Chavaillon, J.; Coppens, Y.; Haesaerts, P.; de Heinzelin, J; and Howell, F. C. 1973a. Situation stratigraphique des localités a Hominidés des gisements plio-pléistocènes de l'Omo en Ethiopie (membres de base, A, B, C, D, and J). *C. R. Acad. Sci. (Paris)*, ser. D, 276:2781-84.

_____. 1973b. Situation stratigraphique des localités à Hominidés des gisements plio-pléistocènes de l'Omo en Ethiopie (Membres E, F, G, et H). *C. R. Acad. Sci. (Paris)*, ser. D. 276:2879-82.

Bonnefille, R.; Chavaillon, J. and Coppens, Y. 1970. Résultats de la nouvelle mission de l'Omo (3ᵉ campagne 1969). *C. R. Acad. Sci. (Paris)*, ser. D, 270:924-27.

Broin, F. de. 1969. Sur la présence d'une tortue, *Pelusios sinuatus* (A. Smith) du Villafranchien inférieur du Tchad. *C. R. Somm. Soc. Géol. France*, fasc. 8, pp. 322-24.

Brown, F. H. 1969. Observations on the stratigraphy and radiometric age of the "Omo Beds," lower Omo basin, southern Ethiopia. *Quaternaria* 11:7-14.

_____. 1971. Radiometric dating of sedimentary formations in the lower Omo valley, southern Ethiopia. In *Calibration of hominoid evolution*, ed. W. W. Bishop and J. A. Miller, pp. 273-87. Edinburgh: Scottish Academic Press; Toronto: University of Toronto Press.

Brown, F. H., and Carmichael, I. S. E. 1969. Quaternary volcanoes of the Lake Rudolf Regions: 1. The basinite-tephrite series of the Korath range. *Lithos* 2:239-60.

_____. 1971. Quaternary volcanoes of the Lake Rudolf region: 2. The lavas of North Island, South Island and the Barrier. *Lithos* 4:305-33.

Brown, F. H.; Croes, M. K.; and Shuey, R. T. 1975. Further data on the magnetostratigraphy of the Shungura Formation, southwestern Ethiopia. *Earth Planet. Sci. Lett.* In press.

Brown, F. H., and Lajoie, K. R. 1971. Radiometric age determinations on Pliocene/Pleistocene formations in the lower Omo basin, southern Ethiopia. *Nature* 229:483-85.

Butzer, K. W. 1969. Geological interpretation of two Pleistocene hominid sites in the lower Omo basin. *Nature* 222:1138-40.

_____. 1970a. Contemporary depositional environments of the Omo delta. *Nature* 226: 425-30.

_____. 1970b. Geomorphological observations in the lower Omo basin, southwestern Ethiopia. In *Argumenta Geographica (Carl Troll Festschrift)*, ed. Wilhelm Lauer, *Colloquium Geographicum* 12:177-92.

_____. 1971a. The lower Omo basin: Geology, fauna and hominids of Plio-Pleistocene age. *Naturwissenschaften* 58:7-16.

_____. 1971b. Recent history of an Ethiopian delta. University of Chicago Department of Geography, Research Paper no. 136:1-184.

Butzer, K. W.; Brown, F. H.; and Thurber, D. L. 1969. Horizontal sediments of the lower Omo valley: The Kibish Formation. *Quaternaria* 11:15-29.

Butzer, K. W., and Thurber, D. L. 1969. Some late Cenozoic sedimentary formations of the lower Omo basin. *Nature* 222:1132-37.

Carr, C. J. 1975. The Dasenitch of southwest Ethiopia: A system of societal/environmental change. University of Chicago Department of Geography, Research Paper.

Carr, C. J. 1976. Riverine ecological studies in the lower Omo basin, Ethiopia. *J. Biogeograph.* 2(4). In press.

Chavaillon, J. 1969. Recherches géologiques dans le Quaternaire de la basse vallée de l'Omo (Ethiopie). In *Palaeoecology of Africa,* ed. E. M. van Zinderen Bakker, 4:59. Cape Town: A. A. Balkema.

_____. 1970. Découverte d'un niveau Oldowayen dans la basse vallée de l'Omo (Ethiopie). *C. R. Soc. Préhist. Franc.* 1:7-11.

_____. 1971*a*. Etat actuel de la prehistoire ancienne dans la vallée de l'Omo (Ethiopie). *Archéologia,* no. 38, pp. 33-43.

_____. 1971*b*. Recherches en Ethiopie. *Sci. Avenir* (special no. *La vie préhistorique),* pp. 78-79.

Cooke, H. B. S., and Coppens. Y. 1975. The fossil Suidae of Omo, Ethiopia. In *Fossil vertebrates of Africa,* vol. 4. In press.

Cooke, H. B. S., and Maglio, V. J. 1972. Plio/Pleistocene stratigraphy in eastern Africa in relation to Proboscidean and Suid Evolution. In *Calibration of hominoid evolution,* ed. W. W. Bishop and J. A. Miller, pp. 303-28. Edinburgh: Scottish Academic Press; Toronto: University of Toronto Press.

Coppens, Y. 1967. L'Afrique équatoriale: Une étape de l'histoire de l'humanité. *Cahiers Explor.,* n.s., no 19, pp. 18-19.

_____. 1968*a*. Esquisse de l'histoire de l'humanité dans le temps et dans l'espace. *Raison Presenté,* no. 7, pp. 91-95.

_____. 1968*b*. La paléontologie en Ethiopie. *Bull. Cent. Reg. Technol. Afr.* (Nairobi), 3(3):70-72.

_____. 1969*a*. Les gisements paléontologiques plio-quaternaires de l'Omo (Ethiopie). *Bull. Post. Sci. Hors Siège,* UNESCO, 4(3):29-33.

_____. 1969*b*. La mission paléontologique internationale de l'Omo (Ethiopie). In *Paleoecology of Africa,* ed. E. M. van Zinderen Bakker, 4:57-58. Cape Town: A. A. Balkema.

_____. 1970*a*. Localisations dans le temps et dans l'espace des restes d'Hominidés des formations plio-pléistocene de l'Omo (Ethiopie). *C. R. Acad. Sci. (Paris),* ser. D, 271:1968-71.

_____. 1970*b*. Les restes d'Hominidés des séries inférieures et moyennes des formations Plio-Villafranchiennes de l'Omo en Ethiopie. *C. R. Acad. Sci. (Paris),* ser. D, 271: 2286-89.

_____. 1971*a*. Les australopithèques réhabilités. *Sci. Avenir* (special no. *La vie préhistorique),* pp. 80-83.

_____. 1971*b*. Les restes d'Hominidés des séries supérieures des formations Plio-Villafranchiennes de l'Omo en Ethiopie. *C. R. Acad. Sci. (Paris),* ser. D, 272:36-39.

_____. 1972. Tentative de zonation du Pliocène et du Pléistocène de'Afrique par les grandes mammifères. *C. R. Acad. Sci. (Paris),* ser. D, 274:181-84.

_____. 1974. Les faunes de vertébrés du Pliocène et du Pléistocène ancien d'Afrique. *Actes du Ve Congrès du Neogène mediterranéen.* Lyon, Septembre 1971, pp. 109-19, Mém. du B.R.G.M. 78.

_____. 1973*a*. Les restes d'Hominidés des séries inférieures et moyennes des formations Plio-Villafranchiennes de l'Omo en Ethiopie (récoltes 1970, 1971 et 1972). *C. R. Acad. Sci. (Paris),* ser. D, 276:1823-26.

_____. 1973*b*. Les restes d'Hominidés des séries supérieures des formations Plio-Villafranchiennes de l'Omo en Ethiopie (récoltes 1970, 1971, et 1972). *C. R. Acad. Sci. (Paris),* ser. D, 276:1981-84.

_____. 1975. La grande aventure paléontologique est-africaine. *Courrier C.N.R.S.,* no. 16 (April 1975):30-37.

Coppens, Y.; Chavaillon, J.; and Beden, M. 1973. Résultats de la nouvelle mission de l'Omo (campagne 1972: Découverte de restes des Hominidés et d'une industrie sur éclats. *C. R. Acad. Sci. (Paris)*, ser. D, 276:161-64.

Coryndon Savage, S., and Coppens, Y. 1973. Preliminary report on Hippopotamidae (Mammalia, Artiodactyla) from the Plio/Pleistocene of the lower Omo basin, Ethiopia. In *Fossil vertebrates of Africa*, ed. L. S. G. Leakey, R. J. Savage, and S. C. Coryndon. 3:139-57. London: Academic Press.

Coryndon, S. C., and Coppens, Y. 1975. Une nouvelle espèce d'hippopotame nain du Plio-Pleistocène du bassin du lac Rudolphe (Ethiopie, Kenya). *C. R. Acad. Sci. (Paris)*. ser. D, 280:1777-80.

Eck, G. G. 1976. Diversity and frequency distribution of Omo Group Cercopithecoidea. *J. Human Evol.* In press.

Eck, G. G., and Howell, F. C. 1972. New fossil *Cercopithecus* material from the lower Omo basin, Ethiopia. *Folia Primatol.* 8:325-55.

Fitch, F. J., and Miller, J. A. 1969. Age determinations on feldspar from the lower Omo basin. *Nature* 222:1143.

Heinzelin, J. de. 1969. Le groupe de l'Omo et l'âge du Pléistocène. *Bull. Soc. Belge Géol. Paléontol. Hydrol.* 78:1-5.

_____. Observations sur la formation de Shungura (vallée de l'Omo, Ethiopie). *C. R. Acad. Sci. (Paris)*, ser. D, 272:2409-11.

_____. 1972. Omo Research Expedition, 1967-1971. *Africa-Tervuren* 19:67-74.

Heinzelin, J. de, and Brown, F. H. 1969. Some early Pleistocene deposits of the lower Omo valley: The Usno Formation. *Quaternaria* 11:31-46.

Heinzelin, J. de; Brown, F. H.; and Howell, F. C. 1970. Pliocene/Pleistocene formations in the lower Omo basin, southern Ethiopia. *Quaternaria* 13:247-68.

Hooijer, D. A. 1969. Pleistocene East African Rhinoceroses. In *Fossil vertebrates of Africa*, ed. L. S. B. Leakey and R. J. Savage, 1:71-98. London: Academic Press.

_____. 1973. Additional Miocene to Pleistocene rhinoceroses of Africa. *Zool. Mededeel., Rijksmuseum Natuurl. Hist., Leiden* 46(11):149-78.

Hooijer, D. A. 1975. Note on some newly found Perissodactyl teeth from the Omo Group deposits, Ethiopia. *Proc. Koninkl. Nederl. Akad. van Wetenschappen, Amsterdam*, ser. B, 78:188-90.

Houin, R.; Bazin, J. C.; and Bolognini, J. 1968. Etude des leishmanioses dans la vallée de l'Omo (Ethiopie). Recherche d'un réservoir de virus sauvage. *Rev. Pathol. Comp. Med. Exp.*, Paris, 68(5-6-7-99):361-63.

Howell, F. C. 1968. Omo Research Expedition. *Nature* 219:567-72.

_____. 1969a. Hominid teeth from White Sands and Brown Sands localities, lower Omo basin (Ethiopia). *Quaternaria* 11:47-64.

_____. 1969b. Remains of Hominidae from Pliocene/Pleistocene formations in the lower Omo basin, Ethiopia. *Nature* 223:1234-39.

_____. 1971a. Hominidae: *Australopithecus*. In *McGraw-Hill yearbook of science and technology*, 1970:220-22. New York: McGraw-Hill.

_____. 1971b. Pliocene/Pleistocene Hominidae in eastern Africa: Absolute and relative ages. In *Calibration of hominoid evolution*, ed. W. W. Bishop and J. A. Miller, pp. 331-68. Edinburgh: Scottish Academic Press; Toronto: University of Toronto Press.

_____. 1972a. Our earliest ancestors. In *Science year: The World Book science annual*, 1973:224-37. Chicago: Field Enterprises.

_____. 1972b. Recent advances in human evolutionary studies. In *Perspectives on human evolution*, ed. S. L. Washburn and P. C. Dolhinow, 2:51-128. New York: Holt, Rinehart and Winston.

Howell, F. C. 1975*a*. Overview of the Pliocene and Earlier Pleistocene of the lower Omo basin, southern Ethiopia. In *African Hominidae of the Plio-Pleistocene*, ed. C. J. Jolly. London: Duckworths.

———. 1975*b*. Overview of the Pliocene and Earlier Pleistocene of the lower Omo basin, southern Ethiopia. In *Human origins: Louis Leakey and the East African evidence*, ed. G. Ll. Isaac and E. Mc Cown. Menlo Park, Calif.: W. A. Benjamin.

Howell, F. C., and Coppens, Y. 1973. Deciduous teeth of Hominidae from the Pliocene/Pleistocene of the lower Omo basin, Ethiopia. *J. Human Evol.* (R. A. Dart Memorial Issue) 2:461-72.

———. 1974. Les faunes de mammifères fossiles de formations plio/pléistocènes de l'Omo en Ethiopie. *C. R. Acad. Sci. (Paris)*, ser. D, 278:2275-78, 2421-24.

Howell, F. C., and Coppens, Y. (with Heinzelin, J. de). 1974. Inventory of remains of Hominidae from Pliocene/Pleistocene formations of the lower Omo basin, Ethiopia (1967-1972). *Am. J. Phys. Anthropol.* 40:1-16.

Howell, F. C.; Fichter, L. S.; and Eck, G. 1969. Vertebrate assemblages from the Usno Formation, White Sands and Brown Sands localities, lower Omo basin, Ethiopia. *Quaternaria* 11:65-88.

Howell, F. C.; Fichter, L. S.; and Wolff, R. 1969. Fossil camels in the Omo Beds, southern Ethiopia. *Nature* 223:150-52.

Howell, F. C., and Wood, B. A. 1974. An early hominid ulna from the Omo basin, Ethiopia. *Nature* 249:174-76.

Landau, I. 1969. Etude au laboratoire sur *Anthemosoma garnhami landau*, Boulard, Houin. *J. Parasitol.* 56(4, sec. 2):199.

Landau, I.; Boulard, Y.; and Houin, R. 1969*a*. *Anthemosoma garnhami* n. g. n. sp., premier Dactylosomidae connu chez un mammifère. *C. R. Acad. Sci. (Paris)*, ser. D, 268:873-75.

———. 1969*b*. Schizogony in a piroplasm of the spiny mouse. *Trans. Roy. Soc. Trop. Med. Hyg.* 63(1):12.

Leakey, M. G., and Leakey, R. E. F. 1973. New large Pleistocene Colobinae (Mammalia, Primates) from East Africa. In *Fossil vertebrates of Africa*, ed. L. S. B. Leakey, R. J. Savage, and S. C. Coryndon, 3:121-38. London: Academic Press.

Leakey, R. E. F.; Butzer, K. W.; and Day, M. A. 1969. Early *Homo sapiens* remains from the Omo river region of southwest Ethiopia. *Nature* 222:1132-38.

Matthey, R. 1968. Cytogénétique et taxonomie du genre *Acomys* A. *Percivali* Dollman et A. *wilsoni* Thomas, espèces d'Abyssinie. *Mammalia* 32(4):621-27.

———. 1969. Chromosomes de Gerbillinae, Genres *Tatera* et *Taterillus*. *Mammalia* 33(3):522-28.

Merrick, H. V. Recent archaeological research in the Plio-Pleistocene deposits of the lower Omo valley, southwestern Ethiopia. In *Human origins: Louis Leakey and the East African evidence*, ed. G. Ll. Isaac and E. Mc Cown. Menlo Park, Calif.: W. A. Benjamin.

Merrick, H. V.; Haesaerts, P.; Heinzelin, J. de; and Howell, F. C. 1973. Archaeological occurrences of Early Pleistocene age from the Shungura Formation, lower Omo valley, Ethiopia. *Nature* 242:572-75.

Morel, P. C., and Rodhain, F. 1972. Contribution à la connaissance des tiques (Ixodina) du Sud de l'Ethiopie, I. *Bull. Soc. Path. Exotique* 65:725-32.

———. 1973. Contribution à la connaissance des tiques (Ixodina) du Sud de l'Ethiopie, II. *Bull. Soc. Path. Exotique* 66:207-15.

Petter, F.; Quilici, M.; Ranque, P.; and Camerlynck, P. 1969. Croisement d'*Arvicanthis niloticus* (Rongeurs, Murides) du Sénégal et d'Ethiopie. *Mammalia* 33(3):540-41.

Rodhain, F. 1970. Les missions françaises de l'Omo. *Rev. Fed. Fr. Soc. Sci. Nat.* 9(39):65-67.

Rodhain, F. 1971. Contribution à l'étude des Culicidés de la basse vallée de l'Omo (Ethiopie), I. *Bull. Soc. Path. Exotique* 64:117-27.

Rodhain, F., and Ovazza, M. 1972. Note sur les Tabanides et les Glossines de la basse vallée de l'Omo (Ethiopie). *Bull. Soc. Path. Exotique* 65:166-69.

Rodhain, F., and Tornay, S. Ethnologie et epidémiologie: A propos d'une enquête pluridisciplinaire auprès de l'ethnic Nyangatem. Hommage au Professeur Baltazard. In press.

Rodhain, F. Contribution à l'étude des Culicidés de la basse vallée de l'Omo (Ethiopie), II. *Bull. Soc. Path. Exotique*. In press.

Shuey, R. T.; Brown, F. H.; and Croes, M. K. 1974. Magnetostratigraphy of the Shungura Formation, southwestern Ethiopia: Fine structure of the lower Matuyama polarity epoch. *Earth Planet. Sci. Letters* 23:249-60.

Tornay, M. M., and Tornay, S. Le jeu de pierres chez les Nyangatom du Sud-ouest éthiopien. *J. Soc. Afr.* In press.

Tornay, S. L'étude de la parenté. L'Anthropologie, science des sociétés primitives. *Denoë* 1:49-111. Paris.

_____. Enquêtes préliminaires chez les Nyangatom (écologie, les grands traits de l'organisation sociale, la carte généalogique d'un village de 150 habitants). *Homme*. In press.

_____. Les noms de couleurs des Nyangatom et des Dassanetch: Critique des thèses de Berlin et Kay (thèses exprimées dans "Basic Color Terms," Berkeley, 1969). In press.

_____. 1974. L'éclipse du 30 juin, 1973 chez les Nyangatom Sud-ouest éthiopien. Laboratoire d'ethnologie et de sociologie comparative, Université de Paris X, Nanterre.

Van Damme, D., and Gautier, A. 1971. Molluscan assemblages from the later Cenozoic of the lower Omo basin, Ethiopia. *Quat. Res.* 2(1):25-37.

5. East Rudolf Research Project

Assembled by G. Ll. Isaac,
from a list prepared by M. G. Leakey

Behrensmeyer, A. K. 1970. Preliminary geological interpretation of a new hominid site in the Lake Rudolf basin. *Nature* 226:225-26.

_____. 1973. The taphonomy and paleoecology of Plio-Pleistocene vertebrate assemblages east of Lake Rudolf. Ph.D. thesis, Harvard University.

_____. 1975. The taphonomy and paleoecology of Plio-Pleistocene vertebrate assemblages east of Lake Rudolf, Kenya. *Bull. Mus. Comp. Zool. Harvard Coll.* 146:473-578.

Bowen, B. E. 1974. The geology of the Upper Cenozoic sediments in the East Rudolf embayment of the Lake Rudolf basin, Kenya. Ph.D. diss., Iowa State University, Ames.

Bowen, B. E., and Vondra, C. F. 1973. Stratigraphical relationships of the Plio-Pleistocene deposits, East Rudolf, Kenya. *Nature* 242:391-93.

Brock, A.; Hillhouse, J.; Cox, A.; and Ndombi, J. 1974. The paleomagnetism of the Koobi Fora Formation, Lake Rudolf, Kenya. *Trans. Am. Geophys. Union* 56:1109 (abstr. GP 15).

Brock, A., and Isaac, G. Ll. 1974. Palaeomagnetic stratigraphy and chronology of hominid-bearing sediments east of Lake Rudolf, Kenya. *Nature* 247:344-48.

Day, M. H. 1974. The early hominids from East Rudolf, North Kenya. *J. Anat.* 117:651 (abstr.).

Day, M. H., and Leakey, R. E. F. 1973. New evidence for the genus *Homo* from East Rudolf, Kenya, I. *Am. J. Phys. Anthropol.* 39:341-54.

_____. 1974. New evidence for the genus *Homo* from East Rudolf, Kenya, III. *Am. J. Phys. Anthropol.* 41:367-80.

Day, M. H.; Leakey, R. E. F.; Walker, A. C.; and Wood, B. A. 1975. New hominids from East
    Rudolf, Kenya, I. *Am. J. Phys. Anthrop.* 42:461-76.

Fitch, F. J.; Findlater, I. C.; Watkins, R. T.; and Miller, J. A. 1974. Dating of the rock
    succession containing fossil hominids at East Rudolf, Kenya. *Nature* 351:213-15.

Fitch, F. J., and Miller, J. A. 1970. Radioisotopic age determinations of Lake Rudolf ar-
    tefact site. *Nature* 226:226-28.

Fitch, F. J.; Watkins, R. T.; and Miller, J. A. 1975. Age of a new carbonatite locality
    in northern Kenya. *Nature* 254:581-83.

Harris, J. M. 1974. Orientation and variability of the ossicones of African Sivatherinae
    (Mammalia: Giraffidae). *Ann. S. Afr. Museum* 65:188-98.

_____. 1975*a*. Pleistocene Giraffidae (Mammalia: Artiodactyla) from East Rudolf, Kenya.
    In *Fossil vertebrates of Africa*, vol. 4. In press.

_____. 1975*b*. Fossil Rhinocerotidae (Mammalia: Perissodactyla) from East Rudolf,
    Kenya. In *Fossil vertebrates of Africa*, vol. 4. In press.

Harris, J. M., and Watkins, R. 1974. New early Miocene vertebrate locality near Lake
    Rudolf, Kenya. *Nature* 252:576-77.

Hurford, A. J. 1974. Fission track dating of a vitric tuff from East Rudolf, Kenya.
    Nature 249:236-37.

Isaac, G. Ll.; Leakey, R. E. F.; and Behrensmeyer, A. K. 1971. Archeological traces of
    early hominid activities, east of Lake Rudolf, Kenya. *Science* 173:1129-34.

Johnson, G. D. 1974. Cainozoic lacustrine stromatolites from hominid-bearing sediments
    east of Lake Rudolf, Kenya. *Nature* 247:520-23.

Leakey, M. D. 1970. Early artefacts from the Koobi Fora area. *Nature* 226:228-30.

Leakey, M. G., and Leakey, R. E. F. 1973. New large Pleistocene Colobinae (Mammalia,
    Primates) from East Africa. In *Fossil vertebrates of Africa*, ed. L. S. B. Leakey,
    R. J. Savage, and S. C. Coryndon, 3:121-38. London: Academic Press.

Leakey, R. E. F. 1970*a*. In search of man's past at Lake Rudolf. *Nat. Geograph.* 137:712-32.

_____. 1970*b*. New hominid remains and early artefacts from northern Kenya. *Nature*
    226:223-24.

_____. 1971. Further evidence of Lower Pleistocene hominids from East Rudolf, North
    Kenya. *Nature* 231:241-45.

_____. 1972*a*. Further evidence of Lower Pleistocene hominids from East Rudolf, North
    Kenya, 1971. *Nature* 237:264-69.

_____. 1972*b*. New evidence for the evolution of man. *Soc. Biol.* 19(2):99-114.

_____. 1973*a*. Australopithecines and hominines: A summary of the evidence from the
    early Pleistocene of eastern Africa. *Symp. Zool. Soc. London* 33:53-69.

_____. 1973*b*. Evidence for an advanced Plio-Pleistocene hominid from East Rudolf,
    Kenya. *Nature* 242:447-50.

_____. 1973*c*. Further evidence of Lower Pleistocene hominids from East Rudolf, North
    Kenya, 1972. *Nature* 242:170-73.

_____. 1973*d*. Skull 1470. *Nat. Geograph.* 143:818-29.

_____. 1974. Further evidence of Lower Pleistocene hominids from East Rudolf, North
    Kenya, 1973. *Nature* 248:653-56.

Leakey, R. E. F., and Isaac, G. Ll. 1972. Hominid fossils from the area east of Lake
    Rudolf, Kenya: Photographs and a commentary on context. In *Perspectives on human
    evolution*, ed. S. L. Washburn and P. Dolhinow, 2:129-40. San Francisco: Holt,
    Rinehart and Winston.

Leakey, R. E. F.; Mungai, J. M.; and Walker, A. C. 1971. New australopithecines from East Rudolf, Kenya. *Am. J. Phys. Anthropol.* 35:175-86.

———. 1972. New australopithecines from East Rudolf, Kenya, II. *Am. J. Phys. Anthropol.* 36:235-51.

Leakey, R. E. F., and Walker, A. C. 1973. New australopithecines from East Rudolf, Kenya, III. *Am. J. Phys. Anthropol.* 39:205-22.

Leakey, R. E. F., and Wood, B. A. 1973. New evidence for the genus *Homo* from East Rudolf, Kenya, II. *Am. J. Phys. Anthropol.* 39:355-68.

———. 1974*a*. A hominid mandible from East Rudolf, Kenya. *Am. J. Phys. Anthropol.* 41:245-50.

———. 1974*b*. New evidence for the genus *Homo* from East Rudolf, Kenya, IV. *Am J. Phys. Anthropol.* 41:237-44.

Maglio, V. J. 1971. Vertebrate faunas from the Kubi Algi, Koobi Fora and Ileret areas, East Rudolf, Kenya. *Nature* 231:248-49.

———. 1972. Vertebrate faunas and chronology of hominid-bearing sediments east of Lake Rudolf, Kenya. *Nature* 239:379-85.

Vondra, C. F.; Johnson, G. D.; Bowen, B. E.; and Behrensmeyer, A. K. 1971. Preliminary stratigraphical studies of the East Rudolf basin, Kenya. *Nature* 231:245-48.

Walker, A. C. 1973. New *Australopithecus* femora from East Rudolf, Kenya. *J. Human Evol.* 2:545-55.

Wood, B. A. 1974*a*. Evidence on the locomotor pattern of *Homo* from early Pleistocene of Kenya. *Nature* 251:135-36.

———. 1974*b*. A *Homo* talus from East Rudolf, Kenya. *J. Anat.* 117:203-4 (abstr.)

———. 1974*c*. Morphology of a fossil hominid mandible from East Rudolf, Kenya. *J. Anat.* 117:652-53 (abstr.)

CONTRIBUTORS

Michel Beden
Laboratoire de paleontologie des vertébrés
   et paléontologie humaine
Faculté des Sciences
Université de Poitiers
40, avenue de Recteur Pineau
86022 Poitiers
France

Dr. A. K. Behrensmeyer
Department of Geology
University of California
Santa Cruz, California 95064

Prof. W. W. Bishop
Department of Geology
Queen Mary College
Mile End Road
London E1, 4NS
England

Noel Boaz
Department of Anthropology
University of California
Berkeley, California 94720

Dr. Raymonde Bonnefille
Laboratoires de Bellevue
C.N.R.S.
1, place A. Briand
92-Bellevue
France

Dr. Bruce E. Bowen
Texaco Research
Bellaire, Texas 74701

Dr. Andrew Brock
Department of Physics
University of Botswana, Lesotho,
   and Swaziland
Roma, Lesotho
Africa

Dr. F. H. Brown
Department of Geology and Geophysics
717 Mineral Science Building
University of Utah
Salt Lake City, Utah 84112

Prof. K. W. Butzer
Departments of Geography and Anthropology
University of Chicago
Chicago, Illinois 60637

Dr. Claudia J. Carr
Kresge College
University of California
Santa Cruz, California 95060

Thure E. Cerling
Department of Geology and Geophysics
University of California
Berkeley, California 94720

Dr. Jean Chavaillon
Laboratoire de géologie
Collège de France
Station Berthelot
Avenue Marcelin Berthelot
92-Meudon
France

Prof. H. B. S. Cooke
Department of Geology
Dalhousie University
Halifax, Canada

Yves Coppens
Musée de l'homme
Palais de Chaillot
75016 Paris
France

Shirley C. Coryndon
Department of Geology
University of Bristol
Bristol
England

D. Crader
Department of Anthropology
University of California
Berkeley, California 94720

Prof. Michael Day
Department of Anatomy
St. Thomas' Hospital Medical School
Lambeth Palace Road
London SE1, 7EH
England

Gerald Eck
Department of Anthropology
University of Washington
Seattle, Washington 98105

Dr. Vera Eisenmann
Institut de paléontologie
Muséum national d'histoire naturelle
8, rue de Buffon
75005 Paris
France

Ian C. Findlater
Geological Research Laboratory
c/o Department of Geology
Birkbeck College
7/15 Gresse Street
London W1P, 1PA
England

Dr. F. J. Fitch
Geological Research Laboratory
c/o Department of Geology
Birkbeck College
7/15 Gresse Street
London W1P, 1PA
England

Dr. A. Gautier
Geologisch Instituut
Rijksuniversiteit Gent
Rozier 44
Gent
Belgium

Dr. A. W. Gentry
British Museum (Natural History)
Cromwell Road
London SW7
England

J.-L. Grattard
Laboratoire de paléontologie des
  vertébrés et de paléontologie
  humaine
4, place Jussieu
Université de Paris VI
75230 Paris
France

Claude Guérin
Laboratoire de paléontologie
  stratigraphique
Département des sciences de la terre
Université Claude Bernard-Lyon 1
15-43, boulevard du 11 Novembre 1918
F 69621 Villeurbane
France

Dr. Paul Haesaerts
Geografisch Instituut
Vrije Universiteit te Brussel
Adolf Buyllaan 87
1050 Brussels
Belgium

Dr. John M. Harris
National Museums of Kenya
P. O. Box 40658
Nairobi
Kenya

J. W. K. Harris
Department of Anthropology
University of California
Berkeley, California 94720

Prof. J. de Heinzelin
Geologisch Instituut
Rijksuniversiteit Gent
Rozier 44
Gent
Belgium

Dr. D. A. Hooijer
Rijksmuseum van Natuurlijke Historie
Raamsteeg 2
Leiden
Netherlands

Prof. F. Clark Howell
Department of Anthropology
University of California
Berkeley, California 94720

Prof. Glynn Ll. Isaac
Department of Anthropology
University of California
Berkeley, California 94720

Dr. J.-J. Jaeger
Laboratoire de paléontologie
Académie de Montpellier
Place Eugène-Bataillon
34060 Montpellier
France

Dr. Donald C. Johanson
Department of Anthropology
Case Western Reserve University
Cleveland, Ohio 44106

Dr. Gary D. Johnson
Department of Earth Sciences
Dartmouth College
Hanover, New Hampshire 03755

Richard E. F. Leakey
National Museums of Kenya
P. O. Box 40658
Nairobi
Kenya

Dr. Meave G. Leakey
National Museums of Kenya
P. O. Box 40658
Nairobi
Kenya

Dr. H. V. and J. P. S. Merrick
Department of Anthropology
Yale University
New Haven, Connecticut 06520

Dr. John A. Miller
Department of Geodesy and Geophysics
Cambridge University
Cambridge
England

Dr. W. P. Nash
Department of Geology and Geophysics
717 Mineral Science Building
University of Utah
Salt Lake City, Utah 84112

Dr. Germaine Petter
Institut de paléontologie
Muséum national d'histoire naturelle
8, rue de Buffon
75005 Paris
France

R. G. H. Raynolds
Department of Applied Earth Sciences
Stanford University
Stanford, California 94305

Dr. Ralph Shuey
Department of Geology and Geophysics
717 Mineral Science Building
University of Utah
Salt Lake City, Utah 84112

Charles Smart
Department of Geology and Geophysics
Princeton University
Princeton, New Jersey 08540

Marcel Splingaer
Institut royale des sciences naturelles
Rue Vautier, 31
B-1040 Brussels, Belgium

Dr. Eitan Tchernov
Department of Zoology
Hebrew University
Jerusalem
Israel

Prof. Carl F. Vondra
Department of Earth Sciences
Iowa State University
Ames, Iowa 50010

Dr. Alan Walker
Department of Anatomy
Medical School
Harvard University
Boston, Massachusetts 02138

H. B. Wesselman
Department of Anthropology
University of California
Berkeley, California 94720

Dr. Bernard Wood
Department of Anatomy
The Middlesex Hospital Medical School
Cleveland Street
London W1P, 6DB
England